Psychiatric
and **Behavioural Disorders**
in **Developmental Disabilities**
and **Mental Retardation**

The problems faced by individuals with developmental disability are all too often heightened by psychiatric or behavioural disorder. These quality-of-life issues have come to attention increasingly over recent years with improved community and social integration. In tune with this mood of concern, Dr Bouras has gathered together a comprehensive dossier of essential facts and concepts for all those involved with the care of the dually diagnosed. Drawing on both clinical experience and the latest research, an international and multi-professional team of contributors provides concise and relevant reviews. The contributors highlight the principles of good clinical practice in assessment, management and services, providing hands-on practical advice for a wide range of mental health professionals including psychiatrists, psychologists, nurses, therapists, social workers, managers and service providers.

NICK BOURAS has many years of experience in mental health and services for people with developmental disabilities and mental retardation. He has published widely, including *Mental Health in Mental Retardation* with Cambridge University Press, and is co-editor of the *Mental Health in Learning Disabilities Training Package and Handbook*. He is the editor of the *Journal of Intellectual Disability Research – Mental Health* and co-founder of the European Association of Mental Health in Mental Retardation. He is currently Chairman of the Mental Retardation Section of the World Psychiatric Association.

Psychiatric
and Behavioural Disorders
in Developmental Disabilities
and Mental Retardation

Edited by
NICK BOURAS
Mental Health in Learning Disabilities Centre,
Guy's – King's College – St Thomas' Hospital
Medical School, Guy's Hospital, London

CAMBRIDGE
UNIVERSITY PRESS

PUBLISHED BY THE PRESS SYNDICATE OF THE UNIVERSITY OF CAMBRIDGE
The Pitt Building, Trumpington Street, Cambridge, United Kingdom

CAMBRIDGE UNIVERSITY PRESS
The Edinburgh Building, Cambridge CB2 2RU, UK
40 West 20th Street, New York, NY 10011–4211, USA
10 Stamford Road, Oakleigh, VIC 3166, Australia
Ruiz de Alarcón 13, 28014 Madrid, Spain
Dock House, The Waterfront, Cape Town 8001, South Africa

http://www.cambridge.org

First published 1999
Reprinted 2001

Printed in Great Britain at the University Press, Cambridge

Typeface Adobe Minion 10.25/12.75pt and FF Dax *System* QuarkXPress®   [SE]

A catalogue record for this book is available from the British Library

Library of Congress Cataloguing in Publication data

Psychiatric and behavioural disorders in developmental disabilities
and mental retardation / edited by Nick Bouras.
    p.   cm/
Includes index.
ISBN 0 521 64395 3 (pbk.)
1. Mentally handicapped–Mental health. 2. Mentally handicapped–
Mental health services. I. Bouras, Nick.
[DNLM: 1. Mental Retardation. 2. Mental Disorders.
3. Developmental Disabilities. 4. Behavior. WM 307.M5P974 1999]
RC451.4.M47P77   1999
616.89–dc21
DNLM/DLC
for Library of Congress   99-38465 CIP

ISBN 0 521 64395 3 paperback

Contents

Contributors

DAVID ALLEN
Honorary Lecturer and Consultant
    Clinical Psychologist
Cardiff Community Healthcare NHS
    Trust
Welsh Centre for Learning Disabilities
University of Wales College of Medicine
Meridian Court
North Road
Cardiff CF4 3BL
UK

BETSEY A. BENSON
Adjunct Associate Professor of Psychology
Nisonger Center
Ohio State University
1581 Dodd Drive
Columbus
Ohio 43210-1296
USA

JOAN BEASLEY
Director
Robert D. Sovner Behavioral Healthcare
    Resource Center
99 Rosewoood Drive
Suite 240
Danvers
Massachusetts 01923
USA

NICK BOURAS
Senior Lecturer
Mental Health in Learning Disabilities
    Centre
York Clinic
Guy's Hospital
47 Weston Street
London SE1 3RR
UK

NANCY N. CAIN
Clinical Associate Professor of Psychiatry
Department of Psychiatry
University of Rochester School of
    Medicine and Dentistry
Box 671
601 Elmwood Avenue
Rochester
New York 14642
USA

PAUL CAMBRIDGE
Senior Lecturer in Learning Disability and
    Service Development Consultant
Tizard Centre
University of Kent at Canterbury
Canterbury
Kent CT2 7LZ
UK

DAVID CLARKE
Senior Lecturer in Developmental
    Psychiatry
University of Birmingham Department of
    Psychiatry
Queen Elizabeth Psychiatric Hospital
Mindelsohn Way
Birmingham B15 2QZ
UK

RICHARD A. COLLACOTT
Consultant Psychiatrist
Western Isles Hospital
Stornoway
Isle of Lewis HS1 2AF
UK

SALLY-ANN COOPER
Consultant in Learning Disabilities
    Psychiatry
Rockingham Forest NHS Trust
St Mary's Hospital
London Road
Kettering
Northants NN15 7PW
UK

ARTHUR J. DALTON
Co-director
Center for Aging Policy Studies
New York State Institute for Basic
    Research in Developmental
    Disabilities
1050 Forest Hill Road
Staten Island
New York 10314
USA

PHILIP W. DAVIDSON
Professor of Pediatrics and Psychiatry
Strong Center for Developmental
    Disabilities
University of Rochester School of
    Medicine and Dentistry
Box 671
601 Elmwood Avenue
Rochester
New York 14642
USA

KENNETH DAY
Honorary Consultant Psychiatrist
Northgate & Prudhoe NHS Trust
Northgate Hospital
Morpeth
Northumberland NE61 3BP
UK

ANTON DOSEN
President
European Association of Mental Health in
    Mental Retardation
Niew Spraeland
Wanssumseweg 14-Oostrum
Postbus 5029
5800 GA Venray
The Netherlands

ELISABETH M. DYKENS
Assistant Professor
Neuropsychiatric Institute
Division of Child and Adolescent
    Psychiatry
University of California
760 Westwood Plaza
Los Angeles
California 90024-1759
USA

ERIC EMERSON
Professor of Clinical Psychology in
    Intellectual Disability
Hester Adrian Research Centre
University of Manchester
Oxford Road
Manchester M13 9PL
UK

DAVID FELCE
Professor of Research in Learning
    Disabilities and Director of Applied
    Research Unit
Welsh Centre for Learning Disabilities
University of Wales College of Medicine
Meridian Court
North Road
Cardiff CF4 3BL
UK

MARK FLEISHER
Assistant Professor of Psychiatry
Creighton-Nebraska Department of
    Psychiatry
Division of Adult Psychiatry
600 South 42nd Street
PO Box 985575
Omaha
Nebraska 68198-5575
USA

ROBERT J. FLETCHER
Executive Director
National Association for the Dually
    Diagnosed (NADD)
132 Fair Street
Kingston
New York 12401-4802
USA

CHRISTOPHER GILLBERG
Professor of Child and Adolescent
    Psychiatry
University of Göteborg
Annedals Clinics
S-413 45 Göteborg
Sweden

ERNEST GRALTON
Senior Registrar
Trecare NHS Trust
57 Pydar Street
Truro
Cornwall TR1 2SS
UK

CHRIS HATTON
Research Fellow
Hester Adrian Research Centre
University of Manchester
Oxford Road
Manchester M13 9PL
UK

SUSAN M. HAVERCAMP
Doctoral Candidate
Nisonger Center
Ohio State University
1581 Dodd Drive
Columbus
Ohio 43210-1296
USA

JESSICA A. HELLINGS
Assistant Professor and Director of Mental
    Retardation/Autism Program in
    Psychiatry
The University of Kansas
Schiefelbusch Institute for Lifespan
    Studies
1052 Dole Human Development Centre
Lawrence
Kansas 66045
USA

JOHN HILLERY
Associate Director
University College Dublin
Centre for the Study of Developmental
    Disabilities
Roebuck Castle
Belfield
Dublin 4
Ireland

ROBERT M. HODAPP
Associate Professor
Graduate School of Education
University of California
405 Hilgard Avenue
Los Angeles
California 90095-1521
USA

JOHN W. JACOBSON
Director
Independent Living in the Capital
    District, Inc.
627 Plymouth Avenue
Schenectady
New York 12308-3507
USA

MATTHEW P. JANICKI
Director
Bureau of Aging and Special Populations
New York State Office of Mental
    Retardation and Developmental
    Disabilities
44 Holland Avenue
Albany
New York 12229-0001
USA

CHRIS KIERNAN
Professor
Hester Adrian Research Centre
University of Manchester
Oxford Road
Manchester M13 9PL
UK

MARY LINDSEY
Consultant Psychiatrist
Trecare NHS Trust
57 Pydar Street
Truro
Cornwall TR1 2SS
UK

JONATHAN MASON
Researcher
Tizard Centre
University of Kent
Canterbury
Kent CT2 7LZ
UK

DANIELLE MORRIS
Clinical Assistant Professor of Psychiatry
Strong Center for Developmental
    Disabilities
University of Rochester School of
    Medicine and Dentistry
Box 671
601 Elmwood Avenue
Rochester
New York 14642
USA

STEVE MOSS
Senior Research Fellow
Hester Adrian Research Centre
University of Manchester
Oxford Road
Manchester M13 9PL
UK

DECLAN MURPHY
Professor of Psychiatry and Brain
    Maturation
Department of Psychological Medicine
Institute of Psychiatry
De Crespigny Park
Denmark Hill
London SE5 8AF
UK

GLYNIS MURPHY
Reader in the Applied Psychology of
    Learning Disability
Tizard Centre
University of Kent
Canterbury
Kent CT2 7LZ
UK

R. MATTHEW REESE
Assistant Professor and Director of
    Training
Child Development Unit
The University of Kansas
Schiefelbusch Institute for Lifespan
    Studies
1052 Dole Human Development Center
Lawrence
Kansas 66045
USA

DENE ROBERTSON
Lecturer
Department of Psychological Medicine
Institute of Psychiatry
De Crespigny Park
Denmark Hill
London SE5 8AF
UK

STEPHEN R. SCHROEDER
Professor and Director
Schiefelbusch Institute for Lifespan
    Studies
The University of Kansas
1052 Dole Human Development Center
Lawrence
Kansas 66045
USA

CHRISSOULA STAVRAKAKI
Professor of Psychiatry
737 Manor Avenue
Ottawa
Ontario K1M 0E4
Canada

PETER STURMEY
Chief Psychologist
San Antonio State School
PO Box 14700-700
San Antonio
Texas 78214-0700
USA

BRUCE J. TONGE
Professor of Developmental Psychiatry
Monash University Centre for
    Developmental Psychiatry
Melbourne
Victoria 3168
Australia

SIEGFRIED TUINIER
Psychiatrist
Department of Biological Psychiatry
Vincent van Gogh Institute for Psychiatry
Stationsweg 46
5803 AC Venray
The Netherlands

WILLEM M. A. VERHOEVEN
Neuropsychiatrist and Director of
    Residency Training
Vincent van Gogh Institute for Psychiatry
Stationsweg 46
5803 AC Venray
The Netherlands

Foreword

Looking back over the past 25 years we can see a huge amelioration of life circumstances of individuals with developmental disabilities and mental retardation. Housing, education, social engagement, work and leisure opportunities have improved dramatically and there have been significant developments in ethical and legal issues. Society now recognizes and appreciates the abilities, skills and needs of people with mental retardation, who are increasingly accepted as full members of the community. Over the last ten years, the process of community and social integration has identified quality of life as an important aspect in relation to the care and support of people with mental retardation. In this context, optimal physical and mental health are essential prerequisites for a satisfactory quality of life for people with mental retardation.

In different countries around the world, professionals in the fields of mental health and mental retardation have emphasized the necessity for a more systematic way to research service provision for people with mental retardation. A decade ago, it was important to prove that psychiatric disorders existed among this population, and that the members of it were entitled, as any other group, to have access to mental health professionals. Currently, attention is focused on the natural process of mental health disorders, their differences and respective treatment approaches.

Professionals, researchers and academics have become aware that the knowledge acquired from studies in the general population is not sufficient to understand the complexities of mental health disorders in people with developmental disabilities and mental retardation. New studies and new methodologies have emerged, targeting specific aspects and groups of people with mental retardation.

There is now a growing recognition of the need to respond more adequately to mental health problems of people with developmental disabilities and mental retardation. A number of countries allocate significant resources to specialist services, and promote training and research. In some countries this interest resulted in the establishment of national and international associations such as the National Association for Dually Diagnosed (NADD) in the USA and the European Association for Mental Health in Mental Retardation (MHMR). These associations have been organizing scientific meetings, professional exchanges and educational activities, and have provided the impetus for the cultivation of ideas resulting in the development of appropriate specialist services for people with mental retardation and mental health needs.

Education and dissemination of modern knowledge relating to mental health problems of people with developmental disabilities and mental retardation are necessary for all disciplines involved in the care of this population, including all mental health professionals.

A number of professional books on this issue have appeared in the last decade. One of these books was *Mental Health in Mental Retardation – Recent Advances and Practice*, published in 1994 and edited by Nick Bouras. The book has been widely read internationally, and four years after its publication Nick Bouras decided to edit a new book dealing with recent progress and developments. In the book you have in your hands, the editor has gathered contributions from distinguished scientists in mental retardation and mental health from Europe, USA, Canada and Australia. This wide-ranging text offers a comprehensive review of all the aspects of the psychiatric and behavioural disorders in developmental disabilities and mental retardation. It is extensively referenced and is divided into five parts.

The first part presents the concept of developmental disabilities and mental retardation in relation to the use of the international classification systems of psychiatric disorders. It also considers recent trends towards alternative approaches to classification of mental disorders. A more focused perspective on the assessment of mental health problems in people with mainly mild developmental disabilities is outlined and directions of future research are highlighted. A rather different approach is offered for the assessment of people with severe developmental disabilities who also have challenging behaviour and may or may not have a mental illness. The high expectations based on the spectacular developments of neuroimaging offer a scientific ground for the future.

The second part deals with some of the specific syndromes that are associated with psychiatric and behavioural problems in people with developmental disabilities. These include autism, behavioural phenotypes and self-injurious behaviour. In all of these areas there has been significant research progress over the last few years. There is also a chapter focusing on dementia in people with developmental disabilities, presenting the current care practices as applied particularly in the USA.

The third part presents a clinical perspective of the broad range of psychiatric diagnoses and psychopathology from childhood to old age in people with developmental disabilities. This is an area in which developments continue to progress and more research is forthcoming. Multiprofessional collaboration based on the concepts and issues discussed in the first part of this book is very promising. An extensive review is provided of issues, literature and the most recent research findings relating to people with developmental disabilities who break the law and offend.

The different therapeutic and treatment approaches for people with developmental disabilities and mental retardation who also have psychiatric and behavioural problems are covered in the fourth part of the book. Clinical management techniques and service responses for the wide range of problems and disabilities are comprehensively covered from different perspectives. Undoubtedly there have been major developments in this area and current research has inspired a flavour of optimism for the use of some of the described techniques for people with severe developmental disabilities and behavioural disorders. Current advances in psychopharmacology are also promising and it is hoped that the ongoing research will confirm their effectiveness as has been happening in other branches of medicine, including general psychiatry.

The final part covers policy and service systems issues for people with developmental disabilities and psychiatric or behavioural problems. This is probably one of the most remarkable areas of progress during this century, with significant advances in community-based services, care management systems, quality and outcomes monitoring and staff and professional training.

In my opinion, Nick Bouras has succeeded in this book in gathering a substantial part of current knowledge of psychiatric disorders among individuals with developmental disabilities and mental retardation. I am sure that the book will fulfil an important task of dissemination of this knowledge among the professionals working in the field of mental health and mental retardation.

This publication will, without doubt, be valued by all who seek an authoritative yet readable account of modern ideas and practices for people with developmental disabilities and mental retardation who also have psychiatric and behavioural problems.

Anton Dosen

Preface

The recent advances in the diagnosis, treatment and delivery of services for people with developmental disabilities and mental retardation who have additional mental health needs require regular documentation and critical appraisal.

This book links research findings with clinical knowledge, thereby placing strong emphasis on the scientific evidence for and against various concepts, theories, treatment methods and practices. Contributors are drawn from the broad international, multiprofessional context of the fields of developmental disabilities, mental retardation and mental health. Some topics are approached from different points of view, offering a variety of perspectives and dimensions.

Though research advances continue constantly to appear in our areas of professional interests, more work is required to bridge the gap between developmental disabilities and psychiatry, psychology, health and social care. More studies using randomized samples for therapeutic and treatment methods are needed to assess clinical effectiveness. Also, vigorous evaluation of service models and international comparative research will facilitate further advances and practices.

The terms developmental disabilities and mental retardation are indiscriminately used throughout the book according to author's preference.

Thanks are owed to all contributors, to Helen Costello for her invaluable assistance in helping me with the editing, and to Dr Jocelyn Foster, of Cambridge University Press, for her support and encouragement.

NICK BOURAS

Part 1 **Concepts, classification and assessment**

1 Classification: concepts, progress and future

PETER STURMEY

Introduction

Classification has long been perceived as a controversial issue: label-ling people, especially people with mental retardation, has often been seen as pejorative. The use of people-first language, the elimination of unnecessary labels, the demedicalization of terminology, and the use of more sensitive language in professional writing all reflect this perspective. Classification is also a marker of professional boundaries. Physicians and some researchers tend to use and value classification. Advocates, behaviour analysts and some non-medical professionals tend to be critical of classification and eschew its use. Throughout the nineteenth and early twentieth centuries, psychiatrists themselves were often opposed to classification. One of the earliest systems of psychiatric classification did not originate from within the medical pro-fession. It came about in 1918 as a method of accounting for the use of hospi-tal beds for the census (Grob, 1991). Psychiatric classification is seen by some as the unnecessary medicalization of life's problems. The development of *The Diagnostic and Statistical Manual*, fourth edition (DSM-IV, American Psychiatric Association, 1994) has been extensively criticised, mainly on the grounds that many psychiatric diagnoses are the creations of committees. When DSM-IV expanded its codes to include 'Other conditions that may be a focus of clinical attention', it encompassed a broad array of problems including relationship problems, abuse and neglect, non-compliance with treatment, academic achievement, occupational, identity, religious, accultu-ration and phase of life problems. Some view expansion of the scope of DSM-IV as a legitimate reflection of psychiatry, whilst others view it as the expansion of billable experiences to include almost all of life's problems. On the other hand, some psychiatrists and researchers regard psychiatric diag-noses as the newly discovered illnesses of the brain. These illnesses are the basis for biological treatment. In defence of this position, some have noted that not all physical illnesses are clearly defined in terms of aetiology. Thus, some of these new brain illnesses may also have the same provisional status of many physical illnesses (Mindham, Scadding & Cawley, 1992).

Functions of classification

Classification of psychiatric disorders serves several purposes. DSM-IV notes that classification is used for medical record keeping, data collection, retrieval and compilation of statistical information, communicating with third parties, such as insurers and governmental agencies, and is the basis for eligibility and reimbursement for psychiatric services. Classification is the basis for communication between different professional groups and non-professionals. It is used in many different contexts such as research, education of the patient and significant others, and between medical staff. Classification also serves the purpose of providing summary labels for multiple presenting symptoms, aetiology and prognosis. It is apparently the basis for pharmacological intervention. Differential diagnosis is the theoretical and professional basis for differential use of psychotropic medication. Classification can also be used for legal purposes, such as treatment consent, determining ability to participate in legal proceedings, and ability to participate in contracts (Bersoff, Glass & Blain, 1994). It can also be used in service planning, monitoring and evaluation.

Issues in classification

General issues

Reliability and validity

A classification scheme must be both reliable and valid. Reliability refers to several related, but distinguishable, properties of a measurement system. Measures that have good reliability are perceived as objective and public; measures that are unreliable are seen as subjective and may merely reflect the opinion of each observer. Inter-rater reliability refers to agreement between two or more independent observers. Test–retest reliability refers to agreement on diagnosis over time. Internal consistency refers to the extent that individual items or criteria that are supposed to measure the same disorder tend to be correlated closely together. For example, if two clinicians agree that nine out of ten people meet the criteria for depression, that eight of ten meet the criteria two weeks apart, and that all the items measuring depression are closely correlated with each other, then the measure of depression would be said to be reliable.

Sturmey (1993) reviewed empirical studies of the reliability of making psychiatric diagnoses using either psychometric checklists or unstructured clinical interviews and record reviews. Extensive data were found on the reliability of checklists of psychiatric symptoms and behaviours in people with mental retardation (Aman, 1991; Sturmey, Reed & Corbett, 1991). Although data were variable, many checklists proved highly reliable in measuring individual symptoms and the total number of symptoms. However, trained raters are often needed to achieve reliability. Furthermore, reliably measuring symptoms is only one step towards making a diagnosis. Typically, checklists measure current symptoms, but do not provide a history or exclude other causes for these symptoms. Reliability data on diagnosis based on unstructured clinical interviews and record reviews were largely absent from the research literature. This is an important omission, since this is typical clinical practice. Clinical interviewing has received relatively little attention, although the Psychiatric Assessment Schedule for Adults with a Developmental Disability (PAS-ADD), an interview schedule for use with adults with mental retardation (Moss et al., 1993), addresses specific obstacles to reliability and validity. Clinical interviewing for people with mental retardation is discussed further in Chapter 2.

Validity is a more subtle quality. It refers to the extent that a measure or concept is psychologically real, meaningful or useful. For example, validity can refer to the degree to which a diagnosis predicts other important variables such as response to psychotropic medication or social behaviour associated with a diagnosis. Validity has generally been neglected in the literature on diagnosis in people with mental retardation (Sturmey, 1993), although some studies on this aspect of validity have been published (Sturmey & Bertman, 1995; Sturmey et al., 1996).

Reliability and validity are closely related as reliability is a necessary, but not sufficient, condition for validity. The interplay of reliability and validity can be illustrated by the example of the transition from DSM-II to DSM-III which was heavily influenced by the criticism that DSM-II was unreliable and subjective (Frances et al., 1990). In response to these criticisms, DSM-III adopted clearer, more operationalized criteria and decision rules. However, this approach has been criticized because, although it may improve reliability, validity can be compromised (Zwick, 1983). The elimination of unreliable items and the rewording of items to enhance reliability can all cumulatively change the meaning or validity of the diagnosis being made. For example, Volkmar et al. (1992) compared the application of DSM-III, DSM-III-R, International Classification of Diseases (ICD-10) and clinical diagnosis of autism. They found that DSM-III-R criteria consistently over-diagnosed autism. Szatmari (1992) reviewed five empirical studies on the application of DSM-III-R criteria for autism and reached similar conclusions. Although three of the five studies had good reliability, as shown by kappas (the proportions of agreement corrected for chance agreement) of greater than 0.6, there was evidence of over-diagnosis of autism with DSM-III-R. A second example relates to the validity of diagnostic criteria for psychotic disorders. Farmer et al. (1992) compared the application of five sets of operationalized diagnostic criteria for psychotic illness. They showed that although reliability was uniformly high, agreement between the five sets of criteria was poor, suggesting that some of the sets of criteria were not valid. Thus, at times validity can be sacrificed on the altar of reliability.

Others have voiced more general concerns related to this operational approach to psychiatric diagnosis (Farmer et al., 1992). Operational definitions narrow the collection of information compared to a regular clinical situation. Important information such as psychiatric history, response to medication and clinical impression is excluded. The predetermined sets of categories may tend to force a significant number of patients into default 'not otherwise specified' categories. Many operationalized criteria do not take into account the severity of the symptoms. Thus, if the severity criteria are set low, many people may inappropriately meet lifetime diagnostic criteria even though their problems are mild and transitory. Thus, operationalizing diagnostic criteria may narrow the clinician's focus of attention away from important facts that might otherwise be attended to.

The issue of the reliability and validity of psychiatric diagnosis – still a live issue in general psychiatry – continues to be of major concern to practitioners and researchers working in the field of dual diagnosis (mental retardation and mental illness). (See Chapter 2 for further discussion regarding validity and reliability.) Key clinical questions such as whether a person's aggressive behaviour is a symptom of mania, impulse control, or a learned behaviour, and the question of the choice between different treatments implied by these differing diagnoses, reflect the uncertainty over diagnostic issues in people with mental retardation.

Diagnosis of mental retardation

Mental retardation is typically defined by some operationalization of three criteria: low intelligence, deficits in adaptive behaviour, and the appearance of these problems during the developmental period. Definitions based on these criteria have been proposed by professional societies, research and law. Over the years, the operationalization of mental retardation has varied radically. For example, in the 1960s the American Association on Mental Retardation changed its intelligence quotient (IQ) criterion from one to two standard deviations below the average; overnight, hundreds of thousands of Americans were no longer mentally retarded! Currently, somewhat differing definitions of mental retardation are available from the American Psychological Association, federal and state laws, and laws from different countries.

A further complication is that the standardization of IQ tests is imperfect. There is a general upward drift of population scores over time (Sattler, 1982; Bower & Hayes, 1995) so that the cut-off of 70 is inappropriately low when the standardization of the test is old. Thus, at times some people with mild mental retardation will not meet the IQ diagnostic criterion because of the drift in test norms. Another corollary of the drift in IQ test norms is that when people are retested using a current re-standardized test, their apparent IQs may drop, sometimes substantially. This is not evidence of dementia. Rather, it reflects the upward drift in the norms of the old test and the more accurate norms on a re-standardized test.

None of these changes affects the diagnosis of severe or profound mental retardation to any significant degree. Most people with severe or profound mental retardation present to services before the age of 5 years because of additional disabilities. Their developmental and educational achievements are clearly delayed compared to average children. However, these factors can greatly affect the diagnosis of mental retardation in people with borderline and mild mental retardation. Typically, people with borderline and mild mental retardation do not present to services until the school years and some do not use services until the early teenage years. On leaving school, a significant proportion of individuals disappear from mental retardation services. Some apparently never use any mental health or mental retardation services again (Richardson et al., 1984). Some may present to mental retardation services, mental health services or the criminal justice system at a later date during periods of stress. Thus, people with borderline and mild mental retardation and additional mental health problems are not found exclusively in mental retardation services. Depending upon the presenting problem, the clinician and a variety of other circumstances, they may or may not be recognized as having a developmental disability. It is unclear which kind of agency should serve this population. Several court cases have found that people with mental retardation in the mental health system have been inappropriately served and have mandated that they should be served in mental retardation service (Calhoun, Dudley & Bradley, 1993). However, there is no professional consensus on this point. The issue of distinguishing between people with and without mental retardation empirically who also have mental health problems has been addressed by Kay (1989). A good developmental and school history can often be helpful in order to evaluate whether or not current problems of low intelligence and adaptive behaviour were evident during the developmental period. Diagnosis of borderline and mild mental retardation, both during development and in adults presenting to services, remains a complex issue.

Development of psychiatric classification

There have been two approaches to developing psychiatric classification: rational and empirical. The rational approach is exemplified by the transition from DSM-III-R to DSM-IV. DSM-IV was developed through a three-stage process (Frances et al., 1990) of literature reviews (Widiger et al., 1990), analysis of unpublished data sets, and field trials (Kline et al., 1993). Committees were established to co-ordinate this effort for each of the major diagnostic areas. This process has been criticized for being open to non-scientific influences such as socio-political pressure to make DSM compatible with the ICD (Malt, 1987; Frances, Widiger & Pincus, 1989; Thompson & Pincus, 1989), possible excessive influence of individual committee members (Frances et al., 1990), and a lack of empirical basis for many committee decisions (Zimmerman, 1988). Some have criticized the development of DSM-IV as being over-hasty and motivated by financial considerations on the part of the American Psychological Association (Zimmerman, 1988; Zimmerman et al., 1991). Others have portrayed the development of DSM as a power struggle between the old psychoanalytic guard and the new biologically oriented psychiatrists (Kirk & Kutchins, 1992). Kirk and Kutchins have argued that the scientific basis for revision of DSM was, in fact, weak and that the science was poorly done, but well sold. Some of these concerns are validated by findings of the opinions and practices of clinicians. A survey of over 500 practitioners showed that about one-third would stop using DSM if they were not required to do so. Most respondents did not use all of the multi-axis diagnostic system and most doubted the validity of some diagnoses. Many reported that their patients did not meet the diagnostic criteria for the diagnoses on their records (Jampala, Sierles & Taylor, 1986). This process is also limited for practitioners in services for people with mental retardation and the field trials did not examine the use of the new diagnostic criteria with this population (Kline et al., 1993; Frick et al., 1994).

A second approach to classification of psychiatric and behavioural disorders is an empirical approach. Empirical approaches attempt to avoid any presupposed ideas of classification based on psychiatric nosologies such as DSM or ICD. Rather, they take assessment of symptoms or behaviours and subject them to statistical analysis to uncover groupings of behaviours or subjects that are present in nature. A good example of this approach comes from Farmer et al. (1994), who used assessments of 862 people living in two administratively defined catchment areas of London. These subjects were assessed on 28 variables, mostly rated on Likert scales, which measured physical and sensory disabilities, adaptive and maladaptive behaviours. The two data sets were subjected to factor analysis. In both cases three factors were revealed. The three factors reflected physical disabilities, general adaptive behaviours and behaviour disorders. Thus, the authors called the three factors Physical, Lack of Skills, and Behaviour. A cluster analysis was performed using the scores on these three factors to group similar subjects together. Cluster analysis revealed ten clusters. These clusters were then validated by comparing the staffing levels and place of residence of the people in that cluster. For example, cluster 10 was identified as the least disabled group with few behavioural problems, few physical disabilities and good skills, whereas cluster 6 was identified as having many physical disabilities, a low level of skill, but few behaviour problems. Nearly 90 per cent of people in cluster 10 needed no supervision or only intermittent supervision, whereas 94 per cent of people in cluster 6 needed full-time supervision.

An empirical classification has some advantages over rational approaches. It tends to be data driven and is more likely to resolve problems using data rather than a committee consensus. This approach may uncover or confirm clinical impressions of new symptom clusters or groupings of subjects. Empirical classification tends to be hypothesis driven, but develops very slowly. This approach requires many studies, often using large data sets and independent replications. On the other hand, an empirical approach also has limitations. It can be limited by the pool of items placed in the analysis. For example, in the study by Farmer et al. (1994), behaviour disorders came out as a single undifferentiated factor. Many empirical studies using a broader range of items have uncovered a more complex factor structure for behavioural and psychiatric symptoms in people with developmental disabilities (Aman, 1991). Another potential limitation of empirical approaches to classification is that many of the statistical analyses require data sets to have certain statistical properties in order for the analyses to be valid. Sometimes these problems compromise the interpretation of the results. Finally, an empirical approach tends to downplay the role of theory. The generation of items includes many important theoretical assumptions related to what might be measured and the purpose of the instrument. For example, a researcher must decide whether a behaviour scale should include only narrow, observable items such as 'cries' that might apparently avoid the issue of the cause of the observed behaviour, or, should they include broader, more inferential items such as 'depressed mood' that might give clues as to the psychiatric basis of the observed behaviour. If one takes the latter course, then one begins to make assumptions about the organization of the observed behaviour.

There have been some occasions on which rational and empirical approaches have converged. Edelbrock and Costello (1988) found good agreement on the presence of attention deficit disorder, conduct disorder, and depression/dysthymia between the Child Behavior Checklist, an empirically derived measure of behaviour, and the National Institute of Mental Health Diagnostic Interview Schedule for Children, which was based upon DSM-III criteria. This finding attests to the construct validity of these diagnoses as they were measured in different ways and were derived from very different sources.

Issues specific to people with mental retardation

Diagnostic process

Sovner (1986) reviewed four processes that can influence the making of a diagnosis when working with people with mental retardation. *Intellectual distortion* refers to concrete thinking and impaired communication skills that can lead to poor communication from the person concerning their own experience. *Psychosocial masking* refers to impoverished social skills and life experiences that can lead to an unsophisticated presentation of a psychiatric disorder that could be missed. Psychosocial masking could also lead to mistaking nervousness or silliness for psychiatric symptoms. *Cognitive disintegration* refers to stress-induced disruption of information processing that can present as bizarre behaviour and psychotic symptoms and be mistaken for schizophrenia. *Baseline exaggeration* refers to a general increase in pre-existing cognitive deficits and maladaptive behaviours that can make interpretation of presenting symptoms difficult.

A fifth diagnostic process is *overshadowing*. The label of mental retardation can overshadow co-existing psychiatric problems and can cause practitioners to miss the presence of psychopathology. For example, a person with profound mental retardation who is very withdrawn and asocial may be less likely to be labelled as depressed than a person with average intelligence. Overshadowing has been reported for diagnoses such as schizophrenia, personality disorder and phobias and may be influenced by factors such as degree of mental retardation, clinician experience and professional background (Spengler, Strohmer & Prout, 1990).

Finally, Hurley (1996) has listed a number of sources of confusion regarding the diagnosis of psychotic disorders, although some of these problems may be more general and not specific to this diagnosis. Hurley notes that developmentally appropriate phenomena such as talking to oneself, solitary fantasy play, and imaginary friends can all be mistaken for psychopathology. She also notes that adults with mental retardation may have a lifetime of learning to try to pass for normal (Edgerton, 1967) and may learn to monitor others for responses that indicate their behaviour is perceived as unusual.

Functional explanations of presenting problems

In services for people with mental retardation, as in child and adolescent psychiatry, the user does not necessarily present the problem. It is more likely that third parties such as family members or staff will present the complaint; and they are not likely to complain about a psychiatric disorder, but about a symptom or behaviour that they find irritating, threatening or discomforting. Thus, a 40-year-old adult with Down syndrome will not present with memory loss and poor concentration due to early Alzheimer's disease. Instead, staff may complain that the person has become non-compliant at the workshop and incontinent. This issue is further complicated because such problems do not clearly indicate a specific psychiatric disorder. The previous example also might reflect depression or an anxiety disorder. Another complication is that these presenting problems may reflect environmental factors leading to a learned behaviour disorder. Thus, the increase in non-compliance and incontinence might reflect a change in trainer at work from a skilled to an unskilled trainer who does not keep the person on task and who inadvertently reinforces the behaviour problems by allowing him not to work when he complains. The change in behaviour may merely reflect a change in work task from a familiar, easy task to an effortful, unfamiliar task. A final complication is that third parties may seek out low-effort solutions, such as a pill and an occasional medical appointment. They are less likely to undertake extensive analysis of the environment, including their own inappropriate practices, that might be contributing to the problem, and subsequently to engage in effortful retraining of the problem behaviour.

The interplay of functional and psychiatric explanations is further complicated because the presence of a clear and valid diagnosis does not exclude functional explanations for presenting problems. For example, Lesch–Nyhan syndrome is as good a medical diagnosis as can be found anywhere. Lesch–Nyhan syndrome is caused by an X-linked recessive gene that results in an inherited, complete deficiency in hypoxanthine–guanine phosphoribosyltransferase that is associated with a syndrome of intellectual impairment, neurological impairments such as hypertonicity, and a characteristic behavioural syndrome of self-injurious behaviour involving biting of the lips and fingers (Baumeister & Frye, 1985). Although there is a good understanding of the organic basis of the disorder, pharmacological interventions are of limited use. Observation of self-injurious behaviour shows that it is under the social control of others. Some people with Lesch–Nyhan syndrome are highly manipulative. Their organically caused self-injurious behaviour is mediated by social processes. Further, it is responsive to behavioural interventions such as time out and positive reinforcement for its absence (Anderson, Dancis & Alpert, 1978; Buzas, Ayllon & Collins, 1981). Even when a psychiatric diagnosis does clearly indicate a pharmacological intervention, psychiatric symptoms can still take on functional significance.

People with severe and profound mental retardation

Many believe that the presentation of mental disorders in people with borderline to moderate mental retardation is broadly similar in form to the way mental disorders present in the general population. There is some evidence and clinical wisdom that the presentation of a disorder may be simpler and more concrete than in the general population. For example, delusions may be simpler and more concrete compared to those of people of average intelligence (Meadows et al., 1991). Thus, there appears to be some agreement that there is no qualitative difference between the presentation of mental disorders in people with borderline to moderate mental retardation and in the general population.

In contrast, the diagnosis of psychiatric disorders in people with severe and profound mental retardation presents special challenges to clinicians. The person's premorbid behaviour may be highly restricted. Many maladaptive behaviours, such as stereotypies, poor social skills, bizarre language and withdrawal, may have been present for extensive portions of the person's life. Further, the person may have no ability to communicate his or her mental state, which may have to be inferred from observation of his or her behaviour, third party reports of behaviour, and their inferences from their observations.

Because of their limited repertoire of behaviour, many people with severe and profound mental retardation cannot meet DSM-IV criteria for mental disorders. There are also many other explanations, such as medical problems, programmatic variables, and functional/learning explanations that have to be considered. For example, the DSM-IV criteria for major depressive disorder require five or more of nine symptoms concurrently for at least two weeks. Depressed mood and loss of interest must be present. Certain alternate diagnoses, physical conditions and bereavement must also be excluded. Finally, the symptoms must cause 'clinically significant distress or impairment' (American Psychiatric Association, 1994). A review of some of the problems of applying the nine criteria to this population is found in Table 1.1. Other problems include judgements concerning 'clinically significant distress or impairment' in people who cannot report distress verbally and whose premorbid level of impairment is already considerable.

One solution to this problem has been the development of behavioural equivalents to psychiatric symptoms that can be used both for diagnosis and to track response to intervention. Lowery and Sovner (1992) developed an observational system to track rapid cycling bipolar disorder in two men with severe mental retardation. Similar uses of multiple observable behaviours to develop clinical hypotheses and track psychiatric disorders in people with severe and profound mental retardation can be found in King (1993) and Bodfish and Madison (1993) for obsessive compulsive disorder, and in Jawed et al. (1993) for depression and pica.

Collecting, processing and using diagnostic information

A diagnosis should serve as a framework for the collection of further assessment information, clinical decision making and intervention. Singh et al. (1991) recommended a six-stage process of collecting information including adaptive behaviour and intellectual functioning; screening on general measures of psychopathology such as the Psychopathology Instrument for Mentally Retarded Adults (PIMRA) (Matson, 1988) or structured interviews; clinical interviews; rating scales and checklists for specific disorders; direct observation and experimental analysis of behaviour; and laboratory measures. Many clinicians note the importance of reviewing previous history and response to previous psychotropic medications as part of an initial diagnostic work-up.

Frequently, diagnostic reformulations are necessary in the light of new information, revision of the validity of existing information, and response to psychotropic medication. Although some attention has been paid to the initial diagnosis, it is also important to be aware of the subsequent role that other factors play in the clinical process. Clinicians are often asked to respond to behavioural crises with medication, and can be caught in a trap of being perceived as 'doing nothing' if they fail to prescribe upon request.

Table 1.1 Some of the potential problems in applying DSM-IV criteria for major depressive disorder to people with severe and profound mental retardation

Criteria	Potential problems
1. Depressed mood by either subjective report or observations by others	Subjective reports not available. Observers have to infer mood from behaviour, which can be unreliable (Clarke, Reed & Sturmey, 1991)
2. Diminished interest or pleasure by subjective report or observations of others	Subjective report not available. Person already has very restricted range of interests. Autistic features may also overshadow depression as explanation for restricted range of interests
3. Significant weight loss when not dieting, or weight gain, or decreased/increased appetite	Medical causes of weight gain must be eliminated. Evaluation of appetite, as a subjective experience, has to be inferred from food refusal or excessive intake. Other explanations such as poor food quality or other aversive aspects of the eating experience should be eliminated
4. Insomnia or hypersomnia	Insomnia may be due to poor staff or parent practices, noise, need to go to the bathroom etc. Daytime sleeping may be due to lack of activities during the day, sedation or physical problems
5. Observable psychomotor agitation	May be due to other psychiatric problems such as mania, hyperactivity, attention deficit disorder etc.; may be learned behaviour, shaped and maintained by parents, staff or peers
6. Fatigue or loss of energy every day	Subjective experience difficult to evaluate and infer from observable behaviour
7. Feelings of worthlessness, excessive or inappropriate guilt	Person cannot report and may not be cognitively able to have these experiences
8. Diminished ability to think or concentrate	Baseline levels already high. Subjective experience cannot be reported and is hard to infer. Other explanations such as sedation and side-effects from other medications such as seizure medications must be eliminated
9. Recurrent thoughts of death, suicide or a suicide plan	May not be able to understand notions of death, suicide, or make a plan

Alternative approaches to diagnostic classification

Psychiatric classification has assumed a very powerful central position within psychiatric and psychological practice, research and media images of psychiatry. Although psychiatric classification is the most commonly used method of communication and guide for intervention, it is not the only approach. In the following section, an alternative model is briefly outlined.

Functional analysis

Haynes and O'Brien (1990, p. 654) define functional analysis as '. . . the identification of important, controllable, causal, functional relationships applicable to a specified set of target behaviours for an individual client . . .'. The identification of variables that are reliably related to a clinically significant problem can identify contingencies, maladaptive practices, provocative situations and inappropriate verbal rules about behaviour. The identification of these variables can be used to guide intervention such as training appropriate, functionally equivalent replacement behaviours, removing stressors, or reprogramming environmental contingencies. Functional analysis has been applied to a wide range of behavioural and psychiatric problems in people with mental retardation and those of average intelligence, including depression, psychosis, anxiety disorders and school refusal (Sturmey, 1996). Functional analysis explicitly eschews consideration of the form of a problem as a guide for intervention. Instead, it uses the function of the problem. Thus, a problem motivated by avoidance of aversive arousal in noisy, crowded situations might be treated by graded exposure, teaching an adaptive, acceptable escape response, or by anxiolytic medication plus exposure to the situation. These treatment strategies would be indicated if the problem was a phobia in a person with autism, or aggression in a chronic psychiatric patient. Functional analysis presents an alternative to traditional classification of psychiatric and behavioural problems in people with mental retardation which disavows any simple mapping of treatment from diagnosis. An example of a functional classification of violence can be found in Eichelman and Hartwig (1993).

Conclusion

Diagnosis and classification of psychiatric disorders in people with mental retardation remain a central area of concern for researchers, clinicians and families alike. Considerable progress has been made in certain areas, such as developing reliable psychometric measures of psychiatric disorders. A beginning has been made in the development of reliable interviews, the application of DSM criteria with people with borderline and moderate mental retardation, the validity of classification and medication usage, and the use of behavioural equivalents of psychiatric disorders in people with severe and profound mental retardation. Other areas remain to be explored. The issues of clinical process, clinical decision making, and the development of standardized diagnostic approaches in people with severe and profound mental retardation continue to be fertile grounds to be explored.

References

Aman, M.G. (1991). *Assessing Psychopathology and Behavior Problems in Persons with Mental Retardation: A Review of Available Instruments.* Rockville, MD: US Department of Health and Human Services.

American Psychiatric Association (1994). *Diagnostic and Statistical Manual of Mental Disorders, Fourth edition.*Washington, DC: American Psychiatric Association.

Anderson, L., Dancis, J. & Alpert, M. (1978). Behavioral contingencies and self-mutilation in Lesch–Nyhan disease. *Journal of Consulting and Clinical Psychology*, **46**, 529–36.

Baumeister, A.A. & Frye, G.D. (1985). The biochemical basis of the behavioral disorder in the Lesch–Nyhan syndrome. *Neuroscience and Biobehavioral Reviews*, **9**, 169–78.

Bersoff, D.N., Glass, D.J. & Blain, N. (1994). Legal issues in the assessment and treatment of individuals with dual diagnosis. *Journal of Consulting and Clinical Psychology*, **62**, 55–62.

Bodfish, J.W. & Madison, J.T. (1993). Diagnosis and fluoxetine treatment of compulsive behavior disorder of adults with mental retardation. *American Journal on Mental Retardation*, **98**, 360–7.

Bower, A. & Hayes, A. (1995). Relations of scores on the Stanford Binet fourth edition of form L-M: concurrent validation study with children who have mental retardation. *American Journal on Mental Retardation*, **99**, 555–63.

Buzas, H.P., Ayllon, T. & Collins, R. (1981). A behavioral approach to eliminate self-mutilative behavior in a Lesch-Nyhan syndrome patient. *The Journal of Mind and Behavior*, **2**, 47–56.

Calhoun, L.M., Dudley, J.R. & Bradley, V.J. (1993). *The Thomas S. Case: Analysis of History, Policy, and Implementation November 1992–February 1993.* Charlotte, NC: University of North Carolina Department of Human Resources.

Clarke, A., Reed, J. & Sturmey, P. (1991). Staff perceptions of sadness among people with mental handicaps. *Journal of Mental Deficiency Research*, **35**, 147–53.

Edelbrock, C. & Costello, A.J. (1988). Convergence between statistically derived behavior problem syndromes and child psychiatric diagnosis. *Journal of Abnormal Child Psychology*, **16**, 219–31.

Edgerton, R.B. (1967). *The Cloak of Competence.* Los Angeles: University of California.

Eichelman, B. & Hartwig, A. (1993). The clinical psychopharmacology of violence. Toward a nosology of human aggressive behavior. *Psychopharmacology Bulletin*, **29**, 57–63.

Farmer, A.E., Wessley, S., Castle, D. & McGuffin, P. (1992). Methodological issues using a polydiagnostic approach to define psychotic illness. *British Journal of Psychiatry*, **161**, 824–30.

Farmer, R., Rhode, J., Bonsall, C. & Emmami, J. (1994). Toward the developmental of a multi – axial classification of people with learning disabilities. *Journal of Intellectual Disabilities Research*, **38**, 587–97.

Frances, A., Pincus, H.A., Widiger, T.A., Davis, W.W., & First, M.B. (1990). DSM-IV: work in progress. *American Journal of Psychiatry*, **147**, 1439–48.

Frances, A.J., Widiger, T.A. & Pincus, H.A. (1989). The development of DSM-IV. *Archives of General Psychiatry*, **46**, 373–5.

Frick, P.J., Lahey, B.B., Applegate, B. et al. (1994). DSM-IV field trials for disruptive behavior disorders: symptom utility estimates. *Journal of the American Academy of Child and Adolescent Psychiatry*, **33**, 529–39.

Grob, G.N. (1991). Origins of DSM – I: a study in appearance and reality. *American Journal of Psychiatry*, **148**, 421–31.

Haynes, S.N. & O'Brien, W.H. (1990). Functional analysis in behavior therapy. *Clinical Psychology Review*, **10**, 649–68.

Hurley, A.D. (1996). The misdiagnosis of hallucinations and delusions in persons with mental retardation: a neurodevelopmental perspective. *Seminars in Neuropsychiatry*, **1**, 122–33.

Jampala, V.C., Sierles, F.S. & Taylor, M.A. (1986). Consumers' views of DSM-II: attitudes and practices of U.S. psychiatrists and 1984 graduating psychiatric residents. *American Journal of Psychiatry*, **143**, 148–53.

Jawed, S.H., Krishnan, V.H.R., Prasher, V.P. & Corbett, J.A. (1993). Worsening of pica as a symptom of depressive illness in a person with severe mental handicap. *British Journal of Psychiatry*, **162**, 835–7.

Kay, S.R. (1989). Cognitive battery for differential diagnosis of mental retardation vs. psychosis. *Research in Developmental Disabilities*, **10**, 251–60.

King, B.H. (1993). Self-injury by people with mental retardation: A compulsive behavior hypothesis. *American Journal of Mental Retardation*, **98**, 93–112.

Kirk, S.A. & Kutchins, H. (1992). *Selling DSM: The Rhetoric of Science in Psychiatry*. White Plains, NY: Aldine de Gruyter.

Kline, M., Snydor-Greenberg, N., Davis, W.W., Pincus, H.A. & Frances, A.J. (1993). Using field trials to evaluate proposed changes in DSM diagnostic criteria. *Hospital and Community Psychiatry*, **4**, 621–3.

Lowery M.A. & Sovner, R. (1992). Severe behavior problems associated with rapid cycling bipolar disorder in two adults with profound mental retardation. *Journal of Intellectual Disabilities Research*, **36**, 269–81.

Malt, U. (1987). DSM–III versus ICD–9 in clinical psychiatric research. *Nord Psyckiatr Tidsskr*, **41**, 437–40.

Matson, J.L. (1988). *The PIMRA Manual*. Overland Park, KS: International Diagnostic Systems.

Meadows, G., Turner, T., Campbell, L. & Lewis, S.W. (1991). Assessing schizophrenia in adults with mental retardation. *British Journal of Psychiatry*, **158**, 103–5.

Mindham, R.H.S., Scadding, J.G. & Cawley, R.H. (1992). Diagnoses are not diseases. *British Journal of Psychiatry*, **161**, 686–91.

Moss, S., Patel, P., Prosser, H. et al. (1993). Psychiatric morbidity in older people with moderate and severe learning disability. *British Journal of Psychiatry*, **163**, 471–80.

Richardson, S.A., Koller, H., Katz, M. & McLaren, J. (1984). Career paths through mental retardation services: an epidemiological perspective. *Applied Research in Mental Retardation*, **5**, 53 –67.

Sattler, J.M. (1982). *Assessment of Children's Intelligence and Special Abilities* 2nd edition. Boston. MA: Allyn & Bacon.

Singh, N.N., Sood, A., Soneklar, N. & Ellis, C.R. (1991). Assessment and diagnosis of mental illness in persons with mental retardation. *Behavior Modification*, **15**, 419–43.

Sovner, R. (1986). Limiting factors in the use of DSM–III with mentally ill/mentally retarded persons. *Psychopharmacology Bulletin*, **22**, 1055–9.

Spengler, P.M., Strohmer, D.C., & Prout, H.T. (1990). Testing the robustness of diagnostic overshadowing. *American Journal on Mental Retardation*, **95**, 204–14.

Sturmey, P. (1993). The use of DSM and ICD criteria in people with mental retardation: a review of empirical studies. *The Journal of Nervous and Mental Diseases*, **181**, 39–42.

Sturmey, P. (1996). *Functional Analysis in Clinical Psychology*. Chichester, UK: Wiley.

Sturmey, P. & Bertman, L.J. (1995). The validity of the Reiss screen for maladaptive behavior. *American Journal on Mental Retardation*, **99**, 201–6.

Sturmey, P., Jamieson, J., Burcham, J.M., Shaw, B. & Bertman, L. (1996). The factor structure of the Reiss Screen for Maladaptive Behaviors in institutional and community populations. *Research in Developmental Disabilities*, **17**, 285–91.

Sturmey, P., Reed, J. & Corbett, J.A. (1991). Psychometric assessment of psychiatric disorders in people with learning difficulty (mental handicap): a review of measures. *Psychological Medicine*, **21**, 143–55.

Szatmari, P. (1992). A review of the DSM–III–R criteria for autistic disorder. *Journal of Autism and Developmental Disorders*, **22**, 507–23.

Thompson, J.W. & Pincus, H. (1989). A crosswalk from DSM–III–R to ICD–9. *American Journal of Psychiatry*, **146**, 1315–19.

Volkmar, F.R., Cicchetti, D.V., Bregman, J. & Cohen, D.J. (1992). Three diagnostic systems for autism: DSM-III, DSM-III-R, and ICD-10. *Journal of Autism and Developmental Disorders*, **22**, 483–92.

Widiger, T.A., Frances, A.J., Pincus, H.A. & Davis, W.W. (1990). DSM–IV literature review: rationale, process and limitations. *Journal of Psychopathology and Behavioral Assessment*, **12**, 189–202.

Zimmerman, M. (1988). Why are we rushing to publish DSM–IV? *Archives of General Psychiatry*, **45**, 1135–8.

Zimmerman, M., Jampala, V.C., Sierles, F.S. & Taylor, M.A. (1991). DSM–IV: a nosology sold before its time? *American Journal of Psychiatry*, **148**, 463–7.

Zwick, R. (1983). Assessing the psychometric properties of psychodiagnostic systems: how do the Research Diagnostic Criteria measure up? *Journal of Consulting and Clinical Psychology*, **51**, 117–31.

2 Assessment: conceptual issues

STEVE MOSS

Introduction

There are many factors that suggest that people with mental retardation are more at risk for developing mental illness than the general population. The potential range of factors is biological, psychological and social, including genetic abnormalities, birth trauma, parental rejection, institutionalization, social stigmatization and lack of friends. Evidence from large-scale studies of morbidity indicates that people with mental retardation have higher rates for psychoses and autism, and a very high rate for challenging behaviour, compared with the general population (Moss, 1995). It is often very difficult to determine the extent to which presenting behaviours are the result of an organic condition, a psychiatric disorder, environmental influences, or a combination of these.

An increasing number of studies is attempting to improve knowledge of the manifestation of mental illness in people with mental retardation, particularly the detection and diagnosis of such conditions. There are, however, a number of important issues concerning (a) the validity of psychiatric classification systems derived for the general population, (b) the validity of a diagnosis when a person has insufficient ability to be interviewed, and (c) the wider social factors that need to be taken into consideration when assessing the complex mental health needs of people with mental retardation.

Case *recognition* is a crucial part of the overall assessment process. Cases that are not detected cannot be assessed and treated. The pathway to psychiatric services places people with mental retardation at a major disadvantage. This is due partly to the inherent difficulty of detecting mental health problems in people with mental retardation, and partly because of the current inadequacy of staff training. Indeed, one of the fundamental limitations of the primary health care system with respect to individuals with mental retardation is that it relies so heavily on a person's ability to recognize and report symptoms of ill-health. People with communication problems may not have the skills to do this, and health care professionals may not have the skills needed to overcome this barrier. Research indicates that there are probably many people with mental retardation who have mental illness but whose problems remain undetected (Patel, Goldberg and Moss, 1993). As a result, they have little prospect of receiving appropriate treatment for their condition.

Assuming the person's mental health problems *have* been recognized, the diagnostic process is still fraught with difficulties. A number of researchers and clinicians have asserted that people with mental retardation manifest the full range of mental health conditions shown by the general population. For example, Eaton and Menolascino (1982) and Reiss (1982) reported surveys of people with mental retardation attending community-based mental health clinics in Nebraska and Chicago, concluding that they are subject to a wide range of emotional disturbances, and that the symptoms of specific psychiatric disturbance are essentially the same for people with and without mental retardation. Sovner and Hurley (1983) similarly concluded that mental illness in this population should not be regarded as fundamentally different from that occurring in non-disabled individuals.

It is apparent, however, that there are many diagnostic issues that have not been sufficiently evaluated to make definitive statements about the prevalence, manifestations, or subjective experiences of mental illness in this population. The linguistic barrier between patient and clinician presents a formidable challenge, and is compounded by the fact that mental disorders often do not have clear-cut definitions. Diagnosis depends on the interaction of a variety of factors: what people say they are experiencing, what others say about them, how they are seen to behave, and the history of their complaint. For many people with mental retardation, the first of these factors is usually limited because of reduced linguistic ability, and is often totally absent. As a result, the diagnostic process becomes reliant on third-party reports and observations. The consequence of this is that the validity of diagnosis for non-verbal people is most uncertain (Moss, 1995; Moss et al., 1996).

Defining mental illness

The definitions of mental illnesses are not at all straightforward. Psychiatric conditions are to a large extent socially defined, and hence highly interactive with the context in which the person lives. Certain social situations seem more able to contain or deal with the psychiatric symptoms than others, whereas other social situations may actually produce or exacerbate such symptoms. Most people have experience of 'things getting on top of them', and feeling that they are no longer able to cope. In most cases, however, people manage to cope with the help of support networks. Falloon and Fadden (1993) have estimated that these support networks are able to manage 90–95 per cent of all cases of mental disorder in the community. Goldberg and Huxley (1980) have discussed the factors that determine whether someone with a neurotic disorder becomes a 'case'. They point out that both interpersonal factors and external social factors may determine whether a given set of symptoms results in presentation to a doctor, but that the severity of symptoms is not necessarily directly related to degree of incapacity or interference with day-to-day life.

In contrast to mental illness, the identification of physical disorders is more straightforward. In simplistic terms, we tend to think of physical illness as something which, in most cases, can be 'fixed'. We go to the doctor, the doctor diagnoses the condition and gives the appropriate treatment. The physician is likely to pronounce you 'healthy' if no physical illness is found. The doctor feels able to say this because, in most cases, physical illness can be clearly diagnosed. Thus, conditions such as tuberculosis, HIV and syphilis are defined by the presence of an organism, injuries by the presence of physical trauma, heart disease by measures of cardiovascular functioning which prove to be abnormal.

Even in the case of physical illness, however, the relationship between subjective and objective perceptions of well-being can be in contradiction. A person may be pronounced free of physical illness, but not *feel well.* The subjective perception of physical health is thus not as straightforward as its objective diagnosis. The distinction between subjective and objective perception of mental illness is much less straightforward than for physical illness, because subjective factors – what people say they feel – play such a major part in the definition and diagnosis of these disorders. Certainly, there are conditions such as dementia that have associated symptoms of mental illness, but these are the result of characteristic brain damage. Similarly, toxic effects due to drugs can produce symptoms of mental disorder, but they often clear up if the toxicity is removed. Usually, however, we speak of 'mental illness' as something far less clear cut. The most common mental disorder in the community, for instance, is a mixture of anxiety and depression. It is, of course, highly likely that some people are more susceptible to depression or anxiety than others, but such conditions often relate to life events and general life conditions, such as loss of a close relative, divorce, or loss of a job. In later life, the sense of increasing vulnerability and reducing status in society can make people particularly sensitive to both depression and anxiety.

Even severe mental disorders such as schizophrenia do not have clear-cut biological bases for their origin. Schizophrenia tends to run in families, but genetic predisposition alone does not ensure that a specific individual contracts the illness. Also, schizophrenia can have so many different symptoms that a non-expert could easily assume that two cases had completely different disorders. This is also true for depression and anxiety. Some people suffer panic attacks, some lose their self-confidence, whereas others lose their ability to do things they once enjoyed. Frequently, people suffer from a wide range of symptoms relating to the same disorders.

Mental illness and challenging behaviour

Achieving consensus on defining mental illness in people with mental retardation is particularly difficult in relation to the uncertain status of problematic (challenging) behaviours. Research has shown that approximately 6 per cent of people with mental retardation show behaviours that (a) had at some time caused more than minor injury to the individuals themselves or to others, or had destroyed their immediate living or working environment; or (b) occurred at least once a week and required the intervention of more than one member of staff to control, or placed them in danger, or caused damage which could not be rectified by care staff, or caused more than one hour's disruption; or (c) occurred at least daily and caused more than a few minutes' disruption (Kiernan & Qureshi, 1993). Such behaviours are more common among people with more severe mental retardation; men; adolescents and young adults; people with additional sensory impairments; people with some specific syndromes associated with mental retardation (e.g. Lesch–Nyhan syndrome, fragile X syndrome); people with epilepsy; people with specific impairments in communication; people in institutional settings; and people with known psychiatric disorders (Emerson, 1995).

Challenging behaviour is the most common reason for referral to a psychiatrist in the UK, accounting for a third of the admissions from the community (Day, 1985). However, these problems are often long-term behaviour patterns, rather than illnesses showing a predictable time course. As such, they often do not fit the established criteria for diagnosable psychiatric conditions (Corbett, 1979). Whatever the grounds for referral, the result is that specialist psychiatric services spend a lot of their time dealing with challenging behaviour, but remain comparatively unaware of the more common mental disorders such as depression and anxiety (Patel et al., 1993). This situation can only change if we introduce more effective strategies for recognizing and referring these mental health problems as they occur.

The relationship between mental illness and challenging behaviour is as yet poorly understood, but there is some evidence that psychiatric disorders may, in some cases, underlie or exacerbate problematic behaviour. Thus, for example, recent evidence suggests that some forms of self-injurious behaviour may be associated with obsessive-compulsive disorder (King, 1993; Bodfish et al., 1995) and that fluctuations in mood associated with affective disorders may provide the motivational basis for other forms of self-injury (Sovner et al., 1993). It is important to detect and diagnose any underlying psychiatric disorder in these cases, although the problems of diagnosis in the presence of challenging behaviour are likely to be even greater than in the presence of mental retardation alone. The relationship between challenging behaviour and mental illness is further discussed in Chapter 3.

Behavioural and psychiatric perspectives

Within general psychiatry, there has tended to be a fairly distinctive division between psychologists and psychiatrists in terms of conceptualizing and assessing mental health problems. Psychologists have tended to favour a behavioural model for assessment and treatment, and have developed skills that are particularly effective in cases in which the modification of the person's behaviour is of paramount importance, e.g. the management of anxiety or the treatment of specific phobias. Behavioural techniques are util-ised outside the mental health sphere, for the training of new skills and the reduction of inappropriate ones, and hence have come to particular promi-nence in the field of mental retardation. Indeed, the rise of the behavioural movement in mental retardation was an important step towards recogniz-ing, firstly, that people with mental retardation could develop new skills if given an appropriate framework within which to learn, and, secondly, that many problematic behaviours were due largely to the circumstances in which people lived, rather than because of inherent faults or limitations in the individuals themselves.

The application of a more traditionally psychiatric approach to the needs of this population has been viewed with some suspicion, not least because it harks back to a time when the needs and problems of people with mental illness were often not distinguished from those of people with mental retar-dation. Today, psychiatrists specializing in mental retardation are often found working in multidisciplinary teams, providing a more co-ordinated approach to the assessment and treatment of mental health problems. Because the mental health needs of this population are often highly complex, it is likely that comprehensive assessment will necessitate a combination of approaches. For this reason, it is vital that we have the best possible clarity of thinking about the assumptions we are making.

Table 2.1 highlights some of the differences in emphasis between behavi-oural and traditional psychiatric approaches to the formulation and assess-ment of mental health problems. It is to be stressed that there is no hard and fast boundary between the two approaches, and practitioners will not exclu-sively use one approach or the other. Nevertheless, the differences are significant, and likely to colour our view of what constitutes a 'mental health problem'. In the broadest terms, psychiatric assessment is concerned with identifying patterns of symptoms and their historical development, and matching these patterns with those of previously defined disorders, such as depression and schizophrenia. A behavioural formulation, on the other hand, is concerned with the behaviours themselves, rather than with iden-tifying an underlying disorder that is thought to drive those behaviours. In this respect, the notion of 'diagnosis' is quite different from the psychiatric use of the term. Many of the problem behaviours exhibited by people with mental retardation fit more comfortably within this perspective than in terms of a psychiatric disorder. The behaviours are often long term, and may not fit the patterns of symptoms normally associated with mental health problems, such as depression or anxiety.

When applied to people with mental retardation, there is no consensus about which problems should be included in the term 'mental health

Table 2.1 Differences in emphasis between behavioural and psychiatric approaches to assessment

Behavioural	Psychiatric
Locus of the problem	
The person's current difficulties are viewed as the end-point of a complex learning history, whose effects have accumulated to provide both the form of the current behaviour, and the significance of the environmental influences on the person's behaviour	The significance of social and psychological factors, and their impact across the life course is recognized. Life events are also regarded as risk factors. However, the resulting problem is regarded as being primarily *within the individual*
Significance of individual symptoms	
The individual behaviours themselves are regarded as the focus for treatment. The pattern of symptoms is *not* regarded as having any particular significance (i.e. the presence of a more global pathological condition such as depression, schizophrenia etc.)	In psychiatric formulation it is the *pattern* of symptoms that is regarded as significant – indicating the nature of the underlying pathology. Many different symptom patterns can produce the same diagnosis
Significance of history	
Diagnosis in behaviour therapy focuses on descriptions of *current* behaviours and environments. History is not regarded as a central aspect of programme development. There is no assumption that historical factors and current factors are necessarily related	Clinical history is regarded as essential to understanding the significance of the current symptoms
Diagnostic formulation	
The behaviour therapist seeks to develop an explanation for the person's behaviour in terms of the current internal and external conditions which contribute to the occurrence of those behaviours – to develop a *functional* explanation (antecedents, behaviours and consequences). Observation and discussions with third parties are the main source of information	The psychiatrist seeks to identify the current *pattern* of symptoms and the history of its development. Diagnosis is made by relating the observed picture to clinically defined disorders. In general psychiatry, the patient interview (including clinical observation) is the main source of information. Discussion with key informants is also important

problem'. Does the fact that many problem behaviours would not be diagnosable within existing psychiatric classification systems mean that they are not mental illnesses, or are the classification systems themselves only of limited application to this particular population? If, as seems likely, all behaviours are to some extent a product of neurological processes and environmental factors, then the distinction may be only artificial. At the present time, our understanding of the genesis of mental disorders through biological, psychological and social factors remains limited. For many people with mental retardation, the limits of language and intellect make it even more difficult to understand these complex interactions than in general psychiatry.

Using ICD-10 and DSM-IV in assessment

The World Health Organization and the American Psychiatric Association, producers of two major classification systems, have shown considerable convergence, up to and including the latest versions (DSM-IV and ICD-10). The use of structured interviews in conjunction with fully operationalised criteria has had a major impact on the overall reliability of the psychiatric diagnosis process. The Research Diagnostic Criteria of Spitzer, Endicott and Robins (1978), for example, have been widely adopted for studying a variety of issues.

In the UK, the Present State Examination and Schedules for Clinical Assessment in Neuropsychiatry have operationalized the ICD-9 and ICD-10 research criteria. Wing et al. (1967), for example, held joint interviews with a series of 172 patients using the Present State Examination, and found a concordance rate of 92 per cent for schizophrenia.

If we are to improve the objectivity of diagnosis in people with mental retardation, the application of rigorous classification systems appears to be a promising avenue. The use of ICD and DSM criteria is frequently adopted in studies of mental health problems in people with mental retardation, as a way of attempting to improve the validity and reliability of diagnoses. However, their use poses a number of questions, which are discussed in Chapter 1.

In order to decide whether specific diagnostic criteria are met, symptoms must be operationalized into a structure for the collection of symptom information that results in valid and reliable diagnoses for the population under consideration. A research clinical interview takes this operationalization to a high level; the manner in which the symptoms are elicited is prescribed, as well as the way in which they are recorded. The questions that the patient is asked are laid down in advance, ratings are made serially as the interview progresses, rather than at the end, and definitions, implicit or explicit, are provided for each item. Some guidelines on order of presentation are also given, although most interviews allow the interviewer to respond to the patient spontaneously reporting a symptom by branching to that item. In a fully structured interview, the exact form of words to be used for each question is stipulated, and corresponding ratings are closely tied to the wording of the patient's replies. In contrast, semi-structured interviews such as the Schedules for Clinical Assessment in Neuropsychiatry (SCAN) (World Health Organization, 1994), and the Psychiatric Assessment Schedule for Adults with Developmental Disability (PAS-ADD) (Moss et al., 1993) provide suggested probes for each item, but allow the clinician to ask other questions if it is felt necessary. The final rating represents the clinician's own judgements, rather than the patient's initial reply to the original probe. Data from structured interviews can be processed to produce computer diagnoses based on a matching between the recorded symptoms and the operationalized criteria.

Although structured interviewing can give impressive reliability, the validity of resulting diagnoses is more difficult to ascertain. Column 1 of Table 2.2 shows the conceptual steps in the construction of a semi-structured interview to produce diagnoses with an established classification system (e.g. ICD-10 or DSM-IV), and column 2 notes some of the issues relating to the validity of these various steps. Let us consider some of the particular validity issues facing the operationalization of ICD-10 and DSM-IV in relation to people with mental retardation.

The relationships between symptoms and criteria

There are many symptom presentations that potentially can fulfil a given diagnostic criterion. Whether an interview developed for the general population is equally valid for people with mental retardation depends on a variety of considerations, including whether the same symptoms are manifested by the general population, whether their prevalence is the same, and whether they cluster within individuals in the same way. Additionally, there is the consideration of the language level of the interview, which is discussed below. Validity needs to be determined, not just by the relation of symptoms to criteria, but also to specific glossary definitions that are the yardstick against which symptom presence and severity are judged. For example, the SCAN's definition of *delusional perception* in the general population is:

> . . . an intrusive, often sudden, knowledge that a common percept has a radically transformed meaning. A normal percept, image or memory takes on an entirely new significance. The initial perception may sometimes be related to a specific experience that makes the effect more dramatic. For example, someone undergoing liver biopsy felt, as the needle was inserted, that he had been chosen by God. A woman getting off a bus on a November night was struck on the forehead by a leaf and immediately knew she had been sent to save the world.

It is quite possible that this definition is valid for people with mental retardation. It is also possible, however, that this symptom, or others that are observed in the general population, is expressed differently when developmental level is lower. If this is the case, then the glossary definitions need to be modified so that interviewers can recognize the symptoms. However, it is very difficult to alter either the selected symptoms for criterion fulfilment or the glossary definitions for people with mental retardation. A major problem is that there is no absolute standard against which the interview results can be validated. Expert clinical judgement is an often-used criterion in these circumstances, as the clinician is often in the best position to have the long-term knowledge of the patient necessary for correctly diagnosing the problem. However, the use of clinical judgement as an ultimate criterion is limited (Termelin, 1968; Cooper et al., 1972), and it seems likely that the level of agreement will be even lower with respondents who have mental retardation.

Table 2.2 Validity status of the steps to operationalizing of ICD criteria

Process step	Validity basis
1. Spectrum of psychiatric symptoms in the population, classified as specific disorders according to ICD-10/DSM-IV criteria	Establishing the validity of ICD-10 has been the focus of extensive investigations, including field trials, and re-analyses of previous studies
2. Each diagnostic criterion is interpreted as a symptom/behaviour, or cluster thereof	Interpretation of the criteria has been largely a process of expert clinical judgement, reflecting the glossary definitions provided with the classification manuals
3. Each symptom or behaviour is embodied in terms of a question or observational item on the schedule	The wording of questions has been based on expert judgement of the best way to obtain valid responses to the particular symptoms being sought. In semi-structured interviews, however, there is an unspecified degree of flexibility in wording allowed. The interviewer must be trained for the interview, and have a good knowledge of psychopathology and its manifestations
4. The test of whether a diagnostic criterion has been fulfilled is made by an algorithm relating together the specific question and observational item codes involved in that criterion	Scoring criteria for each item are set to reflect the various levels of severity which it is considered possible reliably to distinguish, and whose distinctions are considered to have clinical significance. (These are sometimes directly specified by the diagnostic criteria but more often have been decided by an aggregate of clinical opinion.)
	The algorithms which combine item codes to determine whether a specific criterion has been met have also been determined by the clinical judgement of the interview developers. Changes in these algorithms will affect observed prevalence of the symptom, so these will presumably have been set to match (a) the estimated prevalence of the specific symptom within the population, (b) the expected clustering of symptoms and syndromes within the population
5. The final algorithm relates fulfilled criteria to the patterns required for specific diagnoses – i.e. a direct application of the decision rules in ICD-10/ DSM-IV	

Some symptoms may be more reliably detected by structured interview than others; some are definitely more difficult for people with mental retardation to describe, and may be more effectively detected by observation and/or informant interviewing. An unambiguous basis for diagnostic algorithms specifically for people with mental retardation, for clear and detailed comparison of the clustering and/or manifestation of psychiatric symptoms, has yet to be developed.

Asking about symptoms

Once we have decided about specific symptoms to be investigated, formulation of the questions becomes the next step. In the general population, face-to-face interviewing can provide useful information, because most patients can describe symptoms with sufficient clarity for a clinician to determine their existence with reasonable confidence (assuming the patient has sufficient insight at the time of interview). Further, a person in the normal IQ range can usually provide information clear enough to make reliable ratings of severity and duration. However, the actual words used to question a respondent about a particular symptom may have a considerable impact on the answer, and hence, depending on the scoring criteria, on its apparent prevalence. This will apply particularly to fully structured interviews in which the wording is fixed. Semi-structured interviewing is a more sophisticated approach, but can only be done by trained raters with an adequate knowledge of psychopathology. Using semi-structured interviewing with respondents of normal intelligence, quite complex propositions can be presented and discussed using the additional probes and as much additional free-language discussion as is necessary for the rater to code the item. The following item, for example, comes from the SCAN:

> Do you have the feeling that you are being blamed or accused by others because of some action or lapse or deficiency that you yourself feel was blameworthy?
> (How much of the time in [Period] have you been free of the feelings?)
> (How often have you had the feeling that you were being blamed for something really serious?)

This particular item is designed to elicit the symptom 'guilty ideas of reference', responses being judged against the relevant SCAN glossary definition. The sentences in brackets are the suggested probes that may additionally be used. On the basis of the discussion, the interviewer must decide (a) whether the symptom is present, and (b) if so, how frequently and severely it has been present in the previous month. It has been shown that trained raters can make these codings with a good level of reliability with respondents in the general population (Wing et al., 1977).

The questioning of people with mental retardation about their mental state is clearly a major obstacle. However, the development of the PAS-ADD (Moss et al., 1993) has shown that many people with mental retardation can tackle quite complex propositions, provided they are appropriately structured (Moss et al., 1997). For example, in the SCAN question on 'guilty ideas of reference', the main question is very precisely worded, but the vocabulary is sophisticated and there are two essential elements within a single sentence ('Do you feel blamed by others?' and 'Is it because of a lapse or personal deficiency'). In the first prompt, being 'free of a feeling' is a more advanced concept than 'having a feeling'. In the second prompt, the person is being asked two things: whether he or/she feels blamed for something 'really serious', and, if so, how often he or she feels like this. Each of these linguistic complications raises intellectual demands, and increases the probability that a respondent with mental retardation will either not respond, or will respond inappropriately. The PAS-ADD's re-wording is designed to break these propositions down into their component elements:

PAS-ADD: Do you think that you are blamed for something?
      (Has anyone said that you have done something bad?)
      (What do you think you have done?)
      (Is it your fault?)
      (Do you feel guilty?)
      (Do other people say it is your fault?)
      (Do you think you should be punished?)

At the present time, it can only be claimed that the PAS-ADD's language appears to be more appropriate for people with mental retardation in terms of its face validity. A more precise consideration of the validity of specific wordings will need evidence of how responses in the population would change if the items were worded differently, and of how this would affect the coding of PAS-ADD items. One thing that can be said in defence of re-wording, however, is that semi-structured interviewing allows an unspecified amount of flexibility in wording and interview style. Experienced PSE and SCAN interviewers will sometimes depart from specific wordings in order to clarify to the patient what precisely is being asked. Good interviewing thus relies as much on a thorough knowledge of the glossary definitions of psychopathology as on the use of specific linguistic forms. What the PAS-ADD attempts to do is to raise the possibility that the person with mental retardation will understand the questions and thus be in a better position to give a valid answer.

Criteria for symptom severity

Once a symptom has been identified, we need to decide whether it is severe enough to be considered clinically relevant. The algorithms that combine item codes to determine whether a specific criterion is fulfilled have, in the case of sophisticated instruments like the SCAN, been determined through extensive field trials, re-analyses of previous studies, and expert clinical judgement. The setting of these rules has enormous implications for the interview's performance. Changes in these algorithms will affect the observed prevalence of the symptom, so these will presumably have been set to match (a) the estimated prevalence of the specific symptom within the population, and (b) the expected clustering of symptoms and syndromes within the population. In the case of people with mental retardation, reduced verbal ability is likely to make it more difficult to detect symptoms than in the general population, so it may be necessary to develop new algorithms, pro-rating items to allow for this lower probability of symptom detection in a patient interview. As with the development of the ICD and DSM criteria themselves, it is likely that diagnostic algorithms for people with mental retardation will take many years to develop and gain agreement. In the first instance, it is difficult to see any basis for setting the algorithm requirements beyond that of expert clinical judgement. Until or unless external criteria for validation (such as biological markers) can be established, it is unlikely that this situation will change.

Clinical interviewing of people with mental retardation

One of the principal findings from research on clinical interviewing is that there is no simple relationship between symptomatology and diagnosis, even with respect to a single clinician (Wittenborn, Holzberg & Simon, 1953; Freudenberg & Robertson, 1956; Nathan et al., 1969). A psychiatric diagnosis is usually made in a situation in which the clinician:

> armed with a variable amount of background information like the patient's age and occupation and source of referral, holds a free-ranging discussion interview with the patient, lasting anything from twenty minutes to an hour or more. In this interview, the psychiatrist seeks to establish a diagnosis by asking the patient first about his current symptoms and difficulties and then about an ever-widening circle of other experiences and events, past and present. (Kendell, 1975)

Different clinicians show considerable differences in the type and quality of information they try to obtain before making a diagnosis. Some focus mainly on current mental state, some are concerned more with the personality as a whole, whereas others concentrate on the situation in which the symptoms developed and the reasons for the stress which was caused. Gauron and Dickinson (1966) showed that, apart from 'reason for referral', which has the greatest impact on final diagnosis, there was no statistically significant rank ordering among the remaining pieces of information.

Although a good interviewer pays close attention to observable phenomena such as posture and non-verbal cues, it is clear that, whichever focus is adopted, there is a high priority given to the patient's verbal behaviour. Kendell (1973), for example, showed that the accuracy of diagnosis by experienced clinicians was equally high whether the interviews were presented as videotapes, audiotapes or written transcripts, and that their confidence of accuracy was also unchanged. '. . . One is forced to conclude that the behavioural items the videotape raters regarded as important were in fact superfluous. The other implication of this, that the psychiatrists rely almost entirely on what the patient says, rather than on the way he behaves, can be used to justify the use of audiotapes or transcripts for research purposes instead of live interviews, and rebuts the arguments that to do so involves losing vital information' (Kendell, 1975). Obviously, such a conclusion could not apply to the diagnosis of people with mental retardation, many of whom have greatly reduced language abilities. In these cases, non-verbal behaviour and historical information must play a more prominent role. This being the case, it is clear that the comparability of diagnostic categories between people with and without mental retardation becomes questionable.

From a practical perspective, the rules of good interviewing of respondents with mental retardation are not fundamentally different from those applicable to the general population. There are, however, two particularly important points to bear in mind if the validity of the information is to be as high as possible. Firstly, people with mental retardation are more likely to acquiesce to what they believe the interviewer wants to hear. Secondly, they often have a relatively short span of attention. With respect to the latter, it is important to recap frequently and to summarize what the respondent has said. This has two benefits: it re-engages and focuses the respondents' attention, gives them an opportunity to add more detail, and allows respondents to concur with or to refute the interviewer's interpretation of what has been said.

Minimizing the tendency to acquiescence is a skill that has general applicability to any psychiatric interviewing, but is particularly important in relation to people with mental retardation (Sigelman et al., 1981). The attitude of anyone being interviewed, with or without mental retardation, is likely to be determined by their expectations of the interaction. People with mental retardation may have had negative experiences of interviews with professionals that colour their expectations. For example, they may believe that something will happen to them as a result of the interview, that they may be sent away somewhere, given medication, or required to change in some way, or they may believe that confidential information may be given to someone else. It is thus very important for an interviewer to learn the use of appropriate 'framework-giving' comments that can help maximize the respondent's confidence and sense of security.

A wide variety of linguistic and phonological problems can make the respondent's responses difficult to understand. The interviewer should be particularly aware of the more subtle problems that can lead to major misunderstanding, notably, poor grammar and abnormal intonation. Poor grammar can lead to ambiguity, e.g. 'Tonight hair cut mum' actually meant that the man was going to have his hair cut that night, accompanied by his mother. Abnormal intonation can lead, for example, to the following misunderstanding. A respondent was asked if he had pain, and replied 'stomach', which the doctor interpreted as a statement about stomach pain, rather than a request by the respondent for clarification of what the doctor meant. If the respondent had said it with a questioning tone, the interpretation would have been different.

Overall, the clinical interviewing of people with mental retardation is a skill that demands sensitivity and practice to acquire. An extensive discussion of the techniques for good interviewing can be found in Moss et al. (1996).

Respondent and informant perspectives

In general psychiatry, it is often the case that information from a variety of sources is necessary to provide a full clinical picture. Respondents do not always have insight into their condition, or may simply have a different perspective on the problem from key informants. This is equally true for people with mental retardation, but there is the additional factor that, in many cases, the report given by the respondent will be less adequate than the informant's, or indeed absent altogether. In cases in which symptom descriptions rely heavily on third-party reports, there is clearly a question mark over the validity of the resulting diagnosis. Do informants and respondents report the same symptoms, or are there significant differences? Would the absence of a respondent interview (in the case of insufficient linguistic or intellectual ability) tend to produce a significant and predictable bias in diagnosis?

A variety of factors is likely to influence the quality of informant interview responses. Amongst these are: (a) the nature of the relationship between informant and client, (b) the prior existence of a label such as 'challenging behaviour' that could influence the judgement of the informant, (c) diagnostic over-shadowing – the presence of mental retardation tending to decrease the judged significance of accompanying mental illness symptoms, even by experienced observers (Reiss, Levitan & Szyszko, 1982).

In terms of the validity of informant reports, research has shown that care staff are often aware of the presence of symptoms, and of the magnitude of emotional distress suffered by their clients, but are for various reasons unable to decide whether referral to a general practitioner is appropriate (Moss & Patel, 1993). In some cases, however, the magnitude of disagreement between respondent and informant reports can be very large. Those cases in which the respondents demonstrate symptoms on interview while the informants see no problems probably indicate a lack of awareness of the psychiatric problem on the part of the informant. It is not surprising that this type of disagreement can occur, given the difficulty of separating psychiatric symptomatology from behaviour relating to the mental retardation.

Respondents more frequently report symptoms relating to subjective feelings, including autonomic symptoms and various psychotic phenomena whose impact on observed behaviour is often hard for an informant to evaluate. These include autonomic symptoms, hallucinations and delusions. Informants may be aware of a person hearing voices, but they are less likely to know what the *nature* of these voices is (which can be diagnostically crucial). Also, informants are much more likely than respondents to give clear accounts of worry, loss of interest, social withdrawal and irritability (Moss et al., 1996). Validity of diagnosis by informant report alone may thus depend partly on the nature of the condition. Developing interview skills with this population, through practice, discussion and reviewing of videotapes, has shown the importance of experience and training in making reliable and valid diagnoses (Moss et al., 1996).

The development of the PAS-ADD psychiatric interview has shown that the interviewing of both respondents and informants is essential for case detection. In people with mental retardation, around a third of cases are missed if either interview is omitted (Moss et al., 1997). Depending on the exact constellation of symptoms, these differences in perspective may have a crucial impact on the diagnostic conclusions. In relation to ICD-10 criteria, there is a particular problem in achieving diagnoses of panics and phobias, because these require evidence of autonomic symptoms, which informants often miss. Training initiatives may increase awareness of mental health problems in people with mental retardation and hence raise the quality of reporting (Bouras & Holt, 1997).

Comprehensive assessment of mental health needs

It is clear that the assessment of mental health problems in people with mental retardation should not be restricted to a consideration of whether the person meets ICD-10 or DSM-IV criteria on the day of assessment. A whole range of factors needs to be taken into consideration, encompassing not just the individual, but also the wider ecology within which the person lives. Mental health is inextricably bound up with quality-of-life issues. A good quality of life is a powerful influence that can go a long way to protecting the individual from mental illness, and minimizing the severity of illness when it does occur. As discussed earlier, the strength of supportive elements means that the vast majority of mental illness in the community can be dealt with by the sufferers themselves and their carers, and in most cases does not come to the attention of mental health services. Obviously, the more severe and debilitating the condition, the more likely that psychiatric help will be sought. However, there are many factors apart from severity of the condition that determine whether outside help is sought, e.g. the amount and quality of social support that is available to the person, the amount of stress in the person's life, the presence or absence of additional physical illness, and the effectiveness of the person's coping mechanisms.

The complexity of factors influencing the mental health of people with mental retardation needs to be matched by a correspondingly sophisticated approach to assessment. Ideally, this should extend beyond the process of clinical investigation, to include the wider aspects of individuals lives, such as their ability to cope with life transitions, and the adequacy of their support networks. In order to widen the assessment process in this way, it is clearly necessary to gain the participation of staff other than those already involved in mental health service provision. In this respect, one of the fundamental problems that needs to be addressed is that of case identification. The decision to consult a primary care physician (general practitioner) or other professional regarding psychiatric ill-health is not taken by people with mental retardation themselves (Fletcher, 1993; Nezu & Nezu, 1994). Seeking help and treatment for a psychiatric problem is thus dependent upon a third party, firstly, recognizing the signs and symptoms of psychiatric illness and, secondly, understanding their significance and taking action. If the disorder is associated with the development of conspicuous symptoms such as challenging behaviour, case recognition is relatively probable. In the absence of specialized knowledge, however, it is likely that many mental health problems will not be identified. Recent studies confirm that this is indeed the case, many cases of depression and anxiety disorders remaining unrecognized and untreated (Reiss, 1990; Patel et al., 1993).

The problems of case recognition are compounded by the fact that the primary health care system relies so heavily on people's ability to recognize and report symptoms of ill-health. People with communication problems may not have the skills to do this, while health care professionals may not have the skills needed to overcome this barrier. Rodgers (1994) argues that professionals in primary health care in the UK may lack the communication skills needed to give appropriate care to people with mental retardation. Langan, Russell and Whitfield's (1993) survey of 70 GPs in the West of England reports that GPs generally lacked special expertise for dealing with people with mental retardation, and almost half felt further training was appropriate. Similar problems have been found in the USA. Harper and Wadsworth (1992) argue that health care professionals in the USA often lack the opportunity to gain experience interacting with people whose ability to express and understand health care information is limited.

A recent review (Moss & Turner, 1995) suggests there is scope for training programmes for primary care team members, service users and carers, both as separate groups and in terms of co-ordination and communication. There is a growing literature from the USA (Wadsworth and Harper, 1991; Harper & Wadsworth, 1992); focusing on the training of staff in this respect. For example, Harper and Wadsworth (1992) report the evaluation of self-study material (text and video) aimed at developing methods of communicating with patients with mental retardation in medical and dental care settings. Knowledge and skills of physicians, nurses, nursing assistants and medical students were found to have improved after training, and they were more proactive in interviews.

The reasons for unrecognized psychiatric illness are often attributed to the carers' lack of understanding of the cause of behaviours and the need for referral and psychiatric assessment (Borthwick-Duffy & Eyman, 1990). Therefore, support workers and direct care staff working with people who have mental retardation also have a crucial role in recognizing potential symptoms. These are the people who are in the best position to identify significant behaviour change and, potentially, to make appropriate referrals. Immediate carers are the people who are usually first to notice significant signs and symptoms, but they often lack the knowledge or confidence to act on this information. Support workers such as community nurses and social workers often have access to information that is more wide ranging in relation to the person's overall functioning, yet these professionals may also lack the skills to make a truly informed decision about whom to refer for in-depth clinical assessment. A number of recent initiatives have been directed specifically towards capitalizing on this knowledge base. The *PAS-ADD Checklist* (Moss et al., 1997) and the *Mini PAS-ADD* (Prosser et al., 1997) are two schedules designed to help health and social service staff identify mental health problems in the people for whom they care. Training materials (Bouras & Holt, 1997) have been designed to raise the awareness and understanding of staff about a wide range of issues relating to the detection, management and treatment of mental illness in people with mental retardation.

Conclusion

Overall, it is clear that the mental health needs of this population are highly complex. As such, diagnostic classification is likely to provide only partial guidance on the morbidity and quality of life experienced by individuals suffering from mental disorders (Falloon & Fadden, 1993). Indeed, this is also true for the general population, and it is apparent that mental health services are increasingly recognizing this, and are adopting a problem-based, rather that strictly diagnostic, approach to assessment.

An effective service not only deals with disorders as they occur, but also minimizes the likelihood of the disorder recurring. Recurrent episodes are more likely, either because the person's biological vulnerability is increased, and/or because environmental stress overwhelms current coping capacity. An *integrated care* approach emphasizes accurate diagnosis as a crucial step that provides a clear direction for biomedical interventions. Following this, however, the problem-based assessment then provides the framework within which to think about *long-term* prevention of occurrence and maximizing quality of life, rather than simply reducing symptoms in the short term. The adoption of such care models is even more important for people with mental retardation, because the majority of them will need help to develop and maintain strategies for the long-term maintenance of their mental health.

References

Bodfish, J.W., Crawford, T.W., Powell, S.B., Parker, D.E., Golden, R.N. & Lewis, M.H. (1995). Compulsions in adults with mental retardation: prevalence, phenomenology, and comorbidity with stereotypy and self-injury. *American Journal on Mental Retardation*, **100**, 183–92.

BorthwickDuffy, S.A. & Eyman, R.K. (1990). Who are the dually diagnosed? *American Journal on Mental Retardation*, **94**, 586–95.

Bouras, N. & Holt, G. (1997). *Mental Health in Learning Disabilities: a Training Pack for Staff Working with People who have a Dual Diagnosis of Mental Health Needs and Learning Disabilities*, 2nd edn. Brighton: Pavilion.

Cooper, J.E., Kendell, R.E., Gurland, B.J., Sharpe, L., Copeland, J.R.M. & Simon, R. (1972). *Maudsley Monograph No. 20*. Oxford: Oxford University Press.

Corbett, J.A. (1979). Psychiatric morbidity and mental retardation. In *Psychiatric Illness and Mental Handicap*, ed. F.E. James & R.P. Snaith. London: Gaskell Press.

Day, K. (1985). Psychiatric disorder in the middleaged and elderly mentally handicapped. *British Journal of Psychiatry*, **147**, 660–7.

Eaton, L.F. & Menolascino, F.J. (1982). Psychiatric disorders in the mentally retarded: types, problems, and challenges. *American Journal of Psychiatry*, **139**, 1297–303.

Emerson, E. (1995). *Challenging Behaviour: Analysis and Intervention in People with Learning Difficulties*. Cambridge: Cambridge University Press.

Falloon, I.R.H. & Fadden, G. (1993). *Integrated Mental Health Care: a Comprehensive Community Based Approach*. Cambridge: Cambridge University Press.

Fletcher, R.J. (1993). Mental illness-mental retardation in the United States: policy and treatment challenges. *Journal of Intellectual Disability Research*, **37** (Suppl. 1), 25–33.

Freudenberg, R.K. & Robertson, J.P.S. (1956). Symptoms in relation to psychiatric diagnosis and treatment. *Archives of Neurology and Psychiatry*, **76**, 1422.

Gauron, E.F. & Dickinson, J.K. (1966). Diagnostic decision making in psychiatry. I. Information usage. *Archives of General Psychiatry*, **14**, 225–32.

Goldberg, D. & Huxley, P. (1980). *Mental Illness in the Community*. London: Tavistock Publications.

Harper D. & Wadsworth, J. (1992). Improving health communication for persons with mental retardation. *Public Health Reports*, **107**, 297–302.

Kendell, R.E. (1973) Psychiatric diagnoses: a study of how they are made. *British Journal of Psychiatry*, **122**, 437–45.

(1975) *The Role of Diagnosis in Psychiatry*. Oxford: Blackwell.

Kiernan, C. & Qureshi, H. (1993). Challenging behaviour. In *Research to Practice? Implications of Research on the Challenging Behaviour of People with Learning Disability*, ed. C. Kiernan, pp. 53–65. Clevedon, Avon: BILD Publications.

King, B. (1993). Self-injury by people with mental retardation: a compulsive behavior hypothesis. *American Journal on Mental Retardation*, **98**, 93–112.

Langan, J., Russell, O. & Whitfield, M. (1993). *Community Care and the General Practitioner: Primary Health Care for People with Learning Disabilities*. Bristol: Norah Fry Research Centre, University of Bristol.

Moss, S.C. (1995). Methodological issues in the diagnosis of psychiatric disorders in adults with learning disability. *Thornfield Journal* (University of Dublin), **18**, 9–18.

Moss, S.C., Ibbotson, B., Prosser, H., Goldberg, D.P., Patel, P. & Simpson, N. (1997). Validity of the PAS-ADD for detecting psychiatric symptoms in adults with learning disability. *Social Psychiatry and Psychiatric Epidemiology*, **32**, 344–54.

Moss, S.C. & Patel, P. (1993). Prevalence of mental illness in people with learning disability over 50 years of age, and the diagnostic importance of information from carers. *Irish Journal of Psychiatry*, **14**, 110–29.

Moss, S.C., Patel, P., Prosser, H. et al. (1993). Psychiatric morbidity in older people with moderate and severe learning disability (mental retardation). Part I: Development and reliability of the patient interview (the PAS-ADD). *British Journal of Psychiatry*, **163**, 471–80.

Moss, S.C., Prosser, H., Ibbotson, B. & Goldberg, D.P. (1996). Respondent and informant accounts of psychiatric symptoms in a sample of patients with learning disability. *Journal of Intellectual Disability Research*, **40**, 457–65.

Moss, S.C. & Turner, S. (1995). *The Health of People with Learning Disability*. Report to the Department of Heath. Manchester: Hester Adrian Research Centre, University of Manchester.

Nathan, P.E., Gould, C.F., Zare, N.C. & Roth, M. (1969). A systems analytic model of diagnosis: improved diagnostic validity from median data. *Journal of Clinical Psychology*, **25**, 370–5.

Nezu, C.M. & Nezu, A.M. (1994). Outpatient psychotherapy for adults with mental retardation and concomitant psychopathology: research and clinical imperatives. *Journal of Consulting and Clinical Psychology*, **62**, 34–42.

Patel, P., Goldberg, D.P. & Moss, S.C. (1993). Psychiatric morbidity in older people with moderate and severe learning disability (mental retardation). Part II: The prevalence study. *British Journal of Psychiatry*, **163**, 481–91.

Prosser, H., Moss, S.C., Costello, H., Simpson, N. & Patel, P. (1997). *The MINI PAS-ADD: an Assessment Schedule for the Detection of Mental Health Problems in Adults with Learning Disability (Mental Retardation)*. Manchester: Hester Adrian Research Centre, University of Manchester.

Reiss, S. (1982). Psychopathology and mental retardation: survey of a developmental disabilities mental health program. *Mental Retardation*, **20**, 128–32.

Reiss, S. (1990). Prevalence of dual diagnosis in community-based day programs in the Chicago metropolitan area. *American Journal on Mental Retardation*, **94**, 578–85.

Reiss, S., Levitan, G. & Szyszko, J. (1982). Emotional disturbance and mental retardation: diagnostic overshadowing. *American Journal of Mental Deficiency*, **86**, 567–74.

Rodgers, J. (1994). Primary health care provision for people with learning difficulties. *Health and Social Care,* **2,** 11–17.

Sigelman, C.K., Budd, E.C., Spanhel, C.L. & Schoenrock, C.J. (1981). When in doubt say yes: acquiescence in interviews with mentally retarded persons. *Mental Retardation,* **19,** 53–8.

Sovner, R. & Hurley, D.A. (1983). Do the mentally retarded suffer from affective illness? *Archives of General Psychiatry,* **40,** 61–7.

Sovner, R., Fox, C.J., Lowry, M.J. & Lowry, M.A. (1993). Fluoxetine treatment of depression and associated selfinjury in two adults with mental retardation. *Journal of Intellectual Disability Research,* **37,** 301–11.

Spitzer, R.L., Endicott, J. & Robins, E. (1978). Research Diagnostic Criteria: rationale and reliability. *Archives of General Psychiatry,* **35,** 773–82.

Termelin, M.K. (1968). Suggestion effects in psychiatric diagnosis. *Journal of Nervous and Mental Disease,* **147,** 349–53.

Wadsworth, J. & Harper, D. (1991). Training health care professionals to communicate with patients with mental retardation. *Academic Medicine,* **66,** 495–6.

Wing, J.K., Birley, J.L.T., Cooper, J.E., Graham, P. & Isaacs, A.D. (1967). Reliability of a procedure for measuring and classifying 'Present Psychiatric State'. *British Journal of Psychiatry,* **113,** 499–515.

Wing, J., Nixon, J., Von-Cranach, M. & Strauss, A. (1977). Further developments of the `present state examination' and CATEGO system. *Archiv fur Psychiatrische Nervenkrankheit,* **224,** 151–60.

Wittenborn, J.R., Holzberg, J.D. & Simon, B. (1953). Symptom correlates for descriptive diagnosis. *Genetic Psychology Monographs,* **47,** 237301.

World Health Organization (1994). *Schedules for Clinical Assessment in Neuopsychiatry, Version 2.* Geneva: WHO.

3 The relationship between challenging behaviour and psychiatric disorders in people with severe developmental disabilities

ERIC EMERSON, STEVE MOSS AND CHRIS KIERNAN

Introduction

This chapter speculates about the relationship between challenging behaviour and psychiatric disorders in people with *severe* developmental disabilities. Behavioural and neurobiological approaches have made quite separate but undoubtedly significant contributions to our understanding of 'abnormal' behaviours shown by people with severe developmental disabilities (Emerson, 1995). Examining the overlap and relationship between these approaches has potential benefits in advancing our theoretical understanding and identifying new avenues of investigation. More pragmatically, such an exercise may lead to the development of more effective frameworks for designing socially valid approaches to intervention. First, however, it is necessary to clarify the terminology used in this chapter.

Challenging behaviour

The term challenging behaviour, as used here, refers to 'culturally abnormal behaviour of such an intensity, frequency or duration that the physical safety of the person or others is likely to be placed in serious jeopardy, or behaviour which is likely to seriously limit use of, or result in the person being denied access to, ordinary community facilities' (Emerson, 1995).

It is important to keep in mind that, in this definition, challenging behaviours are viewed as *social constructions defined by their social impact.* They are behaviours which transgress social rules. Whether a particular behaviour will be 'challenging' will be based on complex interactions between what the person does, the setting in which it is done and how his or her behaviour is interpreted or given meaning. As such, challenging behaviours, are likely to range widely in their form (topography) and, more importantly, the psychological and/or biological processes which underlie them. The term itself carries no implications (implicit or explicit) about the processes which may underlie challenging behaviour.

Challenging behaviours are shown by 10–15 per cent of users of educational, health or social care services for people with developmental disability, with 'more demanding' challenging behaviours[1] shown by 5–10 per cent of such users (Emerson et al., 1997). Challenging behaviours are the most common reason for referral to a psychiatrist in the UK, accounting for a third of the admissions from the community (Day, 1985).

Psychiatric disorders

The Diagnostic and Statistical Manual of Mental Disorders, fourth edition (DSM-IV: American Psychiatric Association 1994) defines a mental disorder as:

> . . . a clinically significant behavioural or psychological syndrome or pattern that occurs in an individual and that is associated with present distress (e.g., painful symptom) or disability (i.e., impairment in one or more important areas of functioning) or with a significantly increased risk of suffering death, pain, disability, or an important loss of freedom . . . Whatever its original cause, it must currently be considered a manifestation of a behavioral, psychological or biological dysfunction in the individual. Neither deviant behavior (e.g., political, religious or sexual), nor conflicts that are primarily between the individual and society are mental disorders, unless the deviance or conflict is a symptom of a dysfunction in the individual, as described above.

This qualification applies to the diagnoses of conduct disorder and antisocial personality disorder.

Clearly, the above definition is sufficiently broad that many forms of challenging behaviour could be accommodated within it. Self-injurious behaviour would qualify because it implies pain and suffering for the individual, and would in most, if not all, cases be regarded as severely dysfunctional. Aggressive behaviour presents more of a problem. If the behaviour is perceived as being due mainly to a lack of inhibition towards others, then it might be viewed as having no associated distress, or increased risk of suffering (apart from that of other people).

---

1. Defined as challenging behaviours that also met at least one of the following four criteria: (1) they occurred *at least once a day*; (2) they *usually* prevented the person from taking part in programmes or activities appropriate to his or her level of ability; (3) they *usually* required physical intervention by one or more members of staff; (4) they *usually* led to major injury (i.e. injury requiring hospital treatment) to either the individual, carers or other people with intellectual disabilities.

The co-morbidity of psychiatric disorders and challenging behaviour

Given the definitional issues discussed above, it is apparent that there can be no unambiguous estimate of the co-morbidity of challenging behaviour and psychiatric disorders. This is reflected in the huge variations in the reported prevalence of mental health problems among people with developmental disabilities. Campbell and Malone (1991), for instance, reported prevalence rates between 14 per cent and 67 per cent. If aggressive and disruptive 'challenging behaviours' are included as a form of psychiatric disorder, prevalence estimates tend to be high, with a large proportion of people receiving diagnoses of personality disorders. Thus, Reiss (1990) reported an overall prevalence of 39 per cent, Menolascino (1989) 30 per cent, and Iverson and Fox (1989) 36 per cent. Amongst hospital populations, figures as high as 60 per cent have been reported (Leck, Gordon & McKeown, 1967; Craft, 1971; Primrose, 1971; Reid, 1972). However, if people who *only* show challenging behaviour are excluded, then the prevalence of psychosis and neurosis combined appears to be as low as 8–10 per cent (Heaton-Ward, 1977). This discrepancy would tend to be lower in older groups, because older groups demonstrate a lower rate of behaviour problems than younger ones (Day, 1985; Kiernan & Moss, 1990).

One of the few published studies to discuss the statistical relationships between challenging behaviour and mental health problems used information from mental retardation registers in California and New York (Rojahn, Borthwick-Duffy & Jacobson, 1993). Despite the very large number of subjects (89,419 in California and 45,683 in New York), no compelling correlations were found to link aggression, self-injury, destruction or stereotypies to the presence or absence of a psychiatric diagnosis. Unfortunately, because this was a register study, it was not possible to evaluate the quality of the diagnostic information.

Similarly, a large-scale study of challenging behaviour in people with developmental disabilities in the UK asked respondents whether the people identified had a psychiatric disorder diagnosed by a psychiatrist (Kiernan & Qureshi, 1993). Only 89 of the 693 people identified (13 per cent) had such a diagnosis, but the fact that in over 59 per cent of instances respondents said that they did not know if such a diagnosis had been made, opens the possibility of failure to diagnose disorders.

Possible forms of relationship

The remainder of this chapter discusses four possible ways in which psychiatric disorders may be associated with challenging behaviour. First, to be discussed are family factors that may be common to challenging behaviour and conduct disorder. Second is the possibility that challenging behaviours may, in some circumstances, represent the atypical presentation of a psychiatric disorder in people with severe developmental disabilities. Third, is the possibility that challenging behaviours may occur as secondary features of psychiatric disorders among people with severe developmental disabilities. Finally, the possible interaction between psychiatric disorders and behavioural processes in the manifestation of challenging behaviour is discussed.

Family factors associated with the development of challenging behaviour and conduct disorder

Evidence from diverse studies suggests that similar family factors may be implicated in the development of challenging behaviour in children and young people with developmental disability and the development of conduct disorder in children and young people without developmental disability (e.g. Rutter, 1985; McCord, 1990). For example, increased prevalence of conduct disorder or challenging behaviour has been associated with:

- discontinuities in upbringing, care that was below basic level, family discord, and instability or disorganization in the home among young adults with mild developmental disability (e.g. Nihara, Meyers & Mink, 1980; Richardson, 1987);
- poor parental adjustment and parent–child relationships among children with developmental disabilities (e.g. Cunningham et al., 1986; Sloper & Turner, 1993);
- inadequate housing, low income and unemployment among families with a child with Down syndrome (e.g. Sloper & Turner, 1993).

These studies indicate similarities between the aetiology of challenging behaviour and conduct disorder with particular reference to children and young adults with mild developmental disabilities. One crucial question, which has not been addressed in research studies, is whether severe developmental disabilities, especially accompanied by physical impairments, amplify or overshadow the impact of such factors.

Challenging behaviour may be the atypical presentation of a psychiatric disorder in people with severe developmental disabilities

The apparently low prevalence of certain forms of psychiatric disorder raises the possibility that some examples of challenging behaviour among people with severe developmental disabilities may represent the atypical (or unrecognized) presentation of a psychiatric disorder. For example, two sources of circumstantial evidence suggest that some forms of self-injurious behaviour may constitute the atypical presentation of obsessive–compulsive disorder among people with severe developmental disabilities (King, 1993). First, there are clear topographical similarities between obsessive–compulsive disorder and self-injurious behaviour in that both categories of 'challenging' behaviour are repetitive, stereotyped, ritualistic, apparently unrelated to the immediate demands of the person's situation and are extremely resistant to change (Kiernan et al., 1997). Second, there is growing evidence to suggest that serotoninergic agonists or reuptake inhibitors (e.g. fluoxetine, clomipramine) can reduce obsessional compulsive disorders in people without developmental disabilities (Lader & Herrington, 1996) and self-injurious behaviour in people with severe developmental disabilities (Markowitz, 1992; Bodfish & Madison, 1993; Sovner et al., 1993; Lewis, et al., 1996; see also Chapters 7, 15 and 18).

Challenging behaviour may be a secondary feature of psychiatric disorders among people with severe developmental disabilities

It has previously been suggested that a range of challenging behaviours (including aggression and self-injurious behaviour) may occasionally occur as secondary features of affective disorders among people with severe developmental disabilities (Reid, 1982; Sovner & Hurley, 1983). Reid (1982), for example, suggests a variety of clinical features which may be indicative of depression among people whose level of disability makes it difficult to verbalize their feelings. These features include somatic symptoms (e.g. headache and abdominal ache), hysterical fits, agitation, and disturbances of physiological functions such as sleep, appetite and bowel movements.

A number of recent studies have attempted to quantify the diagnostic significance of challenging behaviours and loss of self-care skills in depression. Meins (1995), for example, identified major depression in adults with mental retardation using a two-phase method of screening followed by detailed assessment of potential cases. Additional potential symptoms, including a range of problem behaviours and loss of self-care skills, were also observed. Meins showed that, in people with more severe developmental disabilities, the severity of existing behaviour problems was higher in the presence of depression as defined by DSM-II-R criteria. He points specifically to the diagnostic significance of aggressive and self-injurious behaviour, stereotypies, screaming and spontaneous crying. Similarly, Reiss and Rojahn (1993), using the Reiss Screen, found criterion levels of depression to be evident in four times as many aggressive as non-aggressive subjects.

Psychiatric disorders may establish a motivational basis for the expression of challenging behaviours maintained by (operant) behavioural processes

The preceding section explored the possibility that some forms of challenging behaviour that have traditionally been thought of as being maintained by behavioural processes may instead represent the atypical (or unrecognized) presentation of a psychiatric disorder among people with severe developmental disabilities. A more intriguing possibility is that some examples of challenging behaviour may involve the operation of behavioural process in the context of an underlying psychiatric disorder.

Over recent years there has been a growing interest within the behavioural literature in understanding the motivational basis underlying challenging behaviour (e.g. Carr & Smith, 1995; Gardner & Whalen, 1996) and in beginning to explore the interrelationship between behavioural and neurobiological processes in the expression of challenging behaviour (e.g. Oliver & Head, 1990; Oliver, 1993; Murphy, 1994; Emerson, 1995). Traditionally, such accounts of challenging behaviour have focused almost entirely on the immediate antecedents and consequences of behaviour in an attempt to determine the function of challenging behaviour (e.g. to enable the person to escape from an 'aversive' situation). More technically, behavioural practice and theory have been preoccupied with identifying the contingencies of reinforcement responsible for maintaining challenging behaviour.

While undoubtedly productive, such a focus has largely ignored the effects of contextual factors that exercise functional (motivational) control over these contingencies. This preoccupation is somewhat puzzling because behavioural theory predicts that personal, biological, historical and environmental contexts exert a crucial motivational influence over behaviour by determining or establishing the reinforcing and punishing potential of otherwise neutral stimuli. As such, a comprehensive behavioural analysis needs to address (at least) two distinct questions.

– What are the functions of the person's challenging behaviours?
– What historical and concurrent contextual factors have endowed particular events and activities with a capacity to reinforce or punish the person's challenging behaviours?

The latter question is of crucial importance, because answering it may identify approaches to intervention based on the modification of such 'setting events'[2] rather than the direct modification of the contingencies maintaining behaviour (Emerson, 1995).

To take a recent example, Carr and Smith (1995) have explored the relationship between pain, behavioural processes and challenging behaviour. The data they present suggest that some challenging behaviours that serve a clear behavioural function (escape from instructional demands) may only become apparent when a particular motivational condition (pain) is present (O'Reilly, 1997). That is, it appears that the biological state (pain) created the conditions under which instructional demands became aversive, and that the person's challenging behaviour served to terminate the aversive demands (but not the pain).

Such a conceptualization is clearly distinct from approaches that view challenging behaviour as occurring as a direct consequence of biological

2. The behavioural terminology for dealing with such operations is currently evolving but includes the concepts of setting factors, setting events, establishing operations and establishing stimuli (Bijou & Baer, 1978; Wahler & Fox, 1981; Michael, 1982).

state (i.e. pain is seen as a sufficient condition for the occurrence of challenging behaviour). Instead, it points to the possibility that underlying biological conditions may change the valence of otherwise neutral environmental events, thereby creating the conditions under which (functional) challenging behaviours may occur. The importance of the distinction is that the latter model suggests two complimentary approaches to intervention: (1) change the motivating condition (e.g. by treating the underlying medical condition, c.f. Peine et al., 1995); and (2) change the 'functionality' of the person's challenging behaviour (e.g., by providing a more effective and more socially appropriate way for the person to escape from instructional demands (c.f. Carr et al., 1994).

It seems plausible to suggest that some psychiatric disorders may also operate in this way by similarly changing the valence of otherwise neutral environmental events. For example, depression may be associated with an unwillingness to participate in educational or social activities, thus establishing such activities as negative reinforcers (i.e. events whose termination is reinforcing). If the person has previously learned that challenging behaviours can terminate such aversive events, we would expect an episode of depression to be associated with an increase in challenging behaviour. It is worth noting, that, unlike in the previous section, depression is not seen as 'causing' challenging behaviour (i.e. is not a sufficient condition for the expression of challenging behaviour). Rather, the occurrence of challenging behaviour is determined by the combination of: (1) the motivational influence of depression in establishing negative reinforcers; and (2) the pre-existence in the individual's repertoire of challenging behaviours which have previously served an escape function. Again, such a conceptualization suggests two complementary approaches to intervention: (1) change the motivating condition (e.g. treat the person's depression); and (2) change the 'functionality' of the person's challenging behaviour.

Lowry and Sovner (1992) describe two case studies in which this type of process appeared to be operating. In both cases rapid cycling bipolar mood disorder (assessed through detailed behavioural recording of affect and activity) appeared to be closely associated with variations in self-injury (Case 1) or aggression (Case 2). For both cases, however, anecdotal information was presented to suggest that: (1) specific environmental events (demands from care staff) precipitated episodes of challenging behaviour, but only during particular mood states (depression for Case 1, mania for Case 2); and (2) the person's challenging behaviour may have functioned within such states to terminate or delay such precipitating stimuli.

Conclusion

The preceding sections review the evidence that suggests possible relationships between challenging behaviour and psychiatric disorders in people with severe developmental disabilities. The available data are limited by two main factors: (1) the inherent difficulties in diagnosing psychiatric disorders in this client group; and (2) the quite distinct research traditions, cultures and institutions within which behavioural and psychiatric research is conducted.

The evidence reviewed in this chapter does, however, suggest that at least four types of relationship between challenging behaviour and psychiatric disorders may be of immediate clinical significance. These are that:
- family factors associated with the development of challenging behaviour appear similar to those associated with the development of conduct disorder;
- challenging behaviour (e.g. self-injurious behaviour) may, in some circumstances, represent the atypical presentation of an underlying psychiatric disorder (e.g. obsessive–compulsive disorder) in people with severe developmental disabilities;
- challenging behaviours may occur as secondary features of psychiatric disorders (e.g. depression) among people with severe developmental disabilities;
- psychiatric disorders may establish a motivational basis for the expression of challenging behaviours maintained by (operant) behavioural processes.

The first formulation has clear implications for the understanding of challenging behaviour in terms of historical factors which may have endowed particular events or activities with the capacity to reinforce or punish the person's challenging behaviour, and clear implications for early intervention in the prevention of challenging behaviour. The clinical implications of the second and third formulations are clear and straightforward: the most appropriate approach to intervention will require the diagnosis and treatment of the 'underlying' psychiatric disorder. The fourth formulation, however, suggests that the challenging behaviours displayed by individuals pre-exist in their repertoire as functional and 'adaptive' responses. The role of the psychiatric disorder is to provide a motivational basis within which these pre-existing challenging behaviours are likely to be evoked. Given that it is possible that other setting events (e.g. physical illness) could have a similar motivational impact to the psychiatric disorder (e.g. both pain and depression may serve to increase the aversiveness of carer demands), this points to the possible need for parallel and complementary approaches to intervention. While these will include, as above, the appropriate diagnosis and treatment of the underlying psychiatric disorder, it is probable that intervention efficacy will be increased by the addition of behavioural approaches.

References

American Psychiatric Association (1994). *Diagnostic and Statistical Manual of Mental Disorders*, fourth edition. Washington, DC: American Psychiatric Association.

Bijou, S.W. & Baer, D.M. (1978). *Behavior Analysis of Child Development.* Englewood Cliffs, NJ: Prentice-Hall.

Bodfish, J.W. & Madison, J.T. (1993). Diagnosis and fluoxetine treatment of compulsive behavior disorder of adults with mental retardation. *American Journal on Mental Retardation,* **98**, 360–7.

Campbell, M. & Malone, R.P. (1991). Mental retardation and psychiatric disorders. *Hospital and Community Psychiatry,* **42**, 374–9.

Carr, E.G., Levin, L., McConnachie, G., Carlson, J.I., Kemp, D.C. & Smith, C.E. (1994). *Communication-Based Intervention for Problem Behavior: A User's Guide for Producing Positive Change.* Baltimore: Brookes.

Carr, E.G. & Smith, C.E. (1995). Biological setting events for self-injury. *Mental Retardation and Developmental Disabilities Research Reviews,* **1**, 94–8.

Craft, M. (1971). 'A North Wales experiment in subnormality care'. *British Journal of Psychiatry,* **118**, 199–206

Cunningham, C., Sloper, T., Rangecroft, A. & Knussen, C. (1986). *The Effects of Early Intervention on the Occurrence and Nature of Behaviour Problems in Children with Down's Syndrome.* Manchester: Hester Adrian Research Centre, University of Manchester.

Day, K. (1985) Psychiatric disorder in the middle-aged and elderly mentally handicapped. *British Journal of Psychiatry,* **147**, 660–7.

Emerson, E. (1995). *Challenging Behaviour: Analysis and Intervention in People with Learning Difficulties.* Cambridge: Cambridge University Press.

Emerson, E., Alborz, A., Reeves, D. et al. (1997). *The HARC Challenging Behaviour Project. Report 2: The Prevalence of Challenging Behaviour.* Manchester: Hester Adrian Research Centre, University of Manchester.

Gardner, W.I. & Whalen, J.P. (1996). A multimodal behavior analytic model for evaluating the effects of medical problems on nonspecific behavioral symptoms in persons with developmental disabilities. *Behavioral Interventions,* **11**, 147–61.

Heaton-Ward, A. (1977). Psychosis in mental handicap. *British Journal of Psychiatry,* **130**, 525–33.

Iverson, J.C. & Fox, R.A. (1989). Prevalence of psychopathology among mentally retarded adults. *Research in Developmental Disabilities,* **10**, 77–83.

Kiernan, C. & Moss, S.C. (1990). Behavioural and other characteristics of the population of a mental handicap hospital. *Mental Handicap Research,* **3**, 320.

Kiernan, C. & Qureshi, H. (1993). Challenging behaviour. In ed. C. Kiernan *Research to Practice? Implications of Research on the Challenging Behaviour of People with Learning Disability,* pp. 53–65. Clevedon, Avon: BILD Publications.

Kiernan, C., Reeves, D., Hatton, C. et al. (1997). *The HARC Challenging Behaviour Project. Report 1: Persistence and Change in the Challenging Behaviour of People with Learning Disability.* Manchester: Hester Adrian Research Centre, University of Manchester.

King, B.H. (1993). Self-injury by people with mental retardation: a compulsive behavior hypothesis. *American Journal on Mental Retardation,* **98**, 93–112.

Lader, M. & Herrington, R. (1996). *Biological Treatments in Psychiatry,* 2nd edition. Oxford: Oxford University Press.

Leck, I., Gordon, W.L. & McKeown, T. (1967). Medical and social needs of mentally subnormal patients. *British Journal of Preventative and Social Medicine*, 21, 115–21.

Lewis, M.H., Bodfish, J.W., Powell, S.B., Parker, D.E. & Golden, R.N. (1996). Clomipramine treatment for self-injurious behavior of individuals with mental retardation: a double-blind comparison with placebo. *American Journal on Mental Retardation*, **100**, 654–65.

Lowry, M.A. & Sovner, R. (1992). Severe behavior problems associated with rapid cycling bipolar disorder in two adults with profound mental retardation. *Journal of Intellectual Disability Research*, **36**, 269–81.

Markowitz, P. (1992). Effect of fluoxetine on selfinjurious behavior in the developmentally disabled: a preliminary study. *Journal of Clinical Psychopharmacology*, **12**, 27–31.

McCord, J. (1990). Long term perspectives on parental absence. In *Straight and Devious Paths from Childhood to Adulthood*, ed. L.N. Robins & M. Rutter, pp. 116–34. Cambridge: Cambridge University Press.

Meins, W. (1995) Symptoms of major depression in mentally retarded adults. *Journal of Intellectual Disability Research*, **39**, 41–5.

Menolascino, F.J. (1989). Clinical care update: model services for treatment/management of the mentally retarded–mentally ill. *Community Mental Health Journal*, **25**, 145–55.

Michael, J. (1982). Distinguishing between discriminative and motivational functions of stimuli. *Journal of the Experimental Analysis of Behavior*, **37**, 149–55.

Murphy, G. (1994). Understanding challenging behaviour. In *Severe Learning Disabilities and Challenging Behaviours: Designing High Quality Services*, ed. E. Emerson, P. McGill & J. Mansell, pp. 37–68. London: Chapman and Hall.

Nihara, K., Meyers, C.E. & Mink, I.T. (1980). Home environment, family adjustment, and the development of mentally retarded children. *Applied Research in Mental Retardation*, *1*, 5–24.

Oliver, C. (1993). Self-injurious behaviour: from response to strategy. In *Research to Practice? Implication of Research on the Challenging Behaviour of People with Learning Disabilities*, ed. C. Kiernan pp. 135–88. Clevedon, Avon: British Institute of Learning Disabilities.

Oliver, C. & Head, D. (1990). Selfinjurious behaviour in people with learning disabilities: determinants and interventions. *International Review of Psychiatry*, **2**, 101–16.

O'Reilly, M.F. (1997). Functional analysis of episodic self-injury correlated with otitis media. *Journal of Applied Behavior Analysis*, **30**, 165–7.

Peine, H.A., Darvish, R., Adams, K., Blakelock, H., Jenson, W. & Osborne, J.G. (1995). Medical problems, maladaptive behaviours, and the developmentally disabled. *Behavioral Interventions*, **10**, 149–60.

Primrose, D.A. (1971). A survey of 502 consecutive admissions to a subnormality hospital from 1st January 1968 to 31st December 1970. *British Journal of Mental Subnormality*, **17**, 25–8.

Reid, A.H. (1972). Psychoses in adult mental defectives: II. Schizophrenic and paranoid psychoses. *British Journal of Psychiatry*, 120, 213–18.

Reid, A.H. (1982). *The Psychiatry of Mental Handicap.* Oxford: Blackwell.

Reiss, S. (1990). Prevalence of dual diagnosis in community-based day programs in the Chicago metropolitan area. *American Journal on Mental Retardation,* **94**, 578–85.

Reiss, S. & Rojahn, J. (1993). Joint occurrence of depression and aggression in children and adults with mental retardation. *Journal of Intellectual Disability Research,* **37**, 287–94.

Richardson, S.A. (1987). The ecology of mental handicap. In *Prevention of Mental Handicap: a World View,* ed. G. Hosking & G. Murphy, pp. 95–102. International Congress and Symposium Series, Number 112. London: Royal Society of Medicine Services.

Rojahn, J., Borthwick-Duffy, S.A. & Jacobson, J.W. (1993). The association between psychiatric diagnoses and severe behavior problems in mental retardation. *Annals of Clinical Psychiatry,* **5**, 163–70.

Rutter, M. (1985). Family and school influences on cognitive development. *Journal of Child Psychology and Psychiatry,* **26**, 683–704.

Sloper, T. & Turner, S. (1993). Family factors and parents' report of behaviour problems in 6–14 year old children with Down's syndrome. In *Research to Practice? Implications of Research on the Challenging Behaviour of People with Learning Disability,* ed. C. Kiernan, pp. 69–87. Clevedon, Avon: BILD Publications.

Sovner, R., Fox, C.J., Lowry, M.J. & Lowry, M.A. (1993). Fluoxetine treatment of depression and associated selfinjury in two adults with mental retardation. *Journal of Intellectual Disability Research,* **37**, 301–11.

Sovner, R. & Hurley, D.A. (1983). Do the mentally retarded suffer from affective illness? *Archives of General Psychiatry,* **40**, 61–7.

Wahler, R.G. & Fox, J.J. (1981). Setting events in applied behavior analysis: toward a conceptual and methodological expansion. *Journal of Applied Behavior Analysis,* **14**, 327–38.

4   Brain imaging and behaviour

DENE ROBERTSON AND DECLAN MURPHY

Introduction

A range of neuroimaging techniques has become available that allows clinical and research investigations of in-vivo brain structure and function in people with developmental disabilities. This chapter:

1. describes the available techniques,
2. discusses how these have been used to study normal brain development,
3. describes how they can be used to study the genetic and environmental determinants of normal and abnormal brain development, using Turner's syndrome as a model,
4. describes research findings in three groups of people in whom developmental disability occurs – these are people with autism, fragile X syndrome, and Down syndrome,
5. explores ways in which neuroimaging techniques may be used in a clinical setting to benefit individual patients.

Neuroimaging techniques

Until relatively recently, in-vivo brain imaging was used to examine brain structure but had no capacity to examine function. However, advances in positron emission tomography (PET) and single photon emission tomography (SPET) and the development of functional magnetic resonance imaging (fMRI) have made it possible to examine cerebral metabolism, regional cerebral blood flow, receptor location and density, and the neural correlates of cognitive function and psychiatric disorder.

Current neuroimaging techniques are described under two headings: structural brain studies, and functional brain studies.

Structural brain studies

Computerized tomography scanning

X-ray computerized tomography (CT) was developed from pre-existing X-ray technology in the 1970s. It involves measuring the X-ray attenuation of thin slices of the body from multiple angles, and combining the information using a computer to create images of slices through the body.

Clinically, CT is the investigation of choice for certain acute brain investigations (e.g. haemorrhage or trauma). It demonstrates bone and bleeds with excellent detail, but has several disadvantages when compared to MRI. For example, soft tissue contrast is inferior to that obtained with MRI, CT is particularly poor at the visualization of some brain areas bordering thick bone (e.g. posterior fossa and inferior temporal lobes), and it exposes the patient to ionizing radiation.

Magnetic resonance imaging

The mechanism of action of MRI depends upon a property of biologically abundant atomic nuclei (e.g. ^1H, ^{31}P) with an uneven number of neutrons or protons called *spin*. Because the nuclei of these atoms are positively charged, they act in a similar way to a collection of randomly oriented small bar magnets. An externally applied magnetic field (usually generated by the passage of a large current through a very powerful superconducting magnet) causes the nuclei to align either parallel or antiparallel with this magnetic field. Individual nuclei do not align absolutely perfectly with the field, however, but precess or wobble around the magnetic field's axis slightly, in the same way that the earth precesses around its axis under the gravitational influence of the sun. For a given type of nucleus (for example ^1H), the rate at which this precession occurs is directly proportional to the applied field strength.

Under the influence of the applied magnetic field, there are slightly more nuclei aligned with the magnetic field in a parallel than in an antiparallel direction. The nuclei in each pair pointing parallel and antiparallel to the main magnetic field cancel each other out, but the slight excess of nuclei parallel to the field leads to a net magnetic moment parallel to the field. More nuclei can be excited into the higher energy antiparallel state by the application of a burst of radiofrequency energy at a frequency that matches the precessional frequency of the nuclei. Following the application of this applied radiofrequency magnetic field, the nuclei give off the energy they have absorbed by a process called relaxation, which leads to the emission of extremely weak radio waves. Sensitive radio receivers within the MR system can detect this weak signal. The rate at which the nuclei relax, and the additional effects of small applied magnetic field gradients determine the type of image that is produced. There are two types of relaxation. In spin-lattice relaxation (more commonly known as T_1 relaxation) energy is given off to the surrounding molecules, whilst in spin-spin relaxation (more commonly known as T_2 relaxation) energy is given off to neighbouring non-excited nuclei.

Images are produced by applying a series of radiofrequency and gradient pulses and recording the weak radiofrequency signals emitted by the relaxing nuclei. The timing of these pulses can lead to images that are more or less sensitive to T_1 or T_2 relaxation. 'T_1-weighted' images are excellent at demonstrating anatomy and are characterized by dark cerebrospinal fluid with white matter brighter than grey matter (Fig. 4.1). 'T_2-weighted' images are

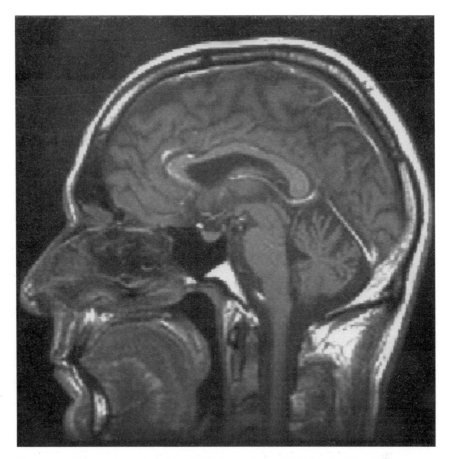

Fig. 4.1 A midline sagittal 'T$_1$-weighted' MR image. 'T$_1$-weighted' images have dark cerebrospinal fluid, brighter white than grey matter, and provide an excellent demonstration of anatomy.

often used to demonstrate pathology because of their sensitivity to changes in water within the brain, such as oedema. They are characterized by bright cerebrospinal fluid with grey matter brighter than white matter (Fig. 4.2). Clinically, T$_1$-weighted and T$_2$-weighted images are often complementary, for example neoplasms appear dark on T$_1$-weighted images and bright on T$_2$-weighted images. A variety of other image types can also be generated by appropriate choice of a variety of acquisition parameters.

The principal strengths of MRI are its excellent soft tissue contrast, ability to acquire images in any arbitrary oblique plane, and total lack of ionizing radiation. Despite the advantages of MRI over CT in research and clinical practice, there are limitations to its application. For example, the magnetic and radiofrequency fields have safety implications in terms of the attraction of metallic objects and the use of radiofrequency pulses for altering the calibration of some implants. Therefore, patients with clips on intracerebral aneurysms, cardiac pacemakers and cochlear implants should not be scanned. Further, patients are required to enter the relatively narrow bore of

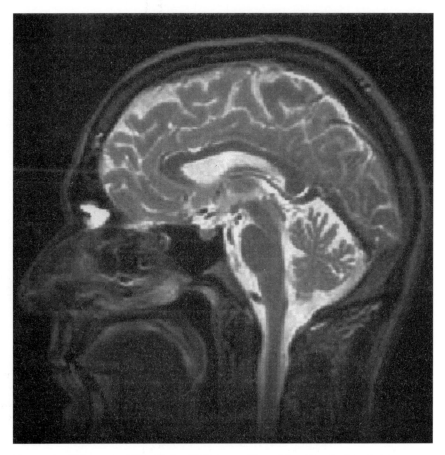

Fig. 4.2 A midline sagittal 'T$_2$-weighted' MR image. 'T$_2$-weighted' images have bright cerebrospinal fluid, brighter grey than white matter, and are often used to demonstrate pathology.

the machine, which can be intimidating for a small number of patients without sedation.

Functional brain studies

Magnetic resonance spectroscopy

Proton magnetic resonance spectroscopy (MRS) is a non-invasive technique that allows measurements of neuronal integrity and metabolism. Using this technique, spectra (rather than images) of the magnetic signals of nuclei such as ^{1}H and ^{31}P are obtained. ^{1}H is biologically abundant, leading to a large-amplitude signal; thus, ^{1}H (or 'proton') MRS is commonly employed, and allows better resolution than is possible with other nuclei. It is proton spectroscopy that is discussed here.

The resonant frequency of a proton depends very subtly on the chemical environment that it finds itself within. Thus, a proton attached to a fat molecule will have a slightly different resonant frequency from one attached to a water molecule. It is this subtle difference in resonant frequency that is the

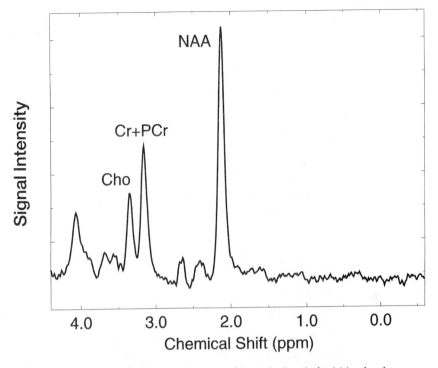

Fig. 4.3 A representative ¹H MR spectrum. Signal intensity (vertical axis) is related to concentration of the metabolite of interest. Chemical shift (horizontal axis) is a proportionality constant, enabling differentiation between protons in different local magnetic environments. Cho, choline; Cr+PCr, creatine and phosphocreatine; NAA, N-acetyl-ʟ-aspartate.

basis of MRS and leads to a spectrum of signal intensity versus frequency (Fig. 4.3). The area under a peak in an MR spectrum is related to the concentration of nuclei within the volume of interest.

Positron emission tomography

The PET technique depends upon the administration of radio-labelled compounds that emit positrons. These positrons travel only a short distance within tissue before colliding with an electron. The particles annihilate each other, producing a pair of photons that travel in opposite directions. These 'annihilation pairs' are detected by a system of photomultiplier tubes behind a collimator array. Computer algorithms similar to those used in X-ray CT then produce an image corresponding to the distribution of the radionuclide. Correction for signal attenuation by the patient's tissues is made by performing a transmission scan with an external ring source immediately prior to the PET scan series. PET images are often 'co-registered' with a detailed anatomical image (e.g. a MR image) so that more precise anatomical information can be gained.

Many different radiotracer compounds have been developed for PET, and their use depends upon their distribution and interactions. These can be conveniently categorized as follows.

1. Receptor location and density estimation. The administration of radio-labelled ligands that interact with receptors enables determination of receptor location and density in vivo. Changes in pathologic states, in disease progression and in response to intervention may also be determined.

2. Resting brain metabolism. Whole (CMRglc) and regional (rCMRglc) brain glucose metabolism can be studied using [^{18}F]2-fluoro-2-deoxyglucose (FDG), a radioisotope with a half-life of approximately two hours, which crosses the blood–brain barrier and is taken up into cells where it is phosphorylated and becomes trapped. Because FDG becomes involved in the same metabolic pathways in the cell as glucose, the resulting images map the pattern of glucose metabolism within the brain.

3. Regional cerebral blood flow. Measurement of relative and absolute cerebral blood flow is possible. Assessment of *absolute* regional cerebral blood flow is relatively difficult because it involves sampling radiopharmaceutical concentrations in arterial blood simultaneously with PET scanning in order to calculate the amount of radiopharmaceutical entering the cerebral artery. However, there is a close relationship between neuronal activity, glucose metabolism and cerebral blood flow (Fox & Raichle, 1986). Thus, when the aim is to compare neurons in an inactive and an active state, *relative* regional cerebral blood flow changes are hypothesized to be proportional to changes in synaptic activity. Measurement of relative regional cerebral blood flow change does not require arterial sampling, and is computationally much less difficult.

Single photon emission tomography

The general principles underlying SPET are similar to those underlying PET. Radiopharmaceuticals are administered intravenously or inhaled, and photons emitted in the brain as a result of radioactive decay are detected by a gamma camera. However, SPET is much cheaper than PET and is more widely available. Images are produced by computational techniques that are similar to those used for PET, and co-registration can be performed in a similar way for anatomical localization. Image resolution is generally lower with SPET than with PET, and SPET is more limited in its range of applications.

Functional magnetic resonance imaging

This provides the highest image resolution of all the functional techniques described here. It relies on small signal changes in a series of rapidly acquired MR images during the performance of the active (on) and control (off) phases of an activation paradigm. These signal changes are due to temporal changes in the magnetic susceptibility of tissue where there is a change in the concentration of deoxyhaemoglobin, an effect called blood oxygen level dependent (BOLD) contrast. Such concentration changes occur as a result of alterations in synaptic activity associated with cortical activity. A typical functional activation paradigm consists of alternating on and off phases (which, respectively, contain the cognitive work in question and a control task) for a period of several minutes; repeated acquisition leads to an effective increase in the signal to noise ratio once analysis is performed. The same caution should be exercised in experimental design and data analysis as described above for PET.

The newest and most rapidly evolving of the functional imaging techniques, fMRI can be performed on the higher performance 1.5T machines that are common in teaching hospitals. Unlike PET, therefore, the hardware exists that will shortly enable many centres to use this technology in both research and clinical practice.

Normal brain development and ageing

It is necessary to know how the brain develops and ages normally in order to understand how abnormalities of brain development affect higher cognitive function and behaviour in people with a developmental disability. Knowledge of normal brain development is also essential if we are to understand the genetic and environmental *determinants* of brain structure and function.

Post-mortem studies of human brain during development demonstrate that brain weight quadruples within the first decade, thereafter undergoing gradual decline (Debakan & Sadowsky, 1978). Myelination occurs at different rates throughout the brain, and some regions are fully myelinated before others. For example, the hippocampus is not fully myelinated until late in the fourth decade of life, and starts to have age-related loss of cells as late as the fifth decade. Therefore, a dynamic relationship exists between changes in whole and regional brain parameters during development and ageing, and it is increasingly recognized that development and ageing of the brain are not discrete biological entities, but form a continuum.

Brain imaging techniques have been used to extend our understanding of age-related changes in brain structure and function derived from such post-mortem data. For example, grey matter, white matter, cerebrospinal fluid and regional brain volumes can be related to whole-brain volume as functions of age and sex. Changes in structure may be related to alterations in brain function.

MRI studies have reported that white matter tracts are identifiable by one year of age, and that myelination continues into adolescence (Holland et al., 1986; Barkowich et al., 1988; Christophe et al., 1990). Whole-brain white matter volume reaches a peak at approximately 20 years of age, and thereafter remains constant throughout adult life (Jernigan et al., 1991a; Pfefferbaum et al., 1994). In contrast, the peak brain grey/white matter ratio occurs at approximately four years of age, and thereafter undergoes gradual decline (Pfefferbaum et al., 1994). Thus, age-related loss of brain tissue may predominantly be of grey matter. In later adult life, there are age-related increases in cerebrospinal fluid that accompany age-related loss of grey matter (Jernigan, Press, Hesselink, 1990; Jernigan et al., 1991a, 1991b; Pfefferbaum et al., 1994). Generally, these whole-brain MRI studies accord with earlier CT studies (DeLeo et al., 1985; Schwartz et al., 1985), and are consistent with post-mortem data (Brody, 1955; Davis & Wright, 1977; Debakan & Sadowsky, 1978; Ho et al., 1980; Hubbard & Anderson, 1981). Regional variation in age-related loss of brain matter has also been examined using MRI. For example, the temporal lobes show less loss of brain tissue than the frontal lobes (DeCarli et al., 1994; Murphy et al., 1992).

CT studies have reported age-associated changes in brain that are gender specific. For example, a precipitous increase in ventricular volume begins in the fifth decade in men and in the sixth decade in women (Kaye et al., 1992), suggesting that brain atrophy begins earlier in men than in women. However, once started, the *rate* of the atrophy process increases with age more rapidly in women (Takeda & Matsuzawa, 1985). MRI studies of sex differences in brain ageing are in disagreement, however. Some find no sex difference (Coffey et al., 1992), whereas others (Cowell et al., 1994; Gur et al., 1991) report that males have a greater age-related loss of whole-brain volume than females, and that age-related atrophy is asymmetric in males but symmetric in females. Only one MRI study has investigated the effects of sex differences on regional brain volumes (Murphy et al., 1996). It reported that the ageing effect was significantly greater in males than females in whole brain, frontal and temporal lobes, whereas it was greater in females than males in hippocampus and parietal lobes. Sex differences in brain ageing strongly suggest a role for the sex chromosomes and/or gonadal hormones in the development and ageing of normal brain.

Functional changes during brain development in childhood are thought to reflect changes occurring at the cellular and synaptic level. Thus, when PET was used to examine the cerebral metabolic rates of children from five days to 15 years (Chugani, Phelps & Mazziota, 1987), a decrease in cerebral metabolism of 50 per cent was found to occur in those older than nine years, possibly as a result of lower synaptic density. The finding has been corroborated by a SPET study that reported maximal metabolism at about five years (Chiron et al., 1992).

Age-related changes in resting glucose metabolism have also been examined in adulthood. An investigation using FDG-PET (Murphy et al., 1996), reported significant sex differences in age-related effects in the temporal and parietal lobes, Broca's area, thalamus and hippocampus. For example, males had no age-related decline in hippocampal metabolism, whereas women did. Further, age-related decline in brain metabolism was greater on the left than on the right side in males, but in females it was generally symmetric. Because these gender differences occur in brain regions associated with cognitive function and neuropsychiatric disease, they may underlie gender differences in the prevalence and symptomatology of neuropsychiatric disorders such as autism, dyslexia, schizophrenia and Alzheimer's disease.

In addition to measuring glucose metabolism of isolated brain regions, functional relationships between areas of the brain can be studied by applying a statistical correlation analysis (Clark et al., 1984; Horwitz, Duara & Rapoport, 1984). The assumption is that if two brain regions are functionally coupled so that activity in one depends on the activity in the other, an increase or decrease in one brain region will be correlated with a similar increase or decrease in the other. This approach was used to compare the regional intercorrelations of glucose metabolic rates in a group of young subjects and a group of older subjects in a PET study (Horwitz, Duara & Rapoport, 1986). The older group had the same general pattern of intercorrelations as the young group, but there were significantly fewer correlations in the old group between metabolic rates in the frontal and parietal regions and between regions within the parietal areas bilaterally. These age-related changes were interpreted as arising from a decrease in the integrated function between these areas, and may be associated with some of the neuropsychological deficits that are seen in the elderly, specifically those that may depend heavily on the integrated function of anterior and posterior brain regions, such as tasks of attention (Mesulam, 1981).

In contrast, functional experiments using PET have suggested that hemispheric lateralization of cognitive function is probably maintained during healthy ageing. For example, when subjects performed recognition tasks for words and faces (Berardi et al., 1990, 1991), performance on the tasks was related to resting metabolic asymmetry in both young and old subjects. Subjects with a better verbal memory performance had greater left than right parietal metabolism, and those with better memory for faces had greater right than left parietal metabolism. Conversely, there is also PET evidence that age-related changes in brain do have functional consequences. In an activation study in which healthy subjects were required to encode and then recognize faces (Grady et al., 1995), young people showed increased regional cerebral blood flow in right hippocampus, left prefrontal and temporal cortices during face encoding that was not present when elderly subjects performed the tasks. Thus, it may be that age-related deficits in memory for faces occur as a result of defective encoding. Also, these may be consequent upon age-related changes in brain structure.

In summary, to understand the abnormal brain development that occurs in developmental disability, we need to know about the normal process. Sex differences in *healthy* brain development and ageing suggest that sex steroids and chromosomes have a crucial part to play. Some studies have investigated the role of such factors (e.g. the X chromosome) in other populations using in-vivo brain imaging, and these are discussed below. The outcome of these studies may be of benefit to the general population as well as to people with a developmental disability.

Turner's syndrome as a model for examining brain development

The X chromosome's importance in regional brain development and ageing is suggested by the studies above and by neuropsychological and brain imaging studies of sex chromosome aneuploidies. For example: 49,XXXXY males have better visuospatial than verbal skills (Borghgraef et al., 1988; Curfs et al., 1990), and girls who are 47,XXX have delayed language and cognitive development (Robinson et al., 1979; Pennington, Puck & Robinson, 1980; Nielsen, Sorenson & Sorenson, 1981; Netley & Rovet, 1987). Turner's syndrome females (45,X) typically have better verbal than visuospatial skills (Murphy et al., 1993). Because women with Turner's syndrome do not produce oestrogen and lack one, or part of one, X chromosome, they provide a model for the investigation of the effects of sex chromosomes and sex steroids on structural brain development. Thus, a quantitative MRI study reported significant bilateral decreases in the volumes of cerebral hemispheric and parieto-occipital brain matter, hippocampus, lenticular and thalamic nuclei compared to controls (Murphy et al., 1993). X chromosome dosage effects were reported in a number of brain regions (right and left cerebral hemisphere, caudate, lenticular and thalamic nuclei) but not in others (hippocampus). Moreover, there were X chromosome dosage effects on some cognitive abilities (e.g. verbal and visuospatial function) but not on others, possibly reflecting the different contributions of the X chromosome and sex steroids to normal brain development.

Using PET and FDG, Murphy et al. (submitted) reported that women with Turner's syndrome had relative bilateral hypometabolism in association neocortices and insulae compared to controls, adding to Clark, Klonoff and Hayden's (1990) report of decreased metabolism in occipital and parietal cortex (Clark et al., 1990; Murphy et al., 1997). Moreover, correlation analyses revealed significant differences in functional associations of pairs of brain regions originating in bilateral occipital cortices, and within the right hemisphere. Left/right asymmetries of brain function correlated with cognitive deficits, and metabolic abnormalities of the insulae may explain the abnormalities of social interaction (e.g. difficulty in interpreting social cues) that occur in Turner's syndrome. Further, X chromosome dosage effects were demonstrated in language ability and left middle temporal lobe metabolism, right/left asymmetry of neuropsychological test scores and parietal lobe metabolism. These effects were mainly due to group differences in verbal function and left parietal metabolism, whereas visuospatial function and right parietal metabolism were decreased to a similar extent in both mosaic and full Turner's syndrome, implying that the X chromosome may be involved in the development of both left and right association neocortices, and that sex steroids may be more crucially involved in the development of the right-sided neocortex.

Fragile X syndrome

Fragile X syndrome is the most common form of inherited developmental disability, and is associated with variable intellectual ability (from normal intelligence to severe developmental disability). However, the neurobiological basis to the variation in cognitive ability of people with this syndrome is unknown. Fragile X syndrome is caused by an expansion of cytosine–guanine–guanine triplet repeats in the *FMR-1* gene on the X chromosome. Healthy normal subjects have up to approximately 50 triplet repeats, premutation carriers have 50–200, and people with the full mutation have more than 200 – causing hypermethylation of the promotor region, inactivation of the *FMR-1* gene and consequently loss of gene expression.

Developmental delay in those with fragile X syndrome varies considerably, from normal levels of intellectual ability through to severe–profound mental handicap. Moreover, there are significant gender differences in the cognitive phenotype of the syndrome. Most males with the fragile X syndrome full mutation have mental retardation – usually in the moderate or severe range (Kemper et al., 1986; Kemper, Hagerman, Altshul-Stark, 1988). The cognitive profile of relative strengths and weaknesses observed in females with fragile X syndrome resembles that found in males but is more severe and less variable (Kemper et al., 1986; Miezejeski et al., 1986; Prouty et al., 1988; Freund & Reiss, 1991). In addition to an overall impairment of intelligence, people with the syndrome have relatively greater deficits in attention, processing of sequential information, short-term memory, visual–spatial abilities, visual–motor co-ordination, and pragmatic language (Kemper et al., 1988; Freund & Reiss, 1991; Sudhalter, Scarborough & Cohen, 1991; Sudhalter, Maranion & Brooks, 1992). Also, some authors report that verbal abilities are less affected than performance (Theobald, Hay & Judge, 1987; Veenema et al., 1987). Thus, in fragile X syndrome, some cognitive skills may be more susceptible to impairment than others, suggesting a possible selective role for the *FMR-1* gene's influence on brain development.

This neuropsychological evidence for abnormal brain development in people with fragile X syndrome is supported by in-vivo experimental evidence of changes in brain structure. Qualitative CT studies have reported mild ventricular dilatation or cerebral atrophy (Rhoades, 1982; Wisniewski et al., 1985; Veenema et al., 1987). Consistent with reports of increased head circumference (Hagerman, 1991), a quantitative CT study of male adults with fragile X syndrome reported significantly increased intracranial volume compared to healthy controls (Schapiro et al., 1995). However, this study did not replicate the qualitative CT reports of cortical atrophy in the syndrome, or the reports of ventricular dilatation. Nevertheless, patients with fragile X syndrome had significantly larger right than left lateral ventricles, suggesting that there are changes in regional as well as whole-brain structure.

Structural MRI studies have reported deviations in the size of the cerebellar vermis, fourth ventricle, hippocampus and caudate volume that correlate with X activation ratio – the percentage of active X chromosomes carrying the fragile X mutation (Reiss et al., 1995). Thus, some cognitive difficulties and abnormalities in brain structure may result from lack of the gene product in brain areas normally having heavy *FMR-1* transcription. For example, the hippocampus is implicated in memory in mammals, and memory and hippocampal morphometry are abnormal in fragile X syndrome (Reiss et al., 1995; Murphy et al., 1997).

People with fragile X syndrome also have altered rCMRglc. Using PET and FDG, Schapiro et al. (1995) reported significantly increased rCMRglc in the vermis (possibly also structurally abnormal in this disorder), calcarine cortex and caudate nucleus compared to controls. Right/left asymmetry in rCMRglc was significantly greater in the parietal lobes in subjects with the syndrome.

The right parietal cortex has been implicated in visuospatial short-term memory and attention (Parasuraman & Haxby, 1993) – aspects of cognition that are impaired in people with fragile X syndrome. Thus, reports of abnormal asymmetry in brain function and structure lend weight to the hypothesis that regionally disordered neuroanatomy and metabolism mediate the reported specific cognitive deficits.

Patients with fragile X syndrome may also undergo increased brain ageing, and it has been reported that decrease in the volume of the superior temporal gyrus and increase in the volume of the hippocampus may be age related (Reiss, Lee & Freund, 1994). Preliminary work (Murphy et al., 1997) using volumetric MRI and PET-FDG has examined female premutation carriers of the disorder, who are known to have an increased prevalence of premature ovarian ageing. Compared to controls, female premutation carriers had relative hypometabolism in association neocortices and differences in right/left asymmetry of language areas – all related to higher cognitive function. Thus, the fragile X premutation affects brain. However, we are unsure whether these changes are *secondary* to abnormalities in brain development or ageing. These findings require replication.

Autism

The nature of the changes in brain in autism is controversial. A number of investigators have reported structural abnormalities in ventricular size and in cerebral hemispheric asymmetry using CT (Lotspeich & Ciaranello, 1993). In MRI studies, which have better resolution, cerebellar hypoplasia is most consistently reported (Gafney et al., 1987; Courchesne et al., 1988; Murakami et al., 1989; Hashimoto et al., 1995); abnormalities have been detected in the cerebellar vermis (lobules VI and VII) (Courchesne et al., 1988) as well as in the cerebellar hemispheres (Murakami et al., 1989). Other studies, however, have failed to replicate these findings (Holttum et al., 1992; Hashimoto et al., 1993). Neuropsychological support for cerebellar abnormalities in autism comes from studies that report an increased latency in the extinction of classical eye-blink conditioning in autistic subjects (Sears, Finn & Steinmetz, 1994) and abnormal motor behaviour (Adrien et al., 1992).

Other brain regions are also reported to be structurally abnormal in people with autism. For example, qualitative MRI studies found widened parietal sulci (implying loss of parietal cortical grey matter; Courchesne, Press & Yeung-Courchesne, 1993), and a decreased cross-sectional area of posterior corpus callosum (Egaas, Courchesne & Saitoh, 1995). These results suggest that there may be a decrease in the number of cortico-cortical axons and hence a deficit in interhemispheric communication between parietal lobes. Although there are post-mortem data that the temporal lobes of people with autism have cellular abnormalities (Bauman & Kemper, 1985, 1993), there are no structural imaging data that show gross abnormality in temporal lobe structure. However, this may reflect the relative insensitivity of structural MRI techniques.

The results of studies that examined resting brain metabolism in people with autism using SPET and PET are in disagreement, and metabolism has been reported as increased (Rumsey et al., 1985; de Volder et al., 1987), unchanged (Herold et al., 1988; Zilbovicius et al., 1992) or decreased (George et al., 1992; Gillberg et al., 1993). However, those studies that examined brain asymmetry and interregional correlations in brain function reported: (1) lack of metabolic asymmetry (Buchsbaum et al., 1992), and (2) significant differences in the pattern of interregional correlations of brain metabolism involving frontal and parietal lobes and subcortical grey matter compared to controls (Horwitz et al., 1988). Also, a SPET study reported a delay in the normal development of patterns of blood flow to the frontal cortex (Zilbovicius et al., 1995). In autistic individuals, blood flow at the age of three was equivalent to flow at one year in controls.

Thus, although the specific nature of the structural and functional findings in autism is not clear, the data are consistent with the hypothesis that people with autism have abnormalities in brain development that affect connectivity between brain regions, and the cognitive and social deficits seen in autistic individuals may arise from these.

Down syndrome and age-related change in brain

People with Down syndrome have a high prevalence (and significant variation in severity) of developmental disabilities, and a high prevalence of age-related cognitive decline and Alzheimer's disease (Haxby, 1989; Shapiro et al., 1989). However, the neurobiological basis to this is unknown. There are a number of possible explanations, but there is compelling evidence that people with Down syndrome have abnormalities in brain structure, neural integrity and metabolism.

A quantitative study of young adults with Down syndrome using CT reported that they have a reduced whole-brain size (Shapiro et al., 1989). However, this may be accounted for by their small stature and their abnormal cranial cavity. Nevertheless, another CT study (Pearlson et al., 1990) reported decreased temporal lobe volume in people with Down syndrome. It is unknown if this is secondary to hypoplasia or atrophy; this is an issue that must be resolved by longitudinal investigation.

A volumetric MRI study of people with Down syndrome has reported a decrease in volume of frontal cortex and cerebellum, together with angulation of the brain stem. Also, there was less sulcal and gyral definition in the Down syndrome brains, together with abnormalities in the volume ratios of the hippocampus:parahippocampal gyrus and hippocampus:temporal cortex volumes (Kesslak et al., 1994). Hippocampal area (even when corrected for head size) was significantly decreased, and was affected by ageing significantly more than in controls. However, it is difficult to tease out changes due to Alzheimer's disease from those due to abnormalities in brain development. A report of an 18-month-old child with Down syndrome suggests that the abnormalities detected in adults may lie at least partly in brain development, as there was significant delay in myelination in most brain regions (Koo et al., 1992).

MRS studies of people with Down syndrome reported no difference in brain N-acetylaspartate, creatine/phosphocreatine and choline (Shetty, et al., 1995), but did find a significant increase in myoinositol (Shonk & Ross, 1995). Also, cerebrospinal fluid (but not plasma) myoinositol concentration is significantly elevated (Shetty et al., 1995). There may be a genetic explanation for this. The human myoinositol transporter gene is localized to band q22 on chromosome 21 (Berry et al., 1995), and people with Down syndrome have an increased myoinositol uptake in skin fibroblasts (Fruen & Lester, 1990). However, these MRS studies were small, did not study areas of brain crucial to higher cognitive function, and intellectual ability was not related to neural integrity. Thus, it is unknown if these increases in myoinositol are related to abnormalities in cognition, brain structure or neural integrity.

Investigations of age-related changes in brain of people with Down syndrome have reported significant increases in relative choline concentration compared to controls – probably reflecting age-related differences in membrane metabolism (Murata et al., 1993). MRS studies of people without Down syndrome but with Alzheimer's disease reported abnormalities in N-acetylaspartate (Bruhn et al., 1992; Ide et al., 1992; Meyerhoff et al., 1992; Miller et al., 1993), choline (Meyerhoff et al., 1992), and myoinositol (Miller et al., 1993). Thus, there is evidence that people with Down syndrome have a significant increase in brain myoinositol concentration and significant age-related abnormalities in membrane metabolism. Also, in people without Down syndrome, abnormalities in neural integrity/metabolism are associated with Alzheimer's disease. However, in people with Down syndrome, it is not known whether these abnormalities as measured by MRS, are associated with developmental disability, change with age, or Alzheimer's disease. Thus, further investigation of the link between Down syndrome and age-related change in brain is likely to prove fruitful in advancing understanding of neuropathological changes in both Down syndrome and Alzheimer's disease.

Conclusion

People with a developmental disability have abnormal brain function, and the cause of this is often unknown. MRI has radically altered the risk/benefit ratio considerations involved in deciding which patients should undergo brain imaging. Thus, the authors propose that MRI should be performed on most patients with developmental difficulties in order to determine if they have abnormalities in brain structure and/or neural integrity that are remediable. All patients who have progressive pathology should have baseline MRI for possible future comparison (should the clinical picture change). Further, certain conditions, such as Down syndrome and fragile X syndrome, are associated with abnormal brain, so people with these conditions should have MRI, especially when there is uncertainty about age-related cognitive decline. A similar case can be made in circumstances in which there is no known cause of developmental disability, or in which there may be organic sequelae of epilepsy, because of the *possibility* of progressive pathology. Patients who have localizing neurological signs, or signs of deficits in neuropsychological function (e.g. memory deficits or signs of frontal lobe damage), should have MRI as it may confirm clinical findings as well as provide a benchmark for future reference.

This leaves patients with no sign of underlying progressive brain pathology and a 'syndromal' cause for developmental disability to be considered. Firstly, patients with morphometrically abnormal brains are at least as likely to suffer further organic insult later in life as members of the wider population. Without a baseline measure, it is difficult to differentiate new pathology from old. Secondly, when a patient has a morphometrically abnormal brain, it is important to know if or how the structure of the brain relates to the behaviour of the individual. MRI performed after change in brain has occurred is less likely to yield the anatomical correlates of new behavioural or cognitive pathology. Finally, many clinicians, carers, patients and relatives find it helpful to know *why* an individual behaves in a particular way, when this is possible. For example, it may be unrealistic to design a treatment programme based upon a neuropsychological function (e.g. memory) when a patient has abnormal memory and hippocampal abnormalities.

The remaining considerations for most clinicians are cost, distress to patients caused by the procedure, and the medical model employed (the 'pathologizing' of patients). Issues to do with finance should not prevent a counsel of clinical perfection, and are not our consideration here. There are, however, some circumstances in which the cost–benefit analysis tilts against scanning – for example, when there are concerns about patient consent, the need for sedation and the distress that may be caused by the procedure.

Although, by its nature, scanning is a medical procedure, and reinforces the medical model, it should be seen as part of an eclectic approach. Now that this technology is available, we have a responsibility to use it, in research as well as clinically, for the benefit of our patients.

References

Adrien, J.L., Perrot, A., Sauvage, D. et al. (1992). Early symptoms in autism from family home movies. Evaluation and comparison between 1st and 2nd year of life using I.B.S.E. scale. *Acta Paedopsychiatrica*, **55**, 71–5.

Barkowich, A.J., Kjos, B.O., Jackson, D.E. & Norman, D. (1988). Normal maturation of the neonatal and infant brain: MR imaging at 1.5T. *Neuroradiology*, **166**, 173–80.

Bauman, M.L. & Kemper, T.L. (1985). Histoanatomic observations of the brain in early infantile autism. *Neurology*, **35**, 866–74.

(1993). The contribution of neuropathologic studies to the understanding of autism. *Neurology Clinics*, **11**, 175–87.

Berardi, A., Haxby, J.V., Grady, C.L. & Rapoport, S.I. (1990). Memory performance in healthy young and old subjects correlates with resting state brain glucose utilization in the parietal lobe. *Journal of Nuclear Medicine*, **31**, 879.

(1991). Asymmetries of brain glucose metabolism and memory in the healthy elderly. *Developmental Neuropsychology*, **7**, 87–97.

Berry, G.T., Mallee, J.J., Moo, H. et al. (1995). The human osmoregulatory Na$^+$/myoinositol co-transporter gene (SLC5A3): molecular cloning and localization to chromosome 21. *Genomics*, **25**, 507.

Borghgraef, M., Fryns, J.P., Smeets, E., Marien, J. & Van Den Berghe, H. (1988). The 49,XXXXY syndrome. Clinical and psychological follow-up data. *Clinical Genetics*, **33**, 429–34.

Brody, H. (1955). Organisation of the cerebral cortex. II. A study of aging in the human cerebral cortex. *Journal of Comparative Neurology*, **102**, 511–56.

Bruhn, H., Stoppe, G., Merboldt, K.D., Michaelis, T., Hanicke, W. & Frahm, J. (1992). Cerebral metabolic alterations in normal ageing and Alzheimer's dementia detected by proton MRS. In *Book of Abstracts*, p. 752. Berkeley, California: Society of Magnetic Resonance in Medicine.

Buchsbaum, M.S., Siegel, B.V., Wu, J.C. et al. (1992). Brief report: attention performance in autism and regional brain metabolic rate assessed by positron emission tomography. *Journal of Autism and Developmental Disorders*, **22**, 115–25.

Chiron, C., Raynaud, C., Maziere, B. et al. (1992). Changes in regional cerebral blood flow during brain maturation in children and adolescents. *Journal of Nuclear Medicine*, **33**, 696–703.

Christophe, C., Muller, M.F., Baleriaux, D. et al. (1990). Mapping of normal brain maturation in infants on phase-sensitive inversion-recovery images. *Neuroradiology*, **32**, 173–8.

Chugani, H.T., Phelps, M.E. & Mazziota, J.C. (1987). Positron emission tomography study of human brain functional development. *Annals of Neurology*, **22**, 487–97.

Clark, C.M., Kessler, R., Buchsbaum, M.S., Margolin, R.A. & Holcomb, H.H. (1984). Correlational methods for determining regional coupling of cerebral glucose metabolism. A pilot study. *Biological Psychiatry*, **19**, 663–78.

Clark, C., Klonoff, H. & Hayden, M. (1990). Regional cerebral glucose metabolism in Turner syndrome. *Canadian Journal of Neurological Science*, **17**, 140–4.

Coffey, C.E., Wilkinson, W.E., Parashos, I.A. et al. (1992). Quantitative cerebral anatomy of the aging human brain: a cross-sectional study using magnetic resonance imaging. *Neurology*, **42**, 527–36.

Courchesne, E., Press, G. & Yeung-Courchesne, R. (1993). Parietal lobe abnormalities detected with MR in patients with infantile autism. *American Journal of Roentgenology*, **160**, 387–93.

Courchesne, E., Yeung-Courchesene, R., Press, G. et al. (1988). Hypoplasia of cerebellar vermal lobules V1 and V11 in autism. *New England Journal of Medicine*, **318**, 1349–54.

Cowell, P.E., Turetsky, B.I., Gur, R.C., Grossman, R.I., Shtasel, D.L. & Gur, R.E. (1994). Sex differences in aging of the human frontal and temporal lobes. *Journal of Neuroscience*, **14**(8), 4748–56.

Curfs, L.M.G., Schreppers-Tijdink, A., Wiegers, A., Borghgraef, M. & Fryns, J.P. (1990). The 49 XXXXY syndrome: clinical and psychological findings in five patients. *Journal of Mental Deficiency Research*, **34**, 277–82.

Davis, P.J.M. & Wright, E.A. (1977). A new method for measuring cranial cavity volume and its application to the assessment of cerebral atrophy at autopsy. *Neuropathology and Applied Neurobiology*, **3**, 341–58.

Debakan, A.S. & Sadowsky, D. (1978). Changes in brain weights during the span of human life: relation of brain weights to body heights and body weights. *Annals of Neurology*, **4**, 345–56.

DeCarli, C.D., Murphy, D.G.M., Gillette, J.A. et al. (1994). Lack of age-related differences in temporal lobe volume of very healthy adults. *American Journal of Neuroradiology*, **15**, 689–96.

DeLeo, J.M., Schwartz, M., Creasey, H., Cutler, N. & Rapoport, S.I. (1985). Computer-assisted categorization of brain computerised tomography pixels into cerebrospinal fluid, white matter, and gray matter. *Computers in Biomedical Research*, **18**, 79–88.

de Volder, A., Bol, A., Michel, C., Cogneau, M. & Goffinet, A.M. (1987). Brain glucose metabolism in children with the autistic syndrome: positron tomography analysis. *Brain Development*, **9**, 581–7.

Egaas, B., Courchesne, E. & Saitoh, O. (1995). Reduced size of corpus callosum in autism. *Archives of Neurology*, **52**, 794–801.

Fox, P.T. & Raichle, M.E. (1986). Focal physiological uncoupling of cerebral blood flow and oxidative metabolism during somatosensory stimulation in human subjects. *Neurobiology*, **83**, 1140–4.

Freund, L.S. & Reiss, A.L. (1991). Cognitive profiles associated with Fra (X) syndrome in males and females. *American Journal of Medical Genetics*, **38**, 542–7.

Fruen, B.R. & Lester, B.R. (1990). Down's syndrome fibroblasts exhibit enhanced inositol uptake. *Biochemical Journal*, **270**, 119.

Gafney, G.R., Tsai, L.Y., Kuperman, S. & Minchin, S. (1987). Cerebellar structure in autism. *American Journal of Diseases in Children*, **141**, 1330–2.

George, M.S., Costa, D.C., Kouris, K., Ring, H.A. & Ell, P. (1992). Cerebral blood flow abnormalities in adults with infantile autism. *Journal of Nervous and Mental Diseases*, **180**, 413–17.

Gillberg, I.C., Bjure, J., Uvebrant, P., Vestergen, E. & Gillberg, C. (1993). SPECT (single photon computed tomography) in 31 children and adolescents with autism and autistic-like conditions. *Childhood and Adolescent Psychiatry*, **2**, 50–9.

Grady, C.L., McIntosh, A.R., Horwitz, B. et al. (1995). Age-related reductions in human recognition memory due to impaired encoding. *Science*, **269**, 218–21.

Gur, R.C., Mozley, P.D., Resnick, S. et al. (1991). Gender differences in age effect on brain atrophy measured by magnetic resonance imaging. *Proceedings of the National Academy of Sciences USA*, **88**, 2845–9.

Hagerman, R.J. (1991). Physical and behavioral phenotype. In *Fragile X Syndrome: Diagnosis, Treatment, and Research*, ed. R.J. Hagerman & A.C. Cronister, pp. 3–68. Baltimore: Johns Hopkins University Press.

Hashimoto, T., Tayama, M., Miyazaki, M., Murakawa, K. & Kuroda, Y. (1993). Brainstem and cerebellar vermis involvement in autistic children. *Journal of Child Neurology*, **8**, 149–53.

Hashimoto, T., Tayama, M., Murakawa, K., Yoshimoto, T., Miyazaki, M. & Kuroda, Y. (1995). Development of the brainstem and cerebellum in autistic patients. *Journal of Autism and Developmental Disorders*, **25**, 1–18.

Haxby, J.V. (1989). Neuropsychological evaluation of adults with Down syndrome: patterns of selective impairment in nondemented old adults. *Journal of Mental Deficiency Research*, **33**, 193–210.

Herold, S., Frackowiak, R.S.J., Couteur, A.L., Rutter, M. & Howlin, P. (1988). Cerebral blood flow and metabolism of oxygen and glucose in young autistic adults. *Psychological Medicine*, **18**, 823–31.

Ho, K., Roessmann, U., Straumfjord, J.V. & Monroe, G. (1980). Analysis of brain weight. 1. Adult brain weight in relation to sex, race, and age. *Archives of Pathology and Laboratory Medicine*, **4**, 635–9.

Holland, B.A., Haas, D.K., Norman, D., Brant-Zawadski, M. & Newton, T.H. (1986). MRI of normal brain maturation. *American Journal of Neuroradiology*, **7**, 201–8.

Holttum, J.R., Minshew, N.J., Sanders, R.S. & Phillips, N.E. (1992). Magnetic resonance imaging of the posterior fossa in autism. *Biological Psychiatry*, **32**, 1091–101.

Horwitz, B., Duara, R. & Rapoport, S.I. (1984). Intercorrelations of glucose metabolic rates between brain regions: application to healthy males in a state of reduced sensory input. *Journal of Cerebral Blood Flow Metabolism*, **4**, 484–99.

(1986). Age differences in intercorrelations between regional cerebral metabolic rates for glucose. *Annals of Neurology*, **19**, 60–7.

Horwitz, B., Rumsey, J.M., Grady, C.L. & Rapoport, S.I. (1988). The cerebral metabolic landscape in autism: intercorrelations of regional glucose utilisation. *Archives of Neurology*, **45**, 749–55.

Hubbard, B.M. & Anderson, J.M. (1981). A quantitative study of cerebral atrophy in old age and senile dementia. *Journal of Neurological Science*, **50**, 135–45.

Ide, M., Naruse, S., Furuya, S. et al. (1992). Some investigations of senile dementia of Alzheimer type (SDAT) by 1H CSI. In *Book of Abstracts*, p. 1930. Berkeley, California: Society of Magnetic Resonance in Medicine.

Jernigan, T.L., Archibald, S.L., Berhow, M.T., Sowell, E.R., Foster, D.S. & Hesselink, J.R. (1991a). Cerebral structure on MRI. Part 1: Localization of age related changes. *Biological Psychiatry*, **29**, 55–67.

Jernigan, T.L., Press, G.A. & Hesselink, J.R. (1990). Methods for measuring brain morphologic features on magnetic resonance images: validation and normal aging. *Archives of Neurology*, **47**, 27–32.

Jernigan, T.L., Salmon, D., Butters, N. et al. (1991b). Cerebral structure on MRI. Part II: Specific changes in Alzheimer's and Huntington's diseases. *Biological Psychiatry*, **29**, 68–81.

Kaye, J.A., DeCarli, C.D., Luxenberg, J.S. & Rapoport, S.I. (1992). The significance of age-related enlargement of the cerebral ventricles in healthy men and women measured by quantitative computed x-ray tomography. *Journal of the American Geriatric Society*, **40**, 225–31.

Kemper, M.B., Hagerman, R.J., Ahmad, R.S. et al. (1986). Cognitive profiles and the spectrum of clinical manifestations in heterozygous fragile-X-females. *American Journal of Medical Genetics*, **23**, 139–56.

Kemper, M.B., Hagerman, R.J. & Altshul-Stark, D. (1988). Cognitive profiles of boys with the fragile-X syndrome. *American Journal of Human Genetics*, **30**, 191–200.

Kesslak, J.P., Nagata, B.S., Lott, M.D. & Nalcoiglu, O. (1994). Magnetic resonance imaging analysis of brain age-related changes in the brains of individuals with Down's syndrome. *Neurology*, **44**, 1039–45.

Koo, B.K.K., Blaser, S., Harwood-Nash, D., Becker, L.E. & Murphy, E.G. (1992). Magnetic resonance imaging evaluation of delayed myelination in Down's syndrome: a case report and review of the literature. *Journal of Child Neurology*, **7**, 417–21.

Lotspeich, L.J. & Ciaranello, R.D. (1993). The neurobiology and genetics of infantile autism. *International Review of Neurobiology*, **35**, 87–129.

Mesulam, M-M. (1981). A cortical network for directed attention and unilateral neglect. *Annals of Neurology*, **10**, 309–25.

Meyerhoff, D.J., MacKay, S., Constans, J.M., Norman, D., Van Dyke, C. & Fein, G. (1992). Axonal injury and membrane alterations in Alzheimer's disease suggested by in vivo proton magnetic resonance spectroscopy imaging. *Annals of Neurology*, **36** (**1**), 40–7.

Miezejeski, C.M., Jenkins, E.C., Hill, A.L., Wisniewski, K., French, J.H. & Brown, W.T. (1986). A profile of cognitive deficit in females from fragile-X families. *Neuropsychologia*, **24**, 405–9.

Miller, B.L., Mouts, R.A., Shonk, T., Ernst, T., Woolley, S. & Ross, B.D. (1993). N-acetyl aspartate is decreased by 11% in mild to moderate Alzheimer's disease. *Radiology*, **187** (**2**), 433–47.

Murakami, J., Courchesne, E., Press, G., Yeung-Courchesne, R. & Hesselink, J. (1989). Reduced cerebellar hemisphere size and its relationship to vermal hypoplasia in autism. *Archives of Neurology*, **46**, 689–94.

Murata, T., Yoshino, Y., Omori, M. et al. (1993). In vivo proton magnetic resonance spectroscopy study on premature aging in adult Down's syndrome. *Biological Psychiatry*, **34**, 290–7.

Murphy, D.G.M., DeCarli, C.D., Daly, E. et al. (1993). X chromosome effects on female brain: a magnetic resonance imaging study of Turner's syndrome. *Lancet*, **342**, 1197–200.

Murphy, D.G.M., DeCarli, C.D., Schapiro, M.B., Rapoport, S.I. & Horwitz, B. (1992). Age related differences in volumes of subcortical nuclei, brain matter, and cerebrospinal fluid in healthy men as measured with MRI. *Archives of Neurology*, **49**, 839–49.

Murphy, D.G.M., McIntosh, A.R., Daly, E. (1996). Sex differences in human brain morphometry and metabolism: an in vivo quantitative MRI and PET study on the effect of aging. *Archives of General Psychiatry*, **53**, 585–94.

Murphy, D.G.M., Mentis, M.J., Grady, C. et al. (submitted). The effect of X chromosome triplet repeats on brain in premutation female carriers of fragile X syndrome.

Murphy, D.G.M., Mentis, M., J., Pietrini, P. et al. (1997). A PET study of Turner's syndrome: effects of sex steroids and the X chromosome on brain. *Biological Psychiatry*, **41**, 285–98.

Netley, C.T. & Rovet, J. (1987). Relations between a dermatoglyphic measure, hemispheric specialization, and intellectual abilities in 47, XXY males. *Brain and Cognition*, **6**, 153–60.

Nielsen, J., Sorenson, A.M. & Sorenson, K. (1981). Mental development of unselected children with sex-chromosome abnormalities. *Human Genetics*, **59**, 324–32.

Parasuraman, R. & Haxby, J.V. (1993). Attention and brain function in Alzheimer's disease: a review. *Neuropsychology*, **7**, 242–72.

Pearlson, G.D., Warren, A.C., Starkstein, S.E. et al. (1990). Brain atrophy in 18 patients with Down syndrome: a computed tomographic study. *American Journal of Nuclear Medicine*, **11**, 811–16.

Pennington, B., Puck, M. & Robinson, A. (1980). Language and cognitive development of 47 XXX females followed since birth. *Behavior Genetics*, **10**, 31–41.

Pfefferbaum, A., Mathalon, D.H., Sullivan, E.V., Rawles, J.M., Zipursky, R.B. & Lim, K.O. (1994). A quantitative magnetic resonance imaging study of changes in brain morphology from infancy to late adulthood. *Archives of Neurology*, **51**, 874–87.

Prouty, L.A., Rogers, R.C., Stevenson, R.E. et al. (1988). Fragile-X syndrome: growth, development, and intellectual function. *American Journal of Medical Genetics*, **30**, 123–42.

Reiss, A.L., Abrams, M.T., Greenlaw, R., Freund, L. & Denckla, M. (1995). Neurodevelopmental effects of the FMR-1 full mutation in humans. *Nature Medicine*, **1**, 159–67.

Reiss, A.L., Lee, J. & Freund, L. (1994). Neuroanatomy of fragile X syndrome: the temporal lobe. *Neurology*, **44**, 1317–24.

Rhoades, F.A. (1982). X-linked mental retardation and fragile X or marker X syndrome. *Pediatrics*, **69**, 668–9.

Robinson, A., Lubs, H.A., Nielsen, J. & Sorensen, K. (1979). Summary of clinical findings: profiles of children with 47,XXY, 47,XXX, and 47,XYY karyotypes. In *Sex Chromosome Aneuploidy: Prospective Studies in Children*, ed. A. Robinson, H. Lubs & D. Bergsma, New York: Alan R. Liss.

Rumsey, J.M., Duara, R., Grady, C. et al. (1985). Brain metabolism in autism. *Archives of General Psychiatry*, **42**, 448–55.

Schapiro, M.B., Murphy, D.G.M., Hagerman, R.J. et al. (1995). Adult fragile X syndrome: neuropsychology, brain anatomy, and metabolism. *American Journal of Medical Genetics – Neuropsychiatric Genetics*, **60**, 480–93.

Schwartz, M., Creasey, H., Grady, C.L. et al. (1985). Computed tomographic analysis of brain morphometrics in 30 healthy men, aged 21 to 81 years. *Annals of Neurology*, **17**, 146–57.

Sears, L.L., Finn, P.R. & Steinmetz, J.E. (1994). Abnormal classical eye-blink conditioning in autism. *Journal of Autism and Developmental Disorders*, **24**, 737–51.

Shapiro, M.B., Luxenberg, J., Kaye, J. et al. (1989). Serial quantitative CT analysis for brain morphometrics in adult Down syndrome at different ages. *Neurology*, **39**, 1349–53.

Shetty, U.H., Shapiro, M.B., Holloway, H.W. & Rapoport, S.L. (1995). Polyol profiles in Down syndrome myo-inositol specifically is elevated in the cerebrospinal fluid. *Journal of Clinical Investigations*, **95**, 542–6.

Shonk, T. & Ross, B.D. (1995). Role of increased cerebral myo-inositol in the dementia of Down syndrome. *Magenetic Resonance in Medicine*, **33**, 858–61.

Sudhalter, V., Maranion, M. & Brooks, P. (1992). Expressive semantic deficit in the production language of males with fragile X syndrome. *American Journal of Medical Genetics*, **43** (1–2), 65–71.

Sudhalter, V., Scarborough, H.S. & Cohen, I.L. (1991). Syntactic delay and pragmatic deviance in the language of fragile X males. *American Journal of Medical Genetics*, **38**, 493–7.

Takeda, S. & Matsuzawa, T. (1985). Age-related brain atrophy: a study with computed tomography. *Journal of Gerontology*, **40**, 159–63.

Theobald, T., Hay, D. & Judge, C. (1987). Individual variation and specific cognitive deficits in the fra(X) syndrome. *American Journal of Medical Genetics*, **28**, 1–11.

Veenema, H., Geraedts, J.P.M., Beverstock, G.C. et al. (1987). The fragile-X-syndrome in a large family. Cytogenic and clinical investigations. *Medical Genetics*, **24**, 23–31.

Wisniewski, K.E., French, J.H., Fernando, S. et al. (1985). Fragile X syndrome: associated neurological abnormalities and developmental disabilities. *Annals of Neurology*, **18**, 665–9.

Zilbovicius, M., Garreau, B., Samson, Y., Remy, P., Syrota, A. & Lelord, G. (1995). Delayed maturation of the frontal cortex in childhood autism. *American Journal of Psychiatry*, **152**, 248–52.

Zilbovicius, M., Garreau, B., Tzourio, N. et al. (1992). Regional cerebral blood flow in childhood autism: a SPECT study. *American Journal of Psychiatry*, **149**, 924–30.

Part 2 **Specific conditions**

5   Autism and its spectrum disorders

CHRISTOPHER GILLBERG

Introduction

Autism with onset in early childhood (infantile autism, childhood autism, autistic disorder) has been conceptualized as a behavioural syndrome with a possibly unique aetiology. This view is reflected in the concern with ever-more precise and refined diagnostic criteria (Volkmar, 1992; World Health Organization, 1993; American Psychiatric Association, 1994) and interview and observation methods for eliciting the highly specific information considered necessary to arrive at an exact diagnosis (Le Couteur et al., 1989; Lord et al., 1989; Gillberg, C., Nordin & Ehlers 1996). However, there is considerable empirical support for the notion of autism as a syndrome – or spectrum disorder (Wing , 1996) – with multiple aetiologies (Gillberg, C. & Coleman, 1992, 1996). This chapter provides a review of what is currently known about the syndrome of autism – and its spectrum disorders – in terms of diagnosis, epidemiology, aetiology, outcome and intervention. The concept of autism underlying the text is one of a set of behavioural syndromes involving severe restriction of reciprocal communication/social interaction, varying in severity (and even, to some extent, in type) and with far-reaching consequences for prognosis and intervention, but with no assumption of a discrete aetiology. Autism is viewed as one of the behavioural syndromes that can be branched off from the autism spectrum; Asperger's syndrome (Wing, 1981a) is another one, as is disintegrative disorder (Volkmar, 1992) and other autistic-like conditions (Steffenburg & Gillberg, 1986).

Diagnosis

The diagnosis of autism – regardless of diagnostic manual used (American Psychiatric Association, 1980, 1987, 1994; World Health Organization, 1993) – rests on the triad of social, communication and imagination–behaviour restriction (Wing, 1981a). Some manuals (American Psychiatric Association, 1980, 1994; World Health Organization, 1993) require that the age of onset be before 30–36 months, whereas others specify only that signs of the triad be present from infancy or childhood (American

Psychiatric Association, 1987). The diagnostic criteria for autism of the DSM-III-R and the DSM-IV are the ones currently most often used; they are listed in Table 5.1. These latter criteria are very similar to those published by the ICD-10. The DSM and ICD use the umbrella term 'pervasive developmental disorders' (PDD) for all the syndromes (autism, Asperger's syndrome etc.) on the autism spectrum. The DSM-IV also lists criteria for Asperger's syndrome, but these have been shown not to correspond to the clinical Gestalt outlined by Asperger (Miller & Ozonoff 1997). The criteria published by Gillberg and Gillberg (1989), which are specifically based on Asperger's own descriptions, are therefore listed instead.

The triad

All current manuals referring to childhood autism concur in requiring the presence of symptoms from the triad of (i) social, (ii) communication and (iii) imagination–behaviour impairment as outlined by Wing and Gould (1979).

The social interaction problems in autism are centred around the typical lack of reciprocity. It is not, as was surmised in many of the early writings, that people with autism cannot be in 'contact' with other people, but rather that they do not know how to reciprocate in an automatic, intuitive give-and-take fashion. They can look other people in the eye – indeed, they may have the same amount of gaze contact as normal people (Mirenda, Donnellan & Yoder, 1983) – but do so in an abnormal, non-reciprocal way. They may enjoy body contact and appreciate the proximity of some people (often those who they know well and who behave in a fashion reasonably predictable to them) and yet sometimes show clearly that they do not understand or like the approaches made for body contact by others than themselves. Furthermore, the lack of reciprocity of social interactions in autism does not reflect a general lack of affect. People with autism often demonstrate overt signs of basic affects, such as happiness and anger, usually at a level appropriate to their general functioning. Therefore, it does not seem reasonable to refer to the social interaction problems encountered in autism as primarily 'affective'. People with autism do not usually, as was once believed, specifically avoid other human beings or actively seek out 'autistic aloneness', nor do they generally demonstrate a 'stand-offish' manner. Such avoidant behaviours seem to be characteristic only of a subgroup, including those with the fragile X-syndrome (Hagerman et al., 1992; Gillberg, C., 1992; Turk, 1994).

The communication problems are also characterized by lack of reciprocity (Wing, 1996). It is not so much that people with autism cannot speak at a level appropriate to their general level of functioning. Indeed, some of the high-functioning cases, including those with Asperger's syndrome, have superficial speech and language skills which are at a level superior to their performance IQ level (Frith, 1991; Ehlers et al., 1997). The major problem

Table 5.1 Diagnostic criteria for autistic disorder according to DSM-III-R* and DSM-IV†

....

DSM-III-R

At least eight of the following sixteen items are present, these to include at least two items from A, one from B, and one from C.

Note. Consider a criterion to be met *only* if the behaviour is abnormal for the person's developmental level.

A. Qualitative impairment in reciprocal social interaction as manifested by the following:
    (The examples within parentheses are arranged so that those first mentioned are more likely to apply to younger or more handicapped, and the later ones to older or less handicapped, persons with this disorder.)
    (1) marked lack of awareness of the existence or feelings of others (e.g., treats a person as if he or she were a piece of furniture; does not notice another person's distress; apparently has no concept of the need of others for privacy)
    (2) no or abnormal seeking of comfort at times of distress (e.g., does not come for comfort even when ill, hurt, or tired; seeks comfort in a stereo-typed way, e.g., says 'cheese, cheese, cheese' whenever hurt)
    (3) no or impaired imitation (e.g., does not wave bye-bye; does not copy mother's domestic activities; mechanical imitation of others' actions out of context)
    (4) no or abnormal social play (e.g., does not actively participate in simple games; prefers solitary play activities; involves other children in play only as 'mechanical aids')
    (5) gross impairment in ability to make peer friendships (e.g., no interest in making peer friendships; despite interest in making friends, demonstrates lack of understanding of conventions of social interaction, for example, reads phone book to uninterested peer)

B. Qualitative impairments in verbal and nonverbal communications, and in imaginative activity, as manifested by the following:
    (The numbered items are arranged so that those first listed are more likely to apply to younger or more handicapped, and the later ones to older or less handicapped, persons with this disorder.)
    (1) no mode of communication, such as communicative babbling, facial expression, gesture, mime, or spoken language
    (2) markedly abnormal nonverbal communication, as in the use of eye-to-eye gaze, facial expression, body posture, or gestures to initiate or modulate social interaction, (e.g., does not anticipate being held, stiffens when held, does not look at the person or smile when making a social approach, does not greet parents or visitors, has a fixed stare in social situations)
    (3) absence of imaginative activity, such as playacting of adult roles, fantasy characters, or animals; lack of interest in stories about imaginary events
    (4) marked abnormalities in the production of speech, including volume, pitch, stress, rate, rhythm, and intonation (e.g., monotonous tone, questionlike melody, or high pitch)
    (5) marked abnormalities in the form of content of speech including stereotyped and repetitive use of speech (e.g., immediate echolalia or mechanical repetition of television commercial); use of 'you' when 'I' is meant (e.g., using 'You want cookie?' to mean 'I want cookie'); idiosyncratic use of words or phrases (e.g., 'Go on green riding' to mean 'I want to go on the swing'); or frequent irrelevant remarks (e.g., starts talking about train schedules during a conversation about sports)
    (6) marked impairments in the ability to initiate or sustain a conversation with others, despite adequate speech (e.g., indulging in lengthy monologues on one subject regardless of interjections from others)

C. Markedly restricted repertoire of activities and interests, as manifested by the following:
    (1) stereotyped body movements, e.g., hand-flicking or -twisting, spinning, headbanging, complex whole-body movements
    (2) persistent preoccupation with parts of objects (e.g., sniffing or smelling objects, repetitive feeling of

Table 5.1 *(cont.)*

texture of materials, spinning wheels of toy cars) or attachment to unusual objects (e.g., insists on carrying around a piece of string)

(3) marked distress over changes in trivial aspects of environment, e.g., when a vase is moved from usual position

(4) unreasonable insistence on following routine in precise detail, e.g., insisting that exactly the same route always be followed when shopping

(5) markedly restricted range of interests and a preoccupation with one narrow interest, e.g., interested only in lining up objects, in amassing facts about meteorology, or in pretending to be a fantasy character

D. Onset during infancy or childhood
Specify if childhood onset (after 36 months of age).

DSM-IV
A. A total of six (or more) items from (1), (2), and (3) with at least two from (1), and one each from (2) and (3):

(1) qualitative impairment in social interaction, as manifested by at least two of the following:
(a) marked impairment in the use of multiple nonverbal behaviours such as eye-to-eye gaze, facial expression, body postures, and gestures to regulate social interaction
(b) failure to develop peer relationships appropriate to developmental level
(c) a lack of spontaneous seeking to share enjoyment, interests, or achievements with other people (e.g., by a lack of showing, bringing or pointing out objects of interest)
(d) lack of social or emotional reciprocity

(2) qualitative impairments in communication as manifested by at least one of the following:
(a) delay in or total lack of the development of spoken language (not accompanied by an attempt to compensate through alternative modes of communication such as gesture or mime)
(b) in individuals with adequate speech, marked impairment in the ability to initiate or sustain a conversation with others
(c) stereotyped and repetitive use of language or idiosyncratic language
(d) lack of varied, spontaneous make-believe play or social imitative play appropriate to developmental level

(3) restricted repetitive and stereotyped patterns of behaviour, interests, and activities, as manifested by at least one of the following:
(a) encompassing preoccupation with one or more stereotyped and restricted patterns of interest that is abnormal either in intensity or focus
(b) apparently inflexible adherence to specific, nonfunctional routines or rituals
(c) stereotyped and repetitive motor mannerisms (e.g., hand or finger flapping or twisting, or complex whole-body movements)
(d) persistent preoccupation with parts of objects

B. Delays or abnormal functioning in at least one of the following areas, with onset prior to age 3 years:
(1) social interaction, (2) language as used in social communication, or (3) symbolic or imaginative play.
C. The disturbance is not better accounted for by Rett's disorder or childhood disintegrative disorder.

Notes:
*American Psychiatric Association (1987).
†American Psychiatric Association (1994).

seems to be that most people with autism do not understand the meaning of language and its function as a tool for communication (and not as a means in itself). Therefore, to a large extent, depending on overall IQ level, many people with autism – about half according to most surveys (Gillberg, 1993) – do not speak at all, whereas some echo words or phrases used by others or by themselves, and some ask endless questions and demand standard answers.

The restriction of the imaginative–behavioural repertoire is possibly best conceptualized as a lack of access to a normal variety of social behaviours. Imagination is restricted and tends to be very concrete. Stereotyped body movements (including hand flapping), adherence to strict routines and various other ritualistic phenomena are part and parcel of the autistic syndrome. However, such behaviours are encountered in other psychiatric syndromes/developmental disorders and in normal people also. The problem in autism is that the behaviours take up all or most of the person's time and that there is no automatic changing from one behaviour to another as may be demanded by the social situation. It is the amount, rigidity and style of adherence to the various behaviours considered typical of autism which constitute the third cornerstone of the triad, not the behaviours as such.

This triad of social, communication and behaviour problems is what constitutes the basis of an autism diagnosis in all current systems. Kanner and Eisenberg (1956) highlighted the 'autistic aloneness' and the insistence on elaborate, repetitive routines as central features of autism, but even though some authorities still emphasize these features, they are not the sine qua non for an autism diagnosis to be made. In common 'clinical parlance', the 'triad' as a diagnostic phrase is sometimes used when discussing cases with severe–profound mental retardation and triad autism symptoms (Wing, 1991). In Asperger's syndrome, language is much better developed than in classic Kanner autism. However, language development is often both delayed and deviant and, even in the very high-functioning group, pragmatic language problems tend to persist into adult life.

Apart from triad symptoms, a plethora of problems are often, but not invariably, associated with a diagnosis of autism. Sleep problems, auditory perceptual abnormalities, abnormal response to pain, touch, heat and cold, motor hyperactivity, food fads and feeding problems, self-injurious behaviours, destructiveness and aggression are all common associated features, but are not seen in all cases of autism.

Differential diagnosis

It was not until the seminal papers of Wing and Gould (1979) and later Garreau and co-workers (1984) that it gradually came to be accepted that autism cases could not be adequately behaviourally subdivided on the basis of the presence or absence of brain damage. Later studies (Ritvo et al., 1990; Steffenburg, 1991) have shown even more clearly that there is no rationale for classifying autism cases into those with and without brain dysfunction.

More often than not, mental retardation coincides with autism (Rutter, 1983; Nordin & Gillberg, 1996). However, this statement has to be tempered by recent prevalence data on Asperger's syndrome suggesting that it may be at least five times more common than so-called autistic disorder according to the DSM-III-R (Ehlers & Gillberg, 1993; Gunnarsdóttir & Magnussón, 1994). Asperger's syndrome is regarded by some as synonymous, or at least largely overlapping, with high-functioning autism (Wolff, 1995). Since Asperger's syndrome is not usually associated with mental retardation, autism may not be as strongly associated with mental retardation as previously purported.

For people with profound mental retardation, as well as for those with superior intelligence, there may be problems in deciding on a diagnosis of autism. Other syndromes/disorders which may cause diagnostic confusion are hyperkinetic/attention disorders (sometimes referred to as deficits in attention, motor control and perception (DAMP) (Gillberg, C., Carlström & Rasmussen, 1983)), obsessive–compulsive disorders (Rapoport, 1989), obsessive–compulsive personality disorder (Gillberg, C. & Coleman, 1992) and occasionally extremes of 'normality', including severe stubbornness. Some of these diagnostic labels should not unreflectingly be taken as true markers of the need for clear differential diagnosis: many times it is a matter of the emperor's new clothes, with divergent labels used for the same syndrome.

It may need emphasizing here that the diagnosis of autism can be made in the presence of almost any other disorder or handicap. Thus, there should no longer be a need to discuss whether a child has blindness or autism, when he or she may have both (Ek et al., 1998). Equally, it would seem to be unreasonable to refrain from a diagnosis of autism in a child with severely autistic behaviour (meeting diagnostic criteria for autism), just because it has been demonstrated that he or she also meets criteria for the fragile X syndrome or Rett syndrome. However, in the case of Rett syndrome, the DSM and ICD have taken a different position and include it as a separate disorder under the general heading of pervasive developmental disorder.

In most of the published autism literature, the presence of an associated disorder (epilepsy, blindness, hypothyroidism) is most likely to lead to clinician/researcher reluctance to make a diagnosis of autism. Often, such cases have been included in a group of autistic-like conditions, 'non-nuclear' cases or even in a 'non-autism' group. This would lead to an underestimate of the prevalence of autism associated with other medical conditions. Also, female sex may serve as a confounder: because girls have better developed superficial social and language skills early in life (and less of the male type of interest patterns associated even in the minds of laymen with autism), the basic disabilities associated with autism tend to go unrecognized for long periods of time. This would lead to an underestimate of the prevalence of autism in girls.

Prevalence

When discussing autism prevalence nowadays, one has to take account of all the various syndromes comprised in the 'autistic continuum' or 'autism spectrum' (Gillberg, I.C. & Gillberg, C., 1989; Wing, 1996).

Autism

It now seems that autism may be considerably more common than previously believed. Recent studies (Steffenburg & Gillberg, 1986; Bryson, Clark & Smith, 1988; Tanoue et al., 1988; Sugiyama & Abe, 1989; Cialdella & Mamelle, 1989; Gillberg, C., Steffenburg & Schaumann, 1991a; Webb et al., 1997; Arvidsson et al., 1997) suggest that, in rural and urban areas alike, autism (infantile autism/autistic disorder) occurs in 7–17 per 10 000 children born, and a few studies have suggested even higher rates. The highest prevalence reported is in school-age children, for whom the rate is 12–20 per 10,000 children born. This prevalence rate is likely to be closer to the true rate in the population than the rate for very young children, given the problems of diagnosing autism in the infancy and pre-school periods.

Autism is much more common in people with mental retardation, with a rate of about 5 per cent in those with an IQ in the 70–50 range and 15 per cent in those with an IQ under 50 (Nordin & Gillberg, 1996). The rates are about twice as high if other autistic-like conditions are included with autistic disorder.

Asperger's syndrome

In a 1991 study from one borough of Göteborg, Asperger's syndrome was present in at least 36 and possibly in 71 of 10 000 children born (Ehlers & Gillberg, 1993). These figures are similar to those reported from Iceland (Gunnarsdóttir & Magnussón, 1994).

Disintegrative disorder

An autistic-like syndrome with onset after the age of 3 years is often referred to as 'disintegrative disorder' (formerly known as Heller syndrome) (Volkmar, 1992). Disintegrative disorder is extremely rare and occurs in no more than 5 to 10 children in one million surviving the first years (Gillberg, C., 1997).

Other autistic-like conditions

The prevalence of other autistic-like conditions appears to be about 2–4 per 10 000 children born. These are children who will show some uncharacteristic traits and yet share most of the symptoms demonstrated by the group with classically autistic traits (Wing & Gould, 1979; Steffenburg & Gillberg, 1986; Cialdella & Mamelle, 1989; Lotter, 1966).

'Autistic traits'

In Lorna Wing's Camberwell studies, 21 in 10 000 children had 'the triad', but only 4.5 met all the criteria for autism (and only 2.0 could be said to have 'classical autism') (Wing & Gould, 1979). In a population-based study in Göteborg, Sweden, Gillberg found 'autistic traits' or 'psychotic behaviour' in 35 out of 10 000 children (Gillberg, C., 1984; Gillberg, I.C. & Gillberg, C., 1989) who did not meet diagnostic criteria for autism or Asperger's syndrome.

Sex ratio

Sex ratios in autism have been the basis of some speculation ever since the 1940s. It is generally accepted that autism and autistic-like conditions affect males more frequently than females. Only recently have there appeared studies trying to tease out what the skewed sex ratio might mean (Wing, 1981b; Tsai, Stewart & August, 1981; Lord, Schopler & Revicki, 1982; Lord & Schopler, 1985; Kopp & Gillberg, 1992). The male:female ratio in autism is often unreservedly reported to be 3–4:1, but the population studies yield a much more variable picture, with figures ranging from 1.4–1.6:1 (Brask, 1972; Bohman et al., 1983) to 5.4:1 (Steffenburg & Gillberg, 1986). There are several reports suggesting that the ratio is lowest in the autism sub-population with severe–profound mental retardation (Wing, 1981b; Gillberg, C., 1984; Nordin & Gillberg, 1996). The boy:girl ratio in Asperger's syndrome is generally believed to be even higher than in autistic disorder (Wing, 1981a; Gillberg, C., 1989; Szatmari, Brenner & Nagy, 1989). However, the only population-based rates that exist (Gillberg, I.C., and Gillberg, C., 1989; Ehlers & Gillberg, 1993) suggest that the ratio may not be higher than 2–3:1 and that the high rates reported may be a result of clinicians being more prone to diagnose Asperger's syndrome in boys than in girls or of girls, with the syndrome only rarely being referred to clinics (or rather to clinicians who use the diagnosis of Asperger's syndrome).

Cognition

In autistic disorder, the rate of mental retardation (defined as IQ under 70) is 75–90 per cent (Gillberg, C., 1990). In Asperger's syndrome, mental retardation is rare, and possibly at the same level as in the general population (Gillberg, I.C., & Gillberg, C., 1989; Ehlers et al., 1997).

Several studies have reported a particular cognitive profile in autism. The test most often used in this context is the WISC-R, which has yielded a fairly consistent autism profile (Frith, 1989), with superior results on block design and extremely poor results on picture arrangement and comprehension. Results of the performance tests are usually generally better than those of the verbal tests. A recent study using the Griffiths Scale (Dahlgren-Sandberg et al., 1993) yielded similar results, with peaks in visuo-spatial domains and troughs in verbal areas. In Asperger's syndrome, verbal scores tend to be better than performance score (although not invariably so) and the typical profile is one with poor results on picture arrangement and object assembly (Ehlers et al., 1997).

Frith (1989) has speculated that the typical autism profile on the WISC could suggest an underlying deficit in the development of a 'theory of mind' and in 'central coherence'.

Epilepsy

Epilepsy occurs at a rate of 25–35 per cent in autism (Gillberg, C., 1991). Conversely, it appears that autism is considerably more common in people with epilepsy than in those without, particularly if there is also mental retardation (Steffenburg, Gillberg & Steffenburg, 1996). Epilepsy may be more common in Asperger's syndrome than in the general population (Gillberg, C., 1989), but the present evidence is insufficient for any conclusions to be drawn. Infantile spasms are strongly associated with autistic behaviour. More than one-third of all cases with infantile spasms (regardless of the presence or absence of other signs of tuberous sclerosis) show autistic behaviour and at least one in six of all cases meet criteria for autism during one phase of development (Riikonen & Amnell, 1981).

It appears that partial complex seizures may be more common in the autism population than in other populations with epilepsy (Gillberg, C., 1991). In the study by Olsson, Steffenburg & Gillberg (1988), three-quarters of all children with autism who also had epilepsy suffered from partial complex seizures (solely or in combination with other types of seizures). Conversely, even though this has not been explicitly stated, it is quite possible that a number of children in the longitudinal Oxford studies of partial complex epilepsy (Ounsted, Lindsay & Richards, 1987) showed autistic behaviour during the course of development.

Hearing deficits

It now seems clear that hearing deficits are common in autism (Steffenburg, 1991; Jure, Rapin & Tuchman, 1991; Rosenhall et al., submitted). One study (Steffenburg, 1991) indicated that moderate–severe hearing loss (>25dB) occurred in at least 20 per cent of a representative sample of young children with autistic disorder/infantile autism.

Ophthalmological problems

At least one in five of all children with autism have reduced visual acuity (Steffenburg, 1991). This is probably higher than in the general population, although no exactly comparable figures are available. Some blind children, particularly those with retinopathy of prematurity, have a very high rate of autism (Ek, et al., 1998). Many children with autism have a squint or other abnormalities of eye movements (Steffenburg, 1991). The appreciation of this type of problem in autism has been rendered particularly difficult because of major problems of co-operation in the evaluation process.

Fundus abnormalities in autism have not been extensively studied, in spite of the fact that fundoscopy holds considerable potential promise in the evaluation of autism aetiology. For instance, fundus hamartomata may be the only diagnostic marker in tuberous sclerosis, which is not an uncommon associated medical disorder in autism. The recent description of autism associated with Goldenhar syndrome (Landgren, Gillberg & Strömland, 1992) and thalidomide (Strömland et al., 1994) highlights the need for ophthalmologic examination in cases of autism.

Associated medical disorders

About one in four of all children with autism in the general population have an associated medical disorder (Gillberg, C., & Coleman, 1996). The rate may be somewhat lower in a specialized child psychiatric clinic setting. Table 5.2 lists those medical conditions that have been reported to be associated with autism in at least two published studies. They range from chromosomal to neurocutaneous disorders and metabolic and infectious diseases. Many of the disorders are genetic in nature. It is possible that the reason why autism is specifically associated with these medical disorders is that they may affect specific neural circuitry in the brain, circuitry necessary for the normal development of communication and social interaction. Some of the disorders are known to affect the temporofrontal areas of the brain (e.g. tuberous sclerosis, herpes encephalitis and the fragile X syndrome), and these areas are the ones now most commonly implicated in the pathogenesis of autism (Gillberg, C., & Coleman, 1992; Baron-Cohen, 1995).

Genetics

There is considerable evidence that in some cases autism has a genetic root (Bolton & Rutter, 1990). Three sets of published twin studies (Folstein & Rutter, 1977; Steffenburg et al., 1989; Le Couteur et al., 1996) on population-based samples of same-sexed twins without a known associated medical disorder have shown that in identical twins concordance is at a high rate (36–89 per cent), whereas in non-identical twin pairs it is low (0 per cent in all of the mentioned studies). In studies of extended families with children with autism, the rate of autism in siblings is considerably raised compared with the general population. Most of the available evidence suggests a 20–100-fold

Table 5.2 Medical disorders possibly related to autism or autistic-like conditions according to review of the literature

Medical condition	Reference
Cytomegalovirus infection	Stubbs (1976)
Duchenne muscular dystrophy	Komoto et al. (1984)
Encephalitis	Greenebaum & Lurie (1948)
Fragile X syndrome	Hagerman (1989)
Haemophilus influenzae meningitis	Ritvo et al. (1990)
Herpes simplex encephalitis	Gillberg, C. (1986)
Hypomelanosis of Ito	Zappella (1992)
Hypothyroidism	Gillberg, I. C. et al. (1992)
Lactic acidosis	Coleman & Blass (1985)
Maternal rubella	Chess et al. (1971)
Multiple congenital anomalies/mental retardation syndrome	Steffenburg (1991)
Moebius syndrome	Ornitz et al. (1977)
Mucopolysaccharidosis	Knobloch & Pasamanick (1975)
Neurofibromatosis	Gillberg, C. & Forsell (1984)
Other autosomal chromosome anomalies	Hagerman (1989)
Other sex chromosome anomalies	Hagerman (1989)
Partial tetrasomy 15 syndrome	Gillberg, C. et al. (1991b)
Phenylketonuria	Friedman (1969)
Purine disorders	Coleman et al. (1976)
Rett syndrome	Coleman et al. (1988)
Sotos syndrome	Zappella (1990)
Tuberous sclerosis	Hunt & Shepherd (1993)
West syndrome	Riikonen & Amnell (1981)
Williams' syndrome	Reiss et al. (1985)

Note:
All conditions included have been reported either in at least one population study plus at least one clinical study, or in at least three clinical studies of autism.

increase (Bolton & Rutter, 1990; Gillberg, C., Gillberg, I.C. & Steffenburg, 1992). There appears to be an accumulation of other neuropsychiatric disorders in families with children with autism and Asperger's syndrome. Manic–depressive illness (DeLong & Nohria, 1994), Tourette syndrome (Comings & Comings, 1990; Ehlers et al., 1997), DAMP (Gillberg C., et al, 1992), dyslexia and other specific language impairments (Bolton & Rutter, 1990) and anorexia nervosa (Gillberg, C., & Rastam, 1992; Comings & Comings, 1990) have all been reported to cluster in families in which at least one member has been diagnosed as suffering from infantile autism or autistic disorder. Finally, several reports have documented the co-existence of autism and elective mutism within the same family tree (Gillberg, C., 1989, 1992).

Neurobiological factors

A host of neurobiological correlations have been demonstrated in autism and autism spectrum problems. These can be subdivided into neurochemical, neurophysiological, neuroimaging and autopsy findings. The area is too vast to cover in a brief overview like the present one, but some recent developments can be highlighted.

An array of biochemical findings exists in the autism literature (Cook, 1990). Very few of these findings have been confirmed by independent groups (Gillberg, C. & Coleman, 1992). A raised level of whole-blood serotonin in a subgroup of individuals with autism seems to be the most robust finding. However, this finding is not specific to autism and could be associated with the degree of mental retardation in autism rather than with autism per se. Other findings include a raised level of cerebrospinal fluid homovanillic acid, the ganglioside GM-1, and GFA-protein (Nordin et al., 1998).

There have been a large number of reports on evoked response examinations in autism. The majority have included auditory brainstem response examinations, and the majority of these have shown abnormal prolongation of brainstem transmission time and abnormal interrelationships between the brainstem waves (Gillberg, C. & Coleman, 1992).

Electroencephalogram (EEG)-studies have consistently shown a high rate of abnormalities in autism, but it is not quite clear to what extent this increase is accounted for by the high prevalence of epilepsy in autism.

The majority of neuroimaging studies (pneumoencephalography, computerized atrial tonography (CAT) scan and magnetic resonance imaging (MRI) scan examinations of the brain) have shown abnormalities in autism, but no typical pattern has emerged. However, structural abnormalities in the region of the brainstem and pons have been most often reported (Gillberg, C. & Coleman, 1992). Also, the ventricular system has been enlarged according to several studies. The temporal lobes have been implicated in a number of studies. The cerebellum was described as rather specifically affected in one autism study (Courchesne et al., 1988), but so far, no other group has been able to replicate the results of that report. Also, in one study (Herold et al., 1988), it appeared that the caudate nucleus might be specifically affected.

Only a few autopsy studies of autism exist. The findings show no consistent pattern. Dense cell packing in the amygdala, abnormal histoanatomy of Purkinje cell fibres, gliosis, and unspecific general atrophy have all been reported (Gillberg, C. & Coleman, 1992; Kemper & Bauman, 1993).

It is likely that autistic behaviour can arise on the basis of abnormal function in several different parts of the brain. The brainstem, temporal lobes and frontal lobes have been the areas most often implicated in autism. The cerebellum has been highlighted by some authors. With social functioning being a very complex process, it should not be unexpected that abnormal social functioning can result from problems in several different parts of the brain.

Obviously, in those cases with an underlying medical disorder, the specific anatomical problems might vary with that disorder. Many of the disorders have fairly distinct patterns or 'predilection'. Thus, for instance, it appears that the frontal lobes may be crucially impaired in the fragile X syndrome, the temporal lobes and diencephalon in tuberous sclerosis, and the brainstem in Moebius syndrome.

The dopamine neurons arising in the brainstem and projecting onto target areas in the temporal and frontal lobes might well be particularly important in autism, as proposed by several authors (Maurer & Damasio, 1982; Gillberg, C. & Coleman, 1992). The Klüver–Bucy syndrome, similar in some respects to autism, can result from bilateral temporal lobe dysfunction, perhaps specifically bilateral dysfunction of the amygdala. Herpes encephalitis destroying the amygdala on both sides can result in a syndrome indistinguishable from autism (DeLong et al, 1981; Gillberg, C., 1986; Gillberg, I.C., 1991). One single photon emission computed tomography (SPECT) study indicated pronounced bitemporal dysfunction in autism (Gillberg, I.C. et al., 1993). Asperger's syndrome has been suggested to be confined to unilateral temporal lobe dysfunction – and right-sided abnormality in particular. However, a recent positron emission tomography (PET) study (Happé et al., 1996) showed a deviant activation pattern in the left medial portion of the frontal lobe in Asperger's syndrome during mentalizing activities. These, and other studies, fit a model for the development of autism involving temporofrontal lobe dysfunction, with the amygdala possibly being crucial. The findings implicating the brainstem also fit this hypothesis. The temporal lobes could be dysfunctional because of primary damage to the temporal regions of the brain, or secondarily because of problems in the brainstem. If both temporal lobes are affected, communication and social skills will suffer equally and autism could result. If only one temporal lobe is dysfunctional, social and communication skills will suffer, but not to the extent encountered in classic autism; in such cases, Asperger's syndrome might seem to be a more appropriate diagnosis (Goodman, 1989).

This, of course, is a highly speculative model for autism pathogenesis, and it should not be assumed that it proposes to account for all autism or Asperger's syndrome cases. Other mechanisms could account for yet other autism/Asperger cases.

Psychological factors

An almost incredible number of psychological theories have been advanced over the years to account for the autism behaviour pattern. One recent theory appears to have opened a new window of the field, providing not only a means of explaining autism phenomena once they have appeared, but also comprising a model for predicting behaviour and communication in autism. According to this so-called theory of mind – or mentalizing – autism theory, people with autism have an abnormality – or delay – in the acquisition of metarepresentational skills. They fail to attribute mental states such as knowing and believing to other people, and hence have to rely only on the observable world (Frith, 1989; Baron-Cohen, 1995) in their efforts to appreciate and evaluate the actions taken by other people. In other words, they do not understand mental states which are not readily observable 'on the outside', they do not form mental concepts which can facilitate the grouping of observable phenomena, and they do not 'mentalize' in response to communication – verbal or non-verbal – from other people. Conversely, they often develop superior skills in dealing with aspects of the observable world (location, jigsaws etc.). In an ingenious set of experiments, Frith's group (Baron-Cohen, 1990) has demonstrated convincingly that several aspects of mentalizing are deficient in autism. However, some studies have failed to confirm these findings convincingly (Prior, Dahlström & Squires, 1990).

Frith (1989) and Happé et al. (1996) have also highlighted the difficulty with central coherence encountered in so many individuals on the autism spectrum. This difficulty shows in the inability to extract meaning from piecemeal information that is typical of autism. Central coherence deficits and mentalizing problems could be parallel phenomena or interacting concepts, and a theory proposing a deficit in one of the areas does not exclude a deficit in the other area also.

Frith (1989) has suggested that this psychological core deficit encountered in autism could have its biological counterpart in the biological core deficit model described in the foregoing.

Social factors

That autism is nothing to do with social class is gradually becoming accepted (Wing, 1980; Gillberg, C., 1995). The old studies suggesting an upper social class bias were based on clinical materials in most cases. The only population study which has ever supported the social class bias was the first epidemiological survey in the field (Lotter, 1966). Perhaps it is this fact that has made the notion persist in the face of at least ten other epidemiological studies not reporting any social class bias (Gillberg, C. & Coleman, 1992).

A number of studies suggest that autism is more common in children born to parents born in cultures geographically distant from those being epidemiologically screened for autism (Wing, 1980; Akinsola & Fryers, 1986; Gillberg, C. et al., 1987; 1991a; Gillberg, I.C. & Gillberg, C., 1996). The reason for this high rate is unclear.

Outcome

The outcome in autism and autistic-like conditions is generally poor as regards social functioning in adult life. Nevertheless, there is great individual variation and the whole range of outcomes, from independent functioning to life in an institution, should be considered in most cases whenever prognosis is discussed. According to a recent review (Nordin & Gillberg, 1998), there is slightly increased mortality in autism, possibly due to the high rate of associated severe brain disorders. About two-thirds of all individuals diagnosed in childhood as suffering from autism will be dependent on other people in adult life, both as regards living and work. About one in four does relatively well in respect of either living independently or work and a few per cent are indistinguishable from normal. IQ above 70 and some communicative speech at age 5–6 years are both predictive of a relatively fair prognosis, whereas IQ under 50 is almost invariably associated with a poor outcome. The outcome in Asperger's syndrome is not well known. However, the available evidence suggests that many people with this syndrome lead so-called normal lives in adulthood. However, it is equally clear that many have a poor psychosocial prognosis and that atypical depression, suicide, paranoia and overall social ineptness are all quite common types of outcome in Asperger's syndrome (Wing, 1981a; Frith, 1991; Gillberg, C., 1992). Asperger's syndrome is probably underdiagnosed at the present time. Some adult psychiatric patients with diagnoses such as 'borderline', 'pseudoneurotic schizophrenia', 'paranoid psychosis' and 'masked depression' have suffered from social impairments and communication deficits from early childhood and a diagnosis of Asperger's syndrome, as we know it today, might have been appropriate.

Intervention

As in any disorder with multiple aetiologies, rational treatment can only be offered on the basis of a proper understanding of the underlying causative mechanisms. Therefore, a comprehensive medical work-up is called for in each case diagnosed as suffering from autism, in order that the best available treatment be offered. A cure for autism is not available in most cases at the present stage. However, autism can be prevented in certain situations: rubella embryopathy, phenylketonuria and hypothyroidism are examples of medical conditions that can either be prevented altogether or are amenable to treatment at a very early age. In such instances, the otherwise high risk for autistic behaviour can be reduced almost to zero.

In lactic acidosis (Coleman & Blass, 1985) and rare cases of epilepsy with autistic behaviour, specific treatments are available.

By and large, however, educational and behavioural modes of intervention remain the best documented methods in the treatment of autism

(Schopler, 1989; Lovaas, Calouri & Jada, 1989; Howlin & Yates, 1989). Behaviour problems, social interaction and communication can all be considerably improved if proper structured training is provided at an early age.

A few medications, such as dopamine blockers (Campbell, 1989) and large doses of vitamin B6 (Gualtieri & Hicks, 1985), have shown promise in ameliorating some of the most conspicuous autism symptoms, but side-effects of neuroleptics prevent them from being widely used. Antiepileptic treatments can sometimes be effective in reducing autistic symptoms (Gillberg, C., 1991), but they can, equally, contribute to the aggravation of such symptoms. Other drugs have not been widely studied in autism, but there are currently many studies of the new serotonin reuptake inhibitors underway, and it is possible that these may find a place in the treatment of some cases with autism.

Conclusion

Given the concept of autism presented, it would seem that the way forward in the field will be to subdivide groups of autism cases according to underlying aetiology. Only by taking this route can we hope to provide better (more rational) treatment in each individual case of autism.

By comparing the behavioural profile in cases of autism with different aetiologies, we may finally arrive at a concept of the 'syndrome' that is different from that originally forwarded by Kanner: there may be no such thing as a distinct autistic syndrome, but rather a wide variety of brain problems which are reflected in varying degrees and types of so-called autistic behaviour.

References

Akinsola, H.A. & Fryers, T. (1986). A comparison of patterns of disability in severely mentally handicapped children of different ethnic origins. *Psychological Medicine*, **16**, 127–33.

American Psychiatric Association (1980). *Diagnostic and Statistical Manual of Mental Disorders*, 3rd edn. Washington, DC: APA.

(1987). *Diagnostic and Statistical Manual of Mental Disorders*, 3rd edition, revised. Washington, DC: APA.

(1994). *Diagnostic and Statistical Manual of Mental Disorders*. 4th edition. Washington, DC: APA.

Arvidsson, T., Danielsson, B., Forsberg, P., Gillberg, C., Johansson, M. & Källgren, G. (1997). Autism in 3–6-year-old children in a suburb of Göteborg, Sweden. *Autism*, **7**, 163–73.

Baron-Cohen, S. (1990). Autism: a specific cognitive disorder of 'mind-blindness'. *International Review of Psychiatry*, **2**, 81–90.

(1995). *Mind Blindness. An Essay on Autism and Theory of Mind*. Cambridge, MA: MIT Press.

Bohman, M., Bohman, I.L., Björk, P. & Sjöholm, E. (1983). Childhood psychosis in a northern Swedish county: some preliminary findings from an epidemiological survey. In *Epidemiological Approaches in Child Psychiatry*, ed. M.H. Schmidt & H. Remschmith, pp. 164–73. Stuttgart: Georg Thieme.

Bolton, P. & Rutter, M. (1990). Genetic influences in autism. *International Review of Psychiatry*, **2**, 67–80.

Brask, B.H. (1972). A prevalence investigation of childhood psychosis. In *Barnepsykiatrisk Förening: Nordic Symposium on the Comprehensive Care of Psychotic Children*, Oslo. pp. 145–53.

Bryson, S.E., Clark, B.S. & Smith, I.M. (1988). First report of a Canadian epidemiological study of autistic syndromes. *Journal of Child Psychology and Psychiatry*, **29**, 433–45.

Campbell, M. (1989). Pharmacotherapy in autism: an overview. In *Diagnosis and Treatment of Autism*, ed. C. Gillberg, pp. 203–18. New York: Plenum Press.

Chess, S., Korn, S.J. & Fernandez, P.B. (1971). *Psychiatric Disorders of Children with Congenital Rubella*. New York: Brunner/Mazel.

Cialdella, P. & Mamelle, N. (1989). An epidemiological study of infantile autism in a French department (Rhone): a research note. *Journal of Child Psychology and Psychiatry*, **30**, 165–75.

Coleman, M. & Blass, J.P. (1985). Autism and lactic acidosis. *Journal of Autism and Developmental Disorders*, **15**, 1–8.

Coleman, M., Brubaker, J., Hunter, K. & Smith, G. (1988). Rett syndrome: a survey of North American patients. *Journal of Mental Deficiency Research*, **32**, 117–24.

Coleman, M., Landgrebe, M. & Landgrebe, A. (1976). Purine autism. In *The Autistic Syndromes*, ed. M. Coleman, pp. 120–8. Amsterdam: North-Holland.

Comings, D.E. & Comings, B.G. (1990). A controlled family history study of Tourette's syndrome. I. Attention deficit hyperactivity disorder and learning disorders. *Journal of Clinical Psychiatry*, **51**, 275–80.

Courchesne, E., Yeung-Courchesne, R., Press, G.A., Hesselink, J.R. and & Jernigan, T.L. (1988) Hypoplasia of cerebellar vermal lobules VI and VII in autism. *New England Journal of Medicine*, **318**, 1349–54.

Cook, E.H. (1990). Autism: Review of neurochemical investigation. *Synapse*, **6**, 292–308.

Dahlgren-Sandberg, A., Nydén, A., Gillberg, C. & Hjelmquist, E. (1993). The cognitive profile in infantile autism – a study of 70 children and adolescents using the Griffiths Mental Development Scale. *British Journal of Psychology*, **84**, 365–73.

DeLong, G.R., Beau, S.C. & Brown, F.R. (1981). Acquired reversible autistic syndrome in acute encephalopathic illness in children. *Archives of Neurology*, **38**, 191–4.

DeLong, R. & Nohria, C. (1994). Psychiatric family history and neurological disease in autism spectrum disorders. *Developmental Medicine and Child Neurology*, **36**, 441–8.

Ehlers, S. & Gillberg, C. (1993). The epidemiology of Asperger syndrome. A total population study. *Journal of Child Psychology and Psychiatry*, **34**, 1327–50.

Ehlers, S., Nydén, A., Gillberg, C. et al. (1997). Asperger syndrome, autism and attention disorders: a comparative study of the cognitive profile of 120 children. *Journal of Child Psychology and Psychiatry*, **38**, 207–17.

Ek, U., Fernell, E., Jacobsson, L. & Gillberg, C. (1998). Relationship between blindness due to retinopathy of prematurity and autistic spectrum disorders. A population study. *Developmental Medicine and Child Neurology*, **40**, 297–301.

Folstein, S. & Rutter, M. (1977). Infantile autism: a genetic study of 21 twin pairs. *Journal of Child Psychology and Psychiatry*, **18**, 297–321.

Friedman, E. (1969). The autistic syndrome and phenylketonuria. *Schizophrenia*, **1**, 249–61.

Frith, U. (1989). Autism and 'theory of mind'. In *Diagnosis and Treatment of Autism*, ed. C. Gillberg, pp. 33–52. New York: Plenum Press.

   (1991). *Autism and Asperger Syndrome.* Cambridge: Cambridge University Press.

Garreau, B.C., Barthelemy, C., Sauvage, D., Leddet, I. & Lelord, G. (1984). A comparison of autistic syndromes with and without associated neurological problems. *Journal of Autism and Developmental Disorders*, **14**, 105–11.

   (1984). Infantile autism and other childhood psychoses in a Swedish urban region. Epidemiological aspects. *Journal of Child Psychology and Psychiatry*, **25**, 35–43.

   (1986). Brief report: onset at age 14 of a typical autistic syndrome. A case report of a girl with herpes simplex encephalitis. *Journal of Autism and Developmental Disorders*, **16**, 369–75.

   (1989). Asperger syndrome in 23 Swedish children. *Developmental Medicine and Child Neurology*, **31**, 520–31.

   (1990). Autism and pervasive developmental disorders. *Journal of Child Psychology and Psychiatry*, **31**, 99–119. (Published erratum (1991) in *Journal of Child Psychology and Psychiatry*, **32**(1), 213.

   (1991). The treatment of epilepsy in autism. *Journal of Autism and Developmental Disorders*, **21**, 61–77.

   (1992). The Emanuel Miller Memorial Lecture 1991. Autism and autistic-like conditions: subclasses among disorders of empathy. *Journal of Child Psychology and Psychiatry*, **33**, 813–42.

Gillberg, C. (1993). Autism and related behaviours. *Journal of Intellectual Disability Research*, **37**, 343–72.

   (1995). The prevalence of autism and autism spectrum disorders. In *The Epidemiology of Child and Adolescent Psychopathology*, ed. F.C. Verhulst & H.M. Koot, pp. 227–57. Oxford: Oxford University Press.

   (1997). *Disintegrativ störning hos barn (Heller syndrom).* Stockholm: Riksföreningen Autism.

Gillberg, C., Carlström, G. & Rasmussen, P. (1983). Hyperkinetic disorders in seven-year-old children with perceptual, motor and attentional deficits. *Journal of Child Psychology and Psychiatry*, **24**, 233–46.

Gillberg, C. & Coleman, M. (1992). *The Biology of the Autistic Syndromes.* Clinics in Developmental Medicine No. 126, p. 317. London, New York: Mac Keith Press.

(1996). Autism and medical disorders. A review of the literature. *Developmental Medicine and Child Neurology*, **38**, 191–202.

Gillberg, C. & Forsell, C. (1984). Childhood psychosis and neurofibromatosis – more than a coincidence? *Journal of Autism and Developmental Disorders*, **14**, 1–8.

Gillberg, C., Gillberg, I.C. & Steffenburg, S. (1992). Siblings and parents of children with autism. A controlled population based study. *Developmental Medicine and Child Neurology*, **34**, 389–98.

Gillberg, C., Nordin, V. & Ehlers, S. (1996). Early detection of autism. Diagnostic instruments for clinicians. *European Child & Adolescent Psychiatry*, **5**, 67–74.

Gillberg, C. & Rastam, M. (1992). Do some cases of anorexia nervosa reflect underlying autistic-like conditions? *Behavioural Neurology*, **5**, 27–32.

Gillberg, C., Steffenburg, S., Börjesson, B. & Andersson, L. (1987). Infantile autism in children of immigrant parents. A population- based study from Göteborg, Sweden. *British Journal of Psychiatry*, **150**, 856–8.

Gillberg, C., Steffenburg, S. & Schaumann, H. (1991a). Is autism more common now than 10 years ago? *British Journal of Psychiatry*, **158**, 403–9.

Gillberg, C., Steffenburg, S. Wahlström, J. et al. (1991b). Autism associated with marker chromosome. *Journal of the American Academy of Child and Adolescent Psychiatry*, **30**, 489–94.

Gillberg, I.C. (1991). Autistic syndrome with onset at age 31 years. Herpes encephalitis as one possible model for childhood autism. *Developmental Medicine and Child Neurology*, **33**, 920–4.

Gillberg, I.C., Bjure, J., Uvebrant, P. & Gillberg, C. (1993). SPECT (single photon emission computed tomography) in 31 children and adolescents with autism and autistic-like conditions. *European Child & Adolescent Psychiatry*, **2**, 50–9.

Gillberg, I.C. & Gillberg, C. (1989). Asperger syndrome – some epidemiological considerations: a research note. *Journal of Child Psychology and Psychiatry*, **30**, 631–8.

(1996). Autism in immigrants. A population-based study from a Swedish rural and urban area. *Journal of Intellectual Disability Research*, **40**, 24–31.

Gillberg, I.C., Gillberg, C. & Kopp, S. (1992). Hypothyroidism and autism spectrum disorders. *Journal of Child Psychology and Psychiatry*, **33**, 531–42.

Goodman, R. (1989). Infantile autism: a syndrome of multiple primary deficits? *Journal of Autism and Developmental Disorders*, **19**, 409–24.

Greenebaum, J.V. & Lurie, L.A. (1948). Encephalitis as a causative factor in behavior disorder in children: analysis of 78 cases. *Journal of the American Medical Association*, **136**, 923–30.

Gualtieri, C.T. & Hicks, R.E. (1985). An immunoreactive theory of selective male afflication. *Behavioral and Brain Science*, **8**, 427–41.

Gunnarsdóttir, K. & Magnussón, P. (1994). The Epidemiology of Autism and Asperger Syndrome in Iceland. A Pilot Study. Nordic Conference on Autistic Disorders, Epidemiology, Biology, Diagnostic Aspects, Oslo, Norway.

Hagerman, R.J. (1989). Chromosomes, genes and autism. In *Diagnosis and Treatment of Autism*, ed. C. Gillberg, p. 105–32. New York: Plenum Press.

Hagerman, R.J., Jackson, C., Amiri, K., Silverman, A.C., O'Connor, R. & Sobesky, W. (1992). Girls with fragile X syndrome: physical and neurocognitive status and outcome. *Pediatrics*, **89**, 395–400.

Happé, F., Ehlers, S., Fletcher, P. et al. (1996). 'Theory of mind' in the brain. Evidence from a PET scan study of Asperger syndrome. *NeuroReport*, **8**, 197–201.

Herold, S., Frackowiak, R.S.J., Le Couteur, A., Rutter, M. & Howlin, P. (1988). Cerebral blood flow and metabolism of oxygen and glucose in young autistic adults. *Psychological Medicine*, **18**, 823–31.

Howlin, P. & Yates, P. (1989). Treating autistic children at home. A London based programme. In *Diagnosis and Treatment of Autism*, ed. C. Gillberg, pp. 307–22. New York: Plenum Press.

Hunt, A. & Shepherd, C. (1993). A prevalence study of autism in tuberous sclerosis. *Journal of Autism and Developmental Disorders*, **23**, 323–39.

Jure, R., Rapin, I. & Tuchman, R.F. (1991). Hearing-impaired autistic children. *Developmental Medicine and Child Neurology*, **33**, 1062–72.

Kanner, L. & Eisenberg, L. (1956). Early infantile autism: 1943–1955. *American Journal of Orthopsychiatry*, **26**, 55–65.

Kemper, T.L. & Bauman, M.L. (1993). The contribution of neuropathologic studies to the understanding of autism. *Neurologic Clinics*, **11**, 175–87.

Knobloch, H. & Pasamanick, B. (1975). Some etiologic and prognostic factors in early infantile autism and psychosis. *Journal of Pediatrics*, **55**, 182–91.

Komoto, J., Udsui, S., Otsuki, S. & Terao, A. (1984). Infantile autism and Duchenne muscular dystrophy. *Journal of Autism and Developmental Disorders*, **14**, 191–5.

Kopp, S. & Gillberg, C. (1992). Girls with social deficits and learning problems: autism, atypical Asperger syndrome or a variant of these conditions. *European Child & Adolescent Psychiatry*, **1**, 89–99.

Landgren, M., Gillberg, C. & Strömland, K. (1992). Goldenhar syndrome and autistic behaviour. *Developmental Medicine and Child Neurology*, **34**, 999–1005.

Le Couteur, A., Bailey, A., Goode, S. et al. (1996). A broader phenotype of autism: the clinical spectrum in twins. *Psychology and Psychiatry*, **30**, 405–16.

Le Couteur, A., Rutter, M., Lord, C. et al. (1989). Autism diagnostic interview: a standardized investigator-based instrument. *Journal of Autism and Developmental Disorders*, **19**, 363–87.

Lord, C., Rutter, M., Goode, S. et al. (1989). Autism diagnostic observation schedule: a standardized observation of communicative and social behavior. *Journal of Autism and Developmental Disorders*, **19**, 185–212.

Lord, C. & Schopler, E. (1985). Differences in sex ratios in autism as a function of measured intelligence. *Journal of Autism and Developmental Disorders*, **15**, 185–93.

Lord, C., Schopler, E. & Revicki, D. (1982). Sex differences in autism. *Journal of Autism and Developmental Disorders*, **12**, 317–30.

Lotter, V. (1966). Epidemiology of autistic conditions in young children. *Social Psychiatry*, **1**, 124–37.

Lovaas, I., Calouri, K. & Jada, J. (1989). The nature of behavioural treatment and research with young autistic persons. In *Diagnosis and Treatment of Autism*, ed. Gillberg, C., pp. 285–305. New York: Plenum Press.

Maurer, R.G. & Damasio, A.R. (1982). Childhood autism from the point of view of behavioral neurology. *Journal of Autism and Developmental Disorders*, **12**, 195–205.

Miller, J.N. & Ozonoff, S. (1997). Did Asperger's cases have Asperger's disorders? A research note. *Journal of Child Psychology and Psychiatry*, **38**, 247–51.

Mirenda, P.L., Donnellan, A.M. & Yoder, D.E. (1983). Gaze behaviour: a new look at an old problem. *Journal of Autism and Developmental Disorders*, **13**, 397–409.

Nordin, V. & Gillberg, C. (1996). Autism spectrum disorders in children with physical or mental disability or both. Part I: Clinical and epidemiological aspects. *Developmental Medicine and Child Neurology*, **38**, 297–313.

(1998). The long-term course of autistic disorders: update on follow-up studies. *Acta Psychiatrica Scandinavica*, **97**, 99–108.

Nordin, V., Lekman, A., Johansson, M., Fredman, P. & Gillberg, C. (1998). Gangliosides in cerebrospinal fluid in children with autism spectrum disorders. *Developmental Medicine and Child Neurology*, **40**, 587–611.

Olsson, I., Steffenburg, S. & Gillberg, C. (1988). Epilepsy in autism and autistic-like conditions: a population-based study. *Archives of Neurology*, **45**, 666–8.

Ornitz, E.M., Guthrie, D. & Farley, A.J. (1977). The early development of autistic children. *Journal of Autism and Childhood Schizophrenia*, **7**, 207–29.

Ounsted, C., Lindsay, J. & Richards, P. (1987). Temporal lobe epilepsy. A biographical study 1948–1986. Clinics in Developmental Medicine No. 103. Oxford: MacKeith Press.

Prior, M., Dahlström, B. & Squires, T.-L. (1990). Autistic children's knowledge of thinking and feeling states in other people. *Journal of Child Psychology and Psychiatry*, **31**, 587–601.

Rapoport, J.L. (1989). *Obsessive–Compulsive Disorder in Children and Adolescents*. Washington, DC: American Psychiatric Association.

Reiss, A.L., Feinstein, C., Rosenbaum, K.N., Borengasser-Caruso, M.A. & Goldsmith, B.M. (1985). Autism associated with Williams syndrome. *Journal of Paediatrics*, **106**, 247–9.

Riikonen, R. & Amnell, G. (1981). Psychiatric disorders in children with earlier infantile spasms. *Developmental Medicine and Child Neurology*, **23**, 747–60.

Ritvo, E.R., Mason-Brothers, A., Freeman, B.J. et al. (1990). The UCLA–University of Utah epidemiologic survey of autism: the etiologic role of rare diseases. *American Journal of Psychiatry*, **147**, 1614–21.

Rosenhall, U., Sandström, M., Nordin, V. & Gillberg, C. (submitted). Autism and hearing loss. *Journal of Autism and Developmental Disorders*.

Rutter, M. (1983). Cognitive deficits in the pathogenesis of autism. *Journal of Child Psychology and Psychiatry*, **24**, 513–31.

Schopler, E. (1989). Principles for directing both educational treatment and research. In *Diagnosis and Treatment of Autism*, ed. C. Gillberg, pp. 167–83. New York: Plenum Press.

Steffenburg, S. (1991). Neuropsychiatric assessment of children with autism: a population-based study. *Developmental Medicine and Child Neurology*, **33**, 495–511.

Steffenburg, S. & Gillberg, C. (1986). Autism and autistic-like conditions in Swedish rural and urban areas: a population study. *British Journal of Psychiatry*, **149**, 81–7.

Steffenburg, S., Gillberg, C., Hellgren, L. et al. (1989). A twin study of autism in Denmark, Finland, Iceland, Norway and Sweden. *Journal of Child Psychology & Psychiatry & Allied Disciplines*, **37**, 785–801.

Steffenburg, S., Gillberg, C. & Steffenburg, U. (1996). Psychiatric disorders in children and adolescents with active epilepsy and mental retardation. *Archives of Neurology*, **53**, 904–12.

Strömland, K., Nordin, V., Miller, M., Akerström, B. & Gillberg, C. (1994). Autism in thalidomide embryopathy: a population study. *Developmental Medicine and Child Neurology*, **36**, 351–6.

Stubbs, E.G. (1976). Autistic children exhibit undetectable hemagglutination-inhibition antibody titers despite previous rubella vaccination. *Journal of Autism and Childhood Schizophrenia*, **6**, 269–74.

Sugiyama, T. & Abe, T. (1989). The prevalence of autism in Nagoya, Japan: a total population study. *Journal of Autism and Developmental Disorders*, **19**, 87–96.

Szatmari, P., Brenner, R. & Nagy, J. (1989). Asperger's syndrome: a review of clinical features. *Canadian Journal of Psychiatry*, **34**, 554–60.

Tanoue, Y., Oda, S., Asano, F. & Kawashima, K. (1988). Epidemiology of infantile autism on Southern Ibaraki, Japan: differences in prevalence rates in birth cohorts. *Journal of Autism and Developmental Disorders*, **18**, 155–66.

Tsai, L.Y., Stewart, M.A. & August, G. (1981). Implication of sex differences in the familial transmission of infantile autism. *Journal of Autism and Developmental Disorders*, **11**, 165–73.

Turk, J. (1994). The Fragile X Syndrome. First Norwegian Congress on Autism, Oslo, Norway.

Volkmar, F.R. (1992). Childhood disintegrative disorder: issues for DSM-IV. *Journal of Autism and Developmental Disorders*, **22**, 625–42.

Webb, E.V.J., Lobo, S., Hervas, A., Scourfield, J. & Fraser, W.I. (1997). The changing prevalence of autistic disorder in a Welsh health district. *Developmental Medicine and Child Neurology*, **39**, 150–2.

Wing, L. (1980). Childhood autism and social class: a question of selection. *British Journal of Psychiatry*, **137**, 410–17.

(1981a). Asperger's syndrome: a clinical account. *Psychological Medicine*, **11**, 115–29.

(1981b). Sex ratios in early childhood autism and related conditions. *Psychiatry Research*, **5**, 129–37.

(1991). The relationship between Asperger's syndrome and Kanner's autism. In *Autism and Asperger syndrome*, ed. U. Frith, pp. 93–121. Cambridge: Cambridge University Press.

(1996). *The Autism Spectrum*. London: Constable.

Wing, L. & Gould, J. (1979). Severe impairments of social interaction and associated abnormalities in children: epidemiology and classification. *Journal of Autism and Developmental Disorders*, **9**, 11–29.

Wolff, S. (1995). Loners. *The Life Path of Unusual Children*. London: Routledge.

World Health Organization (1993). *The ICD-10 Classification of Mental and Behavioural Disorders. Diagnostic Criteria for Research*. Geneva: WHO.

Zappella, M. (1990). Autistic features in children affected by cerebral gigantism. *Brain Dysfunction*, **3**, 241–4.

(1992). Hypomelanosis of Ito is common in autistic syndromes. *European Child & Adolescent Psychiatry*, **1**, 10–7.

6 Behavioural phenotypes: towards new understandings of people with developmental disabilities

ELISABETH M. DYKENS AND ROBERT M. HODAPP

Introduction

Studying behavioural phenotypes presents a paradox. On one hand, interest in different genetic disorders is at unprecedented levels. Over the past 40 years, more than 750 genetic disorders have been identified that are associated with developmental disabilities (Opitz, 1996), and the mechanisms of many of these disorders are becoming increasingly better characterized. Due to advances in molecular and clinical genetics, more syndromes are being identified, and more people with developmental disabilities are receiving genetic diagnoses than ever before. Yet, at the same time, we know precious little about the behavioural phenotypes of most genetic syndromes associated with developmental disabilities (Hodapp & Dykens, 1994). Of all disorders, Down syndrome is the only one which has been the subject of widespread behavioural research over an extended period. Indeed, from 1985 to 1990, Down syndrome alone was the subject of nearly half (46 per cent) of all behavioural studies of genetic developmental disability syndromes (Hodapp, 1996). Although certain aspects of behaviour have also been recently examined in fragile X syndrome, Prader–Willi syndrome, and Williams' syndrome, very few behavioural studies exist for most of the other genetic syndromes associated with developmental disabilities.

This chapter begins by examining some of the reasons for this paradox. The concept of a behavioural phenotype is then defined and an illustration given of how that concept can be profitably used in psychiatric research. As this chapter aims to show, behavioural phenotypes provide a critical starting point for the description, understanding and treatment of psychopathology in individuals with developmental disabilities.

The two cultures

In resolving the paradox of great interest but little behavioural work in genetic disorders, we borrow a metaphor from the British chemist and novelist C.P. Snow (1963). In Snow's experience with both the humanities and the sciences earlier this century, he noted that workers in these two traditions worked in almost total isolation from each other. Indeed, Snow identified sciences versus the humanities as two, rarely overlapping, 'cultures' within British society of the late 1950s.

On a smaller scale, these authors also feel that two cultures characterize behavioural work in the field of developmental disabilities. On one side are social scientists such as clinical psychologists, cognitive psychologists, developmental psychologists, behavioural workers, social workers, special educators, and speech and language therapists. Despite their different training and theoretical backgrounds, these workers engage in a common research practice of examining subjects with mixed aetiologies. Individuals with diverse or even unknown causes for their developmental delay are studied as a single group, and data are analysed by IQ level (e.g. mild, moderate, severe, profound), age, gender, living status, or other variables of interest. These workers generally publish in journals such as the *American Journal on Mental Retardation, Mental Retardation*, and the *Journal of Intellectual Disability Research*.

A second, more biomedically oriented group also studies behaviour in people with developmental disabilities. Mainly consisting of clinical geneticists, paediatricians, and adult and child psychiatrists, these biomedical workers generally publish in journals such as the *American Journal of Medical Genetics, Journal of Child Psychology and Psychiatry*, and the *Journal of the American Academy of Child and Adolescent Psychiatry*. Most importantly, these more biomedical workers divide their research groups on the basis of aetiology. Studies might, for example, examine people with Down syndrome or fragile X syndrome, or compare people with a single genetic disorder to a 'mixed' or 'non-specific' disability group.

Each approach features both strengths and weaknesses. The strength of the first culture – the social scientists who examine mixed aetiological groups – involves their understanding of behaviour. These scientists best understand cognitive, linguistic, adaptive, and social behaviour, family functioning, the many aspects of information processing, and how to conceptualize and evaluate intervention programmes. Conversely, this group shows little appreciation of different aetiologies of developmental disabilities, and questions why one needs to consider aetiological differences (Hodapp & Dykens, 1994; Dykens, 1996).

In contrast, biomedically oriented workers in the second culture are more knowledgeable about genetics and better appreciate the remarkable technical advances in diagnosing people with syndromes. Yet, at the same time, these workers know relatively little about many aspects of behaviour, often thinking that a simple IQ score or superficial behavioural description (e.g. 'sing-songy' language) constitutes a sufficient explanation of behaviour.

Although the two cultures are detailed elsewhere (Hodapp & Dykens,

1994), the focus here is on one outgrowth of these separate cultures: our knowledge of psychopathology. As the present book illustrates, we know much more about psychopathology in the heterogeneous population of people with developmental disabilities than we do about people with distinct syndromes. More often than not, studies emphasize the prevalence of maladaptive behaviour and psychiatric disorders in mixed groups, and how symptoms differ across age, intellectual level, gender and living setting (e.g. Borthwick-Duffy, 1994).

The general inattention to aetiology is reflected in many of the field's leading journals. From 1970 to 1990, these authors counted 375 journal articles in Aman's (1991) comprehensive bibliography of research publications on behavioural, psychiatric and emotional disturbance in people with developmental disabilities. Of these 375 articles, 89 per cent used heterogeneous groups of subjects, and just 11 per cent were devoted to psychiatric or behavioural problems in people with specific genetic syndromes. Although less comprehensive, there were remarkably similar percentages from 1990 to 1995 in the two journals published by the American Association on Mental Retardation. Of the studies on behavioural or psychiatric dysfunction published in the *American Journal on Mental Retardation*, and in *Mental Retardation*, 88 per cent and 89 per cent, respectively, used mixed groups, leaving just 11–12 per cent of articles on specific syndromes, primarily Down syndrome. Given recent genetic advances, the field is thus left with a situation in which many syndromes have been well characterized genetically, but the large majority of these syndromes have not yet been studied psychiatrically or behaviourally.

Behavioural phenotypes

One obstacle to more syndrome-based research may be the lack of an agreed-upon definition of a behavioural phenotype. Workers often differ in their definitions, and at the risk of stirring up these differences, these authors add their own working definition to the mix. For their purposes, a behavioural phenotype 'may best be described as the heightened probability or likelihood that people with a given syndrome will exhibit certain behavioural or developmental sequelae relative to those without the syndrome' (Dykens, 1995). This definition leads to several noteworthy points.

Within-syndrome variability

As behavioural phenotypes involve a probability, not every individual with a given syndrome will exhibit that syndrome's characteristic behaviour. Nor will each individual show that behaviour to the same extent or level of severity, or at the same point in development. Just as only 57 per cent of infants with Down syndrome show that disorder's epicanthal folds

(Pueschel, 1983), so too will individuals with the same syndrome differ in their behaviours. Indeed, that a specific behaviour 'characterizes' a given syndrome means only that significantly more of that behaviour is noted compared to a mixed or non-specific group (Rosen, 1993; Einfeld & Hall, 1994; Dykens, 1995). This probabilistic perspective contrasts with the view that 'a behavioural phenotype should consist of a distinctive behaviour that occurs in almost every case of a genetic or chromosomal disorder...' (Flynt & Yule, 1994). This movement away from absolutes, or 'in almost every case' to 'heightened probability or likelihood', throws interesting complications into studies of within-syndrome differences.

Perhaps the most challenging complication is identifying genetic, psychosocial or other variables that account for within-syndrome behavioural variability. As a complete review of within-syndrome work is beyond the scope of this chapter, a few examples are highlighted instead that demonstrate genetic and other sources of within-syndrome variability. People with 5p− syndrome often show elevated hyperactivity relative to others with developmental delay, yet social withdrawal, disinterest in others, and other autistic features are seen primarily in 5p− cases due to translocations as opposed to deletions (Dykens & Clarke, 1997). In Prader–Willi syndrome, we find preliminary, subtle differences in the frequency and severity of compulsive behaviours across cases with paternal deletion of 15q11–q13 versus those with maternal uniparental disomy of chromosome 15 (Dykens & Cassidy, 1996).

Other innovative work makes more specific correlations between genes and behaviour. Recent examples include work that:
  – links molecular genetic status to cognitive and psychiatric outcomes in fragile X syndrome (Sobesky, Hull & Hagerman, 1994; Reiss et al., 1995);
  – localizes the cat cry in 5p− syndrome to 5p15.3 (Gersh et al., 1995);
  – identifies a candidate gene in Williams' syndrome (LIM-kinase1) that is near the elastin gene deletion on chromosome 7, and that may be responsible for the visual–spatial deficit seen in many people with this disorder (Frangiskakis et al., 1996) .

In addition to genetic status, other characteristics such as IQ and age are emerging as correlates of maladaptive behaviour or psychopathology within syndromes. In Prader–Willi syndrome, IQ level appears unrelated to stubbornness, temper tantrums and non-food compulsivity (Dykens & Cassidy, 1995; Dykens, Leckman & Cassidy, 1996). Yet IQ level in 5p− syndrome is negatively correlated with impulsivity, self-injury and stereotypies (Dykens & Clarke, 1997). Age emerges as a significant correlate of depression and anxiety in Down syndrome children, but not in children with Prader–Willi syndrome (Dykens & Kasari, 1997). In Prader–Willi syndrome, decreased obesity may be associated with heightened anxiety, distorted thinking and depression (Dykens & Cassidy, 1995). In these and other syndromes, then, combinations of genetic, constitutional, developmental, environmental and psychosocial factors need to be identified that help explain within-syndrome behavioural variability.

Total versus partial specificity from one syndrome to another

A second implication of a probabilistic view of phenotypes involves total versus partial specificity. The goal of many behavioural phenotype studies is to discover the unique behaviours of a given aetiology. Indeed, sometimes there appears to be a one-to-one correspondence, such that a particular behaviour appears unique to one and only one genetic aetiology. Although speculative, as comparative studies have yet to be done, examples of potentially unique syndromic behaviours include: hyperphagia in Prader–Willi syndrome (Holm et al., 1993), hand-ringing in Rett syndrome (Van Acker, 1991), self-mutilation in Lesch–Nyan syndrome (Anderson & Ernst, 1994), inappropriate laughter in Angelman's syndrome (Clayton-Smith, 1992), self-hugging in Smith-Magenis syndrome (Finucane et al., 1994), and the infantile cat-cry in 5p− (cri du chat) syndrome (Gersh et al., 1995).

It is more often the case, however, that syndromic behaviours are not unique. Instead, different genetic aetiologies may share a propensity for a particular behaviour. We call this situation 'partial specificity', and it occurs when two or more different syndromes share a predisposition to a particular outcome (Hodapp, 1997). Although totally specific behaviours may exist, research to date suggests that many syndromes are partially specific in their effects. Such thinking follows the developmental psychopathology principle of 'equifinality', the idea that, when considering psychiatric disorders, many roads lead to a single outcome (Cicchetti, 1990; Loeber, 1991). Or, as Opitz (1985, p. 9) notes, 'The causes are many, but the final common developmental pathways are few'.

Partial specificity often shows itself in the maladaptive behaviours and psychopathologies common to different genetic aetiologies. In some cases, a specific aetiological group more often shows a particular behaviour or psychiatric diagnosis compared to mixed or non-specific groups, but the behaviour or diagnosis also occurs in more than one syndrome. For example, hyperactivity and inattention are salient in people with fragile X syndrome (Bregman, Leckman & Ort, 1988), Williams' syndrome (Udwin, Yule & Martin, 1987), and 5p− syndrome (Dykens & Clarke, 1997), even as hyperactivity is less often seen in mixed groups or in other genetic disorders (Prader–Willi syndrome: Dykens et al., 1992a). Or, as shown in a recent comparative study, children with Prader–Willi syndrome and Down syndrome shared a propensity for 'stubbornness' and 'inattention', yet at the same time were different in their rates of obsessions and compulsive behaviour (Dykens & Kasari, 1997). Indeed, people with Prader–Willi syndrome seem particularly vulnerable to non-food obsessions and compulsions relative to others with developmental delay (Dykens et al., 1996; Dykens & Kasari, 1997).

If this field of study is ever to ascertain which behaviours are totally specific and which partially specific, more studies are needed that compare the maladaptive behaviour of various aetiological groups. Between-syndrome studies have important implications for work on mechanisms associated with behavioural phenotypes. These mechanisms can be described on a number of levels, all the way from the production of proteins to the development and functioning of brain structures. Both totally and partially specific effects will be of interest in the search for causal mechanisms. By identifying totally specific effects, researchers will be able to home in on a single pathway, for example, how the lack of imprinted paternal contribution to the Prader–Willi critical region on chromosome 15 (via paternal deletion or maternal uniparental disomy) may lead to hyperphagia. Conversely, evidence that two or more aetiologies lead to a certain behaviour may indicate that researchers need to examine commonalities: what protein has not been produced, or what other mechanism disrupted, that leads to a single outcome across two or more conditions? Although such thoughts must presently remain speculative, both total and partial specificity should eventually aid in the search for the mechanisms leading to psychopathology on any number of levels.

Diversity of behavioural domains

Most work by aetiology-based researchers focuses on maladaptive behaviour and psychiatric disorders, as these are often quite compelling and immediately capture our attention as clinicians. However, other behaviours show fascinating associations to aetiology, as exemplified in Williams' syndrome, Prader–Willi syndrome and Down syndrome. People with Williams' syndrome often show pronounced deficits in specific visual–spatial tasks, especially integrating parts into a whole (Bihrle et al., 1989), even as their recognition for faces seems preserved (Udwin & Yule, 1991; Bellugi, Wang & Jernigan, 1994). Though these individuals may also show relative strengths in expressive language, this profile may not necessarily be widespread in the Williams' syndrome population (Udwin & Yule, 1990; Pober & Dykens, 1996). Many people with Prader–Willi syndrome show relative strengths in specific visual–spatial abilities, including a proficiency with jigsaw puzzles that is so striking it is noted as a 'supportive finding' in the clinical criteria for this disorder (Dykens et al., 1992b; Holm et al., 1993). Children with Down syndrome may have relative weaknesses in expressive versus receptive language abilities (Miller, 1992), and in grammar versus other aspects of language (Fowler, 1990). Although the exact profiles remain unresolved for these and most other syndromes, future phenotypic studies could benefit from a broader behavioural scope that includes cognitive, linguistic, adaptive and other domains.

Indirect behavioural effects

In addition to their direct effects, different genetic disorders may also show indirect effects. These indirect effects may relate to parents, siblings, families, teachers and peers. It may be that certain behavioural features within syndromes literally set the stage for highly characteristic ways of interacting with others. Referred to as evocative genotype–phenotype interactions by Scarr and McCartney (1983), this idea implies that a person's genotype evokes particular environmental responses, and also that people may actively seek environments that reinforce or are compatible with their genotypes. If so, then we would expect predictable environmental differences across various syndromes.

Consider, for example, the relatively low rates of psychopathology among children with Down syndrome relative to children with Prader–Willi syndrome, Smith–Magenis syndrome, or 5p− syndrome (Dykens & Clarke, 1997; Dykens, Finucane & Gayley, 1997; Dykens & Kasari, 1997). Although far from problem free, children with Down syndrome seem to show less prevalent or severe psychopathology than others, and some studies further suggest an engaging, charming Down syndrome personality (Gibbs & Thorpe, 1983). For these and perhaps other reasons, rates of family stress are consistently lower in families with a Down syndrome member compared to families of children with mixed aetiologies, or with Prader–Willi syndrome, Smith–Magenis syndrome or 5p− syndrome. Further, in families with a Prader–Willi, Smith-Magenis or 5p− syndrome child, increased familial stress is best predicted by the affected child's maladaptive behaviours (Hodapp, 1995; Hodapp, Dykens & Masino, 1997; Hodapp, Wijma & Masino, 1997). Preliminary family work thus lends some support to an alternative, indirect way of studying phenotypes: through the differential impact that individuals with syndromes have on their environments.

Effects of developmental and other contexts

Developmental, contextual and 'other genetic' factors must all be considered when one ponders why a particular syndromic behaviour occurs. Thus, different behaviours will become more apparent at some ages than at others. Hyperphagia in Prader–Willi syndrome, for example, has its onset between two and six years of age, dramatically affecting the young child's cognitive and behavioural schema in ways that we have yet fully to appreciate. Children with Down syndrome seem to show age-related increases in internalizing symptoms such as anxiety and sadness that are not seen in children with Prader–Willi syndrome or with mixed or heterogenous causes for their delay (Dykens & Kasari, 1997). Further, males with fragile X syndrome show particular developmental trajectories in both cognition and adaptive behaviour involving a plateau in mental age and decline in standard scores that occurs in late childhood or early adolescence (Dykens, Hodapp &

Leckman, 1994; Dykens et al., 1996). These trajectories differ from patterns of development in Down syndrome, in which many children show slowed development in their earliest years, followed by alternating periods of growth and slowing in cognition (Gibson, 1966), grammatical skills (Fowler, 1988), and adaptive behaviour (Dykens, Hodapp & Evans, 1994). All these examples underscore the importance of adopting a strong developmental orientation in future research on behavioural phenotypes.

Further, certain contexts and practices may alter the prevalence or intensity of particular behaviours. Earlier diagnosis and intervention in Prader–Willi syndrome, for example, is resulting in a new cohort of children and young adults who have never been obese, providing novel opportunities to sort out the differential impact of obesity on Prader–Willi's behavioural phenotype. Finally, though researchers often focus on specific genetic anomalies, behaviour and development are also a function of a person's entire genetic endowment, not just their genetic anomaly. In short, while the direct effects of a particular genetic anomaly are important, they are just one of many genetic and environmental factors that shape behaviour.

Intervention implications

Behavioural phenotypes have important implications for the study and treatment of psychiatric disorders in people with developmental disabilities. One implication concerns aetiology. In particular, it is now well appreciated that people with developmental disabilities in general are at increased risk for behavioural and psychiatric dysfunction. Yet, the exact causes of this increased risk remain unknown, and are probably associated with a combination of psychological, cognitive, social, neurological and genetic factors (Matson & Sevin, 1994). The search for causal mechanisms may be hampered by heterogeneity in subject groupings; indeed, the vast majority of dual diagnosis research uses groups of subjects with mixed or unknown aetiologies (Dykens, 1996). Using homogeneous groups of people with well-delineated syndromes may identify possible genetic contributions to psychiatric vulnerabilities, as well as differentiate genetic from psychosocial risk factors.

Phenotypic research also has implications for clinical and educational treatment. In many ways, phenotypes can guide treatment priorities, providing novel adaptations to more standard clinical care. Consider, for example, the increased risk of non-food compulsivity in people with Prader–Willi syndrome (Dykens et al., 1996). This vulnerability suggests that many people with Prader–Willi syndrome need particular help getting 'unstuck'; these people may benefit particularly from environmental or serotonergic manipulations to help them make the transition from one thought or activity to the next (Dykens & Hodapp, 1997). While many people with developmental disabilities need help with transitions, this seems particularly true in Prader–Willi syndrome. In another example, the verbal skills, sociability and keen interests in others shown by many people with Williams' syndrome may be particularly well suited to verbally oriented group therapies, social skills training, and people-oriented jobs or a team approach at work or school (Dykens & Hodapp, 1997). In contrast, people with fragile X syndrome have a proneness to shyness, gaze aversion, distractibility and social anxieties (Dykens & Volkmar, 1997), and are likely to respond best to more individualized approaches that minimize interpersonal demands.

Not every syndrome is apt to show striking maladaptive behaviours, and some syndromes will thus provide more novel directions to intervention or therapy than others. Even so, diagnosis of a syndrome in itself brings to the forefront many issues of concern. How, for example, does having a specific syndrome affect a person's sense of self? What is the affected individual's understanding of his or her syndrome, and does the person harbour misconceptions about the syndrome? Some people with Prader–Willi syndrome, for example, believe that their syndrome will go away if they achieve their ideal weight, and are disappointed when their adjustment difficulties do not disappear along with their body fat.

In a related way, diagnosis of a syndrome needs to be examined in the context of the family system. In addition to the relief that many families experience when given a known genetic cause for their child's delay, many also receive genetic diagnoses with a sense of guilt or pessimism. Couples may struggle with having 'caused' their child's syndrome, and feel that because the cause is genetic, the prognosis is more guarded. Diagnoses of syndromes and their resultant behavioural phenotypes can thus inform and direct treatment in novel or specific ways, or they can bring up more general issues of therapeutic concern.

Conclusion

This chapter began with a paradox. Geneticists are rapidly uncovering the genetic workings of over 750 different aetiologies of developmental disabilities, yet research on behavioural phenotypes lags far behind. The cause of this discrepancy can be found in the two cultures of behavioural work. On one hand, social scientists focus on mixed aetiological groups, even as they lead the way in measuring the intricacies of behaviour. On the other, biomedical workers know much less about the complexities of behaviour, even as they lead the way in examining different aetiological groups. This cultural divide, though present in many areas, seems especially evident in research on maladaptive behaviour and psychopathology.

Yet, with recent work from many aetiology-based workers, we are now poised to understand better the direct effects of genetic syndromes. These effects may occasionally involve totally specific effects, or one-to-one correspondences, as in the hyperphagia of Prader–Willi syndrome or the infantile cat-cry in 5p– syndrome. Based on research to date, however, it seems more often the case that many outcomes are shared by two or more genetic syndromes. Comparative studies are needed between various syndromes to shed further light on the relative uniqueness of behavioural phenotypes. Only after we have a better sense of behaviours that are shared versus unique does it make sense to combine different syndromes into a common research group. Finally, considerable within-syndrome work also remains, including the search for genetic, developmental and psychosocial mechanisms that mediate the expression of phenotypes and that ultimately help explain within-syndrome individual differences.

Although far from complete, then, a syndrome-based approach to behavioural and psychiatric research will enrich the developmental disability field. Phenotypic research facilitates the search for gene–behaviour relations, helps differentiate genetic from other causes of psychiatric disorders, and leads to more fine-tuned treatments. All of these ultimately contribute to a more precise science of developmental disabilities. Although the study of behavioural phenotypes is only now coming into its own, and genetic work is presently surpassing behavioural work in its amount and sophistication, it is to be hoped that behavioural work will soon catch up.

References

Aman, M.G. (1991). *Working Bibliography on behavioral and Emotional Disorders and Assessment Instruments in Mental Retardation*. Rockville, MD: US Department of Health and Human Services.

Anderson, L.T. & Ernst, M. (1994). Self-injury in Lesch–Nyan disease. *Journal of Autism and Developmental Disorders*, **24**, 67–81.

Bellugi, U., Wang, P. & Jernigan, T. (1994). Williams syndrome: an unusual neuropsychological profile. In *Atypical, Cognitive Deficits in Developmental Disorders*, ed. S.H. Groman & J. Grafman, pp. 23–56. Hillsdale, NJ: Erlbaum.

Bihrle, A.M., Belugi, U., Delis, D. & Marks, S. (1989). Seeing either the forest or the trees: dissociation in visuospatial processing. *Brain Cognition*, **11**, 37–49.

Borthwick-Duffy, S.A. (1994). Epidemiology and prevalence of psychopathology in people with mental retardation. *Journal of Consulting & Clinical Psychology*, **62**, 17–27.

Bregman, J.D., Leckman, J.F. & Ort, S.I. (1988). Fragile X syndrome: genetic predisposition to psychopathology. *Journal of Autism and Developmental Disorders*, **18**, 343–54.

Cicchetti, D. (1990). A historical perspective on the discipline of developmental psychopathology. In *Risk and Protective Factors in the Development of Psychopathology*, ed. J. Rolf, A.S. Masten, D. Cicchetti, K.H. Neuchterlein & S. Weintraub pp. 2–28. New York: Cambridge University Press.

Clayton-Smith, J., (1992). Angelman's syndrome. *Archives of Disease in Childhood*, **67**, 889–91.

Dykens, E.M. (1995). Measuring behavioral phenotypes: provocations from the 'new genetics.' *American Journal on Mental Retardation*, **99**, 522–32.

Dykens, E.M. (1996). DNA meets DSM: the growing importance of genetic syndromes in dual diagnosis. *Mental Retardation*, **34**, 125–7.

Dykens, E.M. & Cassidy, S.B. (1995). Correlates of maladaptive behavior in children and adults with Prader–Willi syndrome. *American Journal of Medical Genetics*, **60**, 546–9.

Dykens, E.M. & Cassidy, S.B. (1996). Prader–Willi syndrome: genetic, behavioral, and treatment issues. *Child and Adolescent Psychiatric Clinics of North America*, **5**, 913–27.

Dykens, E.M. & Clarke, D. (1997). Correlates of maladaptive behavior in persons with 5p- (cri du chat) syndrome. *Developmental Medicine and Child Neurology*, **39**, 752–6.

Dykens, E.M., Finucane, B. & Gayley, C. (1997). Cognitive and behavioral profiles in persons with Smith–Magenis syndrome. *Journal of Autism and Developmental Disorders*, **27**, 203–11.

Dykens, E.M. & Hodapp, R.M. (1997). Treatment issues in genetic mental retardation syndromes. *Professional Psychology: Research and Practice*, **28**, 263–70.

Dykens, E.M., Hodapp, R.M. & Evans, D.W. (1994). Profiles and development of adaptive behavior in children with Down syndrome. *American Journal on Mental Retardation*, **98**, 580–7.

Dykens, E.M., Hodapp, R.M. & Leckman, J.F. (1994). *Behavior and Development in Fragile X Syndrome*. Thousand Oaks, CA: Sage.

Dykens, E.M., Hodapp, R.M., Walsh, K. & Nash, L.J. (1992a). Adaptive and maladaptive behavior in Prader–Willi syndrome. *Journal of the American Academy of Child and Adolescent Psychiatry*, **31**, 1131–6.

Dykens, E.M., Hodapp, R.M., Walsh, K. & Nash, L.J. (1992b). Profiles, correlates, and trajectories of intelligence in Prader–Willi syndrome. *Journal of the American Academy of Child and Adolescent Psychiatry*, **31**, 1125–30.

Dykens, E.M. & Kasari, C. (1997). Maladaptive behavior in children with Prader–Willi syndrome, Down syndrome, and non-specific mental retardation. *American Journal on Mental Retardation*, **102**, 228–37.

Dykens, E.M., Leckman, J.F. & Cassidy, S.B. (1996). Obsessions and compulsions in Prader–Willi syndrome. *Journal of Child Psychology and Psychiatry*, **37**, 995–1002.

Dykens, E.M., Ort, S.I., Cohen, I. et al. (1996). Trajectories of adaptive development in males with fragile X syndrome: multicenter studies. *Journal of Autism and Developmental Disabilities*, **26**, 287–301.

Dykens, E.M. & Volkmar, F.R. (1997). Medical conditions associated with autism. In *Handbook of Autism and Pervasive Developmental Disorders*, 2nd ed. D.J. Cohen & F.R. Volkmar, pp. 388–407. New York: John Wiley.

Einfeld, S.L. & Hall, W. (1994). When is a behavioral phenotype not a phenotype? *Developmental Medicine and Child Neurology*, **36**, 467–70.

Finucane, B.M., Konar, D., Haas-Givler, BV., Kurtz, M. & Scott, C.I. (1994). The spasmodic upper body squeeze: a characteristic behavior of Smith–Magenis syndrome. *Developmental Medicine and Child Neurology*, **36**, 78–83.

Flynt, J. & Yule, W. (1994). Behavioural phenotypes. In *Child and Adolescent Psychiatry: Modern Approaches*, 3rd edition, ed. M. Rutter, E. Taylor, & L. Hersov, pp. 666–87. London: Blackwell Scientific.

Fowler, A. (1988). Determinants of rate of language growth in children with Down syndrome. In *The Psychobiology of Down Syndrome*, L. Nadel, pp. 217–45. Cambridge, MA: MIT Press.

Fowler, A. (1990). Language abilities in children with Down syndrome: evidence for a specific syntactic delay. In *Children with Down Syndrome: A Developmental Approach,* ed. D. Cicchetti & M. Beeghly, pp. 302–28. New York: Cambridge University Press.

Frangiskakis, J.M., Ewart, A.K., Morris, C.A. et al.(1996). LIM-kinase1 hemizygosity implicated in impaired visuospatial constructive cognition. *Cell,* **86,** 59–69.

Gersh, M., Goodart, S.A., Pasztor, L.M., Harris, D.J., Weiss, L. & Overhauser, J. (1995). Evidence for a distinctive region causing a cat-like cry in patients with 5p deletions. *American Journal of Human Genetics,* **56,** 1404–10.

Gibbs, M.V. & Thorpe, J.G. (1983). Personality stereotype of noninstitutionalized Down syndrome children. *American Journal of Mental Deficiency,* **87,** 601–5.

Gibson, D. (1966). Early developmental staging as a prophecy index in Down's syndrome. *American Journal of Mental Deficiency,* **70,** 825–8.

Hodapp, R.M. (1995). Parenting children with Down syndrome and other types of mental retardation. In *Handbook of Parenting.* Vol. 1: *How Children Influence Parents,* ed. M. Bornstein, pp. 233–53. Hillsdale, NJ: Erlbaum.

Hodapp, R.M. (1996). Down syndrome: developmental, psychiatric, and management issues. *Child and Adolescent Psychiatric Clinics of North America,* **5,** 881–94.

Hodapp, R.M. (1997). Direct and indirect behavioral effects of different genetic disorders of mental retardation. *American Journal on Mental Retardation,* **102,** 67–79.

Hodapp, R.M., & Dykens, E.M. (1994). Mental retardation's two cultures of behavioural research. *American Journal on Mental Retardation,* **98,** 675–87.

Hodapp, R.M., Dykens, E.M. & Masino, L.L. (1997). Families of children with Prader–Willi syndrome: stress-support and relations to child characteristics. *Journal of Autism and Developmental Disorders,* **27,** 11–24.

Hodapp, R.M., Wijma, C.A. & Masino, L.L. (1997). Families of children with 5p- (cri du chat) syndrome: familial stress and sibling reactions. *Developmental Medicine and Child Neurology,* **39,** 757–61.

Holm, V.A., Cassidy, S.B., Butler, M.G. et al. (1993). Prader–Willi syndrome: consensus diagnostic criteria. *Pediatrics,* 91, 398–402.

Loeber, R. (1991). Questions and advances in the study of developmental pathways. In *Models and Integrations,* ed. D. Cicchetti & S. Toth, pp. 97–117. Rochester Symposia on Developmental Psychopathology, Vol. 3. Rochester, NY: University of Rochester Press.

Matson, J.L. & Sevin, J.A. (1994). Theories of dual diagnosis in mental retardation. *Journal of Consulting and Clinical Psychology,* **62,** 6–16.

Miller, J. (1992). Lexical development in children with Down syndrome. In *Child Talk: Advances in Language Acquisition,* ed. R.S. Chapman, pp. 202–16. Chicago: Year Book Medical.

Opitz, J.M. (1985). Editorial comment. The developmental field concept. *American Journal of Medical Genetics,* **21,** 1–11.

Opitz, J.M. (1996). Historiography of the causal analysis of mental retardation. Speech to the 29th Annual Gatlinburg Conference on Research and Theory in Mental Retardation and Developmental Disabilities, Gatlinburg, TN.

Pober, B.R. & Dykens, E.M. (1996). Williams syndrome: an overview of medical, cognitive, and behavioral features. *Child and Adolescent Psychiatric Clinics of North America*, **5**, 929–43.

Pueschel, S.R. (1983). Down syndrome. In *Developmental–Behavioral Pediatrics*, ed. M.D. Levine, W.B. Carey & A.C. Crocker, pp. 353–62. Philadelphia: Saunders.

Reiss, A.L., Freund, L.S., Baumgarder, T.L., Abrams, M.T. & Denckla, M.B. (1995). Contributions of the FMR1 gene mutation to human intellectual dysfunction. *Nature Genetics*, **11**, 331–4.

Rosen, M. (1993). In search of the behavioral phenotype: a methodological note. *Mental Retardation*, **31**, 177–8.

Scarr, S., & McCartney, K. (1983). How people make their own environments: a theory of genotype–environment effects. *Child Development*, **54**, 424–35.

Snow, C.P. (1963). The two cultures. In *The Scientist versus the Humanist*, ed. G. Levine & O. Thomas, pp. 1–6. New York: Norton. (Reprinted from the New Statesmen, 1956, Vol. 52).

Sobesky, W.E., Hull, C.E. & Hagerman, R.J. (1994). Symptoms of schizotypal personality disorder in fragile X women. *Journal of the American Academy of Child and Adolescent Psychiatry*, **33**, 247–55.

Udwin, O. & Yule, W. (1990). Expressive language of children with Williams syndrome. *American Journal of Medical Genetics*, **6**, 108–14.

Udwin, O. & Yule, W. (1991). A cognitive and behavioural phenotype of Williams syndrome. *Journal of Clinical and Experimental Neuropsychology*, **13**, 232–44.

Udwin, O., Yule, W. & Martin, N. (1987). Cognitive abilities and behavioral characteristics of children with idiopathic infantile hypercalcaemia. *Journal of Child Psychology and Psychiatry*, **28**, 297–309.

Van Acker, R. (1991). Rett syndrome: a review of current knowledge. *Journal of Autism and Developmental Disorders*, **21**, 381–406.

7 Self-injurious behaviour and people with developmental disabilities

JOHN HILLERY

Introduction

Self-mutilation has been recorded through history, across cultures, and can be culturally congruent (Favazza, 1989). Self-mutilation is the deliberate alteration or destruction of body tissue without conscious suicidal intent. It can be seen as a symptom of psychiatric disorder or as a distinct syndrome. Favazza and Rosenthal (1993) have suggested that it be classified into three basic types: major, superficial and stereotypic. In this classification, major self-mutilation is associated with acute psychiatric illness or severe personality disorder. Superficial self-mutilation is a common behaviour (from 400 to 1400 per 100 000 of population per year) that is a symptom or associated feature of many psychiatric disorders. Stereotypic self-mutilation is most commonly seen in institutionalized people with developmental disabilities, although Favazza admits that not all self-mutilation in people with developmental disabilities is of this type. Indeed, we know that people with developmental disabilities can show myriad forms of self-mutilation. This behaviour is referred to as self-injurious behaviour in people with developmental disabilities. It can be resistant to treatment, has no apparent cause, and can be responsible for much medical, psychological and social morbidity.

Definition

The definition of self-injurious behaviour varies from author to author; this variety has made comparison between epidemiological studies difficult. The definitions used generally include the requirement that the actions cause damage to the self. This tissue damage criterion (Oliver, Murphy & Corbett, 1987) also allows for the fact that people may be wearing protective clothing (e.g. a helmet) by including actions that would cause tissue damage if the person were not wearing such clothing. Oliver et al. (1987) reported that the 'tissue damage' criterion proved robust when judging the ability of different informants to agree on caseness.

Rojahn (1994) makes a strong case for his assertion that the term self-injurious behaviour stands for a heterogeneous group of behaviours with little in common. He suggests that future epidemiological research should be based on definitions specifying the type and topography of the behaviour to be studied and combining topographical and functional information to determine the relationship between the two. However, though this argument has many merits, epidemiological assessment of global self-injurious behaviour still has relevance in establishing prevalence and resource need at a clinical service level.

Consequences of self-injurious behaviour

The consequences of exhibiting self-injurious behaviour may be positive in the short term, but, for the person exhibiting them, in the long term they are usually negative. There can be physical morbidity as a direct result of the behaviour. For example, Mikkelsen (1986) related consequences including sensory deficit, neurological impairments and even death. In a recent study Wieseler, Hanson & Nord (1995) corroborated this consequence of auditory and visual sensory damage, though they did not find a decrease in life expectancy in those with self-injurious behaviour in the population studied. Other authors have pointed out that behaviour disorder is a cause of increased stress to relatives (Quine & Pahl, 1985) and that self-injurious behaviour puts people displaying it at increased risk of suffering physical abuse from carers (Maurice & Trudel, 1982).

Studies of family decision making have shown that behavioural disorder in the person with developmental disabilities is one of the strongest influences on a family deciding to place their relative in residential care (Tausig, 1985; Bromley & Blacher, 1991). Self-injurious behaviour itself puts people at increased risk of institutionalization (Lakin et al., 1983).

Once in residential care, people who display self-injurious behaviour are more likely to be given psychotropic medication (Oliver et al., 1987) and are more likely to be kept on medication (Chadsey-Rusch & Sprague, 1989). Many authors have questioned the appropriateness of much of this prescribing (Emerson et al., 1994) in view of the fact that much of the behaviour involved does not have a proven neurochemical and/or psychopathological basis. Griffen et al. (1986) expressed concern about the high number of people in their survey of self-injurious behaviour who were in physical restraint. Their concern is understandable in view of the possible adverse consequences of restraint, both in the short and the long term, for physical health and independent functioning (Oliver et al., 1987).

Self-injurious behaviour is a common reason for people with developmental disabilities being excluded from community-based educational services and vocational training (Shlalock et al., 1985). Those in residential care who self-injure are probably less likely to receive a day service than those who do not (Oliver et al., 1987). The conclusion from available research is that exhibiting self-injurious behaviour considerably decreases a person's quality of life.

Epidemiology

Comparing epidemiological studies of self-injurious behaviour, one finds widely varying prevalence rates. This is due to differences in the methodology of the studies, the definition used and the populations studied. The last-mentioned have varied in age, level of intellectual ability, type of disability (i.e. single or multiple disability) and in their origin (i.e. geographically based or service based).

Prevalence rates as low as 1.7 per cent (Rojahn, 1986) and as high as 41 per cent (Saloviita, 1988) have been reported. Studies that take place in residential services produce higher prevalence rates than community studies. This is because people who self-injure are more likely to be in residential care. Even with the effort to correct for bias by using geographically based populations (Kebbon & Windahl, 1985, 4.2 per cent; Hillery & Mulcahy, 1997, 14 per cent; Collacott et al., 1997, 16 per cent), there is still a wide variation in prevalence. Rojahn (1994) points out that studies based on service system databases are biased in favour of those who proclaim an urgent need for service and against those who do not take up services, for whatever reason.

It seems apparent from the results given above that for future epidemiological studies to be useful for furthering international approaches to self-injurious behaviour, consensus must occur on parameters for choosing populations for study.

Demographic variables related to self-injurious behaviour

Studies of self-injurious behaviour have generally found an inverse relationship between IQ and the likelihood of a person displaying such behaviour Although studies suggest a relationship between self-injurious behaviour and age, the relationship is not a statistically significant one. However, in a review of studies, Rojahn (1994) reports a curvilinear relationship (i.e. a higher prevalence in adolescents and adults than in young children and the elderly). Rojahn suggests that this may be due to underreporting of self-injurious behaviour in the very young, due either to the behaviours not being fully developed (the 'cocoon' stage) or to a reluctance by informants to label childhood behaviours as self-injurious behaviour even when the topography is the same as that of behaviours which would be labelled as such if they occurred in an adult.

Many authors have reported a connection between gender and self-injurious behaviour that is not statistically significant. The connection is to prevalence (Oliver et al., 1987) or to topography (Maisto, Baumeister &

Maisto, 1978; Griffen et al., 1986; Oliver et al., 1987). However, apart from an association with two X-linked conditions – Lesch–Nyhan syndrome (Lesch & Nyhan, 1964) and fragile X syndrome (Turk, 1992) – no statistically significant relationship with gender has been reported (Rojahn, 1994).

Environmentalists such as Wolfensberger have strongly championed the benefits of de-institutionalization, with the implication that institutional environments are responsible for behavioural disorders such as self-injuri-ous behaviour Winchel and Stanley (1991) stated that self-injurious behavi-our among people with developmental disabilities without Lesch–Nyhan or de Lange syndrome usually appears only after admission to a chronic care facility. These ideas have not been supported by research. Oliver et al. (1987) found that there was no evidence from their study that institutional environ-ments cause self-injurious behaviour. Recently, Hillery and Mulcahy (1997) reported that the occurrence of self-injurious behaviour was not related to environment but that its severity was greater in those living in residential centres. These findings endorse the opinion of Emerson (1992) that little direct evidence exists to support the view that non-normative or institu-tional environments are a major cause of self-injurious behaviour. Emerson refers also to the evidence that self-injurious behaviour leads to people being placed in more restrictive environments.

Finally, efforts to link the occurrence of the behaviour to specific medical diagnoses or known neurobiological disturbances have been disappointing (Murphy, 1994). It has been reported as having greater prevalence in those with an additional disability (Emerson, 1990). Other authors have reported a relationship to blindness (Maisto et al. 1978) and speech problems (Shodell & Reiter, 1968). Self-injurious behaviour has also been associated with certain biologically transmitted conditions such as Cornelia de Lange syn-drome (Bryson et al., 1971), Prader–Willi syndrome (Clarke, Waters & Corbett, 1989; Bhargava et al., 1996), Rett syndrome (Oliver et al., 1987) and Smith–Magenis syndrome (McNaught & Turk, 1993). It has also been reported in people with autistic spectrum disorder, although in many cases both the autistic traits and the self-injurious behaviour could be interpreted as signs of an underlying genetically transmitted condition (Gillberg, 1992)

Theories on the causation of self-injurious behaviour

Available hypotheses on the aetiology of this behaviour remain mostly theoretical and contradictory. The main reason for this is probably the impracticality of attempting to generate one aetiologic theory for a heterogeneous concept whose presentation is a sign of a range of different symptoms (Rojahn, 1994). In the last few years, several authors have sug-gested ways in which available theoretical information can be related to prac-tical experience in order to generate working hypotheses useful for treatment. The long-standing breach between behavioural theories and those relating self-injurious behaviour to underlying mental illness, neuro-chemical imbalance and/or biologically transmitted conditions is fading.

The list of theories as to aetiology includes self-injurious behaviour as a learned behaviour, a result of neurochemical imbalance, a symptom of acute organic illness (e.g. otitis media: Carr & Smith, 1995), a symptom of chronic organic illness (e.g. epilepsy: Gedye, 1989), a symptom of intermittent phys-ical discomfort (e.g. menstruation: Taylor et al., 1993), secondary to self-stimulation in a person with a sensory deficit (Thurrell & Rice, 1970), a symptom of mental illness (e.g. depression: Sovner et al., 1993), a conse-quence of stereotypies (Wieseler et al., 1985), a form of communication (Bird et al., 1989), a compulsive behaviour (King, 1993), a symptom of grief or post-traumatic stress (Sinason, 1992), or due to over-sensitivity to sensory input (Reisman, 1993). It may be part of the phenotype of a biologically transmitted condition (Nyhan, 1971, 1994). Though it is acknowledged that an institutional environment is probably not a cause for self-injury, ecology (the interaction of people with their environment) is an important factor in its initiation and maintenance (Murphy, 1994). A summary of the main the-ories is presented below.

Behavioural theories

Behavioural theories are based on operant conditioning (Oliver, 1993). A behaviour occurs and may be positively reinforced with a reward (e.g. attention) or by the removal of an unwanted demand. The initial beha-viour may be displayed by accident (e.g. as part of a tantrum) or on purpose, but for a reason unrelated to the eventual reinforcer (e.g. as a response to the pain of otitis media). It has been pointed out that there is often a relationship between people displaying self-injurious behaviour and their carers that involves operant conditioning on both sides. So the individual self-injures, the carer gives him or her attention, and then the individual stops self-injur-ing. The self-injury is thus reinforced by the attention from the carer, and the carer's responses are reinforced by the individual's response. A self-perpetu-ating cycle of actions on both sides of the equation has commenced. The individual may increase the intensity of the behaviour if the desired response is not occurring. Obviously, any intervention that requires the carer not to respond to the behaviour may lead to an increase in severity of the behaviour. It may be impossible for the carer not to intervene for fear of individuals inflicting severe damage on themselves. It is obvious that the earlier the intervention, the better.

Neurochemical theories

Neurochemical theories concern three separate types of neurotrans-mitters: dopamine, opiates and serotonin. The dopamine theory postulates that self-injurious behaviour is the result of dopamine receptor over-sensi-tivity (Schroeder, 1996). Post-mortem studies of the brains of people with

Lesch–Nyhan syndrome exhibiting self-injurious behaviour, showed changes in the dopamine system. Animals displayed such behaviour after receiving dopamine agonists (e.g. Pemoline). The D1 receptors are thought to be the principal dopamine receptors involved in the genesis and maintenance of self-injurious behaviour. This has important implications for pharmacotherapy as most neuroleptics have little effect at these receptors. A newer neuroleptic, clozapine, is more active at these receptors and has been successfully used to treat self-injurious behaviour (Schroeder et al., 1995; see also Chapter 18).

Studies showing raised plasma beta-endorphin in people with self-injurious behaviour (Sandman et al., 1990) or a therapeutic behaviour-attenuating response to the administration of opiate-blocking agents (Sandman et al., 1990; Roth, Ostcott & Hoffman, 1996) support hypotheses of raised endogenous opiates as a cause. Two theories have been put forward. The first is that a high level of circulating endogenous opiates allows the person to display self-injurious behaviour without suffering painful consequences, thus the behaviour can be used by the person to influence his or her environment. The second is that when people self-injure, they induce release of endogenous opiates and this serves as a pleasurable positive reinforcer for the behaviour. The initial behaviour may occur for a variety of reasons, but its repetition is encouraged by the opiate feedback. Recently, Sandman and Hetrick (1995) found raised levels of plasma beta-endorphin in individuals directly after they self-injured. The proposal that self-injurious behaviour is secondary to serotonin imbalance is somewhat tenuous (Murphy, 1994). It is supported by findings of hyposerotoninaemia in people who have syndromes associated with self-injurious behaviour such as Cornelia de Lange syndrome (Gillberg & Coleman, 1992) and case reports of a treatment response to serotonin-raising medication such as fluoxetine (Markowitz, 1992) or clomiprimine (Lewis et al., 1996).

It has been generally accepted that no one aetiologic theory can determine assessment and treatment in individual cases. Many people with developmental disabilities are exposed to events that could initiate a response of self-injurious behaviour or have factors that are associated with it, without ever displaying it. Oliver (1993) proposed that some people have factors that make them vulnerable to developing such behaviour, including sensory and physical disability, having a syndrome known to be associated with self-injurious behaviour and/or having an increased degree of developmental disability. There are also mediating factors such as expressive communication problems, operant vulnerability and susceptibility, and pre-existing neurotransmitter disturbance that make occurrence of the behaviour and its maintenance more likely. The first factor refers to the extent to which a person can influence the behaviour of others through verbal or other forms of communication. Operant vulnerability is an increased likelihood that a person will be exposed to an establishing situation or circumstance. Operant susceptibility refers to the enhanced potency of some reinforcers to maintain self-injurious behaviour in susceptible people. The neurotransmitter abnormalities will affect the way that people respond to their environment.

Implications of theory and research for assessment and therapy

Murphy (1994) in reviewing non-pharmaceutical treatment approaches, concluded that effective treatment programmes using up-to-date techniques (functional analysis, constructional approaches and functional communication training) were feasible but that success was not guaranteed. Iwata et al. (1994) stated that the only treatments that have been consistently effective in treating self-injury have been those based on punishment in the form of aversive stimulation but that concerns exist about the appropriateness and safety of their use. Aman (1993), in reviewing the efficacy of psychotropic drugs for self-injurious behaviour, concluded that the available research showed tenuous success for such treatment. It is probable that a combination of approaches aimed at the individual patient is the most likely to succeed. Unless an obvious remediable cause explains the behaviour, assessment should take account of all the aetiologic factors already outlined. Assessment approaches should thus be multidisciplinary.

Recently, several authors have proposed assessment schemes that integrate behavioural and neurochemical theory. Mace and Mauk (1995) outlined a schedule for what they called bio-behavioural diagnosis and treatment. This involved a range of assessments: psychological, paediatric, psychiatric and neurochemical. Patients were placed in a diagnostic category subtype on the basis of this schema. They were then treated according to a treatment plan linked to the diagnostic category with behavioural therapy or psychotropic medication or a combination of each, depending on the subtype. The authors claimed that this procedure had improved the success rate for treatment, and they emphasized the need for transdisciplinary work in dealing with the complex problem of self-injurious behaviour. Gardner and Sovner (1994) proposed what they called a multimodal functional approach. They emphasized the importance of data keeping and review in the context of the possible known aetiologic factors. Thompson et al. (1994) summarized the evidence for the relevance of psychotropic medications to self-injurious behaviour treatment regimes. If treatment takes account of the effects of psychotropics on learning and the neurochemical theories on aetiology, then the interventions are more likely to succeed, and inappropriate use of psychotropic agents can be avoided. In the review quoted above, Aman (1993) recommended that in view of the possible serious side-effects of these drugs, a behavioural programme should always be tried before introduction of medication. A behavioural monitoring programme should remain in place during treatment with psychotropic medication and should combine systematic direct observations and the use of a suitable rating tool.

Different approaches were recommended depending on whether the cause of the patient's developmental disabilities is unknown or known (e.g. Down syndrome in which the serotonergic system may be dysfunctional), or if an organic problem (e.g. epilepsy) or mental illness (e.g. depression) is suggested by assessment.

Conclusion

Self-injurious behaviour causes physical and mental morbidity for the people who display it, stress for their carers, and uses valuable resources of service providers. The importance of early intervention with a proactive approach to prevention (Oliver, 1993) cannot be overemphasized. This should involve screening at all ages for behaviours that may evolve into self-injury, for mild forms of the behaviour, for minor illnesses that may precipitate it, and for environments that do not offer sufficient opportunities for other ways of behaviour to develop. Assessment of self-injurious behaviour must be multi(trans)disciplinary, person centred and take account of up-to-date research on aetiology and intervention. Resources must be provided for behavioural programmes to be implemented consistently. Medication should be used in a rational way that takes account of available neurochemical information.

Acknowledgements

The author wishes to thank the National Association for the Mentally Handicapped of Ireland and the Irish Health Research Board for grants which partly supported this chapter. He is also grateful for the help of the Research Department of the St John of God Brothers of Ireland. Finally, he thanks Dr Michael Mulcahy for his encouragement and guidance.

References

Aman, M.G. (1993). Efficacy of psychotropic drugs for reducing self injurious behaviour in the developmental disabilities. *Annals of Clinical Psychiatry*, **5** (3), 171–88.

Bird, F., Dores, P., Moniz, D. & Robinson, J. (1989). Reducing severe aggressive and self-injurious behaviors with functional communication training. *American Journal on Mental Retardation*, **94** (1), 37–48.

Bhargava, S.A., Putnam, P.E., Kocoshis, S.A., Rowe, M. & Hanchett, J. (1996). Rectal bleeding in Prader–Willi syndrome. *Paediatrics*, **97** (2), 265–7.

Bromley, B.E. & Blacher, J. (1991). Parental reasons for out of home placement of children with severe handicaps. *Mental Retardation*, **29** (5), 275– 80.

Bryson, Y., Sakati, N., Nyhan, W.L. & Fisch, C.H. (1971). Self mutilative behavior in the Cornelia de Lange syndrome. *American Journal of Mental Deficiency*, **76**, 319–24.

Carr, E.G. & Smith, C.E. (1995). Biological setting events for self-injury. *Mental Retardation and Developmental Disabilities Research Reviews*, **1** (2), 94–8.

Chadsey-Rusch, J. & Sprague, R.L. (1989). Maladaptive behaviors associated with neuroleptic drug maintenance. *American Journal on Mental Retardation*, **93**, 607–17.

Clarke, D.J., Waters, J. & Corbett, J.A. (1989). Adults with Prader–Willi syndrome: abnormalities of sleep and behaviour. *Journal of the Royal Society of Medicine*, **82**, 21–4.

Collacott, R.A., Cooper, S., Branford, D. & Mc Grother, C. (1997). Epidemiology of self-injurious behaviour in adults with learning disability in Leicestershire, UK. Unpublished manuscript.

Emerson, E. (1990). Severe self-injurious behaviour: some of the challenges it presents. *Mental Handicap*, **18**, 92–8.

(1992). Self-injurious behaviour: an overview of recent trends in epidemiological and behavioural research. *Mental Handicap Research*, **5**, 49–81.

Emerson, E., Felce, D., Mc Gill, P. & Mansell, J. (1994). Introduction. In 'Severe Learning Disabilities and Challenging Behaviours', ed. E. Emerson, P. McGill & J. Mansell, pp. 3–16. London: Chapman & Hall.

Favazza, A. (1989). Normal and deviant self-mutilation: an essay review. *Transcultural Psychiatry Research Review*, **26** (2), 113–27.

Favazza, A. & Rosenthal, R. (1993). Diagnostic issues in self-mutilation. *Hospital and Community Psychiatry*, **44** (2), 134–40.

Gardner, W.I. & Sovner, R. (1994). *Self-injurious Behaviours; Diagnosis and Treatment: A Multimodal Functional Approach*. Pennsylvania: VIDA Publishing.

Gedye, A. (1989). Extreme self-injury attributed to frontal lobe seizures. *American Journal on Mental Retardation*, **94** (1), 20–6.

Gillberg, C. (1992). Subgroups in autism. Are there behavioural phenotypes typical of underlying medical conditions? *Journal of Developmental Disabilities Research*, **36**, 201–14.

Gillberg, C. & Coleman, M. (1992). Biochemistry. In 'The Biology of the Autistic Syndromes,' 2nd edition, ed. C. Gillberg & M. Coleman, pp. 115–30. London: MacKeith Press.

Griffen, J., Williams, D., Stark, M., Altmeyer, B. & Mason, M. (1986). Self-injurious behavior: a state wide prevalence survey of the extent and circumstances. *Applied Research in Mental Retardation*, **7**, 105–16.

Hillery, J. & Mulcahy, M. (1997). Self-injurious behaviour in persons with a mental handicap: an epidemiological study in an Irish population. *The Irish Journal of Psychological Medicine*, **14** (1), 12–5.

Iwata, B.A., Dorsey, M.F., Slifer, K.J., Bauman, K.E. & Richman, G.S. (1994). Toward a functional analysis of self-injury. *Journal of Applied Behaviour Analysis*, **27**, 197–209.

Kebbon, L. & Windahl, S. (1985). Self-injurious behaviour. Results of a nationwide survey among mentally retarded persons in Sweden. Seventh World Congress of IASSMD.

King, B.H. (1993). Self-injury by people with mental retardation: a compulsive behavior hypothesis. *American Journal on Mental Retardation*, **98** (1), 93–112.

Lakin, K.C., Hill, B.K., Hauber, F.A., Bruininks, R.H. & Heal, I.W. (1983). New admissions and readmissions to a national sample of public residential facilities. *American Journal of Mental Deficiency*, **88**, 13–20.

Lesch, M. & Nyhan, W.L. (1964). A familial disorder of uric acid metabolism and central nervous system dysfunction. *American Journal of Medicine*, **36**, 561–70.

Lewis, M.H., Bodfish, J.W., Powell, S.B., Parker, D.E. & Golden, R.N. (1996). Clomiprimine treatment for self-injurious behavior of individuals with mental retardation: a double-blind comparison with placebo. *American Journal on Mental Retardation*, **100** (6), 654–65.

Mace, C.F. & Mauk, J.E. (1995). Bio-behavioural diagnosis and treatment of self-injury. *Mental Retardation and Developmental Disabilities Research Reviews*, **1**, 104–10.

Maisto, C.R., Baumeister, A.A. & Maisto, A.A. (1978). An analysis of variables related to self-injurious behaviour among institutionalised retarded persons. *Journal of Mental Deficiency Research*, **22**, 27–36.

Maurice P. & Trudel, G. (1982). Self injurious behaviour; prevalence and relationships to environmental events. In *Life-threatening behavior*, ed. J. Hollis & C. Meyers, pp. 81–103. Washington, DC: AAMD. Monograph.

Markowitz, P.I. (1992). Effect of Fluoxetine on self-injurious behaviour in the developmentally disabled: a preliminary study. *Journal of Clinical Psychopharmacology*, **12** (1), 27–31.

McNaught, A. & Turk, J. (1993). Smith–Magenis syndrome mistaken for emotional abuse: a case report. Presentation at the Fourth Annual Meeting of the Society for the Study of Behavioural Phenotypes, Royal Society of Medicine, London.

Mikkelsen, E.J. (1986). Low dose Haloperidol for stereotypic self-injurious behavior in the mentally retarded. *New England Journal of Medicine*, **316**, 398–9.

Murphy, G. (1994). Understanding challenging behaviour. In *Severe Learning Disabilities and Challenging Behaviours: Designing High Quality Services*, ed. E. Emerson, P. Mc Gill & J. Mansell, pp. 37–68. London: Chapman & Hall.

Nyhan, W.L. (1971). Behavioural phenotypes in organic genetic disease. Presidential Address to the Society for Paediatric Research, May 1, 1971. *Paediatric Research*, **6**, 1–9.

(1994). The Lesch–Nyhan disease. In *Destructive Behaviour in Developmental Disabilities. Diagnosis and Treatment*, ed. T. Thompson & D.B. Gray, pp. 181–97. London: Sage Publications.

Oliver, C. (1993). Self-injurious behaviour: from response to strategy. In *Research to Practice? Implications of Research on the Challenging Behaviour of People with Learning Disability*, ed. C. Kiernan, pp. 135–88. Clevedon, Avon: BILD Publications.

Oliver, C., Murphy, G.H. & Corbett, J.A. (1987). Self-injurious behaviour in people with mental handicap: a total population study. *Journal of Mental Deficiency Research*, **31**, 146–62.

Quine, L. & Pahl, J. (1985). Examining the causes of stress in families with mentally handicapped children. *British Journal of Social Work*, **15**, 501–17.

Reisman, J. (1993). Using a sensory integrative approach to treat self-injurious behaviour in an adult with profound mental retardation. *American Journal of Occupational Therapy*, **47** (5), 403–11.

Rojahn, J. (1986). Self-injurious and stereotypic behavior of non-institutionalised mentally retarded people. Prevalence and classification. *American Journal of Mental deficiency*, **91** (3), 268–76.

(1994). Epidemiology and topographic taxonomy of self-injurious behaviour. In *Destructive Behaviour in Developmental Disabilities*, eds. T. Thompson & D.B. Gray, pp. 49–67. London: Sage Publications.

Roth, A.S., Ostrott, R.B. & Hoffman, R.E. (1996). Naltrexone as a treatment for repetitive self-injurious behaviour: an open label trial. *Journal of Clinical Psychiatry*, **57** (6), 233–7.

Saloviita, T. (1988). *Self-injurious Behaviour in an Institution for Mentally Handicapped Persons.* An epidemiological study. Helsinki: Mental Handicap Research Unit.

Sandman, C.A., Barron, J.L., Chicz-DeMet, A. & DeMet, E.M. (1990). Plasma β-endorphin levels in patients with self-injurious behavior and stereotypy. *American Journal on Mental Retardation*, **95** (1), 84–92.

Sandman, C.A. & Hetrick, W.P. (1995). Opiate mechanisms in self-injury. *Mental Retardation and Developmental Disabilities Research Reviews*, **1** (2), 130–6.

Schroeder, S.R., Hammock, R.G., Mulick, J.A., et al. (1995). Clinical trials of D1 and D2 dopamine modulating drugs and self-injury in mental retardation and developmental disabilities. *Mental Retardation and Developmental Disabilities Research Reviews*, **1** (2), 120–9.

Schroeder, S.R. (1996). Dopaminergic mechanisms in self-injury. *Psychology in Mental Retardation and Developmental Disabilities*, **22** (2), 10–3.

Shlalock, R., Harper, R. & Genung, T. (1985). Community integration of mentally retarded adults: community placement and program success. *American Journal of Mental Deficiency*, **89**, 352–61.

Shodell, M.J. & Reiter, H.H. (1968). Self-mutilative behaviour in verbal and non-verbal schizophrenic children. *Archives of General Psychiatry*, **19**, 453–5.

Sinason, V. (1992). Finding meaning without words: self-injury and profound handicap. In *Mental Handicap and the Human Condition, New Approaches from the Tavistock*, ed. V. Sinason, pp. 221–55. London: Free Association Books.

Sovner, R., Fox, C.J., Lowry, M.J. & Lowry, M.A. (1993). Fluoxetine treatment of depression and associated self-injury in two adults with mental retardation. *Journal of Developmental Disabilities Research*, **37**, 301–11.

Tausig, M. (1985). Factors in family decision making about placement for developmentally disabled individuals. *American Journal on Mental Retardation*, **89**, 352–61.

Taylor, D.V., Rush, D., Hetrick, W.P. & Sandman, C.A. (1993). Self-injurious behavior within the menstrual cycle of women with mental retardation. *American Journal on Mental Retardation*, **97** (6), 659–64.

Thompson, T., Egli, M., Symons, F. & Delaney, D. (1994). Neurobehavioural mechanisms of drug action in the developmental disabilities. In *Destructive Behaviour in Developmental Disabilities: Diagnosis and*

Treatment, eds. T. Thompson & D.B. Gray London, pp. 133–80. Sage Publications.

Thurrell, R.J. & Rice, D.G. (1970). Eye rubbing in blind children: application of a sensory deprivation model. *Exceptional Children*, **10**, 325–30.

Turk, J. (1992). The fragile X syndrome. On the way to a behavioural phenotype. *British Journal of Psychiatry*, **160**, 24–35.

Wieseler, N.A., Hanson, R.H., Chamberlin, T.P. & Thompson, T. (1985). Functional taxonomy of stereotypic and self-injurious behavior. *Mental Retardation*, **23** (5), 230–4.

Wieseler, N.A., Hanson, R.H.& Nord, G. (1995). Investigation of mortality and morbidity associated with severe self-injurious behavior. *American Journal on Mental Retardation*, **100** (1), 1–5.

Winchel, R.M. & Stanley, M. (1991). Self-injurious behavior: a review of the behavior and biology of self-mutilation. *American Journal of Psychiatry*, **148** (3), 306–17.

8 Dementia in developmental disabilities

MATTHEW P. JANICKI AND ARTHUR J. DALTON

Introduction

Dementia is a term applied to progressive mental deterioration in adults that is coupled with personality changes in a state of clear consciousness associated with a specific configuration of neuropathological changes in the brain (Reisberg et al., 1989; Berg, Karlinsky & Holland, 1993; American Psychiatric Association, 1997). There are several causes of dementia, each with a somewhat different course and prevalence. Alzheimer's disease is the most common cause, accounting for between 50 and 75 per cent of all dementias (American Psychiatric Association, 1997), but little is known about the causes, treatment and prevention of this disease. It affects between 5 and 8 per cent of the general population older than 65 years of age, and represents a significant risk factor for people with certain forms of developmental disability, specifically those with Down syndrome. Many other types of dementia, including vascular and multi-infarct, are of lower prevalence and to what degree they affect adults with developmental disability is unknown. Clinicians are becoming more aware of the presence of Alzheimer's disease among adults with developmental disability as the number of these older adults increases.

The purposes of this chapter are to review the current status of knowledge about dementia and its relationship to developmental disability, to examine the nature and significance of co-morbid conditions, to summarise the clinical presentation of signs and symptoms of dementia, and to explore contemporary issues related to diagnosis, assessment and care management. Questions of dementia policy and suggestions for training programmes concerned with dementia and developmental disability are also addressed.

Dementia of the Alzheimer type

It has long been known that people with Down syndrome are uniquely susceptible to the development of Alzheimer's disease and that the risk begins at about the age of 40 years. Information about dementia associated with Alzheimer's disease among adults with developmental disability without Down syndrome is sparse. Published longitudinal studies provide indications that the clinical presentation among those adults with developmental disabilities at most, if not all, levels of mental retardation is similar to that of adults without developmental disability. The onset and progression of dementia of the Alzheimer type can be conveniently characterized into a number of stages. Some investigators (e.g. Reisberg et al., 1989) have demarcated seven stages. These refinements are particularly helpful for family members who are caring for an affected relative, and they have substantial advantages from a research perspective. However, experience reveals that it is difficult, if not impossible, to discriminate so many stages for people with developmental disabilities who develop dementia of the Alzheimer type. Consequently, a three-stage model that classifies this type of dementia into early, middle and late stages has received more widespread acceptance; this model has been available for many years (Sim, 1965; Sourander & Sjögren, 1975), and it has been adopted by several organizations (Janicki et al., 1996; American Psychiatric Association, 1997).

Crapper-McLachlan et al. (1984) and Dalton and Crapper-McLachlan (1986) provided a useful description of the clinical presentation of dementia of the Alzheimer type framed within a three-stage model. At the onset of this disorder, psychometric examinations usually reveal that memory performance is impaired prior to psychomotor performance and language performance is least involved. In the early stage, intelligence test scores – such as those derived by the Wechsler Adult Intelligence Scale (WAIS) – decline at variable rates, but on average a change of 8 to 10 IQ points per year is frequently encountered. The date of onset of the illness, as reported by carers, seems to be correlated with the onset of change in the performance score of the WAIS. With progression of the disease, changes in affect and emotional impulse control become apparent, as well as in motivation and general interest. At an early stage, slow waves appear in the electroencephalogram (EEG) and the proportion of the EEG occupied by abnormal slow waves gradually increases as the disease progresses, until there is slow-wave domination of the EEG. When intellectual deterioration is moderately severe and the patient requires supervision, palmomental reflexes may appear. This abnormal reflex often appears about the time that the EEG abnormalities are obvious. With further progression, dyspraxias and agnosias are apparent and, as the adult enters the middle stage of the illness, superficial facial reflexes, including the pout, snout and glabellar reflexes, may be elicited. Towards the end of the middle stage, there is altered muscle tone, often associated with bradykinesia (abnormal slowness of movement).

As the disease progresses, there is frequently a general increase in muscle tone, particularly in the flexor groups and often most pronounced in the upper limbs. Myoclonic jerks or general seizures may occur during the latter stages of the disease. There may also be defective upward gaze with preservation of downward gaze. With loss of useful intellectual and motor function, the sucking and grasp reflexes appear and the palmomental reflex disappears. As the terminal stage of the illness is approached, urinary incontinence and the loss of most motor functions necessitate total nursing care and predispose to the terminal events of cachexia and bronchopneumonia. After a bout of pneumonia or other systemic illness, the plantar response may become extensor and focal neurological signs such as hemianopia, hemiparesis or unilateral tone changes may appear. However, focal neurological signs of this type are not characteristic of the disease, which may have a course as short as 18 months or as long as 27 years. The average duration of illness is about ten years. Recent studies report a high prevalence of psychotic delusions, ranging from 26 per cent (Cooper et al., 1991) to 50 per cent (Cummings et al., 1987) of patients with Alzheimer type of dementia, and hallucinations ranging from 17 per cent (Cooper et al., 1991) to 76.4 per cent (Mendez et al., 1990) through most of the course of the disease.

Dementia in people with developmental disability

The clinical expression of the Alzheimer type of dementia in people with Down syndrome and its relationship to Alzheimer's disease have been the subject of several reviews (e.g. Lott, 1982; Sinex & Merril, 1982; Dalton & Crapper-McLachlan, 1986; Dalton & Wisniewski, 1990; Rabe et al., 1990; Schupf et al., 1990, Lai, 1992a, 1992b; Dalton et al., 1993). Evenhuis (1997) – in a retrospective follow-up study over an 11-year period of 144 people living in the Netherlands with developmental disabilities ranging from mild to profound levels, without Down syndrome, all over the age of 60 years – reported that age-related incidences (7.6 per cent), age at onset (77.7 years), duration (7.3 years, range 4–13 years) and symptoms of dementia were comparable to those in the general population. Zigman and his associates – in a large-scale study of an age-stratified sample of 2534 people with Down syndrome and 16 182 people with developmental disabilities of other aetiologies – reported an estimated prevalence of dementia of 2.4 per cent among the non-Down syndrome group, 61–70 years of age (n = 1840) (Zigman et al., 1995). However, Cooper (see Chapter 13), in a review of three other published epidemiological studies of dementia, cited prevalences of dementia of 22.2 per cent, 21.6 per cent and 23.5 per cent for people with developmental disabilities without Down syndrome at 65 years of age and older. The outcome of an American state survey of 4028 programme sites serving individuals over the age of 40 years has recently been reported by Janicki and Dalton (1997). These authors found about 800 individuals with developmental disabilities who were diagnosed or suspected of having signs or symptoms of dementia, or about 3 per cent of the group aged 40 and older and 6 per cent of the group aged 60 and older. These data are consistent with previously published reports based on clinical samples (Evenhuis, 1997) and with the generally accepted prevalence among ageing people from the general population, but not with the epidemiological studies discussed by Cooper (see Chapter 13).

No doubt careful examination of methodological differences, criteria for selection of subjects, methods for the assignment of dementia status, and data analysis, can explain many of these inconsistencies. Notwithstanding these problems, it is essential to recognize the growing importance of these observations because of the relatively large number of individuals with developmental disabilities who are being detected and diagnosed with dementia. The implications for service provision and clinical practice are readily apparent.

To help illustrate the progression from an applied perspective, the clinical history is presented here of RM, a woman with Down syndrome who died at the age of 64 years with a confirmed neuropathological diagnosis of Alzheimer's disease (Dalton & Janicki, 1999). This history illustrates in detail the characteristics of the onset, progression and ultimate fate of someone affected with the disease. The pattern of functional changes described includes the early subtle changes in a very few functions (e.g. learning and memory), which are gradually followed by an ever-increasing number of signs of possible co-morbid conditions (visual and hearing losses), followed after an interval by a relatively brief three-year period of greatly increased deterioration in many functions that persists until death. The co-occurrence of several age-associated changes illustrates some of the complexities in the clinical presentation and shows how diagnosis can be hampered without neuropathological confirmation of Alzheimer's disease. The subtlety and insidious development of one or only a few symptoms at the start, in the absence of global deterioration in general health and daily living skills until the late stage, are remarkable features of the Alzheimer type of dementia in this person.

The course of functional deterioration for RM revealed substantial individual differences when compared to the course of symptoms of two other individuals with Down syndrome who were residents at the same institution as RM. Post-mortem confirmation of a neuropathological diagnosis of Alzheimer's disease was obtained for all three. Neuropathological results for RM are summarised here and the results for the other two cases have been reported elsewhere (Wisniewski et al., 1985; Dalton & Crapper-McLachlan, 1986). While they differ substantially from each other, the pattern of results for all three cases suggests that individuals with Down syndrome show a pattern of development of dementia of the Alzheimer type similar to those affected by Alzheimer's disease in the general population. These cases highlight the importance of recognising that there are wide individual differences in the nature of the first signs and symptoms to appear, the number and severity of the signs and symptoms, as well as the duration of the functional deterioration prior to death. No comparable data are available at this time for individuals with developmental disabilities without Down syndrome.

The case study of RM

History

RM was born in 1928, following an uneventful, full-term labour without injury to a mother who was 36 years of age at the time. RM was the fifth child in a sibship of six children. In 1934, when she was six years of age, she was admitted to a large institution for people with developmental disabilities located in a rural area of Canada. She lived there throughout her life, until her death in 1992 of respiratory failure and chronic obstructive pulmonary disease at the age of 64 years. Her IQ at the time of her admission was estimated at 21 points, with a mental age of 1.2 years. Psychometric examinations, 40 years later (1973), as well as when she was 48 and 50 years of age, using the Leiter International Performance Scale, yielded similar IQ scores of 19, 25 and 23, respectively (profound to severe mental retardation). No further IQ scores were available between the age of 50 years and her death. RM always had limited speech. She could use a few words combined with gestures, but she was hard to understand.

Medical conditions

RM had the usual childhood illnesses before the age of 10 years including mumps (age 4), measles (age 5 years), German measles (age 7 years), and chicken pox (age 8 years), as well as an early episode of pneumonia (age 8 years). She suffered an acute bout of bronchitis when she was 11 years old, started menorrhoea when she was 16 years of age and menopause when she was 47 years old. A systolic heart murmur (V/VI) was noted when she was 23 years of age and she became edentulous at the age of 42 years. Her heart was considered normal on admission to the institution, but at age 23 a soft systolic murmur was noted for the first time and several times thereafter. An examination when she was 61 years old failed to detect any sign of a heart abnormality or murmur. Electrocardiograms at ages 54, 55 and 59 years were all described as normal. Chromosomal studies conducted when she was 45 and 62 years of age confirmed the presence of classical trisomy-21. At 61 years of age, after notable increase in deterioration, a neurological examination was performed and revealed an alert, co-operative woman with a full range of eye movements including upward and downward gaze. The overall impression at the time was that a minor seizure may have accounted for the changes in her behaviour noted by staff. Deep tendon reflexes were normal, with a very weak early grasp reflex bilaterally and a weak right palmomental reflex without a left palmomental reflex. The snout reflexes were just beginning to appear. There were no sucking or rooting reflexes. Her stance and gait were quite normal at the time, but she was unable to perform tandem gait. A second neurological examination performed four months later resulted in neurological findings that were essentially unchanged except for an occasional myoclonic jerk during the examination. It is noteworthy that RM had

normal thyroid function test results at age 56 years, no evidence of abnormalities in her electrocardiograms and no evidence of malignancies
throughout the period of the study (summarized in Table 8.1). A detailed
review of her physician's prescriptions for medications for the period of
seven years up to the day before her death revealed that no antidepressants,
psychoactive agents, or anxiolytics were ever prescribed, suggesting that she
suffered from no apparent psychiatric symptoms requiring active treatment.

Changes in sensory functions

Sensory changes and deterioration are commonly observed among
normal ageing people as well as among older people with Down syndrome.
Records indicate that formal audiological assessments of RM were conducted at least twice, when she was 47 and 53 years of age. The first evaluation
was inconclusive because of occluded ear canals, a common condition
among institutional residents with developmental disabilities. The second
assessment revealed the presence of speech reception thresholds at 60 dB
bilaterally, bone conduction responses to speech noted at 40 to 45 dB, with a
moderate mixed hearing loss. Acoustic impedance measurements indicated
occluded Eustachian tubes at the time of this assessment. At age 53, she was
fitted with a hearing aid. Shortly thereafter, bilateral myringotomy with
tubes was performed (retraction of both drums with negative middle ear
pressure, chronic serous otitis). Frequent impacted wax in both external ear
canals was regularly observed, leading to severe to profound hearing loss at
about this time. Internal strabismus was noted when she was 40 years old,
with the identification of congenital cataract with left corneal abnormality at
age 46 years; left esotropia was noted at age 47 years, with bilateral kerato-
conus. She was found to be hepatitis B positive for the first time at age 51 years
and continued to have antibodies to hepatitis B. At age 63, tests for malig-
nancy were negative. A CT scan of the brain at age 59 years revealed the presence of cerebellar and cerebral atrophy with partially empty sella turcica. At
age 55 years she was fitted with glasses. Ophthalmologic assessments were
conducted several times. At the age of 56 years, she was diagnosed with congenital cataracts. At 60 years of age, an ophthalmologic examination concluded that she could see gross objects. At age 62 years, she was declared
legally blind.

Cognitive tests for early dementia

At age 44 years, RM's cognitive functions were evaluated seven times,
on an annual basis, beginning in 1972 and continuing through 1983, using
two specially designed matching-to-sample (MTS) tests of learning and two
delayed-matching-to-sample (DMTS) recognition memory tests (Dalton,
Crapper & Schlotterer, 1974). The MTS tests provide an indicator of her abilities to learn simple visual discriminations. Her performances on these tests
provided the earliest sign of deterioration which alerted care providers to the
possibility of dementia. A standard or Z@ score of −2.00 was used as a criter-

Table 8.1 Chronological presentation of signs and symptoms of dementia

First appearance of sign or symptom	*Age (years)*
Internal strabismus	40
Intact memory (DMTS) and learning (MTS) abilities[a]	44
Corneal abnormality	46
Left esotropia with keratoconus	47
First decline in memory (DMTS) and learning (MTS) abilities[a]	49
Hepatitis B positive	51
Moderate to profound hearing loss	53
Visual impairments	55
Continued decline in memory (DMTS) and learning (MTS) abilities[a]	55
Cataracts	56
CT brain scan evidence of atrophy	59
EEG: dysrhythmia with superimposed sharp wave activity	59
12-hour EEG: generalized dysrhythmia; no epileptiform activity	60
Gross visual impairments	60
Confusion	61
Incontinence	61
Wandering	61
Refusal to co-operate	61
Gait impairment	61
Seizures	61
Reflexes hyperactive for first time	61
Requires constant supervision	61
Intact ADL skills for past 12 years, evaluated annually	61
First decline in ADL skills	62
Declared legally blind	62
Myoclonic jerks	62
Respiratory failure and death	64

Notes:
ADL, activities of daily living.
[a] Using slightly different procedures over a 12-year period. Described in Dalton, Crapper & Schlotterer (1974); Dalton & Crapper (1977); Dalton & Crapper-McLachlan (1984).

ion to define suspicion of dementia (based on norms created from the performances of 65 institutionalized individuals with Down syndrome without signs or symptoms of dementia of the Alzheimer type). RM's Z scores on the MTS (circles *vs* squares) learning tests were: −1.74 −0.08, −4.31, −4.31, −4.31, and her Z scores on the DMTS (circles *vs* squares) memory test were: −1.04, +0.58, −3.88, −3.88 and −3.88 at ages 44, 47, 49, 52 and 55 years, respectively. She exceeded the criterion cut-off score at the age of 49 years, raising the suspicion of dementia for the first time. At the same time she was failing on the circles *vs* square test (hard). She successfully met the learning criterion on the coloured pictures MTS (easy) test until the last test at age 55 years. Only mild deterioration on an easier test of memory, the DMTS coloured pictures test, was evident when she reached the age of 55 years.

Skills of daily living

RM's daily living skills were repeatedly evaluated with the two-part Basic Life Skills Scale (BLS) behaviour rating test with 259 items in Part 1, which assesses motor skills, perceptual skills, self-care skills, communication skills, social skills, community living skills, academic skills, and Part 2, with 60 items measuring adaptability, sociability, co-operation, motivation, frustration tolerance, tolerance towards pressure, activity level, emotional maturity, absence of abnormal behaviour and predictability of behaviour (Cibiri & Jackson, 1976). Parts 1 and 2 of the BLS are highly correlated statistically with the AAMR's Adaptive Behavior Scale (ABS). The BLS was used because it was routinely employed with every institutional resident on an annual basis. It makes no assumptions about development and it is more sensitive to the low end of the IQ scale than the ABS. RM's overall Index of Functional Independence (IFI), which is a mean score based on all of Part 1 and 2 of the BLS, did not change significantly at any time for 12 years, when she was between the ages of 49 and 61 years, three years before she died. Her IFI scores for the 10-year annual evaluations ranged between 56 and 59 points, all within five points (on the BLS scale of scores from 0 to 100) of the mean for a sample of 114 adults with Down syndrome and a sample of 691 individuals with developmental disabilities without Down syndrome, all from the same institution. At the age of 62 years, RM's scores fell precipitously, consistent with the appearance of the late stage of dementia of the Alzheimer type.

Neuropathological diagnosis

Permission was obtained for post-mortem removal and examination of brain tissue specimens. Examination of the tissue and the neuropathological diagnosis of Alzheimer's disease was performed. The brain weighed 1010 g after fixation and revealed a marked degree of diffuse cortical atrophy and enlargement of the sulci. Atrophy was marked in the temporal lobes, with severe atrophy of both the amygdala and hippocampus. Sections from 13 regions of the brain were examined microscopically, revealing moderate neuronal loss in nucleus basalis with scattered neurofibrillary tangles. The globus pallidus showed mineralisation of scattered vessels. There were abundant plaques and tangles in the cingulate region, with severe neuronal loss in the amygdala and adjacent entorhinal cortex. Middle temporal gyrus revealed abundant plaques and tangles. The inferior parietal cortex was less involved, with moderate numbers of plaques and tangles. The hippocampus revealed marked cell loss and innumerable plaques and tangles. The substantia nigra was well populated. A rare tangle was observed, but no Lewy bodies. In the medulla, not bodies, mild neuronal loss and gliosis were present in the inferior olive. The thalamus and cerebellum were unremarkable on routine stains. There was no mention of vascular amyloidosis in the brain. The post mortem concluded that the presence of Alzheimer's disease was indicated.

Summary of declines in function

Highlights extracted from the monthly case reports on RM are provided for the last 11 years of her life. At age 53 years, notwithstanding the development of serious hearing losses, she continued to participate in daily activities, including shopping and going to church and working in the institution's laundry. Assays of blood specimens revealed that her thyroid functions were normal, with a weakly positive anti-thyroglobulin titre. At the age of 57 years, she was placed on a diet of soft food to compensate for the gradual loss of her teeth. Throughout, she had an active social life and her two sisters and brother frequently sent her gifts and kept frequent contact with her and the staff of the institution. At the age of 62 years, 24-hour ambulatory EEG studies revealed only moderate abnormality, consisting of generalized dysrhythmia without definite epileptic activity. By 1989, at the age of 61 years, she had began to experience onset of several bouts of incontinence and occasional incidents of crying (which may have been associated with gastrointestinal problems). Also, at this age, she fell and injured herself, but did not break any bones, and she began wandering. During this same time, she continued to be incontinent and also appeared confused. Chest pains were diagnosed as a transient ischaemic attack. Her confusion continued to increase at this time, as did episodes of (urinary) incontinence, and there were instances of improper clothing (wearing pyjamas at inappropriate times) and undressing at inappropriate places. She needed assistance with self-help skills such as dressing. Her eating skills deteriorated (she was reported to pour milk into a bowl of beans and to try to eat soup with a knife). Instances of refusal to co-operate were noted, as well an apparent fear of stairs (which may have been related to her greatly diminished vision). She was placed on dilantin for a time, then valproic acid, to control seizures that started at about this time. At 61 years of age, she became increasingly unsteady in her movements and could climb stairs only with assistance. She was frequently incontinent, undressed inappropriately, and stuffed her clothing in toilets. Staff reported that she needed constant supervision and wandered off. By the age 62 years, RM had to be provided with a wheelchair because of her increased mobility problems. She slept most of the day and could not walk. Late in the same year, there was an incident of smearing faeces on her bed. Staff noted again that she required constant supervision and care. Social contacts with family members, previously regular, decreased by the next year when she was 63 years of age, about 13 months prior to her death. During the last 12 months of her life, monthly staff reports noted that she had occasional incidents of abrupt jerking movements and few behaviour problems other than occasional incidents of stripping off her clothes. She had more seizures and was no longer involved in any programmes. She spent most of her waking time just sitting in her rocking chair and dozing. Her appetite remained good until the last few weeks before her death, although she had to be spoon fed with puréed food. The month before she died she weighed 105 pounds. At the age of 64, she died of respiratory failure and chronic obstructive pulmonary disease.

Other types of dementia

Whereas dementia of the Alzheimer type is the most prevalent form of dementia observed in adults with developmental disabilities, other dementias have also been recognized. Vascular (multi-infarct) dementia is gradually being acknowledged as a more frequent co-morbid condition than previously suspected in people from the general population who have a diagnosis of Alzheimer's disease. It also presents with a different course from and greater impairment than Alzheimer's disease among people with the same general cognitive impairment level (e.g. Sultzer et al., (1993) noted greater degrees of behavioural retardation, depression and anxiety in adults with vascular dementia when compared to matched controls with Alzheimer's disease), but with overall lower frequency with advancing age (American Psychiatric Association, 1997). The course of vascular dementia is characterized by more acute onset and stepwise decline and it may often be present at the same time as Alzheimer's disease. Early treatment for hypertension and vascular disease may serve to prevent further progression (American Psychiatric Association, 1997).

Collacott and his co-workers (Collacott, Cooper & Ismail, 1994) have suggested that evidence of cerebrovascular disease may be overlooked and that multi-infarct dementia may be under-reported in neuropathological studies of individuals with Down syndrome. Unfortunately, the knowledge about individuals with developmental disabilities without Down syndrome is scanty. Recently, Janicki and Dalton (1997), in their survey of some 27 000 older adults with developmental disabilities, reported that about 800 people over the age of 40 years were classified by care-provider staff as having either diagnosed or suspected dementia. Among the group with a diagnosis of dementia, as expected, the adults with Down syndrome were more likely to have a diagnosis of dementia of the Alzheimer type (77 per cent). Adults without Down syndrome were more likely to have diagnoses of a variety of dementias (26 per cent had the Alzheimer type, 34 per cent had dementia not otherwise specified). The duration of dementia also varied. Some 85 per cent of the Down syndrome group had been diagnosed within the past three years, compared with only 55 per cent of the non-Down syndrome group, perhaps reflecting the impact of differences in the prevalence of Alzheimer-type dementia between those with Down syndrome and those without.

Assessment issues

Neuropathological considerations

For more than 60 years since Struwe's first report (Struwe, 1929), nearly all reports of post-mortem examinations of brain tissue specimens from virtually 100 per cent of individuals with Down syndrome who have died over the age of 40 years have shown the characteristic lesions of Alzheimer's disease. Prior to the work of Visser and his colleagues (1997), there were only three known cases of people with Down syndrome who died after the age of 40 years in which post-mortem studies of brain tissue specimens failed to provide evidence of the characteristic lesions of Alzheimer's disease. Visser and his colleagues, in a ground-breaking longitudinal study of dementia, identified a perfect correlation between the presence or absence of clinical dementia when individuals with Down syndrome were followed for periods up to 11 years while alive, and the post-mortem examination of brain tissues using the generally accepted CERAD criteria for neuropathological diagnosis of Alzheimer's disease. They found that all of their 16 cases who were positive for dementia while alive also had a neuropathological diagnosis of Alzheimer's disease whereas three cases who were negative for dementia while alive had no neuropathology consistent with such a diagnosis. These observations suggest that it may be a mistake to assume that the brain lesions of Alzheimer's disease are present in all people with Down syndrome who are about 40 years of age or older.

A thorough review of the current state of knowledge about the similarities and differences in the morphology and microchemistry of the neuropathologic lesions associated with Alzheimer's disease in people from the general population and in those with Down syndrome has recently been published (Mann, 1993). Only rarely have there been any reports of differences in the lesions of Alzheimer's disease and Down syndrome. For example, Mann (1993) failed to observe an interaction of neurofibrillary tangles with lectins in brain tissue specimens from people with Down syndrome, which typically occurs in similarly treated specimens from individuals with Alzheimer's disease from the general population. Mann (1993) concluded that the slight differences, which do exist, may be closely linked to the chromosome 21 alterations that occur in Down syndrome but not in Alzheimer's disease. He singles out for particular attention the overexpression and production of the amyloid precursor protein that is genetically coded on chromosome 21. Yankner (1996) provides an excellent review and summary of recent advances in the molecular genetics and cell biology of Alzheimer's disease and discusses the potential pathogenic mechanisms that emerge, with particular emphasis on the role of the overexpression of amyloid precursor protein in Down syndrome.

The prevalence and incidence of the brain lesions of Alzheimer's disease among ageing people with developmental disabilities with aetiologies other than Down syndrome are not known with certainty. They are generally assumed to be similar to those found in the general population. The neuropathological features of Alzheimer's disease may be much more common in this group than previously suspected (Franceschi et al., 1990).

Diagnosis

Diagnosis of dementia of the Alzheimer type is generally classified into *possible Alzheimer's disease* (that is, suspicion but absent independent confirmation) or *probable Alzheimer's disease* (that is, beyond suspicion and with independent confirmation) (McKhann et al., 1984). A diagnosis of *definite Alzheimer's disease* is only possible upon post-mortem neuropathological evidence of the classical lesions. The assessment of dementia of the Alzheimer type is much more difficult among adults with developmental disabilities because (1) the assessment methods in common clinical use are generally not applicable to people with developmental disabilities, particularly for those whose level of intellectual functioning is in the severe and profound classifications (Gambert et al., 1988; Carlsen et al., 1994; Chicoine et al., 1994, 1995; Aylward et al., 1997), and (2) the subtle, insidious and progressive signs of this type of dementia can be easily concealed when superimposed on the pre-existing limitations in behaviour repertoire, verbal and communication skills. Many of these thorny issues were addressed by the 1994 Minneapolis Colloquium on Alzheimer Disease and Mental Retardation (Janicki, 1994; Deb & Janicki, 1995). From a practical and applied perspective, the starting point of any diagnostic process must involve a carefully developed individual assessment profile. The application of diagnostic standards, such as the National Institute of Neurological and Communicative Disorders and Stroke/Alzheimer's Disease and Related Disorders Association (NINCDS/ADRDA) research criteria (McKhann et al., 1984) for the population in general, and the American Association of Mental Retardation/International Association for the Scientific Study of Intellectual Disability guidelines for diagnosis for people with developmental disabilities (Aylward et al., 1995), have helped to sharpen the approach to diagnostic evaluation.

There are well-recognized problems in assigning an accurate clinical diagnosis of dementia in people with developmental disability because signs of the disease process are superimposed on a life-long background of limited intellectual abilities and behavioural repertoire. In addition, there is no generally accepted definition of dementia specific for individuals with a developmental disability. The existing diagnostic criteria developed in the USA (DSM-IV, American Psychiatric Association, 1994) and the ICD-10 criteria developed in Europe (World Health Organization, 1992) are silent for these individuals. The American Association on Mental Retardation/International Association for the Scientific Study of Intellectual Disability (AAMR/IASSID) Working Group Report has proposed a set of diagnostic criteria and procedures for assessing dementia in adults with developmental disabilities to help overcome such difficulties (Aylward et al., 1995). The ICD-10 diagnostic criteria for dementia have been recommended as the standard to be used for people with developmental disabilities. The recommendation is based on the heavier emphasis that the ICD-10 criteria place on the importance of non-cognitive changes. These are frequently, if not always, the first changes that are noted in this population. In addition, the ICD-10 criteria define an assessment process involving two steps in which the first presence of dementia and then the possible presence of dementia of the Alzheimer type is ascertained. The recommendations also retain the focus on the presence/absence of memory decline, other cognitive functions, awareness of the environment, emotional control, motivation, and social behaviour and duration of symptoms that are features of the diagnostic criteria in both systems of disease classification. Nevertheless, there is no litmus test, and the determination of the presence of dementia of the Alzheimer type is necessarily by a process of exclusion of all other possible causes for the presenting symptoms. Thus, a definitive diagnosis in people with developmental disabilities must be reserved for those instances when autopsy is possible; otherwise, the diagnosis will always remain probable.

Co-morbidity

Knowledge of what medical conditions or diseases occur at the same time in a given individual is essential if we are to improve the management and treatment of people with developmental disabilities who have signs and/or symptoms of dementia. A recent report succinctly reviewed the existing literature and calculated the relative risk that people with Down syndrome have for certain disorders (van Schrojenstein Lantman-de Valk et al., 1997). It reported that congenital heart defects, hypothyroidism, hearing impairment and hepatitis B were the only conditions in which there was a significant odds ratio. In a Dutch study of ageing people with developmental disabilities with clinically diagnosed dementia over the age of 60 years without Down syndrome, Evenhuis (1997) reported that co-morbid conditions were of sufficient frequency and severity as to hamper the interpretation of their losses in cognitive functions.

There is a growing recognition that depression, which may be part of the clinical presentation, has often been neglected or not properly distinguished from the signs or symptoms of dementia (Burt, Loveland & Lewis, 1992; Prasher, 1995e; Prasher & Hall, 1996; Burt, 1999). In addition, it is conceivable that a large, indeterminate proportion of people experience depression of varying severity during the stage (pro-dromal) that immediately precedes or accompanies the appearance of the early cognitive changes associated with dementia of the Alzheimer type. Other psychiatric conditions are also receiving more attention (Prasher, 1995a; Prasher & Day, 1995; Thorpe, 1999). The relatively high prevalence of psychotic delusions and hallucinations associated with Alzheimer's disease in people from the general population has already been mentioned. Cooper (1997), in a recent study, reported that 27.6 per cent of 29 people with dementia experienced at least one type of psychotic symptom: delusions occurred in 20.7 per cent and hallucinations in 20.7 per cent. Similarly, Lantman and co-workers reported that 14.8 per cent of their Dutch sample of people over the age of 60 years with dementia and with developmental disabilities without Down syndrome showed signs or symptoms of other psychiatric disorders (van Schrojenstein Lantman-de Valk et al., 1997).

These findings for people with developmental disabilities without Down syndrome are consistent with observations for affected people from the general population. However, they are in marked contrast to the situation among people with Down syndrome. Delusions and hallucinations are almost never reported for people with Down syndrome who are suffering from dementia, according to a recent review of 86 cases described in 15 reports published between 1948 and 1992 (Prasher, 1999). Another recent, carefully conducted, evaluation of the mental health, physical health and adaptive behaviour of 12 adults aged 50 years and older, with developmental disabilities (five with Down syndrome, seven without Down syndrome), each with a clinical diagnosis of dementia, reported seven areas of significant mental symptoms (sleep difficulty, hypersomnia, irritability, inefficient thought, anhedonia, social withdrawal and anergia) but failed to report any evidence for delusions or hallucinations (Moss & Patel, 1997). It is evident that the clinical presentation of dementia among people with developmental disabilities, particularly those with Down syndrome, may be different from that among similarly affected individuals from the general population. These differences in expression have also been recognized by others (e.g. Holland, Karlinsky & Berg, 1993); their impact is not yet clear. It does suggest, however, that extreme caution is the only responsible course of action to be taken in arriving at a diagnosis of dementia.

Deterioration in sensory functions (Evenhuis et al., 1992; Cronin-Golomb, 1995; Cronin-Golomb, Corkin & Growdon, 1995; Prasher, 1994a, 1995b), the appearance of thyroid abnormalities (Murdoch et al., 1977; Prasher & Krishnan, 1993; Prasher, 1994b, 1995c), seizures (Prasher & Corbett, 1993; McVicker, Shanks & McClelland, 1994; Prasher, 1995d; Johannsen et al., 1996), and other conditions (Prasher, 1994c), frequently occur at the same time as signs or symptoms of dementia. Whether or not these conditions play an active role in the pathogenesis of the underlying disease process or are merely associated conditions is not known.

Evaluation methods

The limitations of existing neuropsychological tests – none of which is sensitive enough to detect changes over time or specific enough for dementia of the Alzheimer type in the presence of pre-existing developmental disabilities – also create an important obstacle. As Burt and Aylward (1999) have indicated, misconceptions regarding the prevalence of dementia in adults with Down syndrome and failure to follow nationally accepted standards for differential diagnosis have resulted in misdiagnoses of Alzheimer's disease. The difficulties in assessment and diagnosis as they arise specifically for people with Down syndrome have been extensively reviewed (Dalton, 1992; Holland et al., 1993; Prasher et al., 1993; Prasher & Chung, 1996).

The absence of a suitable litmus test for this type of dementia requires the development and standardization of new methods for evaluation, a task that is both laborious and time consuming. Standard clinical history, laboratory tests, medical, neurological and radiological studies have been widely utilized in arriving at a diagnosis. However, these methods need to be supplemented by behavioural observations based on carefully constructed interview methods and rating scales that are designed and standardized specifically for this population at risk. Several scales have been developed that purport to be applicable for screening adults for dementia (Aylward et al., 1997). However, most involve administration by highly trained specialists who may not be available at many agencies. Some can be administered by other, less specialized staff, but these have questionable reliability and validity. The most desirable starting point seems to be the development and adoption of an appropriately standardized and normed behaviour scale or measure which could be used with confidence in its reliability at frequent, yearly intervals, starting at an appropriately chosen starting time in the individual's adult life. The AAMR/IASSID guidelines call for the adoption of such a scheme and recommend that the initial evaluations should be done for all adults with Down syndrome at the age of 40 years and for all others at the age of 50 years. Aylward and colleagues (Aylward et al., 1995, 1997) call for the adoption of such measures at an even earlier age to help identify sensory, motor and other age-associated changes that could precede the appearance of any cognitive changes associated with dementia of the Alzheimer type. Adoption of these proposals can provide a more rational basis for reporting the first suspicion of dementia and for making decisions for a more comprehensive diagnostic workup. This combination of an easy-to-administer screen test and a standardised measure of adaptive behaviour appears particularly useful in capturing baseline and follow-up data in the event that signs or symptoms of dementia occur at a later date.

Adaptive behaviour

In anticipating dementia, the assessment of adaptive behaviour in at-risk adults with developmental disability is an important part of the complete assessment of the individual. Many different instruments are available to measure adaptive functioning. Unfortunately, most measures of adaptive behaviour are based on the report of informants, a notoriously unreliable source of information. This is particularly so in institutional and other large settings where test scores from scales measuring adaptive behaviours are frequently used as a basis for allocation of financial and other resources. In addition, staff turnover is high and rotation of staff through different parts of such facilities reduces the length of exposure that most informants have to individuals in their care. It can also be a problem in community settings in which no one informant remains sufficiently familiar with the individual to provide reliable information over time. Thus, a standard behavioural measure should be used that is least affected by these factors.

Notwithstanding these limitations, there is an increasing number of reports that describe age-related changes in adaptive behaviour in adults with developmental disability. In general, the findings suggest that there is a significant impairment and deterioration of skills after the age of 50 years among people with Down syndrome and about a decade later among those without Down syndrome (Zigman et al., 1987, 1995). Declines within individuals over time have been harder to document because most of the literature is cross-sectional and, therefore, cohort effects confound the interpretation of data.

Care management

Immediate family members and care providers often find themselves confronted with agencies poorly equipped to provide practical guidance on management and care of adults with dementia and developmental disability. Physicians with experience in the diagnosis and treatment of older individuals with developmental disabilities are hard to find. Family practitioners, geriatricians and many other health professionals who are accessible may not be aware of the special needs of individuals with developmental disabilities and their impact on care providers. Many people with developmental disabilities are unable to provide verbal self-reports and often cannot follow verbal or spoken instructions readily. These problems hamper the introduction of effective care management strategies.

Moreover, as noted earlier, there are unique problems among older individuals with Down syndrome. They are at higher risk than others for the development of thyroid abnormalities (Percy et al., 1990a), superoxide dismutase abnormalities (Percy et al., 1990b), immune system changes (Mehta et al., 1993), auditory and visual problems (Evenhuis, 1999), and arthrosis and osteoporosis (Haveman, Maaskant & Sturmans, 1989). At the same time, they appear to be less likely to develop other conditions such as delusions and hallucinations (Moss & Patel, 1997; Prasher, 1999), high blood pressure, heart attacks, emphysema, chronic lung disease, and bone fractures (Haveman et al., 1989) than people of comparable age with developmental disabilities of other aetiologies. These are unique problems that require innovative and imaginative approaches to the evaluation of both preserved and deteriorating functions as well as extra thought in the development of appropriate care plans and programmes when dementia is also present (Holland et al., 1993; Holland, 1999).

Many clinicians may not recognize dementia in people with developmental disabilities and many attribute the behavioural changes to other causes. Often, reliable longitudinal information is missing because no one is readily available who has known the individual for any significant period of time. Without specific guidance, providers may offer programmes or services that are inappropriate for this population, or refer them to other care systems too soon. For example, people with developmental disabilities and dementia may be referred to long-term care settings, thereby exposing them to unnecessary and possibly inappropriate or overly restrictive conditions that may hasten or aggravate their functional decline. Janicki and Dalton (1993) have reported that most referrals for diagnosis originally came about as a result of staff suspicions and that staff indicated a high need for training to help them deal more effectively with the complex problems they encounter in providing care for these individuals. Agencies are now seeing greater numbers of individuals in their care who are showing signs of dementia and the staff need much more support to cope with their own feelings as well as with the increasingly heavy demands of providing care (Koenig, 1995; Visser et al., 1997; Hammond & Benedetti, 1999; Udell, 1999).

Useful information regarding assessment and interventions for people affected by dementia in the general population is beginning to emerge from a variety of sources (American Psychiatric Association, 1997), as is such information regarding individuals with developmental disabilities (Marler & Cunningham, 1994; Koenig, 1995; The Arc, 1995). Specific practice guidelines for the care of individuals with developmental disabilities and dementia have been promulgated jointly by the AAMR and the IASSID (Janicki et al., 1995, 1996). These AAMR/IASSID practice guidelines provide specific suggestions for assessment and service provision as well as a rational basis for making clinical decisions and developing programmes that are specifically responsive to the needs of individuals affected with dementia. The guidelines were developed with the following operating assumptions: (1) each person's needs must determine how care is provided; (2) age-associated changes are a normal part of life; (3) people with Down syndrome are at greater risk for Alzheimer's disease; (4) some behavioural changes may look like dementia of the Alzheimer type, but may be due to other causes and be reversible; and (5) the individual's own abilities and levels of function should be the basis for evaluating subsequent changes (Janicki et al., 1996).

The AAMR/IASSID guidelines call for an initial screening for dementia followed by periodic reviews combined with the implementation of care management practices that are tightly coupled to the expected sequence of functional changes as the individual progresses through the stages of dementia. For example, a programme for managing incontinence should be prepared and kept on the shelf to be available when the individual shows signs, so that it can be immediately implemented at the time when it may be most effective and least embarrassing for the affected individual. The AAMR/IASSID practice guidelines (Janicki, et al., 1996) distinguish situations that require only a screening procedure from those that require a more comprehensive assessment. A three-step course of action is recommended: first, recognize changes; second, conduct assessments and evaluations; and third, institute medical and care management.

A number of workers (Newroth & Newroth; 1981; Antonangeli, 1995; Koenig, 1995; May et al., 1996) have provided detailed advice based on the identification of the subtle links between the functional changes of an affected person in the initial stage of dementia with the impact and consequences to the person's friends and staff. This approach is then extended to offer guidance as the affected individual progresses through all of the stages of dementia of the Alzheimer type. A manual published by Newroth and Newroth (1981) represents a pioneering effort in this connection. It utilizes plain language throughout the text and a simple set of tables to help families and human service workers. The manual focuses on the practical, day-to-day judgements of function and advances simple ways to provide the best care possible for the affected individual. However, it also underscores the need for changes in the overall management of resources of the entire agency. For example, it suggests that the key to success in the care of a person with Down syndrome who has this type of dementia is a dedicated team approach in which a number of staff cannot only share the burdens of care but can also have respite for themselves and ways of exploring and dealing with their own feelings towards the affected individual. As this disease will eventually leave the individual totally bedridden and helpless, the provision of care will become a job that cannot be done by just one or two people. It requires a substantial physical and emotional sacrifice on the part of carers, an issue that is seldom addressed in other manuals. Caring for the person with this type of dementia sooner or later becomes a very demanding task that involves a 'primacy of human presence' (Newroth & Newroth, 1981), sensitivity, and stability over technology and organization. It is not easy for staff consistently to maintain devotion to these necessary human qualities over long periods of care. The kinds of problems encountered are best met by an interlocking support system of counselling, training and supportive management.

The guidelines for stage one, modified from Newroth and Newroth (1981) are shown in Table 8.2. To help staff address the demands of care and changing behaviours associated with the progression of dementia of the Alzheimer type, the chart's first column presents a series of physical and psychological symptoms; the second, a list of observed behaviours that are associated with the signs or symptoms; and the third, a list of implications of those behaviours for the individual and for those who render care (be they staff, family, or

Table 8.2 Stage one

Symptoms	Behaviour examples	Implications	Suggestions
1. *Impairment of memory* includes: • diminished ability in decision making and judgement • time disorientation • confusion and general intellectual disorientation	Person cannot remember names of acquaintances or of common objects	Social life becomes limited; person is not satisfying social needs of acquaintances; therefore, people may begin to by-pass the person	Staff should not take behaviour personally; the person may show recognition through other behaviours; people need to expect less interaction, but to stimulate maximum opportunities for socialization, e.g. meals with others, attend parties, etc.
	Forgets words and sentences	Unable to explain personal needs or condition adequately (doctor's visit, banking, etc.)	Provide advocate or 'interpreter'
	Cannot remember what he/she did with familiar articles (gloves, cigarettes, etc.)	Experiences frustration and irritability results	Needs help to find personal possessions; familiar articles should be placed within easy access, in sight
	Loss of interest in personal hygiene and appearance; dresses inappropriately for social functions	May appear unkempt, dirty and smelly and, therefore, less socially acceptable; may draw unfavourable attention to self	Provide supervision to choose appropriate clothing, leaving room for personal preference; eliminate clothing that is difficult to manage (ties, shoe-laces, flies that button, etc.); give reminders to wash, brush teeth, etc., and offer encouragement and direction to maintain appearance and hygiene routines. Supervision should be sensitive and made available only when necessary
	Forgets what time of day it is	Is frequently late for meals, appointments, etc., and upsets routines	Requires frequent reminders

Table 8.2 (*cont.*)

Symptoms	Behaviour examples	Implications	Suggestions
	Apparent loss of sensory feedback re: (1) sleep, (2) appetite, (3) climate		
	(1) Wakes in the middle of the night and dresses	Wakes others, risks injury, loses sleep and further confuses self	Provide someone to supervise at night
	(2) Doesn't know what meal he has just eaten, what meal to expect next (breakfast, lunch or supper – may expect a meal just after finishing one)	Annoys others with inappropriate expectations or questions	Exercise patience and share responsibility for gentle reminders about routines, meal times, time of day, etc.
	(3) Dresses inappropriately for climate	Risk of catching cold	
	Starts to undress at bedtime and forgets what he/she is doing and begins to dress again	Exasperates care providers	
2. *Spatial disorientation* including: • loss of sense of direction	Can't find his/her bedroom, or bathroom, even in familiar home setting; gets lost easily in familiar neighbourhood; tries to enter bus from wrong side	Gets lost easily as daily activities change (especially in strange environment and routine); often late; risks personal injury, therefore others worry and get impatient, which may cause over-reaction in the form of undue restrictions	Be prepared to provide increased supervision and direction within the house, and to provide escorts on neighbourhood outings; outings alone should be limited to daytime and fair weather; avoid radical changes in physical setting (re-decorating, moving furniture), and daily routine
	Difficulty in focusing and successfully grasping, holding fixed object and bringing to desired spot (finding fork, placing food on fork, putting fork in mouth)	Drops food, spills things; mealtimes may become burdensome to others	Person should be adequately supplied with serviette, apron, etc.; simplify tableware (spoon instead of knife and fork, mug instead of cup and saucer)

• unable to place body in correct reference to activity	Sits on half of chair; difficulty in orienting self to place setting at table	May fall or annoy others at table	'Cheerful cleaner-upper': it is important for morale that staff and others do not blame the person for the inconveniences caused by the deteriorating condition
3. *Lack of spontaneity:* • diminished spontaneous movement	Does not initiate activities for self and interest in outside activities diminishes	Not included in mainstream of activity; tendency to become withdrawn, left out; experiences loneliness; not stimulated by surroundings	Encourage increased external motivation from peers or supervisor; make the person central to group activities and offer help to participate and feel 'part of'
	Generally decreased body movement		
	Remains sedentary for long periods		Do not leave the person alone for long periods of time
	General decreased alertness and eye contact	People tend to ignore the value of eye contact and no longer encourage it	Encourage, seek out and maintain eye contact; use bright objects to capture attention
• diminished spontaneous reaction to people	Manifestations of greeting, reception, interest in, and awareness of people's physical presence and emotional states are reduced	May offend others; may not be greeted by others	Increase effort to affirm person's presence; help others to appreciate that this decline is not a personal rejection; try to maintain continuity of relationships
	Inability to respond to simple questions about repetition; misses cues for social interactions	May be avoided by others; friendship and social contacts 'fall off' because colleagues may find the relationship unsatisfactory	Encourage social interaction with others, especially with old friends; friends may require assistance (counselling) to understand why the relationship has changed

Table 8.2 (*cont.*)

Symptoms	Behaviour examples	Implications	Suggestions
4. Physical dysfunction: • increasing drowsiness • tires easily • general slowing of movements • loses balance	Falls asleep at work or home, tires easily; walks, responds, works slowly	Cannot be counted on to produce and, therefore, loses status and employment opportunities as a worker	Should be employed in sheltered work or attend a 'flexible' programme determined by individual's potential
			Should be provided with opportunity to rest during the day at work or home
		Frustrates co-workers and staff	Physical condition needs respect and to be accepted in work environment by staff and co-workers; staff and co-workers should be counselled on the special needs of this person

friends). The fourth, and most important, column provides a list of practical suggestions on how to respond to the needs of those involved.

The occurrence of dementia among individuals with developmental disabilities requires recognition of its profound impact on the quality of life for the affected individuals, their families, friends and carers. Longitudinal and crosssectional studies suggest that people with developmental disabilities are at least as likely to experience symptoms of dementia as the general population. Useful models and training programmes for families and carers of the general population with Alzheimer dementia are much more numerous and widely available now than they were a decade ago. These service models and programmes may be usefully adapted for the population with developmental disabilities suffering from dementia.

However, even with the ready availability of these service models, modifications for people with developmental disabilities must be contemplated. For example, individuals with developmental disabilities are more likely to have difficulties with communication (McCallion, 1998) and to experience problems with everyday activities (Moss & Patel, 1997). Because, there are life-long major limitations of verbal and communication skills, there is a greater likelihood that dementia will be well advanced before a diagnosis is made. However, individuals with this type of dementia still have remaining strengths that can be supported and maintained. The key is the willingness of families and other carers to recognize the significance of supporting those strengths, and to supplement this support with appropriate modifications to the affected person's environment. Patience and sensitivity in all attempts at communication are also essential, particularly as the disease progresses and the affected individual faces increasing social isolation.

There are rapidly growing demands being placed on service agencies, hospitals and clinics to provide effective interventions. At present, and for some time to come, the most effective interventions will be based upon the day-to-day, trial-and-error experiences of care staff. These experiences need to be made available for an informed management strategy. A number of workers have provided case studies viewed from a care management perspective which are instructive (Tyler & Shank, 1996; Davis; 1998; Hammond & Benedetti, 1998; Udell, 1998).

When faced with dementia, many workers have had to make the choice of either developing a specialist programme or tailoring an individual's services within his or her current programme or supports. If specialist programmes are used, how should dementia care management be practised in such settings? Some have begun to delve into this issue (Holland et al., 1993; Noelker & Somple, 1993; Marler & Cunningham, 1994; Antonangeli, 1995; The Arc, 1995; Janicki et al., 1996, Janicki & Dalton, 1998). It is generally agreed that as dementia related to a disease process progresses, significant changes in supports have to be put in place. Dementia-related behavioural changes may include a greater number of chronic health problems and diminished capacity of self-directed activities, as well as significant changes in personality and behavioural control (Moss & Patel, 1997). Such changes will have a significant impact on a care programme because dementia-related changes are perceived as unexpected. The developmental disabilities 'system' expects either static or continued development and ever-growing independence following interventions, supports or programmes, and does not easily accommodate functional decline. Diminishing abilities may create a demand for more staff time and supervision, a change in the level of intensity of programmes or supports, and potentially a change in residence. They also may call for adjustments in the individual's care or programme plan to accommodate expected changes in behaviour and capabilities resulting from the effects of dementia. Whether the developmental disabilities system or the long-term health (dementia) care system is most capable of providing appropriate care is left to each jurisdiction for final determination.

Care providers are faced with the problem of how to handle diminishing abilities constructively among people who have been relatively independent and capable of extensive self-direction for most of their lives. They may find that philosophical and pragmatic considerations may conflict with a need for personal care that becomes more necessary with each year following the onset of progressive dementia. As described by a number of workers (Visser et al., 1997; Davis, 1999; Hammond & Benedetti, 1999; Prasher, 1999; Udell, 1999) adults with Down syndrome can experience a precipitous decline in functions, and care management practices can take a substantial emotional toll on family and staff resources as a result (Whittick, 1989; Service, Lavoie & Herlihy, 1999). Others, with different aetiologies, will have a later onset and longer duration of decline, stretching the responsible care agency resources in different ways. However, in most instances, when the adult has been part of the developmental disabilities care system, staff have come to expect to see progressive increases in skills and independence, and the presentation of a disease course that results in the opposite can be disconcerting. This may present difficulties for the service provider and will call for specialized training for staff to help address the contradiction between the reality that the disease presents and the developmental ideology that has been the basis for the delivery of care in the field of developmental disabilities.

Training and staff development

The Minneapolis Colloquium Report (Janicki, 1994) noted the lack of focus with respect to public policy in the area of Alzheimer's disease and developmental disabilities. There is a definite prospect in the future for a substantial increase in referrals to nursing facilities. The report noted the potential high cost of this type of care if prevention strategies were not adopted within the next few years, special efforts were not set up to support carers, and current programmes were not modified. The best way to address some of these problems is to promote early recognition of signs of functional deterioration through the provision of appropriate training for clinicians, carers and others involved with adults at risk of dementia or who have dementia. Direct care providers and other operational staff should be trained to raise the 'index of suspicion'. That is, everyone should become more aware of the onset of the subtle signs of dementia, such as memory loss and behaviour change, and should be trained to become careful observers who keep detailed notes of their observations. Training should also focus on care management techniques and the specific approaches for coping with functional limitations as the disease progresses to the late stage. As the death of affected individuals becomes imminent, additional supports for the staff become essential (for a related perspective, see Newroth & Newroth, 1981). This training is based on the belief in the individuality of the adult with dementia and a perspective that promotes personal dignity, autonomy, and personal welfare. Such workshops and training courses should provide information on Alzheimer's disease, and diagnostic and treatment practices with particular application to people with developmental disabilities. Workshops and courses should be structured to provide up-to-date information, in print form and other media, on normal and pathological ageing, Alzheimer's disease, recognition of early signs of dementia, methods for conducting periodic assessments and evaluations, available services, supporting carers, general care management and effective practices for interventions for the early, middle and late stage of dementia.

Training programmes should also be supported by the distribution of information geared to help carers. Supports and orientation should be provided to family carers to enable them to maintain their relative's functioning more effectively and to know how to seek needed services. Information about programme supports, such as day services and respite, as well as in-home services should be made available. Families should be connected to support organizations for Alzheimer's disease or for intellectual or developmental disabilities and other community resources. Available diagnostic and practice information should be made widely available throughout the relevant professional community (McLennan, Murdoch & McIntosh, 1993) and to family carers (Marler & Cunningham, 1994; The Arc, 1995).

Conclusion

Five recommendations are offered below to guide effective planning and care of individuals with developmental disabilities who are suspected of being in an early stage of dementia.

1. *Become better informed about the nature of the symptoms of dementia as well as the characteristics of individuals with developmental disabilities.* For example, it is very unlikely that a person 30 years of age or younger with

Down syndrome who is showing symptoms of deteriorating functions has dementia of the Alzheimer type. Individuals with Down syndrome have a high risk of developing hypothyroidism, that is, an underactive thyroid gland. This dysfunction can produce symptoms similar to those associated with this type of dementia.

2. *Be careful behavioural observers:* Understanding that the disease course following onset of Alzheimer's disease among adults with developmental disability requires careful observation of behavioural changes at periodic intervals. Awareness is necessary that the course among adults with Down syndrome is highly variable from person to person, can start at any time after the age of 40 years, but mostly after the age of about 50–55 years, with an average duration of about seven years, ranging from 2 to 28 years. Among adults with other developmental disabilities, the course of Alzheimer dementia may have different consequences. Onset is almost certain to occur after the age of 65 years and it may have a duration of from 10 to more than 20 years. It should be expected that dementia of the Alzheimer type will be less frequently found among these individuals and that other types of dementia may be more common. The functional changes associated with Alzheimer's disease have a profound impact on every aspect of the life of the affected individual and his or her care providers.

3. *Be good programme designers:* the management of planning for individuals with early to middle stage dementia of the Alzheimer type includes providing associated services, such as housing, day services and clinical supports. Planning for late-stage services must include the need for more intensive care, but not necessarily skilled nursing care. Models of care developed through many years of experience by clinics, self-help groups and not-for-profit associations provide an important source of ideas that will be helpful for affected people with developmental disabilities.

4. *Be able to develop and disseminate innovative care management policies based on actual experience.* Clinical interventions should be based upon practices that reflect a growing body of experience as well as a commitment for effective care of people with Alzheimer's disease and developmental disability. The option of referral of an individual to a specialised setting that offers higher levels of care should be based solely upon a reasonably firm diagnosis of mid-stage to late-stage dementia with evidence of distressing symptoms that staff can no longer deal with effectively. Managers should keep abreast of the potential long-term significance of new discoveries in molecular biology and genetics that are leading to the development and marketing of new treatments. The search for biological markers in blood specimens that can be used as a litmus test for the diagnosis of Alzheimer's disease is a very active field of investigation although, as of the time of this writing, such a test still eludes us.

5. *Be prepared to provide training that is responsive to what the staff need and not as a response to preconceived notions of what they ought to know.* Training should be provided in care management techniques and the specific approaches for coping with functional limitations and death. At the most general level, the organizing principle underlying this training is respect

for the individual who is affected with dementia and a perspective that promotes the personal dignity, autonomy and personal welfare of the person. At the practical level, it means asking many questions of direct care providers and listening attentively to their trial-and-error experiences of coping day by day with affected individuals. Sharing of these experiences in a workshop or small-group setting will provide many precise and effective tools for staff, as well as providing a boost to morale and the identification of potential problems before they become unmanageable.

Acknowledgements

The authors express their gratitude to the entire staff and friends of the Huronia Regional Centre, Orillia, Ontario, who provided generous co-operation over a period of more than 20 years, without which it would not have been possible to conduct the longitudinal evaluation of RM before, at the onset, and throughout the progression and development of Alzheimer's disease. The reports and notes in the clinical file also convey a respect and caring concern by all those who made entries in the voluminous record. The preparation of this chapter was also partly supported by the New York State Institute for Basic Research in Developmental Disabilities and the New York State Office on Mental Retardation and Developmental Disabilities.

References

American Psychiatric Association (1994). *Diagnostic and Statistical Manual of Mental Disorders*, 4th edn. Washington, DC: APA.

American Psychiatric Association (1997). Practice guidelines for the treatment of patients with Alzheimer's disease and other dementias of late life. *American Journal of Psychiatry*, **154**, (May Supplement), 1– 39.

Antonangeli, J.M. (1995). *Of Two Minds: A Guide to the Care of People with the Dual Diagnosis of Alzheimer's disease and Mental Retardation*. Malden, MA: Co-operative for Human Services.

Aylward, E.H., Burt, D.B., Thorpe, L.U., Lai, F. & Dalton, A.J. (1995). *Diagnosis of Dementia in Individuals with Intellectual Disability*. Washington DC: American Association on Mental Retardation.

Aylward, E., Burt, D., Thorpe, L., Lai, F. & Dalton, A.J. (1997). Diagnosis of dementia in individuals with intellectual disability. *Journal of Intellectual Disability Research*, **41**, 152–64.

Berg, J.M., Karlinsky, H. & Holland, A.J. (1993). *Alzheimer Disease, Down Syndrome, and their Relationship*. Oxford: Oxford University Press.

Burns, A. (1992). Cause of death in dementia. *International Journal of Geriatric Psychiatry*, **7**, 461–4.

Burt, D.B. (1999). Depression and aging. In *Dementia, Aging and Intellectual Disabilities: a Handbook*, ed. M.P. Janicki & A.J. Dalton, pp. 198–216. Philadelphia: Taylor and Francis.

Burt, D.B. & Aylward, E. (1999). Procedures for diagnosis of dementia. In *Dementia, Aging and Intellectual Disabilities: a Handbook,* ed. M.P. Janicki & A.J. Dalton, pp. 141–56. Philadelphia: Taylor and Francis.

Burt, D.B., Loveland, K.A. & Lewis, K.R. (1992). Depression and the onset of dementia in adults with mental retardation. *American Journal on Mental Retardation,* **96**, 502–11.

Carlsen, W.R., Galluzzi, K.E., Forman, L.F. & Cavalieri, T.A. (1994). Comprehensive geriatric assessment: applications for community residing, elderly people with mental retardation/ developmental disabilities. *Mental Retardation,* **32**, 334–40.

Chicoine, B., McGuire, D., Hebein, S. & Gilly, D. (1994). Development of a clinic for adults with Down syndrome. *Mental Retardation,* **32**, 100–6.

  (1995). Use of the community oriented primary care model for a specialneeds population: a clinic for adults with Down syndrome. *American Journal of Public Health,* **85**, 869–70.

Cibiri, S.M. & Jackson, L.J. (1976). *Training Developmentally Handicapped Persons in Basic Life Skills.* Toronto: Ontario Ministry of Community and Social Services.

Collacott, R.A., Cooper, S-A. & Ismail, I.A. (1994). Multi-infarct dementia in Down's syndrome. *Journal of Intellectual Disability Research,* **38**, 203–8

Cooper, J.K., Mungas, D., Verma, M. & Weiler, P.G. (1991). Psychotic symptoms in Alzheimer's disease. *International Journal of Geriatric Psychiatry,* **6**, 721–6.

Cooper, S-A. (1997). Psychiatric symptoms of dementia amongst elderly people with learning disabilities. *International Journal of Geriatric Psychiatry,* **12**, 662–6.

Crapper-McLachlan, D.R., Dalton A.J., Galin, H., Schlotterer, G. & Daicar, E. (1984). Alzheimer's disease: clinical course and cognitive disturbances. *Acta Neurologica Scandinavica,* Supplement 99, **69**, 83–90.

Cronin-Golomb, A. (1995). Vision in Alzheimer's disease. *Gerontologist,* **35**, 370–6.

Cronin-Golomb, A., Corkin, S. & Growdon, J.H. (1995). Visual dysfunction predicts cognitive deficits in Alzheimer disease. *Optometry and Vision Science,* **72**, 168–76.

Cummings, J.L., Miller, B., Hill, M.A. & Neshkes, R. (1987). Neuropsychiatric aspects of multi-infarct dementia and dementia of the Alzheimer type. *Archives of Neurology,* **44**, 389–93.

Dalton, A.J. (1992). Dementia in Down syndrome: methods of evaluation. In *Alzheimer Disease and Down Syndrome,* ed. L. Nadel & C.J. Epstein, pp. 51–76. New York: Wiley Liss.

Dalton, A.J. & Crapper, D.R. (1977). Down's syndrome and aging of the brain. In *Research to Practice in Mental Retardation: Biomedical Aspects,* Vol. II, ed. P.M. Mittler, pp. 391–400. Baltimore: University Park Press.

Dalton, A.J. & Crapper-McLachlan, D.R. (1984). Incidence of memory deterioration in aging people with Down's syndrome. In *Perspectives and Progress in Mental Retardation: Biomedical Aspects,* Vol II, ed. J.M. Berg, pp. 55–62. Baltimore: University Park Press.

  (1986). Clinical expression of Alzheimer's disease in Down's syndrome. *Psychiatric Clinics of North America: Psychiatric Perspectives on Mental Retardation,* 9, 659–670.

Dalton, A.J. Crapper, D.R. & Schlotterer, G.R. (1974). Alzheimer's disease in Down's syndrome: visual retention deficits. *Cortex,* **10**, 366–77.

Dalton, A.J. & Janicki, M.P. (1999). Aging, dementia and Alzheimer disease. In *Dementia, Aging and Intellectual Disabilities: a Handbook,* ed. M.P. Janicki & A.J. Dalton, pp. 5–31. Philadelphia: Taylor and Francis.

Dalton, A.J., Seltzer, G.B., Adlin, M.S. & Wisniewski, H.M. (1993). Association between Alzheimer disease and Down syndrome: clinical observations. In *Alzheimer Disease, Down Syndrome and Their Relationship,* ed. J.M. Berg, H. Karlinsky, & A.J. Holland, pp. 53–69. Oxford: Oxford University Press.

Dalton, A.J. & Wisniewski, H.M. (1990). Down syndrome and the dementia of Alzheimer disease. *International Review of Psychiatry,* **2**, 43–52.

Davis, D. (1999). A parent's experience. In *Dementia, Aging and Intellectual Disabilities: a Handbook,* ed. M.P. Janicki & A.J. Dalton, pp. 42–53. Philadelphia: Taylor and Francis.

Deb, S. & Janicki, M. (1995). Conference report: international colloquium on mental retardation and Alzheimer's disease. *Journal of Intellectual Disability Research,* **39**, 149–50.

Evenhuis, H.M. (1997). The natural history of dementia in ageing people with intellectual disability. *Journal of Intellectual Disability Research,* **41**, 92–6.

Evenhuis, H.M., van Zanten, G.A., Brocaar, M.P. & Roerdinkholder, W.H.M. (1992) Hearing loss in middle-age persons with Down syndrome. *American Journal on Mental Retardation,* **97**, 47–56.

Evenhuis, H.M. (1999). Associated medical aspects of dementia. In *Dementia, Aging and Intellectual Disabilities: a Handbook,* ed. M.P. Janicki & A.J. Dalton, pp. 103–21. Philadelphia: Taylor and Francis.

Franceschi, M., Comola, M., Piattoni, F., Gualandri, W. & Canal, N. (1990). Prevalence of dementia in adult patients with trisomy 21. *American Journal of Medical Genetics* (Supplement), 7, 306–8.

Gambert, S.R., Crimmins, D., Cameron, D.J. et al. (1988). Geriatric assessment of the mentally retarded elderly. *The New York Medical Quarterly,* **8**, 144–7.

Hammond, B., & Benedetti, P. (1999). Perspectives of a care provider. In *Dementia, Aging and Intellectual Disabilities: a Handbook,* ed. M.P. Janicki & A.J. Dalton, pp. 32–41. Philadelphia: Taylor and Francis.

Haveman, M., Maaskant, M.A. & Sturmans, F. (1989). Older Dutch residents of institutions with and without Down syndrome: comparisons of mortality and morbidity trends and motor/social functioning. *Australian and New Zealand Journal of Developmental Disabilities,* **15**, 241–55.

Holland, A.J. (1999). Down syndrome and the high risk of Alzheimer disease. In *Dementia, Aging and Intellectual Disabilities: a Handbook,* ed. M.P. Janicki & A.J. Dalton, pp. 183–97. Philadelphia: Taylor and Francis.

Holland, A.J., Karlinsky, H. & Berg, J.M. (1993). Alzheimer disease in persons with Down syndrome: diagnostic and management considerations. In *Alzheimer Disease and Down Syndrome: Their Relationships,* ed. J.M. Berg, H. Karlinsky & A.J. Holland, pp. 95–113. Oxford: Oxford University Press.

Janicki, M.P. (ed.). (1994). *Alzheimer Disease among Persons with Mental Retardation: Report from an International Colloquium.* Albany: New York State Office of Mental Retardation and Developmental Disabilities.

Janicki, M.P. & Dalton, A.J. (1993). Alzheimer disease in a select population of older adults with mental retardation. *Irish Journal of Psychology,* **14,** 38–47.

Janicki, M.P. & Dalton, A.J. (1997). Prevalence of dementia among individuals with intellectual disabilities: Report of a statewide survey. Paper presented at International Congress III on the Dually Diagnosed, Montreal, Canada.

(1999). Dementia and public policy considerations. In *Dementia, Aging and Intellectual Disabilities: a Handbook,* ed. M.P. Janicki & A.J. Dalton, pp. 388–414. Philadelphia: Taylor and Francis.

Janicki, M.P. Heller, T., Seltzer, G.B. & Hogg, J. (1995). *Practice Guidelines for the Clinical Assessment and Care Management of Alzheimer and other Dementias among Adults with Mental Retardation.* Washington DC: American Association on Mental Retardation.

(1996). Practice guidelines for the clinical assessment and care management of Alzheimer's disease and other dementias among adults with intellectual disability. AAMRIASSID Workgroup on Practice Guidelines for Care Management of Alzheimer's Disease among Adults with Intellectual Disability. *Journal of Intellectual Disability Research,* **40,** 374–82.

Johannsen, R., Christensen, J.E.J., Goldstein, H., Nielsen, V.K. & Mai, J. (1996). Epilepsy in Down syndrome – prevalence in three age groups. *Seizure,* **5,** 121–5.

Koenig, B.R. (1995). *Aged and Dementia Care Issues for People with an Intellectual Disability: Best Practices.* Brighton, South Australia: MINDA, Inc.

Lai, F. (1992a). Clinicopathologic features of Alzheimer disease in Down syndrome. In *Down Syndrome and Alzheimer Disease,* ed. L. Nadel & C.J. Epstein, pp. 15–34. New York: Wiley-Liss.

(1992b). Alzheimer disease. In *Biomedical Concerns in Persons with Down Syndrome,* ed. S.M. Pueschel & J.K. Pueschel, A., Gupta, K.L., & Escher, J.E. pp. 175–96. Baltimore: Paul H. Brookes.

Lott, I.T. (1982). Down syndrome, aging and Alzheimer's disease: a clinical review. *Annals of the New York Academy of Sciences,* **396,** 15–27.

Mann, D.M.A. (1993). Association between Alzheimer disease and Down syndrome: neuropathological observations. In *Alzheimer Disease, Down Syndrome and Their Relationship,* ed. J.M. Berg, H. Karlinsky & A.J. Holland, pp. 71–92. Oxford: Oxford University Press.

Marler, R. & Cunningham, C. (1994). *Down's Syndrome and Alzheimer's Disease.* London: Down's Syndrome Association (155 Mitcham Road, SW17 9PG).

May, H.L., Fletcher, C., Alvarez, N., Zuis, J. & Cavallari, S.G. (1996). *Alzheimer's Disease and Down Syndrome: A Manual of Care.* Wretham, MA: Alzheimer's Committee of Wrentham Developmental Center.

McCallion, P. (1999). Maximizing and maintaining communication. In *Dementia, Aging and Intellectual Disabilities: a Handbook,* ed. M.P. Janicki & A.J. Dalton, pp. 261–77. Philadelphia: Taylor and Francis.

McKhann, G., Drachman, D., Folstein, M., Katzman, R., Price, D. & Stadlan, E.M. (1984). Clinical diagnosis of Alzheimer's disease: report of the NINCDS-ADRDA Work Group under the auspices of the Department of Health and Human Services Task Force on Alzheimer's Disease. *Neurology,* **34,** 939–44.

McLennan, J.M., Murdoch, P.S. & McIntosh, I.B. (1993). *Dementia touches everyone: a guide for trainers and trainees in general practice.* Stirling, Scotland: Dementia Services Development Centre, University of Stirling.

McVicker, R.W., Shanks, O.E.P & McClelland, R.J. (1994). Prevalence and associated features of epilepsy in adults with Down's syndrome. *British Journal of Psychiatry,* **164**, 528–32.

Mehta, P.D., Dalton, A.J., Percy, M.E., & Wisniewski, H.M. (1993). Increased beta-2 microglobulin and interleukin-6 in sera from older persons with Down syndrome. *Advances in the Biosciences,* **87**, 95–6.

Mendez, M.F., Martin, R.J., Smyth, K.A. & Whitehouse, P.J. (1990). Psychiatric symptoms associated with Alzheimer's disease. *Journal of Neuropsychiatry and Clinical Neurosciences,* **2**, 28–33.

Moss, S. & Patel, P. (1997). Dementia in older people with intellectual disability: symptoms of physical and mental illness, and levels of adaptive behaviour. *Journal of Intellectual Disability Research,* **41**, 60–9.

Murdoch, J.C., Ratcliffe, W.A., McLarty, D.G., Rodger, J.C. & Ratcliffe, J.G. (1977). Thyroid function in adults with Down's syndrome. *Journal of Clinical Endocrinology & Metabolism,* **44**, 453–8.

Newroth, S. & Newroth, A. (1981). *Coping with Alzheimer Disease: A Growing Concern.* Downsview, Ontario: National Institute on Mental Retardation (Kinsmen NIMR Building, York University Campus, 4700 Keele Street, Ontario, Canada, M3J lP3).

Noelker, E.A. & Somple, L.C. (1993). Adults with Down syndrome and Alzheimer's. In *The Elderly Caregiver: Caring for Adults with Developmental Disabilities,* ed. K.A. Roberto, pp. 81–92. Newbury Park: Sage Publications.

Percy, M.E., Dalton, A.J., Markovic, V.D. et al. (1990a). Autoimmune thyroiditis associated with mild subclinical hypothyroidism in adults with Down syndrome: a comparison of patients with and without manifestations of Alzheimer disease. *American Journal of Medical Genetics,* **36**, 148–54.

(1990b). Red cell superoxide dismutase, glutathione peroxidase and catalase in Down syndrome patients with and without manifestations of Alzheimer disease. *American Journal of Medical Genetics,* **35**, 459–67.

Prasher, V.P. (1994a). Screening of ophthalmic pathology and its associated effects on adaptive behavior in adults with Down's syndrome. *European Journal of Psychiatry,* **8**, 197–204.

(1994b). Prevalence of thyroid dysfunction and autoimmunity in adults with Down syndrome. *Down's Syndrome: Research and Practice,* **2**(2), 67–70.

(1994c). Screening of medical problems in adults with Down syndrome. *Down's Syndrome: Research and Practice,* **2**(2), 59–66.

(1995a). Prevalence of psychiatric disorders in adults with Down syndrome. *European Journal of Psychiatry,* **9**(2), 77–82.

(1995b). Screening of hearing impairment and associated effects on adaptive behaviour in adults with Down syndrome. *British Journal of Developmental Disabilities,* **41**, 121–32.

(1995c). Reliability of diagnosing clinical hypothyroidism in adults with Down syndrome. *Australia & New Zealand Journal of Developmental Disabilities,* **20**, 223–33.

(1995d). Epilepsy and associated effects on adaptive behavior in adults with Down syndrome. *Seizure*, **4**, 53–6.

(1995e). Age-specific prevalence, thyroid dysfunction and depressive symptomatology in adults with Down syndrome and dementia. *International Journal of Geriatric Psychiatry*, **10**, 25–31.

(1999). Adaptive behavior. In *Dementia, Aging and Intellectual Disabilities: a Handbook*, ed. M.P. Janicki & A.J. Dalton, pp. 157–81. Philadelphia: Taylor and Francis.

Prasher, V.P. & Chung, M.C. (1996). Causes of age-related decline in adaptive behavior of adults with Down syndrome: differential diagnoses of dementia. *American Journal on Mental Retardation*, **101**, 175–83.

Prasher, V.P. & Corbett, J.A. (1993). Onset of seizures as a poor indicator of longevity in people with Down syndrome and dementia. *International Journal of Geriatric Psychiatry*, **8**, 923–7.

Prasher, V.P. & Day, S. (1995). Brief report: obsessive-compulsive disorder in adults with Down syndrome. *Journal of Autism and Developmental Disorders*, **25**, 453–7.

Prasher, V.P. & Hall, W. (1996). Short-term prognosis of depression in adults with Down's syndrome: association with thyroid status and effects on adaptive behavior. *Journal of Intellectual Disability Research*, **40**, 32–8.

Prasher, V.P. & Krishnan, V.H.R. (1993). Hypothyroidism presenting as dementia in a person with Down syndrome: a case report. *Mental Handicap*, **21**, 147–8.

Prasher, V.P., Krishnan, V.H.R., Clarke, D.J. & Corbett, J.A. (1993). The assessment of dementia in people with Down syndrome: changes in adaptive behaviour. *British Journal of Developmental Disabilities*, **40**, 120–30.

Rabe, A., Wisniewski, K.E., Schupf, N. & Wisniewski, H.M. (1990). Relationship of Down's syndrome to Alzheimer's disease. In *Application of Basic Neuroscience to Child Psychiatry*, ed. S.I. Deutsch, A. Weizman & R. Weizman, pp. 325–340. New York: Plenum Press.

Reisberg, B., Ferris, S.H., DeLeon, M.J., et al. (1989). The stage-specific temporal course of Alzheimer's disease: functional and behavioral concomitants based upon cross-sectional and longitudinal observation. In *Alzheimer's Disease and Related Disorders*, ed. Iqbal, K., Wisniewski, H.M. & Windblad, B., pp. 23–41. New York: Liss.

Schupf, N., Zigman, W.B., Silverman, W.P., Rabe, A. & Wisniewski, H.M. (1990). Genetic epidemiology of Alzheimer's disease. In *Aging Brain and Dementia: New Trends in Diagnosis and Therapy*, ed. L. Battistin, pp. 57–78. New York: Alan R. Liss.

Service, K.P., Lavoie, D. & Herlihy, J.E., (1999). Coping with losses, death and grieving. In *Dementia, Aging and Intellectual Disabilities: a Handbook*, ed. M.P. Janicki & A.J. Dalton, pp. 330–57. Philadelphia: Taylor and Francis.

Sim, M. (1965). Alzheimer's disease: a forgotten entity. *Geriatrics*, **20**, 668–74.

Sinex, F.M., & Merril, C.R. (eds.) (1982). Alzheimer's disease, Down's syndrome, and aging. *Annals of the New York Academy of Sciences*, **396**, 1–199.

Sourander, P., & Sjögren, H. (1975). The concept of Alzheimer's disease and its clinical implications. In *Alzheimer's Disease and Related Conditions*, ed. G.E.W. Wolstenholme and M. O'Connor, pp. 11–36. London: Churchill.

Struwe, F. (1929). Histopathlogische untersuchungen uber entstehung und wesen der senilen plaques. *Zeitschrift fur Neurologie und Psychiatrie,* **122,** 291–307.

Sultzer, D.L., Levin, H.S., Mahler, M.E., High, W.M. & Cummings, J.L. (1993). A comparison of psychiatric symptoms in vascular dementia and Alzheimer's disease. *American Journal of Psychiatry,* **150,** 1806–12.

The Arc (1995). *Developmental Disabilities and Alzheimer Disease: what you should know.* Arlington, Texas: The Arc (500 East Border Street, 76010).

Thorpe, L. (1999). Psychiatric disorders in old age: clinical applications to aging persons with intellectual disabilities. In *Dementia, Aging and Intellectual Disabilities: a Handbook,* ed. M.P. Janicki & A.J. Dalton, pp. 217–31. Philadelphia: Taylor and Francis.

Tyler, C.V. & Shank, J.C. (1996). Dementia and Down syndrome. *Journal of Family Practice,* **42,** 619–21.

Udell, L. (1999). Support people with dementia in small group home settings. In *Dementia, Aging and Intellectual Disabilities: a Handbook,* ed. M.P. Janicki & A.J. Dalton, pp. 316–29. Philadelphia: Taylor and Francis.

van Schrojenstein Lantman-de Valk, H.M., van den Akker, M., Maaskant, M.A. et al. (1997). Prevalence and incidence of health problems in people with intellectual disability. *Journal of Intellectual Disability Research,* **41,** 4251.

Visser, F.E., Aldenkamp, A.P., van Huffelen, A.C., Kuilman, M., Overweg, J. & van Wijk, J. (1997). Prospective study of the prevalence of Alzheimer-type dementia in institutionalized individuals with Down syndrome. *American Journal on Mental Retardation,* **101,** 400–12.

Whittick, J.E. (1989). Dementia and mental handicap: attitudes, emotional distress and caregiving. *British Journal of Medical Psychology,* **62,** 181–9.

Wisniewski, K.E., Dalton, A.J., Crapper McLachlan, D.R., Wen, G.Y. & Wisniewski, H.M. (1985). Alzheimer's disease in Down's syndrome: clinicopathologic studies. *Neurology,* **35,** 957–61.

World Health Organization (1992). *ICD10: International Statistical Classification of Diseases and Related Health Problems,* 10th revision. Geneva: WHO.

Yankner, B.A. (1996). Mechanisms of neuronal degeneration in Alzheimer's disease. *Neuron,* **16,** 921–32.

Zigman, W.B., Schupf, N., Lubin, R.A. & Silverman, W. (1987) Premature regression of adults with Down syndrome. *American Journal of Mental Deficiency,* **92,** 161–8.

Zigman, W.B., Schupf, N., Sersen, E. & Silverman, W. (1995). Prevalence of dementia in adults with and without Down syndrome. *American Journal on Mental Retardation,* **100,** 403–12.

Part 3 **Diagnosis and psychopathology**

9 Psychopathology of children with developmental disabilities

BRUCE J. TONGE

Introduction

There is no doubt that emotional and behavioural problems are a significant extra dimension that burdens the lives of many children with developmental disability and their families and carers. Young people with developmental disabilities have about three times as much psychiatric disturbance as children of average intelligence. Rutter, Tizard, and Whitmore (1970), in their Isle of Wight population study, found that 50 per cent of children with developmental disabilities with an IQ below 70 had a psychiatric disorder, compared with 6.8 per cent of children with an IQ above 70. Corbett (1979), in a study of the urban area of South-East London, found a prevalence rate of psychiatric disorder, of 47 per cent in children aged up to 15 years with IQ below 50.

A recent epidemiological study of developmentally disabled Australian children aged between four and 18 years found that 41 per cent had a clinically significant emotional or behavioural disorder (Einfeld & Tonge, 1996). The study also found that disruptive and antisocial behaviours were more common in young people with mild developmental disabilities but self-absorbed and social relating problem behaviours were more common in those with more severe developmental disability. In contrast to general childhood psychopathology, age and sex did not affect prevalence. Of concern was that fewer than 10 per cent of these children with developmental disabilities had received any specialist mental health services.

Phenomenology

Children with developmental disability can suffer from the full range of psychopathological disorders experienced by children of normal intelligence. Anxiety disorders, depression and bipolar affective disorders, attention deficit hyperactivity disorder, schizophrenia and psychotic disorders have all been described in young people with developmental disability (Matson & Barrett, 1982). Developmental disability is also present in at least

70 per cent of cases of autism (Prior & Tonge, 1990). However, there remains a lack of agreement on a common approach to the classification and diagnosis of the range of disturbed emotions and behaviours exhibited. There are some patterns of disturbed emotions and behaviours in young people with developmental disabilities that cannot be adequately described by current psychiatric diagnostic systems such as the ICD-10 (World Health Organization, 1992) and the DSM-IV (American Psychiatric Association, 1994). The validity of these two major systems of psychiatric diagnosis is yet to be demonstrated when applied to young people with developmental disabilities.

The types of psychopathological disorders in children with mild developmental disabilities are more likely to resemble those found in the general population. As the level of disability becomes more severe, language and communication impairment and the inability to share with others the content of their thinking and emotional experience make it increasingly difficult for the clinician to apply existing diagnostic classifications confidently. A supplement to the ICD-10 has recently been published – *The ICD-10 Guide for Mental Retardation*, (World Health Organization, 1996). This is an important attempt to approach this issue but further research is required in order to establish if certain behavioural problems are more common, or even unique, in people with developmental disability. If this is established, then the development of a new taxonomy of psychiatric syndromes or disorders will be required (McLean, 1990; Rutter, 1991). An example of such a new psychopathological disorder included in ICD-10 is 'over active disorder associated with mental retardation and stereotype movements' (World Health Organization. 1992).

Another approach to the description of emotional and behavioural problems is the quantitative taxonometric model based on the statistical analysis of symptom questionnaires collected on defined populations of young people with developmental disabilities

An example of this approach has recently been provided in a study by Tonge et al. (1996), who used the Developmental Behavior Checklist (DBC), a reliable and valid 96-item questionnaire of emotional and behavioural problems in young people with developmental disability that is completed by parents or carers (Einfeld & Tonge, 1993). Factor analysis of questionnaire data from 1093 children and adolescents with developmental disability derived six factors, which included items describing behaviours and symptoms that were each predominantly consistent with a cohesive dimension of disturbance. Each of these factors or subscales was then labelled with a term chosen to best describe the nature of the symptoms included in that factor. Analysis of DBC questionnaires on 194 children (4–19 years) who were defined as suffering from a clinically significant level of emotional and behavioural problems, from an epidemiological sample of 450 Australian children with developmental disability, revealed that over 80 per cent of

Table 9.1 Distribution of subscale scores (syndromes) of the DBC in an epidemiological sample of Australian children (aged 4–19 years) with clinically significant psychopathology

Subscale	Percentage
Positive score on one subscale	
1 Disruptive	22.7
2 Self-absorbed	13.4
3 Language disturbance	6.7
4 Anxiety	23.2
5 Social relating	10.8
6 Antisocial	3.6
Total positive score on one subscale	80.4
Positive scores on two subscales	14.4
Positive scores on three subscales	3.1
No positive scores	2.1

$n=194$, from a total of $n=450$.

these clinical cases presented with a factor score profile that predominantly focused on one factor or subscale. For example, Table 9.1 shows that 22.7 per cent of the children defined as psychiatric cases had a predominant positive score on the disruptive subscale, indicating that demanding and disruptive behaviours were a key feature of their presentation.

This study also found that 23.2 per cent of the young people who were cases (i.e. 10.1 per cent of the overall epidemiological sample of children with developmental disability aged 4–19 years) had psychopathology in which symptoms of anxiety were the predominant feature. Further study of these data showed that there was no sex difference in the distribution of anxiety but its prevalence decreased significantly with age through to late adolescence. Anxiety was approximately equally distributed through mild and moderate levels of developmental disability but was significantly less prevalent with more severe levels. These findings are in contrast to repeated studies of the general population of young people in whom the prevalence of anxiety disorder is about 2–5 per cent, and amongst whom females are twice as likely as males to suffer anxiety (Tonge, 1988). Although these subscales cannot be regarded at this stage as categorical psychiatric disorders, they are likely to indicate specific groups of problematic disturbance, which might then have implications for research and treatment. Similar groupings of disturbed behaviours and symptoms have been found in other factor analytic studies of descriptive/empirical questionnaires, which tends to support the validity of this approach to the description of patterns of psychopathology in developmentally disabled children (Aman, 1991).

Clinical assessment

The clinical interview is the essential component in diagnosis and assessment and is therefore necessary in the process of deciding on a rational management and treatment plan. The presence and severity of developmental disability in the child necessitates some modification of a routine child psychiatric assessment and mental state examination. Information from the parents or carers and direct observation of the child, preferably in a variety of settings such as at school as well as at the clinician's office, are essential.

Cox and Rutter (1985) have demonstrated that the combined use of non-directive interview techniques together with more directive and structured questions, supplemented by parent and teacher completed checklists, provides the most comprehensive information and significantly improves assessment and diagnosis. This combined, unstructured and structured approach is still effective in promoting rapport and the expression of affect.

This work has been replicated in an analysis of 70 psychiatric assessments of children with developmental disability (Einfeld & Tonge, 1993). The non-directive interview component of the assessment revealed parental concern regarding an average of nine symptoms, compared to an average of 35 symptoms scored by the parents on a DBC they had previously completed (Einfeld & Tonge, 1993). The use of a parent or carer completed checklist such as the DBC clearly enriches the clinical assessment process, and parents reported that they felt the problems they faced had been fully explored and understood.

A framework for the clinical assessment is presented in Table 9.2.

It is useful during part of the assessment to interview the parents or carers and the child together, and if the child can manage the separation, it is essential to see the child individually. Information from others, such as teachers, provides a broader perspective as well as information on contextual elements of the child's emotional or behavioural problems, and more resilient and adaptive behaviour. A comprehensive cognitive assessment is also necessary in order to place the child's behaviour into a developmental perspective and to understand the influence and impact of any cognitive impairments or specific pattern of cognitive performance on behaviour, communication and comprehension. For example, children with autism usually have better visual and performance skills, than verbal and social comprehension skills, which can account for some of their frustration and difficult behaviour and has implications for education and management.

Assessments of communication and motor skills can also add considerable information to the overall picture. To date, there are no standardized general psychiatric assessment interviews validated for use with young people with developmental disability. The parents version of the Anxiety Disorders Interview Schedule (Albano & Silverman, 1996), which provides an algorithm for DSM-IV diagnoses, is being used in some clinical studies of

Table 9.2 Clinical assessment

Interview with parent(s)/carers

Presenting problems: detailed description, antecedents, context, consequences

Mental state: anxieties and worries, fears, mood, anger and aggression, perceptual disturbances and sensitivities

Behavioural review: appetite and eating, sleep, bowel and bladder control, play and interests, family/carer/sibling attachment, socialization and friendships, activity level, learning and school adjustment, concentration and impulsiveness, behavioural control, disruptiveness and compliance, repetitive and compulsive behaviour, response to change, motor skills and co-ordination, sexual behaviours, episodic/cyclical phenomena

Developmental history: pregnancy, birth, attachment behaviour and separations, milestones, cognition and learning, medical illnesses/treatment, communication and socialization, abuse/neglect and alternative care

Family history: (best completed during family meeting), genogram, parental health, mental health and relationship, family illnesses, mental illness, learning problems, genetic disorders, siblings, social and cultural context support and adversity

Parent/carer-completed questionnaires (e.g. DBC)

Interview with child

Rapport building: discussion, play

School experience: friends, learning, play, teasing

Mental state: observation, worries/anxieties, fears, mood, anger, perceptual disturbance (e.g. hallucinations, delusions)

Play: free and structured (e.g. form boards), drawing (squiggle, draw a person, draw a dream), motor skills (catching, hopping, pencil grip)

Medical/neurological examination

Other investigations (as indicated)

Teachers reports

Psychological/cognitive assessment

Medical investigations (e.g. EEG, chromosome analysis, metabolic studies)

Multidisciplinary case conference

Complete multiaxial diagnosis

DSM-IV (American Psychiatric Association, 1994)	ICD-10 (World Health Organization, 1996)
Axis 1: clinical disorders	Axis 1: severity of retardation and problem behaviours
Axis 2: personality disorders and mental retardation	Axis 2: associated medical conditions
Axis 3: general medical conditions	Axis 3: associated psychiatric disorders
Axis 4: psychosocial and environmental problems	Axis 4: global assessment of psychosocial disability
Axis 5: global assessment of functioning scale	Axis 5: associated abnormal psychosocial situations

anxiety disorders in children with moderate or less severe levels of developmental disability. In the specific area of autism spectrum disorders, Lord, Rutter and Le Couteur (1994) have developed the Autism Diagnostic Instrument (ADI), which comprises a structured parental interview and an observation of the child. The ADI provides a reliable and valid diagnosis of pervasive developmental disorders. It requires a skilled clinician to administer and is appropriately time consuming, given the complexity and the serious implications of this diagnosis.

The application of current psychiatric classification becomes more difficult as the severity of developmental disability increases. At profound levels of developmental disability, a form of organic brain syndrome is the only diagnosis that is likely to be made with any reliability.

It is evident that the psychiatric assessment of young people with developmental disability is complex, and requires information from all those involved in their care, as well as detailed mental state, psychological, developmental and physical assessment of the child. This process is usually of necessity a multidisciplinary one, requiring contributions from psychiatrists, psychologists, paediatricians and, when appropriate, others such as speech pathologists, occupational therapists, physiotherapists and special teachers. To be effective, this multidisciplinary assessment requires co-ordination, usually through a case conference in which one of the specialist clinicians is designated as the case manager.

Assessment issues

There is usually a range of contextual problems and factors that influence and complicate the presentation of emotional and behavioural problems in young people with developmental disability, which need to be taken into account in order to achieve a satisfactory assessment diagnosis and a rational treatment plan. (Tonge & Einfeld, 1991).[1]

Developmental level and cognitive ability

The diagnosis of many psychiatric disorders requires an assessment of the person's thought processes and content. This may be possible in a mildly developmentally disabled child with some communication skills, but becomes progessively more difficult as the level of disability becomes more severe. Costello (1982) argues that it is impossible to diagnose schizophrenia in people with an IQ under 45 because their lack of cognitive and verbal ability makes it virtually impossible for thought disorder, delusional thinking, and for any perceptual abnormality such as auditory hallucinations to be assessed. Similar problems apply to the diagnosis of affective disorder, for which impaired communication skill and concrete thinking, even in the

---

1. Parts reproduced with permission of the *Journal of Developmental Disability*.

more able, makes it difficult, if not impossible, for the developmentally dis-abled young people to describe their feelings. The clinician must often rely on observation of behaviour and signs such as changes in appetite, sleep and activity level, as well as observed mood, to make a presumptive diagnosis of affective disorder (Costello, 1982; Sovner, 1986). The developmental level of a child must also be taken into account when assessing the significance of problem behaviours. Normal behaviours in young children, such as separa-tion anxiety or short attention span, may be seen in a much older child with developmental disability who is still functioning at that younger develop-mental level. This is recognised by some of the diagnostic categories in DSM-IV (American Psychiatric Association, 1994) and ICD-10 (World Health Organization, 1992) such as autistic disorder and attention deficit hyper-activity disorder, which indicate that the criteria for these disorders are only met if the behaviour is abnormal for a person of the same mental age and developmental level. The assessment of antisocial, aggressive and defiant behaviour should take into account the child's developmental level when making a diagnosis of conduct disorder. The capacity of the child to under-stand social rules and right from wrong usually excludes children with autism or more severe levels of developmental disability from the diagnosis of conduct disorder. In some children, organic deterioration of cognitive ability, or behavioural consequences of puberty and hormones may also cause psychopathological symptoms and complicate or alter response to treatment.

Multiple disabilities and medical illness

Children and adolescents with developmental disability are more likely than the general population to have a range of physical and sensory impairments and medical illnesses that handicap their lives and complicate the assessment of emotional and behavioural problems (Sovner & Hurley, 1989). For example, deafness may lead to behaviour that is seen in autistic children or children with conduct disorder. Hearing impairment may also aggravate psychiatric disorders such as a separation anxiety. Children with developmental disability are much more likely to have medical illnesses or abnormalities of the brain such as epilepsy. Children in the general popula-tion with chronic illness that affects the brain have a higher prevalence of associated psychiatric disorder (Tonge, 1991). In particular, epilepsy can cause disturbed behaviour and can aggravate existing emotional and behav-ioural problems. Down syndrome is associated with an increased risk of the development of Alzheimer's dementia (Rubin, 1987). Autism is associated with a range of medical conditions such as tuberous sclerosis and other psychiatric conditions such as Tourette syndrome (Prior & Tonge, 1990). Specific patterns of behaviour are also evident as the behavioural phenotypic expression of some genetic disorders associated with developmental disabil-ity, for example shyness in children with fragile X syndrome (Einfeld, Tonge

& Florio, 1994), and insomnia and irrepressibility in children with William's syndrome (Einfeld, Tonge & Florio, 1997). Developmentally disabled children may also not be able to communicate effectively that they are suffering from pain or the symptoms of a fever or physical illness. Instead, they may exhibit disturbed behaviour such as irritability, restlessness, or withdrawal, which may be misunderstood as being due to a psychiatric disorder.

Psychosocial and family factors

Children and adolescents with developmental disability are more likely than the general population to experience a range of psychosocial stresses and environmental experiences that adversely affect their personality development, emotional adjustment and attachment behaviour and can result in impoverished or distorted and inappropriate social behaviour (Sovner, 1986; Aman & Schroeder, 1990). The families of children living in alternative residential care may not be available for interview to provide reliable developmental and family histories. Institutional records often give an unreliable and inadequate account of the person's history. Observation and assessment of the child's interaction with the family, or with staff and residents of the alternative care environment, are essential in order to understand the behaviour and psychosocial context and the contribution that these interactions make to the psychopathology. For example, in response to environmental stress, some children with developmental disability may experience a regression and disintegration of their already impaired cognition, resulting in bizarre and psychotic-like behaviour that can be misdiagnosed as schizophrenia. Another child might be withdrawn, listless and apathetic in response to parental overprotection and lack of stimulation. Environmental deprivation and abuse, and a lack of stimulation and opportunity for play, activity and socialization, aggravate developmental disability, prevent children from reaching their full potential, and lead to a range of attachment, personality, emotional and behavioural problems and handicaps.

Management principles

Successful management begins with the establishment of a positive relationship with the parents and carers and, if possible, the child during the assessment process. A working diagnosis that takes into account the biological, psychological and social contributing factors and context, provides the key to a rational management plan. Treatment is usually multimodal, requiring a combination of parent support and skills training, behavioural interventions, modifications to the social and educational environment, modified psychological treatments and, as a second line of treatment in combination with psychological and supported management, the use of psychoactive medication when indicated (Table 9.3).

Some young people with moderate or less severe levels of developmental

Table 9.3 Approaches to management

Assessment and diagnosis

Behaviour analysis and management

Cognitive–behavioural therapy modified according to level of developmental disability (e.g. relaxation, modelling, behavioural reinforcement, positive statements, social skills)

Communication, motor, sensory–integrative skills training

Special education

Parent education, support and skills training

Family therapy

Social support (e.g. respite care, home help)

Psychotropic drugs, judicious selection, follow-up to monitor compliance, side-effects and response

Consultation and case conferencing with parents, carers and other professionals

disability have sufficient communication skill and understanding of consequences to be able to benefit from a modified form of cognitive behavioural therapy. This involves a combination of relaxation training, modelling and reinforcement of confident and prosocial behaviours, formulating positive self-thoughts and statements instead of negative attributions, and providing a structured experience of rewarding educational and social activities and skills.

There is no evidence that family therapy has a direct effect, but it does reduce family dysfunction and conflict and modify problematic family interactional patterns, such as parental overprotection, which contribute to psychopathology in the child. The provision to the parents of educational information on developmental disability in general, and on the nature of the developmental disability and the psychopathological disorder in their child in particular, helps the parents generate their own adaptive responses and co-operate as partners with a range of services in the management of their child. A co-operative working relationship with the parents does make it more likely that they will feel encouraged to share their grief regarding their child's disability, and this in itself is also therapeutic. Counselling and the provision of psychological and educational interventions for siblings may also be necessary to promote family functioning.

Behaviour management using operant conditioning techniques can be an effective strategy for managing difficult behaviours. The design of an effective behaviour-modification programme requires a detailed behavioural analysis regarding the context, the communication intent of the behaviour, consequences that reinforce the behaviour, the response by others to the behaviour, and the longer term consequences of the behaviour.

There is a secondary role for drug treatment, but it should form part of a broader psychotherapeutic and supportive management plan. Most research on the use of pharmacotherapy in children with developmental disability is focused on aggression and self-injurious behaviours. Controlled trials of haloperidol have shown that it is effective in the treatment of aggression, hyperactivity and stereotypic behaviours, particularly in developmentally disabled children with autism, although this neuroleptic drug is associated with a significant rate of parkinsonism (30 per cent approximately) and other troublesome side-effects (Campbell et al., 1993). Lithium, carbamazepine, beta-blockers such as propranolol and the alpha-2-adrenergic agonist clonidine, have been shown (mostly in open trials) to reduce aggressive, disruptive and agitated behaviour. Opiate agonists and antagonists (e.g. naloxone and naltrexone) may have some role in reducing self-injurious behaviours (Botteron & Geller, 1993). Stimulant drugs such as dexamphetamine and methylphenidate may be useful in the treatment of unequivocal attention deficit and hyperactivity symptoms (Birmaher, Quintana & Greenville, 1988; Dulcan, 1990). A favourable response to stimulant medication in developmentally disabled children and those with autism who also have attention deficit hyperactivity disorder may not be as marked as in children with attention deficit hyperactivity disorder who do not have developmental disabilities. In young people with more severe developmental disability, stimulant drugs may even exacerbate stereotypic and disturbed behaviour. Anxious and obsessional behaviour in developmentally disabled young people, particularly those with autism, may respond to treatment with selective serotonin reuptake inhibitors such as fluoxetine, and the older tricyclic antidepressants such as clomipramine and imipramine, but firm evidence from controlled trials is still required, and it is not clear if these reported therapeutic effects are due to specific effects on serotonin metabolism. Drug treatment requires regular follow-up and monitoring for compliance, the development of side-effects and therapeutic response. It is preferable to document the therapeutic response through the use of behavioural observations and a symptom checklist.

Case examples

The application of the clinical principles outlined in this chapter is highlighted in the following four case studies.

1. Susan, aged seven years

Susan was reported by the school psychologist to have a severe degree of developmental disability and little functional language. She was integrated into a rural primary school. She did not participate in educational or social activities, and sat at the back of the class on a rubber mat because she was incontinent. Susan spent most of her time rocking, being withdrawn and 'nodding off to sleep'. Both the teacher and the school psychologist were concerned that she might have autism or a degenerative condition. Her parents reported that her behaviour was similar at home. Her birth was a complicated forceps delivery due to failure to progress in labour, and there was associated perinatal cerebral anoxia. She was an irritable baby with delayed developmental milestones, but did form a reciprocal attachment with her parents and showed emerging play and social skills. She had a series of grand mal epileptic seizures between 18 months and two years of age, and was placed on anticonvulsant medication. The family then moved to a small country town, and although she remained on a low dose of anticonvulsant medication, a specialist neurologist did not review her epilepsy again. When this was finally reviewed as part of this assessment, it was found on EEG that she was having frequent epileptic activity and complex partial seizures which were associated with incontinence, cognitive impairment and behavioural withdrawal and disturbance. The re-introduction of a therapeutic level of anticonvulsant medication produced a dramatic therapeutic response, with improvements in her cognitive ability, communication and social skills, mood and behaviour, and capacity to enjoy life. Her teacher even jokingly complained that she had become assertive in pushing to join in all the classroom activities. Subsequent cognitive assessment revealed that the level of her developmental disability was in the moderate range.

The next two examples are teenage boys who were referred with the same problem behaviour, that of masturbating in public.

2. Bill, aged 13 years

Bill had a moderate degree of developmental disability, with some basic language skills, and attended a special school. He lived with his mother and father and two younger siblings. The cause of his developmental disability was not known, although he had some dysmorphic features and was a tall, ungainly and clumsy boy for his age. The school and his parents referred him because he was masturbating in public. This activity was solitary and in the context of general social withdrawal, but occurred in public places, such as an isolated corner of the school grounds and the back corner of a supermarket.

The parents completed the DBC, which provided a score of 44 with 38 problem items checked. These comprised 22 emotional disturbance items (internalising symptoms), 1 social relating problem item and 14 disturbed behaviour items (externalising problems). The items that received the highest score – of 2, being very true or often true – related to Bill appearing depressed and unhappy, crying easily, being irritable, lacking self-confidence with poor self-esteem, and loss of appetite (with weight loss of around 2 kg over the past six months). Bill also had frequent temper tantrums and the questionnaire revealed that he was generally distressed and anxious, had some nightmares, had become fearful about going to school and leaving the house and becoming separated from his mother. These behaviours had been getting worse over the preceding 12 months.

Bill presented as a dejected and depressed-looking boy, who was listless and appeared to have no energy. He was generally withdrawn and showed no interest in toys or play activity. He became distressed and anxious when separated from his parents and spent some time crying. His parents claimed that he had told them he wished he was dead, although it was not possible during the assessment to get him to communicate verbally, other than with some occasional monosyllabic answers.

His symptoms and presentation fulfilled the DSM-IV diagnostic criteria for a dysthymic disorder. There were some contributing family factors. His paternal grandmother and a paternal uncle had both been treated for depressive illness. Bill's emotional disorder began about 18 months earlier, at about the time of onset of puberty. Growth and hormonal changes of puberty may have contributed to his depression, but at that time his parents also began to have increasing unresolved parental conflict about a number of interpersonal and financial problems. This marital conflict had led to brief marital separation on two occasions. Therefore, Bill's depressive illness had occurred in the context of a probable genetic predisposition, but was also influenced by the biological and psychological impact of puberty and significant interactional distress, consequent upon parental marital conflict.

Treatment involved the use of a tricyclic antidepressant (imipramine), participation in a social skills training group, and a behavioural programme at school and at home aimed at building self-esteem through setting achievable tasks and rewarding and positively commenting on all achievements, no matter how small. The parents were also keen to seek help for their marital difficulties and were able to resolve these after a few sessions of marital therapy. Bill made a good response to these treatments and within four weeks, was more cheerful and positive, had regained his appetite and was sleeping well, had more energy and was interested in social relationships. He no longer engaged in self-preoccupied masturbation in public.

3. Brian, aged 15 years

Brian had a moderate level of developmental disability and simple language skills. He lived with his parents and attended a special school. His mother suffered toxaemia during the pregnancy. His birth was prolonged and complicated and he may have suffered some degree of cerebral anoxia.

His parents completed the DBC, which revealed a total score of 62. A total of 35 behavioural problems (externalizing) were identified, and 2 emotional problems (internalizing) and 8 social relating problem behaviours were described. Most of the disturbed behaviour items related to disruptive over-active behaviour with associated distractibility and limited attention span. He was noisy and boisterous, particularly in the family meeting, interrupting his parents with a mixture of sounds and simple phrases. He was also aggressive, unco-operative and generally very difficult to manage by both his parents and teachers. His masturbatory behaviour, which led to the referral, was not frequent but occurred as a provocative and threatening act towards his female teacher and also a party of young girls having a picnic in a park near the family home, from which he had run away. Both the parents and the school believed that it might be better for Brian to be cared for in a community residential unit. Brian presented as a wiry boy for his age, who acted as if he was driven by a motor. He could not sit still and focus on any task, particularly when he was together with his parents in a room that contained many toys and other items of interest. In a small, confined room, bare except for table and chairs, he was able to focus better on items such as a form board when these were individually shown to him, although he generally remained easily distracted. Neurological examination revealed some soft neurological signs and clumsiness, more marked on the right side of his body. Further detailed neurological assessment failed to find any specific neurological disorder. He had entered puberty 9–12 months earlier.

Brian was the youngest child in the family, with two older brothers in their early twenties who had not experienced any developmental difficulty. There was no family history of any physical or psychiatric illnesses. His parents had a good and effective relationship and there were no significant interactional difficulties in the family. Brian had always been an overactive and easily distracted boy, but since entering puberty this behaviour had become significantly worse and, with his larger body size, he was more difficult to manage.

Taking his moderate degree of developmental disability into account, his symptoms were still excessive for a child of his mental age, and therefore a DSM-IV diagnosis of attention deficit hyperactivity disorder could be made. It is possible that hormonal and other biological changes of puberty had produced a worsening of his behaviour. Increase in body size and new behavioural problems of a sexual nature made him more difficult to manage at home and school, and created anxiety for both parents and teachers, who had previously been able to contain and manage him. On the basis of this assessment, he received a trial of a stimulant medication (methylphenidate), which produced a rapid and dramatic improvement in his behaviour. He became less active and his attention span improved, particularly in one-to-one or small-group teaching situations in which there was a focused activity and no distractions in the surrounding environment. A behaviour-modification programme, based on a combination of reducing environmental stimulation and providing a range of separate enjoyable tasks for which his performance was rewarded, was instituted. His father also involved Brian in a daily exercise programme of swimming in a private pool, where there were no other distractions, and bicycle riding in a quiet park. These activities were undertaken in consultation with a physiotherapist, who also provided a remedial gymnasium programme at the school. All of these interventions combined to create a significant improvement in Brian's behaviour, which could be contained by his parents and teachers. The use of stimulant medication was kept under review and its effectiveness was tested by occasional periods off the medication.

4. Darren, aged 16 years

Darren was referred because of disruptive behaviour, particularly in the environment of the residential unit in which he lived. Over the past year, he increasingly had arguments with the other residents and, when reprimanded by the staff and put into his bedroom for time out, he would become angry and lose control, smashing furniture, breaking windows, kicking doors and walls. After up to an hour of rage, he would calm down and then usually become remorseful and emotionally upset about the episode. He had a mild degree of developmental disability and attended a special school. His educational progress was not as good as might be expected, given his relatively mild degree of developmental disability documented on psychological assessment. He was socially confident, at times beyond the level of his social competence and skill, and this led to problems. For example, he would abscond and take public transport, claiming he was looking for a relative, but end up getting lost. His father and three younger siblings lived in another state.

The care staff of the residential unit completed the DBC. This revealed a score of 39, with 15 problems in the emotional (internalizing) problem area and 18 items of disturbed behaviour (externalizing) being identified. The major behaviours identified were that he was often downcast and unhappy, with poor self-esteem, and showed frequent mood changes, and that he also frequently had tempers and was irritable. Staff had heard him talk on several occasions about killing himself, after angry outbursts. He was reported to make up stories about what he had been doing and was regarded as untrustworthy by the staff. The record of his past history was inadequate. The record revealed that he had a mild degree of developmental delay and was rather overactive during childhood, but was otherwise no problem for his parents. His mother died in a motor-car accident when Darren was aged nine. His behaviour began to deteriorate in early secondary school and his father requested alternative care for Darren when he was 13. At that time he was reported to be irritable and aggressive, frequently absconded from home and was threatening towards the young children of the woman with whom his father was living and subsequently married. His father, stepmother and all the other children in the family moved to another state shortly after Darren was placed in a residential unit. Since then, he had only occasional contact with his father and had not been given his telephone number or address.

Darren presented as a tall, rather thin young man. He was initially inappropriately overfriendly, demonstrating clumsy social skills. He embellished accounts of events and it was obvious that at times he made up stories to put himself in a favourable light. He had few, if any, friends, although he was very keen to visit places where young people gathered, such as a local shopping centre, and observe and try to participate in the activities of these young people. He became upset when talking of his father and it became clear that he could not understand why his father had gone to live in another state, without taking him with the family. When asked to draw a picture of a bad dream (Tonge, 1982), he produced the drawing in Figure 9.1. He said 'I'm in mum's car on the way from her work. A truck was out of the lane. There was a crash. Mum died.' He spoke with increasing distress about the motor-car accident in which his mother died. He was also in the car, but was lucky to escape uninjured. He observed his mother being covered by a sheet and taken away in the ambulance, never to see her again. He was not allowed to go to the funeral. He claimed that often he would go out to try to look for the cemetery where his mother is buried, although he had no idea where that is. He was asked to draw a picture of himself, showing how he still felt about his mother's death. He drew a picture of himself crying, with a puddle of tears at his feet, saying that he was 'very unhappy 100 per cent'.

Fig. 9.1

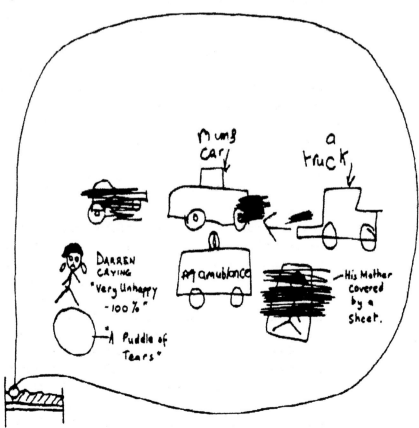

Darren presented with a depressive disorder that fulfilled the DSM-IV criteria for dysthymia. This was in the setting of prolonged psychosocial stress, beginning with the death of his mother. He had not been able to resolve his loss satisfactorily and the process of grief and mourning had been further complicated by rejection from his family and his placement in a residential unit that had frequently changing staff. A number of different treatment approaches was needed in order to help him recover from this complex psychological disorder, from which he had suffered for seven years of his life. A night-time dose of tricyclic antidepressant (imipramine) was prescribed. A behavioural programme was provided that focused on relaxation skills and training for anger management, which included some aspects of cognitive therapy that taught him to say positive things about himself. It was realised that Darren's superficial social confidence covered some significant deficits in social skills, so arrangements were made for him to attend a social skills training group at his school. He attended fortnightly for some brief psychotherapy aimed at helping him ventilate his grief, anger and distress about events in his life such as his mother's death and his father moving away. Arrangements were made for him to visit his mother's grave. The supervisor of the residential unit went to considerable effort to contact the father and, after some initial difficulty, managed to get the father to contact Darren on a regular basis by telephone. Finally, regular holidays with his father were arranged. This treatment process took about 12 months, but at the end of that time Darren had become a co-operative and helpful member of the residential unit, was making significant educational progress at school, and was exhibiting social behaviour more appropriate to a young adolescent.

Conclusion

There is no doubt that psychiatric disorder is a major source of distress, extra handicap and burden for young people with developmental disabilities and their families, carers and teachers. Considerable research is required to understand further the epidemiology, phenomenology, classification, aetiology and treatment of this psychopathology. However, by taking a comprehensive biopsychosocial approach to the assessment of these often complex emotional and behavioural problems, a diagnosis and multidimensional formulation become possible, which then provide the basis for a rational treatment and management plan.

References

Albano, A.M. & Silverman, W.K. (1996). *Anxiety Disorders Interview Schedule for DSM-IV: Clinicians' Manual.* San Antonio: The Psychological Corporation, Harcourt Brace & Company.
Aman, M.G. (1991). Review and evaluation of instruments for assessing emotional

and behavioural disorders. *Australian and New Zealand Journal of Developmental Disabilities,* **17**, 127–45.

Aman, M.G. & Schroeder, S.R. (1990). Specific learning disorders and mental retardation. In *Handbook of Studies on Child Psychiatry,* ed. B J. Tonge, G. D. Burrows & J. Werry, pp 209–24. Amsterdam: Elsevier.

American Psychiatric Association (1994). *Diagnostic and Statistical Manual of Mental Disorders,* 4th edn. Washington, DC: APA.

Birmaher, B., Quintana, H. & Greenville, L.L. (1988). Methylphenidate treatment of hyperactive autistic children. *Journal of the American Academy of Child and Adolescent Psychiatry,* **27**, 248–51.

Botteron, K. & Geller, B. (1993). Disorders, symptoms and their pharmacotherapy. In *Practitioner's Guide to Psychoactive Drugs for Children and Adolescents,* eds Werry J. and Aman M., pp. 179–201. New York: Plenum Medical.

Campbell, N., Gonzales, N.M., Bernst N., Silva R. R., & Werry J.S. (1993). Antipsychotics (neuroleptics) In *Practitioners' Guide to Psychoactive Drugs for Children and Adolescents,* ed. J. Werry M. Aman, pp. 269–96. New York: Plenum Medical.

Corbett, J.A. (1979). Psychiatric morbidity and mental retardation. In *Psychotherapy in the Mentally Retarded,* ed. F.E. James & R.P. Snaith, pp. 28–45. New York: Grune and Stratton.

Costello, A. (1982). Assessment and diagnosis of psychopathology. In *Psychopathology in the Mentally Retarded,* ed. J.L. Matson & R.P. Barrett, pp. 37–52. New York: Grune and Stratton.

Cox, A. & Rutter, M. (1985). Diagnostic appraisal and interviewing. In *Child and Adolescent Psychiatry: Modern Approaches,* 2nd edn, ed. M. Rutter & L. Hersov, pp. 233–47. Oxford: Blackwell Scientific Publications.

Dulcan, M.K. (1990). Using psycho-stimulants to treat behavioural disorders of children and adolescents. *Journal of Child and Adolescent Psychopharmacology,* **1**, 7–20.

Einfeld, S.L. & Tonge, B.J. (1993). *Manual for the Developmental Behaviour Checklist.* Melbourne: Centre for Developmental Psychiatry, Monash University; Sydney: School of Psychiatry, University of New South Wales.

(1996). Population prevalence of psychopathology in children and adolescents with intellectual disability. II Epidemiological findings. *Journal of Intellectual Disability Research,* **40** (2), 99–109.

Einfeld, S.L., Tonge, B.J. & Florio, T. (1994). Behavioural and emotional disturbance in fragile X syndrome. *American Journal of Medical Genetics,* **51**, 386–91.

(1997). Behavioural and emotional disturbance in individuals with Williams syndrome. *American Journal on Mental Retardation,* **102**(1), 45–53.

Lord, C., Rutter, M. & Le Couteur, A. (1994). Autism Diagnostic Interview–Revised: a revised version of a diagnostic interview for caregivers of individuals with possible pervasive developmental disorders. *Journal of Autism and Developmental Disorders,* **24**(5), 659–85.

Matson, J.L. & Barrett, R.P. (eds.) (1982). *Psychopathology in the Mentally Retarded.* New York: Grune and Stratton.

McLean, W.E. Jr (1990). Issues in the assessment of aberrant behaviour among persons with mental retardation. In *Assessment of Behavior Problems in Persons with Mental Retardation Living in the Community,* ed. E. Dibble & D.B. Gray, pp. 135–45. Rockville, MD: NIMH.

Prior, M. & Tonge, B.J. (1990). Pervasive developmental disorders. In *Handbook of Studies on Child Psychiatry,* ed. B.J. Tonge, G.D. Burrows & J.S. Werry, pp 193–208. Amsterdam: Elsevier.

Rubin, L.I. (1987). Health care needs of adults with mental retardation. *Mental Retardation,* **25,** 201–6.

Rutter, M. (1991). Annotation: child psychiatric disorders in ICD-10. *Journal of Child Psychology and Psychiatry,* 30, 499–513.

Rutter, M., Tizard, J., & Whitmore, K. (1970). *Education Health and Behaviour.* London: Longman.

Sovner, R. (1986). Limiting factors in the use of DSM III criteria with mentally ill/mentally retarded persons. *Psychopharmacology Bulletin,* **22,** 1055–9.

Sovner, R. & Hurley, A.D. (1989). Ten diagnostic principles for recognizing psychiatric disorder in mentally retarded persons. *Psychiatric Aspects of Mental Retardation Reviews,* **8,** 9–13.

Tonge, B.J. (1982). Draw a dream: an intervention promoting change in families in conflict. In *The International Book of Family Therapy,* ed. F.W. Kaslow, pp 212–26. New York: Brunnel/Mazel.

(1988). Anxiety in adolescence. In *Handbook of Anxiety* Vol. 2. *Classification, Etiological Factors and Associated Disturbances,* ed. R. Noyes, M. Roth, – G.D. Burrows, pp 269–88. Amsterdam: Elsevier.

(1991). Children with physical impairments. In *Handbook of Studies on General Hospital Psychiatry,* ed. F.K. Judd, G.D. Burrows & D.R. Lipsitt, pp. 195–206. Amsterdam: Elsevier.

Tonge, B.J. & Einfeld, S. (1991). Intellectual disability and psychopathology in Australian children. *Australia and New Zealand Journal of Developmental Disabilities,* 17, (2) 155–67.

Tonge, B.J., Einfeld, S.L., Krupinski J. et al. (1996). The use of factor analysis for ascertaining patterns of psychopathology in children with intellectual disability. *Journal of Intellectual Disability Research,* 40(3), 198–207.

World Health Organization (1992). *The ICD-10 Classification of Mental and Behavioural Disorders.* Geneva: WHO.

World Health Organization (1996). *The CD-10 Guide for Mental Retardation.* Geneva: WHO.

10 Depression, anxiety and adjustment disorders in people with developmental disabilities

CHRISSOULA STAVRAKAKI

Introduction

Depression, anxiety and adjustment disorders are more prevalent amongst people with developmental disabilities than in the general population (Tu & Zellweger, 1965; O'Dwyer, Holmes & Collacott, 1992; Gedye, 1993; Stavrakaki & Mintsioulis, 1995). This has been the case for most psychiatric disorders (Singh et al. 1991; Vitello & Behar, 1992; Einfeld, 1992; King et al., 1994; Gitta & Goldberg, 1995; Sovner & Harley, 1989; Stavrakaki & Mintsioulis, 1997). King et al. (1994) found that the most common diagnoses in individuals with developmental disabilities at the Landerman Developmental Center in California were impulse control disorders, stereo-typical/habit disorders, anxiety disorders and mood disorders. In a similar study in Canada, Gitta and Goldberg (1995) concluded that co-existence of anxiety disorders, adjustment disorders and depression was high in people with developmental disabilities.

This chapter describes the main clinical aspects of depression, anxiety and adjustment disorders and considers the similarities and differences of the three conditions in people with developmental disabilities.

Depression

The current American classification system for mental diseases (DSM-IV, American Psychiatric Association, 1994) includes two types of depressive disorders:
(a) major depressive disorders, and
(b) dysthymic disorders.
Major depressive disorder is characterized by one or more major depressive episodes (i.e. at least two weeks of depressed mood or loss of interest). According to this classification, five or more of the following symptoms of depression must be present during the same two-week period for a diagnosis of major depressive disorder to be made:

- depressed mood most of the day
- markedly diminished interest or pleasure in all activities
- considerable weight loss or gain
- insomnia or hypersomnia
- psychomotor agitation or retardation
- fatigue or loss of energy
- feelings of worthlessness
- diminished ability to think or concentrate
- recurrent thoughts of death.

Dysthymic disorder is characterized by at least two years of depressed mood for more days than not, accompanied by additional depressive symptoms that do not meet the criteria for a major depressive episode. The DSM-IV criteria for dysthymic disorder require that depressed mood should be present for most of the day, more days than not, for at least two years. The presence of two or more of the following symptoms is necessary for the diagnosis of dysthymic disorder to be made:

- poor appetite or overeating
- insomnia or hypersomnia
- low energy or fatigue
- low self-esteem
- poor concentration
- feelings of worthlessness.

Although the diagnostic criteria for depressive disorders in DSM-IV apply to people with developmental disabilities, certain limitations are apparent. One of the main problems is that people with developmental disabilities and either limited or non-verbal communication cannot express subjective feelings such as lack of pleasure. Therefore, there has been concern that depressive disorders are not properly recognized in this population and remain under-diagnosed. King et al. (1994) and Gitta and Goldberg (1995) emphasized the apparent high incidence of depressive disorders in people with developmental disabilities; other studies have described single case studies or have focused on specific subpopulations, i.e. those with pervasive developmental disorder (Ghaziuddin & Tsai, 1991) or Down syndrome (Cooper & Collacott, 1994).

The prevalence of major depressive episode in the general population has been estimated to be from 10 to 25 per cent for women and from 5 to 12 per cent for men. The prevalence of dysthymic disorder has been found to be approximately 8 per cent for both sexes. In a recent study of adults with developmental disabilities attending a psychiatric out-patient clinic, 26 people (9.1 per cent) of a total sample of 285 were found to have a depressive or dysthymic disorder.

Aetiology

The causes of depressive disorders in people with developmental disabilities are similar to the causes in the general population. Although the latter have been extensively studied in recent years, there is a paucity of research for people with developmental disabilities. Collacott, Cooper and McGrother (1992) examined 378 adults with Down syndrome and compared them to an almost equal number of adults with developmental disabilities due to other pathologies. They concluded that Down syndrome patients were more likely to have been diagnosed as having depression with dementia (see also Chapter 12).

Biological and genetic factors have been identified as causing depression in people with Down syndrome (Tu, & Zellweger, 1965; Collacott et al., 1992). Similar factors may be responsible for the higher incidence of depressive disorders in people with pervasive developmental disorders (Ghaziuddin & Tsai, 1991).

The relationship between stressful life events and depressive disorders has been of long-standing interest for clinicians and researchers. This is particularly important for people with developmental disabilities whose lives may be characterized by frequent major adverse life events such as separation from care givers, attending school, and other traumatic events (Stavrakaki & Mintsioulis, 1997). In a recent study of adults with developmental disabilities diagnosed as having depressive disorders, there was a high frequency of life events occurring one to three months prior to the onset of depression (Stavrakaki & Mintsioulis, in preparation). Major depressive disorder was associated with sexual assault, physical assault, parental loss and parental separation. Dysthymic disorder was linked with parental illness, parental separation, divorce and change of residence.

Assessment

Depressive disorders are easier to diagnose in people with mild and moderate developmental disabilities than in those whose disabilities are severe and profound (King et al., 1994; Gitta & Goldberg, 1995; Marston et al. 1997; Stavrakaki & Mintsioulis, 1997). Modified ICD-10 and DSM-IV diagnostic criteria have been used to diagnose depression in people with developmental disorders.

Meins (1993) applied the Children's Depression Inventory (CDI) to diagnose depressive disorders in a sample of adults with developmental disabilities. He concluded that a CDI score of 17 or above was strongly suggestive of depressive disorders (based on DSM-III-R criteria, American Psychiatric Association, 1987): of 54 subjects, 57 per cent were diagnosed as suffering from depressive disorders. The CDI, in an informant-rating version, was also found to be a suitable diagnostic and screening instrument for adults with developmental disabilities.

Meins (1996) also used the developed depression subscale of the Comprehensive Psychopathological Rating Scale (CPRS) to distinguish between depressive and non-depressive individuals and between subgroups of depression in a sample of 51 adults with developmental disabilities. He concluded that the scale was able to distinguish the depressed from the non-depressed group as well as between dysthymia and major depressive disorder. This scale consists of nine items and can be used for almost all people with varying degrees of intellectual disability, including the severely and profoundly disabled. Marston et al. (1997) completed a standard checklist, comprised of 30 symptoms associated with depressive disorder derived from the ICD-10 diagnostic criteria (World Health Organization, 1992), on 82 people with developmental disability. They found that 36 subjects were suffering from depressive disorder as assessed by two raters.

However, the diagnosis of depressive disorders in people with developmental disabilities needs more systematic research in order to develop standardized assessment and diagnostic instruments specifically for this population. The Psychiatric Assessment Schedule for Adults with Developmental Disability (PAS-ADD: Moss et al., 1993) could be a promising development in this respect. Conceptual issues about the assessment and diagnosis of mental health problems including depression are also described in Chapters 2 and 3.

Symptom presentation

The use of strict criteria for the diagnosis of depressive disorders in people with developmental disabilities may exclude potential cases and lead to the under-representation of the problem. Recent research has focused on the presentation of symptoms as they appear in depressed people to ensure a more accurate diagnosis, particularly for those with severe developmental disabilities.

Meins (1995), in his study of 32 adults with developmental disabilities, found that those with severe disabilities presented more atypical symptoms such as irritability, psychomotor agitation, increased behaviour problems and, rarely, a loss of adaptive behaviour. Those with mild disabilities were diagnosed successfully by using the DSM-III-R diagnostic criteria.

Marston et al. (1997) found common and distinct symptoms in the presentation of the depressive disorders in people with developmental disabilities based on their degree of disability. The common symptoms were depressed affect and sleep disturbance. The distinct symptoms based on the degree of disability were:

mild developmental disability
  – tearfulness
  – diurnal mood variation
  – loss of energy
  – loss of interest
  – low self-esteem
moderate developmental disability
  – social isolation
  – self-injurious behaviour

　　　– weight loss
　　severe/profound developmental disability
　　　– screaming
　　　– aggression
　　　– self-injurious behaviour.

It appears from the existing literature that depressive symptoms in adults with developmental disabilities vary according to the degree of their disability: the higher their intellectual ability, the closer their symptoms of depression are to those of the general population. In people with the severe disability, depression seems to be presented with atypical symptoms. However, this is an area that requires further research and exploration.

Anxiety disorders

Anxiety disorders, as defined in DSM-IV, are clinically significant, unpleasant emotions that have the quality of fear, dread and alarm in the presence or absence of an identifiable psychosocial stressor or stresses. The following conditions are described as anxiety disorders in DSM-IV:
　　　– panic disorder with agoraphobia
　　　– panic disorder without agoraphobia
　　　– agoraphobia without panic disorder
　　　– specific phobias
　　　– social phobias
　　　– obsessive–compulsive disorder
　　　– post-traumatic stress disorder
　　　– acute stress disorder
　　　– generalized anxiety disorder.

Aetiology

Various theories have been put forward concerning the aetiology of anxiety disorders in people with developmental disabilities (King et al. 1994; Gitta & Goldberg, 1995; Ryan 1994; Stavrakaki & Mintsioulis, 1997). Whereas some suggest a relationship between anxiety disorders and the underlying pathology responsible for the developmental disability, others have pointed to environmental factors such as physical illness, trauma and abuse to explain the higher incidence of anxiety disorders amongst these people (Ryan, 1994). Prior to post-traumatic stress disorder, post-traumatic stress in people with developmental disabilities was attributed to a number of psychiatric diagnoses. Common diagnoses included autism and intermittent explosive disorder, and less common diagnoses included affective disorders, personality disorders and adjustment. People with developmental disabilities are vulnerable to physical (Gil, 1970) and to sexual abuse (Elvik et al., 1990). Like young children, they may be unable to relate the details of the abusive event. It is, then, very difficult to assess the extent of the abuse, especially because the tools used with non-verbal sexually abused children, such as anatomically detailed dolls, developmentally targeted interviews etc., have not yet been validated for people with developmental disabilities.

Assessment

It is difficult to assess anxiety disorders in people with developmental disabilities. Criteria similar to those applied to the general population can apply, but they have to be modified and are dependent upon the ability of the individuals concerned to communicate their subjective feelings of discomfort. In studies of anxiety in the general population, people are usually asked to self-rate their anxiety on one of the standard assessment tools available for research. The problem with this method when applied to the developmental disabilities group is that it is difficult for people to rate their own anxiety. Some attempts have been made by Lindsay and Michie (1988) to adapt one of the standard anxiety assessment scales for use with this group of people. The Zung Self-Rating Anxiety Scale (SAS; Zung, 1971) has been widely used in the assessment of generalized anxiety and treatment effects because this scale can be adjusted to be more easily understood by people with developmental disabilities by simply indicating presence or absence of anxiety symptoms. However, the main problem inherent in the standard presentation of the responses in the Zung SAS is the complex conceptual awareness of one's own anxiety. For individuals with developmental disabilities, it is almost impossible to categorize and to rate the extent of their anxiety from 'never' to 'some of the time', 'a good part of the time', and 'most or all of the time'. A standardized scale that can be easily understood and has only a positive or a negative response could be a useful assessment tool for people with developmental disabilities.

Gedye developed a compulsive behaviour checklist for people with developmental disabilities in order to assess and to grade the severity of obsessions (A. Gedye, personal communication). This behaviour checklist has yielded good results and has been used extensively by several facilities and services. The PAS-ADD checklist (Moss et al., 1997) referred to above also includes assessment. (see also Chapter 3).

Symptom presentation

A person with developmental disabilities can show signs of anxiety in response to a threat in his or her own environment that do not interfere with their life activities. In some instances, however, especially when the stressors are enduring, symptoms of anxiety may interfere with the person's ability to function.

The presentation of anxiety disorders in this group of individuals is still being explored, in contrast to the vast literature that exists for the general population. In her study of post-traumatic stress disorder in people with developmental disabilities, Ryan (1994) examined the symptoms and reasons for psychiatric referral and found that almost all of her clients were

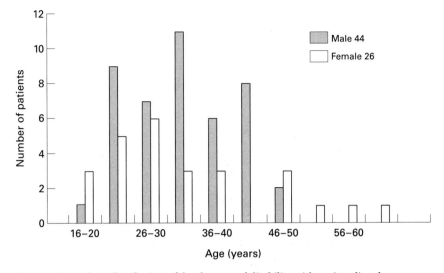

Fig. 10.1 Sex and age distribution of developmental disability with anxiety disorder.

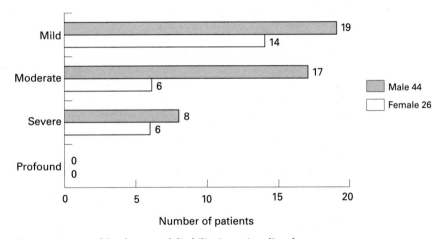

Fig. 10.2 Degree of developmental disability in anxiety disorders.

referred for violent or disruptive behaviours. Stavrakaki and Mintsioulis (1997) found that 70 patients out of a total of 257 (27 per cent) with developmental disabilities suffered from anxiety disorders. The sex, age distribution and degree of developmental disability of this sample are presented in Figures 10.1 and 10.2.

In relation to the symptomatology of the anxiety disorders found in this study, the prevailing common symptoms were: aggression, agitation, obsessive–compulsive phenomena, i.e. self-mutilation, obsessive fears, ritualistic behaviours and insomnia. Specific symptoms for each category were: over-activity, panic attacks, agoraphobia, sexual dysfunction, mood changes, depersonalization and derealization. Stavrakaki and Mintsioulis (1997) also summarized the life events that had preceded the onset of symptoms in the same sample of patients by three to six months. Out of 70 patients, 63 had been exposed to one or more of the following life events:

- rape/sexual assault
- physical assault
- accidents
- illness
- move
- loss of care giver
- change in policy.

Adjustment disorders

Adjustment disorders are partially related to anxiety and partially to the depressive disorders. They are defined on DSM IV criteria as clinically significant emotional or behavioural symptoms in response to identifiable psychosocial stressors. The clinical categories of adjustment disorders are:

- depressed mood
- anxiety
- mixed anxiety and depressed mood
- mixed disturbance of emotions and conduct
- unspecified.

Adjustment disorders can be seen as the precursor of anxiety and depressive disorders, as presented on Figure 10.3. As the diagram indicates, in some instances it is very difficult to disentangle the symptoms associated with adjustment disorders from those of anxiety and depressive disorders. There are, however, incidents in which specific stressors can cause an adjustment disorder with its own characteristic symptomatology that will run its own course and will have a specific prognosis. The stressors may be a single event, multiple stressors and/or stressors that affect a single individual, an entire family or a large group or community.

As already mentioned, the lives of the people with developmental disabilities, are affected by multiple traumas. As a result, the prevalence of adjustment disorders can be significantly increased (Göstason, 1987; Ryan, 1994; Gitta & Goldberg, 1995; Stavrakaki & Mintsioulis, 1997). The symptom presentation of adjustment disorders seems to follow patterns similar to those of anxiety disorders. However, there are, common and specific presentations of the symptoms of the two disorders. Common symptoms between adjustment and anxiety disorders include disruptive behaviours, i.e. aggression, agitation, distractibility, physical and verbal abuse and self-mutilation. Specific symptoms include somatic complaints and biological symptoms, i.e. sleep and appetite disturbance. The specific symptoms have more resemblance to the depressive disorders.

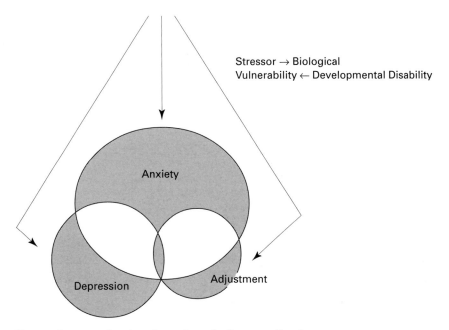

Fig. 10.3 Stressors of anxiety, depressive and adjustment disorders.

Treatment methods

The treatment methods used for people with developmental disabilities and depression, anxiety and adjustment disorders are similar to those used in the general population and include the following.

Pharmacotherapeutic regimes

Pharmacotherapeutic regimes including antidepressants, anxiolytics, neuroleptics, mood stabilizers, anticonvulsants, beta-blockers etc. have been used widely to treat depression and anxiety disorders in people with developmental disabilities over time (see Chapter 19).

Pharmacotherapy should be used cautiously in the treatment of anxiety disorders in this group of people because of the relatively high rate of unwanted side-effects, including increased susceptibility, paradoxical and even toxic reactions (Ryan, 1994; Ratey et al. 1991; Bodfish & Madison, 1993; Stavrakaki & Mintsioulis, 1997). There has been a general agreement that the doses of medication used for the treatment of people with developmental disabilities and anxiety disorders should be kept lower than normal and reviewed at regular intervals.

Behaviour therapies

Behaviour therapies such as progressive relaxation (Jacobson, 1938) and abbreviated progressive relaxation (Bernstein & Borkovec, 1973) have been used to treat a variety of behaviour and cognitive problems, including self-injurious behaviour, inappropriate sexual responses, temper-tantrums, phobic symptoms and psychomotor seizures. These techniques seem to be most successful when applied to individuals with moderate and mild levels of developmental disability. However, these techniques have not produced effective results for people with more severe developmental disabilities (Lindsay, Baty and Michie, 1989).

Environmental factors

Environmental changes are frequently detrimental to people with developmental disabilities and anxiety disorders. Environmental triggers are very important in the development of dissociative phenomena, for example in the cases of post-traumatic stress disorder (Ryan, 1994). Individuals with developmental disabilities can become very anxious and feel threatened in the course of their daily activities by environmental stimuli. In most cases, these problems are preventable. Careful review of living conditions and daily activities of these individuals is necessary to ensure that triggers and other factors that create extensive anxiety and inordinate stress can be ameliorated.

Staff training

Staff training has been highly recommended in the overall treatment of anxiety disorders in people with developmental disabilities (Ryan, 1994; Stavrakaki & Mintsioulis, 1997). More recently, structured staff training techniques have been gaining increasing interest (Bouras & Holt, 1997).

Identification of physical problems

The identification of physical problems is of major importance for people with developmental disabilities. Often, physical discomfort may be expressed as aggressive or agitated behaviour in these individuals. Early recognition and treatment of underlying physical problems will have an overall beneficial effect.

Conclusion

Depression, anxiety and adjustment disorders are more frequent than previously accepted in people with developmental disabilities. Although they are distinct clinical entities, they may also interrelate and overlap with each other. The symptom presentation of each of the three disorders in higher functioning individuals is distinct and follows the generally accepted criteria as they apply to the general population. However, in adults with severe/profound developmental disabilities, the symptoms of the three disorders overlap and tend to include more behavioural disturbances such as aggression, irritability and self-injurious behaviour.

Areas of future research should address the possibility of identifying biological markers related to these disorders. Pharmacological studies including randomised samples should be specifically designed for people with developmental disabilities. The early recognition and identification of depression, anxiety and adjustment disorders, together with appropriate therapeutic interventions, are necessary in order to prevent, modify and ameliorate their clinical impact. There is a great need for specialized services dealing with people with dual diagnosis and their families. These services should offer a holistic approach and address the mental health needs of these people in a manner that enhances the quality of their lives.

References

American Psychiatric Association (1987). *Diagnostic and Statistical Manual of Mental Disorders*, 3rd edition, revised. Washington DC: APA.

American Psychiatric Association (1994). *Diagnostic and Statistical Manual of Mental Disorders*, 4th edition. Washington DC: APA.

Bernstein, D. & Borkovec, T.D. (1973). *Progressive Relaxation Training*. Chicago: Illinois Research Press.

Bodfish, J.W. & Madison, J.T. (1993). Diagnosis and fluoxetine treatment of compulsive behavior disorder of adults with mental retardation. *American Journal on Mental Retardation*, **98**, 360–7.

Bouras, N. & Holt, G. (1997), *Mental Health in Learning Disabilities: Training Package*. Brighton: Pavilion.

Collacott, R.A., Cooper, S.A. & McGrother, C. (1992). Differential rates of psychiatric disorders in adults with Down's Syndrome compared with other mentally handicapped adults. *British Journal of Psychiatry*, **16** (C-AB), 671–4.

Cooper, S.A. & Collacott, R.A. (1994). Clinical features and diagnostic criteria of depression in Down's syndrome. *British Journal of Psychiatry*, **165**, 399–403.

Einfeld, S.L. (1992). Clinical assessment of psychiatric symptoms in mentally retarded individuals. *Australia & New Zealand Journal of Psychiatry*, **26**, 48–63.

Elvik, S.L., Berkowitz, C.D., Nicholas, E., Lindley Lipman, J. & Inkelis, S.H. (1990). Sexual abuse in the developmentally disabled: dilemmas of diagnosis. *Child Abuse and Neglect*, **14**, 497–502.

Gedye, A. (1993), Evidence of serotonergic reduction of self-injurious movements. *The Habilitative Mental Health Care Newsletter*, **12**, 53–6.

Ghaziuddin, M. & Tsai, L. (1991). Depression in autistic disorder. *British Journal of Psychiatry*, **159**, 721–3.

Gil, D.G. (1970). Violence Against Children: *Physical Child Abuse in the United States*. Cambridge, MA: Harvard University Press.

Gitta, M.Z. & Goldberg, B. (1995). Dual diagnosis: psychiatric and physical disorders in a clinical sample, Part II. *Clinical Bulletin of Developmental Disabilities Program*, **6**. 1–2.

Göstason, R. (1987). Psychiatric illness among the mildly mentally retarded. *Upsala Journal of Medicine and Science*, Supplement, **44**, 115–24.

Jacobson, E. (1938). *Progressive Relaxation*. Chicago: University of Chicago Press.

King, B.H., Carlo DeAntonio, B.A., McCracken, J.T., Fomess, S.R. & Ackerland, V.

(1994). Psychiatric consultation in severe and profound mental retardation. *American Journal of Psychiatry*, **151**, 1802–8.

Lindsay, W.R. & Michie, A.M. (1988). Adaptation of the Zung self-rating anxiety scale for people with a mental handicap. *Journal of Mental Deficiency Research*, **32**, 485–90.

Lindsay, W.R., Baty, F.J. & Michie, A.M. (1989). A comparison of anxiety treatments with adults who have moderate and severe mental retardation. *Research in Developmental Disabilities*, **10**, 129–40.

Marston, G.J., Perry, D.W. & Roy, A. (1997). Manifestations of depression in people with intellectual disability. *Journal of Intellectual Disability Research*, **41**, (6), 476–80.

Meins, W. (1993). Assessment of depression in mentally retarded adults: reliability and validity of the Children's Depression Inventory (CDI). *Research in Developmental Disabilities* **14**(4), 299–312.

(1995). Symptoms of major depression in mentally retarded adults. *Journal of Intellectual Disability Research*, **39**, 41–5.

(1996). A new depression scale designed for use with adults with mental retardation. *Journal of Intellectual Disability Research*, 40, 222–6.

Moss, S.C., Patel, P., Prosser, H. et al. (1993). Psychiatric morbidity in older people with moderate and severe learning disability (mental retardation). Part I: Development and reliability of the patient interview (the PAS-ADD). *British Journal of Psychiatry*, 163, 471–80.

Moss, S.C. et al. (1997). *Hester Adrian Research Centre, PAS-ADD Checklist*, Manchester: University of Manchester.

O'Dwyer, J., Holmes, J. & Collacott, R.A. (1992). Two cases of obsessive–compulsive disorder in individuals with Down's syndrome. *Journal of Neurology and Mental Disability*, **180**, 603–4.

Ratey, J., Sovner, R., Parks, A. & Rogentine, K. (1991). Buspirone treatment of aggression and anxiety in mentally retarded patients: a multiple-baseline, placebo lead-in study. *Journal of Clinical Psychiatry*, **52**, 159–62.

Ryan, R. (1994). Posttraumatic stress disorder in persons with developmental disabilities. *Networker*, **3**, 1–5.

Singh, N.N., Sood, A., Somemklar, N. & Ellis, C.R. (1991). Assessment and diagnosis of mental illness in persons with mental retardation: methods and measures. *Behaviour Modification*, **15**, 419–43.

Sovner, R. & Harley, A.D. (1989). Ten diagnostic principles for recognising psychiatric disorders in mentally retarded persons. *Psychiatric Aspects of Mental Retardation Reviews*, **8**, 9–14.

Stavrakaki, C. & Mintsioulis, G. (in preparation). Depressive disorders in a clinic sample of adults with developmental disability.

Stavrakaki, C. & Mintsioulis, G. (1995). Pharmacological treatment of obsessive–compulsive disorders in Down's syndrome individuals: comparison with obsessive–compulsive disorders of non-Down's mentally retarded persons. In *Proceedings of the International Congress II on the Dually Diagnosed*, pp. 52–6. Boston.

(1997). Anxiety disorders in persons with mental retardation: diagnostic, clinical, and treatment issues. *Psychiatric Annals*, **27**, 182–9.

Tu, J.B. & Zellweger, H. (1965). Blood serotonin deficiency in Down's syndrome. *Lancet*, **2**, 715–7.

Vitello, B. & Behar, D. (1992). Mental retardation and psychiatric illness. *Hospital Community Psychiatry*, **43**, 494–9.

World Health Organization (1992). *The International Classification of Mental and Behaviour Disorders – Clinical Descriptions and Diagnostic Guidelines*, 10th Revision (ICD-10). Geneva: WHO.

Zung, W.K. (1971). A rating instrument for anxiety disorders. *Psychosomatics* **XII**, 371–9.

11 Functional psychoses in people with mental retardation

DAVID CLARKE

Introduction

This chapter discusses issues of functional psychoses in relation to mental retardation and the services people who have such disorders may require. Psychoses are more common among this population of people than in the general population, and certain conditions associated with mental retardation may imply particularly high risks.

Non-psychiatric professionals and care staff, therefore, need some knowledge of psychoses and their treatment. They are often better placed than the psychiatrist to communicate with the person concerned and to notice small changes in behaviour or functioning that may indicate the presence of a psychotic disorder, benefits from treatment, or side-effects produced by medication.

Psychoses are forms of mental illness in which contact with reality is lost or seriously impaired. They are characterized by features such as delusions (false beliefs that are not the result of the person's educational, social or cultural background), hallucinations (perceptions that occur with no external stimulus, such as 'voices') and profound changes in mood.

Psychoses are conventionally divided into those for which there is an obvious organic cause (such as delirium related to an infection, or a dementing illness caused by Alzheimer's disease) and 'functional' psychoses in which an organic cause is not apparent (such as schizophrenia). This distinction between organic and functional psychoses is clinically useful because the symptoms are different, and the treatment of organic psychoses is directed at the underlying cause, whereas the treatment of functional psychoses is directed towards the relief of symptoms. However, there is increasing evidence that 'functional' psychoses are associated with organic brain changes (in structure or function). The term 'functional' is therefore not entirely appropriate, but retained in the absence of any better alternative.

Organic psychoses are typically associated with confusion (short-term memory impairments resulting in disorientation in time, place or person, and deficits in transferring information to long-term memory) and clinical features such as visual hallucinations.

The nature of functional psychoses

Functional psychoses have traditionally been divided into affective (mood) disorders and schizophrenia and related disorders. This dichotomy is broadly reflected in current classificatory systems such as the *Classification of Mental and Behavioural Disorders* within the tenth revision of the *International Classification of Diseases* (ICD-10; World Health Organization, 1992). However, some psychoses may encompass symptoms suggestive of both affective and schizophrenic psychoses, and others may involve only one or two symptoms (such as isolated delusions or hallucinations).

Research has failed fully to support the notion that affective and schizophrenic psychoses are entirely distinct and separate disorders; some psychiatrists view them as poles on a continuum. Others have argued that the concept of 'schizophrenia' lacks any single defining principle, and is best regarded as a label for a syndrome reflecting a pattern of brain dysfunction that may have many causes (e.g. Brockington, 1992). Because they are used widely, and are of help in predicting treatment response, this chapter describes the main categories of functional psychosis listed in ICD-10.

It can be argued that the classification of psychoses at present parallels the classification of medical illnesses in the seventeenth or eighteenth century. At that time, fluid retention (oedema) was known as 'dropsy'. William Withering noted the use of foxglove extracts to treat dropsy in folk medicine and employed them in clinical practice. People whose dropsy was caused by heart failure benefited (because of the effect of digoxin and related compounds). Those people whose dropsy was caused by kidney or liver failure or other disorders did not benefit. The causes of dropsy came to be known after treatment effects were noted, and partly as a result of such effects. Schizophrenia may well be a similar syndrome, with several different patterns of causation and treatment response.

Affective disorders

Affective disorders include states of abnormally low mood (depressive disorders) and states in which mood is abnormally elevated (manic states). These disorders differ from ordinary unhappiness or euphoria because the mood state is persistently abnormal, and accompanied by other characteristic features. The term bipolar affective disorder is used to describe recurrent psychoses (two or more episodes, at least one of which was manic). The term recurrent depressive disorder is used to delineate multiple (two or more) episodes of depression.

In hypomanic states, mood is abnormally and persistently elevated, and accompanied by features such as increased activity, restlessness, increased talkativeness, distractibility, decreased need for sleep, increased sexual energy, over-spending or other irresponsible behaviour, disinhibition and over-familiarity. When severe (a manic as opposed to a hypomanic state), other features occur, such as flight of ideas (when thoughts race from one topic to another, reflected in the person's speech), abnormally increased self-esteem or grandiosity, and reckless behaviour. Delusions and/or hallucinations are not uncommonly associated with severe manic states. These are usually mood congruent (consistent with the mood abnormality, such as voices announcing that the person has won a large prize).

Depressive disorders are characterized by low mood, reduced energy and activity, anhedonia (loss of enjoyment and satisfaction), reduced appetite and libido, sleep abnormalities (typically with early morning waking), and ideas of guilt or worthlessness that may be delusional.

Relatively recent research has identified subtypes of affective disorder such as recurrent brief depression and seasonal affective disorder. Some of these disorders are of clinical relevance because they predict different outcomes or treatment responses. For example, people with seasonal affective disorder may respond to treatment by daylight extension using high-intensity lighting.

Schizophrenia

Schizophrenia is characterized by fundamental and characteristic distortions of thinking and perception, and mood states that are inappropriate to the social context or that are flat and unchanging. Typical clinical features are listed in Table 11.1, with brief descriptions and examples of the experiences as perceived by the patient.

Schizophrenic disorders can be either continuous or episodic (with a progressive or stable pattern of deficits), or there may be one or more episodes, with complete or incomplete remission. Schizophrenia is not usually diagnosed if manic or depressive symptoms are prominent. It should not be diagnosed during states of drug intoxication or withdrawal, or 'in the presence of overt brain disease' (ICD-10). As discussed below, the latter exclusion criterion may cause difficulties for clinicians working with people with mental retardation.

Other psychoses

ICD-10 groups schizo-affective disorders (episodic psychoses in which both affective and schizophrenic symptoms are prominent) with schizophrenia, while noting that their relationship to schizophrenia and affective disorders remains to be clarified. Other atypical psychoses include delusional disorders characterized solely or predominantly by abnormal beliefs – for example, the conviction that small louse-like insects have infested the head, leading to regular 'treatment' with paraffin (Winokur, 1977). Cycloid psychoses, or acute and transient psychotic disorders, are characterized by a sudden onset and a shifting, polymorphous pattern of symptoms including agitation, anxiety and mood and/or schizophrenic symptoms (Perris, 1988).

Table 11.1 Clinical features suggestive of schizophrenia	
Clinical feature	*Description*
Thought echo	Thoughts are repeated in audible form (occasionally, thoughts are anticipated rather than repeated)
Thought insertion	Thoughts are suddenly put into the mind, disrupting the train of thought
Thought withdrawal	Thoughts are suddenly withdrawn from the mind, disrupting the train of thought
Thought broadcasting	Thoughts are apparent to others as soon as they occur; the patient may have an 'explanation' such as telepathy or a mind-reading machine
Delusional perception	An ordinary stimulus (such as seeing a fir tree in a garden) leads suddenly to a delusion that seems unconnected (the fir tree means the patient is to be assassinated by an occult organization)
Delusions of control or influence, or 'passivity' experiences	Delusional beliefs that the patient's body or mind is controlled by some external force; an 'explanation' may be linked to other psychopathology ('The BBC make my mind go blank using the transmitter at Droitwich')
Auditory hallucinations ('voices')	The 'voices' are usually of a characteristic nature in schizophrenia; they are often derogatory and may comment on the person in the third person, or make other remarks ('She's turned the tap on. Stupid isn't she?') or argue with each other
Thought disorder	Used to describe disordered speech reflecting underlying thought disorganization; neologisms (non-existent words) may be used, for example, 'I never eat sphericks'

Psychoses among people with mental retardation

Psychoses are not uncommon among the general population: just under 1 per cent will have one or more episodes of schizophrenia in their life (Shields & Slater, 1975) and a similar proportion (0.6–1 per cent) will experience bipolar affective disorder (Weissman & Myers, 1978). Less severe forms of depression are more prevalent, and occur more frequently in women than in men.

Among people with mental retardation, the pooled results of studies suggest rates between 2 and 6 per cent for schizophrenia (usually only diagnosed among people with mild or moderate retardation) and between 3 and 8 per cent for affective disorders. These prevalence rates are about four times higher among people with mental retardation than among the general population. Why should this be?

Social and psychological explanations are often advanced (disadvantage, the effects of low self-esteem and lack of empowerment, etc.). Evidence from child and adolescent populations suggests that such factors play a role.

Rutter et al. (1975) found rates of psychiatric disorder in a disadvantaged area of London to be double those found on the Isle of Wight. However, as with epilepsy and autism, it seems likely that biological factors play an important role in the causation of psychoses associated with mental retardation. Rutter, Tizard and Whitmore (1970) studied 10-year-old and 11-year-old children on the Isle of Wight, and their results illustrate some aspects of the relationship between disability and psychiatric disorder. The authors studied broadly defined psychiatric disorder, rather than psychosis (most diagnoses were of conduct or emotional disorders, as would be expected given the age of the study population). The overall prevalence rate for psychiatric disorder was 6.8 per cent. If a physical disorder not affecting the brain was present, the rate increased slightly to 10.4 per cent. If a brain disorder was present, the rate of psychiatric disorder increased to 34.3 per cent (similar to the prevalence rates of challenging behaviour in many studies of populations of people with mental retardation). The rate of psychiatric disorder was higher among those people with a disorder affecting the brain who also had epilepsy (implying ongoing brain dysfunction) than among those who did not.

Although organic factors contribute to the increased vulnerability to psychosis associated with mental retardation, this does not imply that they are not treatable; it may sometimes be easier to influence brain neurotransmitter activity or to compensate for dysfunctions than to change social conditions such as the consequences of abnormal parenting, isolation or bereavement.

Diagnosis

The diagnosis of psychoses among people with mild mental retardation is not usually problematic for an experienced clinician, although more weight may have to be given to non-verbal clinical features and accounts from carers. If the person has a moderate, severe or profound retardation, with significant problems in communicating, the diagnosis of schizophrenia or related psychoses may be impossible. This reflects the extraordinary nature of the complex subjective experiences involved (see Table 11.1) and the difficulty people have in conveying these experiences to others. Reid (1972) concluded that the diagnosis of schizophrenia was very difficult to establish for people with language development below that seen in children of about seven years old. The diagnosis of affective disorder is often possible even among severely disabled people. The syndromes of depression and mania involve disturbances of vitality and biological functions (such as eating and sleeping) that can be observed, and combined with information about changes in behaviour and social functioning, previous history, family history etc. to produce a probable diagnosis. A presumptive diagnosis of a schizophrenic disorder can often be made on the basis of observable features.

These may include behaviour strongly suggestive of auditory hallucinations (such as shouting back at people not present, social withdrawal, blunted or inappropriate affect and suspiciousness that was not previously part of the person's personality).

Psychoses represent a *change* in mental functioning, and this can be helpful to distinguish them from disorders such as autism if the change is recent. Much care is needed to differentiate functional psychoses from other emotional and behavioural abnormalities seen in association with mental retardation, such as stereotyped movements related to a syndrome such as Rett syndrome (Hagberg et al., 1983) or an autistic disorder. Apparently incongruous affect may result from distractibility or a disorder such as Angelman syndrome (Robb et al., 1989). Unusual preoccupations associated with autistic disorders may be difficult to differentiate from delusions. 'Practice' repetitive vocalizations or talking to an imaginary friend may lead to a suspicion of auditory hallucinations.

Diagnostic instruments have been of limited use (Sturmey, Reed & Corbett, 1991) because they usually rely on a 'snapshot' of the person in the form of lists of clinical features that are rated by a carer. This can cause diagnostic confusion (e.g. confusing autism with chronic schizophrenia), but may be useful as a screening technique for research purposes. Newer instruments such as the Psychopathology Assessment Schedule for Adults with Developmental Disability (PAS-ADD; Moss et al., 1993) appear to have fewer limitations, but have yet to be fully evaluated.

Hucker et al. (1979) used Research Diagnostic Criteria developed by Feighner et al. (1972) with a group of people with mental retardation, and concluded that it was relatively easy to develop criteria for the diagnosis of affective disorders, whereas the criteria for schizophrenia were more problematic and controversial. Brugha et al. (1988) used draft ICD-10 criteria, and found that people with mild mental retardation had little difficulty in reporting symptoms such as delusions and hallucinations. Clarke et al. (1994) used draft Diagnostic Criteria for Research linked to ICD-10, and found these to be relatively easy to apply to populations of people with mental retardation and psychiatric and behavioural disorders, with the exception of schizophrenia.

Origin and clinical features of psychoses associated with mental retardation

Hucker et al. (1979) studied 24 people with mental retardation and schizophrenia, and 40 control subjects. They found higher proportions of people with impaired hearing (8.3 per cent *vs* 5.0 per cent), gestation below 36 weeks (4.2 per cent *vs* 2.5 per cent) and low birth weight (4.2 per cent *vs* 2.5 per cent) in the group with schizophrenia. O'Dwyer (1996) reported higher rates of obstetric complications among 50 people with mental retardation and

schizophrenia than among controls matched for age, sex, severity of retardation and presence or absence of epilepsy.

Sensory impairments are more common among people with mental
retardation, and there is a specific association with psychosis in some cases of
Usher's syndrome, which consists of retinitis pigmentosa, congenital deafness, vestibulo-cerebellar ataxia, mental retardation in about 23 per cent, and
psychosis (usually schizophrenia) in about 15 per cent of cases (Hallgren,
1959). Associations have been suggested, but not established, between psychotic illness and velocardiofacial syndrome (Goldberg et al., 1991) and
Prader–Willi syndrome (Clarke, 1993). Several authors have suggested a vulnerability to affective disorder associated with autism, and cases have been
described (e.g. Wing, 1981; Clarke et al., 1989).

Meadows et al. (1991) studied 25 people with mental retardation and
schizophrenia and 26 controls without mental retardation. The symptomatology of the two groups was very similar, the most common features being
delusions and hallucinations. Little support was found for the view that psychotic disorders occurring in association with mental retardation are characterized by atypical symptoms and much behavioural 'overlay'.

General principles of treatment

Psychoses associated with mental retardation are treated in the same
way as psychoses affecting other groups of people, but drug treatments have
to be tailored to the individuals and the particular problems they have. This
may mean using drugs with a particular adverse effect profile to minimize
the effect on, for example, a concurrent seizure disorder or motor problem.
Sometimes a definite diagnosis cannot be established, but enough information can be gathered to suggest appropriate treatment. In such circumstances, an attempt should be made to monitor the effect of treatment in
some measurable way, for example by using a standardized instrument sensitive to change or by devizing an instrument to quantify target behaviours
or emotional states. The drug treatment of psychoses is discussed in Chapter
19. Counting the frequency, severity and duration of episodes of the target
behaviour can help to assess the effect of medication. Visual–analogue scales
may also be useful (Clarke & MacLeod, 1993).

Non-drug treatments may be used in combination with medication or,
more rarely, alone. As with medication, most of the research into non-
pharmacological approaches to treating functional psychoses has been
carried out on study samples of people without mental retardation. Such
interventions include cognitive techniques to address maladaptive assumptions that may maintain depressive states (Blackburn et al., 1981), the use of
distraction or masking techniques to treat auditory hallucinations,
(Nelson, Thrasher & Barnes, 1991), and interventions to reduce expressed
emotion and help prevent relapse of schizophrenic psychoses (Anderson &
Adams, 1996). Some of these techniques are used in clinical practice with

people with mental retardation, but systematic evaluations are rarely published.

Cognitive approaches appear to be useful for people with mental retardation and depressive states, if they have the linguistic and cognitive skills necessary to utilize such an approach. In practice, this usually means people with mild mental retardation.

Techniques to reduce the impact of auditory hallucinations by masking appear to be applicable to many people with mental retardation, if they are able to tolerate an ear plug or can comply with techniques such as subvocal counting.

Programmes to reduce expressed emotion seem to be applicable to people with mental retardation. The intervention is focused primarily on family members or others in regular face-to-face contact with the person who has a psychotic disorder. Where a person with mental retardation is living in a group home, the standard techniques of working with families may have to be modified to take account of other residents' difficulties with language or with the understanding of concepts such as hostility. A community nurse or psychologist may be able to work with residents and staff members to reduce criticism of the person concerned, but input may have to consist of relatively short discussions spread over a long time period, with refresher visits as necessary. In view of the effectiveness of such interventions in the general population, evaluation of packages to lower expressed emotion, modified for use with people with mental retardation, would appear to be a priority for future research.

Services for people with mental retardation and psychoses

The components of a psychiatric service for people with mental retardation and psychoses will depend to some extent on local expertise and the availability of resources. A hospital admission service will be necessary to assess and treat people detained using mental health legislation. A home treatment or intensive support service may reduce the need for such admissions, and offers a form of assessment that may be more informative than admission in some circumstances (because changes consequent on alterations in the living environment are reduced). For some people, home treatment is not an option (for example, if the person has delusions concerning family members, and may be at risk of acting on the delusions). Access to day and respite services where the staff have some knowledge of severe psychiatric disorders offers an improvement on traditional generic local authority or voluntary sector provision where the behaviour resulting from psychotic illnesses is often misunderstood, and may become an unnecessary cause of concern to staff and other service users. Most people with psychoses can be managed as out-patients or on a domiciliary basis. Adequate out-patient facilities, expertise within community teams, and mechanisms to facilitate liaison with other statutory and voluntary organizations should be in place. The multidisciplinary community team will need expertise in areas such as nursing, social work, psychology, psychiatry, speech therapy and occupational therapy.

Some service users will have behaviours that are dangerous to themselves or others. Often, such behaviour is transient, resolving as the psychotic illness is treated. Staff training in the management of challenging behaviour, and work to address staff perceptions of, and responses to, such behaviour may be valuable. For a small proportion of people with psychoses, such behaviours continue over a prolonged period of time, and special residential provision may be necessary to meet their needs for a stable, homely environment with low expressed emotion.

Some people with mild mental retardation and a psychotic illness may be treated in non-specialist psychiatric services or units. However, there are often issues around diagnosis, treatment (in view of other disabilities) or multidisciplinary management that make such an arrangement unworkable or unacceptable to the service user, or which result in an inferior service being received. Many people with relatively mild retardation are reluctant, or refuse, to be admitted to in-patient services in which people with more severe disabilities receive a service. Such a mix of clientele is often unwise clinically (many people with severe retardation have autistic disorders or severely challenging behaviours unrelated to psychotic illness, and need different forms of management). There is often pressure for integrated services on the basis of policies of normalization and non-segregation (and sometimes cost) that should be resisted if the clinician feels patients will receive a lower standard of care.

Services, especially in-patient services, need to be structured so that beds and staff can be employed flexibly. The service user's individual needs (including non-psychiatric needs such as those resulting from membership of a particular religious or ethnic group) can then be met adequately and cost effectively.

The proportion of resources allocated to the different components of a service for people with psychoses will depend on the availability of other components. An effective day, respite and home treatment service will reduce (but not eliminate) the need for in-patient facilities, and staff training will reduce exclusions from non-specialist day and residential settings.

Conclusion

Psychoses are more common among people with mental retardation than in the general population. The features of psychotic disorders are often extremely distressing, and may lead to behaviours such as self-harm, social withdrawal or aggression.

The diagnosis of psychosis associated with mental retardation requires special expertise because of the relatively high prevalence of communication problems in the population, the effect of cognitive impairment on the assessment of features such as delusions, and the need for knowledge of other disorders associated with mental retardation that may cause diagnostic confusion (such as autistic disorders and epilepsy).

Treatments usually involve the prescription of psychoactive medications, which are effective in relieving positive symptoms of psychosis and associated distress for the majority of affected people. The psychiatrist's role involves a careful balancing of potential risks and benefits from treatment, bearing in mind the presence of other illnesses or disabilities.

Non-drug interventions may be helpful to reduce the impact of environmental determinants of illness, such as expressed emotion. Some biologically based treatments are not pharmacological (for example phototherapy for seasonal affective disorder).

People with chronic psychoses usually need specialist input to day and residential services if their rehabilitation is to be optimized to produce the best quality of life. Specialized assessment and treatment facilities, and intensive support for people in their homes and day settings are necessary. Respite care is valued by many people with psychoses and by their carers, and can be effectively combined with treatment reviews.

Research into the causation, classification and treatment of psychoses associated with mental retardation is urgently required. Much of the information currently used to guide treatment decisions is based on trials that excluded people with mental retardation. The diagnosis of psychoses among people with mental retardation would be helped by the identification of biological markers (such as a serum or blood cell abnormality), thus overcoming the difficulties resulting from communication problems, misinterpretation, diagnostic confusion, etc.

Priorities for research include the evaluation of drug and other treatment strategies specifically for people with psychosis associated with mental retardation, and studies to help practitioners learn more about aetiology. It may be worthwhile to study groups of people with possibly increased risk or atypical symptomatology, such as those with velocardiofacial syndrome or Prader–Willi syndrome. The possible relationship between autism and affective disorder also merits study.

References

Anderson, J. & Adams, C. (1996). Family interventions in schizophrenia: an effective but underused treatment. *British Medical Journal*, **313**, 505–6.

Blackburn, I.M., Bishop, S., Glen, A.I.M., Whalley, L.J. & Christie, J.E. (1981). The efficacy of cognitive therapy on depression: a treatment trial using cognitive therapy and pharmacotherapy, each alone and in combination. *British Journal of Psychiatry*, **139**, 181–9.

Brockington, I.F. (1992). Schizophrenia: yesterday's concept. *European Psychiatry*, **7**, 203–7.

Brugha, T.S., Collacot, R., Warrington, J., Deb, S. & Bruce, J. (1988). Eliciting and reliably rating delusions and hallucinations in the mildly retarded. Paper read at the Eighth Congress of the International Association for the Scientific Study of Mental Deficiency, August 1988, Dublin, Eire.

Clarke, D.J. (1993). Prader–Willi syndrome and psychoses. *British Journal of Psychiatry*, **163**, 680–4.

Clarke, D., Cumella, S., Corbett, J. et al. (1994). Use of ICD 10 research diagnostic criteria to categorise psychiatric and behavioural abnormalities among people with learning disabilities: the West Midlands field trial. *Mental Handicap Research*, **7**, 273–85.

Clarke, D.J., Littlejohns, C.S., Corbett, J.A. & Joseph, S. (1989). Pervasive developmental disorders and psychoses in adult life. *British Journal of Psychiatry*, **155**, 692–9.

Clarke, D.J. & MacLeod, M. (1993). Recurrent brief depression and mild learning disability: successful community management. *Mental Handicap*, **21**, 92–6.

Feighner, J.P., Robins, E., Guze, S.B., Woodruff, R.A., Winokur, G. & Munoz, R. (1972). Diagnostic criteria for use in psychiatric research. *Archives of General Psychiatry*, **26**, 57–63.

Goldberg, R.B., Shprintzen, R.J., Marion, R.W. & Guthrie, E. (1991). Late onset psychosis in the velocardiofacial syndrome. *American Journal of Human Genetics*, Suppl. **149**, 312.

Hagberg, B., Aicardi, J., Dias, K. & Ramos, O. (1983). A progressive syndrome of autism, dementia, ataxia, and loss of purposeful hand use in girls: Rett's syndrome: report of 35 cases. *Annals of Neurology*, **14**, 471–9.

Hallgren, B. (1959). Retinitis pigmentosa combined with congenital deafness; with vestibulo-cerebellar ataxia and mental abnormality in a proportion of cases. A clinical and genetico-statistical study. *Acta Psychiatrica Neurologica Scandinavica*, **24** (suppl. 138), 1–101.

Hucker, S.J., Day, K.E., George, S. & Roth, M. (1979). Psychosis in mentally handicapped adults. In *Psychiatric Illness and Mental Handicap*, ed. P. Snaith, P.E. James, pp. 52–76. London: Gaskell Press.

Meadows, G., Turner, T., Campbell, L., Lewis, S.W., Reveley, M.A. & Murray, R.M. (1991). Assessing schizophrenia in adults with mental retardation: a comparative study. *British Journal of Psychiatry*, **158**, 103–5.

Moss, S., Patel, P., Prosser, H. et al. (1993). Psychiatric morbidity in older people with moderate and severe learning disability. I: Development and reliability of the patient interview (PAS-ADD). *British Journal of Psychiatry*, **163**, 471–80.

Nelson, H.E., Thrasher, S. & Barnes, T.R.E. (1991). Practical ways of alleviating auditory hallucinations. *British Medical Journal*, **302**, 327.

O'Dwyer, J. (1996). Schizophrenia in those with learning disabilities: the role of obstetric complications. Abstract number 21. Tenth World Congress of the International Association for the Scientific Study of Intellectual Disabilities, 8–13 July 1996, Helsinki, Finland.

Perris, C. (1988). The concept of cycloid psychotic disorder. *Psychiatric Developments*, **1**, 37–56.

Reid, A.H. (1972). Psychoses in adult mental defectives. II. Schizophrenic and paranoid psychoses. *British Journal of Psychiatry*, **120**, 213–8.

Robb, S.A., Pohl, K.R.E., Baraitser, M., Wilson, J. & Brett, E.M. (1989). The 'happy puppet' syndrome of Angelman: review of the clinical features. *Archives of Disease in Childhood*, **64**, 83–6.

Rutter, M., Cox, A., Tupling, C., Berger, M. & Yule, W. (1975). Attainment and adjustment in two geographic areas: I. The prevalence of psychiatric disorder. *British Journal of Psychiatry*, **126**, 520–33.

Rutter, M., Tizard, J. & Whitmore, K. (1970). *Education, Health and Behaviour*. London: Longman.

Shields, J. & Slater, E. (1975). Genetic aspects of schizophrenia. In *Contemporary Psychiatry*, ed. J. Silverstone & B. Barraclough. British Journal of Psychiatry Special Publication 9. London: Gaskell.

Sturmey, P., Reed, J. & Corbett, J. (1991). Psychometric assessment of psychiatric disorders in people with learning disabilities (mental handicap): a review of measures. *Psychological Medicine*, **21**, 143–55.

Weissman, M.M. & Myers, J.K. (1978). Affective disorders in a United States urban community. *Archives of General Psychiatry*, **35**, 705–12.

Wing, L. (1981). Asperger's syndrome: a clinical account. *Psychological Medicine*, **11**, 115–29.

Winokur, G. (1977). Delusional disorder (paranoia). *Comprehensive Psychiatry*, **18**, 511–21.

World Health Organization (1992). *The ICD-10 Classification of Mental and Behavioural Disorders: Clinical Descriptions and Diagnostic Guidelines*. Geneva: World Health Organization.

12 People with Down syndrome and mental health needs

RICHARD A. COLLACOTT

Introduction

The overwhelming majority of individuals with Down syndrome have developmental disabilities, with an average developmental age of under 30 months, placing them within the category of individuals with a severe degree of mental retardation. Additional mental disorders occur more frequently amongst individuals with developmental disabilities than in the general population (Rutter, Tizard & Whitmore, 1970; Richardson et al., 1979). The concept of behavioural phenotypes suggests that certain forms of primary developmental disability may predispose such individuals to develop particular mental disorders. The clearest such association is between individuals with Down syndrome and their predisposition to develop Alzheimer's disease. However, the relationship between Down syndrome and other mental disorders is, by contrast, still relatively unexplored. In addition, whilst approximately 95 per cent of individuals with Down syndrome demonstrate a karyotype that includes trisomy 21, the vulnerability of individuals with Down syndrome associated with translocations, mosaicism etc. remains uncertain.

In 1992, Collacott, Cooper and McGrother published their findings of a study of diagnosed mental disorders in 371 adults with Down syndrome. The individuals were matched on the basis of age, sex and residential placement with a similar number of control subjects with developmental disabilities. There were striking differences between the two groups in the rates of associated mental disorder. People with Down syndrome were less likely to receive an additional psychiatric diagnosis. In particular, people with Down syndrome appeared to be protected from conduct and personality disorder, neurotic disorders (other than depression), and schizophrenia. On the other hand, they were considerably more vulnerable to presenile dementia (by a factor of ×16) and depressive disorders (by a factor of ×2–3).

The study could be faulted on the basis that the controls were not matched on the basis of the degree of developmental disability; additionally, in the absence of generally held diagnostic criteria for mental disorders in individuals with developmental disabilities, the diagnoses – which were based on retrospective case-note analysis – were those made clinically. However, the study remains the strongest yet to establish a different vulnerability of people with Down syndrome to develop mental disorders.

Personality stereotype and behaviour

People with Down syndrome have historically been considered to possess characteristic personality and behavioural traits. Langdon Down (1866) commented upon 'powers of imitation', 'mimicry' and a 'humerous and lively sense of the ridiculous', and in a later paper 'obstinacy' and 'amiability' (Down, 1877). Fraser and Mitchell (1876) also described people with Down syndrome as 'cheerful', 'affectionate', 'easily amused', 'mischievous', 'but it is very rare to find him guilty of bad temper or any of the vices or bad habits which characterise so many of the ordinary defectives'. Fraser and Mitchell (1876) also commented on traits of mimicry and musicality. Brousseau and Brainerd (1928) studied 40 people with Down syndrome, and concluded them to be good natured, cheerful, affectionate and docile, and seldom ill-tempered or destructive. However, Rollin (1946), in his study of 73 people with Down syndrome, found 60 per cent to have a history of abnormal behaviours which included antisocial behaviours. Only 44 per cent of this group conformed to the stereotype. Engler (1949) suggested that people with Down syndrome fell into three groups, only one of which coincided with the stereotype. Blaketer-Simmonds (1953) compared the case notes of 140 people with Down syndrome with 100 people with developmental disabilities of other aetiologies. The two groups were similar for most characteristics, and only differed with regard to mischieviousness, solitariness, and docility amongst the Down syndrome group. He further studied 60 people with Down syndrome and 300 people with developmental disabilities of other aetiologies, using an informant-rated questionnaire of personality traits. This study, however, found no differences in personality traits between the two groups.

Moore, Thulin and Laverne Capes (1968) studied 536 people with Down syndrome of average age 21 years and matched controls. They were less likely to show hyperactivity, aggressive, destructive, self-injurious, restless or noisy behaviours. A larger group of 2606 people with Down syndrome, with the same mean age (21 years), also showed differences from controls, with higher rates of socially adaptive and competent behaviours (Johnson & Abelson, 1969). Collacott and his colleagues have recently studied the behavioural characteristics of 360 adults with Down syndrome compared to 1829 adults with developmental disabilities due to other aetiologies (Collacott et al. 1998). The instrument used to define the behaviours was the Disability Assessment Schedule. Despite an equal age and developmental quotient ratio, the Down syndrome group was less likely to demonstrate maladaptive behaviours. The behaviour characteristics of the groups of adults with Down syndrome remained consistent throughout adult life. In addition, individuals with Down syndrome tended to belong to behaviour clusters with limited aberrant behaviours (Smith et al. 1996). Most other studies of the personality and behaviour of people with Down syndrome have focused exclusively on children (Wunsch, 1957; Silverstein, 1964; Domino, Goldschmid & Kaplan, 1964; Domino, 1965; Baron, 1972; Gibbs & Thorpe, 1983; Gunn, Berry & Anderson, 1981; Bridges & Cicchetti, 1982; Gath & Gumley, 1986; Rodgers, 1987; Pueschel, Bernier & Pezzullo, 1991), with conflicting results.

Autism

There have been relatively few case reports of autism occurring in people with Down syndrome. Wakabayashi (1979) and Bregman and Volkmar (1988) have described cases of children with Down syndrome who met the criteria for autism. Additional cases have been reported (Ghaziuddin & Tsai, 1991; Ghaziuddin, Tsai & Ghaziuddin, 1992; Ghaziuddin, 1997). It has been claimed that the association between autism and Down syndrome is uncommon (Rutter & Schopler, 1988). Wing and Gould (1979), in their epidemiological survey of social impairments in 35 000 children under the age of 15 years, found that out of a total of 30 children with Down syndrome, 27 were classified as sociable severely retarded, one was described as aloof, one as passive and odd, and only one as autistic. Ghaziuddin et al. (1992), however, suggested that the association between the two conditions might be more common than has been generally believed.

Autism may be undiagnosed and under-reported amongst people with Down syndrome. Lund (1988) reported that 11.3 per cent of his sample had 'infantile autism': Ghaziuddin et al. (1992) estimated that between 4 per cent and 5 per cent of people with Down syndrome may meet diagnostic criteria for autism. Gath and Gumley (1986) found a prevalence of 1 per cent amongst children and adults. Myers and Pueschel (1991) found three out of 261 people with Down syndrome had autism (1 per cent). Collacott et al. (1992) reported a diagnosed prevalence of 2.2 per cent amongst adults.

Ghaziuddin (1997) has pointed out that in many ways the image of behaviours and social adaptability that people with Down syndrome often project appears incompatible with the presence of autistic symptoms. For example, autistic children suffer from a distinctive pattern of social impairment and are often aloof and isolative, whereas those with Down syndrome are often friendly and sociable. Interestingly, Ghaziuddin (1997) has described three young adults with Down syndrome and autism, each of whom had at least one parent with a history of mild autistic traits whilst not meeting the full criteria for autism. He proposed that autism-specific genetic factors might be important, even when autism co-existed with another disorder, such as Down syndrome.

Depression

Depression in people with developmental disabilities, including those with Down syndrome, has recently been reviewed (Cooper & Collacott, 1996). Several case reports of depression occurring in people with Down syndrome have been described (Roith, 1961; Keegan, Pettigrew & Parker, 1974; Storm, 1990; Lazarus, Jaffe & Dubin, 1990; Ghaziuddin & Tsai, 1991). Warren, Holroyd and Folstein, (1989) described depression, compatible with DSM-III-R criteria, in five individuals with Down syndrome, and drew attention to the importance of accurate diagnosis and the need to differentiate between depression and a presumptive diagnosis of dementia of Alzheimer's type. However, studies of groups of people with Down syndrome are limited.

In an uncontrolled study, Myers and Pueschel (1991) examined the medical records of 164 adult out-patient attenders and determined that 25.6 per cent had a psychiatric disorder: for 6.1 per cent of the total group, this was depression. Collacott et al. (1992), in a case-note study, showed that a past history of depression (using ICD-9 criteria) was present in 11 per cent of adults with Down syndrome compared to 4 per cent of age, sex and residence matched control individuals with developmental disability of aetiology other than Down syndrome.

The presumed increased rate of depression in adults with Down syndrome has been challenged, and Meins (1993) cites studies in support. However, these studies are of children. The one study involving adults with Down syndrome (Lund, 1988) is of very small size, with findings reported on only 44 individuals, and the low rates of mental disorders diagnosed are in keeping with the atypically low rates found in Lund's other studies (Lund, 1985).

Depression in individuals with Down syndrome, as with others, is undoubtedly associated with genetic inheritance, including biochemical milieu, early experiences, personality attributes and life experiences. The specific vulnerability of individuals with Down syndrome compared to other individuals with developmental disabilities may lie within the biochemical arena. Down syndrome studies, particularly those involving blood platelets, suggest that there is a state of relative hyposerotonergia. In particular, blood platelets (which have been used as a proxy for cerebral neurons) appear unable to store serotonin, due to defects in membrane transport mechanisms.

Diagnostic criteria of depression

A major difficulty in studying depression in people with Down syndrome is the lack of generally held diagnostic criteria. Cooper and Collacott (1994a) examined the extent to which the definition of depression in DSM-III-R (American Psychiatric Association, 1987) and Diagnostic Criteria for

Table 12.1 Kettering/Leicester diagnostic criteria for depression

These criteria are for use in adults with developmental disabilities

The symptoms/signs must be present for at least two weeks

The presentation must not be a direct consequence of drugs or organic disorders, e.g. dementia

The symptoms/signs must present a change from the individual's premorbid state

At least four of the following must be present, which must include item 1 or 2:

1. Depressed mood or irritable mood
2. Loss of interest or pleasure in activities, or social withdrawal, or reduction in self-care, or reduction in the quantity of speech
3. Loss of energy
4. Loss of confidence, or increase in reassurance-seeking behaviour
5. Increased tearfulness or hypochondriasis
6. Reduced ability to concentrate/distractibility or increased indecisiveness
7. Increase in aggression or tantrums, or increase in other specific maladaptive behaviour
8. Motor agitation or motor retardation
9. Appetite disturbance or significant weight change
10. Sleep disturbance
11. A past history of mania, or of depression which responded to antidepressant treatment

Research (DCR; World Health Organization, 1993) based on ICD-10 (World Health Organization, 1992) coincides with the clinical presentation of depression, as diagnosed by psychiatrists. The most commonly described symptoms and signs were depressed affect, social withdrawal, anhedonia, tearfulness, reduced energy, psychomotor retardation, loss of appetite, regression of self-care, sleep disorder, hypochondriasis, increase in aggression and reduced speech. Recurrent thoughts of death, worthlessness or guilt are infrequently elicited. The authors questioned the appropriateness of either DSM-III-R or DCR in people with developmental disability. Subsequently, criteria for depression for use in this population have been proposed (Cooper & Collacott, 1996; Table 12.1).

Follow-up studies of adults with Down syndrome who have sustained depressive episodes have revealed the development of significantly impaired adaptive behaviour, as measured by the American Association on Adaptive Behavior Scale (Fogelman, 1975). This is in spite of the resolution of the depressive episode (Collacott & Cooper, 1992; Prasher & Hall, 1996). A particular vulnerability factor appears to be the age at which the depressive episode occurred; a young age for the onset of depression appears to carry a particularly poor prognosis (Cooper & Collacott, 1993). It has been speculated that this relates to a loss of confidence following the illness. Relapse of depression appears to be associated with certain characteristics, including a short duration for the index depressive episode, a clinical profile including biological symptoms and anhedonia. On the other hand, people whose depression becomes recurrent are less likely to have life-events associated with the episode and are less likely to demonstrate irritability or loss of self-care skills during the first episode (Cooper & Collacott, 1994b).

Manic episodes

There have been few systematic studies of hypomania in people with Down syndrome. Indeed, Sovner and Hurley (1983), in reviewing the literature, were unable to find reports of manic episodes in Down syndrome individuals, despite several reports of depressive episodes. Sovner, Hurley and Labrie (1985) concluded that Down syndrome precludes the development of mania: they acknowledged that cases might have gone unnoticed, but viewed this as unlikely, because there had been reports of mania in individuals with developmental disabilities with other aetiologies. However, Cooke and Levanthal (1987) quoted Rollin (1946) who described episodes of behavioural change suggestive of mania, but with insufficient detail to establish the diagnosis retrospectively without doubt.

Subsequently, there have been a number of case reports in the literature of hypomania in individuals with Down syndrome (Singh & Zolese, 1986; Cooke & Levanthal, 1987; McLaughlin, 1987; Sovner, 1991; Cooper & Collacott, 1991; Cooper, Collacott & Hauck, 1994), and a review has been published (Cooper & Collacott, 1993). Collacott et al. (1992) found no difference in the rate of manic disorders in individuals with Down syndrome compared to people with developmental disability due to other causes.

The age of onset of the first manic episode has ranged between 19 and 52 years, with an average of 34 years. To date, the overwhelming majority of reported individuals with manic episodes have been men. Over half the patients have sustained more than one episode. About a third of the reported cases have sustained a rapid-cycling pattern of illness. The majority has also experienced depressive episodes. In no cases described has there been a family history of affective disorder.

The common presenting symptoms have included over-activity, irritable mood, elated mood, noisiness and pressure of speech. The clinical features of mania in individuals with Down syndrome are not considered to differ from those reported in other individuals with developmental disabilities (Reid, 1972; Heaton-Ward, 1977; Hucker et al., 1979).

Observations on the natural history of manic disorders in people with Down syndrome must remain guarded in the light of the few studies undertaken. However, certain features appear to be atypical. In Down syndrome, there is only one report of manic episodes in a woman, suggesting that this may be rare. This is in contrast to findings in other adults with bipolar affective disorder: in the general population there is an equal sex ratio, although women outnumber men in those with a rapid-cycling pattern of illness (Wehr et al., 1988). In people with developmental disabilities due to causes other than Down syndrome, the sex ratio also appears to be equal (Reid, 1972; Naylor et al., 1974; Heaton-Ward, 1977; Hucker et al., 1979; Rivinus & Harmatz, 1979; Sovner, 1989). The absence of a family history of affective disorders in people with Down syndrome and mania also appears to be unusual. Amongst people with developmental disabilities due to causes other than Down syndrome, mania is frequently associated with a family history (Reid, 1972; Heaton-Ward, 1977; Glue, 1989).

Alzheimer's disease

Individuals with Down syndrome appear to be particularly vulnerable to developing the histopathological changes associated with Alzheimer's disease. The association between the two conditions has been admirably reviewed (Berg, Karlinsky & Holland, 1993).

In 1907, Alois Alzheimer described the case of a single individual who developed a paranoid psychosis in association with cognitive decline during the pre-senium, and who, at post-mortem, demonstrated the typical histopathology of what is now known as Alzheimer's disease. In 1929, Struwe described an individual with Down syndrome who demonstrated Alzheimer's pathology, but it was not until 1948 that Jervis emphasized the relationship between the two conditions. The relationship between Down syndrome and Alzheimer's disease is discussed further in Chapter 8.

Less common psychiatric syndromes

The literature on other psychiatric syndromes in association with Down syndrome is sparse and largely confined to case reports. The following syndromes have been described: multi-infarct dementia (Collacott, Cooper & Ismail, 1994); obsessive–compulsive disorder (O'Dwyer, Holme & Collacott, 1992; Prasher & Day, 1995); schizophrenia (Duggirala, Cooper & Collacott, 1995; Cooper, Duggirala & Collacott, 1995); Gilles de la Tourette syndrome (Collacott & Ismail, 1988); de Clerambault's and Fregoli syndrome (Collacott & Napier, 1991); and anorexia nervosa (Szymanski & Biederman, 1984). However, the extent of the association of these disorders with Down syndrome remains unclear.

Conclusion

People with Down syndrome present special mental health needs. Such individuals usually have a severe degree of developmental disability, and their personality and behavioural characteristics generally conform to a distinct behavioural phenotype. They often present with fewer behavioural problems than do others with severe developmental disabilities. Whereas the relationship between Down syndrome and autistic traits requires further exploration, it is clear that people with Down syndrome may present with the full range of mental disorders. However, they do appear to be particularly susceptible to developing affective disorders and Alzheimer's disease, both of which require special management. The precise reasons for this differential susceptibility are, as yet, not completely understood.

References

Alzheimer, A. (1907). Uber eine eigenartige Erkrankung der Hirnrinde. *Allgemeine Zeitschrift fur Psychiatrie und Psychisch-Gerichtliche Medizin*, **64**, 146–48.

American Psychiatric Association (1987). *Diagnostic and Statistical Manual of Mental Disorder*, 3rd edition, revised. Washington, DC: APA.

Baron, J. (1972). Temperament profile of children with Down's syndrome. *Developmental Medicine and Child Neurology*, **14**, 640–3.

Berg, J.M., Karlinsky, H. Holland, A.J. (eds) (1993). *Alzheimer's Disease, Down Syndrome, and their Relationship*. Oxford: OxfordUniversity Press.

Blaketer-Simmonds, D.A. (1953). An investigation into the supposed differences existing between mongols and other mentally defective subjects with regard to certain psychological traits. *Journal of Mental Science*, **99**, 702–19.

Bregman, J.D., & Volkmar, F.R. (1988). Autistic social dysfunction and Down's syndrome. *Journal of the American Academy of Child and Adolescent Psychiatry*, **27**, 440–1.

Bridges, F.A. & Cicchetti, D. (1982). Mothers' ratings of the temperament characteristics of Down's syndrome infants. *Developmental Psychology*, **18**, 238–44.

Brousseau, K. & Brainerd, H.G. (1928). *Mongolism: a Study of the Physical and Mental Characteristics of Mongolian Imbeciles*. London: Balliere, Tindall & Cox.

Collacott, R.A., & Cooper, S-A. (1992). Adaptive behaviour after depression in Down's syndrome. *Journal of Nervous and Mental Disease*, **180**, 468–70.

Collacott, R.A., Cooper, S-A, Branford, D., & McGrother, C. (1998). Behaviour phenotype for Down syndrome. *British Journal of Psychiatry*, **172**, 85–9.

Collacott, R.A., Cooper, S-A, & Ismail, I.A. (1994). Multi-infarct dementia in Down syndrome. *Journal of Intellectual Disability Research*, **38**, 203–8.

Collacott, R.A., Cooper, S-A, & McGrother, C.A. (1992). Differential rates of psychiatric disorders in adults with Down's syndrome compared with other mentally handicapped adults. *British Journal of Psychiatry*, **161**, 671–4.

Collacott, R.A., & Ismail, I.A. (1988). Tourettism in a patient with Down's syndrome. *Journal of Mental Deficiency Research*, **32**, 163–6.

Collacott, R.A., & Napier, E.M. (1991). Erotomania and Fregoli-like state in Down's syndrome: dynamic and developmental aspects. *Journal of Mental Deficiency Research*, **35**, 481–6.

Cooke, E.D. & Leventhal, B.L. (1987). Down's syndrome with mania. *British Journal of Psychiatry*, **150**, 249–50.

Cooper, S-A. & Collacott, R.A. (1991). Manic episodes in Down's syndrome: two case reports. *Journal of Nervous and Mental Disease*, **179**, 635–6.

(1993). Mania and Down's syndrome. *British Journal of Psychiatry*, **161**, 739–43.

(1994a). Clinical features and diagnostic criteria of depression in Down's syndrome. *British Journal of Psychiatry*, **165**, 399–403.

(1994b). Relapse of depression in adults with Down's syndrome. *British Journal of Developmental Disability*, **40**, 32–7.

(1996). Depressive episodes in adults with learning disabilities. *Irish Journal of Psychological Medicine*, **13**(3), 105–13.

Cooper, S-A., Collacott, R.A. & Hauck, A. (1994). Late onset mania in Down's syndrome. *Journal of Intellectual Disability Research*, **38**, 73–8.

Cooper, S-A., Duggirala & C. & Collacott, R.A. (1995). Adaptive behaviour after schizophrenia in people with Down's syndrome. *Journal of Intellectual Disability Research*, **39**, 201–4.

Domino, G. (1965). Personality traits in institutionalised mongoloids. *American Journal of Mental Deficiency*, **69**, 568–70.

Domino, G., Goldschmid, M. & Kaplan, M. (1964). Personality traits of institutionalised mongoloid girls. *American Journal of Mental Deficiency*, **68**, 498–502.

Down, J.H.L. (1866). *Observations on an Ethnic Classification of Idiots.* Clinical lectures and reports. London: London Hospital. Reprinted in Payne, R. (1965). The centenary of 'mongolism'. *Journal of Mental Science*, **11**, 89–92.

(1877). Mental Afflictions of Childhood and Youth. London: Churchill.

Duggirala, C., Cooper, S-A. & Collacott, RA (1995) Schizophrenia and Down's syndrome *Irish Journal of Psychological Medicine*, **12**, (1), 30–3.

Engler, M. (1949). Mongolism Baltimore: Williams & Wilkins.

Fogelman, C.J. (1975). *AAMD Adaptive Behavior Scale Manual.* Washington, DC: American Association on Mental Deficiency.

Fraser, J. & Mitchell, A. (1876). Kalmuc Idiocy *Journal of Mental Science*, **22**, 169–79.

Gath, A. & Gumley, D. (1986). Behaviour problems in retarded children with special reference to Down's syndrome *British Journal of Psychiatry*, **149**, 156–61.

Ghaziuddin, M. (1997). Autism in Down's syndrome: family history correlates. *Journal of Intellectual Disability Research*, **41**, 87–91.

Ghaziuddin, M. & Tsai, L. (1991). Depression in autistic disorder (depressive illness in a patient with Down's syndrome and autism). *British Journal of Psychiatry*, **159**, 721–3.

Ghaziuddin, M., Tsai, L.Y. & Ghaziuddin, N. (1992). Autism in Down's syndrome: presentation and diagnosis. *Journal of Intellectual Disability Research*, **36**, 449–56.

Gibbs, M.V. & Thorpe, J.G. (1983). Personality stereotype of non-institutionalised Down syndrome children. *American Journal of Mental Deficiency*, **87**, 602–5.

Glue, P. (1989). Rapid cycling affective disorders in the mentally retarded. *Biological Psychiatry*, **26**, 250–6.

Gunn, P., Berry, P. & Anderson, R.J. (1981). The temperament of Down syndrome infants: a research note. *Journal of Child Psychiatry and Psychiatry*, **22**, 189–94.

Heaton-Ward, A. (1977). Psychosis in mental handicap. *British Journal of Psychiatry*, **130**, 525–33.

Hucker, S.J., Day, K.A., George, S. et al. (1979). Psychosis in mentally handicapped adults. In *Psychiatric Illness and Mental Handicap* (ed. E.E. James & R.P. Snaith), pp.27–35, London: Gaskell Press.

Johnson, R.C. & Abelson, R.B. (1969). Intellectual, behavioral and physical characteristics associated with trisomy, translocation and mosaic types of Down's syndrome. *American Journal of Mental Deficiency*, **73**, 852–5.

Keegan, D.L., Pettigrew, A. & Parker, Z. (1974). Psychosis in Down's syndrome treated with amitryptiline. *Canadian Medical Association Journal*, **110**, 1128–9.

Lazarus, A., Jaffe & R.L., Dubin, V.V.R. (1990). Electroconvulsive therapy and major depression in Down's syndrome. *Journal of Clinical Psychiatry*, **51**, 422–5.

Lund, J. (1985). The prevalence of psychiatric morbidity in mentally retarded adults. *Acta Psychiatrica Scandinavica*, **72**, 563–70.

  (1988). Psychiatric aspects of Down's syndrome. *Acta Psychiatrica Scandinavica*, **78**, 369–74.

McLaughlin, M. (1987). Bipolar affective disorder in Down's syndrome. *British Journal of Psychiatry*, **151**, 116–7.

Meins, W. (1993). Prevalence and risk factors for depressive disorders in adults with intellectual disability. *Australia and New Zealand Journal of Developmental Disabilities*, **18**, 147–56.

Moore, R.B., Thulin, H.C. & Laverne Capes, A.B. (1968). Mongoloid and non-mongoloid retardates: a behavioural comparison. *American Journal of Mental Deficiency*, **73**, 433–6.

Myers, B.A. & Pueschel, S.M. (1991). Psychiatric disorders in people with Down's syndrome. *Journal of Nervous and Mental Disease*, **179**, 609–13.

Naylor, G.J., Donald, J.M. & LePoidevin, D. et al. (1974). A double-blind trial of long-term lithium therapy in mental defectives. *British Journal of Psychaitry*, **124**, 52–7.

O'Dwyer, J., Holme, J. & Collacott, R.A. (1992). Obsessive-compulsive disorder in adults with Down's syndrome. *Journal of Mental and Nervous Dsease*, **180**, 603–4.

Prasher, V.P. & Day, S. (1995). Brief report: obsessive compulsive disorder in adults with Down's syndrome. *Journal of Autism and Developmental Disorders*, **25**, 342–458.

Prasher, V.P. & Hall, W. (1996). Short-term prognosis of depression in adults with Down's syndrome: association with thyroid status and effects on adaptive behaviour. *Journal of Intellectual Deficiency Research*, **40**, 32–8.

Pueschel, S.M., Bernier, J.C. & Pezzullo, J.C. (1991). Behavioural observations on children with Down's syndrome. *Journal of Mental Deficiency Research*, **35**, 502–11.

Reid, A.H. (1972). Psychoses in adult mental defectives I: Manic depressive psychosis. *British Journal of Psychiatry*, **120**, 205–12.

Richardson, S.A., Katz, M., Koller, H. et al. (1979). Some characteristics of a population of mentally retarded young adults in a British city: a basis for estimating some service needs. *Journal of Mental Deficiency Research*, **23**, 276–86.

Rivinus, T.M. & Harmatz, J.S. (1979). Diagnosis and lithium treatment of affective disorders in the retarded: 5 case studies. *American Journal of Psychiatry*, **136**, 551.

Rodgers, C. (1987). Maternal support for the Down's syndrome stereotype: the effect of direct experiences of the condition. *Journal of Mental Deficiency Research*, **31**, 271–78.

Roith, A.I. (1961). Psychotic depression in a mongol. *Journal of Mental Subnormality*, **7**, 45–7.

Rollin, H.R. (1946). Personality in mongolism with special reference to the incidence of catatonic psychosis. *American Journal of Mental Deficiency*, **51**, 219–37.

Rutter, M. & Schopler, E. (1988). Autism and pervasive developmental disorders. In: *Assessment and Diagnosis in Child Psychopathology*, ed. M. Rutter, A.H. Tuma & I.S. Lann pp. 408–34. London: David Fulton.

Rutter, M., Tizard, J., & Whitmore, K. (1970). *Education, Health and Behaviour*. London: Longman.

Silverstein, A.B. (1964). An empirical test of the mongoloid stereotype. *American Journal of Mental Deficiency*, **68**, 493–7.

Singh, I. & Zolese, G. (1986). Is mania really incompatible with Down's syndrome? *British Journal of Psychiatry*, **148**, 613–14.

Smith, S., Branford, D., Collacott, R.A., Cooper & S-A, & McGrother, C. (1996). Prevalence and cluster typology of maladaptive behaviour in a geographically defined population of adults with learning disabilities. *British Journal of Psychiatry*, **169**, 219–27.

Sovner, R. (1989). The use of valproate in the treatment of mentally retarded persons with typical and atypical bipolar disorders. *Journal of Clinical Psychiatry*, **50**, (Suppl. 3), 40–3.

(1991). Divalproex-responsive rapid cycling bipolar disorder in a patient with Down's syndrome: implications for the Down's syndrome – mania hypothesis. *Journal of Mental Deficiency Research*, **35**, 171–3.

Sovner, R. & Hurley, D.A. (1983). Do the mentally retarded suffer from affective illness? *Archives of General Psychiatry*, **40**, 319–20.

Sovner, R., Hurley, D.A. & Labrie, R. (1985). Is mania incompatible with Down's syndrome? *British Journal of Psychiatry*, **146**, 319–20.

Storm, W. (1990). Differential diagnosis and treatment of depressive features in Down's syndrome: a case illustration. *Research in Developmental Disabilities*, **11**, 131–7.

Struwe, F. (1929). Histopathologische Untersuchungen uber Entstehung und Wesen der senilen Plaques. *Zentralblatt fur die gesante Neurologie und Psychiatrie*, **122**, 291–307.

Szymanski, L.S. & Biederman, J. (1984). Depression and anorexia nervosa in persons with Down syndrome. *American Journal of Mental Deficiency*, **89**, 246–51.

Wakabayashi, S. (1979). A case of infantile autism associated with Down's syndrome. *Journal of Autism and Developmental Disorders*, **9**, 31–6.

Warren, A.C., Holroyd, S. & Folstein, M.F. (1989). Major depression in Down's syndrome. *British Journal of Psychiatry*, **155**, 202–5.

Wehr, T.A., Sack, D.A., Rosenthal, W.E. et al. (1988). Rapid cycling affective disorder: contributing factors and treatment responses in 51 patients. *American Journal of Psychiatry*, **145**, 179–84.

Wing, L. & Gould, J. (1979). Severe impairment of social interaction and associated abnormalities in children: epidemiology and classification. *Journal of Autism and Developmental Disorders*, **9**, 11–29.

World Health Organization (1992). *The ICD-10 Classification of Mental and Behavioural Disorders: Clinical Description and Diagnostic Guidelines.* Geneva: World Health Organization.

(1993). *The IQ-10 Classification of Mental and Behavioural Disorders: Diagnostic Criteria for Research.* Geneva: World Health Organization.

Wunsch, W.L. (1957). Some characteristics of mongoloids evaluated in a clinic for children with retarded mental development. *American Journal of Mental Deficiency*, **62**, 122–30.

13 Psychiatric disorders in elderly people with developmental disabilities

SALLY-ANN COOPER

Introduction

People with developmental disabilities form a small proportion of the whole population, but because of their special needs, they require suitable attention and services. Elderly people form only a small proportion of all people with developmental disabilities. However, it is important to focus on this group because the needs of elderly people with developmental disabilities differ from the needs of younger adults, and yet services have not yet adapted to meet the challenge of caring for them. (Most services are still designed to meet the needs of children or young adults with developmental disabilities.) Additionally, the number of people with developmental disabilities who will reach old age is increasing.

Population changes

Amongst the general population, the proportion of elderly people is increasing. This is due to changing birth rates, for example those in the post-war baby boom cohort of the 1940s are now in their 50s. This affects equally people with developmental disabilities and people of average ability. People are also living longer than they did in the past, and this particularly affects people with developmental disabilities. This relates in part to changing attitudes and lifestyles, more individualised and improved quality of care, and access to medical treatments that used to be denied, such as treatments for respiratory infections and congenital heart disease.

Dayton et al. (1932) reported that only 28 per cent of ten-year-old children with developmental disabilities would survive to be 60 years of age. Forty years later, this figure was shown to have risen to 46 per cent (Balakrishnan & Wolf, 1976). Institutional studies have all shown increases in the lifespan of people with developmental disabilities (Carter & Jancar, 1983; Tait, 1983; Lubin & Kiely, 1985; Wolf & Wright, 1987), as have community studies (McCurley, Mackay & Scally, 1972; Miller & Eyman, 1978). The less severe a person's developmental disabilities, the greater his or her life expectancy

(Jacobson, Sutton & Janicki, 1985; Wolf & Wright, 1987). The greatest life expectancies are for women who are ambulatory, do not have Down syndrome, have mild rather than severe developmental disabilities, and who have remained living in the community (Jacobson et al., 1985). Although the life expectancy of a person with Down syndrome is less than that of the average person with developmental disabilities of other causes, people with Down syndrome are also living longer (Richards & Siddiqui, 1980; Carter & Jancar, 1983; Fryers, 1984; Baird & Sadovnick, 1987).

Some researchers have attempted to quantify the number of middle-aged and elderly people with developmental disabilities (Janicki & MacEachron, 1984; Moss et al., 1992; Hand, 1994; Ashman et al., 1994). However, it is difficult to draw comparisons between these studies due to the differing age groups investigated and the differing research methodologies. Although the number of individuals is small, it will increase in the near future, for the reasons given above.

Dementia

Dementia is a disease that is associated with old age. There are many causes of dementia, but the most common types are dementia in Alzheimer's disease and vascular dementia. A recent analysis of all comprehensive European studies revealed the European general population prevalence rates for dementia in five-year age groups from 60 to 94 years as: 1.0, 1.4, 4.1, 5.7, 13.0, 21.6 and 32.2 per cent respectively (Hofman et al., 1991). Amongst people with developmental disabilities, the prevalence of dementia is considerably higher than for the age-matched general population. This is particularly true for people with Down syndrome, but also for people with developmental disabilities of other causes. The relationship between Down syndrome and dementia has been reviewed in detail (Oliver & Holland, 1986; Holland & Oliver, 1995), and is considered further in Chapter 8.

Dementia has also been recognized for many years to occur in people with developmental disabilities of causes other than Down syndrome (Bleuler, 1924; Kaplan, 1956; Heaton-Ward, 1967). Corbett (1979) suggested that there is a 'probable earlier appearance of dementia' in people with developmental disabilities, but did not quote actual rates in his study. Studies of the prevalence of dementia have focused on different populations, and used differing methodologies, which makes comparisons difficult. Some studies have drawn their subjects from people resident in institutions (Reid & Aungle, 1974; Tait, 1983; Day, 1985, 1987; Sansom et al., 1994), whereas others have studied epidemiological samples from the community and institutions (Lund, 1985), or whole populations living in a defined area (Moss & Patel, 1993; Cooper, 1997a). Some studies have relied on taking information/diagnoses from existing medical case notes (Day, 1985), whereas others included comprehensive psychiatric assessment and clearly defined diagnostic

Table 13.1 Prevalence of dementia in people with developmental disabilities

	n		*Age (years)*	*Percentage*
Clinical studies				
Reid & Aungle (1974)	133	Hospital residents	45–64	6.0
	22		65+	13.6
Tait (1983)	81	Hospital residents	65+	11.1
Lund (1985)	67	Epidemiological	45–64	6.0
	27		65+	22.2
Day (1985)	357	Hospital residents	40+	3.3
Day (1987)	99	Hospital residents	65+	12+15[a]
Moss & Patel (1993)	105	Epidemiological	50+	11.4
Sansom et al. (1994)	124	Hospital residents	60+	12.9
Cooper (1997b)	134	Epidemiological	65+	21.7
	—	Epidemiological	50+	13.0
Neuropathological studies (non-Down syndrome)				
Barcikowska et al. (1989)	70		65+ at death	31
Popovitch et al. (1990)	385		23–49 at death	9.5
			50–65 at death	54
			66–75 at death	76
			76–90 at death	87

Note:
[a] Late-onset behaviour change, not diagnosed.

criteria (Sansom et al., 1994; Cooper, 1997a). The studies have examined different age groups: those aged 40 years and over (Day, 1985), 45 years and over (Reid & Aungle, 1974), 50 years and over (Moss & Patel, 1993), 60 years and over (Sansom et al., 1994), and 65 years and over (Day, 1987; Cooper, 1997a). Lund (1985) studied adults of all ages, and consequently had only a small number of people in his 65 years and over age band. These studies are summarized in Table 13.1.

All existing studies show the prevalence of dementia to be considerably higher in elderly people with developmental disabilities, when compared with the age-matched general population, and epidemiological studies provide similar findings. Lund (1985) reported 22.2 per cent and Cooper (1997a) reported 21.6 per cent of people aged 65 years and over to have dementia. People with Down syndrome do not yet usually live beyond the age of 65 years, and so these two studies refer almost exclusively to people with developmental disabilities of causes other than Down syndrome. In the study by Cooper (1997a), only five out of the 134 elderly people had Down syndrome; three out of these five people had dementia, compared with 26 out of the 129 people with other underlying causes of their developmental disabilities. Moss and Patel (1993) found 11.4 per cent of people aged 50 years and over to have dementia. This included four out of the nine people in the study with Down syndrome, and eight out of the 96 people with developmental disabilities of other causes. The inclusion of a comparison group of younger adults with developmental disabilities in the study reported by Cooper (1997a), together with a known size of the total population through prior ascertainment using active case-finding methods, means that an estimated rate of dementia amongst people aged 50 years and over can be calculated from this study. This yields a rate of 13.0 per cent, which compares very closely with the 11.4 per cent reported by Moss and Patel (1993). Hence, all of the three existing epidemiological studies provide similar rates for the prevalence of dementia, and show this rate to be considerably higher than that in the general population.

The prevalence of dementia increases with age: 15.6 per cent in those aged 65–74 years; 23.5 per cent in the 75–84-year age group; and 70.0 per cent for those aged 85–94 years (Cooper, 1997a). People with dementia have also been demonstrated to be more likely to be female, with more poorly controlled epilepsy and a larger number of additional physical disorders, and less likely to be smokers, compared with those without dementia (Cooper, 1997a).

Psychiatric disorders other than dementia

The existing literature regarding psychiatric disorders amongst elderly people with developmental disabilities is even more limited than it is for dementia, and it is difficult to compare studies (Cooper, 1992). Studies of people living in institutions include that of Day (1985), who reported the diagnoses documented in the case notes of 357 hospital residents aged 40 years and over, and found 109 (31 per cent) to have a documented psychiatric diagnosis. Subsequently Day interviewed staff to determine that one-fifth of the 99 hospital residents aged 65 years and over had a psychiatric disorder (diagnostic criteria were not defined) (Day, 1987). Sansom et al. (1994) examined 124 hospital residents aged 60–94 years with developmental disabilities, and found 8.9 per cent to meet DSM-III-R (American Psychiatric Association, 1987) criteria for affective disorders, and 6.5 per cent to meet DSM-III-R criteria for schizophrenia. (They did not study anxiety disorders or behaviour disorders.)

Psychiatric studies that have encompassed people living in the community as well as in an institution include that of Corbett (1979), who employed ICD-8 criteria (World Health Organization, 1968) and interviewed the carers of subjects in a two-stage process. One hundred and ten subjects were aged 60 years or over, of whom 62.9 per cent were free from psychiatric disorders (not including dementia). Schizophrenia was found in 5.4 per cent, depression in 1.8 per cent, manic depressive psychosis in 2.7 per cent, childhood psychosis in 3.6 per cent and personality/behaviour disorder in 22.7 per cent. Patel, Goldberg and Moss (1993) used a semi-structured interview to study the whole population of people aged 50 years and over with moderate and profound developmental disabilities and living in Oldham, UK (n=105). Twelve people were determined to have a psychiatric diagnosis meeting DSM-III-R criteria (excluding dementia); two other people were reported to have schizophrenia that could not be detected by the rating scale that was used – bringing the total to 14 out of 105. Surprisingly, no-one was reported to have behaviour disorders (it is unclear whether this is due to the diagnostic criteria that were employed). Of the 105 people, three were found to have agoraphobia, two had panic disorder, three had generalized anxiety disorder, five had major depression, one had dysthymia and one had hypomania.

Cooper (1997b) studied the whole population of people aged 65 years and over with developmental disabilities living in Leicestershire, UK, using a semi-structured psychiatric rating scale ($n = 134$). She used Diagnostic Criteria for Research (the operational criteria of ICD-10) (World Health Organization, 1993) to diagnose disorders, modified where necessary. Modifications were due to a lack of reliable informants for developmental histories from early childhood for people who presented at the time of the study with the symptoms and signs of autism, and to take account of the impossibility of assessing 'insight' in non-verbal people who presented at the time of the study with symptoms and signs of anxiety disorders. The Kettering/Leicester criteria for depression were used (Cooper & Collacott, 1994a, 1996). Criteria for behaviour disorders were also clearly defined. A psychiatric diagnosis (defined to include dementia and past history of affective disorder) was found in 68.7 per cent. Schizophrenia/delusional disorder was present in 3.0 per cent; a current diagnosis of depression was present in 6.0 per cent; a past history of affective disorder in 15.7 per cent; generalized anxiety disorder in 9.0 per cent; agoraphobia in 3.7 per cent; other phobia in 3.0 per cent; behaviour disorder in 14.9 per cent; and autism in 6.0 per cent. This study also examined a younger cohort of adults with developmental disabilities, and found the elderly group to have higher rates of depression and anxiety disorders, but equal rates of schizophrenia/delusional disorders, autism and behaviour disorders in the two groups.

By the same method as previously described for dementia, it was possible to calculate from this study the estimated rates of psychiatric disorders for people aged 50 years and over. This shows the prevalence rates for psychiatric disorders to be higher in those aged 65 years and over, compared with those aged 50 years and over (Cooper, 1997b). The difference found between age groups accounts for the apparent difference in findings between the studies of Patel et al. (1993) and Cooper (1997b). When the age adjustment is made, comparable rates are found for the prevalence of depression and anxiety disorders, although the lack of reported behaviour disorder in the study of Patel et al. (1993) is at odds with the finding of 14.9 per cent of those aged 65 years and over with behaviour disorders and an estimated rate of 11.5 per cent for those aged 50 years and over by Cooper (1997b), and also the high rates found by Corbett (1979). Due to the number of subjects involved, it is not possible to age adjust the results of Cooper (1997b) to estimate rates for a 60 years and over group, which would be required to compare rates with the study of Corbett (1979).

It is not surprising that higher rates of psychiatric disorders are found in elderly when compared with younger adults with developmental disabilities. Adults with developmental disorders have all the usual risk factors for psychiatric disorders that are present amongst the general population (e.g. genetic predisposition, associations with physical health, psychological predisposition, social factors and life events). Additionally, they have the risk factors for psychiatric disorders that are specific to developmental disorders (e.g. behaviour phenotypes, associations with epilepsy and physical disabilities, disadvantaged backgrounds more likely to result in damaged psychological development and hence predisposition, limited social networks, restricted social circumstances and stigma, developmental factors). Elderly people with developmental disabilities are at risk of these factors and also further factors associated with ageing (e.g. physical frailty, bereavement and loss of previous role such as work at the day centre, reduction in social network). Additionally, the current cohort of elderly people with developmental disabilities was raised at a time when prejudice and discrimination existed against people with developmental disabilities, and these individuals were more likely to have grown up in an institution, rather than within families, with all the disadvantages that are acquired as a result.

Psychopathology

There are similarities in the psychopathology of psychiatric disorders in people with developmental disorders compared with the general population, but also some important differences. Differences include the common occurrence of some symptoms in the presentation of psychiatric disorders in people with developmental disorders, that are unusual in the general population. Examples include increase in specific maladaptive behaviours, or onset of maladaptive behaviours (such as aggression), reduction in adaptive skills, reduction of speech and reassurance-seeking behaviour (Reiss & Rojahn, 1993; Sturmey, 1993; Cooper & Collacott, 1994b). Alternatively, the degree of symptom subdivision in people of average ability can often be determined with considerable sophistication, whereas such subdivision becomes impossible with someone of limited or no verbal skills. This is particularly true with regard to psychotic symptoms. For example, delusions and hallucinations may be elicited in a person with developmental disabilities, and it may be possible to subdivide auditory hallucinations into second or third person; but it is extremely unlikely that passivity phenomena (the experience of replacement of will) could be distinguished from the belief of being controlled or influenced, or that thought interference could be distinguished from delusions of mind reading, or that delusional perception could be confidently determined. It is also difficult in people with developmental disorders to elicit the cognitions that are characteristic (in people of average ability) of other psychiatric disorders. Examples of this include depressive cognitions (guilt, hopelessness, suicidal intent, worthlessness), obsessional thoughts and the insight that occurs in anxiety disorders.

A further consideration in eliciting psychopathology amongst people with developmental disabilities is the importance of distinguishing between trait and state finding, i.e. of demonstrating that a change has occurred. For example, if a person has been socially withdrawn, all his or her life, then this is a normal finding for that person, and is not a symptom of psychiatric illness. However, when social withdrawal occurs in a person who was previously sociable, then this does indicate psychiatric disorder. If a person with lifelong social withdrawal becomes more socially withdrawn than is usual for him or her, then this, too, indicates psychiatric illness. This is an important point, because many symptoms of psychiatric disorders can be present as lifelong traits in people with developmental disorders (as an integral part of the developmental disorder), whereas this is unusual in people of average ability. Some symptoms are always abnormal and therefore always indicate psychiatric disorder, e.g. delusions and hallucinations.

For many people with developmental disabilities, psychopathology is elicited through observation of the person rather than from self-reports of symptoms. The necessity of this is inversely proportional to the person's level of verbal and intellectual abilities. Even when working with people with verbal skills, clinicians require skill and experience in eliciting history items, in view of the well-recognized phenomenon of compliant answers, the possibility of the person mixing up the sequencing of events and their time scale, poor concentration spans, and the need to avoid complex, and use developmentally appropriate, language.

Some studies have examined the psychopathology of dementia in people with developmental disabilities. Cooper (1997c) found that 27.6 per cent of 29 people with dementia experienced at least one type of psychotic symptom: delusions occurred in 20.7 per cent and hallucinations in 20.7 per cent. All delusions were persecutory, with the most common type being delusions of money and other items being stolen from the subject, occurring in 10.3 per cent. The most common type of hallucination was that of visual hallucinations of strangers in the person's house, occurring in 13.8 per cent, followed by visual hallucinations of relatives in 6.9 per cent and second person auditory hallucinations in 6.9 per cent. Non-psychotic psychiatric symptoms were also common, particularly changed sleep pattern (69.0 per cent), loss of concentration (69.0 per cent), worry (41.4 per cent), reduced quantity of speech (41.4 per cent), change in appetite (31.0 per cent) and onset of, or increase in verbal aggression (31.0 per cent). Onset of, or increased, physical aggression occurred in 24.1 per cent. Almost everyone experienced forgetfulness, impaired understanding, confusion and reduced self-care skills. Forgetting people's names was also common (58.6 per cent), as was geographical disorientation (55.2 per cent) and temporal disorientation (44.8 per cent). The rates of psychotic symptoms found in this study fall within the range that is quoted for such symptoms amongst people with dementia from the general population; the types of psychotic symptoms that are found are also similar.

Other researchers have not studied psychotic symptoms in dementia, but have examined non-psychotic symptoms. Moss and Patel (1995) examined 12 people with developmental disabilities and dementia, compared with people with developmental disabilities but without dementia. They found those with dementia to have higher levels of sleep difficulty, hypersomnia, irritability, inefficient thought and loss of interests, which are similar to the findings of Cooper (1997c).

Some studies have specifically examined people with Down syndrome and found overlap of symptoms of depression and dementia (Burt, Loveland & Lewis, 1992; Prasher, 1995; Prasher & Filer, 1995).

Some of the psychopathology of dementia can cause a significant management problem for carers, and so assumes great importance and may influence the viability of a person's place of residence. In addition to the study of Cooper (1997c), it has previously been suggested that aggression can be a feature of dementia in people with developmental disabilities (Reid & Aungle, 1974; Day, 1985). Other symptoms, such as sleep disturbance, may also influence a carer's ability to continue to care. Hence, such symptoms are important in terms of the necessary service requirements for this population. Some of the psychopathology of dementia can be responsive to pharmacotherapy (e.g. psychotic symptoms), environmental manipulation (e.g. disorientation) or behavioural therapy (e.g. sleep disturbance), and so identification of these symptoms is of clinical significance.

There are no existing studies that report comparisons of psychopathology of different psychiatric disorders between elderly and younger adults with developmental disabilities. This area requires further research because such differences have been reported to occur between elderly and younger adults of average ability. It is of clinical relevance because an accurate knowledge of the presentation of psychiatric disorders is required in order to achieve accurate diagnosis, which in turn informs and directs the management plan.

Assessment and diagnosis

Comprehensive assessment is essential in order to achieve an accurate diagnosis from which the treatment/management care plans can be derived. The assessment must be thorough enough to include full details of the descriptive psychopathology and also to derive an aetiological formulation.

This requires listening carefully and clarifying all of the information that is presented, but also specifically asking about psychopathology, present circumstances and background information, which might not have been volunteered. The following examples demonstrate the importance of this. If an elderly person with developmental disabilities, who has previously always been well, starts to become physically aggressive at home, then this is probably the problem that will be presented to the health care team. However, aggression can occur as a symptom of several psychiatric disorders. It would, therefore, be inappropriate to assume that it is due to a behaviour disorder without first specifically enquiring about all the other symptoms that are a feature of dementia, schizophrenia, depression and anxiety disorders. Only by doing this will the correct diagnosis be established, and hence the correct treatment/management care plan embarked upon. Similarly, a full assessment of the descriptive psychopathology alone is inadequate. For example, the descriptive psychopathology may indicate a depressive episode, but the management plan would differ for a person who has a long history of bipolar affective episodes and a family history of bipolar disorder, but no apparent psychological predisposition, social disadvantages or recent life events except discontinuation of their lithium, when compared with that for a person who has recently been bereaved of a parent and consequently moved into residential care and lost contact with his or her previous neighbourhood.

Psychiatrists in the UK who specialize in developmental disabilities are trained to conduct assessments in a standard way. This includes taking a full history from an informant who has known the person long enough to have knowledge of his or her usual premorbid personality and traits, as well as interviewing the person with developmental disabilities. Information is collected regarding the descriptive psychopathology, the time scale and sequence of events, and any associated factors, including recent life events and changes in the care environment; past episodes of psychiatric disorders, their presentation, duration and successes/failures of treatments; past and current medical disorders and epilepsy history; details of current and past drugs that are taken for psychiatric and physical conditions (as some drugs can cause psychiatric disorders, and some drug side-effects can mimic psychiatric disorders), the use of alcohol and illegal/street drugs; psychiatric disorders and developmental disabilities that are present in family members; details of the individual's personal history, which indicates the way in which his or her personality has been shaped and coping strategies; details of the person's social circumstances and social network; a developmental history, including the underlying cause of the person's developmental disabilities and the current level of adaptive functioning; details of forensic history and past offences. A mental state examination is undertaken throughout the duration of the interview. A physical examination should then be undertaken in order to exclude any physical causes of the psychiatric disorder and, similarly, routine blood tests should be done, including full blood count, urea and electrolytes, liver function tests and thyroid function tests. Thyroid dysfunction, in particular, can mimic and/or precipitate all of the more common types of psychiatric disorders. Any previous medical case notes about the person should be checked for additional relevant information. Additional investigations may well be required, but this is dependent upon the findings from the initial assessment.

If the individual presents with the descriptive psychopathology suggestive of dementia, more detailed physical investigations are required in order to eliminate any reversible/treatable causes. This will necessitate additional blood tests to measure serum B12 and red cell folate, syphilis serology and the erythrocyte sedimentation rate. A urine sample should be checked for infection, and an electrocardiogram and chest X-ray taken. A cranial computed tomography or magnetic resonance imaging scan may be required to exclude other treatable causes of dementia, such as space-occupying lesions. These scans are not usually helpful in the diagnosis of dementia (other than to exclude other pathology), unless there has been a previous scan taken at some point in the past with which they can be compared (as scan findings are often abnormal in people with developmental disabilities, regardless of the presence of psychiatric disorders). Recommendations have been made regarding the necessary investigations for research projects of dementia amongst people with developmental disabilities (Zigman et al., 1995).

Several members of the multidisciplinary team will often contribute to the assessment, e.g. psychiatrists, psychologists, nurses and occupational therapists. Carers from the person's usual residential and day places will also contribute to this process, as will family members, if there are any: very few elderly people with developmental disabilities live with their families (Cooper, 1997d). In some special cases, it may be necessary to admit the person into a psychiatric admission unit in order to undertake more detailed multidisciplinary assessments in a setting in which there are qualified nurses present 24 hours a day.

Traditionally, services for people with developmental disabilities have focused on children and young adults, with an emphasis on learning and development. Such approaches and settings are less relevant to elderly people. Consequently, in some cases, people may benefit from receiving additional care from the old-age psychiatric team. The most effective outcomes are likely to be achieved when the two psychiatric health care teams work flexibly and in collaboration to care for the individual and advise the primary health care team. In this way, their differing expertise can be pooled so that the provision of treatment/management plans can be tailored to best meet the needs of each individual (Royal College of Psychiatrists, 1997).

Conclusion

The lifespan of people with developmental disabilities is increasing, and many can now expect to live to their middle and old age. Psychiatric disorders are common amongst elderly people with developmental disabilities because they have the additional risk factors associated with developmental disorders as well as those associated with old age. Dementia, in particular, occurs commonly: the prevalence is four times higher in people with developmental disabilities aged 65 years and over than it is in the age-matched general population. This finding is independent of the strong association that also occurs between people with Down syndrome and dementia. Anxiety disorders and depression also occur commonly in elderly people: schizophrenia/delusional disorders, behaviour disorders and autism occur at a rate similar to that found in younger adults with developmental disabilities. The psychopathology of dementia has been studied, and many symptoms are common, including sleep disturbance, delusions and hallucinations, and aggression. It is important to determine these symptoms because many can be treated or modified; they are also a potential source of stress for carers and may affect the viability of people continuing to live at their usual residence.

Further research is required into differences in the psychopathology of different psychiatric disorders between elderly and younger adults with developmental disabilities: an accurate knowledge of the presentation of disorders is required in order to achieve accurate diagnosis, which in turn informs and directs the treatment/management plan. Comprehensive psychiatric assessment is essential in all cases in which the individual has changed in some way, in order to determine the diagnosis and aetiological formulation (and from there to plan treatment/management). This assessment is often undertaken in a multidisciplinary way. Services need to develop in order to meet the challenge of caring for this special population, which will grow in size in coming years.

References

American Psychiatric Association (1987). *Diagnostic and Statistical Manual of Psychiatric Disorders*, 3rd edn, revised. Washington, DC: APA.

Ashman, A., Suttie, J., Bramley, J. & Suttie, A. (1994). Older Australians with intellectual disability: the survivors. *Australian and New Zealand Journal of Developmental Disabilities*, **19**, 25–43.

Baird, P.A. & Sadovnick, A.D. (1987). Life expectancy in Down's syndrome. *Journal of Pediatrics*, **110**, 849–54.

Balakrishnan, T.R & Wolf, L.C. (1976). Life expectancy of mentally retarded persons in Canadian institutions. *American Journal on Mental Deficiency*, **80**, 650–62.

Barcikowska, M., Silverman, W., Zigman, W. et al. (1989). Alzheimer–type neuro-pathology and clinical symptoms of dementia in mentally retarded people without Down's syndrome. *American Journal on Mental Retardation*, **93**, 551–7.

Bleuler, E. (1924). *Lehrbuch der Psychiatrie*, translated as *Textbook of Psychiatry* by A.A. Brill, New York: Macmillan.

Burt, D.B., Loveland, K.A. & Lewis, K.R. (1992). Depression and the onset of dementia in adults with mental retardation. *American Journal on Mental Retardation*, **96**, 502–11.

Carter, G. & Jancar, J. (1983). Mortality in the mentally handicapped: a fifty year survey at the Stoke Park Group of hospitals (1930–1980). *Journal of Mental Deficiency Research*, **27**, 143–56.

Cooper, S.A. (1992). The psychiatry of elderly people with mental handicaps. *The International Journal of Geriatric Psychiatry*, **7**, 865–74.

(1997a). High prevalence of dementia amongst people with learning disabilities not attributed to Down's syndrome. *Psychological Medicine*, **27**, 609–16.

(1997b). Epidemiology of psychiatric disorders in elderly compared with younger adults with learning disabilities. *British Journal of Psychiatry*, **170**, 375–80.

(1997c). Psychiatric symptoms of dementia amongst elderly people with learning disabilities. *International Journal of Geriatric Psychiatry*, **12**, 662–6.

(1997d). Deficient health and social services for elderly people with learning disabilities. *Journal of Intellectual Disability Research*, **41**, 331–8.

Cooper, S-A. & Collacott, R.A. (1994a). Standardised diagnostic criteria for depression in people with learning disabilities. Abstracts of the Mental Handicap Section of the Royal College of Psychiatrists Annual Meeting.

(1994b). Clinical features and diagnostic criteria of depression in Down's syndrome. *British Journal of Psychiatry*, **165**, 399–403.

(1996). Depressive episodes in adults with learning disabilities. *Irish Journal of Psychological Medicine*, **13**, 105–13.

Corbett, J.A. (1979). Psychiatric morbidity and mental retardation. In: *Psychiatric Illness and Mental Handicap*, ed. F.E. James, and R.P. Snaith, pp. 11–25. London: Gaskell Press.

Day, K. (1985). Psychiatric disorder in the middle-aged and elderly mentally hand-icapped. *British Journal of Psychiatry*, **147**, 660–7.

Day, K.A. (1987). The elderly mentally handicapped in hospital: a clinical study. *Journal of Mental Deficiency Research*, **31**, 131–46.

Dayton, N.A., Doering, C.R., Hilferty, M.M., Maher, H.C. & Dolan, H.H. (1932). Mentality and life expectation in mental deficiency in Massachusetts: anal-ysis of the fourteen year period 1917–1930. *New England Journal of Medicine*, **206**, 550–70.

Fryers, T. (1984). *The Epidemiology of Severe Intellectual Impairment: The Dynamics of Prevalence*. New York: Academic Press.

Hand, J.E. (1994). Report of a national survey of older people with lifelong intel-lectual handicap in New Zealand. *Journal of Intellectual Disability Research*, **38**, 275–87.

Heaton-Ward, W.A. (1967). *Mental Subnormality,* 3rd edn. Bristol: John Wright and Sons.

Hofman, A., Rocca, W.A., Brayne, C. et al. (1991). The prevalence of dementia in Europe: a collaborative study of 1980–1990 findings. *International Journal of Epidemiology,* **20**, 736–48.

Holland, A.J. & Oliver, C. (1995). Down's syndrome and the links with Alzheimer's disease. *Journal of Neurology, Neurosurgery and Psychiatry,* **59**, 111–15.

Jacobson, J.W., Sutton, M.S. & Janicki, M.P. (1985). Demography and characteristics of aging and aged mentally retarded persons. In: *Aging and Developmental Disabilities, Issues and Approaches,* ed. M.P. Janicki, H.M. Wisniewski, pp. 115–41. Baltimore: P.H. Brooks.

Janicki, M.P. & MacEachron, A.E. (1984). Residential, health and social service needs of elderly developmentally disabled persons. *The Gerontologist,* **24**, 128–37.

Kaplan, O.J. (1956). In: *Psychiatric Disorders in Later Life.* Oxford: Oxford University Press.

Lubin, R.A & Kiely, M. (1985). Epidemiology of aging in developmental disabilities. In *Aging and Developmental Disabilities, Issues and Approaches,* ed. M.P. Janicki, & H.M. Wisniewski, pp. 95–113. Baltimore: P.H. Brooks.

Lund, J. (1985). The prevalence of psychiatric morbidity in mentally retarded adults. *Acta Psychiatrica Scandinavica,* **72**, 563–70.

McCurley, R., Mackay, D.N. & Scally, B.G. (1972). The life expectation of the mentally subnormal under community and hospital care. *Journal of Mental Deficiency Research,* **16**, 57–66.

Miller, C. & Eyman, R. (1978). Hospital and community mortality rates among the retarded. *Journal of Mental Deficiency Research,* **22**, 137–45.

Moss, S, Hogg, J. & Horne, M. (1992). Demographic characteristics of a population of people with moderate, severe and profound intellectual disability (mental handicap) over 50 years of age: age structure, I.Q. and adaptive skills. *Journal of Intellectual Disability Research,* **36**, 387–401.

Moss, S & Patel, P. (1993). The prevalence of mental illness in people with intellectual disability over 50 years of age, and the diagnostic importance of information from carers. *The Irish Journal of Psychology,* **14**, 110–29.

(1995). Psychiatric symptoms associated with dementia in older people with learning disability. *British Journal of Psychiatry,* **167**, 663–7.

Oliver, C. & Holland, A.J. (1986). Down's syndrome and Alzheimer's disease: a review. *Psychological Medicine,* **16**, 307–22.

Patel, P., Goldberg, D. & Moss, S. (1993). Psychiatric morbidity in older people with moderate and severe learning disabilities II: The prevalence study. *British Journal of Psychiatry,* **163**, 481–91.

Popovitch, E.R., Wisniewski, H.M., Barcikowska, M. et al. (1990). Alzheimer neuropathology in non-Down's syndrome mentally retarded adults. *Acta Neuropathologica,* **80**, 362–7.

Prasher, V.P. (1995). Age specific prevalence, thyroid dysfunction and depressive symptomatology in adults with Down syndrome and dementia. *International Journal of Geriatric Psychiatry,* **10**, 25–31.

Prasher, V.P. & Filer, A. (1995). Behavioural disturbance in people with Down's syndrome and dementia. *Journal of Intellectual Disability Research*, **39**, 432–6.

Reid, A.H. & Aungle, P.G. (1974). Dementia in ageing mental defectives: a clinical psychiatric study. *Journal of Mental Deficiency Research*, **18**, 15–23.

Reiss, S. & Rojahn, J. (1993). Joint occurrence of depression and aggression in children and adults with mental retardation. *Journal of Intellectual Disability Research*, **37**, 287–94.

Richards, B.W. & Siddiqui, A.Q. (1980). Age and mortality trends in residents of an institute for the mentally handicapped. *Journal of Mental Deficiency Research*, **24**, 99–105.

Royal College of Psychiatrists (1997). *Meeting the Mental Health Needs of People with Learning Disability*. Part 2: *Elderly People with Learning Disability*. Council Report CR56. London: Royal College of Psychiatrists.

Sansom, D.T., Singh, I., Jawed & S.H., Mukherjee, T. (1994). Elderly people with learning disabilities in hospital: a psychiatric study. *Journal of Intellectual Disability Research*, **38**, 45–52.

Sturmey, P. (1993). The use of DSMIIIR and ICD diagnostic criteria in people with mental retardation: a review of empirical studies. *Journal of Nervous and Mental Disease*, **181**, 38–41.

Tait, D. (1983). Mortality and dementia among ageing defectives. *Journal of Mental Deficiency Research*, **27**, 133–42.

Wolf, L.C. & Wright, R.E. (1987). Changes in life expectancy of mentally retarded persons in Canadian institutions: a 12 year comparison. *Journal of Mental Deficiency Research*, **31**, 41–59.

World Health Organization (1968). *Eighth Revision of the International Classification of Diseases: Glossary of Psychiatric Disorders*. Geneva: WHO.
(1993). *The ICD-10 Classification of Mental and Behavioural Disorders: Diagnostic Criteria for Research*. Geneva: WHO.

Zigman, W., Schupf, N., Haveman, M. et al. (1995). *Epidemiology of Alzheimer Disease in Mental Retardation: Results and Recommendations from an International Conference (Report of the AAMD-IASSID Workgroup on Alzheimer Disease)*. Washington DC: American Association on Mental Retardation.

14 People with developmental disabilities who offend

GLYNIS MURPHY AND JONATHAN MASON

Introduction

It has long been recognized, in North America and Europe, that people with mental health needs and/or developmental disabilities who break the law should be dealt with differently from those without such needs. Thus, as early as the thirteenth century in the UK, people were sometimes pardoned for crimes as a result of such difficulties and there was some recognition that mental health needs ('madness') and developmental disabilities ('idiocy') were different (Walker & McCabe, 1968; Fitch, 1992). By the seventeenth century in the UK, people who had committed crimes and who had mental health needs could be sent to hospital (Forshaw & Rollins, 1990) and the 1840s saw the introduction of the McNaughton rules in the UK, and similar grounds for acquittal (the so-called 'right–wrong' test) due to 'insanity' in the USA (Quen, 1990; Fitch, 1992). No doubt, initially, this 'special treatment' for people with mental health needs and/or developmental disabilities relied on the whim and perspicacity of those involved in up-holding the law, but gradually special provisions were enshrined in law, to ensure that those with developmental disabilities and/or mental health needs were fairly treated. So, for example, by 1913 England had introduced a Mental Deficiency Act under which people with 'arrested or incomplete development of mind', if they were convicted of an imprisonable offence, could be sent to hospital rather than to prison (and in 1920, for example, 183 people were sent to hospital in this way, according to Walker & McCabe, 1973). Similarly, in parts of the USA, under the Durham Rule of 1954, the accused could be held to be not criminally responsible if his or her unlawful act was the 'product of a mental disease or defect' (Fitch, 1992).

Nevertheless, despite this understanding that people with mental health needs and/or developmental disabilities should not be treated like the rest of the population if they broke the law, there was a strong belief that these people were especially *likely* to break the law, and some startling assertions were made during the eugenics era, both in the UK and in the USA:

> *We have discovered that pauperism and crime are increasing at an enormous rate . . . even a superficial investigation shows us that a large percentage of these troubles come from the feeble-minded* (Goddard, 1912).

Similarly, Clark (1894, quoted in Brown & Courtless, 1971) asserted that children who were developmentally disabled and who 'portrayed viciousness (in early life) . . . should be kept from society as we would keep poison from food'.

These beliefs probably led to a great many people with developmental disabilities and/or mental health needs being incarcerated in hospitals and prisons for unjustifiably long periods (indeed, some of the people detained probably should not have been there at all). At times, this became alarmingly clear, as in the well-known Baxstrom case: in 1966, the US Supreme Court ruled that 967 people detained in two hospitals for the 'criminally insane' in New York State should be released. The mean length of custody for the group was over 13 years and all had been detained for longer than the maximum sentence for their original conviction or for the crime with which they were charged when originally considered incompetent to stand trial (Steadman & Halfon, 1971). Mostly, these people were in their 30s and 40s and there were disproportionate numbers of black southern migrants. Following release to civil hospitals, most were later discharged to the community and extremely few re-offended, only 21 of the 967 people being returned to the secure hospitals in the first four years (Steadman & Halfon, 1971). Cases such as these, together with the advent of normalization (Emerson, 1992) and the 'ordinary life' philosophy (Kings Fund Centre, 1980), have led to a changing attitude to people with developmental disabilities and/or mental health needs who break the law. This chapter addresses, the progress in the recognition of people with developmental disabilities within the criminal justice system, together with recent developments in the understanding of their needs.

Prevalence

Whether a larger proportion of people with developmental disabilities commit crimes than might be expected from the general population crime rates can really only be investigated through total population studies. Several such studies exist and they throw some light on the issue of prevalence of criminal offending in people with developmental disabilities, though they are by no means conclusive. West and Farrington's long-term follow-up of working-class boys, born in 1953 and living in London, is probably the most instructive, because it involved a total population of 411 boys and was prospective in nature (West & Farrington, 1973; Farrington, 1995). It transpired that over one-third of the participants were convicted of criminal offences in the period up to age 32 years, and that the peak age for offences was 17 years, rates decreasing thereafter. Those with convictions were more likely to have developmental difficulties and to be achieving poor results at school, as well as being physically smaller, lighter, more hyperactive and impulsive at ten years; they were more likely to have come from larger, poorer families in which harsh or erratic discipline was employed and to have had parents who had separated or were in constant conflict and who had been convicted themselves. By the age of 32, 6 per cent of the sample had committed half of all the offences (Farrington & West, 1993), and these 'chronic offenders' could be remarkably well predicted from age 8–10 by 'troublesome' child behaviour, economic deprivation, lower cognitive ability, a convicted parent and poor child-rearing (Farrington, 1985).

A different research strategy was adopted by Hodgins (1992), who examined convictions for a Swedish birth cohort of 15 117 people born in Stockholm in 1953 who were followed up for 30 years. Evidence of developmental disability was taken from registers of the children who were placed in special classes at school, as a result of developmental disabilities (this included 1.5 per cent of the men and 1.1 per cent of the women). Hodgins reported that the likelihood of conviction for a man with developmental disabilities was three times as high as for those without disabilities. For women with developmental disabilities, the likelihood was nearly four times as high as for women without disabilities. The odds ratios were even more extreme for violent offences (five times higher for men with developmental disabilities and 25 times higher for women).

A further study by Hodgins et al. (1996) of a total population in Denmark of over 300 000 people, born between 1944 and 1947, followed up at age 43 years, gave similar results: people with developmental disabilities (excluding those with serious mental illness), who had had admissions to psychiatric wards, had an increased risk of committing offences of various kinds compared to people who had never been admitted (risk ratios were 5.5 and 6.9 for women and men, respectively, for crimes entered onto the computerized criminal record system, which came into operation in 1978 in Denmark). There was no particular pattern to the crimes, according to Hodgins et al. (1996).

The extent to which these figures result from differences in arrest/conviction patterns rather than differences in criminal behaviour per se is uncertain, however; it may just be that people with disabilities are less good at evading the police (Robertson, 1988) and/or more 'visible' or vulnerable to arrest (and even to wrongful conviction). Moreover, retrospective surveys like Hodgins' are not able to distinguish cause from effect (this does not apply to the prospective West and Farrington study). It may be, for example, that being given special schooling (Hodgins, 1992) or being admitted to a psychiatric ward (Hodgins et al., 1996) is more likely if the person shows challenging or antisocial behaviour, so that people with developmental disabilities who have been in special schools or hospital wards are biased samples of the total population of people with developmental disabilities and are more likely to commit offences for reasons which may be unrelated to their disabilities.

Where all the people within developmental disability services in a particular area have been studied, it appears that somewhere between 2 per cent and 5 per cent of them have been in contact with the police as potential suspects over the previous year, according to Lyall, Holland and Collins (1995a) in Cambridge and McNulty, Kissi-Debrah and Newsom-Davies (1995) in London. In the Cambridge study, the contacts with police were for a range of offences (including assault and sexual offences) but none of the individuals was prosecuted and only one was formally cautioned, whereas in the London study, most were cautioned and about one-third were charged (however, the numbers in both studies were very small). In all probability, though, these kinds of studies miss a number of people with mild developmental disabilities who become involved in the criminal justice system but are not known to disability services.

Several recent UK studies have examined the numbers of people with developmental disabilities appearing at police stations. For example, Gudjonsson et al. (1993) assessed the intellectual ability of 156 people appearing at two London police stations, using a short form of the Weschler Adult Intelligence Scale – Revised) (WAIS-R). Nine per cent of the total sample had an IQ score below 70, and 34 per cent had a score below 75 (representing the bottom 5 per cent of the general population), suggesting that a significant proportion of those detained by the police have an intellectual impairment (Gudjonsson et al. did not assess social functioning). Similar findings were reported by Lyall et al. (1995b), who screened 251 people appearing at a Cambridge police station for questioning. Participants were screened for the presence of a developmental disability using a brief questionnaire (adapted from Clare & Gudjonsson, 1993), consisting of questions about the individuals' reading and writing skills, whether they had received extra help at school and/or if they had attended a special needs school. Five per cent of the 251 people arrested and screened had attended a school for children with mild or severe developmental disabilities (Lyall et al. did not assess individuals formally), and a further 10 per cent had attended schools for children with emotional/behavioural difficulties or a learning support unit within a mainstream school. Again, the results suggested that substantial numbers of those appearing at police stations have developmental disabilities.

Very few studies have been conducted which have assessed all those appearing before a court but, in two cohort studies, Hayes (1993, 1996a) has looked at the prevalence of people with a developmental disability appearing before magistrates' courts in New South Wales, Australia. In the first, she assessed 113 people appearing before four local (two urban and two rural) NSW magistrates' courts: 14 per cent of the sample were found to score below IQ 70, a further 9 per cent scored between IQ 70 and 79, meaning that 23 per cent of those tested were found to be functioning at a borderline level or below (Hayes, 1993). In the second study, Hayes (1996a) concentrated solely on two rural courts (thus incorporating a large aboriginal population) and demonstrated that 21 per cent of those tested scored below IQ 70, and a further 36 per cent scored between IQ 70 and 79. Thus, in rural courts containing a high number of aboriginal defendants, 57 per cent of those tested had a score in the borderline range of intelligence or below. In both studies, however, Hayes used the Matrices section of the Kaufman Brief Intelligence Test (K-BIT) on the grounds that it was a culture-fair test (Hayes, 1996b), and it seems possible that this is not entirely the case.

Following appearance in court, people with developmental disabilities may be released unconvicted, or may be convicted and subject to a variety of consequences, including imprisonment, hospitalization, probation or more minor consequences. There has been little research in some of these areas, such as probation, but far more in other areas, such as imprisonment.

Studies of people with developmental disabilities in the prison system have a long history. (Woodward (1955), for example, quoted an analysis by Sutherland of over 300 studies conducted between 1910 and 1928 in the USA.) The numerous investigations have led to a number of divergent opinions as to the approximate number of people with developmental disabilities in the prison system, some asserting that in the USA, for example, 10 per cent is the correct prevalence figure (e.g. Brown & Courtless, 1971), while others argue that this simply reflects poor methodology (MacEachron, 1979). Figures from some of the most recent studies are summarized in Table 14.1. Generally, it seems that studies from American prison populations produce higher prevalence rates than those from prisons in the UK and this may reflect the increased diversion from custody which is possible in the UK (see below). It also seems that geographical differences exist within some countries, such that some states in the USA record far higher prevalence rates than others (Noble & Conley, 1992). Variations in prevalence rates may also come about as a result of the use of different tests, the administration of the tests by personnel with varying degrees of training, the time at which the tests are administered (for example whether these are done at times when individuals may be highly stressed), the type of institution (it may be that some prisons are more prone to receive offenders with developmental disability than others) and the methodology employed in the study (Noble & Conley, 1992).

Probably one of the least restrictive consequences following conviction is a sentence requiring the individual to report to a probation officer. The probation service, both in the UK and USA, provides for the supervision of offenders within the community. Little research has been done on the prevalence of mental disorder amongst those on probation, but it is likely that a number of those with a developmental disability who pass through the criminal justice system will turn up in the probation service. Government policy in the UK emphasises the least restrictive alternative and community-based treatment whenever possible (Home Office, 1990, 1995a; Department of Health and Home Office, 1992; Department of Health, 1993) and, in the USA, the American Bar Association's *Criminal Justice Mental Health Standards* (1986) also acknowledge the least restrictive environment principle (Laski,

Table 14.1 Prevalence of offenders with developmental disabilities in prisons

Reference	Location of study	Number of participants	Test(s) used in study	Percentage of prisoners with developmental disabilities
Brown & Courtless (1971)	Inmates in USA prisons	90 000 (80 per cent of prison population)	Large variety	9.5
MacEachron (1979)	Inmates in 2 USA prisons	436 of the 3938 total population	Variety	1.5–5.6 (depending on how measured)
Denkowski & Denkowski (1985)	20 prisons in USA[a]	191 133	WAIS-R	0.2–5.3 (state to state variations)
Coid (1988)	1 prison in England	Retrospective study: 10 000	None specified	0.34
Gunn et al. (1991)	16 prisons; 9 YOIs in UK	404 youths, 1365 men	None specified	0.4
Murphy et al. (1995)	1 London prison (remand only)	157 men	WAIS-R	$0 < IQ\,70$ $5.7 < IQ\,75$
Birmingham et al. (1996)	1 prison, northern UK (remand only)	569 men	None specified	1
Brooke et al. (1996)	13 prisons and 3 YOIs in UK	750 youths and men	Quick Test	1

Notes:
YOI, Young Offender Institution.
[a]Denkowski and Denkowski also look at IQ scores on group tests in 16 other institutions. These have been omitted.

1992). Consequently, it may be the case that people with developmental disabilities are increasingly appearing before the probation service rather than being sent to hospital or prison, and this has been confirmed by Mason (1997) who, in a preliminary study of 70 probationers in the south of England, found a prevalence rate of 6 per cent for those with an IQ under 70 and a deficit in social functioning, with a further 11 per cent scoring under IQ 75. Interestingly, an earlier US study reported a similar rate of 6–7 per cent of people on probation and parole in Missouri with developmental disabilities (Wood, 1976, quoted in Noble & Conley, 1992).

Characteristics of people with developmental disabilities who offend

It is clear from the studies discussed above that, although the characteristics of people with developmental disabilities who offend are likely to vary with the setting in which the individuals are studied, nevertheless, it is broadly true that very few people with *severe* developmental disabilities are to be found within any part of the criminal justice system. For example, only one of the Lyall et al. (1995b) sample had severe disabilities, and most other studies seem to have identified very few people or no-one with severe disabilities (Noble & Conley, 1992). Given the estimates of the prevalence rates of some challenging behaviours that tend to occur across the ability range, such as aggression (estimated to occur in 18 per cent of all those with developmental disabilities in touch with services, according to Harris, 1993), this may be surprising. However, it almost certainly results, at least in part, from the requirement in law, in both the UK and USA, that the court must show not just *actus reus* but also *mens rea* on the part of an individual before conviction. Moreover, in the UK and the USA, for state/federal prosecutions, decisions are made by the Crown Prosecution Service (CPS) or the District Attorney (DA) about whether cases should go to court on a number of criteria, including the likelihood of conviction and public interest. It is probable that, when staff or carers do call the police when someone with severe developmental disabilities engages in potentially criminal behaviour, either the police themselves or the CPS/DA judge it not to be in the public interest to proceed.

The vast majority of people with developmental disabilities who are convicted of offences are young and male, though no more so than might be expected when compared to other offender populations without disabilities (Noble & Conley, 1992). Most studies, however, have shown an over-representation of people from ethnic minorities with developmental disabilities in courts/prisons, more than would be predicted from other suspects or offenders without disabilities (Noble & Conley, 1992; Hayes, 1993, 1996a), though quite why this occurs is unclear.

The kinds of crimes which people with developmental disabilities commit have been a matter of dispute for years. Early assertions, drawn from Walker and McCabe's (1973) data on people detained under the Mental Health Act 1959 in a particular year, claimed that sexual offences and arson were particularly common amongst people with developmental disabilities (Prins, 1980; Robertson, 1981). In fact, of course, this did not follow from Walker and McCabe's data: all that their figures showed was that a disproportionate number of the sexual and arson offences *of their sample* was committed by the proportion of people detained under 'mental subnormality' and 'severe mental subnormality' (as they were then termed). However, this could not be interpreted as having any implications for the proportion of all sexual and arson offences committed because, in both cases, it is known that only a minority of such offenders are diverted into hospitals under the Mental Health Act in the UK (Murphy & Holland, 1993). Similar arguments have been put by Noble and Conley (1992) in relation to data from various studies in the USA, and similarly more recent assertions of the same kind, drawn from assessments of people referred for forensic evaluations (Hawk, Rosenfield & Warren, 1993; Rasanen, Hakko & Vaisanen, 1995) can be subject to the same criticism.

The only way to derive a true picture of the types of crimes committed by people with a developmental disability would be through the offence records for a total population sample (and even then, only *documented* offences would be counted). In fact, this is a difficult task: it is well known that, following school leaving age, the number of people with mild degrees of developmental disabilities in touch with services drops by three-quarters to two-thirds, as people 'blend' into the 'ordinary' community, apparently needing no further services (Richardson & Koller, 1985). In the absence of a total population sample, the most that can be said is that, when the types of offences of people with developmental disabilities have been analysed, the range seems similar to those of other offenders (Hodgins et al., 1996). MacEachron (1979), for example, compared the offenders with developmental disabilities to those with borderline abilities in two USA prisons and found no significant differences in the severity of the most recent offence, the length of current sentence, the degree of recidivism, participation in rehabilitation programmes, recommendations for parole, degree to which parole had ever been revoked, and the use of probation as a juvenile. The only significant distinction found was that those with disabilities had fewer violent incidents in prison than the comparison group.

Little further information can be considered to provide a reliable guide to offences committed by people with developmental disabilities. Studies conducted in police stations, courts and prisons, examining all suspects and/or offenders, have obtained only small samples of people with developmental disabilities on the whole (see above), so very little can be deduced from them about the kinds of crimes committed by people with developmental disabilities. Similarly, reports from treatment facilities for people with developmental disabilities usually describe only small numbers of people (usually around 20) and these people are usually a highly selected sample, as they are all considered in need of psychological and/or psychiatric treatment in secure settings, so that they tend to include disproportionately serious offenders (for example, 40 per cent of Day's (1988) sample had been convicted of sex offences and 10 per cent had been convicted of arson).

It appears that the social backgrounds of people with developmental disabilities who have offended are often characterized by social deprivation. Most of the investigations referred to above, if they collected information on the social background of individuals, reported a high incidence of social deprivation and family breakdown/disorder in childhood (Day, 1988; Winter, Holland & Collins, 1997), long histories of antisocial or 'challenging behaviour' (Day, 1988; Winter et al., 1997) and high rates of adult unemployment (Murphy et al., 1995). Nevertheless, relatively few of the studies have included comparison groups of non-disabled offenders, so that any findings are difficult to interpret. MacEachron (1979), however, in her study of people in prison in Maine and Massachusetts, found that, compared to people in the borderline range for IQ, those with developmental disabilities were on average older (in their thirties), less well educated, less likely to be abusing drugs, and were from larger families (the average number of children was seven). Otherwise, the groups were very similar (for example, both groups were highly likely to be unemployed, equally likely to have other disabilities, and equally unlikely to be married). Moreover, in attempts to predict offence severity and length of sentence from intellectual, social and legal variables, MacEachron found few differences between the disabled and non-disabled groups and she concluded that the intellectual differences between the two groups were fairly immaterial, with the social and legal variables 'more germane to the problem of being an offender than . . . intelligence'.

It also seems likely that there is a high prevalence of mental health needs amongst people with developmental disabilities who have committed offences (Noble & Conley, 1992; McGee & Menolascino, 1992). Studies from specialist treatment units and from prisons in the UK and the USA have reported very high rates of dual diagnosis (Steiner, 1984; Day, 1988; Murphy et al., 1991). While this may not be surprising in health service facilities and prisons, it remains to be seen whether the same holds true for people who are questioned at the police station but who are living in the community (recent studies, such as Winter et al. (1997), have included samples too small to determine this accurately).

Vulnerabilities of people with developmental disabilities in the criminal justice system

In a number of countries, the disadvantages that people with developmental disabilities suffer in the criminal justice system are beginning to be documented. Some of these disadvantages are reflected in the legal process: for instance, Brown and Courtless (1971) found 8 per cent of defendants with developmental disabilities were not represented by a lawyer. Some disadvantages are more subtle, however, and relate to the suspects' understanding of their rights in detention and their understanding of the legal process.

In the UK, on arrest, the police are required to 'caution' individuals. The exact words of the caution change from time to time and in England they were altered in 1994, when the right to silence was modified. Thus, the current words are:

> You do not have to say anything. But it may harm your defence if you do not mention when questioned something which you later rely on in court. Anything you do say may be given in evidence.

Several studies in the UK have demonstrated that many people with developmental disabilities did not fully understand the old caution and are even more likely not to understand the new one to anything like the degree that people without developmental disabilities do (Clare & Gudjonsson, 1991; Clare, Gudjonsson & Harari, 1998). Indeed, the middle sentence of the latest English caution is so complex that many of the police are unable to give a full account of its meaning (Clare et al., 1998).

In addition, in the UK, when suspects arrive at the police station, they are given a written 'Notice to Detained Persons', which reiterates the caution and also tells them that they have a right to have someone informed of their arrest, to have a legal representative and to consult the Codes of Practice (Home Office, 1995b). However, analysis of the written 'Notice' has shown that it requires a reading age which people with developmental disabilities are very unlikely to attain (Gudjonsson, 1991), and it contains such complex wording that many people with developmental disabilities cannot understand it, even if they have it read to them, which the police are not obliged to do. As a result, Clare and Gudjonsson (1992) developed an experimental version of the 'Notice' with simplified wording and demonstrated that it was far easier to understand than the version in use in police stations (the Home Office has declined to adopt the new version, however).

Similarly, in the USA, since the Miranda *vs* Arizona case of 1966, suspects have to be warned before interrogation that they have a right to remain silent, that what they do say may be used in court and that they have a right to a lawyer (the so-called 'Miranda rights'). Suspects are allowed to waive these rights if the waiver is made 'voluntarily, knowingly and intelligently' (Fulero & Everington, 1995). Much as in the case of the UK 'Notice to Detained Persons', the written form of the Miranda warning is too complex in wording and reading level for people with developmental disabilities to be able to comprehend it (Fulero & Everington, 1995). Moreover, when tested on the Grisso (1981) scales designed to assess understanding of the Miranda rights, Fulero and Everington (1995) found that even people with mild developmental disabilities obtained very poor scores, compared to both juvenile and adult samples tested by Grisso (1981). They concluded that most people with developmental disabilities would not have been competent to waive their rights.

It is well established that people with developmental disabilities tend to be more suggestible and acquiescent than people without such disabilities (Heal & Sigelman, 1995). In the police station, this means that there is a danger that people with developmental disabilities will be more likely than other people to acquiesce to suggestions made to them by the police and to be led by leading questions into self-incrimination (Clare & Gudjonsson, 1993), so that it would be expected that people with developmental disabilities would be particularly likely to make false confessions, as indeed appears to be the case (Perske, 1991; Gudjonsson, 1992). This is likely to be exacerbated by the fact that many people with developmental disabilities may misunderstand legal terms that are basic to the legal process: Smith (1993), for example, found that about 20 per cent of the people referred for pre-trial competency assessments in South Carolina did not understand the terms 'guilty' and 'not guilty', such that some actually had the meanings of the words reversed. Some people with developmental disabilities may also misunderstand the likely events in the criminal justice process, thinking, for example, that if they make a false confession to a murder in the police station they will be allowed to go home and will be able to correct it later in court (Clare & Gudjonsson, 1995).

In the UK, in recognition of some of these vulnerabilities of people with developmental disabilities, some special provisions were brought in, under the Police and Criminal Evidence Act 1984, in particular the audiotaping of police interviews (so that the manner of police questioning could be analysed) and the provision of an 'appropriate adult' for 'vulnerable' suspects (including those with developmental disabilities). The 'appropriate adults' role in the police station is to protect vulnerable suspects from their tendency to 'provide information which is unreliable, misleading or self-incriminating' (Home Office, 1995b). However, there appear to have been two main problems with the scheme. In the first place, it is difficult for the police to evaluate when someone may have a developmental disability (see below), so that many people are not provided with an 'appropriate adult', even though they are entitled to one (Bean & Nemitz, 1994). Secondly, 'appropriate adults', who may be parents, carers or social workers who have never met the individual in question, often do not speak during the police interview and seem unclear about their role (Pearse & Gudjonsson, 1996).

Diversion out of the criminal justice system

In most countries, diversion out of the criminal justice system can occur at a number of points. For example, the police may decide not to proceed with a case involving a person with developmental disabilities (see above) or, following an appearance in court, the person might be referred to community-based services for people with developmental disabilities or sent to hospital, either on remand or once convicted (Denkowski, Denkowski & Mabli, 1983; Laski, 1992; James, 1996).

In England and Wales, courts can only divert people to hospital if it has been established in court that the individual is unfit to plead (see below) or if he or she falls within the broad category of 'mental disorder' (for admission for assessment) or the specific categories of 'mental illness', 'psychopathic disorder', 'mental impairment' or 'severe mental impairment' of the Mental Health Act 1983. Normally, those with developmental disabilities would be admitted under 'mental impairment' or 'severe mental impairment', which require the presence of a developmental disability and 'abnormally aggressive or seriously irresponsible conduct'. People diverted from courts into hospitals who are classified under 'mental illness' far outnumber those classified under 'mental impairment' or 'severe mental impairment' in hospitals in England and Wales, however. While the numbers of those with mental illness diverted from courts and detained under the Mental Health Act are increasing, the numbers with mental impairment and severe mental impairment are decreasing, amounting to only 58 new orders in 1996 (Mason, 1998).

In the UK and the USA, people with developmental disabilities can be found 'unfit to plead' (UK) or 'not competent to stand trial' (USA) and can be diverted out of the criminal justice system (Rasch, 1990; Bonnie, 1992b). In the UK, under the Criminal Procedure (Insanity) Act 1964, people who were found unfit to plead were detained in hospital (often in high security hospitals) and were supposed to return to court once they became fit to plead. In fact, this happened relatively rarely for people with developmental disabilities. Grubin (1991a), in a survey of the 286 people found unfit to plead between 1976 and 1988, reported that 21 per cent had developmental disabilities (the remainder had serious mental health needs). However, a disproportionate number of those with disabilities remained in hospital without ever returning to court for a trial: 40 per cent of those people who still remained in hospital without a trial by 1989 had developmental disabilities (Grubin, 1991b). This, of course, had major civil rights implications, particularly because the evidence that the person had committed the crime was often unclear (Grubin, 1991b), and there has since been a change in the law in the UK, such that the facts of the case now have to be tried. Nevertheless, relatively few people with developmental disabilities have been found unfit to plead since, perhaps because diversion from the criminal justice system through use of the Mental Health Act 1983 often allows more flexibility.

In the USA, in contrast, 'competence' hearings are relatively common and are estimated to arise in between 2 and 8 per cent of felony cases (Hoge et al., 1992). Trial judges are required to order competence evaluations whenever significant doubts are raised as to the defendant's mental competence, and failure of defence lawyers to consider such an evaluation can invalidate subsequent conviction if competence is later established as an issue (Bonnie, 1992a). Defendants who are considered 'incompetent to stand trial' may not be held involuntarily, unless there is a likelihood of their regaining competence in the future (though Petrella (1992) found that very few people found 'incompetent' in this way probably were restorable to competency). Failing to conduct competence evaluations at all, however, can involve loss of liberty for people with developmental disabilities despite their innocence, because they may be wrongly convicted due to their vulnerabilities in the criminal justice system (see below). Nevertheless, it is thought that competence has often been overlooked as an issue (Bonnie, 1992b), as some studies have shown that as few as 2 per cent of defendants with developmental disabilities have pre-trial evaluations (Brown & Courtless, 1971), though recent figures suggest this has improved somewhat (Smith & Broughton, 1994). Most commonly, competence is judged on the 'Dusky' criterion: 'whether the defendant has sufficient present ability to consult with his lawyer with a reasonable degree of rational understanding and whether he has a rational as well as factual understanding of the proceedings against him' (Dusky *vs* United States, 1960). In practice, competence to stand trial has often been assessed by informal interview, although a number of formal test protocols have been developed for the purpose (Grisso, 1986), including at least one that is highly sophisticated (Hoge et al., 1997). Only two measures have been designed specifically for people with developmental disabilities, however, one being a brief screening test (Smith & Hudson, 1995) and the other a more thorough assessment (Everington & Luckasson, 1987; Everington, 1990).

When competence is assessed in those referred for evaluation, it appears that about 35 per cent are judged not competent to stand trial (Petrella, 1992; Smith & Broughton, 1994). For example, an analysis of a five-year cohort of the 160 people thought to have developmental disabilities, who were evaluated for competence (and/or culpability, see below) in South Carolina, found that they were typically male (93 per cent), mostly black (66 per cent) and young (mean age 28 years) and had frequently spent many months in detention before evaluation and/or court appearances (Smith & Broughton, 1994). Approximately 34 per cent were judged not competent to stand trial (this group had a lower mean IQ of 58, compared to those judged competent, who had a mean IQ of 64). Those judged not competent were far less often sent to jail (0 per cent, as opposed to 55 per cent of those judged competent), less often put on probation (13 per cent, compared to 31 per cent) and mostly were dismissed back home (47 per cent, compared to 7 per cent) or referred to the Department of Mental Retardation (40 per cent, as compared to 7 per cent of those judged competent).

In addition to 'competence' in the USA, 'culpability' or criminal responsibility may be assessed. Essentially, the former refers to whether the defendant understands the charges and court proceedings and can instruct his or her lawyer, while the latter refers to whether the defendant knew right from wrong at the time of the offence (Smith & Broughton, 1994). Criminal responsibility is usually judged by the McNaughten Rule, which states that a person is not legally responsible if he or she was 'labouring under such a defect of reason from disease of the mind, as not to know the nature and quality of the act he was doing; or, if he did know it, that he did not know what he was doing was wrong' (Grisso, 1986). Mental health professionals have often been accused of confusing competence to stand trial and culpability (Johnson, Nicholson & Service, 1990), and a number of investigations have addressed the extent to which the two characteristics co-occur in particular individuals (Johnson et al., 1990; Petrella, 1992; Smith & Broughton, 1994). In general, for people with developmental disabilities, it appears that it is rarer to be judged not criminally responsible than to be judged not competent to stand trial and, amongst those judged not responsible, most will have also been judged not competent (though these relationships are different for people with mental health needs – see Johnson et al., 1990).

Improvements in practice

At present, people with a developmental disability who break the law generally enter the criminal justice system much as other people would, though perhaps with more confusion and less appreciation of their circumstances than most. Essentially, their treatment within the criminal justice system depends on the extent to which their disability is recognised by those coming into contact with them, as it is this factor which will often determine their course through the system. Most research, though, has demonstrated that the identification of people with developmental disabilities in the criminal justice system is poor in the pre-trial phase: according to Brown and Courtless (1971), in the US only 2 per cent of such defendants had a pre-trial psychological assessment, while Denkowski and Denkowski (1985) reported that 38 per cent of US states did not attempt to identify defendants with developmental disabilities. Similarly, in England, where some special provisions exist for people with developmental disabilities and/or mental health needs in the police station, Gudjonsson et al. (1993) found that only about one-fifth of the people who needed this special help were identified, and others have suggested even lower rates of identification nationally (Bean & Nemitz, 1994).

Similarly, reports from court diversion schemes in the UK (James, 1996) have shown that very few people assessed in these projects have developmental disabilities, implying that many cases may simply be missed. Cooke (1991), for example, reported that in a consecutive series of 150 offenders referred for psychological/psychiatric treatment before prosecution (so-called 'primary diversion'), none appeared to have developmental disabilities; and Joseph and Potter (1993), in a London diversion scheme operating at two magistrates' courts, found only four people (2 per cent) had developmental disabilities (formal assessment was not employed). Moreover, *after* conviction, McAfee and Gural (1988), in their survey of the states' Attorneys General, concluded that protections for people with developmental disabilities were also very poor, with many states providing little in the way of treatment or training (Denkowski et al., 1983), and they were forced to conclude that the criminal justice system 'appears to have adopted an informal, inconsistent and inequitable response' to the problems of individuals with mental retardation who are accused of a crime.

Nevertheless, special protections before and during trials do exist, and there is some evidence that they are being increasingly recognized and more often used, though not yet to anything like their full extent. Thus, for example, in some police stations in the UK, people brought in for questioning are screened by the custody sergeant in order to try to ensure that the protections available at the police station are made available (I.C.H. Clare, personal communication). Similarly, brief screening tests for competence to stand trial have been developed in the USA (Smith & Hudson, 1995), in order to allow rapid screening of all those who will appear in court and may need a full competency assessment. In addition, there is beginning to be an increase in the willingness of agencies in the criminal justice system and health services to work together, to provide support for those proceeding through the criminal justice system (Hollins et al., 1997a, 1997b) and to ensure treatment for those people with developmental disabilities who may otherwise be likely to remain at risk of offending (Churchill et al., 1997; Clare & Murphy, 1998).

Conclusion

It seems clear that people with developmental disabilities are liable to break the law from time to time but are less likely to do so than used to be supposed in the early 1900s. The precise prevalence of people with developmental disabilities in the criminal justice system varies with the laws, social policy and the presence of alternative rehabilitative systems in place in the area studied. However, increasingly, in the UK, USA and Australia, it seems to be accepted that people with developmental disabilities should not be in prison, at least partly because of their increased risk of victimization there. Moreover, it is increasingly recognized that people with developmental disabilities are especially vulnerable in the police station and the courts and that they need special provisions there. In a number of jurisdictions, protections for people with developmental disabilities have been set up, but it seems that everywhere the identification and operation of the protective features of the system fall well short of the ideal. There is a long way to go, therefore, but some improvements in practice can be seen which suggest that there is a growing awareness of the difficulties of the person with developmental disabilities both in the criminal justice system and in mental health/disability services.

References

American Bar Association (1986). *Criminal Justice Mental Health Standards*. Washington, DC: American Bar Association.

Bean, P. & Nemitz, T. (1994). *Out of Depth and Out of Sight*. London: Mencap.

Birmingham, L., Mason, D. & Grubin, D. (1996) Prevalence of mental disorder in remand prisoners: consecutive case study. *British Medical Journal*, **313**, 1521–4.

Bonnie, R.J. (1992a). The competence of criminal defendants: a theoretical reformulation. *Behavioural Sciences and the Law*, **10**, 291–316.

(1992b). The competency of defendants with mental retardation to assist in their own defence. In *The Criminal Justice System and Mental Retardation*, ed. R.W. Conley, Luckasson, R. & G.N. Bouthilet, pp. 97–120. Baltimore: Paul H. Brookes.

Brooke, D., Taylor, C., Gunn, J. & Maden, A. (1996). Point prevalence of mental disorder in unconvicted male prisoners in England and Wales. *British Medical Journal*, **313**, 1524–7.

Brown, B.S. & Courtless, T.F. (1971). *The Mentally Retarded Offender*. Department of Health Education and Welfare Publication No. 72–90–39. Washington DC: US Government Printing Office.

Churchill, J., Brown, H., Craft, A. & Horrocks, C. (1997). *There are no Easy Answers: the Provision of Continuing Care and Treatment to Adults with Learning Disabilities who Sexually Abuse Others*. Chesterfield: ARC/NAPSAC.

Clare, I.C.H. & Gudjonsson, G.H. (1991). Recall and understanding of the caution and rights in police detention among persons of average intellectual ability and persons with a mental handicap. *Proceedings of the First DCLP Annual Conference*, **1**, 34–42. Issues in Criminological and Legal Psychology Series, No. 17. Leicester: British Psychological Society.

(1992). *Devising and Piloting an Experimental Version of the 'Notice to Detained Persons'*. The Royal Commission on Criminal Justice, Research Study No. 7. London: HMSO.

(1993). Interrogative suggestibility, confabulation, and acquiescence in people with mild learning disabilities (mental handicap): implications for reliability during police interview. *British Journal of Clinical Psychology*, **32**, 295–301.

(1995). The vulnerability of suspects with intellectual disabilities during police interviews: a review and experimental study of decision-making. *Mental Handicap Research*, **8**, 110–28.

Clare, I.C.H., Gudjonsson, G.H. & Harari, P.M. (1998). Understanding of the current police caution (England and Wales). *Journal of Community and Social Psychology*, **8**, 323–9.

Clare, I.C.H. & Murphy, G. (1998). Working with offenders or alleged offenders with intellectual disabilities. In *Clinical Psychology and People with Intellectual Disabilities*, ed. E. Emerson, A. Caine, J. Bromley & C. Hatton, pp. 154–76. Chichester: John Wiley and Sons.

Coid, J. (1988). Mentally abnormal prisoners on remand – rejected or accepted by the NHS? *British Medical Journal*, **296**, 1779–82.

Cooke, D.J. (1991). Treatment as an alternative to prosecution: offenders diverted for treatment. *British Journal of Psychiatry*, **158**, 785–91.

Day, K. (1988). A hospital-based treatment programme for male mentally handicapped offenders. *British Journal of Psychiatry*, **153**, 636–44.

Denkowski, G.C. & Denkowski, K.M. (1985). The mentally retarded offender in the state prison system: identification, prevalence, adjustment and rehabilitation. *Criminal Justice and Behaviour*, **12**, 55–70.

Denkowski, G.C., Denkowski, K.M. & Mabli, J. (1983). A 50-state survey of the current status of residential programmes for mentally retarded offenders. *Mental Retardation*, **21**, 197–203.

Department of Health and Home Office (1992). *Review of Health and Social*

Services for Mentally Disordered Offenders and Others Requiring Similar Services (Chairman: Dr J. Reed). London: HMSO.

Department of Health (1993). *Services for People with Learning Disabilities and Challenging Behaviour or Mental Health Needs.* (Chairman: Professor Jim Mansell). London: HMSO.

Emerson, E. (1992). What is normalisation? In *Normalisation: a Reader for the Nineties,* ed. H. Brown & H. Smith, pp. 1–18. London: Routledge.

Everington, C.T. (1990). The competence assessment for standing trial for defendants with mental retardation (CAST-MR). *Criminal Justice and Behaviour,* **17**, 147–68.

Everington, C. & Luckasson, R. (1987). *Competence Assessment for Standing Trial for Defendants with Mental Retardation: CAST-MR.* Oxford, Ohio: Miami University, Department of Educational Psychology.

Farrington, D.P. (1985). Predicting self-reported and official delinquency. In *Prediction in Criminology,* ed. D.P. Farrington & R. Tarling, pp. 150–73. Albany, New York: State University of New York Press.

(1995). The development of offending and anti-social behaviour from childhood: key findings from the Cambridge study in delinquent development. *Journal of Child Psychology and Psychiatry,* **360**, 929–64.

Farrington, D.P. & West, D.J. (1993). Criminal, penal and life histories of chronic offenders: risk and protective factors and early identification. *Criminal Behaviour and Mental Health,* **3**, 492–523.

Fitch, W.L. (1992). Mental retardation and criminal responsibility. In *The Criminal Justice System and Mental Retardation,* ed. R.W. Conley, Luckasson, R. & G.N. Bouthilet, pp. 121–36. Baltimore: Paul H. Brookes.

Forshaw, D. & Rollins, H. (1990). The history of forensic psychiatry in England. In *Principles and Practice in Forensic Psychiatry,* ed. R. Bluglass and P. Bowden, pp. 61–101. London: Churchill Livingstone.

Fulero, S.M. & Everington, C. (1995). Assessing competence to waive Miranda rights in defendants with mental retardation. *Law and Human Behaviour,* **19**, 533–43.

Goddard, H.H. (1912). How shall we educate mental defectives? *The Training School Bulletin,* **9**, 43.

Grisso, T. (1981). *Juveniles' Waiver of Rights: Legal and Psychological Competence.* New York: Plenum Press.

(1986). *Evaluating Competencies: Forensic Assessments and Instruments.* New York: Plenum Press.

Grubin, D.H. (1991a). Unfit to plead in England and Wales 1976–1988, a survey. *British Journal of Psychiatry,* **158**, 540–8.

(1991b). Unfit to plead, unfit for discharge: patients found unfit to plead who are still in hospital. *Criminal Behaviour and Mental Health,* **1**, 282–94.

Gudjonsson, G.H. (1991). The 'Notice to Detained Persons', PACE Codes and reading ease. *Applied Cognitive Psychology,* **5**, 89–95.

(1992). *The Psychology of Interrogations, Confessions and Testimony.* Chichester: John Wiley and Sons.

Gudjonsson, G., Clare, I.C.H., Rutter, S. & Pearse, J. (1993). *Persons at Risk During Interviews in Police Custody: the Identification of Vulnerabilities.*

The Royal Commission of Criminal Justice, Research Study No. 12. London: HMSO.

Gunn, J., Maden, A. & Swinton, M. (1991). Treatment needs of prisoners with psychiatric disorders. *British Medical Journal,* **303**, 338–41.

Harris, P. (1993). The nature and extent of aggressive behaviour amongst people with learning difficulties (mental handicap) in a single health district. *Journal of Intellectual Disability Research,* **37**, 221–42.

Hawk, G.L., Rosenfield, B.D. & Warren, J.I. (1993). Prevalence of sexual offences among mentally retarded criminal defendants. *Hospital and Community Psychiatry,* **44**, 784–6.

Hayes, S. (1993). *People with an Intellectual Disability and the Criminal Justice System: Appearances Before the Local Courts.* Research Report No. 4. Sydney: New South Wales Reform Commission Report.

Hayes, S.C. (1996a*). People with an Intellectual Disability and the Criminal Justice System: Two Rural Courts.* Research Report No. 5. Sydney: NSW Law Reform Commission.

Hayes, S. (1996b). Recent research on offenders with learning disabilities. *Tizard Learning Disability Review,* **1**, 7–15.

Heal, L.W. & Sigelman, C.K. (1995). Response biases in interviews of individuals with limited mental ability. *Journal of Intellectual Disability Research,* **39**, 331–40.

Hodgins, S. (1992). Mental disorder, intellectual deficiency and crime: evidence from a birth cohort. *Archives of General Psychiatry,* **49**, 476–83.

Hodgins, S., Mednick, S.A., Brennan, P.A., Schulsinger, F. & Engberg, M. (1996). Mental disorder and crime. *Archives of General Psychiatry,* **53**, 489–96.

Hoge, S.K., Bonnie, R.J., Poythress, N. & Monahan, J. (1992). Attorney–client decision-making in criminal cases: client competence and participation as perceived by their attorneys. *Behavioural Sciences and the Law,* **10**, 385–94.

Hoge, S.K., Bonnie, R.J., Poythress, N., Monahan, J., Eisenberg, M. & Feucht-Haviar, T. (1997). The MacArthur adjudicative competency study: development and validation of a research instrument. *Law and Human Behaviour,* **21**, 141–79.

Hollins, S., Clare, I.C.H., Murphy, G. & Webb, B. (1997a). *You're Under Arrest.* London: Gaskell Press.

Hollins, S., Murphy, G., Clare, I.C.H. & Webb, B. (1997b). *You're On Trial.* London: Gaskell Press.

Home Office (1990). *Provisions for Mentally Disordered Offenders (Circular 66/90).* London: Home Office.

(1995a). *Mentally Disordered Offenders: Inter-Agency Working (Circular 12/95).* London: Home Office.

(1995b). *Police and Criminal Evidence Act 1984. Codes of Practice,* Revised Edition. London: HMSO.

James, A. (1996). *Life on the Edge: Diversion and the Mentally Disordered Offender.* London: Mental Health Foundation.

Johnson, W.G., Nicholson, R.A. & Service, N.M. (1990). The relationship of competency to stand trial and criminal responsibility. *Criminal Justice and Behaviour,* **17**, 169–85.

Joseph, P.L.A. & Potter, M. (1993). Diversion from custody. I: Psychiatric assessment at the magistrates' court. *British Journal of Psychiatry*, **162**, 325–30.

King's Fund Centre (1980). *An Ordinary Life: Comprehensive Locally-based Residential Services for Mentally Handicapped People.* London: King's Fund Centre.

Laski, F.J. (1992). Sentencing the offender with mental retardation: honouring the imperative for intermediate punishments and probation. In *The Criminal Justice System and Mental Retardation*, ed. R.W. Conley, Luckasson, R. & G.N. Bouthilet, pp. 137–52. Baltimore: Paul H. Brookes.

Lyall, I., Holland, A.J. & Collins, S. (1995a). Offending by adults with learning disabilities: identifying need in one health district. *Mental Handicap Research*, **8**, 99–109.

Lyall, I., Holland, A.J., Collins, S. & Styles, P. (1995b). Incidence of persons with a learning disability detained in police custody: a needs assessment for service development. *Medicine, Science and the Law*, **35**, 61–71.

Mason, J. (1997). People on probation with a learning disability: identification, prevalence and characteristics. Paper given at Seventh DCLP Annual Conference, Cambridge.

(1998). People with learning disabilities (mental impairment) detained under part 3 of the Mental Health Act 1983 over the last 13 years. *Tizard Learning Disability Review*, **3**, 42–5.

McAfee, J.K. & Gural, M. (1988). Individuals with mental retardation and the criminal justice system: the view from States' Attorneys General. *Mental Retardation*, **26**, 5–12.

MacEachron, A.E. (1979). Mentally retarded offenders: prevalence and characteristics. *American Journal of Mental Deficiency*, **84**, 165–76.

McGee, J.J. & Menolascino, F.J. (1992). The evaluation of defendants with mental retardation in the Criminal Justice System. In *The Criminal Justice System and Mental Retardation*, ed. R.W. Conley, Luckasson, R. & G.N. Bouthilet, pp. 55–77. Baltimore: Paul H. Brookes.

McNulty, C., Kissi-Debrah, R. & Newsom-Davies, I. (1995). Police involvement with clients having intellectual disabilities: a pilot study in south London. *Mental Handicap Research*, **8**, 129–36.

Murphy, G., Harnett, H. & Holland, A.J. (1995). A survey of intellectual disabilities amongst men on remand in prison. *Mental Handicap Research*, **8**, 81–98.

Murphy, G. & Holland, T. (1993). Challenging behaviour, psychiatric disorders and the law. In *Challenging Behaviour and Intellectual Disability: a Psychological Perspective*, ed. R.S.P. Jones & C. B. Eayrs, pp. 195–223. Clevedon, Avon: BILD Publications.

Murphy, G., Holland, A.J., Fowler, P. & Reep, J. (1991). Mental Impairment Evaluation and Treatment Service (MJETS): a service option for South East Thames Region. I. The philosophy, the service and the clients. *Mental Handicap Research*, **5**, 41–66.

Noble, J.H. & Conley, R.W. (1992). Toward an epidemiology of relevant attributes. In *The Criminal Justice System and Mental Retardation*, ed. R.W. Conley, R. Luckasson & G.N. Bouthilet, pp. 17–53. Baltimore: Paul H. Brookes.

Pearse, J. & Gudjonsson, G.H. (1996). How appropriate are Appropriate Adults? *Journal of Forensic Psychiatry*, **7**, 570–80.

Perske, R. (1991). *Unequal Justice?* Nashville: Abingdon Press.

Petrella, R.C. (1992). Defendants with mental retardation in the forensic services system. In *The Criminal Justice Sytem and Mental Retardation,* ed. R.W. Conley, R. Luckasson & G.N. Bouthilet, pp 79–96. Baltimore: Paul H. Brookes.

Prins, H. (1980). *Offenders, Deviants or Patients? An Introduction to the Study of Socio-Forensic Problems.* London: Tavistock Publications.

Quen, J. (1990). The history of law and psychiatry in America. In *Principles and Practice in Forensic Psychiatry,* ed. R. Bluglass & P. Bowden, pp. 111–16. London: Churchill-Livingstone.

Rasanen, P., Hakko, H. & Vaisanen, E. (1995). The mental state of arsonists as determined by forensic psychiatric examinations. *Bulletin of the American Academy of Psychiatry and Law, 23,* 547–53.

Rasch, W. (1990). Criminal rsponsibility in Europe. In *Principles and Practice in Forensic Psychiatry,* ed. R. Bluglass & P. Bowden, pp. 299–305. London: Churchill-Livingstone.

Richardson, S.A. & Koller, H. (1985). Epidemiology. In *Mental Deficiency: the Changing Outlook,* ed. A.M. Clarke, A.D.B. Clarke & J.M. Berg, pp. 356–400. London: Methuen.

Robertson, G. (1981). The extent and pattern of crime amongst mentally handicapped offenders. *Apex: Journal of the British Institute of Mental Handicap,* **9,** 100–3.

Robertson, G. (1988). Arrest patterns among mentally disordered offenders. *British Journal of Psychiatry,* **153,** 313–6.

Smith, S.A. (1993). Confusing the terms 'guilty' and 'not guilty': implications for alleged offenders with mental retardation. *Psychological Reports,* **73,** 675–8.

Smith, S.A. & Broughton, S.F. (1994). Competency to stand trial and criminal responsibility: an analysis in South Carolina. *Mental Retardation,* **32,** 281–7.

Smith, S.A. & Hudson, R.L. (1995). A quick screening test of competency to stand trial for defendants with mental retardation. *Psychological Reports,* **76,** 91–7.

Steadman, H.J. & Halfon, A. (1971). The Baxstrom patients: backgrounds and outcomes. *Seminars in Psychiatry,* **3,** 376–85.

Steiner, J. (1984). Group counselling with retarded offenders. *Social Work,* **29,** 181–2.

Walker, N. & McCabe, S. (1968). *Crime and Insanity in England,* Vol. 1. Edinburgh: Edinburgh University Press.

(1973). *Crime and Insanity in England,* Vol. 2. Edinburgh: Edinburgh University Press.

West, D.J. & Farrington, D.P. (1973). *Who becomes Delinquent?* London: Heinemann.

Winter, N., Holland, A.J. & Collins, S. (1997). Factors predisposing to suspected offending by adults with self-reported learning disabilities. *Psychological Medicine,* **27,** 595–607.

Woodward, M. (1955). The role of low intelligence in delinquency. *British Journal of Delinquency,* **5,** 281–303.

Part 4 **Treatment and management**

15 Treatment methods for destructive and aggressive behaviour in people with severe mental retardation/developmental disabilities

R. MATTHEW REESE, JESSICA A. HELLINGS AND
STEPHEN R. SCHROEDER

Introduction

People with severe and profound mental retardation/developmental disabilities including autism are increasingly being supported in community living programmes. A challenge in community support is to assess and treat effectively such behavioural difficulties as property destruction, aggression and self-injurious behaviour. In the last 15 years, the treatment of aggressive and destructive behaviour in people with severe mental retardation/developmental disabilities has resulted in greater emphasis being placed on understanding the causes of such behaviour in any particular individual. Behavioural, medical and neuropsychiatric knowledge has developed rapidly, as have psychopharmacologic treatments. Thus, any treatments must be based on thorough, ongoing interdisciplinary evaluations (Schroeder et al., 1997).

To begin this chapter, it is important to review the different types of behaviours that are considered destructive and aggressive in the severe mental retardation/developmental disabilities population. Bates and Wehman (1977) describe aggression as including: (a) verbal aggression such as shouting, cursing or yelling, (b) physical aggression such as biting, choking, or hitting others, (c) property aggression such as throwing objects, and (d) self-aggression including head banging, self-biting, scratching or gouging, and voluntary falling.

The purposes of this chapter are to propose an integrated approach for assessment and treatment and to review medical and behavioural approaches for destructive and aggressive behaviour in people with severe mental retardation/developmental disabilities. Firstly, some of the often-missed physical illnesses and neuropsychiatric conditions that can precipitate or worsen destructive and aggressive behaviour are briefly described.

The treating clinician is dependent to a great extent on observations made in this regard by care givers of the person, and clinicians need to take a thorough medical, medication and neuropsychiatric history. Not much research is available in this regard, but it should be given priority in the future.

Secondly, behavioural assessment and treatment for destructive and aggressive behaviour are reviewed. It is emphasized that researchers and clinicians using the behavioural approach are joining forces with medical and neuropsychiatric professionals in this field. In the final section of this chapter, a model is proposed for effectively establishing treatment protocols for an individual with this disorder who exhibits destructive and aggressive behaviour.

Medical perspective

Early treatment of any reversible underlying medical condition is essential, as this may obviate the need for any further intervention if the condition contributed or led to the person's behavioural crisis. Because people with severe autism or mental retardation/developmental disabilities are more likely to be non-verbal or to have restricted or repetitive language, they often cannot relate feelings of illness or pain, or answer specific illness-related questions. If they are pressured to get out of bed, eat or perform their usual tasks when feeling ill, these individuals may become aggressive and destructive. Additionally, the person may co-operate poorly with a formal physical examination by a doctor during the period of the behavioural crisis. Thus, vigilance for acute, intermediate or chronic signs of physical illness in the person concerned is essential so that diagnosis and treatment can be tailored to the underlying condition, and will be more likely to succeed. Some, but by no means all, of the important clinical signs are described as examples of the authors' medical approach. These include intercurrent infections, allergies and medication side-effects, which commonly occur but are often missed by care-givers and general clinicians.

Firstly, gastrointestinal disturbances are commonly overlooked, and may manifest as food refusal, self-induced vomiting after meals, or the repeated discarding of food at mealtimes. Such disturbances, as well as appetite change, constipation or diarrhoea, may also be due to medication side-effects. Dental or periodontal disease may disturb eating and behavioural functioning. The possibility of silent intestinal obstruction, such as due to pica (eating of non-food items), or other missed abdominal crises underscores the need for specialist referral in any case that is not settling.

In the not infrequent case of intercurrent infections, for example of the gastrointestinal, respiratory or genitourinary systems, flushing of the face associated with sweating or fever may have been missed. Treatment may simply involve a few days of bed rest, monitoring of fluid intake, and antibiotics for bacterial infections. Some detectable but often-missed physical signs of respiratory tract infections may include hoarseness, cough, or a nasal or ear discharge. Recurrent pulling on or self-hitting of an ear, the head or face may occur in persons with infections of the ears, sinuses, nose or throat, with aggression when redirected to stop the behaviour. Some individuals may insert objects into their ears in the presence of ear infections. Infections of the bladder or kidneys may present as a new onset of repeated day or night-time wetting. The person may cry in pain when urinating or appear preoccupied with touching the genital region. Foul-smelling urine may be noted. Various dermatological problems may cause behavioural problems in association with generalised discomfort, persistent itching or irritation. Examples of conditions due to infection include scabies, impetigo and fungal infections of skin folds. Most medications can cause skin rash as an allergic reaction; in some cases, this may be due to colouring dyes rather than the active drug.

Seasonal allergies such as hay fever may cause restlessness and behavioural agitation. Signs of allergies may include persistent redness, rubbing or running of the eyes and nose. At the same time, antihistamines and combination cold or allergy preparations used as treatments may also cause behavioural deterioration. Electrolyte and metabolic disturbances require correction, and this in turn may dramatically decrease associated behavioural problems. Examples of such disturbances include thyroid and parathyroid underactivity or overactivity, and pancreatic insulin-producing tumours. A low serum sodium affecting mental status may be due to treatment with the anticonvulsant medication carbamazepine (Kastner, Friedman & Pond, 1992). Medication side-effects may include aggression, and other maladaptive behaviours, and can occur in association with medications of many classes. It is worth stating that a carefully taken, detailed treatment history is essential to identify any potential drug-related cause of the problem. In such cases, the behavioural deterioration dates back to around the time the drug was started. Substituting the suspect medication, for example phenobarbital or phenytoin prescribed for epilepsy, with a newer antiseizure agent such as valproate or carbamazepine, may eliminate the aggression (Trimble, 1990). The same principle applies to cough and cold medicines, antihypertensive preparations, especially those containing reserpine, hormone preparations such as the contraceptive pill, and many others. Benzodiazepines are recognized to cause behavioural disinhibition in this population and are generally avoided.

Neuropsychiatric perspective

People with any congenital mental retardation syndrome, including Down syndrome, fragile-X syndrome Prader–Willi syndrome and the rarer syndromes such as Rubinstein Taybi syndrome, can present with aggressive or destructive behaviour related to medical or psychiatric illness, or to seizures. It should be borne in mind that behavioural deterioration may occur during or between seizure episodes, or may be due to side-effects of certain anticonvulsant medications (Blumer, 1984; Trimble, 1990; Umbrick et al., 1995). Although the task is a more difficult one when the individual involved is non-verbal, it may be possible to diagnose and thus treat psychiatric conditions using DSM-IV or ICD-10 based criteria other than speech (Sovner & Fogelman, 1996). For example, the manic-like signs of euphoria, irritability, overactivity, pacing, insomnia and hypersexuality, co-occurring with rapid flaring to aggression, may respond well to mood stabilizers such as valproate and lithium (Lowry, 1997). Low-dose serotonin reuptake inhibitors such as sertraline may prove useful in many cases, though controlled studies are needed (Hellings & Warnock, 1994; Hellings et al., 1996). A full discussion of the use of pharmacotherapeutic agents is provided in Chapter 18.

Behavioural perspective

Historically, the behavioural perspective assumes that problem behaviours such as destruction and aggression are learned, and are largely affected by environmental antecedents and consequences. A current trend in behavioural treatment is for practitioners to conduct a functional assessment of problem behaviours prior to beginning an intervention. Functional assessment generally refers to a collection of procedures that are used to assess the relationship between physiological and environmental events and problem behaviours. Functional assessment includes operationally defining the behaviour and measuring its frequency, intensity and duration, examining the physiological and environmental variables that may relate to behaviour problems, and identifying the function or reinforcers for challenging behaviours. The expansion of functional analysis methodology to examine medical and neuropsychiatric conditions, and how these conditions interface with learning-appropriate and learning-inappropriate behaviours, provides a possible link between medical and behavioural models. Recently, there has been interest in looking at quality-of-life variables that may affect problem behaviours when conducting a functional assessment. The next section of this chapter examines important environmental and physiological setting events, potential functions, and quality-of-life variables that may affect aggressive and destructive behaviours in people with severe mental retardation/developmental disability.

Setting events

Setting events are conditions that precede and surround behaviour and affect the stimulus–response or response–consequence relationships that influence it (Kantor, 1959; Bijou & Baer, 1978; Wahler & Fox, 1981).

Environmental setting conditions might include group size, population density, staff ratio, noise level, and room temperature (Reese & Leder, 1990). Physiological setting events might include illness, hunger, behavioural state, pain or psychiatric irritability due to depression (Guess & Carr, 1991; Lowry, 1992; Rojahn, Borthwick-Duffy & Jacobson, 1993; Carr & Smith, 1995; Reese, 1997). Social setting events might include demands, unpredictable schedule changes, confrontational interchanges, and interaction styles (Horner et al., 1996).

Consequence analysis

As noted above, the purpose of a functional assessment is to identify the reinforcers for problem behaviours such as aggression and destruction. Over the years, there has been accumulating evidence that problem behaviours may have different functions, and that the same behaviour may have multiple functions in the same individual (Neef, 1994). Carr (1994) has described attention, escape, sensory reinforcement and obtaining tangible events as key potential functions for aggressive and destructive behaviours. O'Neill et al. (1990) developed a matrix of possible functions of problem behaviours. The matrix included two broad categories: obtain or escape/avoid. In each of these categories, there is a subdivision of biological events, or external environmental events. Thus, the person may exhibit problem behaviours to obtain attention, tangible items, or sensory reinforcement. Similarly, the behaviours may be used to escape difficult tasks, demands, undesirable events, pain or undesirable sensory stimulation.

Identifying the functions and the potential reinforcers for the problem behaviour is extremely important in developing treatment procedures. For example, Carr and Durand (1985) demonstrated that problem behaviours may have a communicative function, and that the individual may be better served by learning communicative strategies that could replace problem behaviours in obtaining reinforcement. For example, an individual may be taught to initiate an interaction if the behaviour is attention seeking, or to ask for help when presented with difficult tasks.

Quality-of-life analysis

Risley (1996) has described a third level of analysis beyond what is typically done in a functional assessment. He indicates that we must also consider life arrangement, and that some individuals need to 'get a life' as an effective treatment for their problem behaviours. Risley states that it is important to ask questions such as, 'How is the person doing overall, over-time?' 'Is the person happy, satisfied and safe in their environment?' 'Does the person have a stable home, family, and friends in which to base his or her life and future?' 'Is the person productive and developing new interests, friends and skills over time?' Sprague and Horner (1995) and Kincaid (1996) propose similar analyses.

Functional assessment methods

There are a number of methods to collect functional assessment data. One of the simplest methods is to conduct a behavioural interview (Bailey & Pyles, 1989; O'Neill et al., 1990). The purpose of this interview is to obtain information regarding the topography of the behaviour problem, potential trigger, stimuli and setting events, consequence events, and other variables that may be maintaining the behaviour. A behaviour interview may be all that is possible, but it is to be hoped that the interview may structure a more direct approach at observing the individual and the behaviour problems. Lennox and Miltenberger (1989) have pointed out some limitations of only using interviews. For example, the interview does not allow direct access to the behaviour and potential controlling variables. There may be faulty recollection of events, observer bias and observer expectations when conducting the interview.

Another method is to use behaviour rating scales, checklists and questionnaires. For example, answers to the 16-question Motivational Assessment Scale (Durand & Crimmins, 1988) can provide information about the potential functions or reinforcers that are maintaining the problem behaviour. Major drawbacks with these scales are reliability and validity (Sprague & Horner, 1995). Because of this, direct observation methods are often preferable to interviews and checklists. A useful observation method that can be used to examine contextual variables that may be related to the behaviour problem is a scatter plot (Touchette, MacDonald & Langer, 1985). A scatterplot is a two-sided matrix with space for behaviour codes recorded across multiple days. The scatter plot is used to determine times in which the behaviour problem occurs at a high rate, and also times in which the behaviour does not occur at all. O'Neill et al. (1990) have developed one of the most sophisticated direct observation techniques. The data sheet involves a matrix in which episodes of the target problem behaviours are recorded. This matrix provides a scatterplot, and observers are asked to judge the function of the target behaviour. Other direct observation techniques include using hand-held computers to examine relationships between antecedent conditions, consequences and problem behaviours (Mace & Lalli, 1991). The problem with this direct observation methodology, however, is that only correlational relationships between antecedent and consequence events and behaviour problems is provided. Manipulation of antecedent and consequent conditions, either in analogue situations (e.g. Iwata et al., 1982) or natural situations (Mace & Lalli, 1991) may be necessary in order to examine the functional relationships between environmental events and the behaviour problem.

Functional assessment and treatment

The purpose of a functional assessment is to lead to treatment options. It is no longer appropriate to ask the question, 'What do we do about aggressive and destructive behaviours?' A more appropriate question is 'What do we do about aggression that serves the function of recruiting attention in the context of a group teaching situation?' An important first step to designing a treatment programme is to improve quality of life. Many individuals need to 'get a life' (Risley, 1996), or to become less vulnerable to specific antecedents or consequences that create aggressive and destructive behaviours. With respect to personal competencies, Saunders and Spradlin (1991) have argued that we often arrange treatment schedules and activities for people with severe mental retardation/developmental disability that consist of tasks the person is unable to do. The activity schedule is therefore arranged so that the person will experience limited success and require a great deal of instruction and assistance. Modifying the schedule to consist of enabling activities and events, which produce competence and fluency, has proven to be an effective methodology for decreasing problem behaviours. A second step in treatment is to modify those environmental conditions that relate to problem behaviours. As noted above, setting conditions including noise, crowding, unpredictable schedules, etc. may be targets for intervention. A third step is to teach and/or reinforce skills that serve the same function as the problem behaviours. The next section provides a step-by-step, interdisciplinary approach to the treatment of aggressive and destructive behaviour.

Biobehavioural assessment and treatment: a step-by-step approach

Historically, treatment of aggressive and destructive behaviours in people with severe mental retardation/developmental disability has been addressed from either a behavioural or a medical point of view. Research literature has reflected either a medical or a behavioural perspective, with little overlap (Gardner, Graeber & Cole, 1996). As noted above, adequate treatment requires an interdisciplinary team approach with emphasis on data-based assessment and measuring the effects of treatment. Ideally, this treatment team should consist of a behavioural psychologist, developmental physician, or neurologist and psychiatrist, all familiar with mental retardation/developmental disability. Other team members who may be useful in such interdisciplinary collaboration include those experienced in speech and language pathology, special education and occupational therapy.

Step one: diagnosis

Step one is a diagnostic task. For the developmental physician, and neurologist, this task includes testing for medical disorders, as outlined in the previous section. The primary role of the psychiatrist is to assess the presence of possible psychiatric disorders. As with medical conditions, it is important to define operationally behaviours that suggest the person is experiencing psychiatric symptoms or biological distress.

The behavioural psychologist has a number of functions. One function is to define operationally the target behaviours. The behavioural psychologist then begins to assess, through interview, the possible effects of various setting and antecedent conditions. Potential functions for the target behaviour are also assessed. With interview and checklist data regarding setting and antecedent events, and potential functions of the target behaviour, the behavioural psychologist sets up a data collection system. At the same time, client skills and characteristics, particularly communication skills, are assessed. The interdisciplinary team working with the individual also assesses quality of life, including personal preferences, relationships, choices, opportunities for participation in a variety of environments, meaningful roles, etc.

Step two: level one interventions

Level one interventions involve several aspects. One is to improve the quality of life for the individual. They also involve arranging programme schedules so that there are frequent opportunities for success and preferred activities. Additionally, level one interventions should provide the individual with opportunities to visit a number of different types of environments, to assess lifestyle preferences. Finally, they involve improving the health of the individual, particularly intercurrent illnesses that may worsen aggressive and destructive behaviours, and treating any identifiable psychiatric disorders.

Step three: re-assessment

As level one interventions are occurring, there is ongoing assessment of setting conditions, behaviours, consequence and potential functions of behaviour. The interdisciplinary team continues to assess treatment effects. At some point in treatment, it may be necessary to re-assess whether level one interventions are producing socially significant changes that are satisfying to the individuals involved (Wolf, 1978).

Step four: level two interventions

Level two interventions involve changing specific environmental setting conditions that may be related to the aggressive and destructive behaviours. Since there has been ongoing data collection, and exposure of the individual to a variety of environments, scatterplots of the target behaviours, which reflect times in which there are high and low rate of behaviour, may be of assistance. Activity schedules can be arranged in which there is low probability of behaviour. At this point, manipulations can be planned to examine the functional relationships between environmental conditions and aggressive and destructive behaviours, and functionally equivalent replacement skills can be targeted.

Additionally, it may be of benefit to begin teaching coping skills. For example, if the behaviour occurs in situations in which there is a great deal of emotional agitation or fear, relaxation skills can be taught. If the behaviour occurs to escape or avoid the lack of predictability of transitions and changes in the programme schedule, a visual schedule might be set up, and the person might be taught to self-manage this schedule. Finally, level two interventions may include the use of medications. Now that more data have been collected, there may be hypotheses about other possible psychiatric conditions.

Step five: re-assessment

It is important continually to assess treatment. If the manipulation of setting events and the teaching of alternative responses are not successful, it may be necessary to use a more microlevel type of behaviour analysis (Risley, 1996). Risley defines elements of this approach as the identification of powerful reinforcers, precise contingencies using these reinforcers, precise shaping of new response contingencies, programming of behaviour chains and response classes. This step may be used earlier for extreme forms of behaviour. The reason these procedures are recommended as a final alternative is because of the staff or parent skill level that is required to carry them out (Risley, 1996), potential problems of contextual fit of these procedures in the natural environment (Albin et al., 1996), and problems with generalization and maintenance (Horner, Dunlap & Koegel, 1988; Huguenin, Weidenman & Mulick, 1991).

Step six: use of applied behaviour interventions

The use of microlevel behaviour modification interventions has been extensively described (Matson, 1981; Matson & Mulick, 1991; Van Houten & Axelrod, 1993; Singh, Osborne & Huguenin, 1996). These procedures are typically divided into techniques for increasing behaviours, which include positive reinforcement, shaping, stimulus control, and techniques to decrease behaviour, including differential reinforcement of other behaviour, differential reinforcement of alternative behaviour, differential reinforcement of incompatible behaviour or differential reinforcement of low rate behaviour. These procedures also consist of extinction and punishment, including response cost, contingent aversive stimulation, overcorrection, and time out (Singh et al., 1996). Behaviour modification also needs to be based on a functional assessment. For example, time out may reinforce aggressive and destructive behaviour that functions to escape situations. Also, identifying the function of the aggressive and destructive behaviour may help in reinforcement selection (Durand et al., 1989). There should be careful scrutiny of the use of punishment procedures. Numerous clinical decision-making models have been advanced in the past (Van Houten, et al., 1988; Axelrod et al., 1993; see also Chapter 16).

Conclusion

Schroeder et al., (1997) indicate that severe behaviour problems in mental retardation/developmental disability are often multiply caused and multiply affected. Fifteen years ago, there was a paucity of research that was hypothesis driven regarding the cause or treatment of aggressive and disruptive behaviour in this population. Today, there are a number of hypotheses to consider; however, few present an integrated developmental approach. An interdisciplinary approach to research and treatment is certainly needed. Behavioural researchers must take into account biological risk factors, and psychopharmacological researchers must begin conducting functional assessments. Lack of such an integrated approach will only increase the fragmentation process in medical and behavioural models. Schroeder et al. (1997) point out that a natural methodology for examining an integrated approach involves drug/behaviour interaction studies. Schroeder, Lewis and Lipton (1983) reviewed this research over 15 years ago. Since then, very little work has been done in the severe mental retardation/developmental disability population. The authors' contention is that more drug/behaviour interaction research will lead to better integrated models.

Acknowlededgments

This chapter and the preparation of the manuscript were supported by NICHD grants numbers 02528, 26927, 23042, as well as by MCH grant number MCJ944 and ADD grant number 07DD0365.

References

Albin, R.W., Lucyshyn, J.M., Horner, R.H. & Flannery, K.B. (1996). Contextual fit for behavior support plans: a model for 'Goodness of fit'. In *Positive Behavioral Support: Including People with Difficult Behavior in the Community,* ed. L.K. Koegel, R.L. Koegel, & G. Dunlap, pp. 81–9. Baltimore: Paul H. Brooke.

Axelrod, S., Spreat, S., Berry, B. & Moyer, L. (1993). A decision-making model for selecting the optimal treatment procedure. In *Behavior Analysis and Treatment,* ed. R. Van Houten & S. Axelrod, pp. 183–202. New York: Plenum Press.

Bailey, J.M. & Pyles, O.A.M. (1989). Behavioral diagnostics. In *The Treatment of Severe Behavior Disorders,* ed. E. Cipiani, pp. 85–107. Washington, DC: American Association on Mental Retardation.

Bates, P. & Wehman, P. (1977). Behavior management with the mentally retarded: an empirical analysis of the research. *Mental Retardation,* **15,** 9–12.

Bijou, S.W. & Baer, D.M. (1978). *Behavior Analysis in Child Development.* Englewood Cliffs, NJ: Prentice-Hall.

Blumer, D. (1984). *Psychiatric Aspects of Epilepsy.* Washington, DC: American Psychiatric Press.

Carr, E.G. (1994). Emerging themes in the functional analysis of problem behavior. *Journal of Applied Behavior Analysis,* **27**, 393–9.

Carr, E.G. & Durand, V.M. (1985). Reducing behavior problems through functional communication training. *Journal of Applied Behavior Analysis,* **18**, 111–26.

Carr, E.G. & Smith, C. (1995). Biological setting events for self-injury. *Mental Retardation and Developmental Disabilities Research Review,* **1**, 94–8.

Durand, V.M., & Crimmins, D.B. (1988). Identifying the variables maintaining self-injurious behavior. *Journal of Autism and Developmental Disorders,* **18**, 99–117.

Durand, V.M., Crimmins, D.B., Caulfield, M. & Taylor, J. (1989). Reinforcer Assessment I: Using problem behavior to select reinforcers. *Journal of the Association for Persons with Severe Handicaps,* **14**, 113–26.

Gardner, W.I., Graeber, J.C. & Cole, C.L. (1996). Behavior therapies: a multimodal diagnostic and intervention model. In *Manual of Diagnosis and Professional Practice in Mental Retardation,* ed. J. Jacobson & J. A. Mulick, pp. 355–70. Washington, DC: APA Books.

Guess, D. & Carr, E. (1991). Emergence and maintenance of stereotype and self-injury. *American Journal on Mental Retardation,* **96**, 299–320.

Hellings, J.A., Kelley, L.A., Gabrielli, W.F., Kilgore, E. & Shah, P. (1996). Sertraline response in adults with mental retardation and autistic disorder. *Journal of Clinical Psychiatry,* **57**: 333–6.

Hellings, J.A. & Warnock, J.K. (1994). Self-injurious behavior and serotonin in Prader–Willi syndrome. *Psychopharmacology Bulletin,* **2**, 245–50.

Horner, R. H., Dunlap, G. & Koegel, R. L. (1988). *Generalization and Maintenance.* Baltimore: Paul H. Brooke.

Horner, R.H., Vaughn, B.J., Day, M. & Narde, W.R. (1996). The relationship between setting events and problem behavior: expanding our understanding of behavioral support. In *Positive Behavioral Support: Including people with Difficult Behavior in the Community,* ed. L.K. Koegel, R.L. Koegel, G. Dunlap, pp. 381–402. Baltimore: Paul H. Brooke.

Huguenin, N. H., Weidenman, L. E., & Mulick, J. A. (1991). Programmed instruction. In *Handbook of Mental Retardation,* 2nd edn, ed. J. L. Matson & J. A. Mulick, pp. 451–67. Elmsford, NY: Pergamon Press.

Iwata, B., Dorsey, M., Slifer, K. et al. (1982). Toward a functional analysis of self-injury. *Analysis and Intervention in Developmental Disabilities,* **2**, 3–20.

Kantor, J.R. (1959). *Interbehavioral Psychology: A Sample of Scientific System Construction.* Chicago: Principia.

Kastner, T., Friedman, D.L. & Pond, W.S. (1992). Carbamazepine-induced hyponatrenia in patients with mental retardation. *American Journal of Mental Retardation,* **96**, 536–40.

Kincaid, D. (1996). Person-centered planning. In *Positive Behavioral Support: Including People with Difficult Behavior in the Community,* ed. L.K. Koegel,

R.L. Koegel, & G. Dunlap, pp. 425–38. Baltimore, MD: Paul H. Brookes.

Lennox, D.B. & Miltenberger, R.G. (1989). Conducting a functional assessment of problem behavior in applied settings. *Journal of the Association for People with Severe Handicaps*, **14**, 304–11.

Lowry, M.A. (1992). Assessment and treatment of mood disorders and associated behavior problems in adults with profound and severe mental retardation. Paper presented at American Psychological Association. Washington, DC.

Lowry, M.A. (1997). Unmasking mood disorders: recognizing and measuring symptomatic behaviors. *The Habilitative Mental Healthcare Newsletter*, **16**(1),1–6.

Mace, F.C. & Lalli, J.S. (1991). Linking descriptive and experimental analysis in the treatment of bizarre speech. *Journal of Applied Behavior Analysis*, **24**, 553–62.

Matson, J.L. (1981). A controlled outcome study of phobias in mentally retarded adults. *Behavior Research and Therapy*, **19**, 101–7.

Matson, J.L. & Mulick, J.A. (eds.) (1991). *Handbook of Mental Retardation*, 2nd edn. Elmsford, NY: Pergamon Press.

Neef, N.A. (1994). Functional analysis approaches to behavior assessment and treatment. Special issue. *Journal of Applied Behavior Analysis*, **2**.

O'Neill, R.E., Horner, R.H., Albin, R.W., Storey, K. & Sprague, J.R. (1990). *Functional Analysis of Problem Behavior: A Practical Assessment Guide*. Pacific Grove, CA: Brooks/Cole.

Reese, R.M. (1997). A biobehavioral analysis of self-injurious behavior in a person with profound handicaps. *Focus on Autism and Other Developmental Disabilities*, **12**(2), 87–94.

Reese, R.M., & Leder, D. (1990). An ecobehavioral setting event analysis of residential facilities for people with mental retardation. In *Ecobehavioral Analysis and Developmental Disabilities: The Twenty-First Century*, ed. S.R. Schroeder, pp. 82–93. New York: Springer-Verlag.

Risley, T. (1996). Get a life! Positive behavioral intervention for challenging behavior through life arrangement and life coaching. In *Positive Behavioral Support: Including People with Difficult Behavior in the Community*, ed. L.K. Koegel, R.L. Koegel, & G. Dunlap, pp. 425–38. Baltimore, MD: Paul H. Brookes.

Rojahn, J., Borthwick-Duffy, S.A. & Jacobson, J.W. (1993). The association between psychiatric diagnosis and severe behavior problems in mental retardation. *Annual of Clinical Psychiatry*, **5**, 163–70.

Saunders, R.R. & Spradlin, J.E. (1991). A supported routine approach to active treatment for enhancing independence, competence, and self-worth. *Behavioral Residential Treatment*, **6**, 11–37.

Schroeder, S.R., Lewis, M.A. & Lipton, M.A. (1983). Interactions of pharmacotherapy and behavior therapy among children with learning behavioral disorders. In *Advances in Learning and Behavioral Disabilities*, Vol. 2, ed. K.D. Gadow & I. Bialer, pp. 179–225. Greenwich, CT: JAI.

Schroeder, S.R., Tessel, R.E., Loupe, P. & Stodgell, C. (1997). Severe behavioral problems in developmental disabilities. In *Handbook of Mental Deficiency*, 3rd edn, ed. W.E. MacLean, pp. 439–65. Hillsdale, NJ: Lawrence Erlbaum Associates.

Singh, N.N., Osborne, J.G. & Huguenin, N.H. (1996). Applied behavioral interventions. In *Manual of Diagnosis and Professional Practice in Mental Retardation*, ed. J. Jacobson & J.A. Mulick, pp. 341–54. Washington, DC: APA Books.

Sovner, R. & Fogelman, S. (1996). Irritability and mental retardation. *Seminars in Clinical Neuropsychiatry*, **2**, 105–14.

Sprague, J.R. & Horner, R.H. (1995). Functional assessment and intervention in community settings. *Mental Retardation and Developmental Disabilities Research Review*, **1**, 89–93.

Touchette, P.E., MacDonald, R.F. & Langer, S.N. (1985). A scatterplot for identifying stimulus control of problem behavior. *Journal of Applied Behavior Analysis*, **23**, 343–51.

Trimble, M. (1990). Anti-convulsants in children and adolescents. *Journal of Child Adolescent Psychopharmacology*, **1**, 107–24.

Umbrick, D., Degree, F.A., Barr, W.B., Lieberman, J.A., Pollack, S. & Schaul, N. (1995). Postictal and chronic psychoses in patients with temporal lobe epilepsy. *American Journal of Psychiatry*, **152**, 224–31.

Van Houten, R. & Axelrod, S. (eds.) (1993). *Behavior Analysis and Treatment*. New York: Plenum Press.

Van Houten, R., Axelrod, S., Bailey, J.S. et al. (1988). The right to effective behavioral treatment. *Journal of Applied Behavior Analysis*, **21**, 381–4.

Wahler, R.G. & Fox, J.J. (1981). Setting events in applied behavior analysis: toward conceptual and methodological expansion. *Journal of Applied Behavior Analysis*, **14**, 327–38.

Wolf, M.M. (1978). Social validity: the case for subjective measurement on how behavior analysis is finding its heart. *Journal of Applied Behavior Analysis*, **31**, 203–14.

16 Behavioural approaches to treatment: principles and practices

BETSEY A. BENSON AND SUSAN M. HAVERCAMP

Introduction

Behavioural interventions have played a prominent role in the habilitation of people with developmental disabilities since the 1960s. Prior to the introduction of behavioural techniques, individuals with developmental disabilities were placed in institutions where they received custodial care and psychotropic drugs to manage disruptive or harmful behaviour. Behavioural techniques offered a way to improve daily-living skills and to reduce maladaptive behaviour. Hundreds of studies have been published that demonstrate the effectiveness of behavioural techniques in decreasing harmful behaviour and teaching self-care skills such as dressing, toileting, eating and grooming (Matson, 1990). Behavioural interventions were found to obtain positive outcomes with individuals of all ages and all levels of intellectual functioning. The results generated a positive outlook among professionals regarding the potential of individuals with developmental disabilities to learn new behaviours and become more independent.

A complete review of behavioural interventions with people who have developmental disabilities is beyond the scope of this chapter; however, numerous excellent resources are available for further information (e.g. Matson, 1990; Singh, Osborne & Huguenin, 1996). This chapter is divided into two main sections: first, behaviour principles and techniques are briefly described, and then applications of behavioural techniques to diagnostic categories or problem behaviours are presented.

Principles

Several assumptions are made in adopting a behavioural approach to assessment and intervention. Most importantly, it is assumed that behaviour is primarily affected by the conditions existing in the person's environment, rather than by intrapsychic dynamics. The focus is on current behaviour and specific behaviour–environment interactions. Through these interactions, the individual learns how his or her behaviour affects the environment (i.e.

the behaviour of parents, siblings, etc.). The goal of behavioural intervention is to change (either increase or decrease) one or more specific behaviours. For example, the goal may be to decrease Jane's hitting or to increase Johnny's shirt-buttoning skill.

The hallmarks of a behavioural approach to intervention include an operational definition of the target behaviour (to be increased or decreased), behaviour analysis, and data collection as an ongoing part of assessment and intervention. Essential elements in the analysis of behaviour are defining the antecedent conditions and the consequences of the behaviour as well as the setting or context in which the behaviour occurs. Behavioural interventions focus on systematically changing one or more of these elements. Treatment goals and strategies are described in detail in a behaviour plan. Once the plan is in place, data continue to be recorded on the effectiveness of the plan, which is modified, when appropriate, to achieve the desired effect on the target behaviour.

Parents, teachers, staff, peers, or the individuals themselves may carry out the behaviour plan. In many cases, the parents, teachers or staff are asked to change *their* behaviour because that is expected to change the target individual's behaviour. To be effective, the behaviour plan must be carried out consistently. For this reason, implementation often involves training several care givers (parents, teachers, etc.) in the details of the plan (Reid & Green, 1990).

In recent years, leaders in the field have recommended that a biopsychosocial approach to assessment and intervention be adopted in which consideration is given to biological influences on the individual's behaviour, as well as to the person's skills and needs, and their physical and social environment (Gardner, Graeber & Cole, 1996). A behavioural intervention could be the primary intervention or could be one part of a plan that also includes pharmacotherapy or other interventions.

No attempt is made here to address the many behavioural techniques, but rather brief descriptions are given of those that are relevant to the practice section of the chapter. Further information can be found in basic texts of applied behaviour analysis and behaviour modification, such as Martin and Pear (1996) and Miltenberger (1997).

Reinforcement

A positive reinforcer is an event that increases the probability that the response that directly precedes it will occur again (Singh et al., 1996). For example, getting paid for walking the neighbour's dog increases the probability that I will agree to walk that dog in the future. In negative reinforcement, the occurrence of a behaviour is followed by the removal of an aversive stimulus or a decrease in the intensity of a stimulus, and results in a strengthening of the behaviour (Miltenberger, 1997). When a temper tantrum is followed by cessation of work demands, for example, the tantrum behaviour may be negatively reinforced. The reinforcing value of an event varies from individual to individual and from time to time and therefore must be established empirically (Singh et al., 1996).

Determining what will function as a reinforcer for a given individual can be a difficult task, particularly with people who have problems making their preferences known (Ivancic & Bailey, 1996). A choice assessment procedure was developed as a way to identify preferences for various stimuli among individuals with severe and profound mental retardation (Fisher et al., 1996; Piazza et al., 1996). Stimuli are either placed in view of the individual or are demonstrated by the therapist (for example hand clapping). Each stimulus in the assessment is paired with every other stimulus, and approach responses to the stimuli are noted. An approach response is interpreted as evidence of a preference. The choice assessment procedure was found to be an effective way of predicting the relative reinforcing value of various stimuli for individuals with severe to profound disabilities (Piazza et al., 1996).

Behaviour shaping

If the desired response is not in the person's repertoire, it cannot be reinforced. One procedure that can be used to teach a new behaviour is shaping. Shaping of behaviour occurs when a reinforcer is provided for behaviour that is increasingly similar to the target behaviour. Reinforcement is then presented differentially for responses that more closely match the desired behaviour, or successive approximations, until the desired response is performed. Once the desired response occurs, it alone is reinforced, to the exclusion of lesser approximations (Martin & Pear, 1996).

Differential reinforcement

Variations of differential reinforcement procedures are used to reduce the frequency of undesirable behaviours. Differential reinforcement of other behaviour is a procedure in which reinforcement is contingent on the non-occurrence of a behaviour during a specified period of time. Any behaviour other than the target behaviour is reinforced. In one example, three women with severe self-injury and either severe or profound mental retardation earned access to a preferred reinforcer for five seconds if they had not self-injured for the preceding 15 seconds (Mazaleski et al., 1993). In differential reinforcement of a prespecified incompatible behaviour, behaviours that physically cannot co-occur with the undesirable behaviour are reinforced (Jones & Baker, 1989); whereas, in differential reinforcement of low rates of behaviour, reduced rates of the undesirable behaviour are reinforced (Cipani, 1990).

Extinction

When a previously reinforced behaviour is no longer reinforced, a process of extinction occurs in which the behaviour reduces in frequency. By design, any reinforcement programme also involves extinction because certain behaviours are reinforced while others are not (Singh et al., 1996).

Lovaas and Simmons (1969) found that for some children, self-injurious behaviour decreased from more than 2000 acts during the first session to no self-injurious acts in the tenth session once all sources of social reinforcement were removed.

Punishment

Punishment is a procedure in which a behaviour is followed by a consequence that decreases the future probability of that behaviour re-occurring. There are several behavioural procedures that can function as punishment, including removal of reinforcement, physical restraint, and electrical shock. In a meta-analysis of behavioural interventions, Scotti et al. (1991) concluded that while punishment procedures were effective in suppressing maladaptive behaviour, their effects were enhanced when combined with reinforcement procedures.

Overcorrection

Overcorrection involves either repeatedly restoring a setting (or individual) to its previous state (before the occurrence of an undesirable behaviour) or the positive practice of behaviour that is incompatible with the undesired response (Singh et al., 1996). For example, an individual who overturns a chair in a lounge area could be first manually guided and then instructed to arrange all the chairs in the room. Azrin and Wesolowski (1975) eliminated habitual and disruptive vomiting by requiring the woman to clean up the vomit (including changing her soiled clothes or bed sheets) and also to engage in 15 practice trials in the correct manner of vomiting (positive practice) each time inappropriate vomiting occurred. The use of positive practice successfully eliminated the dangerous behaviour of aerophagia (pathological air swallowing) in a 22-year-old man who had engaged in this behaviour since the age of five despite a variety of treatment efforts (Holburn & Dougher, 1985).

Time out

Time out from positive reinforcement involves interrupting the reinforcement obtained by the individual contingent on undesirable behaviour. Time out can be exclusionary, in which the individual is removed from the setting for a period of time, or it can be non-exclusionary, in which the individual remains in the setting but potential reinforcers are removed (Singh et al., 1996). The absence of the problem behaviour is usually required to reinstate the previous reinforcing conditions. Hamilton, Stephens and Allen (1967) report the successful use of time out with five women who had severe mental retardation and such behaviours as head banging (sometimes breaking windows), undressing, and aggression towards other residents.

Response-contingent aversive stimulation

Response-contingent aversive stimulation involves presenting an aversive stimulus following the undesirable response. Aversive stimuli that have been used with people with developmental disabilities include water misting, unpleasant tastes, brief physical restraint, and electric shock (Singh et al., 1996). This procedure is avoided except in extreme circumstances (Linscheid et al., 1994; Jacob-Timm, 1996) because of ethical concerns about the misuse of aversive stimuli (Matson & Kazdin, 1981; Landau, 1993).

Stimulus control and stimulus generalization

A behaviour is under stimulus control when its occurrence can be predicted by knowing whether or not a stimulus (a particular person, for example) is present in the environment (Cipani, 1990). When a behaviour is under stimulus control, there is a high probability that it will occur given that the stimulus is present. Stimulus generalization occurs when a behaviour is observed in the presence of stimuli that have not previously been reinforced. Generalization across settings takes place when a behaviour acquired in school, for example, occurs at home under similar conditions.

Modelling

Learning that occurs by observing others perform behaviours is called observational learning or modelling (Bandura, 1969). The observer does not have to perform a behaviour or receive reinforcement directly in order to learn it. Models of appropriate behaviour can be presented live or on film or videotape. In participant modelling, an individual such as a peer, parent or therapist models the desired behaviour and then participates by helping the individual perform the behaviour while offering encouragement and support. Participant modelling has been found to be more effective than live or filmed modelling (Ollendick & Cerny, 1981).

Further considerations

A few basic principles and procedures of behavioural interventions are described above. It is important to note, however, that many behavioural treatments involve combinations of techniques. For example, overcorrection may be combined with a 'differential reinforcement of other behaviour' procedure, or modelling may be used with positive reinforcement of desired behaviour. Matson (1982a) provided behavioural treatment involving a combination of techniques to three men with mild mental retardation who displayed repetitive clothes checking or body checking. A 'differential reinforcement of other behaviour' procedure was instituted in which reinforcement was given for not performing the checking behaviour while the men completed work tasks. Tokens were provided for each minute out of 30 that the behaviour did not occur. The tokens could be exchanged later for snacks (positive reinforcement). When clothes or body checking occurred during the training session, an overcorrection procedure was used in which a set routine of hand and arm movements was repeated. Both self-reported anxiety and obsessive–compulsive behaviours decreased following treatment.

Although there are many behavioural interventions that could be incorporated into a behavioural treatment plan, a task force recommended that the selection of interventions proceed by choosing the least restrictive, effective technique from among those available to deal with that particular problem behaviour (Van Houten et al., 1988). Further, an analysis of risks and benefits of treatment procedures should be conducted (Axelrod et al.,1993).

Practices

Skill building

Relaxation training

Relaxation training is a group of anxiety-reduction techniques (Smith, 1985). The methods range from progressive muscle relaxation, in which several muscle groups are individually tensed and relaxed (Bernstein & Borkovec, 1973), to imagery-based procedures and meditation. For each, the goal is to reduce tension and to produce a calm state in body and/or in mind. Relaxation training can be a primary intervention used to reduce general anxiety levels or it can be one part of a treatment 'package'. In systematic desensitization, a fearful person trained in relaxation skills imagines, or experiences in vivo, a series of anxiety-provoking situations, starting with the least anxiety provoking (Ollendick & Cerny, 1981). In anger management training (Benson, 1992), relaxation training is included to reduce arousal associated with anger-provoking situations.

Among the modifications used to enhance relaxation training for people with mental retardation are the use of simplified language, physical prompts and guidance, behaviour shaping of the response, biofeedback, and positive reinforcement for practice (Harvey, 1979). The addition of modelling and physical guidance to relaxation training helps individuals functioning in the severe range of mental retardation to discriminate between tense and relaxed states (Lindsay et al., 1989). The procedure also improved performance on laboratory learning tasks (Lindsay & Morrison, 1996). Adapting relaxation training procedures for individuals with special needs is the subject of a manual (Cautela & Grodin, 1979) and a videotape (Grodin, Cautela & Grodin, 1989).

Treatment of anxiety

For individuals with mental retardation who have difficulty expressing themselves, an act of refusal is one way to communicate. Some instances in which individuals are considered non-compliant could be due to anxiety or fear concerning the activity (Benson, 1990b). When non-compliance seems associated with a particular type of activity, rather than a general pattern of refusal, further inquiry may be in order to determine if the avoidance is anxiety based. The greatest number of published studies of behavioural

approaches to treatment of anxiety and fear in people with mental retardation has dealt with specific phobias (Jackson, 1983; Benson, 1990b). A few
examples are described here to illustrate different treatment approaches to
reduce fears that interfered with community integration.

Fear of riding in a car or bus was successfully treated with systematic
desensitization and reinforcement (Mansdorf, 1976; Luiselli, 1978). Luiselli
(1978) reported on the treatment of a boy with autism who had tantrums
when asked to get on the school bus and cried continuously while riding. The
behavioural intervention included in-vivo exposure in which the boy's
mother sat with him on the stationary bus for brief periods and then reinforced him with food and praise. Time on the bus was gradually increased,
and the mother's involvement gradually faded out over several days
(shaping), until the boy was riding the bus to and from school without incident. Mansdorf (1976) reported success using a similar treatment plan with a
woman with mild mental retardation residing in an institution who refused
to ride in a car to a workshop or to other community activities.

Interpersonal skills

Several of behaviourally based interventions that focus on improving
social skills of persons with mental retardation have been developed. Social
skills deficits are noted in many people with mental retardation due to their
adaptive behaviour deficits, and are a particular concern for those with
psychiatric or behaviour disorders because of the association observed
between poor social skills and psychopathology (Benson et al., 1985). An
example of the use of social skills training in the treatment of psychosis is
provided, as well as a description of two notable programmes for improving
social skills of adults with mental retardation: Stacking the Deck (Foxx &
McMorrow, 1983) and Home-of-Your-Own Co-operative Living Training
Programme (Tassé, Havercamp & Reiss, 1997). Additional interventions are
described in Benson and Valenti-Hein (1999).

Stacking the Deck

Stacking the Deck (Foxx & McMorrow, 1983) is designed to be used with a
board game. Players move their game pieces around the board by correctly
answering questions of a social skills nature. The playing cards are organized
by skill areas such as compliments, social interaction, politeness, criticism,
social confrontation, and question and answers. Correct responses are
praised and when an incorrect response occurs, the facilitator models a
correct answer. The facilitator keeps a record of the questions answered correctly and incorrectly and charts each player's progress and/or the player may
self-monitor performance.

Home-Of-Your-Own Co-operative Living Training Program

The Co-operative Living Training Program (Tassé, Havercamp & Reiss,
1997) is a curriculum that incorporates behavioural techniques to improve

skills required for sharing a residence. The skills are broadly defined as those that facilitate living and getting along with others, and include borrowing and lending, sharing chores, respecting privacy, and resolving conflicts. The curriculum is designed to be used in groups of adults with mental retardation over ten one-hour sessions. The behavioural techniques used in each session include: instruction, discussion, modelling, role-playing (participant modelling), and feedback (positive reinforcement). The authors field-tested and revised the curriculum over the course of two years, based on their experience with 15 different groups of over 100 individuals who had mental retardation. The Co-operative Living Skills Scale (CooLS) was developed to measure the specific skills taught in the curriculum and it has been demonstrated that scores improved after participation in the curriculum.

Treatment of psychosis
Behavioural techniques have been used to improve the social skills of individuals diagnosed with psychotic disorders. Stephens et al. (1981) worked with three residents of an institution who had been diagnosed with chronic schizophrenia. In the first study, a woman with mild mental retardation was described as talking excessively and repeatedly changing the subject. She was said to perseverate in talking about past problems and used nonsense phrases and inappropriate words. The behavioural treatment included practising role-played scenes of common problems encountered by patients. The techniques used were instructions, audiotaped feedback, modelling by the therapist, and rehearsal of appropriate responses. Rapid improvements were reported. In a second study, two subjects diagnosed with schizophrenia participated, one with moderate and one with severe mental retardation. One individual was withdrawn and spoke little, whereas the other was excessively loud with inappropriate responses. The intervention techniques were similar to those of the first study. Conducting test sessions with an unfamiliar adult and obtaining behaviour ratings from ward staff provided an assessment of the generalization of treatment effects. Both patients improved, and the results generalized across settings. At a two-month follow-up, the treatment gains were maintained.

Liberman, DeRisi and Mueser (1989) were the authors of an excellent manual describing social skills training for psychiatric patients. Although designed for patients without mental retardation, a number of the activities would be appropriate for individuals functioning in the mild range of mental retardation.

Decreasing maladaptive behaviour

Maladaptive or disruptive behaviour in people with mental retardation is frequently defined as including aggression against others, self-injury, and property destruction (Thompson & Gray, 1994). This group of behaviour problems is of great concern because of the potential for serious harm as well as because the behaviours interfere with attention, learning, and social and intellectual development. An overview of selected interventions for disruptive behaviours is provided here. Additional information can be found in Benson and Aman (in press) and Thompson and Gray (1994).

It has long been recognized that even the most destructive behaviours are often learned because they are reinforced in some way (Ferster, 1961; Carr, 1977). For example, Carr proposed that self-injurious behaviour is learned, operant, and maintained by either positive social reinforcement or by the termination of an aversive stimulus (negative reinforcement). He also reviewed a self-stimulation hypothesis that suggests that self-injurious behaviour may be a means of providing visual, tactile or auditory sensory stimulation (Vollmer, 1994). Other researchers recognized the purposeful nature of other types of challenging behaviour such as aggression (Sigafoos & Saggers, 1995), property destruction (Gardner & Cole, 1990) and stereotypy (Rojahn & Sisson, 1990).

Functional assessment

Iwata et al. (1982) developed Carr's environmental hypothesis into an assessment technology called functional assessment. This methodology was designed to assess functional relationships between maladaptive behaviour and specific reinforcers. In this technique, subjects are repeatedly exposed to a series of analogue conditions to assess whether or not the behaviour is maintained by (1) sensory stimulation, (2) escape from demand, (3) social attention, or (4) tangible reinforcement (i.e. a preferred toy). The frequency of self-injurious behaviour is measured during each condition. When a child's self-injury is most frequent during the escape from demand condition, this indicates that the behaviour is maintained by negative reinforcement by permitting the child to escape from demands. Figure 16.1 shows a sample functional analysis graph of an individual's aggressive behaviour. This graph indicates that the aggression is maintained primarily by social attention. Iwata et al. provided direct empirical evidence for the function of various sources of reinforcement in the maintenance of aberrant behaviour. Functional analysis has been found useful for prescribing specific treatments, even in a brief, 90-minute out-patient setting (Northup et al., 1991; 1994).

Functional assessment can also be accomplished using naturalistic observation by recording each instance of the behaviour together with its antecedents and consequences (Mace & Lalli, 1991). For example, does Jason strike out whenever he is asked to do some work? Does Jenny's eye gouging always result in expressions of concerns (social attention) from her family or caretakers? More recently, rating forms have been developed to identify the function of aberrant behaviour (Sturmey, 1994).

Functional analysis is widely used in clinical practice, applied settings (i.e. classrooms), and research (Iwata et al., 1994; Northup et al., 1994, 1995;

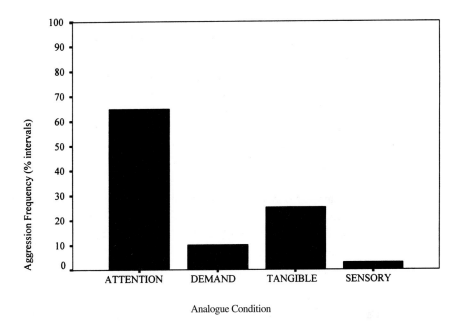

Fig. 16.1 Sample functional analysis graph.

Sigafoos & Saggers, 1995; Vollmer & Smith, 1996). In fact, some service providers mandate a functional assessment before a treatment plan can be implemented. Recently, other functional properties of challenging behaviour have been addressed, such as social context, sequence of tasks and activities, presence or absence of certain individuals, and biological factors such as physical illness, exercise and drugs (Gardner & Graeber, 1993; Carr, 1994).

Functional communication training

Challenging behaviour may be considered a form of communication (Carr & Durand, 1985). For example, if a child's self-injury is maintained by attention (positive reinforcement), the self-injury can be interpreted as a request for attention. The purpose of functional assessment is to determine the function that the behaviour serves for the individual. Intervention can then be tailored to the function by teaching an appropriate communication technique. For example, once it is determined that Jenny misbehaves to obtain attention, then she can be taught a more appropriate means of getting attention (communication training). If her misbehaviour is then consistently ignored (extinction), Jenny will learn that the only way to get the attention she wants is to ask for it appropriately. We would expect her misbehaviour to be replaced by the communicative alternative. Appropriate communication is more likely to generalize to new environments and to maintain for long periods of time (Durand & Carr, 1992). Recently, more comprehensive multimodal treatment packages have been developed that include functional communication training, choice making, building tolerance for delay of reinforcement, as well as biological or medical treatments (Carr & Carlson, 1993; Gardner & Graeber, 1993; Steed et al., 1995; see also Chapters 1 and 15).

Self-management

Assuming that aggressive behaviour is at least partially the result of skill deficits, systematic training in self-management has the potential to reduce conduct problems (Gardner & Cole, 1990). The self-management skills of self-monitoring, self-evaluation and self-consequation were included in a training programme to improve behaviour in a vocational programme (Cole, Gardner & Karan, 1985). Adults with mild to moderate mental retardation and severe conduct problems were taught to identify and self-reinforce 'good worker behaviour' versus 'not good worker behaviour'. The intervention resulted in a significant decrease in aggression and an increase in work productivity that was maintained at follow-up testing several months later.

Treatment of depression

The behavioural treatment of depression in people with mental retardation has focused on verbal statements and non-verbal behaviours occurring in social interactions (Benson, 1990a). A variety of behavioural techniques has been applied, including self-management. Matson, Dettling and Senatore (1979) worked with a man with borderline to mild mental retardation and a long history of depression. The intervention included modelling, praise (reinforcement), self-evaluation and self-reinforcement (self-management). The target behaviours were negative self-statements, suicide statements, and lack of participation in activities. In individual training sessions, the man was praised for positive self-statements and he was asked to praise himself as well. If he made a negative self-statement, the therapist modelled an appropriate statement and the subject rehearsed the modelled statement. Homework assignments were given that required tallying positive statements and noting participation in activities. Positive statements and participation in activities increased following the treatment. Using a similar intervention, Matson (1982b) reported the treatment of somatic complaints, negative self-statements and grooming in four adults with mental retardation and depression. Following a range of 10 to 35 individual sessions, the four participants improved in verbal and non-verbal behaviours and in self-reported depression.

Anger management training

Designed for individuals functioning in the mild to moderate range of mental retardation, the goal of anger management training is to improve self-control skills of individuals with aggressive behaviour (Benson, 1992; Benson, Rice & Miranti, 1986). The multicomponent group or individual therapy programme includes training in identification of emotions

(Benson, 1995b), relaxation training, self-instructional training, and problem-solving skills (Benson, 1995a). Techniques of training include lecture, discussion, modelling, role-playing, feedback and homework. Benson et al. (1986) reported improvements in supervisor ratings of behaviour, self-report and role-play measures at post-test and follow-up for adults who participated in anger management training.

Conclusion

Behavioural interventions have in many ways succeeded in fulfilling their early promise to improve the independence and quality of life of individuals with developmental disabilities. In addition, the emphasis on operational definitions of behaviour, systematic observation, and continuous data collection has provided a methodology by which to evaluate the effects of interventions generally, both behavioural and other approaches.

Remaining challenges include staff training in the functional analysis of behaviour and in the implementation of behavioural treatment plans. Some evidence suggests that staff's immediate response to challenging behaviour is counter to recommended behavioural approaches (Hastings, 1996). Thus, training must not only educate staff in specific procedures, but must overcome responses that appear 'natural' to workers in the setting.

Several areas of treatment have been somewhat neglected. Tremendous attention has been focused on behavioural interventions for disruptive behaviours, while the treatment of anxiety, mood and psychotic disorders has been relatively neglected. Positive results have been obtained, however, and await further application and refinement.

Greater emphasis on involving the individual in the development of his or her behaviour plans would be welcomed in the current zeitgeist of empowering individuals with mental retardation. Behavioural interventions that increase self-management skills are consistent with this philosophy.

The co-ordination of behavioural interventions with other approaches to treatment is also necessary. Pharmacotherapy is a likely partner for behavioural interventions in the treatment of people with developmental disabilities. Evaluating the individual and joint effects of these different treatments is a complex task that requires multidisciplinary co-operation.

Although behavioural interventions have had a short history, their impact has been enormous in raising expectations for what is possible for people with developmental disabilities. Behavioural treatments have the potential to teach new behaviours previously thought beyond the capability of individuals with mental retardation. In addition, they can be used to treat severe maladaptive behaviour, thus opening doors to community integration.

References

Axelrod, S., Spreat, S., Berry, B. & Moyer, L. (1993). A decision-making model for selecting the optimal treatment procedure. In *Behavior Analysis and Treatment*, ed. R. Van Houten & S. Axelrod, pp. 183–202. New York: Plenum Press.

Azrin, N.H. & Wesolowski, M.D. (1975). Eliminating habitual vomiting in a retarded adult by positive practice and self-correction. *Journal of Behavior Therapy and Experimental Psychiatry*, **6**, 145–8.

Bandura, A. (1969). *Principles of Behavior Modification*. New York: Holt, Rinehart & Winston.

Benson, B.A. (1990a). Behavioral treatment of depression. In *Depression in Mentally Retarded Children and Adults*, ed. A. Dosen & F. J. Menolascino, pp. 309–29. Leiden, Netherlands: Logon Publications.

(1990b). Emotional problems I: Anxiety disorders and depression. In *Handbook of Behavior Modification with the Mentally Retarded*, 2nd edn, ed. J.L. Matson, pp. 391– 420. New York: Plenum Press.

(1992). *Teaching Anger Management to Persons with Mental Retardation.* Worthington, OH: IDS Publishing.

(1995a). Problem solving skills training. *Habilitative Mental Healthcare Newsletter*, **14**, 13–7.

(1995b). Resources for emotions training. *Habilitative Mental Healthcare Newsletter*, **14**, 55–8.

Benson, B.A. & Aman, M.G. (in press). Disruptive behavior disorders in children with mental retardation. In *Handbook of Disruptive Behavior Disorders*, ed. H.C. Quay & A.E. Hogan, New York: Plenum Press.

Benson, B.A., Reiss, S., Smith, D.C. & Laman, D. (1985). Psychosocial correlates of depression in mentally retarded adults: II. Poor social skills. *American Journal of Mental Deficiency*, **89**, 657–9.

Benson, B.A., Rice, C.J. & Miranti, S.V. (1986). Effects of anger management training with mentally retarded adults in group treatment. *Journal of Consulting and Clinical Psychology*, **54**, 728–9.

Benson, B.A. & Valenti-Hein, D. (1999). Cognitive and social learning treatments. In *The treatment of mental illness and behavior disorders in mentally retarded children and adults*, ed. A. Dosen & K. Day. Washington, DC: American Psychiatric Press.

Bernstein, D.A. & Borkovec, T.D. (1973). *Progressive Relaxation Training: A Manual for the Helping Professions*. Champaign, IL: Research Press.

Carr, E.G. (1977). The motivation of self-injurious behavior: A review of some hypotheses. *Psychological Bulletin*, **84**, 800–16.

(1994). Emerging themes in the functional analysis of problem behavior. *Journal of Applied Behavior Analysis*, **27**, 393–9.

Carr, E.G. & Carlson, J. I. (1993). Reduction of severe behavior problems in the community using a multicomponent treatment approach. *Journal of Applied Behavior Analysis*, **26**, 157–72.

Carr, E.G. & Durand, V.M. (1985). Reducing behavior problems through functional communication training. *Journal of Applied Behavior Analysis*, **18**, 111–26.

Cautela, J.R. & Grodin, J. (1979) *Relaxation: A Comprehensive Manual for Adults, Children, and Children with Special Needs.* Champaign, IL: Research Press.

Cipani, E. (1990). Principles of behavior modification. In *Handbook of Behavior Modification with the Mentally Retarded,* ed. J. L. Matson, pp. 123–38. New York: Plenum Press.

Cole, C.L., Gardner, W.I. & Karan, O.C. (1985). Self-management training of mentally retarded adults presenting severe conduct difficulties. *Applied Research in Mental Retardation,* **6,** 337–47.

Durand, V.M. & Carr, E.G. (1992). An analysis of maintenance following functional communication training. *Journal of Applied Behavior Analysis,* **25,** 777–94.

Ferster, C.B. (1961). Positive reinforcement and behavioral deficits of autistic children. *Child Development,* **32,** 437–56.

Fisher, W.W., Piazza, C.C., Bowman, L.G. & Amari, A. (1996). Integrating caregiver report with a systematic choice assessment to enhance reinforcer identification. *American Journal on Mental Retardation,* **101,** 15–25.

Foxx, R.M. & McMorrow, M.J. (1983). *Stacking the Deck: A Social Skills Game for Adults with Developmental Disabilities.* Champaign, IL: Research Press.

Gardner, W.I. & Cole, C.L. (1990). Aggression and related conduct difficulties. In *Handbook of Behavior Modification with the Mentally Retarded,* 2nd edn, ed. J. L. Matson, pp. 225–51. New York: Plenum Press.

Gardner, W.I. & Graeber, J.L. (1993). Treatment of severe behavioral disorders in persons with mental retardation: a multimodal behavioral treatment model. In *Mental Health Aspects of Mental Retardation: Progress in Assessment and Treatment,* ed. R.J. Fletcher & A. Dosen, pp. 45–69. New York: Lexington Books.

Gardner, W.I., Graeber, J.L. & Cole, C.L. (1996). Behavior therapies: a multimodal diagnostic and intervention model. In *Manual of Diagnosis and Professional Practice in Mental Retardation,* ed. J. W. Jacobson & J. A. Mulick, pp. 355–69. Washington, DC: American Psychological Association.

Grodin, J., Cautela, J.R. & Grodin, G. (1989). Relaxation techniques for people with special needs: breaking the barriers (Video). Champaign, IL: Research Press.

Hamilton, J., Stephens, L. & Allen, P. (1967). Controlling aggressive and destructive behavior in severely retarded institutionalized residents. *American Journal of Mental Deficiency,* **71,** 852–6.

Harvey, J.R. (1979). The potential of relaxation training for the mentally retarded. *Mental Retardation,* **17,** 71–6.

Hastings, R.P. (1996). Staff strategies and explanations for intervening with challenging behaviours. *Journal of Intellectual Disability Research,* **40,** 166–75.

Holburn, C.S. & Dougher, M.J. (1985). Behavioral attempts to eliminate air-swallowing in two profoundly mentally retarded clients. *American Journal of Mental Deficiency,* **89,** 524–36.

Ivancic, M.T. & Bailey, J.S. (1996). Current limits to reinforcer identification for some persons with profound multiple disabilities. *Research in Developmental Disabilities,* **17,** 77–92.

Iwata, B.A., Dorsey, M.F., Slifer, K.J., Bauman, K.E. & Richman, G.S. (1982).

Toward a functional analysis of self-injury. *Analysis and Intervention in Developmental Disabilities*, **2**, 3–20.

Iwata, B.A., Pace, G.M., Dorsey, M.F. et al. (1994). The functions of self-injurious behavior: an experimental-epidemiological analysis. *Journal of Applied Behavior Analysis*, **27**, 215–40.

Jackson, H.J. (1983). Current trends in the treatment of phobias in autistic and mentally retarded persons. *Australia and New Zealand Journal of Developmental Disabilities*, **9**, 191–208.

Jacob-Timm, S. (1996). Ethical and legal issues associated with the use of aversives in the public schools: the SIBIS controversy. *School Psychology Review*, **25**, 184–99.

Jones, R.S.P. & Baker, L.J.V. (1989). Reducing stereotyped behaviour: a component analysis of the DRI schedule. *British Journal of Clinical Psychology*, **28**, 255–66.

Landau, R.J. (1993). Legislation and regulation in the age of new aversives. Special Issue: Aversives. *Child and Adolescent Mental Health Care*, **3**, 19–29.

Liberman, R.P., DeRisi, W.J. & Mueser, K. T. (1989). *Social Skills Training for Psychiatric Patients*. New York: Pergamon Press.

Lindsay, W.R., Baty, F.J., Michie, A.M. & Richardson, I. (1989). A comparison of anxiety treatments with adults who have moderate and severe mental retardation. *Research in Developmental Disabilities*, **10**, 129–40.

Lindsay, W.R. & Morrison, F.M. (1996). The effects of behavioural relaxation on cognitive performance in adults with severe intellectual disabilities. *Journal of Intellectual Disability Research*, **40**, 285–90.

Linscheid, T.R., Pejeau, C., Cohen, S. & Footo-Lenz, M. (1994). Positive side effects in the treatment of SIB using the Self-Injurious Behavior Inhibiting System (SIBIS): implications for operant and biochemical explanations of SIB. *Research in Developmental Disabilities*, **15**, 81–90.

Lovaas, I.O. & Simmons, J.Q. (1969). Manipulation of self-destruction in three retarded children. *Journal of Applied Behavior Analysis*, **2**, 143–57.

Luiselli, L.K. (1978). Treatment of an autistic child's fear of riding a school bus through exposure and reinforcement. *Journal of Behaviour Therapy and Experimental Psychiatry*, **9**, 169–72.

Mace, F.C. & Lalli, J.S. (1991). Linking descriptive and experimental analyses in the treatment of bizarre speech. *Journal of Applied Behavior Analysis*, **24**, 553–62.

Mansdorf, I.R. (1976). Eliminating fear in a mentally retarded adult by behavioural hierarchies and operant techniques. *Journal of Behaviour Therapy and Experimental Psychiatry*, **7**, 189–90.

Martin, G. & Pear, J. (1996). *Behavior Modification: What it is and How to do it*. Upper Saddle River, NJ: Prentice-Hall.

Matson, J.L. (1982a). Treating obsessive–compulsive behavior in mentally retarded adults. *Behavior Modification*, **6**, 551–67.

  (1982b). The treatment of behavioral characteristics of depression in the mentally retarded. *Behavior Therapy*, **13**, 209–18.

  (ed.) (1990). *Handbook of Behavior Modification with the Mentally Retarded*, 2nd edn. New York: Plenum Press.

Matson, J.L., Dettling, J. & Senatore, V. (1979). Treating depression of a mentally retarded adult. *British Journal of Mental Subnormality*, **16**, 86–8.

Matson, J.L. & Kazdin, A.E. (1981). Punishment in behavior modification: pragmatic, ethical, and legal issues. *Clinical Psychology Review*, **1**, 197–210.

Mazaleski, J.L., Iwata, B.A., Zollmer, T.R., Zarcone, J.R. & Smith, R.G. (1993). Analysis of reinforcement and extinction components in DRO contingencies with self-injury. *Journal of Applied Behavior Analysis*, **26**, 143–56.

Miltenberger, R. (1997). *Behavior Modification: Principle and Procedures*. Pacific Grove, CA: Brooks/Cole.

Northup, J., Broussard, C., Jones, K., George, T., Vollmer, T.R. & Herring, M. (1995). The differential effects of teacher and peer attention of the disruptive classroom behavior of three children with a diagnosis of attention deficit hyperactivity disorder. *Journal of Applied Behavior Analysis*, **27**, 227–8.

Northup, J., Wacker, D.P., Berg, W.K., Kelly, L., Sasso, G. & DeRaad, A. (1994). The treatment of severe behavior problems in school settings using a technical assistance model. *Journal of Applied Behavior Analysis*, **27**, 22–47.

Northup, J., Wacker, D.P., Sasso, G. et al. (1991). A brief functional analysis of aggressive and alternative behavior in an outclinic setting. *Journal of Applied Behavior Analysis*, **24**, 509–21.

Ollendick, T.H. & Cerny, J.A. (1981). *Clinical Behavior Therapy with Children*. New York: Plenum Press.

Piazza, C.C., Fisher, W.W., Hagopian, L.P., Bowman, L.G. & Toole, L. (1996). Using a choice assessment to predict reinforcer effectiveness. *Journal of Applied Behavior Analysis*, **29**, 1–9.

Reid, D.H. & Green, C.W. (1990). Staff training. In *Handbook of Behavior Modification with the Mentally Retarded*, 2nd edn, ed. J.L. Matson, pp. 71–90. New York: Plenum Press.

Rojahn, J. & Sisson, L.A. (1990). Stereotyped behavior. In *Handbook of Behavior Modification with the Mentally Retarded*, 2nd edn, ed. J.L. Matson, pp. 181–217. New York: Plenum Press.

Scotti, J.R., Evans, I.M., Meyer, L.H. & Walker, P. (1991). A meta-analysis of intervention research with problem behavior: treatment validity and standards of practice. *American Journal on Mental Retardation*, **96**, 233–56.

Sigafoos, J. & Saggers, E. (1995). A discrete-trial approach to the functional analysis of aggressive behaviour in two boys with autism. *Australia and New Zealand Journal of Developmental Disability*, **20**, 287–97.

Singh, N.N., Osborne, J.G. & Huguenin, N.H. (1996). Applied behavioral interventions. In *Manual of Diagnosis and Professional Practice in Mental Retardation*, ed. J.W. Jacobson & J.A. Mulick, pp. 341–53. Washington, DC: American Psychological Association.

Smith, J.C. (1985). *Relaxation Dynamics: A Cognitive Behavioral Approach to Relaxation*. Champaign, IL: Research Press.

Steed, S.E., Bigelow, K.M., Huynen, K.B. & Lutzker, J.R. (1995). The effects of planned activities training, low-demand schedule, and reinforcement sampling on adults with developmental disabilities who exhibit challenging behaviors. *Journal of Developmental and Physical Disabilities*, **7**, 303–16.

Stephens, R.M., Matson, J.L., Westmoreland, T. & Kulpa, J. (1981). Modification of psychotic speech with mentally retarded patients. *Journal of Mental Deficiency Research*, **25**, 187–97.

Sturmey, P. (1994). Assessing the functions of aberrant behaviors: a review of psychometric instruments. *Journal of Autism and Developmental Disorders*, **24**, 293–304.

Tassé, M.J., Havercamp, S.M. & Reiss, S. (1997). *Home-Of-Your-Own Cooperative Living Training Program*. Santa Barbara, CA: James Stanfield.

Thompson, T. & Gray, D.B. (eds.) (1994). *Destructive Behavior in Developmental Disabilities: Diagnosis and Treatment*. Thousand Oaks, CA: Sage Publications.

Van Houten, R., Axelrod, S., Bailey, J.S. et al. (1988). The right to effective behavioral treatment. *The Behavior Analyst*, **11**, 111–14.

Vollmer, T.R. (1994). The concept of automatic reinforcement: implications for behavioral research in developmental disabilities. *Research in Developmental Disabilities*, **15**, 187–207.

Vollmer, T.R. & Smith, R.G. (1996). Some current themes in functional analysis research. *Research in Developmental Disabilities*, **17**, 229–49.

17 Service responses to challenging behaviour

DAVID ALLEN AND DAVID FELCE

Introduction

Challenging behaviour is socially defined in two senses. Firstly, forms of behaviour that are atypical and regarded as socially inappropriate or dysfunctional may be defined by society as aberrant: stereotypy, self-injury, aggression to other people, destruction of property, the breaking of social or sexual conventions or taboos, and so on. Investigators may then go on to estimate the prevalence of challenging behaviour by counting how many people with developmental disabilities exhibit such behaviours. The epidemiology of challenging behaviour in this sense has been well described (Kiernan, 1993). Secondly, different behavioural acts or classes of acts may be viewed as more or less problematic. In other words, the classification of the severity of challenging behaviour is also socially determined. Agreement that a person has severe challenging behaviour is arguably the first service response. Research that sheds light on what is perceived as severe is reviewed in the first section of this chapter.

Historically, engaging in severe challenging behaviour has made people particularly vulnerable to exclusion from families, communities and ordinary settings (Lakin et al., 1983; Borthwick-Duffy, Eyman & White, 1987). Moreover, as community alternatives to institutional care have become more common, people with challenging behaviour have tended to be overlooked until the later stages of resettlement (Welsh Office, 1988; Department of Health, 1989). Admissions to long-stay hospitals in the UK have not ceased entirely, and severe challenging behaviour constitutes one of the prime reasons for their continued occurrence (All Wales Advisory Panel on the Development of Services for People with Mental Handicaps, 1991). Research that sheds light on what is required to provide successful, high-quality residential services is reviewed in the second section of this chapter.

Challenging behaviours are, of course, not unique to institutional provision. As one of the main factors causing parents to seek residential placement for their son or daughter, they must first arise in the community. Indeed, Eyman, Borthwick and Miller (1981) and Hill and Bruininks (1984) have commented on the similarity of challenging behaviour in community and institutional settings and of staff or carer response to it. Challenging behaviours are a major contributor to carer stress (Quine & Pahl, 1985; Hubert, 1991), they tend to be chronic (Eyman et al., 1981; Kiernan & Alborz, 1996) and not 'cured' by de-institutionalisation (Emerson & Hatton, 1994; Felce, Lowe & de Paiva, 1994). As Eyman et al. (1981) noted: 'whatever mal-adaptive behaviour was present at the time . . . did not significantly change . . . (in institutional or community services) . . . over a two-year period' (p. 476). Kiernan and Alborz (1996) also showed a 'considerable persistence in indi-vidual challenging behaviours over the five-year period' (p. 190).

Such evidence suggests that there is a need for specialist treatment and support services that work with individuals and their carers over long periods of time. These services may have a number of aims: to assess individ-uals and their behaviour, to bring about behavioural change, to advise carers on how to respond to challenging behaviour, and to provide help or relief at times of crisis. Research on service options for supporting carers and ameli-orating challenging behaviour is reviewed in the third section of this chapter.

Defining challenging behaviour as severe

Compared to the pervasive prevalence of challenging behaviour among people with developmental disabilities, severe challenging behaviour is relatively limited. Qureshi and Alborz (1992) and Emerson et al. (1987) have defined severe challenging behaviour. Their definitions share a common characteristic, namely that severity of challenge reflects the level of impact the behaviour has on the person's outside world. The work of Emerson and his colleagues arose from the South East Thames Regional Health Authority initiative to establish a Special Development Team to advise constituent districts on how to resettle people with severe develop-mental disabilities with the most severe challenging behaviours from institu-tional to community placements. A total of 83 people were referred to the team (Emerson et al., 1987), of whom 31 were accepted: 81 per cent showed aggression to others, 52 per cent damage to the environment, 26 per cent self-injury, 16 per cent severe non-compliance, 16 per cent persistent absconding, 16 per cent faecal smearing, 10 per cent persistent screaming, and lesser pro-portions other behaviours. The disparity in representation of physical assault upon others and self-injury compared to the relative similarity in their prevalence rates implied that severely challenging behaviours were those behaviours that resulted in major organizational problems for services (Emerson et al., 1987).

Such a conclusion is supported by Lowe and Felce (1995), who explored the association between carer reports of the occurrence of problem behavi-ours and the level of management problem the behaviours posed. Their study sample of 92 people was assessed eight times between 1981 and 1985 using the Disability Assessment Schedule (Holmes, Shah & Wing, 1982). The relationship between behavioural category and severity of management problem was analysed by exploring whether occurrences of behaviour were typically considered to pose severe, lesser or no management problems. Instances of one category (Wanders Away) were mostly rated as posing severe management problems at most assessment points whether they occurred frequently or occasionally. This was also true of Sexual Delinquency, but its occurrence was limited. Three categories (Aggression, Temper Tantrums and Disturbing Noises) were considered to pose severe management problems at three-quarters or more of the assessment points when behaviours occurred frequently. Occurrences of all other categories of behaviour, including self-injury, were generally considered to pose lesser management problems, even when frequent. The results suggested that categories of behaviour can be arranged in a hierarchy according to the challenge posed to carers.

These results are consistent with findings from a study of challenging behaviour in special schools (Kiernan & Kiernan, 1994). The behavioural categories discriminating difficulty of challenging behaviour among independently mobile children were in order of descending factor loadings: attacks (would have caused harm), interrupts/physical disruption, attacks (actual harm), social disruption, frequent violent temper tantrums, destructive behaviours (breakage), attacks (but prevented) and non-compliant/negativistic. A similar analysis for non-independently mobile children implicated: frequent violent temper tantrums, social disruption, attacks (but prevented), attacks (actual harm), self-injury and interrupts/physical disruption.

Lowe, Felce and Blackman (1995) compared the characteristics of people referred to and accepted onto the caseloads of two specialist services for people with severely challenging behaviour with those of a stratified random sample of other people in the same districts who were also known as having challenging behaviour but were not referred as a priority for intervention. No significant differences between the samples were found with respect to age, gender, adaptive skills, and presence of the triad of social impairments or mental health status. However, the referred sample had significantly higher scores on the Aberrant Behavior Checklist (Aman & Singh, 1986) than the comparison sample. Two domains, Irritability and Hyperactivity, accounted for this difference. The Irritability domain comprises 15 items, of which four relate to aggression to self or others, seven to temper tantrums or making disturbing noises, and four to moody or complaining behaviour. Hyperactivity comprises 16 items concerned with overactivity, disruptiveness and non-compliance. Many of the behaviours reported in these domains were rated at the highest level of problem. The ratings on the other three domains, Lethargy, Stereotypy and Inappropriate Speech, were similar for both samples. Virtually no behaviours in these domains were accorded the highest level of problem.

Taken together, then, these findings suggest that behaviours that created the biggest social impact or implication for the duty of care carried by carers were those rated as presenting severe management problems. Other behaviours that may constitute a very considerable challenge to the achievement of developmental progress, community integration and a more desirable social status (e.g. withdrawal, inactivity, engagement in repetitious movements or speech and even self-injury) were not rated as posing an equivalent challenge. Readers may feel that this conclusion is hardly surprising. However, the fact that it is the particular nature of the behaviour that seems the salient issue does have a number of implications. First, other diagnostic classifications were not shown to be as important. Level of developmental disability as measured by adaptive behaviour, degree of social impairment and mental health status was not a discriminative factor, a finding that is reinforced by a study by Allen and Kerr (1994), which failed to find differences between the clienteles of specialist challenging behaviour and dual diagnosis services. A required ability to respond to challenging behaviour cuts across the way services are often diagnostically organized. Second, the implicated behaviours are only axiomatically the most challenging if social disruption is the basis for the judgement of their seriousness. However, if impact on the developmental chances or quality of life of the person is adopted as a reference point, then other behaviours that do no direct harm to the person, other people or the fabric of the environment, such as stereotypic behaviours, social withdrawal, tendencies towards self-isolation, and lack of responsiveness to people and activities, could be viewed as severely challenging. Third, the categorization of severity does not necessarily reflect aetiology, function, or the difficulty of either discerning aetiology and function, or bringing about behavioural improvement. The need for specialist diagnostic and treatment skills and the categorization of severe challenging behaviour are not synonymous. An ability to react to and defuse aggression and other forms of disruption safely and with confidence is the most clearly implied required competence.

Designing high-quality residential services

Historically, there have been doubts about the feasibility of community provision for people with more severe developmental disabilities. These have gradually lessened with the results of research (Felce, Kushlick & Smith, 1980; Felce, 1989; Lowe & de Paiva, 1991) and with growing experience as reform has become widespread (Ward, 1982; Towell, 1988). However, lack of experience of providing well for people with severely challenging behaviour has resulted in such doubts being maintained for this particular group. Traditionally, people with challenging behaviour were grouped together within institutional settings, founding an account of their specialism on the notion that a specially designated service results in the development of specialist and experienced staff and the ability to concentrate professional back-up (Royal College of Psychiatrists, 1986; Newman & Emerson, 1991; Lowe, Felce & Orlowska, 1993). Alternatively, the case for desegregation, individualization of approach, and the creation of a social milieu which is not dominated by challenging behaviour, all within an ordinary community and domestic context, has been made if services are to achieve the range of quality-of-life goals commonly stated (Blunden & Allen, 1987; Felce, 1993).

A widespread picture of deprivation in institutions emerges from the research literature: low levels of staff-initiated contact with individuals, low levels of resident engagement with their material or social world, and isolation from the community (Hemming, Lavender & Pill, 1981; Beail, 1985; Rawlings, 1985; Felce, de Kock & Repp, 1986; Firth & Short, 1987; Bratt & Johnston, 1988; de Kock et al, 1988; Lowe et al., 1993). Despite the rhetoric about the concentration of professional treatment expertise, people were unlikely to receive psychological or other therapeutically based help for their challenging behaviours (Oliver, Murphy & Corbett, 1987). In mitigation, it would be hard to believe that treatment effects could outweigh the impoverishment of the institutional environment. Thus, the argument in favour of specialist provision is not necessarily invalidated. The contemporary case combines more advantageous environmental provision with specialist groupings, staffing and professional input. Such an arrangement may create a concentration of relevant expertise, clear operational policies and working methods, and a collective identity that defines and accepts full ownership of the challenge without recourse to referral elsewhere. Specialist staff may readily gain a greater tolerance to cope with challenging behaviour and casework experience which may further reinforce capability. Moreover, the specialist service may more easily become the focus for professional development, research and further training (Newman & Emerson, 1991; Lowe et al., 1993).

Research evidence in support of specialist groupings is, however, almost non-existent. Emerson et al. (1992) collected data on two new specialist units for people with severe developmental disabilities and challenging behaviour provided in two detached houses situated near to each other on the edge of a hospital campus. Data on process and outcome showed the settings to be typical of previously evaluated institutions, providing low levels of stimulation and activity to the people who lived there. Residents received staff assistance to participate in activity for an average of only 3 per cent of time. They spent only about a sixth of their time engaged in some form of constructive activity. Nonetheless, the appeal of the specialist unit logic among service providers is strong and has been reinforced by the division between health and social care. Where health has retained a role as commissioner or provider of residential provision for people with severely challenging behaviour, specialist groupings are likely to result. In more recent research, which surveyed people with the most severe challenging behaviour in Wales, all of the 17 people in community housing lived in settings in which all residents have either severely challenging behaviour, autism or mental illness (Lowe et al., 1997).

A number of researched special development projects have also sought to establish the competence within mainstream services to cater for people with severely challenging behaviour. The NIMROD (Lowe & de Paiva, 1991) and Andover projects (Felce, 1989) pursued similar policies to provide comprehensive services that would include people with severe challenging behaviour within ordinary housing services for adults with severe developmental disabilities. Later, the Special Development Team replicated the approach for a specially selected group of people with the most severe challenging behaviours living in or coming from the South East Thames Region (Emerson et al., 1987). Even though the identified people were specially designated, they were not treated as a specialist group to be separated out and served separately. Many of the services developed – 16 out of 26 (Emerson, 1990) – provided for the identified individuals with another person or small group of others who did not have such challenging behaviour. In addition, the service option put forward for eight people involved living alone with support.

Research evidence from the NIMROD, Andover, and Special Development Team projects shows a picture of positive benefit derived from transfer from hospital to ordinary housing services (Felce, 1989; Lowe & de Paiva, 1991; Emerson, McGill & Mansell, 1994). Moreover, levels of staff support for resident activity and resident engagement in activity were shown to be considerably higher than in the specialist units described above and in studies of other mainstream staffed community housing services (Felce, 1996). A possibly distinguishing feature of the three projects was a strong emphasis on specific working methods and staff training, which may have given the services a different character from those ordinarily provided. This emphasis has come to be termed 'active support' (Felce, 1993, 1996; McGill & Toogood, 1993; Emerson & Hatton, 1994). Active support provides a structure for staff to plan opportunities for resident participation in activity and give the kind of help (explicit verbal instruction, gestural or physical prompting, demonstration and hand-over-hand physical guidance) which Repp, Barton and Brulle (1981) found to be most effective in helping people participate successfully. Planning also establishes staff responsibilities for working with residents, and usually results in staff working alone with residents as opposed to being in the company of other members of staff. This has been shown to be more important to increasing staff interaction with residents than increasing the number of staff (Harris et al., 1974; Mansell et al., 1982; Seys & Duker, 1988; Duker et al., 1991; Felce et al., 1991).

There is insufficient research evidence to isolate the impact and therefore wisdom of specialist groupings as a service design variable. What is clear is that specialist groupings in and of themselves do not guarantee specialism and high-quality process and outcome. Certain demonstration projects have shown high-quality process and outcome while choosing to establish mixed groupings. However, such services also devoted considerable independent effort to developing such specialism, which cannot be disregarded. It is possible that a combination of specialist groupings and a well-organized approach to staff training, working methods and quality assurance would prove superior. Evidence from a different set of specialist concerns, namely those relating to people with dual developmental and sensory disabilities, showed specialist small community settings to be better than small community settings with mixed groupings (and specialist institutional settings: Hatton et al., 1995). However, the separate effect of groupings and working approach could still not be separated because, whereas the specialist settings appeared to operate something akin to active support, the mainstream settings evidenced no particular organizational methods at all. One can conclude that it is desirable to introduce some form of active support in services for people with severe developmental disabilities with or without severe challenging behaviours (Jones et al., 1997). The question of specialist or mixed groupings is still an open one.

Providing effective specialist support

According to the Mansell Report (Department of Health, 1993), the development of services for people who challenge should aim 'to develop and expand the capacity of local services for people with developmental disabilities to understand and respond to challenging behaviour' and 'to provide specialist services locally which can support good mainstream practice as well as directly serve a small number with the most challenging needs' (p.17). The former is clearly a major objective, as it is the competence and capacity within mainstream services to manage severely disruptive behaviours that will ultimately determine the numbers of people who are defined as 'challenging'. There are, however, also clear advantages in establishing specialist support services (as opposed to specialist client groupings). Given the frequent exclusion of challenging individuals from services, such developments clearly demonstrate a commitment to serving the client group. They also allow for the accumulation of knowledge and the development of an expertise in managing challenging behaviours, can act as a focus for research and the development of clinically effective practices, and also serve an advocacy function on behalf of individuals with challenging behaviour (Newman & Emerson, 1991).

Specialist support services fall into two basic types – residential treatment units and peripatetic support teams – although there may be considerable variations within both models and services that feature both components. The theoretical advantages and disadvantages of both options have been outlined by a number of authors (Vischer, 1982; Keene & James, 1986; Blunden & Allen, 1987; Newman & Emerson, 1991;). Within the last decade, a number of studies has emerged which permit a more empirically based analysis of the respective strengths and weaknesses of these two approaches.

Whereas some of most positive reports on the effectiveness of residential treatment units are based largely on subjective data (Day, 1988), a number of more objective evaluations also exists. Units have been shown to be capable of bringing about short-term behavioural change (Fidura, Lindsey & Walker, 1987; Hoefkens & Allen, 1990; Dockrell, Gaskell & Rehman, 1992), can result in an improved quality of life (Murphy, Estien & Clare, 1996), and may be viewed positively by unit staff (Dockrell et al. 1992), referring agents (Maguire & Piersel, 1992) and, to a lesser extent, by clients (Murphy et al., 1996). Behaviour change is not guaranteed though and further deterioration may even occur during admission (Hoefkens & Allen, 1990; Murphy & Clare, 1991), behavioural deterioration may be evident upon returning to the client's normal environment (Hoefkens & Allen, 1990), receiving environments may be unable or unwilling to implement recommended interventions (Dockrell et al., 1992), and some people may be subject to multiple placements or admitted to highly restrictive placements after leaving the unit (Murphy et al., 1996), which is obviously suggestive of on-going problems post-discharge. Despite claims for the role of residential treatment units as centres of excellence, they are frequently staffed by predominantly unqualified personnel (Newman & Emerson, 1991). Silting up, as a consequence of an inability to discharge residents, is also a clear problem (Smith, 1984; Hoefkens & Allen, 1990; Newman & Emerson, 1991).

The use of peripatetic teams has been promoted by the King's Fund Centre (Blunden & Allen, 1987) in the UK and via the Rehabilitation, Research and Training Center on Positive Behavioral Support (Anderson et al., 1996) in the USA. Emerson et al. (1993) identified three basic types of structure within UK teams: uniprofessional (i.e. drawn from a single profession), multiprofessional (i.e. team members occupy different professional roles), and transdisciplinary (i.e. different professionals may be employed but share common job descriptions and are selected according to personal competence). Several teams also employed unqualified staff who worked under the supervision of their senior members. Nurses (50 per cent) and psychologists (10–24 per cent of whom were psychology assistants) made up the bulk of team members. Despite the considerable overlap between dual diagnosis and challenging behaviour (Allen & Kerr, 1994), only 1 per cent of teams had psychiatrists as members.

A survey of 46 teams (Emerson et al., 1996) indicated that 71 per cent categorised their overall therapeutic approach as being behavioural. Teams also described themselves as 'eclectic' (38 per cent), cognitive behavioural (24 per cent), psychotherapeutic (9 per cent), and psychoanalytic (4 per cent). These figures exceed 100 per cent, as some teams claimed multiple orientations. Team caseloads formed a bimodal distribution, 49 per cent of teams having caseloads between one and six cases and 51 per cent having seven or more cases; the caseload range was between one and 25. These results reflect the fact that some teams operated by providing very intensive inputs to a small number of clients at a time, while others provide interventions of varying intensity to larger numbers (McBrien, 1994). Emerson et al. (1996) estimated that only 48 per cent of people with severely challenging behaviour were on current team caseloads; equivalent estimates for residential treatment units are not available.

It has been shown that teams can bring about significant changes in severe challenging behaviours within natural settings (Donnellan et al., 1985; Parmenter & Gray, 1990; Hudson et al., 1995a, 1995b) and that such changes can be maintained or improved upon over time (Scorer et al, 1993; Lowe, Felce & Blackman, 1996). Team intervention may also bring about improvements in quality of life (Toogood et al., 1994), help improve clients' adaptive skills (Hudson et al., 1995a, 1995b), prove popular with carers (Donnellan et al. 1985; Maguire & Piersel, 1992; Colond & Wieseler, 1995; Hudson et al., 1995a, 1995b; Lowe et al., 1996;), improve carer skills and capacity to work with challenging individuals (Toogood et al., 1994; Davidson et al., 1995), reduce institutional admissions (Colond & Wieseler, 1995; Allen, 1998), may require less intervention time than residential units (Magiure & Piersel, 1992) and can be more cost-effective than institutional-based services (Donnellan et al., 1985; Allen & Lowe, 1995; Colond & Wieseler, 1995; Hudson et al., 1995a, 1995b).

However, very different rates of effectiveness may be evident both within (Emerson et al., 1996) and across different teams (Lowe et al., 1996), they too may be prone to the problem of silting up (and hence fail to provide the coverage of specialist support required) (Emerson et al., 1996), may experience high rates of turnover of personnel (Parmenter & Gray, 1990; Lowe et al., 1996), and may be unable to prevent placement breakdown in a percentage of referred cases (Emerson et al. 1996; Allen, 1998).

These mixed results may be related to the fact that some of the community services within which teams deliver their interventions appear qualitatively indistinct from the institutional settings that they were designed to replace. Furthermore, team services are typically advisory in nature; a high percentage of outcome variance will therefore be determined by factors not under the control of the team. As Lowe & Felce (1994) state: 'Ultimately, the long-term consequence of the intervention depended on the collaboration of the natural settings, their commitment to the individual with challenging behaviour and their willingness to adopt effective strategies suggested by specialist personnel' (p. 135). Similarly, team interventions cannot be expected to compensate for basic deficiencies in resources such as day care (Allen, 1994). Intensive support also represents a harder option for referring agencies, which may have easy access to non-local, less risky, more restrictive, albeit more expensive, alternatives. Finally, success will be dependent on the teams' utilization of clinically effective assessment and intervention procedures; in this respect, it is of some concern that several of the teams studied by Emerson et al. (1996) were apparently employing clinical practices that have little or no empirical support (Welsh Health Planning Forum, 1992).

While hard evidence in this area is generally lacking, research and anecdotal accounts of team activity suggest that the independent variables that determine effective team intervention include a broad skill base that can effectively respond to a range of diverse behavioural and psychiatric challenges (Hill-Tout, Doyle & Allen, 1991; Bering, Tupman & Jacques, 1993); the ability to offer long-term support (in view of chronicity of challenging behaviour) (Allen, 1995); a clear conceptual model for intervention based on clinically proven procedures (Donnellan et al., 1985; Lowe & Felce, 1994); an epidemiological basis to service development that allows for intensive support and the delivery of services to all those who require them (Allen, 1995); the ability to train staff in both proactive behaviour change and reactive behaviour management strategies (Allen et al., 1997); a single line of management and clearly separated functions such that services provide both community support teams and acute admission services (Hill-Tout et al., 1991; Bering et al., 1993); and the ability to deploy skilled staff to model interventions. Although the last point is perhaps self-evident, it is a view not necessarily shared by all teams (Lowe & Felce, 1994). Being a member of a specialist support team is a complex job, and one that requires staff to be good at 'hands-on' work, to be able to remain calm under fire, to possess didactic/participative teaching skills, to be effective role models, to be experienced at group work, and to be effective behaviour analysts (Allen, 1995). This is not a readily occurring combination, and a considerable investment in training team members will therefore be required. Credibility, confidence and competence in high-stress situations are generally of more value than academic qualifications at this level, and staff may need to be trained in consultation skills as well as behavioural methods if optimum results are to be obtained (Shore et al., 1995). Thus, as Bering et al. (1993) and Lowe and Felce (1994) found, there may also be considerable advantages to employing staff with track records of working in 'devalued' settings, even though prior expectations might suggest otherwise.

Conclusion

In summary, mixed results have been obtained for both residential treatment units and peripatetic teams but, in general, many of the projected strengths and problems of both approaches have been substantiated in practice. No direct studies of comparative treatment effectiveness exist though, and many of the studies on single specialist services contain major methodological weaknesses. More convincing demonstrations of the clinical effectiveness of both approaches are required, and the research focus also needs to be expanded to include alternative services, such as private residential services or psychiatric services. Despite the continued willingness of many health and social care purchasers to continue to invest in the latter, evidence for their clinical effectiveness is totally lacking. At present, while there appears to be an onus on 'developers' (Department of Health, 1993) to demonstrate the worth of the services they support and promote, 'containers' and 'removers' do not seem to be bound by the same principles.

References

All Wales Advisory Panel on the Development of Services for People with Mental Handicaps (1991). *Challenges and Responses.* Cardiff: Welsh Office.

Allen, D. (1994). Toward meaningful daytime activity. In *Severe Learning Disabilities and Challenging Behaviours. Designing High Quality Services,* ed. E. Emerson, P. McGill, & J. Mansell, pp. 157–78. London: Chapman & Hall.

  (1995). What makes a support service successful? Reviewing helpful characteristics. Paper presented at Welsh Centre for Learning Disabilities Conference, Gregynog, Wales. How effective are challenging behaviour support services? Lessons from practice and research?

  (1998). Changes in admissions to a hospital for people with learning disabilities following the development of alternative community services. *Journal of Applied Research in Intellectual Disabilities,* **11**, 156–65.

Allen, D. & Kerr, M. (1994). A survey of referrals to specialist services for people with learning disabilities who have a dual diagnosis or challenging behaviour. *British Journal of Learning Disabilities,* **22**, 144–7.

Allen, D. & Lowe, K. (1995). Providing intensive community support to people with learning disabilities and challenging behaviour: A preliminary cost–benefit analysis. *Journal of Intellectual Disability Research,* **39**, 67–82.

Allen, D., McDonald, L., Dunn, C. & Doyle, T. (1997). Changing care staff approaches to the management of aggressive behaviour in a residential treatment unit for persons with mental retardation and challenging behaviour. *Research in Developmental Disabilities,* **18**, 101–12.

Aman, M. G. & Singh, N.N. (1986). *The Aberrant Behavior Checklist.* New York: Slosson Educational Publications.

Anderson, J.L, Russo, A., Dunlap, G. & Albin, R.W. (1996). A team training model for building the capacity to provide positive behavioral supports in inclusive settings. In *Positive Behavioural Support: Including People with Difficult Behavior in the Community,* ed. L.K. Koegel, R.L. Koegel & G. Dunlap, pp. 467–90. Baltimore: Paul H. Brookes.

Beail, N. (1985). The nature of interactions between nursing staff and profoundly multiply handicapped children. *Child: Care, Health and Development,* **11**, 113–29.

Bering, S. Tupman, C. & Jacques, R. (1993). The Liverpool specialist support service: meeting challenging needs in practice. In *People with Learning Disability and Severe Challenging Behaviour. New Developments in Services and Therapy,* ed. I. Fleming & B.S. Kroese, pp. 57–82. Manchester: Manchester University Press.

Blunden, R. & Allen, D. (1987). *Facing the Challenge: An Ordinary Life for People with Learning Difficulties and Challenging Behaviours.* London: King's Fund.

Borthwick-Duffy, S.A., Eyman, R.K. & White, J.F. (1987). Client characteristics and residential placement decisions. *American Journal of Mental Deficiency*, **92**, 24–30.

Bratt, A. & Johnston, R. (1988). Changes in lifestyle for young adults with profound handicaps following discharge from hospital care into a 'second generation' housing project. *Mental Handicap Research*, **1**, 49–74.

Colond, J.S. & Wieseler, N.A. (1995). Preventing restrictive community placements through community support services. *American Journal on Mental Retardation*, **100**, 201–6.

Davidson, P.W., Cain, N.N., Sloane-Reeves, J.E. et al. (1995). Crisis intervention for community-based individuals with developmental disabilities and behavioural and psychiatric disorders. *Mental Retardation*, **33**, 21–30,

Day, K. (1988). A hospital-based treatment programme for male mentally handicapped offenders. *British Journal of Psychiatry*, **153**, 635–44.

de Kock, U., Saxby, H., Thomas, M. & Felce, D. (1988). Community and family contact: an evaluation of small community homes for severely and profoundly mentally handicapped adults. *Mental Handicap Research*, **1**, 127–40.

Department of Health (1989). *Needs and Responses : Services for Adults with Mental Handicap who are Mentally Ill, who have Behaviour Problems or who Offend.* London: HMSO.

(1993). *Services for People with Learning Disabilities and Challenging Behaviour or Mental Health Needs.* London: HMSO.

Dockrell, J., Gaskell, G. & Rehman, H. (1992) *Community Care and Challenging Behaviour: Practices and Policies. The MIETS Evaluation.* London: London School of Economics.

Donnellan, A.M., La Vigna, G.W., Zambito, J. & Thvedt, J. (1985). A time-limited intensive intervention program model to support community placement for persons with severe behaviour problems. *Journal of the Association for Persons with Severe Handicaps*, **10**, 123–31.

Duker, P., Seys, D., Leeuwe, J.V. & Prins, L.W. (1991). Occupational conditions of ward staff and quality of residential care for individuals with mental retardation. *American Journal on Mental Retardation*, **95**, 388–96.

Emerson, E. (1990). Designing individualised community-based placements as an alternative to institutions for people with a severe mental handicap and severe behaviour problem. In *Key Issues in Mental Retardation Research*, ed. W. Fraser, pp. 395–404. London: Routledge.

Emerson, E., Barrett, S., Bell, C. et al. (1987). *Special Development Team Annual Report, 1987.* Canterbury: Institute of Social and Applied Psychology, University of Kent at Canterbury.

Emerson, E., Beasley, F., Offord, G. & Mansell, J. (1992). An evaluation of hospital-based specialised staffed housing for people with seriously challenging behaviours. *Journal of Intellectual Disability Research*, **36**, 291–307.

Emerson, E., Cambridge, P., Forrest, J. & Mansell, J. (1993). Community support teams for people with learning disabilities and challenging behaviours. In *Research to Practice? Implications of Research on the Challenging Behaviour of People with Learning Disability*, ed. C. Kiernan, pp. 229–43. Clevedon, Avon: BILD Publications.

Emerson, E., Forrest, J., Cambridge, P. & Mansell, J. (1996). Community support teams for people with learning disabilities and challenging behaviours: results of a national survey. *Journal of Mental Health*, **5**, 395–406.

Emerson, E. & Hatton, C. (1994). *Moving Out: Relocation from Hospital to Community*. London: HMSO.

Emerson, E., McGill, P. & Mansell, J. (1994). *Severe Learning Disabilities and Challenging Behaviours: Designing High Quality Services*. London: Chapman and Hall.

Eyman, R.K., Borthwick, S.A. & Miller, C. (1981). Trends in maladaptive behavior of mentally retarded persons placed in community and institutional settings. *American Journal of Mental Deficiency*, **85**, 473–77.

Felce, D. (1989). *Staffed Housing for Adults with Severe and Profound Mental Handicaps: the Andover Project*. Kidderminster: BIMH Publications.

(1993). Ordinary housing: a necessary context for meeting service philosophy and providing an effective therapeutic environment. In *Challenging Behaviour and Intellectual Disability: A Psychological Perspective*, ed. R. Jones and C. Earys, pp. 121–47. Clevedon, Avon: BILD Publications.

(1996). The quality of support for ordinary living: staff: resident interactions and resident activity. In *Deinstitutionalization and Community Living: Intellectual Disability Services in Britain, Scandinavia and the USA*, ed. J. Mansell & K. Ericcson, pp. 117–33. London: Chapman and Hall.

Felce, D., de Kock, U. & Repp, A. (1986). An eco-behavioural analysis of small community-based houses and traditional large hospitals for severely and profoundly mentally handicapped adults. *Applied Research in Mental Retardation*, **7**, 393–408.

Felce, D., Kushlick, A. & Smith, J. (1980). An overview of the research on alternative residential facilities for the severely mentally handicapped in Wessex. *Advances in Behaviour Research and Therapy*, **3**, 1–4.

Felce, D., Lowe, K. & de Paiva (1994). Ordinary housing for people with severe mental handicaps and challenging behaviours. In *Severe Learning Disabilities and Challenging Behaviour: Designing High Quality Services*, ed. E. Emerson, P. McGill & J. Mansell, pp. 97–118. London: Chapman and Hall.

Felce, D., Repp, A. C., Thomas, M., Ager, A. & Blunden, R. (1991). The relationship of staff: client ratios, interactions and residential placement. *Research in Developmental Disabilities*, **12**, 315–31.

Fidura, J.G., Lindsey, E.R. & Walker, G.R. (1987). A special behaviour unit for treatment of behaviour problems of persons who are mentally retarded. *Mental Retardation*, **25**, 107–11.

Firth, H. & Short, D. (1987). A move from hospital to community: evaluation of community contacts. *Child: Care, Health and Development*, **13**, 341–54.

Hatton, C., Emerson, E., Robertson, J., Henderson, D. & Cooper, J. (1995). *An Evaluation of the Quality and Costs of Services for Adults with Severe Learning Disabilities and Sensory Impairments*. Manchester: Hester Adrian Research Centre, University of Manchester.

Harris, J.M., Veit, S.W., Allen G.J. & Chinsky, J.M. (1974). Aide-resident ratio and ward population density as mediators of social interaction. *American Journal of Mental Deficiency*, **79**, 320–6.

Hemming, J., Lavender, T. & Pill, R. (1981). Quality of life of mentally retarded adults transferred from large institutions to new small units. *American Journal of Mental Deficiency*, **86**, 157–69.

Hill, B.K. & Bruininks, R.H. (1984). Maladaptive behaviour of mentally retarded individuals in residential facilities. *American Journal of Mental Deficiency*, **88**, 380–7.

Hill-Tout, J., Doyle, T. & Allen, D. (1991). Challenging behaviour service, South Glamorgan. In *Meeting the Challenge. Some U.K. Perspectives on Community Services for People with Learning Disabilities and Challenging Behaviour*, ed. D. Allen, R. Banks & S. Staite, pp. 40–4. London: King's Fund.

Hoefkens, A. & Allen, D. (1990). Evaluation of a special unit for people with mental handicaps and challenging behaviour. *Journal of Mental Deficiency Research*, **34**, 213–28.

Holmes, N., Shah, A. & Wing, L. (1982). The Disability Assessment Schedule: A brief screening device for use with the mentally retarded. *Psychological Medicine*, **2**, 879–90.

Hubert, J. (1991). *Home-bound*. London: King's Fund.

Hudson, A., Jauernig, R., Wilken, P. & Radler, G. (1995a). Behavioural treatment of challenging behaviour: a cost-benefit analysis of a service delivery model. *Behaviour Change*, **12**, 216–26,

Hudson, A., Wilken, P., Jauernig, R. & Radler, G. (1995b). Regionally based teams for the treatment of challenging behaviour: A three-year outcome study. *Behaviour Change*, **12**, 209–15.

Jones, E., Perry, J., Lowe, K. et al. (1997). *Opportunity and the Promotion of Activity among Adults with Severe Learning Disabilities Living in Community Housing: The Impact of Training Staff in Active Support*. Cardiff: Welsh Centre for Learning Disabilities Applied Research Unit, University of Wales College of Medicine.

Keene, N. & James, H. (1986). Who needs hospital care? *Mental Handicap*, **14**, 101–3.

Kiernan, C. (1993). *Research to Practice? Implications of Research on the Challenging Behaviour of People with Learning Disability*. Clevedon, Avon: BILD Publications.

Kiernan, C. & Alborz, A. (1996). Persistence and change in challenging and problem behaviours of young adults with intellectual disability living in the family home. *Journal of Applied Research in Intellectual Disabilities*, **9**, 181–93.

Kiernan, C. & Kiernan, D. (1994). Challenging behaviour in schools for pupils with severe learning difficulties. *Mental Handicap Research*, **7**, 177–201.

Lakin, K.C., Hill, B.K., Hauber, F.A., Bruininks, R.H. & Heal, L.W. (1983). New admissions and readmissions to a national sample of public residential facilities. *American Journal of Mental Deficiency*, **88**, 13–20.

Lowe, K. & de Paiva, S. (1991). *NIMROD: an Overview*. London: HMSO.

Lowe, K. & Felce, D. (1994). *Challenging Behaviour in the Community: An Evaluation of Two Specialist Support Services*. Cardiff: Welsh Centre for Learning Disabilities Applied Research Unit, University of Wales College of Medicine.

(1995). How do carers assess the severity of challenging behaviour? A total population study. *Journal of Intellectual Disability Research*, **39**, 117–27.

Lowe, K., Felce, D. & Blackman, D. (1995). People with learning disabilities and challenging behaviour: the characteristics of those referred and not referred to specialist teams. *Psychological Medicine*, **25**, 595–603.

(1996). Challenging behaviour: the effectiveness of specialist support teams. *Journal of Intellectual Disability Research*, **40**, 336–47.

Lowe, K., Felce, D. & Orlowska, D. (1993). Evaluating services for people with challenging behaviour. In *People with Severe Learning Difficulties who also Display Challenging Behaviour in the UK*, ed. I. Fleming and B. Stenfert-Kroese, pp. 115–40. Manchester : Manchester University Press.

Lowe, K., Felce, D., Perry, J., Baxter, H. & Jones, E. (1997). *Challenging Behaviour: Residential Situations, Service Processes, Costs and Outcomes.* Cardiff: Welsh Centre for Learning Disabilities Applied Research Unit, University of Wales College of Medicine.

Maguire, K.B. & Piersel, W.C. (1992). Specialized treatment for behaviour problems of institutionalized persons with mental retardation. *Mental Retardation*, **30**, 227–32.

Mansell, J., Felce, D., Jenkins, J. & de Kock, U. (1982). Increasing staff ratios in an activity with severely mentally handicapped people. *British Journal of Mental Subnormality*, **28**, 97–9.

McBrien, J. (1994). The Behavioural Services Team for people with learning disabilities. In *Severe Learning Disabilities and Challenging Behaviours. Designing High Quality Services*, ed. E. Emerson, P. McGill & J. Mansell, pp. 179–205. London: Chapman and Hall.

McGill, P. & Toogood, A. (1993). Organising community placements. In *Severe Learning Disabilities and Challenging Behaviours: Designing High Quality Services*, ed. E. Emerson, P. McGill & J. Mansell, pp. 232–59. London: Chapman and Hall.

Murphy, G. & Clare, I. (1991). MIETS: a service option for people with mild mental handicaps and challenging behaviour and/or psychiatric problems. 2. Assessment, treatment and outcome for service users and service effectiveness. *Mental Handicap Research*, **4**, 180–206.

Murphy, G., Estein, D. & Clare, I. (1996). Services for people with mild intellectual disabilities and challenging behaviour: service-user views. *Journal of Applied Research in Intellectual Disabilities*, **9**, 256–83.

Newman, I. & Emerson, E. (1991). Specialised treatment units for people with challenging behaviours. *Mental Handicap*, **19**, 113–19.

Oliver, C., Murphy, G.H. & Corbett, J.A. (1987). Self-injurious behaviour in people with mental handicap : a total population study. *Journal of Mental Deficiency Research*, **31**, 147–62.

Parmenter, T.R. & Gray, C. (1990). *Evaluation of a Training Resource Unit for Children and Adolescents with Severe Behavioural and Intellectual Disabilities.* Macquarie, NSW: Macquarie University.

Quine, L. & Pahl, J. (1985). Examining the causes of stress in families with mentally handicapped children. *British Journal of Social Work*, **15**, 501–17.

Qureshi, H. & Alborz, A. (1992). Epidemiology of challenging behaviour. *Mental Handicap Research*, **5**, 130–45.

Rawlings, S. (1985). Behaviour and skills of severely retarded adults in hospitals and small residential homes. *British Journal of Psychiatry*, **146**, 358–66.

Repp, A.C., Barton, L.E. & Brulle, A.R. (1981). Correspondence between effectiveness and staff use of instructions for severely retarded persons. *Applied Research in Mental Retardation*, **2**, 237–45.

Royal College of Psychiatrists (1986). Psychiatric services for mentally handicapped adults and young people. *Bulletin of the Royal College of Psychiatrists*, **10**, 321–2.

Scorer, S., Cale, T., Wilkinson, L., Pollock, P. & Hargan, J. (1993). Challenging Behaviour Project Team. A six month pilot project evaluation. *Mental Handicap*, **21**, 49–53.

Seys, D. & Duker, P. (1988). Effects of staff management on the quality of residential care for mentally retarded individuals. *American Journal on Mental Retardation*, **93**, 290–99.

Shore, B., Iwata, B., Vollmer, T.R., Lerman, D.C., & Zarcone, J.R. (1995). Pyramidal staff training in the extension of treatment for severe behaviour disorders. *Journal of Applied Behaviour Analysis*, **28**, 323–32.

Smith, G.S. (1984). Monitoring and evaluation of an intensive therapy unit for the mentally handicapped. Unpublished paper.

Toogood, S., Bell, A., Jacques, H., Lewis, S., Sinclair, C. & Wright, L. (1994). Meeting the challenge in Clwyd: the Intensive Support Team, part 2. *British Journal of Learning Disabilities*, 22, 46–52.

Towell, D. (1988). *An Ordinary Life in Practice: Developing Comprehensive Community-based Services for People with Learning Disabilities*. London: King's Fund.

Vischer, J.C. (1982). Problem analysis in planning a community-based behaviour management program. *Journal of Practical Approaches to Developmental Handicap*, **6**, 22–8.

Ward, L., (1982). *People First: Developing Services in the Community for People with Mental Handicap*. London: King's Fund.

Welsh Health Planning Forum (1992). *Protocol for Investment in Health Gain: Mental handicap (Learning Disabilities)*. Cardiff: Welsh Office.

Welsh Office (1988). *All Wales Mental Handicap Strategy: Planning and Progress Review and Financial Allocation Timetable for 1988/89 Onwards*. Cardiff: Welsh Office.

18 The psychopharmacology of challenging behaviours in developmental disabilities

WILLEM M.A. VERHOEVEN AND SIEGFRIED TUINIER

Introduction

The term challenging behaviour is frequently used for a wide spectrum of behavioural disturbances and conduct disorders, some of which are likely to reflect covert neuropsychiatric diseases. Challenging behaviour cannot be attributed to a nosological entity, a syndrome, a genetic factor or a developmental issue without a thorough neuropsychiatric assessment; current knowledge on psychopathology risks and the prevalence of behavioural abnormalities in specific syndromes is also necessary (Aman, 1991; Brunner et al., 1993a, 1993b; Einfeld & Aman, 1995; Flint, 1995; Tuinier et al., 1995a; Dykens, 1995a, 1995b; Franke et al., 1996; Verhoven & Tuinier, 1997).

Psychiatric diseases occurring in people with developmental disabilities are often characterized by atypical presentation. Meins (1995) described several features of major depressive states such as aggressive behaviour, self-injury, psychomotor agitation and irritable mood that are not covered by the classification system of DSM. In addition, classical depressive symptoms such as reduced energy, fatigue and depressed mood have been shown to occur infrequently in people with developmental disabilities. King (1993), suggested that a similar atypical presentation might exist for some forms of obsessive–compulsive disorders, in that features such as self-injury, stereotypic movements and anxiety may dominate the clinical picture of an obsessive–compulsive disorder. Regarding bipolar affective disorders, whose existence and presentation were first described at the turn of the century, Reid (1972) emphasized the unusual symptomatology, especially features such as perplexity, lability and irritability. Whether this atypical symptomatology belongs to the domain of bipolar affective disorders with or without a rapid cycling course (Glue, 1989) or, for example, to cycloid psychoses according to ICD-10, is still a matter of debate. The latter is enhanced by the low interrater agreement in the assessment of manic–depressive disorders in people with developmental disabilities (Einfeld & Wurth, 1989). Interestingly, two recent reports mention the high prevalence of mood disorders in a population of patients with developmental disabilities who were referred for psychiatric consultation (King et al, 1994; Verhoeven & Tuinier, 1997). These findings are in line with the original observations by Duncan (1936), who stressed the considerable degree of emotional instability that could not be considered as typical for bipolar affective disorder. It is therefore worthwhile to postulate a concept of unstable mood disorder in cases characterized by an episodic pattern of disturbed mood or behaviour anxiety.

The expression of all behaviours, including those with a neurological aetiology, can be modified by environmental factors. Psychopharmacological treatment strategies for challenging behaviours should, therefore, whenever possible, be aimed at discrete behavioural components with a putative neurobiological substrate, e.g. disordered stress regulation, anxiety, impulsivity and hypersensitivity to sensory stimuli. This approach is in agreement with the dimensional psychopharmacological approach of general psychiatry (Van Praag & Leijnse, 1965; Van Praag, 1990, 1996). This procedure can be regarded as complementary to the classical concept of psychopharmacological treatment of psychiatric disorders such as psychoses, depressive states or obsessive–compulsive disorders.

However, psychopharmacological treatment for people with developmental disabilities is hampered by the underestimation of atypical psychopathological manifestations of specific psychiatric disorders, and the paucity of methodologically sound clinical studies. This chapter addresses both the dimensional and the classical psychopharmacological approaches for people with developmental disabilities and challenging behaviour.

Dimensional approach

One of the key principles of this strategy is the idea that psychotropic compounds should induce specific effects on certain target symptoms with a putative neurobiological substrate, without interfering with adaptive behaviours and thus leading to sedation, locomotor impairment, lowering of activity, reduced cognitive functioning etc. Several lines of research have been pursued over the last decades, including opiate antagonists, serotonin-modulating compounds and beta-blocking agents.

Opiate antagonists

Endogenous opioids have been implicated in the pathophysiology of autism and self-injurious behaviour. In autism, opiate blockers may antagonise excessive brain opioid activity that has been hypothesized to underlie social, communicative and attentional disturbances. In self-injurious behaviour, three rationales have been put forward for treating this behavioural disturbance with opiate antagonists: (1) they may block the addictive properties of endorphin release in the brain stimulated by the self-injurious behaviour; (2) they may normalize elevated sensory thresholds that precipitate aberrant self-stimulation; and (3) they may regulate opioid-mediated stress responses (Sandman et al., 1998).

Panksepp et al. (1978) postulated that endorphins might be involved in the mediation of feelings of social conflict as opioids reduce distress vocalizations in animals. They claimed that excessive opioid activity causes social withdrawal, inability to convey emotions, reduced crying, attentional dysfunctions, labile affect and aggressiveness. Thus, several investigators since have studied the effects of the opiate antagonist naltrexone in people with autism. Although most results are equivocal, some early reports mention increases in aspects of social behaviour such as verbal production and social proximity (Sandman et al., 1998). In three recent reports, a total of 66 people with autism was treated with naltrexone daily for two to four weeks (50–150 mg). In a placebo-controlled design, virtually no beneficial effects were established (Campbell et al., 1993; Borghese et al., 1993; Willemsen-Swinkels et al., 1995a, 1996). Comparable results were reported by Percy et al. (1994) on a double-blind placebo-controlled crossover study with 1 mg naltrexone per kg body weight in 25 individuals with Rett syndrome. In addition to these studies, Bouvard et al. (1995) found, in another placebo-controlled design, only marginally greater therapeutic effects for naltrexone on item scores including social behaviour. Thus, at present, there is no clear-cut evidence that manipulation of the endogenous opioid system by using opiate antagonists is of any therapeutic value in improving social behaviour.

The strongest association between opiate receptor blockers and behaviour in people with developmental disabilities is based on the observation that both naloxone and naltrexone may attenuate and sometimes eliminate self-injurious behaviour. Davidson et al. (1983) described the beneficial effects of naloxone in this respect. Since then, the total number of individuals treated with naltrexone and reported in the literature exceeds 100. The results are summarized in several reviews, which indicate that beneficial treatment effects are mostly achieved in non-blind studies dealing with small numbers of people (Willemsen-Swinkels et al., 1995a; Sandman et al., 1998; Verhoeven & Tuinier, in press). In addition to the efficacy of naltrexone in reducing self-injurious behaviour, in about one-third of the people studied so far, this compound is also reported to reduce hyperactivity and irritability (Willemsen-Swinkels et al., 1995b). These results indicate that the original hypotheses about an excessive activity of endogenous opioids in self-injurious behaviour are probably too elementary, in that increased release of endorphins may be secondary to changes in stress responsivity (McCubbin, 1993; Tuinier & Verhoeven, 1995).

Several other explanations can be given for these differential treatment effects. First, the context within which the treatment is given may be of crucial importance in that environmental factors have been shown to influence test results. This factor may be responsible for the different outcome in small, non-blind versus large controlled studies. Secondly, covert and treatable psychiatric disorders associated with self-injurious behaviour should be excluded in order to circumvent the formation of biologically heterogenous samples. Finally, lack of responsivity may be the result of time-related changes in the neurobiological substrate underlying the behaviour. In line with data from animal experiments, it can be speculated that opiate antagonists are effective in the early stages of the development of self-injurious behaviour only, and that different mechanisms related to dopaminergic neurotransmission are involved in the maintenance phase of the behaviour (Kennes et al., 1988). Thus, taking into account that most, if not all, people included in the opiate antagonists studies were highly resistant to any form of treatment, and the relative safety of a compound like naltrexone, this treatment strategy is still worthwhile from a clinical point of view. Support for this assumption can be derived from the retrospective study by Casner, Weinheimer and Gualtieri (1996), who reported unequivocal beneficial effects in at least 25 per cent of the patients treated with 25–300 mg naltrexone daily over an average period of three years. The data obtained so far, however, do not allow identification of responders in advance.

Serotonin-modulating compounds

Since the mid-eighties increasing attention in psychiatry has been focused on serotonergic mechanisms underlying self-injurious behaviour, obsessive–compulsive disorder panic disorder and behavioural disinhibition (Verhoeven, Tuinier & Sijben, 1993; Markovitz, 1995). The rationale for the potential efficacy of monoamine reuptake inhibitors in challenging behaviours parallels closely the discussion about the involvement of serotonin in a variety of normal and abnormal behaviours such as stress responsivity, impulsivity, anxiety, obsessive–compulsive symptoms and tendency for suicide associated with endogenous depression. Abnormal functioning of monoaminergic metabolism may be related to specific features of such disorders, particularly anxiety, impulsivity, aggression, hedonic functions and goal-directed motivation and motor behaviour (Van Praag et al., 1990; Van Praag, 1996). In addition, increasing evidence is available for the involvement of altered basal ganglia functioning in abnormal stereotyped behaviour (Saint-Cyr, Taylor & Nicholson, 1995; Lewis et al., 1996c).

In line with this functional concept, recent reports have suggested that some forms of challenging behaviour such as stereotypies, self-injurious behaviour and obsessive–compulsive disorder spectrum symptoms may be responsive to treatment with serotonin-modulating compounds (King, 1993; Lewis et al., 1995, 1996a). The principle applies for challenging behaviours related to anxiety and mood disorders. Thus, treatment strategies have been followed using either monoamine reuptake inhibitors with a preferential effect on 5-hydroxytryptamine (5-HT) neurotransmission such as clomipramine, and selective serotonin reuptake inhibitors (SSRIs) or $5-HT_1$ agonists, such as buspirone and eltoprazine.

Monoamine reuptake inhibitors

In 1986, O'Neal et al. first reported beneficial effects on disruptive and aggressive behaviour of treatment with the monoamine reuptake inhibitor trazodone in combination with tryptophan in a patient with Cornelia de Lange syndrome. Since then, several studies have been published, using clomipramine and the SSRIs fluoxetine, sertraline or paroxetine for the treatment of challenging behaviours e.g. self-injurious behaviour, aggression, irritability, stereotypy and compulsive behaviours. As can be seen in Table 18.1, beneficial effects were observed in a majority of the patients in almost all studies.

In the studies by Markowitz (1992), Bodfish and Madison (1993) and Cook et al. (1992) (cited in Tuinier & Verhoeven, 1994), fluoxetine was administered to a total of 53 people, of whom half displayed clear psychiatric co-morbidity, mostly anxiety, mood or obsessive–compulsive disorders. Three other studies comprising 29 individuals, including eight people with autism, used clomipramine in a dosage up to 225 mg daily (Garber et al., 1992, cited in Tuinier & Verhoeven, 1994; Lewis et al., 1995, 1996a). Both studies by Lewis and co-workers followed a placebo-controlled crossover design and assessed changes in behaviour abnormalities in different social situations. Apart from beneficial effects on the target behaviours of stereotypy and self-injurious behaviour, they reported a larger degree of improvement on non-targeted outcomes, i.e. affective and social responsiveness were enhanced. Similar observations were reported earlier by Bodfish and Madison (1993, cited in Tuinier & Verhoeven, 1994) in their study with fluoxetine. These findings strengthen the necessity to make a dimensional diagnosis of challenging behaviour instead of a merely nosological one, and to assess the behavioural profile of a particular compound. Thus, the results of the studies as depicted in Table 18.1, can be interpreted as indicative for the efficacy of monoamine reuptake inhibitors on behavioural dimensions such as anxiety, mood, stress reactivity, response latency, stereotypies and compulsive behaviour.

5-HT$_1$ agonists

The involvement of 5-HT$_1$ subreceptors in the control of aggression has been extensively demonstrated in animal experiments. Compounds such as the 5-HT$_{1a}$ agonist buspirone and the 5-HT$_{1a,b}$ agonist eltoprazine are particularly effective in reducing aggressive behaviour under conditions that promote changing offensive types of aggression without adversely affecting non-aggressive components of the behavioural repertoire (Miczek et al., 1994; Mak et al., 1995).

Eltoprazine

Eltoprazine was developed as a specific anti-aggressive compound – a so-called serenic – and affects the 5-HT$_{1a}$, 5-HT$_{1b}$ and 5-HT$_{1c}$ receptor

Table 18.1 Clinical studies with serotonergic antidepressants in people with developmental disabilities and challenging and self-injurious behaviour

Author	Number of patients	Additional targets	Compound, daily dose; duration of treatment	Number of patients with psychiatric co-diagnosis	Number of responders and results[c]
O'Neil et al. (1986)[a]	1	Aggressive behaviour	Trazodone, 200 mg; 4 weeks	Cornelia de Lange syndrome: 1	Marked reduction in SIB and aggression
Markowitz (1990)[a]	8	—	Fluoxetine, 20–40 mg; >1 month	Schizophrenia: 1	Reduction in SIB and stereotypy: 7
King (1991)[b]	1	—	Fluoxetine, 40 mg; >2 months	—	Temporary effect on SIB
Dech and Budow (1991)[b]	1	Trichotillomania	Fluoxetine, 20–80 mg; 6 months	Prader–Willi syndrome	Moderate reduction
Bass and Beltis (1991)[b]	1	—	Fluoxetine, 40 mg; >2 year	—	Long-lasting marked decrease of SIB
Garber et al. (1992)[b]	11	Stereotypy	Clomipramine, 25–125 mg; 1–12 months	Autism: 4	Marked reduction: 10
Cook et al. (1992)[b]	16	Stereotypy	Fluoxetine, 20–80 mg; >3 months	Depression: 6; psychosis: 1; anxiety disorder: 1; obsessive–compulsive disorder: 2	Moderated to marked reduction: 10
Markowitz (1992)[b]	21	Agitation	Fluoxetine, 20–40 mg; >3 months	Psychosis: 2; major affective disorder: 2; obsessive–compulsive disorder: 2	Decrease in SIB, restlessness and agitation: 19
Warnock and Kestenbaum (1992)[b]	2	—	Fluoxetine, 20–60 mg; >1 year	Prader–Willi syndrome: 2	Marked reduction
Sovner et al. (1993)[b]	2	—	Fluoxetine, 20–40 mg; 5–9 months	Major depression: 2	Decrease to near zero

Study	n	Target behaviour	Drug, dose; duration	Diagnosis	Outcome
Ricketts et al. (1993)[b]	4	—	Fluoxetine, 20–60 mg; 6–12 months	—	Marked decrease: 3
Bodfish and Madison (1993)[b]	16	Stereotypy, aggression, compulsive behaviour	Fluoxetine, 40–80 mg; 5–7 months	Obsessive–compulsive disorder: 10	Reduction in SIB and stereotypy: 7
Singh (1993)[b]	3	—	Fluoxetine, 20–60 mg; >6 weeks?	—	Substantial improvement
Benjamin and Buot-Smith (1993)[b]	1	Skin-picking and compulsive eating	Fluoxetine, 60 mg; >1 year	Prader–Willi syndrome: 1	Global improvement
Wiener and Lamberti (1993)[b]	1	Violent behaviour, anxiety	Sertraline, 50 mg; 2 months	Obsessive–compulsive disorder: 1	Less anxious and fewer verbal outbursts
Frankenburg and Kando (1994)	1	Aggression, hyperactivity, mood lability	Sertraline, 25 mg; >4 months	Attention deficit hyperactivity disorder	Decrease in temper outbursts
Hellings and Warnock (1994)	3	Skin-picking and stereotypies	Fluoxetine, 20–60 mg; >1 year	Prader–Willi syndrome: 3	Improvement in target symptoms and sociability
Hagerman et al. (1994)	35	Anxiety, mood lability, compulsive behaviour	Fluoxetine, 10–40 mg; 1–30 months	Fragile X syndrome: 35	Significant improvement
Snead, Boon and Presberg (1994)	1	Anxiety, aggressive behaviour	Paroxetine, 20 mg; 2 weeks	Autism: 1	Significant reduction of aggression
Buck (1995)	2	Aggression	Sertraline, 100 mg; 8 months	Autism: 1	Decrease in aggressive outbursts
Lewis et al. (1995)	10	Stereotyped and compulsive behaviour	Clomipramine, 3 mg/kg; 5 months	Autism: 4	Reduction in stereotypies and related behaviour: 6
Campbell and Duffy (1995)	1	Irritability, aggression	Sertraline, 100 mg; 3 months	—	Marked decrease

Table 18.1 (*cont.*)

Author	*Number of patients*	*Additional targets*	*Compound, daily dose; duration of treatment*	*Number of patients with psychiatric co-diagnosis*	*Number of responders and results*[c]
Troisi et al. (1995)	19	Aggressive acts	Fluoxetine, 20 mg; 2 months	—	Increase of aggressive behaviour: 17
Hellings et al. (1996)	9	Aggressive behaviour	Sertraline, 25–150 mg; 1–7 months	Autism: 5; psychosis: 1; depression: 1	Reduction of aggression: 8
Lewis et al. (1996a)	8	—	Clomipramine, 3 mg/kg; 5 months	—	Clinical relevant improvement: 6

Notes:
SIB = self-injurious behaviour.
[a]Tuinier and Verhoeven (1994).
[b]Verhoeven and Tuinier (1996).
[c]Number of responders given only when they differ from the number of patients included in the study.

subtypes. Preclinically, the affinity of this compound for the 5-HT$_{1b}$ postsynaptic receptor appeared to be responsible for its inhibitory effects on offensive components of agonistic interactions, suggesting potential efficacy on aggression. In species lacking the 5-HT$_{1b}$ receptor, such as humans, the effects of eltoprazine are most likely to be mediated via the 5-HT$_{1a}$ receptor, and it therefore resembles the azapirones such as buspirone. Concerning the latter, preclinical experiments have yielded clear anti-aggressive properties, although the mode of action of buspirone is rather complicated because it is a partial agonist postsynaptically and a full agonist at the presynaptic somatodendric sites. The clinical efficacy therefore depends on the individual serotonergic tone (De Vrij, 1995).

Results from small open studies on the clinical effects of eltoprazine were initially promising. In the authors' own study, the effects of eltoprazine in a daily oral dosage up to 60 mg were investigated in ten males with developmental disabilities with challenging behaviour, including self-injurious behaviour. In four people, a temporary reduction of self-injurious behaviour was observed, while in others, mood and non-targeted behaviours, such as sociability and general activity, improved (Tuinier et al., 1995b). In a large, placebo-controlled study, however, the no further treatment effects of eltoprazine could be demonstrated, although post-hoc analyses revealed some anti-aggressive effects in a subgroup of patients characterized by high levels of aggressive behaviour (De Koning et al., 1994). Due to the lack of efficacy in this study and the occurrence of psychotic-like side-effects (Moriarty et al., 1994), the further clinical development of this compound was discontinued prematurely.

Buspirone

Ratey et al. (1989, 1991, cited in Verhoeven & Tuinier, 1996) demonstrated, in two studies comprising a total of 20 individuals, a reduction of aggression and agitation upon treatment with 15–45 mg buspirone daily. In the study by King and Davanzo (1996), a differential effect of buspirone was found: in about one-third of the non-autistic people, aggression and anxiety diminished, whereas in those people with autism, the reverse occurred. This partial and ambiguous effect may be explained by the well-known hyperserotonergic status in people with autism or by the mode of action and relatively high doses of buspirone used (Blier & De Montigny, 1990; Tunnicliff et al., 1992). In the authors' study, following a baseline controlled design, eight individuals with symptoms of behavioural disinhibition were treated with at least 20 mg buspirone daily (Verhoeven & Tuinier, 1996). In five people, improvement of sociability was observed that coincided in four of them with a reduction of self-injurious or aggressive behaviour.

As can be seen in Table 18.2, all studies using buspirone found a reduction of challenging behaviour, particularly in relation to aggression, arousal, anxiety and stress responsivity. The beneficial effects of buspirone may,

Table 18.2 The effects of 5-HT$_1$ agonists on impulse and aggression regulation disorders in people with developmental disabilities

Author	Key symptoms (number of patients)	Study design	Daily dosage; duration of treatment	Results
Eltoprazine				
Verhoeven et al. (1992)[a] Tuinier et al. (1995b)	Self-destructive behaviour (n=10)	Open	Up to 60 mg; 12 months	Transient reduction of self-injurious behaviour in 4 patients
Kohen (1993)	Aggressive and self-injurious behaviour (n=8)	Double-blind placebo-controlled	20 mg; 6 weeks	No improvement
Tiihonen et al. (1993)[a]	Aggression (n=6)	Open	30–60 mg; 12 weeks	Improvement in 3 patients
Tyrer and Moore (1993)	Aggressive behaviour and self-injury (n=8)	Open	20 mg; 8 weeks	Reduction of aggression in 6 patients
De Koning et al. (1994)	Aggression and self-injurious behaviour (n=160)	Placebo-controlled	20–30 mg; 8 weeks	No difference between eltoprazine and placebo
Buspirone				
Ratey et al. (1989)[b]	Aggressive and self-injurious behaviour (n=14)	Open	15–45 mg; >12 months(?)	Reduction of aggression and agitation in 9 patients
Realmuto et al. (1989)[b]	Hyperactivity and obsessive ideation (n=4)	Open-blind	15 mg; 4 weeks	Improvement of hyperactive behaviour in 2 patients
Gedye (1991)[b]	Aggressive outbursts (n=1)	Partial blind	20–40 mg; 10 weeks + serotonergic diet	Reduction of aggression, potentiated by serotonergic diet

Study	Behaviour	Design	Dose; duration	Outcome
Ratey et al. (1991)[b]	Aggression, self-destruction and anxiety (n=6)	Multiple-baseline, placebo lead-in	15–45 mg; 11 weeks	Decrease of aggression in 5 patients
Colella et al. (1992)[b]	Paramenstrual aggression (n=1)	Open	10–45 mg >6 months	Marked decrease of aggressive incidences and injurious assaults
Ricketts et al. (1994)	Self-injurious behaviour, anxiety (n=5)	Baseline controlled	45–60 mg; >12 months	Dose-related clinically relevant reduction of self-injuries in 4 patients
King and Davanzo (1996)	Aggressive impulsivity, self-injurious behaviour (n=26)	Baseline controlled	25–60 mg; 2–6 months	Reduction of aggression and anxiety, especially in non-autistic patients
Verhoeven and Tuinier (1996)	Impulsivity, aggression, self-injurious behaviour (n=8)	Baseline controlled	20–50 mg; 3–6 months	Decrease of aggressive behaviour in 5 patients

Notes:
[a]Tuinier et al. (1995b).
[b]Verhoeven and Tuinier (1996).

therefore, be secondary to changes in the biological stress regulatory systems. Extensive animal experiments have clearly demonstrated that the 5-HT_{1a} subreceptors play a crucial role in the ability to cope with stress, and consequently may be involved in the pathogenesis of stress-related disorders in humans including anxiety, hyperarousal and impulsivity (De Kloet et al., 1996). Furthermore, there is compelling evidence that challenging behaviours such as stereotypies, aggression, self-injurious behaviour and obsessive–compulsive disorder features can be considered to serve a de-arousing purpose. Thus, a significant treatment response to buspirone can be expected in those people who exhibit impaired coping with stress and hyperarousability.

Beta-blocking agents

Already in the mid-sixties, it had been observed that the beta-blocking agent propranolol reduced somatic symptoms of anxiety. The subsequent reported beneficial effects of propranolol on symptoms of schizophrenia are, in retrospect, most likely to result from its ability to enhance plasma concentrations of neuroleptics. Over the past 20 years, propranolol has been used for a variety of behavioural disorders with dysregulated impulse control in the context of diverse neuropsychiatric diseases. Finally, propranolol has been demonstrated to reduce symptoms of neuroleptic-induced akathisia.

Several hypotheses have been formulated concerning the mode of action of beta-blockers, of which peripheral dampening of sympathic signals and de-arousing potency seem to be the most prevalent at present (Lader, 1988; Haspel 1995). The effects on hyperarousal and anxiety states may be mediated via an interaction with central somatodendric $5\text{-}HT_1$ autoreceptors, resulting ultimately in an enhanced availability of serotonin (Artigas, 1995; Romero et al., 1996).

However, a limited number of studies with only small samples has been published during the period 1982–1992 regarding the effects of beta-blockers on challenging behaviour in people with developmental disabilities. As can be seen in Table 18.3, only one study followed a placebo-controlled design (Ratey & Lindem, 1991, cited in Verhoeven et al., 1993). The paucity of publications since 1992 warrants skepticism about the efficacy or clinical usefulness of these compounds.

Conventional approach

Although antipsychotics are widely used for the treatment of people with developmental disabilities and challenging behaviour, the evidence suggesting efficacy on specific symptoms is very limited (Tuinier & Verhoeven, 1994). Apart from their well-known effects on psychotic symptoms that are thought to be related mainly to blockade of dopamine

Table 18.3 Clinical studies with beta-blockers in people with developmental disabilities and challenging behaviours

Author	Number of patients	Study design	Compound, daily dose; duration of treatment	Psychiatric comorbidity	Treatment effects
Williams et al. (1982)	13 out of 30	Open, retrospective	Propranolol, 50–960 mg; 1–30 months	Not specified	Decrease of aggressive incidents
Ratey et al. (1986)[a]	12	Open	Propranolol, 120 mg; 3–18 months	Not specified	Impressive reduction of self-injury
Polakoff, Sorgi and Ratey (1986)	1	Case report	Propranolol, 120–200 mg or nadolol 80 mg; >1 year	Not mentioned	Dramatic decrease in assaultive and impulsive behaviour
Ratey et al. (1987)	8	Open	Propranolol, 100–420 mg ($n=7$), nadolol, 120 mg ($n=3$); 1–12 months	Autism	Marked reduction of aggressive incidents and self-injurious behaviour
Jenkins and Maruta (1987)	4 out of 8	Open, retrospective	Propranolol, 80–300 mg; >6 months?	Specified	Substantial improvement of impulsivity and aggression in 3 patients
Kuperman and Stewart (1987)	8	Open	Propranolol, 80–280 mg; at least 3 months	Autism ($n=3$); Attention deficit disorder ($n=2$)	Reduction of aggressive outbursts in 6 patients
Luchins and Dojka (1989)[a]	6	Open, retrospective	Propranolol, 90–360 mg; 3 months	Not specified	Decrease of self-injury in 5 patients
Sims and Galvin (1990)	7	Open, retrospective	Propranolol, 30–150 mg; 1–20 months	Specified	Moderate to marked reduction of aggressiveness in 4 patients

Table 18.3 (*cont.*)

Author	Number of patients	Study design	Compound, daily dose; duration of treatment	Psychiatric comorbidity	Treatment effects
Rudrich et al. (1990)[a]	1	Case report	Propranolol, 60–120 mg; >1 year	Microcephalia; motor seizures	Reduction of aggressive incidents
Calamari et al. (1990)	1	Case report	Propranolol, 30–400 mg; >1 year	Not specified	Dramatic decrease in aggression and improvement of self-injury
Ratey and Lindem (1991)[a]	28	Open (n=14)	Pindolol, 10–40 mg; 4 months (n=14)	Autistiform disorder?	Reduction of assaultive behaviour and self-injury
		Double-blind, placebo-controlled (n=14)	Nadolol, 40–120 mg; 4 months (n=14)		

Notes:

[a]Verhoeven et al. (1993).

receptors, controlled studies in the 1990s on the efficacy of conventional anti-psychotics in behavioural disturbances in general are virtually restricted to one report about zuclopenthixol (Singh & Owino, 1992) and two other publications about zuclopenthixol and placebo or haloperidol (Izmeth et al., 1988; Malt et al., 1995). With respect to the atypical antipsychotics, two studies have been published using risperidone (Vanden Borre et al., 1993) and clozapine (Cohen & Underwood, 1994). The add-on study with risperidone followed a double-blind, placebo-controlled crossover design comprising a total of 37 patients with persistent behavioural disturbances such as hostility, aggressiveness, irritability, agitation, self-injury and hyperactivity. Evaluation of potential treatment effects was assessed by using the Aberrant Behavior Checklist (ABC), Clinical Global Impression (CGI) and a Visual Analogue Scale (VAS) for target behaviours. Although the authors reported beneficial effects of risperidone superior to placebo, more careful analysis of their study does not allow such a positive conclusion. In fact, neither of the evaluation instruments disclosed clear treatment results. Moreover, premature discontinuation of risperidone was necessary in four patients because of serious side-effects, including sedation and hypotension, and adverse reactions such as sedation and drowsiness were quite frequent.

The study with clozapine included six case reports and followed a non-blind design using naturalistic, not formalized, assessment procedures. Behavioural disturbances comprising aggression and self-injury were present in all people, and psychotic symptoms in three out of the six. Treatment with clozapine in dosages up to 600 mg daily resulted in a reduction of aggressive and self-injurious incidents and psychotic features. Although the authors concluded that clozapine is effective in these types of behavioural disturbances, its efficacy may be associated with the well-documented sedative effects of this atypical antipsychotic.

Thus, reviewing the literature, no specific effects of antipsychotics on challenging behaviour can be inferred. Most probably, their presumed efficacy is restricted to suppressing behaviour in general. As reviewed by Baumeister, Todd and Sevin (1993), some evidence is available that low dosages of neuroleptics may selectively reduce stereotyped behaviour. Lewis and co-workers (1996b, 1996c), however, warned against the deleterious long-term effects of neuroleptics for this indication, in that they may induce striatal dopamine depletion, which can be a key element in the pathophysiology of stereotyped movement disorder. Thus, there are several reasons to restrict the use of neuroleptics to the short-term treatment of challenging behaviour, especially as animal experiments have clearly demonstrated the emergence of tolerance for the anti-aggressive properties of haloperidol and even the development of rebound aggression (Mos et al., 1996).

Mood stabilizers, including lithium, and anticonvulsants, such as carbamazepine and valproic acid, have not been found to be clearly effective in reducing challenging behaviour unless there is an underlying mood disorder

(Verhoeven et al., 1993; Verhoeven & Tuinier, in press). On the contrary, it should be emphasized that anticonvulsants may be the causal factor underlying challenging behaviours (Kalachnik et al., 1995). Lithium, however, has shown some positive results in reducing aggression (Baumeister et al., 1993; Bregman, 1995).

Conclusion

In spite of the fact that challenging behaviour may be co-morbid with neuropsychiatric disorders, it should be stressed that the neurobiological rubric of psychopathology is dimensional rather than categorical. According to the dimensional psychopharmacological approach, the efficacy of opiate antagonists, serotonin-modulating compounds and beta-blocking agents has to be regarded as part of a broad spectrum of effects on behavioural components whether targeted or not, such as anxiety, stress regulation, repetitive motor activity, sociability and mood regulation. Such an approach demands a detailed assessment of the behavioural profile of psychotropic compounds as well as a refined description of the several elements of abnormal behaviour. Because serotonin is nowadays thought to be essential for homeostatic control of an array of basic psychological and behavioural functions, it is not surprising that a variety of normal or abnormal behaviours can be influenced by pharmacological agents that affect the functional status of this neurotransmitter system (Dubovsky & Thomas, 1995; Petty et al., 1996). According to this concept, non-responsiveness to the above-mentioned groups of compounds may be brought about not only by diagnostic failures but also by the emergence of a 'tardive behavioural disorder'. Elegant research from different groups has demonstrated the central role of striatal dopamine systems in the maintenance of, and in the possibilities of re-organizing, such behaviours (Saint-Cyr et al., 1995; Lewis et al., 1996c). This implies that the dopaminergic system becomes progressively involved in the behavioural reactivity of the organism. Such a mechanism may underly the resistance to any treatment regimen of long-lasting challenging behaviours such as self-injury, stereotypies and aggression (Tuinier & Verhoeven, 1995; Willemsen-Swinkels et al., 1995a; Sivam, 1995, 1996). Some support for this idea may be derived from recent observations that plasma concentrations of the major dopamine metabolite homovanillic acid are decreased in people with developmental disabilities and long-lasting stereotyped behaviour (Lewis et al., 1996b).

Long-term administration of antipsychotics for indications other than psychoses should therefore be avoided because it may induce supersensitivity of dopaminergic receptor systems and consequently tardive challenging behaviours. This situation is no different from that in general psychiatry, in which neuroleptic treatment is not especially suitable for maintenance treatment of aberrant behaviour.

References

Aman, M.G. (1991). *Assessing Psychopathology and Behaviour Problems in Persons with Mental Retardation: a Review of Available Instruments.* Rockville, MD: US Department of Health and Human Services.

Artigas, F. (1995). Pindolol, 5-hydroxytryptamine, and antidepressant augmentation. *Archives of General Psychiatry,* **52,** 969–70.

Baumeister, A.A. Todd, M.E. & Sevin & J.A. (1993) Efficacy and specificity of pharmacological therapies for behavioral disorders in persons with mental retardation. *Clinical Neuropharmacology,* **16,** 271–94.

Blier, P. & De Montigny, C. (1990). Differential effect of gepirone on presynaptic and postsynaptic serotonin receptors: single-cell recording studies. *Journal of Clinical Psychopharmacology,* **10,** 13S-20S.

Borghese, I.F., Herman, B.H., Anselmi, L.S. et al. (1993). Effects of acutely and chronically administered naltrexone on social behaviour and language of children with autism. *Society of Neuroscience Abstracts,* **19,** 1785.

Bouvard, M.P., Leboyer, M., Launay, J.M. et al. (1995). Low-dose naltrexone effects on plasma chemistries and clinical symptoms in autism: a double-blind, placebo-controlled study. *Psychiatry Research,* **58,** 191–201.

Bregman J.D. (1995). Psychopharmacologic treatment of neuropsychiatric conditions in mental retardation. *Child and Adolescent Psychiatric Clinics of North America,* **4,** 401–33.

Brunner, H.G., Nelen, M., Breakefield, X.O., Ropers, H.H. & Van Oost, B.A. (1993a). Abnormal behaviour associated with a point mutation in the structural gene for monoamine oxidase A. *Science,* **262,** 578–80.

Brunner, H.G., Nelen, M.R., Van Zandvoort, P. et al. (1993b). X-linked borderline mental retardation with prominent behavioural disturbance: phenotype, genetic localization, and evidence for disturbed monoamine metabolism. *American Journal of Human Genetics,* **52,** 1032–9.

Buck, O.D. (1995). Sertraline for reduction of violent behavior. *American Journal of Psychiatry,* **152,** 953.

Calamari, J.E., Mc.Nally, R.J., Benson, D.S. & Babington, D.M. (1990). Case study: use of propranolol to reduce aggressive behaviour in a woman who is mentally retarded. *Behavioural Residential Treatment,* **5,** 287–96.

Campbell, J.J. & Duffy, J.D. (1995). Sertraline treatment of aggression in a developmental disabled patient. *Journal of Clinical Psychiatry,* **56,** 123–4.

Campbell, M., Anderson, L.T., Small, A.M., Adams, P., Gonzalez, N.M. & Ernst, M. (1993). Naltrexone in autistic children: behavioural symptoms and attentional learning. *Journal of the American Academy of Child and Adolescent Psychiatry,* **32,** 1283–91.

Casner, J.A., Weinheimer, B. & Gualtieri, Th. (1996). Naltrexone and self-injurious behavior: a retrospective population study. *Journal of Clinical Psychopharmacology,* **16,** 389–94.

Cohen, S.A. & Underwood, M.T. (1994). The use of clozapine in a mentally retarded and aggressive population. *Journal of Clinical Psychiatry,* **55,** 440–4.

Davidson, P.W., Kleene, B.M., Carroll, M. & Rockowitz, R.J. (1983) Effects of naloxone on self-injurious behaviour. A case study. *Applied Research on Mental Retardation,* **4,** 1–4.

De Kloet, E.R., Korte, M., Rots, N.I. & Kruk, M.R. (1996). Stress hormones, genotype and brain organization. Implications for aggression. *Annals of the New
York Academy of Sciences*, **794**, 179–91.

De Koning, P., Mak, M., De Vries, M.H. & Allsopp, L.F. (1994). Eltoprazine in
aggressive mentally handicapped patients: a double-blind, placebo- and
baseline-controlled multi-centre study. *International Clinical
Psychopharmacology*, **9**, 187–94.

De Vrij, J. (1995). 5-HT(1a) receptor agonists: recent developments and controversial issues. *Psychopharmacology*, **121**, 1–26.

Dubovsky, S.L. & Thomas, M. (1995). Beyond specificity: effects of serotonin and
serotonergic treatments on psychobiological dysfunction. *Journal of
Psychosomatic Research*, **39**, 429–44.

Duncan, A. G. (1936). Mental deficiency and manic–depressive insanity. *Journal of
Mental Sciences*, **82**, 635–47.

Dykens, E.M. (1995a). Measuring behavioral phenotypes: provocations from the
'new genetics'. *American Journal of Mental Retardation*, **99**, 522–32.

(1995b). Adaptive behaviour in males with fragile X-syndrome. *Mental
Retardation Developmental Disabillity Research Review*, **1**, 281–85.

Einfeld, S.L. & Aman, M. (1995). Issues in the taxonomy of psychopathology in
mental retardation. *Journal of Autism and Developmental Disorders*, **25**,
143–67.

Einfeld, S.L. & Wurth, P. (1989). Manic–depression disorder in mental handicap.
Australian and New Zealand Journal of Developmental Disabilities, **15**, 155–6.

Flint, J. (1995). Pathways from genotype to phenotype. In *Behavioural Phenotypes*,
ed. O'Brien, G. & Yule, W., pp. 75–89. Cambridge: Cambridge University
Press.

Franke, P., Barbe, B., Leboyer, M. & Maier W. (1996). Fragile X-syndrome. II.
Cognitive and behavioural correlates of mutations of the FMR-1 gene.
European Psychiatry, **11**, 233–43.

Frankenburg, F.R. & Kando, J.C. (1994). Sertraline treatment of attention deficit
hyperactivity disorder and Tourette's syndrome. *Journal of Clinical
Psychopharmacology*, **14**, 359–60.

Glue, P. (1989). Rapid cycling affective disorders in the mentally retarded.
Biological Psychiatry, **26**, 250–6.

Hagerman, R.J., Fulton, M.J., Leaman, A., Riddle, J., Hagerman, K. & Sobesky, W.
(1994). A survey of fluoxetine therapy in fragile X syndrome.
Developmental Brain Dysfunction, **7**, 155–64.

Haspel, T. (1995). Beta-blockers and the treatment of aggression. *Harvard Review
of Psychiatry*, **2**, 274–81.

Hellings, J.A. & Warnock J.K. (1994). Self-injurious behaviour and serotonin in
Prader–Willi syndrome. *Psychopharmacology Bulletin*, **30**, 245–50.

Hellings, J.A., Kelley, L.A., Gabrielli, W.F., Kilgore E. & Shah, P. (1996). Sertraline
response in adults with mental retardation and autistic disorder. *Journal of
Clinical Psychiatry*, **57**, 333–6.

Izmeth, M.G., Khan, S.Y., Kumarajeewa, D.I., Shivanathan, S., Veall, R.M. &
Wiley, Y.V. (1988). Zuclopenthixol deconate in the management of behavioural disorders in mentally handicapped patients. *Pharmatherapeutica*, **5**,
217–27.

Jenkins, S.C. & Maruta, T. (1987). Therapeutic use of propranolol for intermittent explosive disorder. *Mayo Clinic Proceedings*, **62**, 204–14.

Kalachnik, E., Hanzel, T.E., Harder, S.R., Bauernfeind, J.D. & Engstrom, E.A. (1995). Anti-epileptic drug behavioral side effects in individuals with mental retardation and the use of behavioral measurement techniques. *Mental Retardation*, **33**, 374–82.

Kennes, D., Odberg, F., Bouquet, Y. & De Rycke, P.H. (1988). Changes in naloxone and haloperidol effects during the development of captivity-induced jumping stereotypy in bank voles. *European Journal of Pharmacology*, **153**, 19–24.

King, B.H. (1993). Self-injury by people with mental retardation: a compulsive behavior hypothesis. *American Journal on Mental Retardation*, **98**, 93–112.

King, B.H. & Davanzo, P. (1996). Buspirone treatment of aggression and self-injury in autistic and nonautistic persons with severe mental retardation. *Developmental Brain Dysfunction*, **9**, 22–31.

King, B.H., Deantonio, C., McCracken, J.T., Forness, S.R. & Ackerland, V. (1994). Psychiatric consultation in severe and profound mental retardation. *American Journal of Psychiatry*, **151**, 1802–8.

Kohen, D. (1993). Eltoprazine for aggression in mental handicap. *Lancet*, **341**, 628–9.

Kuperman, S. & Stewart M.A. (1987). Use of propranolol to decrease aggressive outbursts in younger patients. *Psychosomatics*, **28**, 315–19.

Lader, M. (1988). ß-adrenoceptor antagonists in neuropsychiatry: An update. *Journal of Clinical Psychiatry*, **49**, 213–23

Lewis, M.H., Bodfish, J.W., Powell, S.B. & Golden, R.N. (1995). Clomipramine treatment for stereotypy and related repetitive movement disorders associated with mental retardation. *American Journal on Mental Retardation*, **100**, 299–312.

Lewis, M.H., Bodfish, J.W., Powell, S.B., Parker, D.E. & Golden, R.N. (1996a). Clomipramine treatment for self-injurious behavior of individuals with mental retardation: a double blind comparison with placebo. *American Journal on Mental Retardation*, **100**, 654–65.

Lewis, M.H., Bodfish, J.W., Powell, S.B., Wiest, K., Darling, M. & Golden, R.N. (1996b). Plasma HVA in adults with mental retardation and stereotyped behavior: biochemical evidence for a dopamine deficiency model. *American Journal on Mental Retardation*, **100**, 413–27.

Lewis, M.H., Gluck J.P., Bodfish, J.W., Beauchamp, A.J. Mailman R.B. (1996c). Neurobiological basis of stereotyped movement disorder. In *Stereotyped Movements; Brain and Behaviour Relationships*, ed. R.L. Sprague & K.M. Newell, pp. 37–68. Washington DC: American Psychological Association.

Mak, M., De Koning, P., Mos, J. & Olivier B. (1995). Preclinical and clinical studies on the role of 5-HT receptors in aggression. In *Impulsivity and Aggression*, ed. E. Hollander & D. Stein, pp. 289–312. New York: John Wiley & Sons.

Malt, U.F., Nystad, R., Bache, T. et al. (1995). Effectiveness of zuclopenthixol compared with haloperidol in the treatment of behavioural disturbances in learning disabled patients. *British Journal of Psychiatry*, **166**, 374–77.

Markovitz, P. (1995). Pharmacotherapy of impulsivity, aggression and related disorders. In *Impulsivity and Aggression*, ed. E. Hollander & D.J. Stein, pp. 263–88. New York: John Wiley & Sons.

McCubbin, J.A. (1993). Stress and endogenous opioids: behavioral and circulatory interactions. *Biological Psychology*, **35**, 91–122.

Meins, W. (1995). Symptoms of major depression in mentally retarded adults. *Journal of Intellectual Disability Research*, **39**, 41–5.

Miczek, K.A., Weerts, E., Haney, M. & Tidey, J. (1994). Neurobiological mechanisms controlling aggression: preclinical development for pharmacotherapeutic interventions. *Neuroscience and Biobehavioural Reviews*, **18**, 97–110.

Moriarty, J., Schmitz, B., Trimble, M.R. & De Koning, P. (1994). A trial of eltoprazine in the treatment of aggressive behaviours in two populations: patients with epilepsy or Gilles de la Tourette syndrome. *Human Psychopharmacology*, **9**, 253–8.

Mos, J., Van Aken, H.H., Van Oorschot, R. & Olivier, B. (1996). Chronic treatment with eltoprazine does not lead to tolerance in its anti-aggressive action, in contrast to haloperidol. *European Neuropsychopharmacology*, **6**, 1–7.

O'Neal, M., Page, N., Atkins, W.N., Eichelmann, B. (1986). Tryptophan–trazadone treatment of aggressive behaviour. *Lancet*, **ii**, 859–60.

Panksepp, J., Herman, B., Conner, R., Bishop, P. & Scott, J.P. (1978). The biology of social attachments: opiates alleviate separation distress. *Biological Psychiatry*, **13**, 607–18.

Percy, A.K., Glaze, D.G., Schultz, R.J. et al. (1994). Rett Syndrome: Controlled study of an oral opiate antagonist, naltrexone. *Annals of Neurology*, **35**, 464–70.

Petty, F., Davis, L.L., Kabel, D. & Kramer, G.L. (1996). Serotonin dysfunction disorders: a behavioural neurochemistry perspective. *Journal of Clinical Psychiatry*, **57**, S11–16.

Polakoff, S.A., Sorgi, P.J. & Ratey, J.J. (1986). The treatment of impulsive and aggressive behaviour with nadolol. *Journal of Clinical Psychopharmacology*, **6**, 125–6.

Ratey, J.J., Mikkelsen, E., Sorgi, P. et al. (1987). Autism: the treatment of aggressive behaviours. *Journal of Clinical Psychopharmacology*, **7**, 35–41.

Reid, A.H. (1972). Psychoses in adult mental defectives: I. Manic depressive psychosis. *British Journal of Psychiatry*, **120**, 205–12.

Ricketts, R.W., Goza, A.B., Ellis, C.R. et al. (1994). Clinical effects of buspirone on intractable self-injury in adults with mental retardation. *Journal of the American Academy of Child and Adolescent Psychiatry*, **33**, 270–6.

Romero, L., Artigas, F., De Montigny, C. & Blier, P. (1996). Effect of pindolol on the function of pre- and postsynaptic 5-HT$_{1a}$ receptors: in vivo microdialysis and electrophysiological studies in the rat brain. *Neuropsychopharmacology*, **15**, 349–60.

Saint-Cyr, J.A., Taylor A.E. & Nicholson, K. (1995). Behaviour and the basal ganglia. *Advances in Neurology*, **65**, 1–28.

Sandman, C.A., Thompson, T., Barrett, R.P., Verhoeven, W.M.A., McCubbin, J.A. & Hetrick, W.P. (1998). Opiate blockers. In: *Psychotropic Medications and Developmental Disabilities. The International Consensus Handbook*, ed. S. Reiss & M.G. Aman, pp. 291–303. Columbus, Ohio: The OSU Nosonger Centre.

Sims, J. & Galvin, M.R. (1990). Pediatric psychopharmacologic uses of propranolol. *Journal of Child and Adolescent Psychiatric Mental Health Nursing*, **3**,
18–24.

Singh, I. & Owino, W.J.E. (1992). A double-blind comparison of zuclopenithixol
tablets with placebo in the treatment of mentally handicapped in-patients
with associated behavioural disorders. *Journal of Intellectual Disability
Research*, **36**, 541–9.

Sivam, S.P. (1995). GBR-129-9-induced self-injurious behaviour: role of dopamine. *Brain Research*, **690**, 259–63.

(1996), Dopamine, serotonin and tachykinin in self-injurious behaviour. *Life
Sciences*, **58**, 2367–75.

Snead, R.W., Boon, F. & Presberg, J. (1994). Paroxetine for self-injurious behavior.
Journal of American Academy of Child and Adolescent Psychiatry, **33**, 909–10.

Troisi, A., Vicario, E., Nuccetelli, F., Ciani, N. & Pasini, A. (1995). Effects of
fluoxetine on aggressive behaviour of adult patients with mental retardation and epilepsy. *Pharmacopsychiatry*, **28**, 73–6.

Tuinier S. & Verhoeven W.M.A. (1994). Pharmacological advances in mental retardation: a need for reconceptualization. *Current Opinion in Psychiatry*, **7**,
380–6.

(1995). Stress and stereotypy; reflections about its relationship and neurobiological substrate. In *Proceedings of the International Congres II NADD*, ed.
R.J. Fletcher, D. Menelis, L. Fusaro, pp. 57–61. New York: NADD.

Tuinier, S., Verhoeven, W.M.A., Pepplinkhuizen, L., Scherders, M.J.W.T. & Fekkes
D. (1995a). Neuropsychiatric and biochemical characteristics of X-linked
MAO-A deficiency syndrome. *New Trends in Experimental and Clinical
Psychiatry*, **11**, 99–107.

Tuinier, S., Verhoeven, W.M.A., Van den Berg, Y.W.M.M., De Witte-van der
Schoot, E.P.P.M. & Pepplinkhuizen, L. (1995b). Modulation of serotonin
metabolism in self-injurious behaviour; an open study with the 5-HT$_1$
agonist eltoprazine in mental retardation. *European Journal of Psychiatry*,
9, 226–37.

Tunnicliff, G., Brokaw, J.J., Hausz, J.A., Matheson, G.K. & Whitem G.W. (1992).
Influence of repeated treatment with buspirone on central 5–hydroxytryp-
tamine and dopamine synthesis. *Neuropharmacology*, **31**, 991–5.

Tyrer, S.P. & Moore, P.B., (1993). Eltoprazine improves autistic symptoms in self-
injurious mentally handicapped patients. *European
Neuropsychopharmacology*, **3**, 384.

Vanden Borre, R., Vermote, R., Buttiëns, M.et al. (1993). Risperidone as add-on
therapy in behavioural disturbances in mental retardation: a double blind
placebo-controlled cross-over study. *Acta Psychiatrica Scandinavica*, **87**,
167–71.

Van Praag, H.M. (1990). Two-tier diagnosing in psychiatry. *Psychiatry Research*,
34, 1–11.

(1996). Serotonin-related, anxiety/aggression-driven, stressor-precipitated
depression. A psycho-biological hypothesis. *European Psychiatry*, **11**, 57–67.

Van Praag, H.M. & Asnis, G.M., Kahn, R.S. et al. (1990). Monoamines and abnormal behaviour. A multi-aminergic perspective. *British Journal of
Psychiatry*, **157**, 723–34.

Van Praag, H.M. & Leijnse, B. (1965). Neubewertung des Syndroms. Skizze eine funktionellen Pathologie. *Psychiatrie, Neurologie und Neurochirurgie*, **68**, 50–66.

Verhoeven W.M.A. & Tuinier S. (1996). The effect of buspirone on challenging behaviour in mentally retarded patients; an open prospective multiple case study. *Journal of Intellectual Disability Research*, **40**, 502–8.

(1997). Neuropsychiatric consultation in mentally retarded patients; a clinical report. *European Psychiatry*, **12**, 242–8.

(in press). *Pharmacotherapy in Aggressive and Auto-aggressive Behavior*. Washington DC: American Psychiatric Press.

Verhoeven, W.M.A., Tuinier, S. & Sijben, A.E.S. (1993). Biological and pharmacological aspects of self-injurious behaviour. In: *Mental Health Aspects of Mental Retardation*, ed. R.J. Fletcher & A. Dosen, pp. 291–324. New York: Lexington Books, Free Press McMillan.

Williams, D.T., Mehl, R., Ydofsky, S., Adams, D. & Roseman, B. (1982). The effects of propranolol on uncontrolled rage outbursts in children and adolescents with organic brain dysfunction. *Journal of the American Academy of Child Psychiatry*, **21**, 129–35.

Willemsen-Swinkels, S.H.N., Buitelaar J.K., Nijhof, G.J. & Van Engeland, H. (1995a). Failure of naltrexone hydrochloride to reduce self-injurious and austistic behaviour in mentally retarded adults. *Archives of General Psychiatry*, **52**, 766–73.

Willemsen-Swinkels, S.H.N., Buitelaar J.K., Weijnen, F.G., Thijssen, J.H.H. & Van Engeland, H. (1996). Plasma beta-endorphin concentrations in people with learning disability and self-injurious and/or autistic behaviour. *British Journal of Psychiatry*, **168**, 105–9.

Willemsen-Swinkels, S.H.N., Buitelaar J.K., Weijnen, F.G. & Van Engeland, H. (1995b). Placebo-controlled acute dosage naltrexone study in young autistic children. *Psychiatry Research*, **58**, 203–15.

19 The psychopharmacology of mental illness in developmental disabilities

MARK FLEISHER

Introduction

The psychopharmacology for people with mental illness and developmental disabilities should take into consideration specific issues that impact diagnoses, treatments and outcomes. A discussion on medication use that also offers the rationale for such use can lead to treatment regimens that are more likely to be safe, tolerable and effective. There are several principles that lie at the heart of medication decision making. Some of these are adaptations to this population, whereas others address specific problems. The complex presentation of patients in this treatment group makes it imperative to have diagnostic and therapeutic paradigms in place before starting medications.

This chapter presents some important guidelines on specific behavioural patterns that may require pharmacological intervention, but the details given should not be considered sufficient for any particular treatment or clinical situation.

The clinical presentation

An appropriate treatment regimen can flow from an appropriate diagnostic formulation. For most people with mental retardation, all diagnoses of mental illnesses are possible. Old notions of being protected by mental retardation are as wrong as the overdiagnosis of schizophrenia. If there is evidence of mental illness, then the severity and degree to which it impacts the person's life must be considered. The availability of treatment programmes, specialized care and expertise for aftercare must also be considered. A psychiatrist's advice has little chance of being effective if the patient's home environment cannot support the treatment plan. The use of medication must be a therapeutic treatment element that is part of a larger plan, and not a tool to create a convenient respite for medical personnel or for care givers.

Behavioural problems will often be an initial focus of treatment. These behaviours, in the sense of observable human responses, should be addressed by behavioural interventions whenever possible. Differentiating behavioural problems from chronic or acute mental illnesses is at the crux of effective treatment.

Physical illnesses can mimic mental illness or can create new symptoms of mental illness, exacerbate existing symptoms, or create new maladaptive behaviours. In these situations, the psychiatrist as physician must be able to begin the diagnostic and treatment process while considering these co-morbid variables.

Few therapeutic regimens have a chance of working without the support of whatever varied social support exists. Often, the clinician's role is to help align these resources in support of the treatment plan. This may require care-giver education, consultations, dealing with legal aspects such as guardian-ship, or community-wide education.

Diagnostic considerations

There are several factors that contribute to the diagnosis of mental illness and mental health problems in people with mental retardation. These are covered in Chapters 1, 2 and 3 of this book. Given the inherent risks for many of the medications we use, it is important to consider seriously the impact of the diagnosis for people with mental retardation. An incorrect psychiatric diagnosis may begin an endless cycle of using neuroleptic medication without a positive outcome. Diagnostic errors will also skew information and prevalence data that are important to the planning of services.

Treating the patient's state

An important issue has been conceptualized as state versus trait. The patient's state is the current focus of attention and is considered amenable to treatment. It will include the patient's own repertoire of behaviours, personality traits, and symptoms of mental and emotional status. This state may prove to be pharmacologically responsive, pharmacologically unresponsive, or responsive enough to allow a window of opportunity to alter behaviour through therapy or interventions.

Traits are easier to conceptualize as hard-wired phenomena. They are unlikely to respond to treatment. Hair and eye colour are traits. Mental retardation can be similarly conceptualized. One can improve the quality of life and adaptive skills, perhaps occasionally improve cognitive functioning slightly, but the trait will remain.

Indications for therapy

Presenting complaints can represent mental illness, stereotypic beha-viours, behavioural problems, personality traits, personality disorders, misperceptions, or even malignant intentions. Once analysed, it is the product of this human equation that is crucial. If the patient or anyone else is at risk for injury, then an immediate medication intervention may be necessary.

If a safe environment can be maintained while a viable treatment programme is established, that would be ideal. However, sometimes clinicians are forced to opt for the least desirable alternative. That is, to treat a dangerous behaviour in a non-specific manner until safety can be maintained. An obvious example of this situation would be the use of traditional antipsychotic agents to treat aggressive behaviours that are not caused by psychosis or dopaminergic dysregulation. In this circumstance, the antipsychotic is used as a major tranquillizer to diminish dangerous behaviours and to allow one time to establish other treatment options.

The clinical indications and applications for pharmacotherapy in people with mental retardation are built on the same fundamental tenets of general psychiatric practice. Differences include a greater number of uses for some drug classes, a greater variety among the most common diagnoses, and a greater vigilance for unexpected medication effects.

Depressive disorders

Affective illnesses, if accurately diagnosed, can often be treated with the same medications one would consider for the general population. However, as is often the case, the degree of cognitive impairment appears to have a role in the presenting symptoms. There are few well-controlled studies that demonstrate superior efficacy for most agents, but a sampling of some reports suggests that differences between classes of antidepressants do exist. For most individuals with mental retardation and depressive symptoms, selective serotonin reuptake inhibitors (SSRIs) are at least as effective or more effective, and are safer and easier to manage than tricyclics or heterocyclic medications.

In one double-blind, placebo-controlled crossover study, Aman et al. (1986) used imipramine in ten people with profound mental retardation. Two groups of patient data were obtained that separated those with primarily depressive-like symptoms from those with acting-out behaviours. The results indicated that, in both groups, behaviours deteriorated. In 1992, Langee and Conlon were able to identify a group of institutionalized people with profound mental retardation who, over a ten-year period, did respond to heterocyclics after other therapies had failed. They also attempted to identify symptoms as predictors of responsiveness.

The literature regarding the use of SSRIs offers many case reports that demonstrate this class of medications (with the possible exception of clomipramine) as being specifically efficacious and safe for the treatment of depressive disorders. Clinical experiences have also demonstrated depressive symptoms respond about equally well to the most widely used SSRIs (fluoxetine, paroxetine, sertraline and fluvoxamine). The relatively safe side-effect profile of these agents, as well as their ease of administration, make them a first-line choice. Additionally, given the high degree of co-morbidity for affective states and other disorders such as obsessive–compulsive disorders or stereotypy movement disorder, SSRIs clearly become the agents to choose first for these groups of patients. Which agent to choose often rests upon individual patient responses, pharmacokinetics, or the availability of some drugs as liquid solutions as opposed to tablets.

Other choices for affective states and disorders include lithium, especially for mania or to augment antidepressants, buproprion, select heterocyclics such as trazodone or, in unusual circumstances, tricyclics. It is difficult to consider using tricyclics as a first choice given their side-effect profiles. Any agent for any purpose that requires phlebotomy for serum concentrations may be problematic if the person does not tolerate the needle sticks.

For many affective disorders that include hypomanic or manic states, the use of lithium or certain select anticonvulsants may be warranted. During the last decade, many articles have been published that detail the efficacy and relative safety of lithium products for many affective symptoms across all levels of mental retardation. Lithium is far from being a benign drug, but its benefit often outweighs its risks. The effects of lithium on the body can be complex and even fatal in overdose or toxicity. The side-effect potential has been reported as roughly the same as in the general population, about two out of every three individuals (Pary, 1991). Clinicians must be well versed in the problems inherent in the use of this very common medication.

An alternative to lithium may be the use of anticonvulsants. Many papers have been published dealing with the use of anticonvulsants– primarily carbamazepine and valproic acid preparations – for affective symptoms that range from aggression to the more overt cycling mood patterns. This is true for children and adolescents (Freeman & Jan, 1996) as well as for adults. Sovner has written extensively on the use of these agents for cyclic disorders (Sovner, 1988; 1990), as have many other authors. Clearly, there is a strong role, alone or in combination, for these drugs in the treatment of mood disorder for people with mental retardation.

For depressive symptoms associated with dementia in aged patients, the most common treatments have recently been the SSRIs or a mixed function antidepressant such as buproprion or nefazodone. For these medications, the choices are often only distinguished by side-effects, tolerance, or perhaps the patient's treatment medication history.

Psychotic disorders

Antipsychotic agents as a class have been extensively studied for the treatment of psychotic disorders or psychosis related to dementia. Individual agents have been shown to be effective for hallucinations and delusions, with variable results. Side-effects can be a significant problem, especially those relating to anticholinergic effects and movement disorders.

Antipsychotic agents can be divided into 'traditional' and 'atypical' classes. For our purposes, 'traditional' antipsychotic agents are those drugs whose effects follow the dopamine hypothesis of psychotic behaviours. That is, an excess or dysregulation of the dopamine neurotransmitter system is at the core of this disorder. Agents such as chlorpromazine, thioridazine and haloperidol are clearly of the 'traditional' class. 'Atypical' agents are defined here as those drugs that attempt to control psychotic symptoms by blocking both dopamine and serotonin receptors. These agents were produced in response to the notion that serotonin (primarily 5-hydroxytryptamine$_2$: 5-HT$_2$) dysregulation as well as dopamine (primarily D$_2$) dysfunction are both responsible for the psychotic symptoms of schizophrenic and other psychotic disorders.

There are at present, four 'atypical' drugs: risperidone, olanzapine, sertindole and clozapine. In the USA, sertindole has not been released, although it has been approved for release by the Food and Drug Administration (FDA). Olanzapine has been recently released and has the potential to be effective for some individuals. There are, as yet, no reports of its use in people with mental retardation. It may be relatively more effective for negative rather than for positive symptoms. Its anticholinergic side-effects may make it problematic in older adults and undesirable in cognitively impaired adults of any age.

Clozapine remains an option, but it is not considered to be a first choice for any psychotic disorder. It is limited by its side-effects, particularly its potential for fatal agranulocytosis. For that reason, the FDA requires blood to be drawn weekly for white cell counts. Clozapine is believed to act somewhat selectively on limbic dopamine receptor sites and somewhat less selectively for the striatum. Its effects on prolactin levels are minor and thus galactorrhoea or gynaecomastia is not usually seen with chronic use.

Risperidone is a potent serotonin 5-HT$_2$ and dopamine D$_2$ receptor blocker, for which there are limited reports available for people with developmental disabilities. It had been shown to have some efficacy in people with pervasive developmental disorders, but the results are scattered and not specific (Purdon et al., 1994). It has been shown to be safer and more effective than traditional agents for psychosis associated with dementia (Goldberg & Goldberg, 1996), and for mood and thought disorders associated with psychosis in the elderly (Madhusoodanan et al., 1995). The side-effects of motor restlessness and elevated prolactin levels seem to be related to higher doses and are rarely cause for treatment discontinuation. There is no appreciable anticholinergic effect, and long-term problems are considered to be substantially less frequent than with traditional agents. The safety and side-effect profile make it a far better initial treatment choice than traditional antipsychotics. There has been one published study of the use of risperidone as an add-on psychotropic agent for people with mental retardation (Vanden Borre et al., 1993).

Dementia

Clearly, the most common dementia for this patient population will be a non-senile dementia associated with individuals with Down syndrome. Symptomatically, except for the age of onset, this disorder is essentially the same as senile dementia of the Alzheimer's type. This form of Alzheimer's disease associated with Down syndrome does not affect all people with this genetic disorder, but remains a significant possibility.

The exact relationship between Alzheimer's disease, senile dementia of the Alzheimer type and Down syndrome is not clearly elucidated. Genetically, Alzheimer's disease in people with Down syndrome is related to sections of chromosome 21. It may very well be that other chromosomal factors are involved. Nevertheless, the presence of amyloid plaques and neuritic tangles, and the symptoms related to cholinergic deficiency, place the dementia of Down syndrome as essentially equal to senile dementia of the Alzheimer type (see Chapter 8).

It has been estimated that about 90 per cent of patients with Alzheimer's disease demonstrate behavioural changes at some point during the disease process (Tariot & Blazina, 1994). The most typical severe behavioural problems include agitation, aggression, affective lability and psychosis.

The core diagnostic symptoms relate to cognitive loss associated with diminished cholinergic function. It is known that a paucity of cholinergic markers correlates with plaque densities and clinical levels of dementia. It may also be that reduced cholinergic activity is related to the formation of plaques, and that a relatively heightened cholinergic state is related to enhanced neuronal development. Thus the hypothesis that appropriate stimulation of cholinergic activity can have a significant impact on impaired cognition. One focus of this agonism has been through the use of cholinesterase inhibitors.

Until recently in the USA there has only been one drug available to address this deficiency. Tacrine hydrochloride, the first drug available, is poorly tolerated and has limited effectiveness. A new drug, donepezil hydrochloride, is now available and is a cholinesterase inhibitor that is highly specific to the central nervous system and reported to be more selective and potent for type of esterase as well as tissue substrate, to have a more favourable side-effect profile, and greater tolerability and efficacy.

Although donepezil has had no reported clinical use for patients with Alzheimer's disease and Down syndrome in the USA, its safety, tolerability and efficacy in a geriatric population argue strongly for conducting clinical trials. The areas of improved functioning include the large domains of memory, cognition, concentration, apathy, aggression, agitation, mood and behaviour.

Specific agents or classes

Beta-blockers

Beta-blockers, specifically propranolol and nadolol, have been shown to be effective for aggressive behaviours. The relative ease of administration and dosing makes them attractive choices in healthy individuals.

Beta-blockers are beta-adrenergic receptor antagonists. For aggression, the effective daily dose may be as low as 30 mg/day to 50 mg/day but can be two to three times that amount. The obvious hypothesis is that blocked beta receptors directly alter behaviour. However, propranolol at high doses may also act as a 5-HT1 receptor agonist and it is tempting to suggest that the well-known role of serotonin in aggression may be a factor. However, nadolol does not cross a mature blood-brain barrier and has been employed by clinicians and reported through studies to decrease violence (Yudofsky, Silver & Schneider, 1987). This suggests that a peripheral mechanism must also exist.

Non-selective beta antagonism may cause significant side-effects in at least four areas: hypotension, bronchospasm, altered glucose metabolism and an increase in triglycerides. Central nervous system side-effects can include vivid dreams, disturbed sleep, diminished memory and concentration, and even hallucinations. The long-held belief that beta-blockers can cause depression has questionable scientific support.

These side-effects can appear early and at low to moderate doses. Drug–drug interactions also exist. There is a long list of medications that either increase or decrease the effects of propranolol and of those whose effects are magnified by beta-blockers.

Buspirone

Buspirone is a non-benzodiazepine anxiolytic, and its major contribution for people with mental retardation may be its ability to modulate aggressive or self-injurious behaviour. Whereas it is believed to act primarily through 5-HT$_{1A}$ agonism, as demonstrated by a high affinity in vitro, several other transmitter systems are also affected to some degree. The other systems that may be involved include the D$_1$ and D$_2$, norepinephrine, and gamma amino butyric acid (GABA) systems.

It has been repeatedly shown that some dysregulation of serotonin neurotransmission is related to aggression, self-injury and impulsiveness. However, several studies have demonstrated that the most likely agonists able to suppress aggressiveness are the 5-HT$_{1A}$ and 5-HT$_{1B}$ subtypes. As early as 1989, some investigators were reporting some success using buspirone for these problem behaviours (Ratey et al., 1989, 1991). Others have reported varying degrees of success with buspirone in children and adults – including some reports involving autistic individuals – for aggression, self-injury and overarousal behaviour (Verhoeven & Tuinier, 1996). This drug's relatively safe pharmacological and side-effect profiles make it a reasonable choice for many individuals with these behavioural problems.

Electroconvulsant therapy

Electroconvulsant therapy (ECT), while not a pharmacological intervention, can be effective by mediating neurotransmitter function with an end-result similar to the goal of antidepressant drug therapies. Both try to correct mood disorders by correcting deficiencies or inefficiencies in neurotransmitter neuron to neuron pathways.

ECT is well documented as a relatively safe and effective treatment for mood disorders and other select disorders in which pharmacotherapy is not a reasonable or effective alternative. The literature supporting the use of ECT in people with mental retardation and major depressive disorders is scant but pertinent (Lazarus, Jaffe & Dubin, 1990). It may be that, with recent advances in drug therapy, its use is waning in people with mental retardation. It may also be that myths and preconceptions continue to limit its use. Its use may be limited by the ethical issues involving people with diminished intellectual capacity acting as their own guardians, who may be seen as lacking the ability to give informed consent. Well-controlled research comparing issues of safety and efficacy is difficult to perform in the USA due to the required protections of vulnerable subjects as mandated by federal laws and local institutional policies.

Effective treatment with ECT for severe dysthymia and periods of major depression in two cases of individuals with mental retardation was reported by Jancar and Gunaratne (1994). Both individuals suffered dysthymic periods and occasional overlying depression that was treatment refractory, and demonstrated suicidal thinking, aggression and delusions.

ECT as maintenance therapy was discussed by Puri et al. (1992) in a report of its use in a 32-year-old man. This patient was diagnosed with mild mental retardation and severe, recurrent psychotic depression. He either could not tolerate or was resistant to treatment with available drug regimens.

The use of ECT in an out-patient setting for a man with a moderate degree of mental retardation (IQ of 40) with treatment-resistant depression was reported by Karvounis, Holt and Hodgkiss (1992). After a series of 11 treatments, the patient was doing very well and was maintained on 40 mg of fluoxetine for three months at the time of their report.

These reports demonstrate that ECT can be a safe, effective, and cost-saving approach to the treatment of major depressive disorders in people with mental retardation. For those individuals not responsive to or intolerant of pharmacological treatments, ECT is a valuable alternative.

Conclusion

This chapter serves to offer a framework from which rational pharmacological strategies can be devised, alternative treatment options considered, and clinical pitfalls avoided. This should be the beginning of the clinician's search – not the final word. In this era of explosive growth in our understanding of human behaviour and medical science, no one should think we are near an end. We have barely finished the first chapter.

References

Aman, M.G., White, A.J., Vaithianathan, C. & Teehan, C.J. (1986). Preliminary study of imipramine in profoundly retarded residents. *Journal of Autism and Developmental Disorders.* **16**(3), 263–73.

Freeman, R.D. & Jan J.E. (1996). Rapid cycling disorders in mentally retarded children. *Seminars in Clinical Neuropsychiatry* **1**(2), 134–41.

Goldberg, R. & Goldberg, J. (1996). Antipsychotics for dementia-related behavioral disturbances in elderly institutionalized patients. *Clinical Geriatrics,* **42**, 58–68.

Jancar J. & Gunaratne, I. (1994). Dysthymia and mental handicap. *British Journal of Psychiatry,* **164** (5), 691–3.

Karvounis, S., Holt, G. & Hodgkiss, A. (1992). Out-patient ECT for depression in a man with moderate learning disability. (Letter), *British Journal of Psychiatry,* **161**, 426–7.

Langee, H.R. & Conlon, M. (1992). Predictors of response to antidepressant medications. *American Journal on Mental Retardation* **97**(1), 65–70.

Lazarus, A., Jaffe, R. & Dubin, W. (1990). Electroconvulsive therapy and major depression in Down's syndrome. *Journal of Clinical Psychiatry,* **51**, 422–5.

Madhusoodanan, S., Brenner, R., Araujo, L. & Abaza, A. (1995). Efficacy of risperidone treatment for psychoses associated with schizophrenia, schizoaffective disorder, bipolar disorder, or senile dementia in 11 geriatric patients: a case series. *Journal of Clinical Psychiatry,* **56**(11), 514–8.

Pary, R. (1991). Side effects during lithium treatment for psychiatric disorders in adults with mental retardation. *American Journal on Mental Retardation* **96**(3), 269–73.

Purdon, S.E., Lit, W., Labelle, A. & Jones, B.D. (1994). Risperidone in the treatment of pervasive developmental disorder. *Canadian Journal of Psychiatry,* **39**(7), 400–5.

Puri, B., Langa, A., Coleman, R. & Sigh, I (1992). The clinical efficacy of maintenance electroconvulsive therapy in a patient with a mild mental handicap. *British Journal of Psychiatry,* **161**, 707–9.

Ratey J., Sovner, R., Mikkelsen, E. & Chmielinski, H. (1989). Buspirone therapy for maladaptive behavior and anxiety in developmentally disabled persons. *Journal of Clinical Psychiatry,* **50**, 382–4.

Ratey J., Sovner, R., Parks, A. & Rogentine, K. (1991). Buspirone treatment of aggression and anxiety in mentally retarded patients: a multiple-baseline, placebo lead-in study. *Journal of Clinical Psychiatry,* **52**, 159–62.

Sovner, R. (1988). Anticonvulsant drug therapy of neuropsychiatric disorders in mentally retarded persons. In *Use of Anticonvulsants in Psychiatry,* ed. S.L. McElroy & H.G. Pope, pp. 169–81. Clifton, NJ: Oxford Health Care.

(1990). Rapid cycling bipolar disorder. (Behavioral Psychopharmacology Update). *Habilitative Mental Healthcare Newsletter* **9**(3), 25–6.

Tariot, P.N. & Blazina, L. (1994). The psychopathology of dementia. In: *Handbook of Dementing Illnesses*, ed. J.C. Morris, pp. 461–75. New York: Marcel Dekker.

Vanden Borre, R., Vermote, R., Buttiens, M. et al. (1993). Risperidone as add-on therapy in behavioural disturbances in mental retardation: a double-blind placebo-controlled crossover study. *Acta Psychiatrica Scandinavica*, **87**(3), 167–71.

Verhoeven, W. & Tuinier, S. (1996). The effect of buspirone on challenging behaviour in mentally retarded patients: an open prospective multiple-case study. *Journal of Intellectual Disability Research*, **40**, 502–8.

Yudofsky, S., Silver, J. & Schneider, S. (1987). Pharmacologic treatment of aggression. *Psychiatric Annals*, **17**, 397–406.

Part 5 **Policy and service systems**

20 Dual diagnosis services: history, progress and perspectives

JOHN W. JACOBSON

> Particularly when a field is expanding and changing rapidly by virtue of events external to it – for example, in the form of available government support for facilities, training, and research – it frequently happens that increased activity is confused with progress, publications with enlightenment, and past efforts and thoughts with obvious irrelevance. (SARASON & DORIS, 1969)

> All systems, as they become outmoded and outdated, stagnate and cease to provide the type of treatment and care that is required in contemporary society. We would do well to remember this, since the particular forms of treatment and training that we provide at this point in time will very quickly be seen as inappropriate, in some degree, to the future system of education and treatment that is required. (BROWN, 1984)

> The philosophical basis for deinstitutionalisation is fragile and subject to the fickleness of political winds, particularly in times of inflationary stress. (BACHRACH, 1981)

Introduction

The history of dual diagnosis services bears some relation to the historical development of the concepts of mental disorder and mental retardation. This history is not necessarily synonymous with the activities of psychiatry or psychology in service to people with mental retardation, although these activities are relevant. The focus in this chapter is on the services that have been made available during several eras for people with dual diagnosis.

The development of services is assumed to be a function of available financial and human capital in substantial excess of requirements for basic societal productive needs, and the establishment of mechanisms for perpetuation of services (e.g. capacity to train a health and human services work force), as well as the influence of academically based movements (Harris, 1979). For example, understanding of the prospects for future development of dual diagnosis services can be informed by recognition of competition among human and other public services for funds and policy developments.

The focus of this chapter is also upon services that have been made available for, primarily, people with mild to moderate mental retardation and emotional problems, acute and chronic mental disorders, or with severe or profound mental retardation and behaviour problems.

Dual diagnosis services are largely a phenomenon of the post-modern period. They reflect growth in the financial resources directed via public policy to support and treat people with mental retardation in developed nations during the second half of the twentieth century. The development of formal systems of care for people with mental retardation before the 1950s was largely a function of economic and related political developments in industrialized nations. Thus, the major content of this chapter reflects services that have been established in these developed nations. Establishment of dual diagnosis services also reflects – as do other health and human services developments – the population growth of these nations. As one example, the general population of the USA grew from 78 million people in 1900 to 152 million in 1950, and to 250 million in 1990. This presumably includes a roughly threefold increase in the number of people with dual diagnosis. A pragmatic estimate of 0.25 per cent for unweighted population prevalence for dual diagnosis in the USA suggests an increase from 195000 cases in 1900 to 380000 in 1950, and to 625000 in 1990.

The pre-modern period: before the nineteenth century

Although most writers date the Western history of mental retardation from about 1790 (Meyers & Blacher, 1987), earlier services did exist. These earlier services include the founding of an asylum by St Vincent de Paul in Austria (Barr, 1904/1973); the establishment of a hospital in Cairo in the middle ages; a form of group care in thirteenth-century Gheel, Belgium; residential programmes in the early seventeenth century in Thuringen, Bavaria, and Austria; and the founding of a mental hospital as a sanctuary at Epidauros, during about sixth century BC, that remained in operation for 800 years (Kane & Rojahn, 1981; Meyers & Blacher, 1987).

Information from ancient times through the eighteenth century suggests that societal response to mental retardation (and mental disorders) has been highly variable. Some societies in the past, such as in the New Hebrides or in Egypt, and the Spartans, provided little support for deprived individuals with disabilities. In other societies (e.g. the Roman Empire) and in the middle ages, attitudes regarding care of people with severe disabilities fluctuated over time (Meyers & Blacher, 1987). Such variations in practice within cultures over time should not be surprising in the context of the remarkable changes in social policy on mental retardation from 1900 to the present.

Moreover, there are also societal variations in care practices among today's developing nations that are consistent with their cultural history and customs. It cannot be assumed that people with disabilities are able more readily to adapt and assume occupational roles in agrarian, subsistence, or non-industrialized societies. As Meyers and Blacher (1987) note:

> There are societies in which economic jeopardy may require drastic
> measures. Individuals who do not contribute, such as those who are lame,
> blind, elderly and helpless, or mentally impaired, may be abandoned or dis-
> carded . . . Yet such treatment is not universal, even in the most impover-
> ished societies . . .

The modern period: 1800–1900

Foundations

At the juncture of the eighteenth and nineteenth centuries, there were several key figures who contributed towards subsequent developments in mental retardation and mental health. Phillipe Pinel, a Parisian physician, was appointed to the directorship of the Bicetre mental facility (for males) in 1793 and of the Salpetrière facility (for females) in 1796. He found the physical and social conditions unacceptable, and is remembered for the implementation of moral management that included a safe environment, characterized by humane vigilance, planned treatment, recreation and vocational preparation, and the elimination of abuse, chains and indignities (Scheerenberger, 1983). At the turn of the eighteenth century, these reforms were remarkable in their magnitude. In Pinel's work we find the precursors of facility-based or programme based habilitative practice.

In the newly formed USA, Benjamin Rush of Pennsylvania promoted humane concepts of programming for patients with mental disorders or mental retardation, using a mixture of treatments founded on 'enlightenment and tradition' (Scheerenberger, 1983). Although Rush did not propose special treatment or training for people with mental retardation, his work did bring this condition to the attention of the American medical community (Scheerenberger, 1983), which would set the stage for the first major developments in services in the USA.

Back in France, Jean Itard worked over a period of five years with a feral boy (one of 11 known cases, as enumerated by Barr, 1904/1973), and published a book describing the progress achieved by the boy. Although he was disappointed by the extent of the boy's development, Itard was hailed by the French Academy of Science for demonstrating that people with, at that time, poorly understood and marked delays could grow and develop (Murray, 1988). His findings were in marked contrast to expectations based on the nativist perspectives held by Pinel and Esquirol, which would have predicted that these gains could not have been achieved (Barr, 1904/1973; Murray, 1988).

Edouard Seguin, a protégé of Itard, generalized and expanded upon Itard's work (Meyers & Blacher, 1987), and developed a more extensive instructional methodology based on stimulation and training of the senses. Itard and Seguin are generally recognized as the progenitors of modern special education. Itard used '. . . experiences which were based upon reinforcements and rewards . . . evaluated failure in terms of developmental readiness, and . . . attempted to teach needed skills that appeared to be underdeveloped' (Balthazar & Stevens, 1975). Seguin, the founder of the first educational programme for people with mental retardation in France, would also become a noted founder of services in the USA.

Precursors of institutions

Following Itard's publication of his work with the Wild Boy of Averyon in 1801, 'an almost religious movement, spread by evangelistic apostles, developed in the subsequent decades' (Meyers & Blacher, 1987). 'Seguin, Guggenbuhl, Howe and the other "pace setters" of the time appear to have been people with a strong and clear vision of what they wanted to achieve. Their religious convictions seem to have given them the energy and conviction to work toward their goals with missionary zeal' (Murray, 1988). These goals consisted of the establishment of residential schools or educational facilities for people with mental retardation, with the anticipation that, generally, students would become able to re-enter society as productive citizens. During the first half of the nineteenth century, Guggenbuhl founded the first residential centre in Switzerland (using a colony model); sheltered and church-sponsored homes were set up in Germany (Kane & Rojahn, 1981); Wilbur founded the first private school in the USA; and Howe founded the first public programme (Meyers & Blacher, 1987). Programmes were founded by Saegert in Germany, by Guggenmoos in Salzburg, and by Reed in England.

This trend was unabated at mid-century. In Europe, 'no fewer than 32 training schools for idiots were founded within a period of 35 years, from 1846 to 1881' (Barr, 1904/1973 p. 41). In the 1850s 'the number of people catered for by the special schools and establishments of the time was, on the whole, very small . . . the vast majority of people with disabilities was still being catered for in almshouses, asylums, poorhouses, or simply not being catered for at all' in Europe and North America (Murray, 1988). People with mental retardation and mental illness and the poor had been 'served indiscriminately in almshouses, hospitals, prisons' because 'industrialisation and urbanisation undermined (earlier) informal care provisions' (Meyers & Blacher, 1987). In Canada, a mental handicap building at a mental hospital was completed at London, Ontario, in 1870 (Greenland, 1963) because overcrowding of town jails had 'reached a chronic state and out of concern for properly retributive law enforcement' a facility was required (Gibson, Frank & Zarfas, 1963).

Between 1850 and 1900, community schools were founded in Germany and Sweden, and compulsory education statutes including some, but not all, children with mental retardation were enacted in Norway and Saxony (Barr, 1904/1973; Kane & Rojahn, 1981). In the 40 years following Howe's founding of a school in Boston in 1848, 15 state institutions were established in the USA. Mental deficiency hospitals in England were constructed generally in the period between 1880 and 1910 (O'Connor, 1981).

The growth of institutions

This period tended to be characterized in both Europe and North America, by continued increases in the number of places and people with mental retardation. For example, one German facility served 100 patients in 1871 and 920 in 1902 (Barr, 1904/1973). The stimulus for development came largely from medical sources in the USA, and mostly from non-medical, educational sources in Europe (American Psychiatric Association, 1966). Many of the places that eventually became institutions began as small, community-related service settings.

Moral treatment flourished during 1820 to 1860 (Murray, 1988). By 1880, the philanthropic foundation of services had changed to more scientific perspectives founded in medical practice and related social scientific developments (Lakin, Bruininks & Sigford, 1981). From the 1840s (when the USA government began a census of people with mental retardation), it was common for developed nations to recognize mental retardation as a social or public health issue. An 1861 census reported 7033 people with mental retardation (Barr, 1904/1973), but the 1880 USA census enumerated 77000 such people. Of these, only 2429 resided in institutions and an additional 809 received special services (Lakin et al., 1981).

Social, political and economic factors

During the nineteenth century, the directors of the growing institutional programmes were the leading proponents of services for people with mental retardation. These directors often found that larger political and social factors, such as the Civil War and expansion to the West in the USA, economic depressions in the USA and Europe, and invested European interests in colonies around the world, diminished prospects for expanded services in favour of increased numbers of residents in existing facilities. In the wake of the popularization of Darwin's theory of evolution and natural selection, and combined impacts of industrialization, imperialism, capitalism and nationalism on political systems in the last quarter of the nineteenth century, leaders in the field embraced social Darwinism – a concept that implied the survival of the fittest in relation to groups and nations. The derivative of social Darwinism was eugenics, with the implementation of social policy intended to 'improve' a population's genetic status. Some embraced these movements as complementary to medical and sociological perspectives about moral imbecility, others more pragmatically as a competitive strategy to obtain public resources (Trent, 1994).

The notion of moral imbecility – that people with mental retardation were predisposed to engage in morally offensive acts such as crime, sexually proscribed acts, or giving birth to children out of wedlock – had begun to develop prior to the flowering of social Darwinism and eugenics per se, and set the stage for adopting perceptions that people with mental retardation presented a danger, both personally and in the aggregate, to society: '. . . the attention of the public is constantly aroused to the necessity for the segregation and permanent sequestration of these unfortunates. . . .' (Barr, 1904/1973). This segregation was heightened when, by 1890, inmates laboured in production work or to support their residential units as farms (Meyers & Blacher, 1987). Balthazar and Stevens (1975) addressed the factors that were conducive to the professional acceptance of eugenic notions:

> In America, obviously, and even in England, there was at the bottom of the discussion of moral insanity the question of accountability and the idea of sin. Moral insanity, emotional insanity, affective insanity . . . referred to a disorder or disease in which there is a temporary or protracted absence or loss of control over 'baser propensities'.

Professional developments

While at the heart of social Darwinism and eugenics was the notion of bad heredity, the clinical interest was directed towards bad heredity embodied in pseudogenetic studies (Dugdale, 1877; Smith, 1985). Towards the end of the nineteenth century, these ideas also stimulated the mental hygiene movement. In turn, the mental hygiene movement presaged the emergence of community child psychiatry and more conventional professional activity relevant also to dual diagnosis that also occurred during this time.

In 1886, the first legal distinction between psychosis and mental retardation was established in England (Balthazar & Stevens, 1975). Instances of 'dual diagnosis' were described by Seguin in 1866 (e.g. hypokinetic and hyperkinetic types), Griesinger in 1867, Ireland in 1877, Hurd in 1888, Phelps in 1897, and by Clouston (Balthazar & Stevens, 1975; Reid, 1989). Donaldson and Menolascino (1977) cited the importance of the Parisian school of psychiatry and neurology in the 1890s, emphasizing that retardation was generally understood to be 'an expression of some form of brain pathology' suggestive of renewed pessimism about rehabilitative prospects for people with mental retardation. Moreover, although clear distinctions had been made between mental retardation and mental disorder by 1900 (Reid, 1989), there was still considerable uncertainty in the interpretations of relationships between these conditions (Balthazar & Stevens, 1975).

The modern period: 1900–1960

Prior to World War I, social Darwinism had begun to affect public opinion and to stimulate social policies that embodied eugenics. Although some geneticists and biologists questioned the rationales underlying eugenics, other influential professionals strongly advocated eugenic policies, especially in relation to mental retardation. Some of these, such as Goddard in the USA (Goddard, 1912) were later to recant their positions. Nonetheless, eugenics overtook both the public interest and public policy. Eugenic policies and treatment for moral insanity initially converged upon segregation of moral imbeciles (many of whom did not meet contemporary criteria of mental retardation but displayed immoral behaviour). It became apparent that even with the development of new facilities, directors could not hope to manage the growing numbers of people who were admitted under their care. Return to the community of some residents was necessary, and sterilization was adopted as a eugenic strategy to prevent, so it was proposed, procreation or childbearing by former institutional residents.

Social control without social reform

In the USA, the first state sterilisation law was enacted in 1907. By 1926, 23 states had such laws (Meyers & Blacher, 1987). Internationally, schools, institutions or mixed purpose facilities had been established in most industrialised nations. At that time there were 21 states in the USA with at least one institution, serving 10000 people nationally, of an estimated total of 100000 people with mental retardation in a general population of 78 million (Barr, 1904/1973). Similar developments were evident in England. The Mental Deficiency Act 1913 emphasized hospital care, influenced by the eugenics movement and by the substantial numbers of recruits rejected in the 1902 screening for service in the Boer War (O'Connor, 1981).

Although institutional services continued to grow prior to World War I, and new educational services were developed, there remained considerable variation in the extent to which service development was sustained. For example, in Canada in 1902, the training schools that had been in operation for about 15 years were closed due to funding cutbacks associated with a larger political movement to decrease salaries of government employees (Greenland, 1963). During this period, an educational movement led to ungraded classes and special classes in, for example, New York City (Lakin et al., 1981) and Toronto (Greenland, 1963). The Binet Intelligence Scale was translated and adapted for American use in 1908–1910 by Goddard (Balthazar & Stevens, 1975) The advent of intelligence testing was to have a variety of unforeseen effects that diminished the enthusiasm of psychiatrists for work in the field, as measured intelligence became a recognized diagnostic criterion for mental retardation (Donaldson & Menolascino, 1977).

Although many leaders in the field of mental retardation continued to promote eugenics and sterilization (Goddard, 1912), by World War I there was some 'citizen and legal resistance' (Lakin et al., 1981) by some geneticists (Trent, 1994). Institutional directors continued to stress the protection of society from people with mental retardation after the war, but it was clear that such positions were not on very sound footing. In a 1919 study, known as the Waverley follow-up study, Fernald followed outcomes for males who were discharged from one state institution in the USA between 1890 and 1915: 'About two thirds . . . demonstrated no dependency on society or proven delinquency' (Lakin et al., 1981). Moreover, the results of the army (intelligence) tests in World War I suggested that about half of the USA population could satisfy a definition of mental retardation set at a mental age below 13 years (Sarason & Doris, 1969). By 1920, 'the studies that had purported to demonstrate that feeblemindedness was the basis of crime, alcoholism, prostitution, and pauperism' (Sarason & Doris, 1969) had been severely undermined. Nevertheless, the impacts of social Darwinism and eugenics were to be felt well into the first half of the century, with conceptions promoted earlier in the USA and England (Sarason & Doris, 1969; Sloan & Stevens, 1976; Smith & Nelson, 1989; Trent, 1994) being adopted later in other nations. By 1930 in Germany, 'special education teachers were advised to stop working with those individuals who could not be made socially effective' (Kane & Rojahn, 1981).

Unfortunately, because substantial proportions of the people who entered public institutions were from poor families (Trent, 1994), it was not readily apparent until the 1950s, when middle-class parents became politically and socially active, that mental retardation reached well into all social classes. In both North America and England, eugenic perspectives such as declining national intelligence remained 'a respectable psychological opinion' into the 1950s (O'Connor, 1981).

During the 1910s and 1920s in the USA, the total number of people discharged from public institutions grew substantially, from 1009 to 4165 (Lakin et al., 1981). Shortly before the great depression in the USA, Bernstein, an institutional director, had recognized adverse effects of institutionalization and began a concerted programme of community placement, entailing the use of colonies, work placements and foster care placements (Lakin et al., 1981; Trent, 1994). Within the next ten years, community placement efforts became common. These efforts complemented sterilization practices that 'permitted' the option of return to the community in the context of increasing referrals of people with mental retardation to institutions as the natural consequence of general population growth.

Community placement during the 1920s and 1930s provided a safety valve, entailing return to the community of both people with mild mental retardation and some people who had been institutionalized on moral or circumstantial grounds, and the institutional population came to be increasingly more severely disabled (Lakin, et al., 1981). Placement efforts were impeded by the economic depression (Trent, 1994). Concerns also emerged regarding the quality of community placements (Lakin, et al., 1981), but were not to resurface until the major thrust of de-institutionalization over 45 years later.

The period immediately after World War I, until about 1950 or 1960, has been characterized as a time when little was occurring in the field of mental retardation in most nations (Greenland, 1963; Donaldson & Menolascino, 1977). Nonetheless, this was a time of, if not social change, then at least of consequential events in the field. Most industrialized nations experienced economic depressions during the interbellum years that destabilized the work force and sorely pressed the capacity of community health and human services.

Professional developments

Although detailed information is not available regarding the mental state of residents from the turn of the century to post-World War II, those with dual diagnosis were probably considered to have poor prospects for what community placement or release opportunities did exist. During 1920–1939, institutional staff reported the presence of people with dual diagnosis, but there was little agreement in the professional literature about whether people with mental retardation were prone, or even susceptible, to mental disorders and whether or how treatment should be offered (Scheerenberger, 1983):

> Means for effectively treating and/or coping with severe mental illness among mentally retarded persons were not discussed, short of arguing whether the affected should be programmed in an institution of mentally retarded persons or in a mental hospital
>
> A controversy that has persisted, with some modifications, to the present (Day, 1993).

Reid (1989) reported continuing psychiatric and mental health interest in dual diagnosis during 1900 to 1950, manifested in work by Tredgold in 1908, Berkley in 1915, Gordon in 1916, Prodeaux in 1921, Neustadt in 1928, Rohan in 1936, Hayman in 1939, Herskovitz and Pleset in 1941, Penrose (the Colechester Survey of 1938), Larson and Sjogren in 1954, and Hallgren and Sjogren in 1959. Craft (1959) reviewed studies reporting the occurrence of dual diagnosis conducted in state schools, clinics, or mental hospitals from 1928, 1938, 1940, 1941, and 1944. Dual diagnosis rates were 16 – 44 per cent, and Craft reported that 'In the present survey patients with mental disorder suffered at least as much from disorder as their defect' (Craft, 1959).

After about 1940, 'few argued that mental retardation either precluded emotional disturbance or automatically predicted antisocial development' (Scheerenberger, 1983). In line with the pre-eminent importance of psychoanalytic vantages at the time, early childhood aetiologic factors were stressed, an emphasis underscored by Kanner's report on autism in 1943 (Kanner, 1948). With the growing recognition of dual diagnosis warranting treatment, a range of psychotherapeutic approaches were attempted by the 1950s, with variable success (Fisher & Wolfson, 1953; Sarason, 1959; Snyder & Sechrest, 1959). In the 1950s, there was also debate concerning the curability of mental retardation or the conception of psychogenic or pseudo-retardation, a notion linked not only to issues of aetiology but also to dual diagnosis (Cantor, 1955; Clarke & Clarke, 1955). There was also growing recognition that the aetiology of mental disorders in people with mental retardation involved, among other factors, inadequate provision by society for 'maximal adjustment of the mental defective in the community' (Robinson & Pasewark, 1951; Pasamanick, Knobloch & Lillenfield, 1956; Garfield, Wilcott & Milgram, 1961; Menolascino, 1965, 1966; Halpern, 1970).

Politicization of mental retardation

In addition to growing interest among some professionals about dual diagnosis, a variety of events in the field during the 1950s was to set the stage for service development and reform. In 1950, the prevalence of mental retardation in the USA (and its status as a public health problem) was estimated at five million people, with an annual incidence of 126000 affected births (American Medical Association, 1965). In India, the first scientific study of mental retardation was conducted in 1951 in the process of standardizing the Binet Intelligence Test, and 4 per cent of children were found to have mental retardation (Sen, 1981). Such work identified the dimensions of the population issues associated with mental retardation that were to be taken up by social and political action organizations.

The ARC/USA (a parents' organization, originally the Association for Retarded Children) was founded in the USA in 1954, joining the American Association on Mental Retardation (AAMR, founded 1876), and the Council for Exceptional Children (CEC, founded 1922) (Schroeder & Schroeder, 1981). The Australian Association for the Mentally Retarded was formed in 1954, and parent organizations began their work during this decade (Birnbrauer & Leach, 1981). In England, the Mental Health Act 1959 furthered movement towards community care by Local Health Authorities to people with mental retardation (O'Connor, 1981; Day, 1994), and represented a continuation of principles in the National Health Service Act 1946 (Hutchinson, 1970). In the Republic of Ireland, public funds became available to support the work of religious groups and parents and friends groups in serving people with mental retardation (Hillery, 1993). Mental retardation and mental health clinics affiliated with medical–psychiatric services were established in 1958 in California and Nebraska (Menolascino, 1965; Philips & Williams, 1975).

The post-modern period: 1960–1990

The advent of affirmative policy

From the time of the great depression to 1960, there was a building movement towards social reform in the USA (Sarason & Doris, 1969; Bachrach, 1981) and many other industrialized nations. In 1960, USA voters elected a reform candidate as president who, incidentally, had a family interest in mental retardation – John F. Kennedy. The Kennedy administration, through key enabling legislation such as the Maternal and Child Health and Mental Retardation Planning Amendments 1963 and The Mental Retardation Facilities and Community Mental Health Centers Construction Act 1963, established policy precedents in the USA and mechanisms for a federal role in the financing of mental retardation services.

As a result of these policies, University Affiliated Programs (professional training, research, and service centres), Mental Retardation Research Centers, and the National Institute of Child Health and Human Development at the National Institutes of Health were established. Between 1960 and 1985, federal spending for services rose from nil to nearly $4.67 billion in constant 1950 US dollars, with spending in the millions for construction, peaking in 1967, and spending for research and training peaking in the early 1970s (Alexander, 1988). Subsequent administrations in the USA have maintained or modestly increased the total level of fiscal effort.

De-institutionalization

The 'resident population in United States mental retardation institutions peaked in 1967, at 193 183 and decreased to 148 752' within the ten following years, a decrease of 23 per cent (Bachrach, 1981). However, in 1976 there were '18 226 people with a primary diagnosis of mental retardation' living at state mental hospitals (Bachrach, 1981). Thus, together with people who continued to live at mental retardation institutions, 164 978 people with mental retardation remained institutionalized ten years after de-institutionalization had begun in the USA The picture would change much more dramatically over the 20 years following 1977. Highlights include:

> By 1995, institutional usage in the USA had declined to 63 258 people (a decrease of 67.3 per cent since 1967), and four states no longer operated institutional programmes (Lakin et al., 1996).
>
> From 1960, there were 348 state mental retardation institutions or special units in combined mental health–mental retardation institutions in operation, and by 1996 130 had been closed (Lakin et al., 1997).
>
> By 1992, there were 203 000 families of people with mental retardation who were receiving a range of family support services, including respite (Hemp et al., 1994).
>
> From 1977, the annual average increase in per person spending in large state institutions in the USA was 11 per cent, with these expenditures more than doubling between then and 1993 in constant 1967 dollars (Lakin Braddock, & Smith, 1994).
>
> In 1995, there was a total of 305 178 people with mental retardation participating in speciality residential services in the USA, one-half of whom lived in residential settings for six or fewer people (Prouty, Lakin & Smith, 1996). This represented a 58.0 per cent increase in provision of residential accommodation to people with mental retardation since 1967.

These trends are illustrative of the changes in mental retardation policy that have occurred since the 1970s in most industrialized nations. For example, Hatton, Emerson and Kieman (1995), using varying criteria for institutions depending upon national context and history, have summarized changes in institutional utilization among nations during the period 1981 to 1991. They reported rates of utilization for combined public or private institutional residences (serving more than 16, 20 or 50 people each) from 3.1/10 000 to 9.7/10 000 among four Scandinavian countries; from 4.7 to 20.9

among eight countries in the European Community; from 6.1 to 13.8 among three Eastern European countries, and of 4.5/10000 for the USA, based on 1991 to 1993 use. Rates of annual decrease in the use of institutions, according to these definitions, were from −1.6 per cent to −5.9 per cent in Scandinavia, from +0.4 per cent to −5.0 per cent in the European Community, +0.6 per cent in Eastern Europe, and −3.3 per cent in the USA during recent 10–13-year periods.

Although data are not uniformly available, presumably decreases in the utilization of larger residential settings have been offset by increases in the utilization of smaller residential settings and, in at least some nations, increases in the total numbers of people with mental retardation who participate in residential services. Hatton et al. (1995) attribute higher rates of changes in institutional use to the adoption of the principle of normalization (Wolfensberger, 1969, 1972). However, because the adoption of normalization as a guiding perspective in service system development is common among many European and the Scandinavian nations, variation may be due more to long-standing social and disability policies and the proportions of gross national products historically allocated to education health, and human services.

Separate but inadequate services

With the beginnings of de-institutionalization, the divergence of services for people with mental retardation and other individuals with dual diagnosis increased. Although the development of community services for people with mental retardation has been the hallmark of efforts in the field since the 1960s or 1970s in most industrialized nations, contemporary longitudinal research indicates that dual diagnosis is a risk factor for re-institutionalization even when the espoused policy is non-institutionalization (Kearney & Smull, 1992).

Even in the context of large and comprehensive de-institutionalization programmes, people with dual diagnosis are more likely to be retained in institutional settings, or the most restrictive available community settings (Jacobson, 1982, 1988). Community mental health services, which are often separately administered (Gettings, 1988), are utilized at low rates by people with mental retardation (Jacobson & Ackerman, 1988; Windle, et al., 1988) and, when accessed, provide less comprehensive services to people with mental retardation than to others (Dorn & Prout, 1993). Access to community mental health services for people with dual diagnosis in the USA is a long-standing problem that has resisted easy or straightforward solutions (Savino et al., 1973). For example, passage of a 1975 legislative mandate for USA community mental health centres to serve people with mental retardation (Donaldson & Menolascino, 1977) had no reported impact on their utilization.

During the 1960s, there were continuing signs of psychiatry's schism with mental retardation services. The American Medical Association reported in

1965 that more than 100 specialized clinics serving people with mental retardation had been established in the USA since 1949 through the USA Children's Bureau, and that people with mental retardation were served in some of the country's 1400 psychiatric clinics (many of which were child psychiatric services; Evans, 1966).

However, although community mental retardation services were relatively narrow in scope and primarily served school-aged children, the organization of these services was becoming multidisciplinary rather than psychiatric in nature, with such models dominant by 1975 to 1980. Nevertheless, the American Medical Association (1965) position paper directed to community primary care physicians stressed that, while recognizing the contributions of teams, 'Retardation is . . . still a medical problem. . . . The health, happiness, and success of the individual retarded child . . . will always depend on the devotion, knowledge, and skills of the primary physician and his relationships with other professional groups and agencies in the community'. This position paper also stressed that the physician must be the co-ordinator of a total life plan for the individual, a commitment that most community practitioners were probably unable or unwilling to make.

In 1966, the American Psychiatric Association also issued a statement on mental retardation. The statement continued to portray mental retardation services as medical facilities, rather than as educational–habilitative and allied health service settings. The report advocated integration of mental retardation with community mental health services. Psychiatry should take the lead in these efforts, in collaboration with other organizations (but not other professions), to develop standards of care and to avoid establishing duplicative services for people with mental retardation and mental disorders. An important facet of this statement was the inclusion of mental retardation aspects in medical training and the exposure of clinicians to interdisciplinary training. These recommendations were later to be largely realized in the training sequences for medical fellows provided by University Affiliated Programs.

On the other hand, the American Psychiatric Association (1966) noted that 75 per cent of mental retardation institutional psychiatric or paediatric physicians were not board certified. In the positions and recommendations of the American Medical Association and American Psychiatric Association we can see the precursors of what were to become widely acknowledged problems in community mental health services. These included new and diverse multiple federal agency requirements for reimbursement, the impacts of unionization, competitions and frictions regarding local resources and financing with special education: 'An inadequate range of treatment services, fragmentation and lack of co-ordination in treatment services, inaccessibility of treatment services, questionable quality of care' (Bachrach, 1981), and the core problem of the lack of special services tailored to people with dual diagnosis (Marcos, Gil & Vazquez, 1986).

Experiences in the UK appear to have paralleled those in the USA. Day (1994) noted that movement away from institutions began in the 1950s, and that government actions in support of this movement included a White Paper published in 1971 – 'Better Services for the Mentally Handicapped' – the Mental Health Act 1983, the Special Education Amendment 1984, the Disabled Persons Act 1987, and the 1987 new initiative 'Care in the Community', under which responsibility and resources for services were shifted to Local Authorities from the Health Authorities that operated the mental handicap hospitals (Hutchinson, 1970). The development of community services in the UK has not kept pace with institutional reductions. During the period 1976 to 1984, community residential services in the UK grew by 100 per cent and day services by 40 per cent, and there was a 25 per cent reduction in mental handicap hospital utilization, together with a 150 per cent increase in community spending and a 50 per cent increase in hospital spending (Day, 1994).

In contrast to developments in the UK, in 1974 in Ontario, mental retardation services were segregated from mental health services by the Developmental Services Act 1974, a re-alignment that took place throughout Canada at about that time, partly due to a restructuring of the federal financing mechanisms (Puddephatt & Sussman, 1994). Since that time, special service teams have been fielded in one province, in another there is a directory of willing providers, and there are community services teams associated with institutions which help in maintaining community placements.

Prevalence and public health

During 1960 to 1975, a number of dual diagnosis prevalence studies were conducted, involving referred or placed groups: Chess (1962), Philips (1967), Menolascino (1969), Berstein and Rice (1972), and Philips and Williams (1975). Between 1975 and 1987, there were seven community epidemiological studies of behaviour disorders, and during 1970 to 1987 there were nine comparable studies of mental disorders among people with mental retardation (Gostason, 1985; Lund, 1985; Gillberg, et al., 1986; Jacobson, 1990). Despite notable difficulties in the application of established diagnostic criteria developed for use with the general population (Bregman, 1991), most sources cite a 25 per cent minimum rate for the prevalence of mental and behavioural disorders among people with mental retardation. This rate (25 per cent of an administrative rate for mental retardation of 1 per cent) is applied to the populations of a variety of industrialized nations in Table 20.1. The population figures in Table 20.1 suggest that, in all these nations, the numbers of adults with dual diagnosis significantly outnumber the numbers of children with dual diagnosis, and that the numbers of people projected with dual diagnosis in most nations are sufficient to justify policy development and specialized services.

Table 20.1 Estimated populations with dual diagnosis in selected developed nations

| Country | General population 1990 (millions) | Estimated number of people with dual diagnosis | |
		0–19 years old	*20+ years old*
Australia	17.033	12 200	30 400
Austria	7.718	4 500	14 800
Belgium	9.962	6 000	19 000
Canada	26.620	18 200	48 400
Denmark	5.141	3 000	9 800
Finland	4.986	3 200	9 300
France	56.484	36 600	104 600
Germany	79.357	42 600	155 800
Greece	10.123	6 000	19 300
Hungary	10.352	6 800	19 100
Ireland	3.508	2 900	5 800
Italy	57.661	30 700	113 500
Netherlands	14.952	9 100	28 300
New Zealand	3.299	2 500	5 700
Norway	4.242	2 700	7 900
Russia	148.081	106 100	264 100
South Africa	37.191	43 100	49 800
Spain	38.793	23 900	73 000
Sweden	8.559	5 200	16 200
Switzerland	6.779	3 900	13 100
United Kingdom	57.418	36 500	107 000
United States	249.913	180 100	444 700

Population data from the US Bureau of the Census (1997).

Professional developments

During the period 1962 to 1980, there was growing interest in research on treating a range of conditions with various psychotherapeutic approaches, but 'little effort was expended to pursue these procedures on a broad scale' (Scheerenberger, 1987). Instead, emphasis emerged on psycho-pharmacology, and on applied behaviour analysis techniques, especially in the USA (O'Connor, 1981; McGee, 1988; Jacobson, 1993). Psycho-pharmacological treatment was recognized as 'effective and worthwhile in some cases' (Scheerenberger, 1987), but also as posing hazards due to side-effects, particularly for the treatment of behaviour disorders (Gualtieri & Keppel, 1985; Jacobson, 1988; National Institutes of Health, 1991; Pary, 1995; Poling & LeSage, 1995).

These trends and controversies have largely continued into the 1990s.

Whereas the efficacy of some specific psychotherapeutic approaches has not been well supported during this period (e.g. Mudford, 1995), comprehensive behaviour therapeutic approaches incorporating both behavioural analytic and cognitive–behavioural component strategies have demonstrated effectiveness with a range of behaviour disorders and mental disorders, especially among people with mild or moderate mental retardation (Fletcher et al., 1989; Dosen, 1993; Gardner, Graeber & Cole, 1996; Gardner & Whalen, 1996).

Model services

During the post-1960 period, a variety of model services was established in the USA such as at the Langley Porter Institute (San Francisco) Clinic (Philips & Williams, 1975), and the Developmental Evaluation Clinic of Children's Hospital Medical Center in Boston (Szymanski, 1977; Menolascino, 1994). Other model programmes and prominent practitioners associated with them included ENCOR community services in Nebraska (Frank Menolascino), UCLA services (George Tarjan), the University of Illinois Mental Retardation–Mental Health Clinic (Steven Reiss), Rock Creek Foundation individualized services (Michael Smull), Ulster County New York day services (Robert Fletcher), and the work of Robert Sovner and Anne D. Hurley in assuring the availability of modern information on mental health practice in mental retardation (see also Chapter 21). This period has also been marked by the founding of two professional membership organizations dedicated to the improved understanding of and service provision in the area of dual diagnosis – the National Association for the Dually Diagnosed (founded in the USA) and the European Association for Mental Health and Mental Retardation.

Despite the existence of these model programmes, related evaluation efforts have been descriptive in form and there have been few opportunities for comparative studies of the relative benefit of different approaches to the provision of similar services and care. Moreover, these limitations apply to some other noteworthy recent evaluations of services targeted to people with dual diagnosis (Fidura, Lindsey & Walker, 1987; Sandford, Elzinga & Grainger, 1987; Gold et al., 1989; Galligan, 1990; Hoefkens & Allen, 1990; Davidson et al. 1994). Fletcher et al. (1989) aptly summarized the programme evaluation as one in which, in the USA and in other developed countries; 'There are still few clinics and few training programs; there is limited public awareness; minimal federal research support; and little programmatic research'. Programme developments in a variety of developed nations are summarized in Table 20.2. As these summaries indicate, in most nations there are serious concerns about dual diagnosis services, their uneven accessibility and lack of resources.

Table 20.2 Status of dual diagnosis service development post-1980

Nation	Source	Dual diagnosis service issues or status
Australia	Parmenter (1988)	Paucity of trained medical personnel, disproportionate resources spent on diagnosis relative to treatment, separation of diagnostic and treatment services, lack of co-ordination between relevant governmental agencies, serious shortfall of provisions for those with moderate or mild mental retardation
Belgium (Flanders)	Van Walleghem (1988)	In Flanders there has been some enrichment of staffing for service to children with dual diagnosis; generic mental hospitals serve people with dual diagnosis, but there is a general lack of psychiatric interest in such services; lack of psychiatric expertise in severe mental retardation and dual diagnosis, and lack of specially trained personnel on wards or in psychiatric clinics serving people with mental retardation
	Van Walleghem & Van Dun (1993)	In Flanders, people with dual diagnosis are served in mental handicap institutions, and in temporary placements in psychiatric institutions; generally , '. . . there is no special type of service for these people; and there is no specific knowledge of how to treat them' (p. 49).
Canada	Zarfas (1988)	Variation among services in different provinces, services generally reported by government agencies to be insufficient to meet demand even when otherwise of high or suitable quality, lack of resources and lack of expertise, jurisdictional disputes among departments or ministries, and area given a low priority
Chile	Sacristan (1988)	Legislation with regard to mental retardation services is precarious; there are generic psychiatric hospitals and two state institutions serving people with mental retardation, with services based primarily on behavioural principles
Croatia	Igric (1993)	'The rate of employment and integration into society of adults with learning disabilities has fallen dramatically as a result of major economic difficulties and the general rise of unemployment in Croatia . . . People with learning disabilities have a right to training, and they attend schools and training centres' (p. 55). There are no special dual diagnosis services, but some rehabilitation programmes are in development and will be tested
Denmark	Dupont (1993)	The Danish psychiatric care system is hampered by great decline to 8.7 beds/10 000 general population; hospitals are not geared or prepared to serve people with dual diagnosis and opportunities for specialization of physicians in mental retardation practice are not available
France	Ross et al. (1993)	In 1975 legislation integration was set forth as a major public policy priority with respect to people with mental retardation; but large numbers of people are served in specialized adult

Table 20.2 (*cont.*)

Nation	Source	Dual diagnosis service issues or status
France (*cont.*)		medico–educative residential centres and 'far too many' people with severe or profound mental retardation are still living at psychiatric hospitals
Germany	Bradl & Hennicke (1993)	People with severe or profound mental retardation and behaviour disorders have been excluded from services, and there are few institutions providing dual diagnosis services; there are no special community centres for the treatment of people with dual diagnosis
Greece	Xeromeritou (1993)	The Greek Constitution of 1975 guarantees a right to education for all Greek citizens, including children with disabilities, but existing mental retardation services are primarily private, and this source does not indicate the presence of specialized services for people with dual diagnosis in this country
Hungary	Vetro, Kalman & Szucs (1993)	Suitable services and living places for people with dual diagnosis are lacking; presently 10 139 people with mental retardation are served as out-patients in mental health services and 698 are served as in-patients
India	Sen (1981)	As of 1981, there were 150 institutions providing 8000 beds; many states and cities do not have any facilities; illiteracy, malnutrition and poverty are problems for large proportions of the population and hence there is a correspondingly strong focus on primary prevention of mental retardation
Republic of Ireland	Hillery (1993)	Services are provided by generic psychiatric teams nationwide or, for people with moderate, severe or profound mental retardation, by multidisciplinary mental handicap teams; there is only one dual diagnosis services unit, but it is anticipated that mental health centres will be established within mental handicap services, and with associated community services
Mexico	Sacristan (1988)	There are neither specific projects nor services for dual diagnosis; generic psychiatric services are used
The Netherlands	Dosen (1988)	There is a shortage of specialized units to serve people with dual diagnosis (although special units were created in 1983), lack of specialist psychiatrists, and lack of knowledge of dual diagnosis among general psychiatrists; multidisciplinary teams lack a knowledge of psychiatry, and there are no specialized services for out-patients or follow-up care
	Klapwijk (1993)	There are no specialized dual diagnosis institutional services and there is a lack of trained psychiatrists and a lack of adequate day programmes for more than 60 per cent of people in need; mental health care systems for people with mental retardation are non-existent

Table 20.2 *(cont.)*

Nation	Source	Dual diagnosis service issues or status
New Zealand	Singh & Aman (1981)	'... New policies such as normalisation, mainstreaming, and early intervention (to name only a few) are adopted wholesale and without prior evaluation ... This is a major problem in New Zealand as it is elsewhere in the world ... Unfortunately, too many organisations and professionals have shown no inclination to test their theories' (p. 125). Historically, psychoactive medications have been the treatment of choice for behaviour problems; time-limited (2 to 3 weeks) intensive intervention services have been established in communities, but evaluation findings regarding these services have been 'largely uninterpretable'
Spain	Sacristan (1988)	There is a cultural tendency to avoid recognition of specific psychiatric pathology in people with mental retardation; professionals are interested in these issues, but not the government; services that are provided are generally from the mental health system, but there are three university centres at which research on dual diagnosis is conducted
	Salvador & Martinez-Maroto (1993)	There are no special dual diagnosis services in Spain
Sweden	Melin (1988)	'The dominating ideologies upon which the whole field of mental retardation rests are normalisation, humanism, and psychodynamic theory, none of which has been known to generate immediate solutions of an immediate nature' (p. 37). Most problems in service provision are addressed by increasing staff or re-organizing services; given the benchmark of normalization practices, the tendency is for people with dual diagnosis to use regular mental health services with back-up from the system of supports for people with mental retardation
	Kebbon (1993)	Normalization and integration are stated objectives of public policy; Sweden has had a 'broad, tax-supported welfare and security system, where about one-third of the gross national product was redistributed. The economic recession of the first years of the nineteen-nineties has brought this system under discussion ...' (p. 63). Slightly more than one-third of people with mental retardation are considered to have psychiatric problems and one-half of these can be cared for within ordinary services; for the rest, some sort of specialized psychiatric care is needed; the model recommended is forging of linkages among group homes, supported living arrangements, and local medical and psychiatric practitioners
Switzerland	Strasser (1993)	In some regions there are social–psychiatric associations; large numbers of people with dual diagnosis are living in psychiatric

Table 20.2 (*cont.*)

Nation	Source	Dual diagnosis service issues or status
		institutions: 'The permanent integration of people with a mental handicap in psychiatric hospitals is not satisfactory. They need privacy, shelter and a more natural environment, not therapies and medical care' (p. 61)
(Former) Union of Soviet Socialist Republics	Kozlova & Smirnov (1993)	Rehabilitation and correction (e.g. employment) were introduced in the past 10 years, but employment opportunities have declined with the establishment of a free market economy; out-patient rehabilitation and correction services are used by an estimated 50 per cent to 60 per cent of people with mental retardation, but people with more severe mental retardation or dual diagnosis tend to be placed in hospitals; mental handicap is included in medical school training, and psychiatric training, and medical care is typically provided by general psychiatrists
United Kingdom	Day (1988)	Dual diagnosis was historically dealt with within mental handicap services, as an established specialist category for psychiatrists; with hospital closures, there is no clear national dual diagnosis policy; there are controversies between behavioural practitioners and psychiatric organically oriented practitioners; specialized units have been generally in mental handicap hospitals; there are a few locally based units but these remain dependent on the support of larger mental handicap hospitals
	Day (1993)	There is a 'lack of appreciation of the size and nature of the problem . . ., the assumption . . . that the majority of behaviour disorders are a direct consequence of institutionalisation and would be largely eradicated by the new approaches to care . . . the situation has been masked by selective resettlement programmes . . . and it is believed that the generic mental health services can and should cope' (p. 7)
	Bouras (1993)	'. . . there has been ambiguity, fragmentation of responsibilities, lack of clarity, and contradictions on several initiatives' (p. 57); public policy regarding 'provision of specialised services, including psychiatric ones, remains unclear' (p. 59)
United States	Reiss (1988)	'For every mentally retarded person in the United States who needs treatment for a severe behaviour disorder, there are ten who need training in social skills and two who need treatment for depression' (p. 43). Most states have started special projects for dual diagnosis, often entailing special, temporary residential services; by virtue of their own performance, community mental health centres have not emerged as a viable mechanism for serving people with dual diagnosis
	Fletcher (1993)	Problems include difficulties negotiating bureaucratic system boundaries; a 'coherent social policy' is needed

Acknowledgement of service needs

For decades, many professionals were taught that behavioural and mental disorders in adults with mental retardation were largely the consequences of institutional deprivations (Lakin et al., 1981). Although there is little doubt that long-term deprivation of stimulation and socialization in total institutional environments can induce mental and behavioural disorders, at the same time it is clear that de-institutionalization does not uniformly alleviate such disorders, and that children and adults with mental retardation who have never lived apart from family and friends are not immune to the onset of such problems (Gravestock & Bouras, 1997; Kon & Bouras, 1996, 1997) . Yet, in the field of mental retardation, it is not uncommon to hear that the provision of greater choice, such as movement from group homes to more individualized living situations, results in the alleviation of mental or behavioural disorders. Such effects probably occur for some people (Reiss, 1994), but not necessarily for people with severe and complex mental or behavioural disorders who do not have mental retardation, for whom effective treatments are required (Anthony, 1977; Anthony, Cohen & Danley, 1988; Shern, Surles & Waizer, 1989; Willer et al., 1992; Burchard, Atkins & Burchard, 1996). 'Despite the widespread belief that institutionalisation is a causative factor in problem behaviour, this is not supported by the research evidence . . .'(Lowe, Paiva & Felce, 1993). Chung (1996) also noted, 'Philosophy, no matter how sound in principle, is clearly insufficient to effect positive change in problem behaviours . . . (in the absence of) intensive, individualised programming'.

Conclusion

There has been considerable debate in the literature regarding whether specialized dual diagnosis services should be established or existing mental health service providers should serve this population. However, it is clear that whatever strategy is undertaken should be based on high professional standards, involve the use of least-restrictive environments and appropriate treatments, assure the adequacy of staffing and the expertise of staff, assure the provision of individually tailored necessary services, and use standardized diagnostic and assessment methods of mental retardation and mental and behavioural disorders (Leismer, 1989; Nezu, Nezu, & Gill-Weiss, 1992). Correspondingly:

> The present economic and political climate has become associated with a need to cut rather than increase expenditure, and has given rise to a need for new kinds of community care which can combine low capital investment with a high degree of flexibility and adaptability.' (Tufnell et al., 1985),

and

> Health policy planners need treatment outcome data to determine appropriate levels of reimbursement for clinical services and to establish priorities

J.W. JACOBSON
350

for the allocation of scarce resources such as money or expensive new treatments . . . Third-party payers need outcome data to answer the question 'What are we paying for?' . . . Mental health professionals need reliable outcome data to ensure rational decision making . . . (Mirin & Namerow, 1991).

More often than not, dual diagnosis services are provided in a crisis context that greatly amplifies the expenses for care, confounds prospective methods of funding and quality assurance (Nezu et al., 1992), and challenges mental health services (Menolascino, Gilson & Levitas, 1986). In order to become more effective and accessible, dual diagnosis services will have to address both individual needs and service systems complexities for children, adolescents and adults with mental retardation and mental health problems (Bouras, Brooks & Drummond, 1994; Bouras, Holt & Gravestock, 1995; Bouras & Holt, 1997). The challenge for the immediate future, in many nations, will be to work towards the reconciliation of philosophical positions that have hindered the provision of high-quality dual diagnosis services with the evident needs of a meaningful proportion of the population of people with mental retardation, and to do so within the increasing financial constraints that exist internationally.

References

Alexander, D. (1988). The impact of national policies on research in mental retardation – A United States perspective. *Australia and New Zealand Journal of Developmental Disabilities,* 14, 183–8.

American Medical Association (1965). Mental retardation: a handbook for the primary physician. *Journal of the American Medical Association,* 191, 183–232.

American Psychiatric Association (1966). Psychiatry and mental retardation. *American Journal of Psychiatry,* 122, 1302–14.

Anthony, W.A. (1977). Psychological rehabilitation: a concept in need of a method. *American Psychologist,* 32, 658–62.

Anthony, W.A., Cohen, M.R. & Danley, K.S. (1988). The psychiatric rehabilitation model as applied to vocational rehabilitation. In *Vocational rehabilitation of Persons with Prolonged Psychiatric Disorders,* ed. J. A. Ciardello & M. D. Bell, pp. 59–80. Baltimore: The Johns Hopkins University Press.

Bachrach, L.L. (1981). A conceptual approach to deinstitutionalization of the mentally retarded: a perspective from the experience of the mentally ill. In *Deinstitutionalization and Community Adjustment of Mentally Retarded People,* ed. R.H. Bruininks, C.E. Meyers, B.B. Sigford, & K.C. Lakin, pp. 51–67. Washington, DC: American Association on Mental Deficiency.

Balthazar, E.E. & Stevens, H.A. (1975). *The Emotionally Disturbed Mentally Retarded: a Historical and Contemporary Perspective.* Englewood Cliffs, NJ: Prentice-Hall.

Barr, M.W. (1904/1973). *Mental Defectives, their History, Treatment, and Training.* New York: Arno Press.

Berstein, N. & Rice, J. (1972). Psychiatric consultation in a school for the retarded. *American Journal of Mental Deficiency*, **76**, 718–25.

Birnbrauer, J.S. & Leach, D.J. (1981). A progress report on Australian practice and research in intellectual handicap. *Applied Research in Mental Retardation*, **2**, 165–81.

Bouras, N. (1993). The European services: UK. *Journal of Intellectual Disability Research*, **37**, Suppl. I, 57–60.

Bouras, N., Brooks, D. & Drummond, K. (1994). Community psychiatric services for people with mental retardation. In *Mental Health in Mental Retardation*, ed. N. Bouras, pp. 293–9. Cambridge: Cambridge University Press.

Bouras, N. & Holt, G. (1997). Meeting the needs of people with learning disabilities would unblock acute beds. Letter to the Editor. *British Medical Journal*, **314**, 1278–9

Bouras, N., Holt, G. & Gravestock, S. (1995). Community care for people with learning disabilities: deficits and future plans. *Psychiatric Bulletin*, **19**, 134–7

Bradl, C. & Hennicke, K. (1993). The European services: Germany. *Journal of Intellectual Disability Research*, **37**, Suppl. I, 41–4.

Bregman, J.D. (1991). Current developments in the understanding of mental retardation Part II: psychopathology. *Journal of the American Academy of Child and Adolescent Psychiatry*, **30**, 861–72.

Brown, R.I. (1984). The field of developmental handicap – The development of rehabilitation education. In *Integrated Programmes for Handicapped Adolescents and Adults*, ed. R.I. Brown, pp. 1–22. London: Croom-Helm.

Burchard, J.D., Atkins, M. & Burchard, S.N. (1996). Wraparound services. In *Manual of Diagnosis and Professional Practice in Mental Retardation*, ed. J.W. Jacobson & J.A. Mulick, pp. 403–12. Washington, DC: American Psychological Association.

Cantor, G.N. (1955). On the incurability of mental deficiency. *American Journal of Mental Deficiency*, **60**, 362–5.

Chess, S. (1962). Psychiatric treatment of the mentally retarded child with behavior problems. *American Journal of Orthopsychiatry*, **32**, 863–9.

Chung, M.C. (1996). The evaluation of residential services for people with learning difficulties: an overview of United Kingdom research. *Adult Residential Care Journal*, **10**, 115–36.

Clarke, A.D.B. & Clarke, A.M. (1955). Pseudo-feeblemindedness – Some implications. *American Journal of Mental Deficiency*, **59**, 505–9.

Craft, M. (1959). Mental disorder in the defective: a psychiatric survey among in-patients. *American Journal of Mental Deficiency*, **63**, 829–34.

Davidson, P.W., Cain, N. N., Sloane-Reeves, J.E. et al. (1994). Crisis intervention for community-based individuals with developmental disabilities and behavioral and psychiatric disorders. *Mental Retardation*, **33**, 21–30.

Day, K. (1988). Services for psychiatrically disordered mentally handicapped adults – a UK perspective. *Australia and New Zealand Journal of Developmental Disabilities*, **14**, 19–25.

(1993). Mental health services for people with mental retardation: a framework for the future. *Journal of Intellectual Disability Research*, **37**, Suppl. I, 7–16.

(1994). Psychiatric services in mental retardation. Generic or specialised provision? In *Mental Health in Mental Retardation*, ed. N. Bouras, pp. 275–292. Cambridge: Cambridge University Press.

Donaldson, J.Y. & Menolascino, F.J. (1977). Past, current, and future roles of child psychiatry in mental retardation. *Journal of the American Academy of Child Psychiatry*, **16**, 38–52.

Dorn, T.A. & Prout, H.T. (1993). Service delivery patterns for adults with mild mental retardation at community mental health centers. *Mental Retardation*, **31**, 292–6.

Dosen, A. (1988). Community care for people with mental retardation in the Netherlands. *Australia and New Zealand Journal of Developmental Disabilities*, **14**, 15–8.

(1993). Diagnosis and treatment of psychiatric and behavioural disorders in mentally retarded individuals: the state of the art. *Journal of Intellectual Disability Research*, **37**, Suppl. I, 1–7.

Dugdale, R. L. (1877). *The Jukes: a Study in Crime, Pauperism, Disease, and Heredity*. New York: Putnam.

Dupont, A. (1993). The European services: Denmark. *Journal of Intellectual Disability Research*, **37**, Suppl. I, 37–9.

Evans, R. (1966). Integration of a mental retardation program into a service of child and adolescent psychiatry in a general hospital. *American Journal of Psychiatry*, **122**, 1235–8.

Fidura, J. G., Lindsey, E.R. & Walker, G.R. (1987). A special behavior unit for treatment of behavior problems of persons who are mentally retarded. *Mental Retardation*, **25**, 107–11.

Fisher, L. & Wolfson, I. (1953). Group therapy of mental defectives. *American Journal of Mental Deficiency*, **57**, 463–76.

Fletcher, R. (1993). Mental illness-mental retardation in the United States: policy and treatment challenges. *Journal of Intellectual Disability Research*, **37**, Suppl. I, 25–33.

Fletcher, R.J., Holmes, P.A., Keyes, C.B. & Schoss, P.J. (1989). Linking research and practice: An integrated approach to the treatment of the dually diagnosed. In *Mental Retardation and Mental Illness: Assessment, Treatment and Service for the Dually Diagnosed*, ed. R.J. Fletcher & F.A. Menolascino, pp. 59–68. Lexington, MA: Lexington.

Galligan, B. (1990). Serving people who are dually diagnosed: a program evaluation. *Mental Retardation*, **28**, 353–8.

Gardner, W.I., Graeber, J.I. & Cole, C.L. (1996). Behavior therapies: a multimodal diagnostic and intervention model. In *Manual of Diagnosis and Professional Practice in Mental Retardation*, ed. J.W. Jacobson & J.A. Mulick, pp. 355–70. Washington, DC: American Psychological Association.

Gardner, W.I. & Whalen, J.P. (1996). Discussion: a multimodal behavior analytic model for evaluating the effects of medical problems on nonspecific behavioral symptoms in persons with developmental disabilities. *Behavioral Interventions*, **11**, 147–63.

Garfield, S.L., Wilcott, J.B. & Milgram, N.A. (1961). Emotional disturbance and suspected mental deficiency. *American Journal of Mental Deficiency,* **66**, 23–9.

Gettings, R. M. (1988). Service delivery trends: a state-federal policy perspective. In *Mental Health and Mental Retardation,* ed. J.A. Stark, F.J. Menolascino, M.H. Albarelli & V.C. Gray, pp. 385–93. New York: Springer-Verlag.

Gibson, D., Frank, H.F. & Zarfas, D.E. (1963). Public mental retardation services in Canada: evolution and trends. *Canadian Psychiatric Journal,* **8**, 337–43.

Gillberg, C., Persson, E., Grufman, M. & Themner, U. (1986). Psychiatric disorders in mildly and severely mentally retarded urban children and adolescents: epidemiological aspects. *British Journal of Psychiatry,* **149**, 68–74.

Goddard, H. (1912). *The Kallikak Family: A Study in the Heredity of Feeble-Mindedness.* New York: MacMillan.

Gold, I.M., Wolfson, E.S., Lester, C.M., Ratey, J.J. & Chmielinskih, E. (1989). Developing a unit for mentally retarded mentally ill patients on the grounds of a state hospital. *Hospital and Community Psychiatry,* **40**, 836–40.

Gostason, R. (1985). Psychiatric illness among the mentally retarded. A Swedish population study. *Acta Psychiatrica Scandinavia,* **71**, Suppl. 318, 1–117.

Gravestock, S. & Bouras, N. (1997). Survey of services for adults with learning disabilities. *Psychiatric Bulletin,* **21**, 197–9.

Greenland, C. (1963). The treatment of the mentally retarded in Ontario: an historical note. *Canadian Psychiatric Journal,* **8**(5), 328–36.

Gualtieri, C.T. & Keppel, J.M. (1985). Psychopharmacology in the mentally retarded and a few related issues. *Psychopharmacology Bulletin,* **21**, 304–9.

Halpern, A.S. (1970). Some issues concerning the differential diagnosis of mental retardation and emotional disturbance. *American Journal of Mental Deficiency,* **74**, 796–800.

Harris, M. (1979). *Cultural Materialism: The Struggle for a Science of Culture.* New York: Random House.

Hatton, C., Emerson, E. & Kieman, C. (1995). People in institutions in Europe. *Mental Retardation,* **33**, 132.

Hemp, R., Braddock, D., Lakin, K.C. & Smith, G. (1994). The growth of family support. *Mental Retardation,* **32**, 319.

Hillery, J. (1993). The European services: Republic of Ireland. *Journal of Intellectual Disability Research,* **37**, Suppl. I, 67–70.

Hoefkens, A. & Allen, D. (1990). Evaluation of a special behaviour unit for people with mental handicaps and challenging behaviour. *Journal of Mental Deficiency Research,* **34**, 213–28.

Hutchinson, A. (1970). Community care services for the mentally retarded in Britain. *American Journal of Public Health,* **60**, 56–63.

Igric, L.J. (1993). The European services: Croatia. *Journal of Intellectual Disability Research,* **37**, Suppl. I, 54–6.

Jacobson, J.W. (1982). Problem behavior and psychiatric impairment in a developmentally disabled population I: Behavior frequency. *Applied Research in Mental Retardation,* **3**, 121–39.

(1988). Problem behavior and psychiatric impairment in a developmentally disabled population III: Psychotropic medication. *Research in Developmental Disabilities*, **9**, 23–38.

(1990). Assessing the prevalence of psychiatric disorders in a developmentally disabled population. In *Assessment of Behavior Problems in Persons with Mental Retardation Living in the Community*, ed. E. Dibble & D.B. Gray, pp. 20–70. Washington, DC: National Institute of Mental Health.

(1993). Public policy and the punishment of the powerless. *Child and Adolescent Mental Health Care*, **3**, 7–8.

Jacobson, J.W. & Ackerman, L.J. (1988). An appraisal of services for mental retardation and psychiatric impairments. *Mental Retardation*, **26**, 377–80.

Kane, J.F. & Rojahn, J. (1981). Development of services for mentally retarded people in the Federal Republic of Germany: a survey of history, empirical research, and current trends. *Applied Research in Mental Retardation*, **2**, 195–210.

Kanner, L. (1948). Feeblemindedness: absolute, relative, and apparent. *Nervous Child*, **7**, 363–97.

Kearney, F.J. & Smull, M.W. (1992). People with mental retardation leaving mental health institutions: Evaluating outcomes after five years in the community. In *Community Living for People with Developmental and Psychiatric Disabilities*, ed. J.W. Jacobson, S.N. Burchard & P.J. Carling, pp. 183–96. Baltimore: The Johns Hopkins University Press.

Kebbon, L. (1993). The European services: Sweden. *Journal of Intellectual Disability Research*, **37**, Suppl. I, 61–5.

Klapwijk, E. Th. (1993). The European services: the Netherlands. *Journal of Intellectual Disability Research*, **37**, Suppl. I, 44–6.

Kon, Y. & Bouras, N. (1996). The use of the Mental Health Act in learning disabilities. *Psychiatric Bulletin*, **20**, 596–8.

(1997). Psychiatric follow-up and health services utilisation for people with learning disabilities. *British Journal of Developmental Disabilities*, **XLIII**(1), 20–6.

Kozlova, I.A. & Smirnov, Y. (1993). The European services: the former USSR. *Journal of Intellectual Disability Research*, **37**, Suppl. I, 52–4.

Lakin, K.C., Braddock, D. & Smith, G. (1994). Expenditures for care in large state-operated MR/DD facilities. *Mental Retardation*, **32**, 381.

Lakin, K.C., Bruininks, R.H. & Sigford, B.B. (1981). Early perspectives on the community adjustment of mentally retarded people. In *Deinstitutionalization and Community Adjustment of Mentally Retarded People*, ed. R.H. Bruininks, C.E. Meyers, B.B. Sigford, & K.C. Lakin, pp. 28–50. Washington, DC: American Association on Mental Deficiency.

Lakin, K.C., Prouty, B., Anderson, L. & Sandlin, J. (1997). Nearly 40% of state institutions have been closed. *Mental Retardation*, **35**, 65.

Lakin, K.C., Prouty, B., Smith, G. & Braddock, D. (1996). Nixon goal surpassed – twofold. *Mental Retardation*, **34**, 67.

Leismer, J. (1989). Systemic needs for a responsible future. In *Mental Retardation and Mental Illness: Assessment, Treatment and Service for the Dually Diagnosed*, ed. R.J. Fletcher & F.A. Menolascino, pp. 265–84. Lexington, MA: Lexington.

Lowe, K., Paiva, D. & Felce, D. (1993). Effects of a community-based service on adaptive and maladaptive behaviours: a longitudinal study. *Journal of Intellectual Disability Research,* **37**, 3–22.

Lund, J. (1985). The prevalence of psychiatric morbidity in mentally retarded adults. *Acta Psychiatrica Scandinavia,* **75**, 563–70.

Marcos, L.R., Gil, R.M. & Vazquez, K.M. (1986). Who will treat the psychiatrically disturbed developmentally disabled patients? A health care nightmare. *Hospital and Community Psychiatry,* **37**, 171–4.

McGee, J. (1988). Issues related to applied behavioral analysis. In *Mental Retardation and Mental Health: Classification, Diagnosis, Treatment, Services,* ed. J.A. Stark, F.J. Menolascino, M.H. Albarelli & V.C. Gray, pp. 203–10. New York: Springer-Verlag.

Melin, L. (1988). Services and provisions for persons with mental retardation in Sweden. *Australia and New Zealand Journal of Developmental Disabilities,* **14**, 37–42.

Menolascino, F.J. (1965). Emotional disturbance and mental retardation. *American Journal of Mental Deficiency,* **70**, 248–56.

(1966). The facade of mental retardation. *American Journal of Psychiatry,* **122**, 1227–35.

(1969). Emotional disturbances in mentally retarded children. *American Journal of Psychiatry,* **126**, 168–76.

(1994). Services for people with dual diagnosis in the USA. In *Mental Health in Mental Retardation,* ed. N. Bouras, pp. 343–52. Cambridge: Cambridge University Press.

Menolascino, F.J., Gilson, S.F. & Levitas, A. (1986). Issues in the treatment of mentally retarded patients in the community mental health system. *Community Mental Health Journal,* **22**, 314–27.

Meyers, C.E. & Blacher, J. (1987). Historical determinants of residential care. In *Living Environments and Mental Retardation,* ed. S. Landesman, P.M. Vietze & M.J. Begab, pp. 3–16. Washington, DC: American Association on Mental Retardation.

Mirin, S.M. & Namerow, M.J. (1991). Why study treatment outcome? *Hospital and Community Psychiatry,* **42**, 1007–13.

Mudford, O.C. (1995). Review of the gentle teaching data. *American Journal on Mental Retardation,* **99**, 345–55.

Murray, P. (1988). The study of the history of disability services: examining the past to improve the present and future. *Australia and New Zealand Journal of Developmental Disabilities,* **14**, 93–102.

National Institutes of Health. (1991). *Treatment of Destructive Behaviors in Persons with Developmental Disabilities.* NIH Publication No. 91–2410. Bethesda, MD: NIH.

Nezu, C.M., Nezu, A.M. & Gill-Weiss, M.J. (1992). *Psychopathology in Persons with Mental Retardation: Clinical Guidelines for Assessment and Treatment.* Champaign, IL: Research Press.

O'Connor, N. (1981). British applied psychology of mental subnormality. *Applied Research in Mental Retardation,* **2**, 97–113.

Parmenter, T.R. (1988). Analysis of Australian mental health services for people with mental retardation. *Australia and New Zealand Journal of Developmental Disabilities*, 14, 9–13.

Pary, R.J. (1995). Discontinuation of neuroleptics in community-dwelling individuals with mental retardation and mental illness. *American Journal on Mental Retardation*, 100, 207–12.

Pasamanick, B., Knobloch, H. & Lillenfield, A. (1956). Socioeconomic status and some precursors of neuropsychiatric disorders. *American Journal of Orthopsychiatry*, 26, 264–71.

Philips, I. (1967). Psychopathology and mental retardation. *American Journal of Psychiatry*, 124, 29–35.

Philips, I. & Williams, N. (1975). Psychopathology and mental retardation: a study of 100 mentally retarded children. *American Journal of Psychiatry*, 132, 139–45.

Poling, A. & LeSage, M. (1995). Evaluating psychotropic drugs in people with mental retardation: where are the social validity data? *American Journal on Mental Retardation*, 100, 193–200.

Prouty, R.W., Lakin, K.C. & Smith, G.A. (1996). Growth in residential settings of 6 or fewer individuals with MR/DD. *Mental Retardation*, 34, 130.

Puddephatt, A. & Sussman, S. (1994). Developing services in Canada: Ontario vignettes. In *Mental Health in Mental Retardation*, ed. N. Bouras, pp. 353–64. Cambridge: Cambridge University Press.

Reid, A.H. (1989). Psychiatry and mental handicap: a historical perspective. *Journal of Mental Deficiency Research*, 33, 363–8.

Reiss, S. (1988). Dual diagnosis in the United States. *Australia and New Zealand Journal of Developmental Disabilities*, 14, 43–8.

(1994). *Handbook of Challenging Behavior.* Worthington, OH: IDS Publishing Corporation.

Robinson, R.G. & Pasewark, R. (1951). Behavior in intellectual deficit. *American Journal of Mental Deficiency*, 55, 598–607.

Ross, N., Robin, O., Bogliolo, A. & Deverne, A. (1993). The European services: France. *Journal of Intellectual Disability Research*, 37, Suppl. I, 65–7.

Sacristan, J.R. (1988). Mental health in Spanish-speaking mentally retarded people: the state of the art. *Australia and New Zealand Journal of Developmental Disabilities*, 14, 27–30.

Salvador, L. & Martinez-Maroto, A. (1993). The European services: Spain. *Journal of Intellectual Disability Research*, 37, Suppl. I, 34–7.

Sandford, D.A., Elzinga, R.H. & Grainger, W. (1987). Evaluation of a residential behavioral treatment program for behaviorally disturbed mentally retarded young adults. *American Journal of Mental Deficiency*, 91, 431–4.

Sarason, S. (1959). *Psychological Problems in Mental Deficiency* 3rd edn. New York: Harper & Row.

Sarason, S.B. & Doris, J. (1969). *Psychological Problems in Mental Deficiency* 4th edn. New York: Harper & Row.

Savino, M., Stearns, P., Merwin, E. & Kennedy, R. (1973). The lack of services to the retarded through community mental health programs. *Community Mental Health Journal*, 9, 158–68.

Scheerenberger, R.C. (1983). *A History of Mental Retardation.* Baltimore: Paul H. Brookes.

(1987). *A history of Mental Retardation: a Quarter Century of Promise.* Baltimore: Paul H. Brookes.

Schroeder, C.S. & Schroeder, S.R. (1981). Mental retardation in the United States: assessment, program development, and applied research. *Applied Research in Mental Retardation*, **2**, 181–94.

Sen, A.K. (1981). Care, prevention and assessment of mental retardation in India. *Applied Research in Mental Retardation*, **2**, 129–37.

Shern, D.L., Surles, R.C. & Waizer, J. (1989). Designing community treatment systems for the most seriously mentally ill: a state administrative perspective. *Journal of Social Issues*, **45**, 105–17.

Singh, N.N. & Aman, M.G. (1981). Mental retardation: state of the field in New Zealand. *Applied Research in Mental Retardation*, **2**, 115–27.

Sloan, W. & Stevens, H.A. (1976). *A Century of Concern: A History of the American Association on Mental Deficiency – 1876–1976*. Washington, DC: American Association on Mental Deficiency.

Smith, J.D. (1985). *Minds Made Feeble: The Myth and Legacy of the Kallikaks.* Rockville, MD: Aspen Press.

Smith, J.D. & Nelson, R.K. (1989). *The Sterilization of Carrie Buck.* Far Hills, NJ: New Horizon Press.

Snyder, R. & Sechrest, L. (1959). Directive group therapy with defective delinquents. *American Journal of Mental Deficiency*, **64**, 117–23.

Strasser, U. (1993). The European services: Switzerland. *Journal of Intellectual Disability Research*, **37**, Suppl. I, 60–1.

Szymanski, L. (1977). Psychiatric diagnostic evaluation of mentally retarded individuals. *Journal of the American Academy of Child Psychiatry*, **16**, 67–87.

Trent, J.W. (1994). *Inventing the Feeble Mind: A History of Mental Retardation in the United States.* Berkeley, CA: University of California Press.

Tufnell, G., Bouras, N., Watson, J. & Brough, D. (1985). Home assessment and treatment in a community psychiatric service. *Acta Psychiatrica Scandinavia*, **72**, 20–8.

Van Walleghem, M. (1988). Survey of principal care facilities for people with mental retardation in Belgium. *Australia and New Zealand Journal of Developmental Disabilities*, **14**, 31–5.

Van Walleghem, M.J. & Van Dun, K. (1993). The European services: Belgium. *Journal of Intellectual Disability Research*, **37**, Suppl. I, 46–9.

Vetro, A., Kalman, J. & Szucs, P. (1993). The European services: Hungary. *Journal of Intellectual Disability Research*, **37**, Suppl. I, 39–41.

Willer, B.S., Guastaferro, J.R., Zankiw, I. & Duran, R. (1992). Applying a rehabilitation model to residential programs for people with severe and persistent mental disorders. In *Community Living for People with Developmental and Psychiatric Disabilities*, ed. J. W. Jacobson, S.N. Burchard & P.J. Carling, pp. 37–52. Baltimore: Johns Hopkins University Press.

Windle, C., Poppen, P.J., Thompson, J.W. & Marvelle, K. (1988). Types of patients served by various providers of outpatient care in CMHCs. *American Journal of Psychiatry*, **145**, 457–63.

Wolfensberger, W. (1969). The origin and nature of our institutional models. In *Changing Patterns in Residential Services for the Mentally Retarded*, ed. R.

Kugel & W. Wolfensberger, pp. 59–177. Washington, DC: President's Committee on Mental Retardation.

Wolfensberger, W. (1972). *The Principle of Normalization in Human Services.* Toronto: National Institute on Mental Retardation.

Xeromeritou, A. (1993). The European services: Greece. *Journal of Intellectual Disability Research, 37*, Suppl. I, 49–52.

Zarfas, D.E. (1988). Mental health systems for people with mental retardation: a Canadian perspective. *Australia and New Zealand Journal of Developmental Disabilities,* **14,** 3–7.

21 Community services for people with developmental disabilities and psychiatric or severe behaviour disorders

PHILIP W. DAVIDSON, DANIELLE MORRIS AND NANCY N. CAIN

Introduction

The presence of severe behaviour or psychiatric disorders in people with developmental disabilities is one of the leading reasons for either loss of community placements or retention in residential environments more restrictive than otherwise required. Behavioural or psychiatric disorders that may have been accepted by institutional staff are often not tolerated in community placements. Hence, the presence of a dual diagnosis is a principal threat to social integration (Pagel & Whitling, 1978; Crawford, Aiello & Thompson, 1979; Hill & Bruininks, 1984; Bruininks et al., 1987; Borthwick, 1988; Bruininks, Hill & Morreau, 1988). As a consequence, such disorders impair the quality of life of people with developmental disabilities (Schalock & Keith, 1993), or cause regression of adaptive or intellectual functioning (Russell & Tanguay, 1981). They may also create unnecessary escalation of family stressors and impair family functioning (Reiss, 1990).

The design of services for individuals with dual diagnosis did not emerge as a major issue until the start of the de-institutionalization movement in the latter third of the twentieth century. Until that point, people with developmental disabilities who developed severe behavioural problems lived in institutional settings and their disorders were managed by physical or pharmacological restraints. Those with recognized psychiatric illnesses were often removed from the developmental disabilities system and maintained in psychiatric hospitals.

As more and more institutional beds were closed, people with dual diagnoses found themselves moving to less restrictive environments, or remaining longer with their families. In such community settings, it became clear that services from both the developmental disabilities network and the mental health system were required. However, few districts have community-based programmes that provide comprehensive, integrated mental health and developmental disabilities services that are fully accessible to people with these disabilities. Sometimes, certain appropriate mental health services may not exist. More often, individuals with developmental disabilities may be excluded from existing generic community-based mental health services. This may be due to organizational issues, such as restrictions on providing services to people with low IQs, or lack of expertise in addressing the needs of those with dual diagnoses. Exclusion may also stem from the belief by mental health professionals that people with developmental disabilities may not benefit from mental health interventions, due either to an impaired ability to process information or to a lack of competence to participate in a therapeutic process.

In the last 20 years, there has been an expansion of specialized community-based services for people with dual diagnoses. The purposes of this chapter are to posit some benchmarks for such services, and to review the few service models that have been field tested and published and assess them against the benchmarks.

Examples of community-based services

Attention to the growing need for services for people with dual diagnosis has led to the development of community models for this population. The specifics of these models and the services offered vary from community to community. The following discussion describes some everyday community models. The list is not exhaustive. Although the authors are aware of many more projects, they have chosen to focus only on programmes for which established peer-reviewed material is available.

The Greater Boston START Model

The START Model finds its roots in the philosophy that no one specific diagnosis or treatment modality will work with all clients (Beasley, Kroll & Sovner, 1992). START is an acronym for systemic, therapeutic, assessment, respite and treatment. It is a crisis intervention and prevention service and is funded by the Massachusetts Department of Mental Retardation in the northern region of Greater Boston. The programme provides emergency assessments and respite care for people with developmental disabilities who are evidencing acute behavioural and emotional experiences. Staffing for the clinical team includes a part-time psychiatrist, three full-time masters-degreed clinicians, and six full-time bachelor-degreed clinicians. Doctoral-degree psychology consultants and licensed social workers are available to provide consultation regarding their field, such as behavioural psychology, neuropsychology and family advocacy.

Each referral receives a comprehensive clinical assessment. This is achieved via the crisis team members collecting the historical information from and then working with community care givers to collect the necessary behavioural data. Ideally, the crisis team serves as a facilitator for the diagnostic process by co-ordinating data collection and networking with the clinicians involved in the case. The team is also available to co-ordinate out-patient services. Respite is available to referrals and can serve several functions: it can diffuse crises that stem from environmental stressors; it can stabilize a client who is too disturbed to remain at home; and it can be used to help clients make the transition from in-patient settings to the community. In-patient mental health services are facilitated by the crisis team members including discharge planning. Additional services provided by the crisis team include educating community care providers and clinicians regarding the mental health needs of people with developmental disabilities. Workshops and training on various topics such as psychiatric diagnosis, positive behaviour programming and psychotropic drug therapy are provided.

The Toronto MATCH Project

The Metro Agencies Representatures' Council (MARC) in Toronto implemented the Continuum of Service for People with Dual Diagnosis or MATCH programme (Puddephatt & Sussman, 1994). MATCH stands for the Metro Agencies Treatment Continuum for Health, and MARC is an association of over 40 agencies in the Metro Toronto area with commitments to providing services for people with developmental handicaps. This model for providing services for individuals with developmental disabilities and mental health needs began as a pilot project. The project was funded jointly through the Ministry of Community and Social Services and the Ministry of Health. It was designed specifically to serve the needs of people with dual diagnosis. Assessment and treatment planning are a main focus for the programme. Services are provided across a continuum covering: prevention/early intervention in the form of education and training; assessment and treatment planning provided in in-patient, out-patient and crisis-response settings; crisis intervention to secure containment and for stabilization; treatment in community-based out-patient settings, day treatment programmes, specialized residential treatment and in-patient psychiatric care; long-term care and support provided via high levels of support to residential community living settings, appropriate day treatment and vocational programmes, family support networks, and respite services for parents.

The Rochester Crisis Intervention Model

The model developed in Rochester, New York, emerged through a series of planning stages, including a formal needs assessment, a survey of existing resources, and a community-based consensus planning conference (Davidson et al., 1995). The model was implemented based on the recommendations developed at the consensus planning conference. Services offered through the Rochester model include: an interdisciplinary crisis intervention team; acute in-patient psychiatric services; out-patient services provided through a specialized mental retardation/developmental disabilities psychiatric clinic; specialized residential services; family support services, including residential respite; prevention services providing staff education and training; and family-centred case management.

Funding for the crisis intervention component of this programme comes from annual grants from the New York State Office of Mental Retardation and Developmental Disabilities (OMRDD). The programme is a joint effort between the University of Rochester Medical Centre and OMRDD's local district office. The treatment team consists of a programme director, two behaviour modification specialists, a part-time licensed psychologist, and a part-time consulting psychiatrist. People eligible for services are individuals with developmental disabilities living with families or living in community-based supervised or independent living situations in the Monroe County Area of New York. There is no fee for service. Services may also be accessed by agencies providing services for these individuals such as schools, sheltered workshops, day treatment programmes, supported work programmes and supported living programmes.

Crisis intervention services are available on a 24-hour per day basis for acute behavioural crises. Specific services available from the crisis team cover a continuum including: case management; participation in in-patient treatment and discharge planning; follow-up consultation to developmental service agencies and families; identification of at-risk consumers; in-home counselling to families of at-risk individuals; consultation to community agencies serving at-risk individuals; and staff training for all involved parties.

The Ulster County Comprehensive Mental Health Model

Community agencies working with individuals with mental retardation in Ulster County, New York, worked in conjunction with Ulster County Mental Health Services to develop a multi-year, comprehensive plan to address the needs of the dually diagnosed population that began with a comprehensive needs assessment (Landsberg, Fletcher & Maxwell, 1987). The model for services included a continuum of residential facilities from supervised living programmes to independent living situations, comprehensive mental health out-patient services from diagnosis to day treatment, and access to short-term and long-term in-patient psychiatric care. Occupational and vocational treatment and experience (sheltered employment, placement, vocational testing), training and education for staff of mental health and mental retardation agencies, and a mechanism to co-ordinate and guide programme development are also provided.

For a continuum of residential facilities to be available in Ulster County, there was a need to create more specialized residential beds. For this purpose, ten beds were set aside in existing community residences for the dually diagnosed and a 14-bed specialized facility was developed. To increase mental health clinical services, the county mental health out-patient programme was asked to seek additional staffing to increase out-patient services and to provide services at work sites. In addition to these, the establishment of a specialized day treatment programme was needed. Specifically, a 40-client day treatment facility with the county mental health centre providing specialized care and consultation was suggested.

The Interface Model

Interface, the name for the collaborative undertaking of the Hamilton County Community Mental Health Board and the University Affiliated Cincinnati Center for Developmental Disorders, set forth to develop multisystem services for individuals with dual diagnosis (Woodward, 1993). This joint effort is funded by the Hamilton County Community Mental Health Board and administered by the University Affiliated Cincinnati Center for Developmental Disorders. This arrangement removes the focus of responsibility away from both the mental health board and the mental retardation/developmental disabilities office. Community service committees were convened to develop and implement individual service plans, obtain needed mental health and mental retardation services, maintain networking and team characteristics, and gather data. Mental health and mental retardation professionals work together on the committees.

Three outcomes resulted: (1) there was an increase in community mental health services; (2) a mental health intermediate care facility/mental retardation community residential setting was built and run collaboratively by county mental health and mental retardation boards; and (3) a multisystem community and in-patient crisis intervention system was developed. The crisis intervention system consisted of three behaviour management specialists with expertise in mental retardation, with services available seven days a week. This community mobile crisis team has links to out-patient psychiatric emergency services, in-patient psychiatric wards, and hospitalization discharge follow-up.

The Eastern Virginia Mental Retardation and Emotional Disturbance Project

Eastern State Hospital, the Southeastern Virginia Training Center, the Community Services Division of the Virginia Department of Mental Health and Mental Retardation, and nine community services boards in eastern Virginia began discussions around the Mental Retardation and Emotional Disturbance Project (Parkhurst, 1984). They identified the following objectives: to develop a survey of the mental retardation/emotional disturbance population in the area who have sought, but not received, services; to conduct a region-wide needs assessment; to survey existing service components that could be expanded; to survey programmes for people with dual diagnosis; to develop a service system to co-ordinate services at the community and institutional levels accessible for both rural and urban populations; to estimate costs, personnel requirements, location and potential funding sources; to develop legislative and policy recommendations for the delivery of services to this population; and to gather data and service information to develop the public education and prevention component.

Outcomes consisted of recommendations for crisis centres, accessible throughout eastern Virginia, for people with dual diagnosis, for special staff training for the treatment of dual diagnosis, and to address the lack of community living arrangements by developing community-based residences.

The Rock Creek Model

This comprehensive community support system was developed over a decade ago by the Rock Creek Foundation in the Metropolitan Washington, DC, area (Smull, Fabian & Chanteau, 1994). It endorses the developmental model and views mental health problems as conditions separate and distinct from mental retardation. It values the recognition of basic human worth and dignity and endorses normalization.

Services involve many different components. Psychotherapeutic services include medication evaluation; individual, group, family and behaviour therapy; psychiatric and psychological evaluations; and expressive arts therapies. Day treatment programmes have both psychiatric and behavioural programming. Out-patient psychotherapeutic services and 24-hour crisis services are available. Social survival services include life skills training in dealing with money, time, communication and public transportation. Vocational services include both prevocational and vocational development. Psychosocial rehabilitation programmes exist for those who still need structure but do not need intensive day treatment. Residential services have the capacity to programme for maladaptive behaviour within the residential setting.

Programming begins in a treatment habilitation and planning process in which the client is viewed within the context of the environment and service system. Programmes are adapted to the individual needs of the client. The surrounding community works with the treatment team to develop strategies for integration. The client gives feasible meaningful input into the plan. Variable and creative funding sources are obtained in order to enable the programme to develop in response to the individual needs of the client.

The Eastern Region Diversion and Support Program

The Eastern Region Diversion and Support Team is a collaborative effort among the State of North Carolina Department of Human Resources, 13 area mental health programmes, and the Department of Psychiatric Medicine at East Carolina University (Antonacci et al., 1996). This programme embraces a person-centred approach to treatment. Services strive to be flexible, accessible, mobile and integrated. The programme serves a predominantly rural area in which interagency collaboration is essential.

Services include interdisciplinary team intervention. The team consists of a full-time psychiatrist, a clinical social worker, a psychologist and a behaviour specialist. It provides support to existing community systems via comprehensive integrated assessments and recommendations. Crisis stabilization is provided and co-ordinated. The crisis is defined through functional assessment. The individual is advocated for and support is provided to the systems involved. The team is not administratively tied to any one system in the region.

In-patient psychiatric services are accessed in the community in which the individual lives. The team is available for consultation and training for any hospital in North Carolina that provides treatment for people with developmental disabilities and mental illness. A specialized psychiatric in-patient unit was established via a collaborative effort between the Department of Psychiatric Medicine at the Eastern Carolina University and the University Medical Center of Eastern Carolina Pitt County. The unit is staffed by a team separate from the consultation team.

On-going training and education are provided to those who provide services for individuals with dual diagnosis. Training and education are approached via providing general education around specific cases or by providing broader-based educational in-service training and workshops.

The ENCOR Program

The Eastern Nebraska Community Office of Retardation in Omaha, Nebraska, has demonstrated that it is both possible and cost beneficial to serve individuals with mental retardation and mental illness in their home communities (Menolascino, 1994). The programme was developed over two decades and its design included community involvement and citizen advocacy. It is prepared to serve all individuals, regardless of their level of mental retardation. The specialized clinical staff also provides direct teaching to care givers. The programme makes use of existing community services, including family support services, and integrated job placements, which have been encouraged through liaison with local industries.

A Developmental Maximation Home for the more severely retarded/multiply handicapped exists at one end of the continuum of services (Menolascino, 1989). Other services include integrated preschool services, in-home teachers, crisis assistance programmes, specialized group homes, alternative living units, and work stations in industry.

ENCOR's clients are grouped into three different levels of involvement. Level I includes people who present daily behavioural management problems, Level II those who display occasional behavioural problems, and Level III those who have only infrequent behavioural problems. The classification of clients by levels as opposed to specific diagnoses allows for accurate assessment of the types of personnel, supports and back-up services required to provide appropriate services for the individual.

ENCOR is governed at the community level by five elected county commissioners, providing a direct link to parents, neighbours, employers and the public at large. There is also a well-organized and active parent advisory committee. The managerial system has public accountability; this facilitates constant improvements in service models, quality of care and opportunities for integration.

The Fairbanks, Alaska, Program

A pilot project was begun within the Fairbanks community utilizing the existing primary mental health agency (Rambow & Arnold, 1996). A partnership between mental health and developmental disabilities service providers was the goal of this project. By utilizing the existing agency in the community, the pilot project was provided with cost-effective administrative support and clinical supervision. A collaboration with integrated psychiatric care to prescribe and monitor any needed psychotropic medications was provided as well. A commitment was made to serve all those with developmental disabilities and mental health needs. Services are systematically designed to meet the individual needs of the client. Having a single/central comprehensive service plan outlining all of the services needed for a given individual is emphasized and safeguards against duplication of service. The model supports prevention and early intervention strategies.

Funding sources are combined from both the mental health and the developmental disabilities budgets. Clients' needs are met via an interdisciplinary team that is selected by the consumer. Individuals are directly involved in designing their services. In this model, the role of the clinician is expanded to include advocacy, case management, staff training, community relations and consultation. The clinician has the ability to offer long-term individual therapy rather than being limited to brief therapy or group models. Therapy is provided in community settings such as the consumers' homes, the local mental health centre, or in other providers' agencies. The continuum of services and supports that an individual receives is often co-ordinated by a case manager working in another agency.

The Community Specialist Psychiatric Service

In South East London, community interdisciplinary teams were formed by the National Health Service to facilitate the development of residential services for people with developmental disabilities and to support those already living in the community (Bouras, Brooks & Drummond, 1994). No clear plans for mental health and mental retardation needs were made until the Community Specialist Psychiatric Service (CSPS) was formed. CSPS integrated with general mental health services in order to access existing expertise and facilities while providing specialist input. CSPS's role is clinical and consultative. It provides assessment and treatment of adults with mental illness and developmental disabilities, management of behavioural problems, work with offenders, and treatment of epilepsy.

All referrals receive detailed assessment and are discussed at weekly community clinical meetings at which an intervention plan is formed. Types of treatment include home-based services, out-patient care, and in-patient psychiatric admission. Other services involve regular consultation and support to multidisciplinary community teams, social services, voluntary and private organizations, day centres, service managers, relatives and care staff. Training and workshops are also available.

The Queensland (Australia) Model

The Queensland Model began with the conducting of a survey on the nature and distribution of disruptive behaviour among the registered clients of the Intellectual Disability Services, which is the state agency for people with mental retardation in Queensland (Attwood & Joachin, 1994). The survey identified a range of factors that included overcrowding, lack of privacy, frustration stemming from poor communication skills, lack of stimulation, lack of attention and affection, poor interpersonal skills, institutionalization effects, and behaviours related to specific conditions.

A small working party was formed to provide recommendations on the prevention and management of seriously disruptive incidents. The recommendations were training programmes for all staff, protective actions to minimize injuries to staff, administrative review after each seriously disruptive incident, and strategies to reduce the risk of a similar incident occurring again. Due to the fact that staff and services span over 200 km, a 'train the trainer' approach was adopted.

Characteristics of community-based comprehensive services

Barriers to comprehensive community services for people with dual diagnosis

In most of the community projects described above, there were both conceptual and operational gulfs between mental health and developmental disabilities service systems. As a result, interagency communication was not well established and access to services across systems was limited. Reiss (1994) identified seven barriers to services for people with challenging behaviours. His list begins with a lack of community commitment to establishing special services, attributed to limited consumer advocacy, and a dearth of momentum-generating support from professional organizations. This lack of commitment may be at the top of a cascade that limits access to existing systems of services and supports, fiscal resources, and organizational resistance to change. It may confine dual diagnosis to a low status among priorities to be addressed by governments and private voluntary groups.

Overcoming the barriers: characteristics of an idealized model

Established by consensus

Despite the presence of barriers to comprehensive care and supports, most of the models described successfully implemented community-based programmes. These programmes have overcome the barriers by different measures. Taken together, however, one can summarize these measures in terms of an idealized model programme. A number of models emphasized the need for consensus among providers, individuals and funders in establishing a comprehensive service network for individuals with dual diagnosis. Unless all sectors of the community agree on the need for such services and supports, what ensues may not achieve credibility, or it may not gain access to all components of the service system with which interfaces are required. Facilitating a consensus can be achieved by bringing all stake-holders together to sanction the need for, and the characteristics of, the service programme before it is established (Davidson et al., 1989).

Establishing cross-system access

People with dual diagnosis and their families may be primarily served by one service system (e.g. the developmental disabilities system) and may not be known to other systems (the mental health or the social services system). For example, the initial presentation in the mental health system for such people may be when they appear at a psychiatric emergency room. If an acute psychiatric disorder requiring in-patient treatment cannot be diagnosed, the emergency room staff may only be able to provide temporary stabilization of the behavioural component of the individual's problem (Beasley et al., 1992). Yet, discharge to the original community setting may be complicated by an unwillingness of the developmental disabilities agency staff to accept the consumer's on-going behaviour problems, thus complicating the position (Marcos, Gil & Vasquez, 1986). Effective discharge planning may require a blending of resources and expertise through cross-system access and communication. This characteristic of co-ordinated, comprehensive, community-based mental health care for people with developmental disabilities is documented by the CSPS (Bouras & Drummond, 1989, 1990; Bouras, Kon & Drummond, 1993). Cross-system access may be enhanced by staff trusted by both mental health and developmental disabilities system personnel, who may act as an ombudsman.

Comprehensive interdisciplinary services

Challenging behaviours and mental disorders in people with developmental disabilities require an interdisciplinary approach by a team of professionals who can address both biomedical and environmental interventions, case management, and supports to families and consumers (Tufnell et al., 1985). The team should include members capable of consulting to generic service elements, including a psychiatric emergency department, an in-patient unit, a community mental health centre, a psychiatric day treatment programme, a developmental disabilities community residence or day treatment programme, or a sheltered workshop programme with equal facilities.

Community based with tertiary links

Long-term resolution of behavioural or psychiatric disorders in people with developmental disabilities requires community-based activities because most or all of the resources for habilitative and therapeutic services are community based. However, resolution of an acute crisis may require tertiary psychiatric or behavioural resources, often available only on a regional basis. Tertiary centres such as university hospitals may offer such resources, including in-patient acute psychiatric evaluation and treatment service, specialized ambulatory psychiatric service, emergency respite service, or emergency behaviour stabilization services.

Credibility

Credibility with providers in both developmental disabilities and mental health systems must be maintained in order to ensure cross-system access. The staff must be well trained and experienced in both developmental disabilities and mental health systems, and the programme must be structured to permit them easily to access and provide effective service in both systems. The administrative structure should promote the staff's role as credible brokers, and should not impose any regulatory or bureaucratic constraints that upset the balance between mental health and developmental disabilities systems. The service location will depend upon a consensus among the constituent stake-holders.

Direct funding

Beasley et al. (1992) have made the point that some elements of the idealized service must depend upon direct funding as third parties may not cover such services. Components such as crisis intervention, respite or public education may be too costly to remain viable in a fee-for-service or capitated system of reimbursement.

Conclusion

This chapter reviews a number of innovative model programmes that have been developed to achieve community-based mental health services for people with dual diagnosis. It is clear that the reported prevalence of dual diagnosis would suggest that, as institutional closures progress, such programmes will be necessary in all communities in which people with developmental disabilities will reside. The alternative to such programmes may be numerous failures of community integration due to lack of appropriate treatment and supports.

The models reviewed all fall short of achieving the idealized hypothetical mental health programme proposed. At the same time, there has never been a test of a hypothetical model community-based service addressing dual diagnosis. Of those models reported, very few data were available measuring their impact on consumers, families and service systems. The field would profit from more research that ascertains outcomes following intervention in any of these models.

There is also a need for the dissemination of model programme ideas that, as yet, have not been published. The authors are aware of numerous local efforts to establish and operate community-based programmes for people with dual diagnosis for which no literature exists.

Finally, the field will advance only if comparative studies are undertaken that evaluate side by side the effectiveness of interdisciplinary, integrated community models and traditional mental health alternatives. It is on the basis of such comparisons that the rationale for change will be identified.

Acknowledgements

The preparation of this chapter was supported by a UAP Core grant to the University of Rochester from the US Administration on Developmental Disabilities. Dr Morris's participation was supported by a LEND grant to the University of Rochester from the Maternal and Child Health Bureau, US Public Health Service.

References

Antonacci, D.J., Hurley, G., Johnson, G., Rota, J. & White, S. (1996). Crisis prevention and community support for individuals who are dually diagnosed: a model programme for open systems consultation. In *Conference proceedings of the National Association for the Dually Diagnosed – Through the Lifespan*, ed. R. Friedlander & D. Sobsey, pp. 137–41. November 13–16, Kingston, NY: National Association for the Dually Diagnosed.

Attwood, T. & Joachin, R. (1994). The prevention and management of seriously disruptive behavior in Australia. In *Mental Health in Mental Retardation: Recent Advances and Practices*, ed. N. Bouras, pp. 365–74. Cambridge: Cambridge University Press.

Beasley, J., Kroll, J. & Sovner, R. (1992). Community-based crisis mental health services for persons with developmental disabilities: The S.T.A.R.T model. *The Habilitative Mental Healthcare Newsletter*, 11 (9), 55–7.

Borthwick, S. (1988). Maladaptive behavior among the mentally retarded: the need for reliable data. In *Mental Retardation and Mental Health: Classification, Diagnosis, Treatment Services*, ed. J. Stark, F. Menolascino, M. Albarelli & V. Gray, pp. 30–40. New York: Springer-Verlag.

Bouras, N., Brooks, D. & Drummond, K. (1994). Community psychiatric services for people with mental retardation. In *Mental Health in Mental Retardation Recent Advances and Practices*, ed. N. Bouras, pp. 293–9. Cambridge: Cambridge University Press.

Bouras, N. & Drummond, C. (1989). Community psychiatric service in mental handicap. *Health Trend*, **21**, 72.

(1990). Diagnostic and treatment issues for adults in community care. In *Treatment of Mental Illness and Behavior Disorder in the Mentally Retarded*, ed. A. Dosen, A. Van Gennep & G. Zwanikken, pp. 479–84. Proceedings of the International Congress, May 3–4. Amsterdam: Logon Publications.

Bouras, N., Kon, Y. & Drummond, C. (1993). Medical and psychiatric needs of adults with a mental handicap. *Journal of Intellectual Disability Research*, **37**, 177–82.

Bruininks, R., Hill, B. & Morreau, L. (1988). Prevalence and implications of maladaptive behaviors and dual diagnosis in residential and other service programmes. In *Mental Retardation and Mental Health: Classification, Diagnosis, Treatment Services*, ed. J. Stark, F. Menolascino, M. Albarelli & V. Gray, pp. 3–29. New York: Springer-Verlag.

Bruininks, R., Rotegard, L., Lakin, K. & Hill, B. (1987). Epidemiology of mental retardation and trends in residential services in the United States. In *Living Environments and Mental Retardation*, ed. S. Landesman & P. Veitze, pp. 17–42. Washington, DC: American Association on Mental Retardation.

Crawford, J., Aiello, J. & Thompson, D. (1979). Deinstitutionalization and community placement: clinical and environmental factors. *Mental Retardation*, **17**, 59–63.

Davidson, P., Peloquin, L.J., Salzman, L., Zielinski, S., Gross, M. & Roberts, K. (1989). Planning and implementing comprehensive crisis intervention for people with developmental disabilities. In *Strengthening Families: New Directions in Providing Services to People with Developmental Disabilities and Their Families*, ed. J. Levy, P. Levy & B. Nivis, pp. 203–10. New York: YAI Press.

Davidson, P.W., Cain, N.N., Sloane-Reeves, J.E. et al. (1995). Crisis intervention for community-based individuals with developmental disabilities and behavioral and psychiatric disorders. *Mental Retardation*, **33**(1), 21–30.

Hill, B. & Bruininks, R. (1984). Maladaptive behavior of mentally retarded people in residential facilities. *American Journal of Mental Deficiency*, **88**, 380–7.

Landsberg, G., Fletcher, F. & Maxwell, T. (1987). Developing a comprehensive community care system for the mentally ill/mentally retarded. *Community Mental Health Journal*, **23**(2), pp. 137–42.

Marcos, L., Gil, R. & Vasquez, K. (1986). Who will treat psychiatrically disturbed developmentally disabled patients? A health care nightmare. *Hospital and Community Psychiatry*, **37**(2), 171–4.

Menolascino, F. (1989). Model services for treatment/management of the mentally retarded-mentally ill. *Community Mental Health Journal*, **25**(2), 145–55.

Menolascino, F.J. (1994). Services for people with dual diagnosis in the USA. In *Mental Health in Mental Retardation Recent Advances and Practices*, ed. N. Bouras, pp. 343–52. Cambridge: Cambridge University Press.

Pagel, S.E. & Whitling, C.A. (1978). Readmissions to a state hospital for mentally retarded persons: reasons for community placement failure. *Mental Retardation*, **16**, 164–6.

Parkhurst, R. (1984). Need assessment and service planning for mentally retarded-mentally ill persons. In *Handbook of Mental Illness in the Mentally*

Retarded, ed. F.J. Menolascino & J.A. Stark, pp. 83–91. New York: Plenum Press.

Puddephatt, A. & Sussman, S. (1994). Developing services in Canada: Ontario vignettes. In *Mental Health in Mental Retardation Recent Advances and Practices*, ed. N. Bouras, pp. 353–64. Cambridge: Cambridge University Press.

Rambow, T.R. & Arnold, M. (1996). Individualized/homogenized/cost effective service model: 'It's time for a professional awakening'. *NADD Newsletter*, **13** (6), 1–4.

Reiss, S. (1990). Prevalence of dual diagnosis in community-based day programmes in the Chicago metropolitan area. *American Journal of Mental Retardation*, **94** (6), 578–85.

(1994). *Handbook of Challenging Behaviors: Mental Health Aspects of Mental Retardation.* Worthington, OH: IDS Publishing Corporation.

Russell, A.T. & Tanguay, P.E. (1981). Mental illness and mental retardation: cause or coincidence. *American Journal of Mental Deficiency*, **85**, 570–4.

Schalock, R.L. & Keith, K.D. (1993). *Quality of Life Questionnaire Manual.* Worthington, OH: IDS Publishing Corporation.

Smull, M.W., Fabian, E.S. & Chanteau, F.B. (1994). Value-based programming for the dually diagnosed the Rock Creek model. In *Handbook of Mental Illness in the Mentally Retarded*, ed. F.J. Menolascino & J.A. Stark, pp. 235–48. New York: Plenum Press.

Tufnell, G., Bouras, N., Watson, J. & Brough, D. (1985). Home assessment and treatment in a community psychiatric service. *Acta Psychiatrica Scandianvia*, **72**, 20–8.

Woodward, H.L. (1993). One community's response to the multi-system service needs of individuals with mental illness and developmental disabilities. *Community Mental Health Journal*, **29** (4), pp. 347–59.

22 Support service systems for people with dual diagnosis in the USA

ROBERT J. FLETCHER, JOAN BEASLEY AND JOHN W. JACOBSON

Introduction

During the past three decades, there has been a dramatic shift in policy from institutional care to a community-based service system in the USA (Finch, 1985; Gettings, 1988; Fletcher & Menolascino, 1989; Reiss, 1994). State and federal legislation, litigation and judicial decisions, and advances in treatment methods have shaped social policy towards the development of community-based individualized programmes, to provide an array of interventions and support services to people with mental retardation who were or were not previously institutionalized. This social policy shift has highlighted the challenges in the service delivery systems for people with a dual diagnosis of mental retardation and mental illness.

In reviewing and assessing community, residential and vocational service developments for people with dual diagnosis in the USA, it is important to recognise that successful development requires a comprehensive and collaborative service structure. In spite of many innovative developments in service delivery for people with disabilities, success for people with dual diagnosis has lagged behind that for other groups. This is a result of the continued existence of structural barriers, created in part as a result of existing policies and, in some cases, divergent policy development in the mental health and mental retardation fields.

This chapter addresses the policy issues that have stimulated planning initiatives in residential and vocational service delivery. The state of the art in programme planning takes into account the importance of accessible, appropriate and accountable services that provide for choice, productivity and integration.

Policy issues affecting service development

In the USA, in the 1960s and into the 1970s, the development of community services was primarily driven by federal financing initiatives (Jacobson & Schwartz, 1991). Programmes, funding and the bureaucracies that regulated services and eligibility were developed for specific groups of people (Fletcher, 1988; Gettings, 1988; Reiss, 1994). With few exceptions in the USA, state mental retardation systems have an administrative framework, funding sources, regulations, treatment approaches, admission criteria and methods of service delivery, separate from those of the mental health service system (Menolascino & McCann, 1983; Gettings, 1988; Reiss, 1994). Access to either community-based service system is generally based on diagnostic criteria of either a psychiatric disorder or a developmental disability (Fletcher, 1993a).

The presence of separate service structures has important consequences for people who need both types of services, creating jurisdictional challenges for people with mental retardation and mental health needs (Reiss, 1994). In many systems, there is a lack of clearly articulated policy for addressing the specific needs of people diagnosed with mental retardation and mental illness (Fletcher, 1993a). The result has been a diffusion of responsibility, resulting in a lack of services and, when services are available, fragmentation of service and supports (Boggs, 1988; Leismer, 1989).

One training and implementation strategy that has been proposed to alleviate these problems involves the delivery of mental health services regardless of other disability considerations (Szymanski & Grossman, 1984). More generally, it has been proposed that to enable the dual-diagnosed population to benefit from the technologies found in both service systems, co-operative policy initiatives should be developed, fostering clinical integration, model flexibility, and consistency in service delivery (Menolascino & Stark, 1984; Fletcher, 1993b; Rambow & Arnold, 1996).

Although the creation of a specialized system to address the mental health service needs of people with mental retardation is one possible policy initiative, a discrete system of this type presents its own set of dilemmas. There is currently sufficient technology to address the complex needs of people with a dual diagnosis; existing service structures have the essential components required to provide a full array of community services and supports for people with mental retardation and mental health needs. The fundamental issue is the ability to transcend bureaucratic boundaries in order to deliver services and supports with a focus on better definitions of service effectiveness (Beasley, 1997a). In order to accomplish this, there is a need for a comprehensive approach to diagnosis and treatment planning, service delivery and development, crisis intervention, personnel training in the mental health and mental retardation fields, and improved accountability through research to test current assumptions (Reiss, Levitan & McNally, 1982).

In service planning for individuals with dual diagnosis, a policy that fosters structural linkages between the mental health and mental retardation systems can be developed. This may require the elimination of eligibility based on the concept of a primary diagnosis or disability. The concept of dual diagnosis was introduced by Frank Menolascino as an alternative to the concept of primary versus secondary disabilities (Reiss, 1994). Services would be provided based on need rather than on the existence of a primary diagnosis, such as mental illness or mental retardation. Services can be delivered in the context of two co-existing disabilities allowing for more appropriate treatment and support service planning and development (Reiss, 1994). The resulting policy would be to create a partnership between the mental health and mental retardation service structures to ensure responsive supports and treatments for previously underserved or mis-served groups of individuals (Rambow & Arnold, 1996).

Integrated, collaborative policy can form the basis of a cross-boundary, interdisciplinary, team approach that uses both prevention and proactive strategies to provide a holistic approach to services and support systems (MARC Mental Health Committee, 1995). Community-based services such as assessment, treatment, housing, respite, vocational and day programmes, as well as generic community support systems, may be included in service development (MARC Mental Health Committee, 1995). A 'clinical safety net', which incorporates the use of preventative services as well as specialized back-up supports providing assessment, treatment, training or in-patient care for people with complex service needs, may be essential to a comprehensive community approach (Beasley, Kroll & Sovner 1992; Woodward, 1993). Further, the utilization of a cross-system team approach (i.e. across mental health and retardation systems) in the development of needed services can promote a co-ordinated, integrated, comprehensive method of addressing service needs for people with a dual diagnosis (Rambow & Arnold, 1996).

In the case of housing and vocational accommodation for people with dual diagnosis, there may also be compelling reasons for re-organizing services around the person. This may entail a variety of specialist teams comprised of trained and qualified staff providing clinical services as and when required (Burchard, Atkins & Burchard, 1996).

Policy initiatives in the USA (county, community, or provider agency)

Policy planning can take place on the national, state or local level. Recent initiatives on the state and local levels offer the best hope for improvements in policy regarding service structure and planning on behalf of people with dual diagnosis. In addition to the targeted dual diagnosis initiatives mentioned below, policy planning can also be potentially informed by organizational development and supported housing innovations in community psychiatric rehabilitation services (Carling, 1992; Nagy & Gates, 1992).

At the national level, there have been several attempts to achieve consensus on policy and to begin to set a national agenda. In 1975, the National

Institute of Child Health and Human Development (NICHD) and the National Institute for Mental Health (NIMH) convened an advisory group that made specific recommendations to improve research, training and services in relation to the mental health aspects of mental retardation (Tarjan et al.,1977). The recommendations of this group were not adopted. Shortly thereafter, in 1978, the Liaison Task Panel on Mental Retardation of the President's Commission on Mental Health (PCMH) reported that neither the mental health nor the mental retardation systems had taken responsibility for services for people with both mental illness and mental retardation (President's Commission on Mental Health, 1978). However, no national planning initiatives to respond to the needs of this population were formulated by that panel.

In 1985, the President's Committee on Mental Retardation (PCMR), along with other federal agencies, sponsored the National Strategy Conference on Mental Retardation and Mental Health in Washington, DC. The purpose of this conference was to bring together the nation's leadership in the areas of mental retardation and mental health in order to delineate the state of the art in relation to diagnosis, care and treatment, as well as to chart a national course for the support and integration of people with these disabilities (Stark et al., 1988). Although significant themes emerged and service delivery systems were critically analysed, no national agenda was implemented.

National initiatives have been limited to needs' assessment and the review of service models, and nationally accepted demonstration programmes have not been provided. However, there have been several important state-initiated projects in which developmental disabilities service and mental health service providers collaborated and worked co-operatively together (Rambow & Arnold, 1996; see also Chapter 21).

Effective planning for services and supports for people with dual diagnosis has occurred frequently at the local level. A local-level task force model can be useful in changing attitudes and formulating planning initiatives that respond to the needs of people with mental illness and mental retardation (Fletcher, 1993b). The stake-holders in the task force model should represent both mental health and mental retardation systems and include social welfare, protective services, and educational or vocational services, as well as consumers, advocates and parents (Fletcher, 1988). For example, Benson and Hunter (1993) have articulated specific recommendations for how mental health and mental retardation systems could co-operate and respond to the needs of people with dual diagnosis based on the work of the 'Metro-Area Dual Diagnosis Task Force' for the Chicago metropolitan area. As another example, Fletcher (1988) reported on the Ulster County (New York) systems model of planning for a local comprehensive service system utilizing the mental health service system to respond to the individual needs of people with a dual diagnosis.

Both administrative experience and the nature of co-ordinative initiatives indicate that the lack of a structural response by the service system to meet the needs of people with dual diagnosis has resulted in reduced community service and community living opportunities. In spite of positive developments in housing and vocational training and employment, people with dual diagnosis (as well as others with more severe disabilities) have not received the same access to newer habilitative service models as those who are less severely impaired (Mank, 1994). Planning and development efforts continue to be needed in order to improve the degree of consistency with which community living opportunities are made available across all service recipient populations, regardless of disability.

Factors that contribute to the planning and development of service options for people with dual diagnosis

Since the beginnings of the de-institutionalization movement in the early 1960s, some residential and vocational programme development for people with dual diagnosis has evolved. For example, early attempts at housing people with dual diagnosis in the community failed. In fact, studies show that people with dual diagnosis have been at greater risk of return to institutional living, in spite of policy to the contrary, than their counterparts with mental retardation who are not dually diagnosed with mental illness (Kearney & Smull, 1992). State-of-the-art programme models offer some guidance to policy planners as they seek to develop effective housing options for people with dual diagnosis.

Guiding principles for successful service development and implementation

1. Services designed to be effective in accomplishing established goals. Access, appropriateness and accountability are essential to the development of an effective service system (Beasley, 1997a). In the case of residential planning, housing must be located in an acceptable community setting that offers opportunities for community integration (access); it must be designed to provide services and supports to meet the needs and desires of the person residing in the setting (appropriate); and it must provide an affordable, safe and comfortable setting (accountable). Vocational services should offer work in integrated settings in a person's community (access), opportunities and supports that are manageable and productive for the worker and the workplace (appropriate), and adequate salary compensation (accountable).
2. Co-ordination of provided services. A co-ordinated service structure must include mechanisms for communication, collaboration and continuity of service provision (Leroy, 1997). In the case of housing and vocational development, services can and should be part of a co-ordinated community

integration and rehabilitation effort. Providers should be able to collabo-
rate with each other in increasing the system's ability to provide for the
needs of the person being served in the least restrictive manner possible.

3. **A comprehensive array of services must be available.** In addition to vocational and housing services for people with dual diagnosis, planning
   should also encompass clinical treatment, applied behaviour analysis, psychiatry and psychopharmacology (Phadt, 1996). Services must be designed
   to accommodate the individual needs of people who are being served and
   changes in these needs, and they must be interconnected with the other
   services in which the person participates.

Integrated employment and vocational services

During the past ten years, there have been significant changes in
employment and vocational services for people with disabilities in the USA
(Rusch, Chadsey-Rusch & Johnson, 1991; Rusch et al., 1992; Johnson &
Rusch, 1994). Many people with disabilities have moved over the course of
the past decade from placement in traditional workshop settings to integrated support employment. Supported employment, a systemic methodology for achieving and maintaining successful paid employment for people
with disabilities through the provision of workplace supports, has emerged
as a growing practice. Research conducted in typical workplaces has indicated that people with severe disabilities can benefit socially, vocationally
and financially from, and be productive in, supported employment situations (Vogelsberg, 1986; Ellis et al., 1990).

Johnson and Rusch (1994) outlined four basic assumptions underlying
supported employment services. First, an effective way to prepare for
working is to work in actual employment situations. Second, integration is a
hallmark of supported employment and a right and responsibility for individuals with disabilities. Third, people with disabilities have a right to be paid
a decent wage. Fourth, individuals with disabilities are capable of achieving
successful employment, given the proper types and ranges of support. The
extent that people with dual diagnosis are engaged in supported employment and their ability to maintain stable work have not yet been fully ascertained. However, in comparison to other supported workers, the types of job
coach, situational and procedural supports that are required for many
people with dual diagnosis will usually be more diverse, extended in duration, or entail specific interventions (Jacobson, 1996).

Several supported placement models have emerged. These are individual,
enclave, work crew and entrepreneurial approaches (Rusch & Hughes, 1990).
The individual model generally involves one person or several people at a
work site with the support of a job coach or employment specialist. This
model often involves a planned fading of support by the job coach as the
employee's job performance increases, and natural supports are expected to

strengthen, leading to increased integration and independence. In an important variation of individual placement – intensive individual placement – job coach, adjustment, prosthetic and social supports may be provided for extended periods of time, or with the expectation that supports may continue indefinitely. Such may be the case for those people with dual diagnosis who manifest particular social behaviours or self-control difficulties that interfere with their own productivity or that of co-workers.

The other models of placement are essentially group arrangements. The enclave model entails several workers doing the same job, with assistance as needed from a job coach, and may consist of a specific work site within a larger commercial enterprise. In a work crew model, several employees are transported to various locations to complete subcontract work. In the entrepreneurial model, workers are employed by companies to provide a specific task or service. Employees are provided by an agency to the company, which subcontracts with the sponsoring agency. In all of these models of integrated employment, supervision, training and support are provided by the job coach for as much time as needed, but in the least amount necessary. The purpose is to assist the person with a disability, in a natural work environment, to promote integration, productivity and independence through work.

Correspondingly, it may be valuable to organize individual planning for supported work around these three primary goals as touchstones, with a view to compensatory or supportive interventions to maintain effective work performance. Effective supported work provision must be responsive to employers' expectations, and for this reason productivity is an especially important criterion for intermediate and long-term retention in the workplace.

Research findings indicate that the majority of supported employment placements have been in the service sector (Shafer, Revell & Isbister, 1991), consistent with shifts towards entry and low skills jobs in the national employment market. Individual placement (as opposed to work crew participation) has had the greatest positive effect on wages (Thompson, Powers & Houchard, 1992), and supported employment has enhanced quality-of-life outcomes for supported workers (McCaughrin et al., 1993).

Although there is an acceptance in society that people with mild levels of disabilities can be gainfully employed, traditional views of the capabilities of people with severe disabilities continue to be major obstacles to their access to the most progressive contemporary, educational and rehabilitation practices (Johnson & Rusch, 1990). Historically, people with severe and complex disabilities have not been considered to be employable, which also appears to be the case today. The number of people with disabilities engaged in supported work and funding for supported employment models have increased dramatically, but participation by people with severe or multiple disabilities has lagged behind that of people with less severe disabilities (Schalock et al., 1993).

A large proportion of funding for vocational services continues to support congregate sheltered workshops (McGaughey et al., 1991), offering a range of services, including vocational training assessment and evaluation, training in activities of daily living, and sheltered employment. These findings in supported employment may indicate that sheltered workshops may become segregated vocational training sites for people with multiple and/or severe disabilities. However, research has indicated that although some rehabilitation goals (i.e. in terms of skill development) may be achieved in sheltered work settings, the outcomes are frequently poor, including low, non-competitive rates of pay, and dissatisfaction among consumers and providers of services (Bellamy et al., 1988).

People with dual diagnosis may be under-represented in both the sheltered and the supported employment work forces. The results of a 1994 study in 42 states of people with mental illness or mental retardation receiving supported employment services, showed that people with mild mental retardation represented 62.8 per cent of supported workers, but that only 22.2 per cent of the supported employment work force had severe mental illness (Revell et al., 1994). In another study of 643 programmes throughout the U.SA, 83 per cent of the workers had mild to moderate mental retardation, but only 8 per cent were categorized as having 'emotional problems' (Schalock et.al., 1993). Neither study addressed dual diagnosis directly, but the findings indicate that individuals with emotional and/or behavioural difficulties are under-represented in progressive vocational options, especially people who also have multiple or severe problems.

Another study, that did measure participation of people with dual diagnosis, found that dual diagnosis was reported in 16 per cent of supported workers with developmental disabilities in one state's vocational training work force. These rates are lower than expected, indicating that the presence of mental illness may be a factor that interferes with obtaining and maintaining supported work for people with mental retardation and mental health needs (Jacobson, 1996). The findings show that difficulties associated with behaviour that is perceived as difficult to manage may affect opportunities for entry into supported work, and longevity in supported work settings (Jacobson, 1996). These data indicate that between 25 per cent and 33 per cent of sheltered workers are reported to be unable to make the transition to supported work due to behaviour problems.

Difficulties in performance attributed to behaviour problems can be adequately addressed if accessible and appropriate assessment and treatment interventions are utilised, and training is provided to support staff to help manage difficulties. In general, however, sheltered work settings lack the appropriate resources and expertise to alleviate mental health problems. As a consequence, only a selected proportion of individuals with dual diagnosis without major problems is likely to be served in sheltered work and to progress to supported work. As contemporary funding and individual planning innovations permit greater flexibility in designing personal supports, it is becoming possible to blend habilitative services and supported work on an individual basis, and to assure that needed clinical services are made available to sheltered workers. The capacity to implement these changes in organizational structures and resource use should permit provider agencies more readily to achieve integrated supported work involvements for people with dual diagnosis.

There are very few programmes in the USA utilizing integrated clinical and training approaches to improve support services. One such model uses a community mental health centre that employs mental health/mental retardation practitioners who provide outreach services in vocational environments (Fletcher, 1988). Another model includes vocational rehabilitation counselling techniques to support adults with mental retardation (Hurley, 1996). A third noteworthy model trains vocational staff in methods to assist people with dual diagnosis in the development of proper social and coping skills, in order to enhance job performance (Hurley, 1996).

Issues in residential services development

The following are some of the main principles to be considered in developing residential services for people with dual diagnosis.

1. **The importance of tenant input in housing development**. This is an essential factor and it is often overlooked in the planning of residential services (Drake & Noordys, 1994). Unfortunately, clinical or treatment considerations are often used as the main criteria in residential design and placements (Beasley, 1997a).

   Case example

   Sally was a 21-year-old female with a background of aggression and non-compliance in the community residential setting in which she had lived since the age of 16. Sally was diagnosed with paranoid schizophrenia and mild mental retardation, which disrupted her ability to interact with others. She had been placed in a high staff-to-resident ratio apartment programme for four women who were considered to have similar needs. Not long after being placed, some of Sally's past behaviours recurred and she became verbally abusive and disturbed, throwing objects and slamming doors. In addition, she became withdrawn, refusing to leave her room for long periods of time and causing a great deal of concern about her well-being. When she was willing to communicate, Sally would simply say that she was not leaving her room until she got her own apartment. At first her support staff found this behaviour to be 'manipulative' and 'inappropriate', but after some time and consultation, they explored the possibility of helping Sally to move into her own apartment. Several months later, Sally was able to find her own apartment with assistance, and staff provide services to her when they are needed. Sally continues to be somewhat isolated and anxious, but she has been complying with treatment and goes to work each day, and she allows contact with support staff on a daily basis. Sally has the skills to care for herself, and her self-esteem has improved immensely. She no longer becomes disturbed and verbally abusive, as she did in other residential settings.

2. **How many people should live together.** A number of community residential models has been designed for people with mental retardation, including those with dual diagnosis (Braddock & Mitchell, 1992). Since the development of residential programmes in the 1970s and 1980s, intermediate care facilities for people with mental retardation, funded through federal, state and local Medicaid, have become the most prevalent residential prototype. Large, 16-plus-person facilities continue to be the prevalent residential model, housing 47.5 per cent of the total residential service recipient population as of 1992 (Braddock & Mitchell, 1992). Since that time, an increasing number of small residential services has been developed for four or fewer people with mental retardation to live together.

Although the intermediate care facilities have offered the opportunity for people with mental retardation to dwell in the community, the operational practices of these settings have continued to reflect the legacy of the types of segregated specialized care provided by institutional settings (Bradley, 1994). In recent years, revised regulations for these facilities have redirected priorities for outcomes on social and lifestyle issues. As alternative funding sources, accompanied by less detailed regulatory content, have become widely available, the impetus to focus on individualized outcomes in group living has increased. Nonetheless, there remain concerns that group living, by its nature, may inhibit the development of more individual and tailored lifestyle support. Many argue for smaller, more individualized residential programming that creates opportunities for inclusion and integration (Hill et al., 1989; Lakin et al., 1992; Abery & Fahnestock, 1994; Bradley, 1994). At minimum, it has become clear that people need private living space and the opportunity to be alone when desired.

During the early 1990s, the Greater Lynn Mental Health and Retardation Association (MHRA) in Massachusetts converted all but one of its apartment programmes of four or more individuals with dual diagnosis into one-person and two-person programmes (Beasley, 1996). These changes were made in response to high mental health hospitalization rates and failed placements. Since that time, all new programme development has been limited to smaller settings, and the rate of successful housing stability has improved dramatically. For people with dual diagnosis, it appears that smaller, less stimulating settings may offer the greatest opportunities for success. The Greater Lynn MHRA, as a single agency, is a provider of both mental health and mental retardation services and, prior to the development of these smaller housing options, it had the organizational capability to deploy mental health services to support people with dual diagnosis living in group homes. Despite this capability, hospitalization rates and residential instability occurred frequently. Provider agencies that do not contract to provide both mental health and mental retardation services may be even more prone to the instability of group living for people with dual diagnosis.

3. **The use of staffing to solve social problems.** The inability of service delivery systems to adapt to the needs of individuals can sometimes be recast as the responsibility of the individual, who is seen as putting too many demands on the system (Beasley & Kroll, 1992). This can be observed in several residential programmes for people with dual diagnosis, in which many believe that the solution to problems is to increase staffing levels. In practice, this is costly and can also become restrictive. Problem behaviours are viewed as being part of the individual's profile. This may not be the case. In some cases, problem behaviour is a way of communicating issues that stem from the nature of the residential environment itself. When problem behaviours arise, they may be viewed as potentially or probably unresponsive to treatment, characteristic of the person's functioning, and likely to persist indefinitely or episodically. In most instances, whereas recurrence of problem behaviours remains an important clinical concern, and one that should be addressed in tailoring clinical intervention, palliative, ameliorative or curative alternatives are available to address most problem behaviours or adjustment problems that are socially significant in nature (Jacobson, 1996).

4. **Linkages with day and other services.** Residential planning for housing requires a collaborative effort between all parties involved in service delivery. For people with dual diagnosis, services often may be co-ordinated amongst multiple providers, including crisis prevention and intervention services, in order to ensure that residential provisions are successful (Beasley & Kroll, 1992; Woodward, 1993). Residential programmes without linkages with other agencies and providers are vulnerable to instability when problems and crises occur.

5. **Socialization with friends, family and familiar community.** Residential providers need to support and encourage individuals to maintain and build natural relationships with friends, co-workers, relatives and other community members. These are very important relationships and should be supported based on the service user's wishes.

6. **The need for qualified and properly paid staff.** Many residential programmes are designed to provide care for people who live in the community that is less expensive than congregate care. As a result, staff may be inexperienced, untrained and overworked, and they often receive lower wages than their counterparts who work in institutional settings. Employment practices for residential settings are often no different from those for large institutions, in spite of the fact that the residence is intended to be the service user's *home*. Staff working in a person's home should be acceptable to the person being supported. In addition, staff need to be valued and given the opportunity to contribute to plans for enhancing the user's skills.

7. **Flexibility in the daily expectations of residents.** One of the major problems with traditional community residential settings for people with dual diagnosis has been that these settings have offered little flexibility in daily service provision schedules, and daily routines, resulting in failed placements. Inflexible staffing patterns, constraints upon choice associated with

group living, and requirements for participation in congregate or non-pre-
ferred day programmes are but a few of the expectations that may result in
difficulties.

The practice of placing people in available residential spaces rather than
considering the compatibility of a person's needs and living environment has
often resulted in failed placements. Successful community placement
requires a degree of flexibility in the day-to-day support programme. This is
probably one of the main reasons why people with dual diagnosis have often
been considered 'too difficult' to be supported in community living situations.

State of the art housing programmes

Although many still live in group home settings, smaller, more individualized settings are now the trend in new community residential service
design. Sometimes called supported housing, residential programme development now focuses on individually designed programmes for people in
which supports in daily living are provided in the person's own apartment
(Felce & Perry, 1995), and where the person may live with one or several
room-mates. Unlike large group settings, the person living in a supported
living setting often owns or co-owns furnishings, chooses his or her room-
mates (and whether or not to have one), and takes an active role in the hiring
of support staff. Some supported living settings offer 'foster families',
wherein a person moves into a home and lives with a family in the community. Another option is that a couple or family may live in the home of the
person with a disability and provide companionship and support services in
exchange for housing and salaried compensation. In most cases, professional
or clinical services associated with mental health care and rehabilitation are
provided in community settings outside of the person's home. However,
staffing assignments, complements and expertise are developed in relation
to the person's preferences and needs, and may include the capability to
provide clinical supports or treatment in the housing situation if required.

The use of community support services

The availability of community support services also enhances opportunities for successful community housing for people with dual diagnosis, as
well as vocational training and job development success. For example, in
some locations, both in-home and out-of-home respite is available so that
people may get a break from each other if needed, or more intensive services
can be provided during periods of difficulty in order to avoid hospitalization
(Davidson et. al., 1995). In such an approach, a community support team
may provide the expertise and resources needed to support an individual
and his or her residential provider in times of difficulty. This may include

availability for 24 hours a day, combined with resources to fill in existing service delivery gaps when necessary (Beasley et al., 1992).

The need for further research

Over the past 15 years, the focus of research for people diagnosed with mental retardation and mental illness has been on epidemiology, assessment and, to a lesser degree, on programme operation and review. Programme evaluation has been almost non-existent in the professional literature. Thus far, the few studies that have been published are based on single and particular programme models (Fletcher, 1988; Reiss, 1988; see also Chapters 20 and 21). There are no multisite cross-sectional or longitudinal studies that sample a diversity of clinical activities or organizational approaches in a comprehensive manner (Jacobson, 1996). Programme evaluation (as well as policy formulation) has not moved substantially forward due to the lack of an impetus to field comparative and longitudinal demonstrations of services and supports, as well as to the failure to bring to bear the range of contemporary clinical technologies that are already in hand (Jacobson, 1996).

There is a need to conduct research to identify the extent to which individualized housing and vocational services, as typically provided, address both shared and disparate needs of people with dual diagnosis. Further, research is needed to help inform practitioners and support personnel about the primary skills and supports that are associated with the stability of housing and long-term residence in preferred housing situations. Finally, demonstration and technology transfer projects are needed to assess the relative effects, success in general and specific terms, and outcomes for people with dual diagnosis of service and support arrangements that are predominantly organized along the lines of progressive mental health or developmental disabilities services, in order to suggest organizational features of successful provider agencies.

Conclusion

Current policy directions point to the development of smaller, supported living settings as an alternative to the larger group living models of the last two decades. In addition to empowering individuals with dual diagnosis, smaller settings, organized to respond to a wide range of needs particular to one or a few people, appear to offer the best environment for the prevention of behavioural difficulties that have jeopardized community living situations in the past. However, no one model will necessarily meet the needs of all individuals with dual diagnosis. Some people may become isolated and lonely in one-person or two-person settings, or have difficulties that cannot be managed in housing in which additional staff or clinical support is not readily available. Some people may simply prefer to live in a supervised group living situation rather than in supported living, and they should be given the opportunity to live in a place in which they prefer to live.

Residential services should include a full range of alternatives to enhance an individual's capacity for community living. The individual receiving residential services should be allowed to have as much comfort, ownership and autonomy as possible. Although group homes remain the most prevalent residential service provided, the trend is to develop much smaller, individualized settings.

As an alternative to residential group homes that often provide a diverse array of needed services, it is recommended that residential programme design develop cost-effective, more individualized housing for service recipients. Unlike the intermediate care facilities for people with mental retardation, where services are comprehensive and facility based, there may be value to a housing development focus on individual's basic needs and desires and the provision of clinical support outside of the home itself. When this occurs, housing can offer a wide range of options for individuals, and maximize opportunities for community integration and personal independence. As an alternative to clinical treatment provided in-house, community support services should work in collaboration with residential providers to provide clinical support and a safety net when difficulties arise. However, individualization also recognizes that when in-house clinical supports are required, the organizational flexibility to provide such supports should be present.

Current policy directions also point towards greater individualization in vocational and lifestyle options. For people with dual diagnosis, the feasibility of persistent community presence and the longevity of supported or integrated vocational situations are greatly influenced by the individualization and flexibility of the support process and the available clinical and support skills (Bouras, Holt & Gravestock, 1995). As in the development of appropriate residential supports, the benefits of day, vocational and therapeutic activities, as well as social and community presence, will be greatly influenced by the capability of organizations and clinicians to provide timely, individually responsive, and minimally restrictive, but clinically sufficient and appropriate, direct staff support and therapeutic services. The delivery of supports and services in this manner represents one of the most important challenges to organizational and clinical effectiveness in services for people with dual diagnosis today.

References

Abery, B.H. & Fahnestock, M. (1994). Enhancing the social inclusion of people with developmental disabilities. In *Challenges for a Service System in Transition: Ensuring Quality Community Experiences for People with Developmental Disabilities,* ed. M.F. Hayden & B.H. Abery, pp. 83–120. Baltimore: Paul H. Brookes.

Beasley, J. (1996). Residential models. Paper presented at the 13th Annual NADD Conference, Vancouver, BC.

(1997a). Factors which contribute to planning and development of housing options for individuals with dual diagnosis (MI/MR). *Habilitative Mental Healthcare Newsletter*, **16** (5), 89–93.

(1997b). The three A's in policy development to promote effective mental healthcare for people with developmental disabilities. *Habilitative Mental Healthcare Newsletter*, **16**(2), 31–3.

Beasley, J. & Kroll, J. (1992). Who is in crisis, the consumer or the system? *NADD Newsletter*, **9**(6), 1–5.

Beasley, J., Kroll, J. & Sovner, R. (1992). Community-based crisis mental health services for people with developmental disabilities: the START model. *Habilitative Mental Healthcare Newsletter*, **11**(9), 55–7.

Bellamy, G.T., Rhodes, L.E., Mank, D.M. & Albin, J.M. (1988). Strategies for change in facility based programmes. In *Supported Employment: a Community Implementation Guide* pp. 139–50. Baltimore: Paul H. Brookes

Benson, B.A. & Hunter, R.H. (1993). Summary recommendations of the Metro-Area Dual Diagnosis Task Group. Unpublished report to the Illinois Department of Mental Health and Developmental Disabilities.

Boggs, E.M. (1988). The role of legislation. In *Mental Retardation and Mental Health Classification, Diagnosis, Treatment, Services,* ed. J.A. Stark, F.J. Menolascino, M.H. Albarelli & V.C. Gray, pp. 317–25. New York: Springer-Verlag.

Bouras, N., Holt, G. & Gravestock, S. (1995). Community care for people with learning disabilities: deficits and future plans. *Psychiatric Bulletin*, **19**, pp. 134–7.

Braddock, D. & Mitchell, D. (1992). Compensation and turnover of direct care staff. In *Challenges for a Service System in Transition: Ensuring Quality Community Experiences for Persons with Developmental Disabilities,* ed. M.F. Hayden & B.H. Abery, pp. 289–312. Baltimore: Paul H. Brookes.

Bradley, V.J. (1994). Evolution of the new service paradigm. In *Creating Individual Supports for People with Developmental Disabilities: a Mandate for Change at Many Levels,* ed. V.J. Bradley, J.W. Ashbaugh & B.C. Blaney, pp. 11–32. Baltimore: Paul H. Brookes.

Burchard, J.D., Atkins, M. & Burchard, S.N. (1996). Wraparound services. In *Manual of Diagnosis and Professional Practice in Mental Retardation,* ed. J.W. Jacobson & J.M. Mulick, pp. 403–12. Washington, DC: American Psychological Association.

Carling, P.J. (1992). Community integration of people with psychiatric disabilities: emerging trends. In *Community Living for People with Developmental and Psychiatric Disabilities,* ed. J.W. Jacobson, S.N. Burchard & P.J. Carling, pp. 20–36. Baltimore: Johns Hopkins University Press.

Davidson, P., Cain, N., Sloane-Reeves, J. et al. (1995). Crisis intervention for community-based individuals with developmental disabilities and behavioral and psychiatric disorders. *Mental Retardation*, **33**, 21–30.

Drake, R.E. & Noordys, D.L. (1994). Case management for people with co-existing severe mental disorder and substance use disorder. *Psychiatric Annals*, **24**(8), 427–31.

Ellis, E., Rusch, F.R., Tu, J. & McCaughrin, W. (1990). Supported employment in Illinois. In *Supported Employment: Models, Methods and Issues,* ed. F. R. Rusch, pp. 31–44. Sycamore, IL: Sycamore Publishing.

Felce, D. & Perry, J. (1995). The extent of support for ordinary living provided in staffed housing: the relationship between staffing levels, resident characteristics and resident activity patterns. *Social Science Medicine,* **40,** 799–810.

Finch, E.S. (1985). Deinstitutionalization: mental health and mental retardation services. *Psychosocial Rehabilitation Journal,* **8**(3), 36–48

Fletcher, R.J. (1988). A county systems model: comprehensive services for the dually diagnosed. In *Mental Retardation and Mental Health: Classification, Diagnosis, Treatment, Services,* ed. J.A. Stark, F.J. Menolascino, M.H. Albarelli &V.C. Gray, pp. 254–64. New York: Springer-Verlag.

(1993a). Mental illness–mental retardation in the United States: policy and treatment challenges. *Journal of Intellectual Disability Research,* **37** Suppl. 1, 25–33.

(1993b). *Developing a Policy for the Dually Diagnosed: a Policy Management Model for Providing Mental Health Services to the Mentally Ill-Mentally Retarded.* Ann Arbor: University of Michigan Dissertation Services.

Fletcher, R.J. & Menolascino, F.J. (1989). *Mental Retardation and Mental Illness: Assessment, Treatment and Service for the Dually Diagnosed.* New York: Lexington Books.

Gettings, R.M. (1988). Service delivery trends: a state–federal policy perspective. In *Mental Retardation and Mental Health: Classification, Diagnosis, Treatment, Services,* ed. J.A. Stark, F.J. Menolascino, M.H. Albarelli & V.C. Gray, pp.385–93. New York: Springer-Verlag.

Hill, P.K., Lakin, K.C., Bruninks, R.H., Amado, A.N., Anderson, D.J. & Copher, J. (1989). *Living in the Community: a Comparative Study of Foster Homes and Small Group Homes for People with Mental Retardation.* Report No. 29. Minneapolis: University of Minnesota, Center for Residential and Community Services.

Hurley, A. (1996). Vocational rehabilitation counseling approaches to support adults with mental retardation. *Habilitative Mental Healthcare Newsletter,* **15**(2), 29–33.

Jacobson, J.W. (1996). Rehabilitation services for people with mental retardation and psychiatric disabilities: dilemmas and solutions for public policy. *Journal of Rehabilitation.* **62,** 11–22.

Jacobson, J.W. & Schwartz, A.A. (1991). Evaluating living situations of persons with developmental disabilities. In *Handbook of Mental Retardation,* ed. J.L. Matson & J.A. Mulick, 2nd edn, pp. 35–62. Elmsford, NY: Pergamon Press.

Johnson, J.R. & Rusch, F.R. (1990). Analysis of hours of direct training provided by employment specialists in supported employees. *American Journal on Mental Retardation,* **94,** 674–82.

(1994). Integrated employment and vocational services for youth and adults with disabilities in the United States. In *Mental Health in Mental Retardation: Recent Advances and Practices,* ed. N. Bouras, pp.300–18. Cambridge: Cambridge University Press.

Kearney, F.J. & Smull, M.W. (1992). People with mental retardation leaving mental health institutions. In *Community Living for People with Developmental and Psychiatric Disabilities*, ed. J. Jacobson, S.N. Burchard & P.J. Carling, pp. 183–96. Baltimore: Johns Hopkins University Press.

Lakin, K.C., Burwell, B.O., Hayden, M.F. & Jackson, N.E. (1992). *An Independent Assessment of the Minnesota Home and Community Based Service Waiver Program* Project Report No. 37. Minneapolis: University of Minnesota, Center for Residential and Community Services.

Leismer, J. (1989). Systemic needs for a responsible future. In *Mental Retardation and Mental Illness: Assessment, Treatment, and Service for the Dually Diagnosed,* ed. R. Fletcher & F. Menolascino, pp 263–84. New York: Lexington Books.

Leroy, L. (1997). Supportive cancer care: the patient's perspective. *The Picker Institute,* 51–9.

Mank, D. (1994). The underachievement of supported employment: a call for investment. *Journal of Disability Policy Studies,* **5**(2), 1–24.

MARC Mental Health Committee (1995). Dual diagnosis: defining the dynamics, determining the dimensions. *University of Western Ontario Clinical Bulletin of the Developmental Disabilities Program,* **6**(4), 1–9.

McCaughrin, W.B., Ellis, W.K., Rusch, F.R. & Heal, L.W. (1993). Cost-effectiveness of supported employment. *Mental Retardation,* **31**, 41–8.

McGaughey, M.J., Kiernan, W.E., Lynch, S.A., Schalock, R.L. & Morganstern, D.R. (1991). *National Survey of Day and Employment Programmes for Persons with Developmental Disabilities: Results from State MR/DD Agencies.* Boston: Children's Hospital, Developmental Evaluation Center.

Menolascino, F.J. & McCann, B.M., eds. (1983). Overview: bridging the gap between mental retardation and mental illness. In *Mental Health and Mental Retardation: Bridging the Gap,* pp. 1–64. Baltimore: University Park Press.

Menolascino, F.J. & Stark, J.A., eds. (1984). *Handbook of Mental Illness in the Mentally Retarded.* New York: Plenum Press.

Nagy, M.P. & Gates, H.M. (1992). Decongregating residential programmes in mental health: The impact on the staff and clients. In *Community Living for People with Developmental and Psychiatric Disabilities,* ed. J.W. Jacobson, S.N. Burchard & P.J. Carling, pp. 201–18. Baltimore: Johns Hopkins University Press.

Phadt, A. (1996). A social ecological perspective on challenging behavior. *Habilitative Mental Healthcare Newsletter,* **15**(6), 119–22.

President's Commission on Mental Health (1978). *Liaison Task Panel on Mental Retardation,* Vol. **4**, pp. 2001–6.

Rambow, T.R. & Arnold, M. (1996). Individualized/homogenized/cost effective service model: 'It's time for a professional awakening!'. *NADD Newsletter,* **13**(6), 1–4.

Reiss, S. (1988). Dual diagnosis in the United States. *Australia and New Zealand Journal of Developmental Disabilities,* **14**, 43–8.

(1994). *Handbook of Challenging Behavior: Mental Health Aspects of Mental Retardation.* Worthington, OH: IDS Publishing Corporation.

Reiss, S., Levitan, G.W. & McNally, R.J. (1982). Emotionally disturbed mentally retarded people: an under served population. *American Psychologist*, **37**, 361–7.

Revell, W.G., Wehman, P., Kregel, J., West, M. & Rayfield, R. (1994). Supported employment for persons with severe disabilities: positive trends in wages, models, and funding. *Education and Training in Mental Retardation and Developmental Disabilities*, **29**, 256–64.

Rusch, F.R. Chadsey-Rusch, J. & Johnson, J.R. (1991). Supported employment: emerging opportunities for employment integration. In *Critical Issues in the Lives of People with Severe Disabilities*, ed. L.H. Meyer, C.A. Peck & L. Brown, pp. 146–69. Columbus, OH: Charles E. Merrill.

Rusch, F.R., DeStefano, L., Chadsey-Rusch, J., Phelps, L.A. & Szymanski, L. (1992). *Transition from School to Adult Life: Models, Linkages and Policy*. Sycamore, IL: Sycamore Publishing

Rusch, F.R. & Hughes, C. (1990). Historical overview of supported employment. In *Supported Employment: Models, Methods and Issues*, ed. F. R. Rusch, pp. 5–14. Sycamore, IL: Sycamore Publishing.

Schalock, R.L., Kiernan, W.E., McGaughey, M.J., Lynch, S.A. & McNally, L.C. (1993). State MR/DD agency information systems and available data related to day and employment programmes. *Mental Retardation*, **31**, 29–34.

Shafer, M.S., Revell, W.G. & Isbister, F. (1991). The national supported employment initiative: a three-year longitudinal analysis of 50 states. *Journal of Vocational Rehabilitation*, **1**, 9–23.

Stark, J.A., Menolascino, F.J., Alberelli, M.H. & Gray, V.C. eds. (1988). *Mental Retardation and Mental Health: Classification, Diagnosis, Treatment, Services*. New York: Springer-Verlag.

Szymanski, L. & Grossman, H. (1984). Dual implications of 'dual diagnosis'. *Mental Retardation*, **22**, 155–6.

Tarjan, G., Dornbusch, S.M., Fenichel, G., Graham, F., Richmond, J. & Zigler, E. (1977). Federal research activity in mental retardation: A review with recommendations for the future. Unpublished report to Directors of NICHD/NIMH.

Thompson, L., Powers, G. & Houchard, B. (1992). The wage effects of supported employment, *Journal of the Association for Persons with Severe Handicaps*, **17**, 87–94.

Vogelsberg, R.T. (1986). Competitive employment in Vermont. In *Competitive Employment Issues and Strategies*, ed. F.R. Rusch, pp. 35–49. Baltimore: Paul H. Brookes.

Woodward, H. (1993). One community's response to the multi-system service needs of individuals with mental illness and developmental disabilities. *Community Mental Health Journal*, **29**, 347–51.

23 The state of care management in services for people with mental retardation in the UK

PAUL CAMBRIDGE

Introduction

This chapter begins with a brief overview of the original British care management experiments. It then reviews subsequent experience of care management in services for people with mental retardation, with a focus on the mainstreaming of care management since its introduction in 1990 community care reforms. The term care management is consistently used in preference to case management because of its current policy and practice relevance in Britain. The temptation to define care management is resisted, because of the variety of models and approaches that have emerged. This is also the case internationally, as a sample of definitions suggests the significance of a range of defining characteristics, including process, policy aims, service co-ordination and user-centred arrangements viz. 'the movement of each individual client from application status to case closure' (Henke, Connolly & Cox, 1975); 'the lynch pin of an individual needs led service' (Audit Commission, 1989); 'the glue that binds otherwise fragmented services into arrangements that respond to changing needs' (Freedman & Moran, 1984); and 'the organisation of information, resources and worker responsibility around the needs and wants of individual service users' (Cambridge, Hayes & Knapp, 1994).

British experimental approaches

Two primary considerations should inform an analysis of care management, namely the features of the care management model itself and the nature of the care systems in which it operates.

The care management model

The Personal Social Services Research Unit at the University of Kent conducted the original care management experiments, which were essentially diversion projects in that older people who were assessed as needing residential care, instead got flexible care packages in their own homes, arranged and purchased by a care manager (Challis & Davies, 1986; Davies & Challis, 1986; Challis et al., 1990). Each care manager was responsible for between 20 and 30 people and had a budget that could be used to buy supplementary services and support, limited to two-thirds of the cost of residential care. Other defining features included an operational policy, a service menu and costs, resource co-ordination and a single agency care management team (with mixed backgrounds). This model was later replicated in mental retardation (Knapp et al., 1992), using a user-centred approach with the additional features of a charter of user rights, contracts (agreements) with users/advocates, and individual service planning co-ordination. Other studies also used care-managed rationales for service design or analysing the characteristics of services (Qureshi, Challis & Davies, 1989: Davies, Bebbington & Charnley, 1990).

In these early models, the care management process comprised a series of core tasks, which stressed an individualized approach (Challis and Davies, 1986), to be modified later by the Department of Health in *Caring for People* (1989). These were:
- case finding and referral
- assessment and selection
- care planning and service packaging
- monitoring and reassessment
- case closure.

The projects were evaluated using an experimental design. Service costs and outcomes were compared with a matched control group of older people who entered residential care. The results indicated that care management was cost effective. It was both productive (producing better outcomes) and efficient (overall, service costs were less than for the control group).

The service system in which care management is introduced

This is a vital consideration because the original projects were specifically designed to work in a particular organizational environment. The concept of care management was adapted from North American approaches that were developed to co-ordinate care better, with the care manager as a sort of broker working for the service user and accessing a care market (see reviews by Renshaw, 1987; Renshaw et al., 1988; Davies, 1992a: Onyett, 1992; Challis, 1994a: Petch, 1996; Sturges, 1996). The conditions prevailing in Britain then, and to a lesser degree now, meant that the agencies involved in funding and providing social and health care found it difficult to work together to develop integrated services at the strategic level and flexible needs-led care packages at the individual level. Agencies tended to cost-shunt, and there were perverse incentives to providing residential care. Care management offered an attractive solution as it by-passed agency and professional divides by providing a single budget, helping service co-ordination and continuity.

Policy and practice overview

The late 1980s and early 1990s witnessed a significant reassessment of British social care policy and practice, including services for people with mental retardation, a major influence being the evaluation of the 12 Government-funded pilot projects that aimed to explore ways of moving people and resources from mental handicap hospitals to community care (Knapp et al., 1992; Cambridge et al., 1994). The costs and outcomes of new services were evaluated one and five years after people moved out of hospital, and a ten-year follow up is now underway. Care management was a condition of funding, and projects had to identify targeting and entry criteria (needs groups) and systems of assessment and case review. Various arrangements emerged and this variety began to be interpreted using four micro-organizational models (Knapp et al., 1992: Cambridge, 1992; see Box 23.1).

Box 23.1

Care management models from the care in the community projects
Operational models
These were designed to help services manage change, tailored specifically to local conditions, demands and circumstances, such as continuity of professional support and records during the deinstitutionalization process

Value-based models
These were characterized by philosophies such as normalization and service principles and goals, challenging the location of power within and between organizations or between organizations and service users

Consumerist models
The principles of user involvement and users as consumers were built into some care management arrangements. In Maidstone, for example, 'clients were supported by case managers who advocated on their behalf and counselled them through the transitional period'

Economic models
Care management arrangements in which cost management was used to purchase and construct service packages from the mixed economy of care, usually with devolved budgets or using shadow cost information

---

This was also the period when the philosophies and values associated with normalisation and social role valorization (Wolfensberger, 1980, 1984) and an ordinary life (King's Fund, 1980) were feeding into practice methodologies (O'Brien, 1987) and impacting on care management.

The different organizational and operational aspects of care management were also scrutinized. Organization was found to be split between a variety of team arrangements, enhanced key-working in residential services, locality-based approaches, and a few examples of quasi-brokerage or independent arrangements. Moreover, the inclusion of a range of operational variables, such as frequency and intensity of contact, resulted in a wide variety of arrangements, contrasting with the tightly prescribed form of the original experiments with services for older people (Cambridge, 1992; Knapp, et al., 1992). These key dimensions provide a blueprint for comparing and reviewing care-managed systems and have been used for generic and international comparisons by Challis (1994b, 1995). Challis (1994b) has also examined the influence of intrinsic and extrinsic factors on different care management models:

> The combination of these two factors may well indicate the extent to which variations in care management systems represent a locally derived judgement of the potential of a particular set of arrangements for specific outcomes within the local context.   (Challis, 1994b, p. 19).

Constructing a simple organizational and management map of care management is useful for helping to understand how well care management fits with divisional, management and commissioning structures. Comparisons of systems in Somerset and Kent in the early 1990s (Fig. 23.1) illustrate fundamental differences in superficially similar patterns. In-house care management in Somerset was aimed at managing an internal market, with decentralization to four divisions – an internal variant of locality purchasing (Ham, 1992). In Kent, care management explicitly related to divisional commissioning structures, with semi-generic teams, large case loads and purchasing from an external market.

Throughout the late 1980s, the Audit Commission promoted care management alongside the emerging policy themes of single budgets and devolved purchasing for delivering individualized and needs-led services (see the Audit Commission reports 1986, p. 75; 1987, p. 8; 1989, p. 16). The 1988 Griffiths report (HMSO, 1988) heralded a change in terminology (from case to care management) and differences in form and function. The concept of care management was reconstructed as a device for resource allocation and accountability at higher management or locality levels, rather than at the individual service user level. The mainstreaming of care management with the 1990 Community Care Reforms related care management as an instrument for other policy aims such as lead agencies for community care planning, the separation of purchasing and providing, consumerism, needs-led provision and the contract, highlighting important links with macro-organization.

Instead of being contained in relatively small and isolated experiments, care management became a general micro-organizational device – effectively, a huge natural experiment. No one model or approach promoted case management:

> Where an individual's needs are complex or significant levels of resources are involved, the Government sees merit in nominating a 'case manager' to take responsibility for ensuring that individuals' needs are regularly reviewed, resources are managed effectively and that each service user has a single point of contact. (Department of Health, 1989, p. 21)

With hindsight, this lack of specificity was a big mistake, as it allowed for deviation from proven methodologies in response to organizational and management expediencies. Even the guidance material brought out by the Department of Health and Social Services Inspectorate (1991) outlined a range of different care management models, each with its own advantages, disadvantages and associated values. Single care manager models on teams, social entreprenuership, shared core task, administrative and user models were identified, as were different interagency models of care management. However, the last-mentioned were extrapolated from wider experience of interagency working rather than from experience with care management (Knapp et al., 1992; see Box 23.2).

Box 23.2

Organizational models from the care in the community projects (Knapp et al., 1992), subsequently adapted by the Department of Health and Social Services Inspectorate (1991).

Lead agency model: one agency in lead role

Unitary agency model: controlled by one agency with minimal input from other agencies

Joint agency model: designated workers drawn from two key agencies, single worker or shared arrangements for user groups or in teams

Multi-agency model: multiple agency involvement across a mixed economy of care

Independent agency models: located in a special external agency or semi-independent arm

---

Care management in Kent's organizational structure

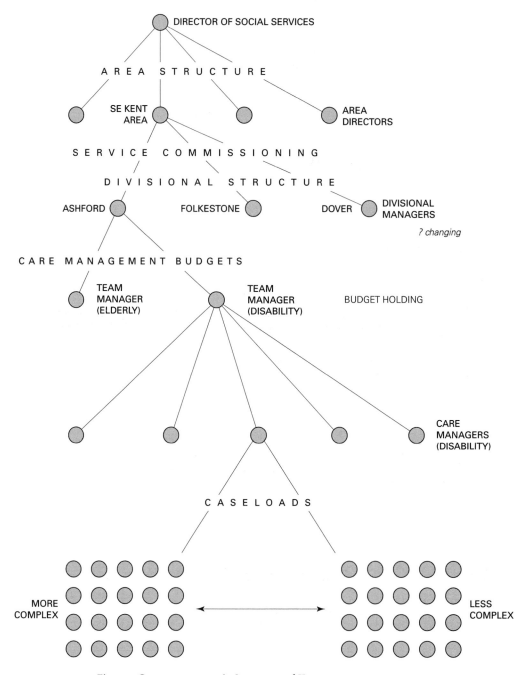

Fig. 23.1 Care management in Somerset and Kent.

Line management levels in Somerset's care and case management structure

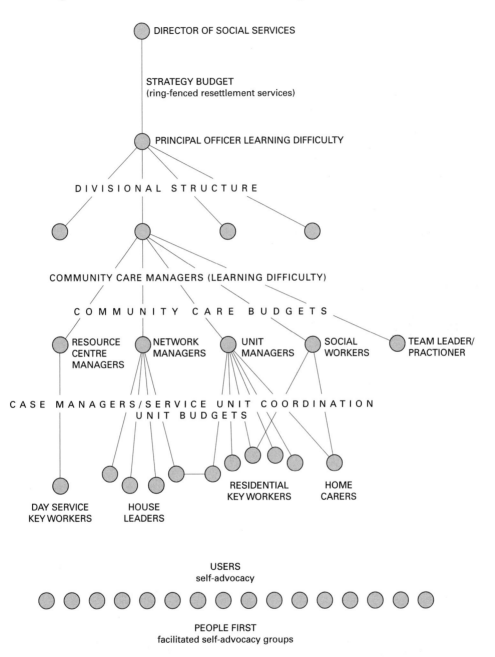

DIRECTOR OF SOCIAL SERVICES

STRATEGY BUDGET
(ring-fenced resettlement services)

PRINCIPAL OFFICER LEARNING DIFFICULTY

D I V I S I O N A L   S T R U C T U R E

COMMUNITY CARE MANAGERS (LEARNING DIFFICULTY)

C O M M U N I T Y   C A R E   B U D G E T S

RESOURCE CENTRE MANAGERS

NETWORK MANAGERS

UNIT MANAGERS

SOCIAL WORKERS

TEAM LEADER/ PRACTIONER

C A S E   M A N A G E R S / S E R V I C E   U N I T   C O O R D I N A T I O N
U N I T   B U D G E T S

DAY SERVICE KEY WORKERS

HOUSE LEADERS

RESIDENTIAL KEY WORKERS

HOME CARERS

USERS
self-advocacy

PEOPLE FIRST
facilitated self-advocacy groups

Analysis and interpretation were also complicated by the different care management arrangements that were emerging more widely in Britain (Beardshaw & Towell, 1990), and from individual initiatives and service innovations (Banks & Kerr, 1988; Pilling, 1988, 1992; Hampshire Social Services and Winchester District Health Authority, 1989; Richardson & Higgins, 1990; National Development Team, 1991). The central policy interest in care management was maintained in the 1990s, recurring as a theme of Audit Commission reports (1992a, 1992b).

Critical review

The remaining sections of this chapter provide a critical review of the performance of care management for people with mental retardation in Britain.

Organizational considerations and structural efficiency

Organizational, management and funding structures should inform the development and review of care management. The introduction of care management risks duplication of function, the emergence of two-tier arrangements and split accountability. Davies (1992a) has identified obstacles to the attainment of policy and practice goals and the resistance of professionals and agencies to change, due in part to the technological difficulties of producing adequate co-ordinative mechanisms. Evidence from mainstream implementation suggests a tendency to fit care management into existing structures or to bolt it onto existing systems, risking inefficiencies:

> ... an inevitable danger is a tendency to identify the new ideas with the familiar, to under-estimate how difficult it will be to use present opportunities to achieve long-run excellence ... to try to pour too much of the heady new wine into rigid old bottles. (Davies, 1992b, p. 32)

Some social services departments have simply redefined the role of social workers (Lewis & Glennerster, 1996), the managers of individual residential services or client key-workers to approximate care management in services for people with mental retardation. Alternatively, community mental retardation or support teams have adopted a quasi-care management role without redefining wider working methodologies or responsibilities (Forrest et al., 1995).

Hospital re-provision and the development of a mixed economy of provision highlighted the complexity of agency and funding responsibilities in some localities. An example was in Camden (Cambridge et al., 1994), where, without care management, tied to a service development and funding strategy, responsibilities and accountability were confused and a number of clients ultimately returned to hospital. With locally agreed social services or joint lead responsibility for services for people with mental retardation, fragmented accountability and confused responsibility are less likely. With fragmented accountability, it would be rational to locate care management in joint agency teams, linked to joint commissioning (Cambridge, 1997a). As has been observed:

> Both health commissioners and local authority commissioners … must have a role in setting the strategic framework within which care management will operate. Many localities lack a coherent service strategy for learning disability and challenging behaviour (Greig, Cambridge & Rucker, 1996, p. 9)

Relationships with service planning and development

The Somerset and Maidstone examples point to the need to attend to organizational process when developing care management. Considerations include the performance of higher level functions, including service planning and commissioning, market management and the driving political values and objectives. Knapp and Wistow (1992) identified the critical place for care management in the commissioning process. Tactical purchasing by care managers will not easily effect changes in the choice, availability or quality of services outside a wider planning and purchasing strategy, so funders, planners and purchasers need to work in tandem with care managers to ensure strategic changes relate to and are informed by tactical demands stemming from a needs-led approach. New mechanisms will be needed to ensure that an implementation gap does not open between strategy and tactics, and that respective behaviours are mutually informed. Steering and liaison mechanisms have successfully been put in place in community mental health services (Cambridge et al., 1996) and there are many examples of the potential co-ordinating role provided by community mental health teams (Onyett, 1992; Ovretveit, 1993).

Arrangements in mental retardation are different, but the need to develop a co-ordinated development strategy is as strong. For example, many localities lack a coherent strategy for challenging behaviour. This should comprise prevention, early intervention, the provision of technical and practical support, and the development of alternative placements (Mansell, McGill & Emerson, 1994). The assessment and quasi-care management role performed by specialist community support teams (Forrest et al., 1995; Emerson et al., 1996) could provide the individual information required. Central policy guidance (HMSO, 1993) has also stressed the importance of an individualized approach for commissioning services for people with mental retardation and challenging behaviours in the context of 'developing' local competence instead of 'removing' or 'containing' the needs of people with challenging behaviours. Mansell (HMSO, 1993, p. 14) also stressed the importance of prioritizing individuals with the greatest needs:

> People with learning disabilities and challenging behaviour present the most complex and difficult problems, both at clinical and service organization levels. Although their numbers may be relatively small, unless services respond well, they occupy a disproportionate amount of time and money

Care management can target needs by establishing eligibility and entry criteria. The needs pyramid (Audit Commission, 1993) provides a model for matching resources to the needs of populations, an essential responsibility of commissioners (Knapp & Wistow, 1992). Figure 23.2 illustrates this concept in relation to the needs of local populations of people with mental retardation. As most such needs are long term, a logical approach would be to include those in the top three tiers of the pyramid in care management. Moreover, the episodic nature of some challenging behaviours and the development of independent living suggest that people will move between tiers, with the intensity of care management varying in response. This arrangement would mirror the tiered care programme approach in mental health (Department of Health, 1994a), helping ensure vertical target efficiency (Davies, 1992a).

In the recent past, peculiar pressures and service changes, such as those associated with hospital re-provision, have sometimes lead to two-tier case management. Historical factors, such as access to financial transfers (dowry payments) and change imperatives such as de-institutionalization, have determined who gets care management (Cambridge, 1988; Cambridge et al., 1994). One of the biggest remaining challenges is the increasing inequities between, as well as within, authorities – different political complexions and

Fig. 23.2 The learning disability needs pyramid.

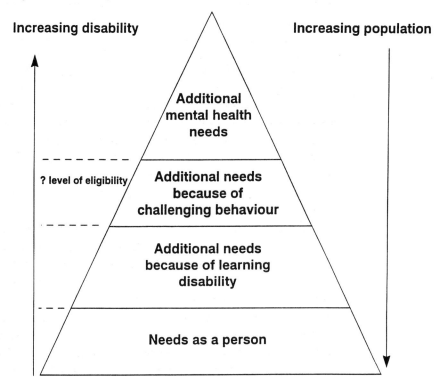

resource constraints have shifted but maintained territorial injustices (see the discussion of horizontal target efficiency in Davies, 1992a). This means that care management will need to be robust enough to manage resource decline in some places, making for difficult rationing decisions. Whether coverage should be maintained at the expense of intensity is a political and professional judgement, but there is a strong case for targeting resources on high-quality interventions which effect significant changes in service quality and appropriateness.

Information for effective management and practice decision making

To achieve the above, effective management and practice information systems are required. The simplest approaches to care management need information on individual services used and needed, generated by the core tasks of assessment and individual service planning. Care management with devolved budgets and purchasing additionally requires information on the costs of services and their likely productivity. This information is required for effective purchasing and service substitution by care managers, but also by managers, planners and purchasers at the macro-level. Agencies and commissioners are also accountable for spending and resource allocation and need to be in an informed position to bid confidently for resources or to justify switching resources between competing needs or target criteria. This requirement demands not only complex information systems on needs, but devolved commitment and forward commitment accounting systems:

> If we have devolved budgets of whatever size, we need proper financial information systems. Anyone putting in a devolved budget without a financial information system will be put through the shredder by the auditors. (Browning, 1992, p. 42).

Experience within care-managed services suggests critical difficulties associated with developing and operating such systems. This was the experience with the original Maidstone Care in the Community project, reported by the Audit Commission (1989, p. 18), remaining as a deficit with the mainstreaming of care management in Kent. The lesson is to invest in developing information technology systems in advance of devolving purchasing within care management.

Equally important is the capacity to integrate diverse information in an informed and consistent way. Quality–cost comparisons and cost-effectiveness judgements are difficult enough to make without information that lacks comprehensiveness and comparability (Knapp & Cambridge, 1997). Financial pressures are increasingly demanding a new set of competencies for care managers that include explicit business skills (Mares, 1996). Care managers need to be in a position to understand the reasons for cost variations when purchasing services or considering substitution, and this will often relate to a combination of user and service characteristics:

> ... cost information should generally not stand in isolation from other relevant evidence, particularly outcome data. Reliance on cost information alone could be dangerous, just as it is inadvisable to neglect costs in policy and practice discussions and decisions.   (Knapp & Cambridge, 1997).

Taking due account of systems level costs and outcomes

Care management will clearly bring one-off and recurring costs. The crucial question is whether the administrative and transactional costs of care management and the accompanying information systems exceed outcome or efficiency gains. As has been observed in the context of the social care market:

> There are costs which arise from operating a market system. The fundamental issue is whether authorities can avoid incurring a level of transaction costs ... which exceeds the efficiency savings ... In addition other costs arise from inspection, accreditation and other regulatory mechanisms.
>
> (Wistow et al., 1993, p. 174)

It is essential to ensure that care management does not raid resources from direct services for people with mental retardation by imposing additional costs with only marginal benefits. It is equally important that the process of rationing that will inevitably occur does not result in costs being off-loaded onto informal carers (Parker, 1990). Yet, we know very little about the costs of care management in long-term care (Kane et al., 1991), pointing to the need not only to codify care management in organizational culture but also to include an awareness of its costs, especially since its organization varies significantly from the original British experiments.

Contracting-in-care-management is one process or intermediate outcome that can help ensure care management systems achieve quality and effectiveness gains, particularly in relation to individualization – helping shift the emphasis from block purchasing and providing to needs-led service specification and provision. With devolved financial accountability or even shadow budgets or cost information, it is possible for care managers to develop individual contracts with different providers to meet user needs. These will effect tactical shifts in service utilization and efficiency that are also value led (with due regard to resources). Cambridge and Brown (1997) have identified the elements of individual service specifications and contracts that could be used to help make the market work better for people with mental retardation:

> Despite the inherent problems of contracting as a mechanism for planning comprehensively for, and maintaining standards in services for people with learning disabilities, there are ways in which the process can be used to promote best practice and harness support for the rights and interests of those who use services and their carers   (Cambridge & Brown, 1997, p. 42)

This means that care managers should also consider specifying radical service models, building commitment to equal opportunities, retaining capital assets in the public domain, incorporating advocacy and counter-controls, and maintaining the capacity to recognize and detect abuse early and close abusive services. Rarely, for instance, is sexuality or HIV risk referenced in contracts with providers (Cambridge, 1996a), and care managers may need to purchase specialist educational or therapeutic interventions, which may need pump-priming. Similar deficits are identifiable in recognizing and responding to sexual and physical abuse and in services and supports that are sensitive to culture and ethnicity (Cambridge, 1998a). Abuse enquiries have often referenced poor care management assignments, will ill-defined responsibility for case co-ordination and accountability (Cambridge, 1998b)

Working agency and market divides

This is the question most posed in Britain, and although lead responsibility has been with social services departments since 1990, this does not always happen (HMSO, 1993). Many community support teams contacted as part of a national survey indicated that they had had to work with providers who also undertook assessments and/or developed individual programmes or interventions (Emerson et al., 1996).

Managers and practitioners have sometimes avoided addressing this question because the answers would have consequences for stake-holding, agency and professional empires and the economic empowerment of service users. The most common arrangement to emerge has therefore been various shared core task models, with health or social care professionals leading the process and undertaking assessment and individual service planning (such as social workers or challenging needs workers if not care managers per se), with service managers or key-workers in provider organizations contributing to assessment or leading case review.

Although this is a perfectly respectable arrangement, which has formed a crucial dimension to a number of approaches (Qureshi et al., 1989; Dant & Gearing, 1990), the fundamental question about where care management responsibilities should lie in relation to service purchasing or providing is not answered. Some providers have initiated key-worker models of care management, but this is similar to ex-public sector provision in arms' length provider units or trusts, even with management walls built between providing and care management. Considering abuse and exploitation can also come from staff, this is a potentially dangerous model, risking the isolation of users and conflicts of interest on the part of key-workers. Others agree that this is inappropriate from a best-management or professional perspective (Bannerman & Robertson, 1996).

There are also legal constraints, as social services departments are unable to devolve powers of assessment to semi-independent agencies or their workers, such as care managers working for joint commissioning bodies. (See Cambridge (1997a) for an analysis of the Lewisham Partnership model, and Department of Health (1995) for related legal considerations.)

Assessment and the performance of the core tasks

Assessment is arguably the most important core task of care management because the information it produces feeds directly into informing service planning. It represents a microcosm of care management and provides an indicator of performance. Moreover, it has received particular political and practice attention in mental retardation because it exposes the mismatch between resources and needs, and highlights user rights, raising questions about inclusion and empowerment.

Some social services departments have tried to re-invent the wheel and have ended up with the Star Ship Enterprise. Holistic assessment forms can run to ten pages but tell you nothing about the person, his or her life or experience – all essential features for an interpretative understanding of the nature of need. They suggest dominant administrative interests, referenced in the time spent designing forms (Lewis & Glennerster, 1996). Others (Payne, 1995) have reviewed the plethora of potential and actual headings utilised in assessment, but underlined the importance of subjective techniques such as observation and interviewing. Meyer (1993) goes further, identifying stages in assessment including exploration and study and drawing inferences. Care managers *need* to 'get to know' people with mental retardation. This view is supported by McLean (1996), who, when talking about the process of assessment itself, stresses it is essentially about an understanding that takes place within the context of a relationship between the practitioner and the service user.

Assessment, therefore, highlights what can be an ambiguous approach to the concept of need:

> Assessments involve decisions which are highly significant; both for the user or carer faced with personal crisis or difficulties and for the practitioner
> with front line responsibility for targeting scarce resources on those with the greatest needs. Much is likely to depend on the meaning attached to need . . .
> (Richards, 1994, p. 5).

In *Getting the Message Across* (Social Services Inspectorate, 1991), assessment was presented as a task that could be formulated and conducted using a checklist of points and issues. It was strong on suggestions about what to do, but did not address the sticky issue of matching resources to needs and rationing, reflected in the variability of the use of comprehensive assessment for referrals (Department of Health, 1994b). Seed and Kaye (1994) unpack the process from assessment to placement packages from a baseline of quality-of-life assessment. The market has, however, shifted the nature of the dependent processes, and Figure 23.3 reformulates the core tasks of care management based on a market approach.

Ideally, the performance of each task should be co-ordinated by a care manager, but this rarely happens in practice as providers and voluntary organizations may develop lead responsibilities under certain conditions (Maxwell & Titterton, 1996). Charnley and Davies (1986) have identified

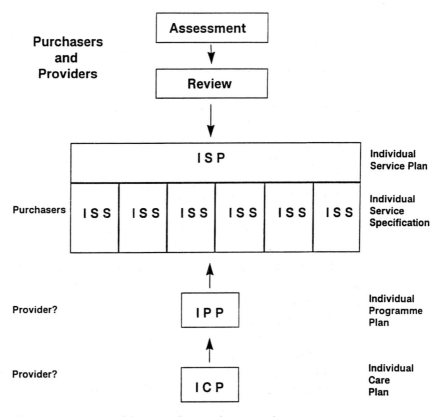

Fig. 23.3 Assessment and the core tasks: a market approach.

potential blockages in the performance of the core tasks and a direct relationship with efficiency. Cameron and Freeman (1996) consider approaches to core task performance and stress the ongoing nature of assessment. In many care-managed systems, assessment has become a megalithic one-off task because of large case loads and time constraints.

Maximizing user involvement and rights

Market models based on consumerism include brokerage, in which service brokers or care managers have responsibility for negotiating and accessing services for people with mental retardation. Such arrangements were promoted in the late 1980s (Brandon & Towe, 1989) and some pilot projects have worked for people with physical disabilities. Others have been tried out for people with mental retardation (see VIA, 1994; Dowson, 1995; Dook, Honess & Senker, 1997), but have usually met organizational resistance. In Britain, brokers can approximate the role provided in North America, which is more explicitly commercial (MacLean, Carpenter & Marlett, 1988):

> The project sets out to support change in service delivery based on the individual's needs and wishes. It enables the service user to take greater control

> ... Service Brokerage works to change the way support is given and to inves-
> tigate and develop new and creative services.   (Dook et al., 1997, p. 3)

Independent care management agencies (Banks & Kerr, 1988) have largely failed because of legal constraints and the mixed economy. Similarly, user-centred approaches identified by the Department of Health (Department of Health and Social Services Inspectorate, 1991) have been little utilized. Users and their advocates can be routinely involved in assessment, service planning and case review (Croft & Beresford, 1990), but this would demand the intensive involvement of the care manager and some quasi-independent or professional advocacy role. The ultimate answer lies with individualized funding, but pilot work is needed to identify the challenges and pitfall of such arrangements, particularly between the interests of users and their families and carers. There would also need to be special safeguards for people who do not have contact with relatives or who are relatively dependent on professionals. More than anything, political commitment to the economic empowerment of people with mental retardation (and their carers) is required:

> Labour believes that anybody with any type of disability may be suitable and
> should be eligible for direct payments rather than services   (Milburn, 1996).

A start should be made as soon as possible to explore solutions and ways forward.

Two challenges remain for care management in relation to developing user-centred arrangements. The first is the participation of people with severe mental retardation and challenging behaviours and those with limited expressive or receptive communication. Steps should be taken to ensure that translators or citizen advocates are present to represent the views or interests of these individuals. The second concerns the rights of people with mental retardation living with their parents or in home care placements, where there may be conflicts of interest and issues of control. Care management will need to ensure that the wishes and interests of the individual are both heard and represented in service planning.

Conclusion

There is no blueprint for best care management in services for people with mental retardation, as each service system has unique demands, presenting complex change scenarios (Beckhard & Harris, 1987). However, the evidence from the original care management experiments in Britain and from the mainstreaming of care management points to the advantages of smaller case loads of between 20 and 30 to allow care managers to develop the relationship, frequency of contact and personal knowledge of the individuals and their physical and social environments needed to design effective interventions. Moreover, if care management operates in a mixed economy of care or a quasi-market, then it will need to balance these considerations with functional demands, such as contracting and individual service specification. Whereas an understanding of the technological aspects of care management is essential, it is important not to be blinkered by methodological complexities or dazzled by assessment. Attention should always focus on individuals and their relationship with care managers.

Care management can easily be introduced at the expense of the professional advocacy role previously provided by social workers (Atkinson, 1989), and sight should not be lost of proven approaches for resolving political and practice conflicts caused by role ambiguity and overlap between care management and social work (Payne, 1995; Lewis & Glennerster, 1996). Care management will also need the capacity to navigate changing patterns of needs, particularly those relating to ageing (Walker, Walker & Ryan, 1996) and the cohorts of people with mental retardation who left long-stay institutions in Britain in the late 1980s and early 1990s. Similar observations can be made in relation to other complex needs such as those relating to HIV (Cambridge, 1996b), raising consideration of the relative benefits of specialist and generic care management, or the capacity to manage potential tensions and conflicts between professionals, user rights and wider political considerations (Cambridge, 1997b). Ultimately, the success of care management will be judged on the extent to which it helps bring welfare, quality-of-life and rights and empowerment gains to people with mental retardation who use community and social care services.

References

Atkinson, D. (1989). *Someone To Turn To: the Social Worker's Role and the Role of Front Line Staff in Relation to People with Mental Handicaps.* Kidderminster: BIMH Publications.

Audit Commission (1986). *Making a Reality of Community Care.* London: HMSO.
  (1987). *Occasional Paper Number 4.* London: HMSO.
  (1989). *Occasional Paper Number 9.* London: HMSO.
  (1992a). *Community Care: Managing the Cascade of Change.* London: HMSO.
  (1992b). *The Community Revolution: Personal Social Services and Community Care.* London: HMSO.
  (1993). *Taking Care.* London: HMSO.

Banks, P. & Kerr, V. (1988). *The CHOICE Model of Case Management: Standards for Quality.* Portsmouth: Shepherds.

Bannerman, L. & Robertson, B. (1996). Care management: a manager's perspective, In *Planning and Costing Community Care*, ed. C. Clark and I. Lapsley, pp. 75–90. London: Jessica Kingsley.

Beardshaw, V. & Towell, D. (1990). *Assessment and Case Management: Implications for the Implementation of Caring for People.* Briefing Paper No. 10. London: King's Fund.

Beckhard, R. & Harris, R. (1987). *Organizational Transitions: Managing Complex Change.* London: Addison-Wesley.

Brandon, D. & Towe, N. (1989). *Free to Choose: an Introduction to Service Brokerage*, Community Living Monograph. London: Good Impressions.

Browning, D. (1992). Looking to the future. In *Case Management: Issues in Practice*, ed. S. Onyett and P. Cambridge, P, pp. 40–3. Canterbury: PSSRU, University of Kent at Canterbury.

Cambridge, P. (1988). *Beyond the Hospital Fringe: Social Justice and Care in the Community*. PSSRU Discussion Paper No. 588. Canterbury: University of Kent at Canterbury.

(1992). Case management in community services: organizational responses *British Journal of Social Work*, **22**, 495–517.

(1996a). Assessing and meeting needs in HIV and learning disability. *British Journal of Learning Disabilities*, **24**, pp. 52–57.

(1996b). Men with learning disabilities who have sex with men in public places: mapping the needs of services and users in south east London. *Journal of Intellectual Disability Research*, **40**(3), 241–51.

(1997a). Joint commissioning: searching for stability in an unstable world. *Tizard Learning Disability Review*, 2(1), 26–30.

(1997b). How far to gay? The politics of HIV in learning disability. *Disability and Society*, **12**, (3), 427–53.

(1998a). The physical abuse of people with learning disabilities and challenging behaviours: lessons for commissioners and providers. *Learning Disability Review*, **3**, (1), 18–26.

(1998b). The first hit: a case study of the physical abuse of people with learning disabilities and challenging behaviours in a residential service. *Disability and Society*, **12**(3), 427–53.

Cambridge, P. & Brown, H. (1997). Making the market work for people with learning disabilities: an argument for principled contracting. *Critical Social Policy*, **17**, 27–52.

Cambridge, P., Hayes, L., & Knapp, M. (1994). *Care in the Community: Five Years On*. Ashgate, Aldershot: Arena.

Cambridge, P., Sangster, A., Carpenter, J., & Ring, C. (1996). *Issues in the Development of Somerset's Mental Health Services: a Discussion Paper*. Report No. VII. University of Kent at Canterbury: Tizard Centre.

Cameron, L. & Freeman, I. (1996). Care management: meeting different needs. In *Planning and Costing Community Care*, ed. C. Clark and I. Lapsley, pp. 91–107. London: Jessica Kingsley.

Challis, D. (1994a). Case management: a review of UK developments and issues. In *Caring for People in the Community: the New Welfare*, ed. M. Titterton, pp. 91–112. London: Jessica Kingsley.

(1994b). *Care Management: Factors Influencing its Development in the Implementation of Community Care*. London: Department of Health.

(1995). Care management around the world. *Care Plan*, **June, 10–14**.

Challis, D., Chessum, R., Chesterman, J., Luckett, R. & Traske, K. (1990). *Case Management in Social and Health Care*. Canterbury: PSSRU, University of Kent at Canterbury.

Challis, D. & Davies, B. (1986). *Case Management in Community Care*. Aldershot: Gower.

Charnley, H. & Davies, B. (1986). *Blockages and the Performance of the Core Tasks of Case Management.* PSSRU Discussion Paper No. 473. Canterbury: University of Kent at Canterbury.

Croft, S. & Beresford, P. (1990). *From Paternalism to Participation: Involving People in Social Services.* London: Joseph Rowntree Foundation.

Dant, T. & Gearing, B. (1990). Key-workers for elderly people in the community: case managers and care co-ordinators. *Journal of Social Policy,* **19**(3), 331–60.

Davies, B. (1992a). *Care Management, Equity and Efficiency: the International Experience.* Canterbury: PSSRU, University of Kent at Canterbury.

(1992b). Lessons for case management. In *Case Management: Issues in Practice,* ed. S. Onyett & P. Cambridge, pp. 32–9. Canterbury: PSSRU, University of Kent at Canterbury.

Davies, B., Bebbington, A & Charnley, H. (1990). *Resources, Needs and Outcomes in Community Based Care.* Aldershot: Avebury.

Davies, B. & Challis, D. (1986) *Matching Resources to Needs in Community Care.* Aldershot: Gower.

Department of Health (1989). *Caring for People.* London: HMSO.

(1994a). *Key Area Handbook: Mental Illness,* 2nd edn, London: HMSO.

(1994b). *Implementing Caring for People: Care Management* London: Department of Health.

(1995). *Practical Guidance on Joint Commissioning for Project Leaders.* London: HMSO.

Department of Health and Social Services Inspectorate (1991). *Care Management and Assessment: Managers' Guide.* London: HMSO.

Dook, J., Honess, J. & Senker, J. (1997). *Making Changes: Service Brokerage in Southwark.* London: Choice Press.

Dowson, S (1995). Service brokerage: the alternative to care management? *Values into Action Newsletter,* **81**, 6–7.

Emerson, E., Forrest, J., Cambridge, P. & Mansell, J. (1996). Community support teams for people with learning disabilities and challenging behaviours: results of a national survey. *Journal of Mental Health,* **5**(4), 395–406.

Forrest, J., Cambridge, P., Emerson, E. & Mansell, J. (1995). Community support teams for people with learning disabilities and challenging behaviour. In *Challenging Behaviour: What we Know,* pp. 20–32. London: Mental Health Foundation.

Freedman, R. & Moran, A. (1984). Wanderers in a promised land: the chronically mentally ill and deinstitutionalisation. *Medical Care,* **22**(12), Supplement.

Greig, R., Cambridge, P. & Rucker, L. (1996). Care management and joint commissioning. In *Purchasing Services for People with Learning Disabilities, Challenging Behaviour and Mental Health Needs,* ed.J. Harris, pp. 5–20. Kidderminster: British Institute of Learning Disabilities.

Ham, C. (1992). *Locality Purchasing.* HSMC Discussion Paper No. 30. Birmingham: University of Birmingham.

Hampshire Social Services and Winchester District Health Authority (1989). *Andover Project of Case Management of Services for People with a Mental Handicap.* Winchester: Hampshire Social Services Department.

Henke, R., Connolly, S., & Cox, J. (1975). Caseload management: the key to effectiveness. *Journal of Applied Rehabilitation Counselling*, **6**(4), 217–27.

HMSO (1988). *Community Care: Agenda for Action*. London: HMSO.

(1993). *Services for People with Learning Disabilities and Challenging Behaviour or Mental Health Needs*. London: HMSO.

Kane, R., Penrod, J., Davidson, G., Moscovice, I & Rich, E. (1991). What cost case management in long-term care? *Social Service Review*, June, pp. 281–303.

King's Fund (1980). *An Ordinary Life*. King's Fund Project Paper No. 24. London: King's Fund Centre.

Knapp, M. & Cambridge, P. (1997). The cost dimension in commissioning and providing services for people with learning disabilities. In *Commissioning and Providing Services for People with Learning Disabilities*, ed. N. Boras and P. Donlan, pp. 71–80. Brighton: Pavilion.

Knapp, M., Cambridge, P., Thomason, C., Beecham, J., Allen, C. & Darton, R. (1992). *Care in the Community: Challenge and Demonstration*. Aldershot: Ashgate.

Knapp, M. & Wistow, G. (1992). *Joint Commissioning for Community Care*. Canterbury: PSSRU, University of Kent at Canterbury.

Lewis, J. & Glennerster, H. (1996). *Implementing the New Community Care*. Buckingham: Open University.

Mansell, J., McGill, P. & Emerson, E. (1994). Conceptualising service provision. In *Severe Learning Disabilities and Challenging Behaviours*, ed. E. Emerson, P. McGill and J. Mansell, pp. 69–93. London: Chapman Hall.

Mares, P. (1996). *Business Skills for Care Management: a Guide to Costing, Contracting and Negotiating*. London: Age Concern.

Maxwell, S. & Titterton, M. (1996). Assessing and managing care: what future for the independent sector? In *Planning and Costing Community Care*, ed. C. Clark and I. Lapsley, pp. 19–32. London: Jessica Kingsley.

MacLean, H., Carpenter, S. & Marlett, N. (1988). *Funding Alternatives that Foster Empowerment*. Toronto: Canadian Association for Independent Living Centres.

McLean, T. (1996). The assessment process. In *Planning and Costing Community Care*, ed. C. Clark and I. Lapsley, pp. 54–74. London: Jessica Kingsley.

Meyer, C. (1993). *Assessment in Social Work Practice*. New York: Columbia University Press.

Milburn, A. (1996). *Why Labour Supports Direct Payments for People with Learning Disabilities*. Values into Action, Funding Freedom, 14 March 1996.

National Development Team (1991). *The Andover Case Management Project*. Manchester: NDT.

O'Brien, J. (1987). A guide to lifestyle planning. In *The Activities Catalogue*, ed. B. Willcox & G. Bellamy, Baltimore: Paul H. Brookes.

Onyett, S. (1992). *Case Management in Mental Health*. London: Chapman and Hall.

Ovretveit, J. (1993). *Co-ordinating Community Care: Multi-disciplinary Teams and Care Management*. Buckingham: Open University.

Parker, G. (1990). Whose care? Whose cost? Whose benefit? A critical review of research on case management and informal care. *Ageing and Society*, **10**, 459–67.

Payne, M. (1995). *Social Work and Community Care*. London: Macmillan.

Petch, A. (1996). Care management: putting the principles into practice. In *Planning and Costing Community Care*, ed C. Clark and I. Lapsley, pp. 4–18. London: Jessica Kingsley.

Pilling, D. (1988). *The Case Manager Project: Report on the Evaluation*. London: City University.

(1992). *Approaches to Case Management for People with Disabilities*. London: Jessica Kingsley.

Qureshi, H., Challis, D. & Davies, B. (1989). *Helpers in Case-Managed Community Care*. Aldershot: Gower.

Renshaw, J. (1987). Care in the community: individual care planning and case management. *British Journal of Social Work*, **18**, 79–105.

Renshaw, J., Hampson, R., Thomason, C., Darton, R., Judge, K. & Knapp, M. (1988). *Care in the Community: the First Steps*. Aldershot: Gower.

Richards, S. (1994). Making sense of needs assessment. *Research, Policy and Planning*. **12**(1), 5–9.

Richardson, A. & Higgins, R. (1990). *Case Management in Practice: Reflections on the Wakefield Case Management Project*. Leeds: NIHSS.

Seed, P. & Kaye, G. (1994). *Handbook for Assessing and Managing Care in the Community*. London: Jessica Kingsley.

Social Services Inspectorate (1991). *Getting the Message Across: a Guide to Developing and Communicating Policies, Principles and Procedures on Assessment*. London: HMSO.

Sturges, P. (1996). Care management practice: lessons from the USA. In *Planning and Costing Community Care*, ed. C. Clark and I. Lapsley, pp. 33–53. London: Jessica Kingsley.

VIA (1994). Choice and no choice. *Values into Action Newsletter*, **79**, London.

Walker, A., Walker, C. & Ryan, T. (1996). Older people with learning difficulties leaving institutional care – a case study of double jeopardy. *Ageing and Society*, **16**, 125–50.

Wistow, G., Knapp, M., Hardy, B., Forder, J., Manning, R. & Kendall, J. (1993). *Social Care Markets: Progress and Prospects*. Canterbury: PSSRU/Nuffield Institute, University of Kent at Canterbury.

Wolfensberger, W. (1980). The definition of normalisation: update, problems, disagreements and misunderstandings. In *Normalisation, Social Integration and Community Services*, ed. R. Flynn and K. Nitsch. Baltimore: University Park Press.

(1984). A reconception of normalisation as social role valorisation. *Mental Retardation* (Canadian), **34**, 22–5.

24 Measuring the outcomes of services

MARY LINDSEY AND ERNEST GRALTON

Introduction

An outcome is a consequence, result or effect. The definition of outcome that is used in this chapter is 'the effect of an intervention, service or policy on a target person or population'. This is similar to that used by Qureshi (1996). The relationship between the outcome and the objectives of an intervention will determine its effectiveness. Hence, there are four key variables that will influence findings from outcome studies (Fig. 24.1):

the target person, problem or population;
the intervention, service or policy being evaluated;
the objectives and expectations of change;
the outcomes selected and the measurements used.

Objectives and outcomes are viewed differently by people with different vested interests (Fig. 24.2). For example, service users and carers are usually more concerned with the quality of their experience when using the service

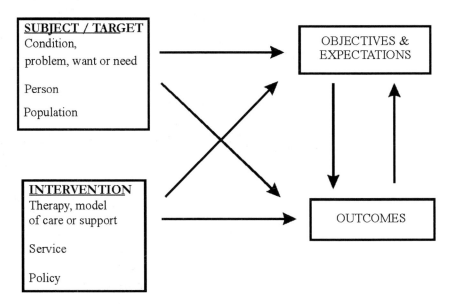

Fig. 24.1 The key variables to be taken into account in outcome studies.

and, if this is good, may be far more willing to accept or value outcomes viewed by professionals as desirable (Bainton, 1992).

The subject or target

A desired change in a person, problem or population (Fig. 24.3) is generally the reason for an intervention, although maintenance of the status quo and prevention of unnecessary suffering are also valid aims.

There is a wide range in the severity of developmental disabilities, and whereas habilitative and educative interventions are likely to enable most people with a mild developmental disability to achieve full independence in self-care and in domestic skills, the same interventions are unlikely to have such an impact on people with a severe or profound degree of developmental disability. Similarly, the engagement of individuals in purposeful activity becomes much more difficult as the degree of developmental disability increases.

In addition, there are many other disabilities and disorders that occur with developmental disability far more frequently than by chance. These include autism, cerebral palsy, epilepsy, sensory impairments, psychiatric disorders and challenging behaviours. Developmental disability services frequently target their interventions at these associated problems, that also vary in severity. Furthermore the severity of one disability may impact on the

Fig. 24.2 The different expectations and views of services and their outcomes.

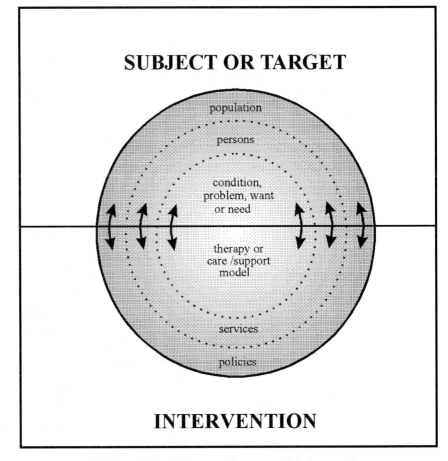

Fig. 24.3 A model of the relationship between the target and the intervention.

prognosis for another. For example, it has been shown that the outcomes for people with autism are heavily dependent on the presence and severity of developmental disability (Lotter, 1974).

Even when one problem is being addressed, there may be much variation in severity, type and causes. For example, the definition of challenging behaviour can vary, as can its manifestation and severity. Also, there are several potential causes such as communication problems, autism and mental illness. Therefore, it is not surprising that an intervention that is effective for one person with challenging behaviour may not work for another. The quality of the assessment may then be the best predictor of success (McGill, Clare & Murphy, 1996), and accurate assessment may be regarded as an intermediate proxy outcome. There are many other variables that may modify the probability of achieving a particular outcome. These include demographic factors such as age, sex, culture and family circumstances.

When comparing one service with another, it is most important that the service users are similar. Unless they have been randomly allocated to two or

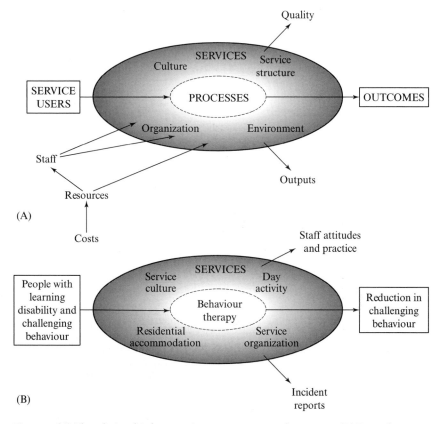

Fig. 24.4 (A) The relationship between inputs, processes and outcomes. (B) Examples as applied to people with learning disability and challenging behaviour.

more interventions or services, there is likely to be referral and selection bias towards those people who are thought to be most likely to benefit. In addition to studying the effect of interventions on service users, there may also be a need to take into account the impact on families and carers. The size of the population studied is also important in order to learn from work with individuals. Studies have to include enough subjects to prove, using statistical tests, that the findings are not just due to chance.

The intervention, service or policy

An effective intervention can be described as one that alters the natural course of events for the better. The scale of an intervention can vary from that of a single treatment for an individual, a service for a group of people, or a policy designed to have an effect on an entire population (Fig. 24.3). When selecting the intervention to be evaluated, it is often recommended that priority should be given to common, high-risk, problem-prone or high-cost activities.

In the past, the difficulty of collecting outcome information led to inputs and processes being used as proxy measures for outcomes (Shaw, 1989; Fig. 24.4). For example, the time spent in therapy was assumed to relate to outcome. It is now recognized that the focus should primarily be on outcomes in terms of gains in well-being or optimal well-being. However, when research has shown a strong probability that, for a particular problem, a specific protocol will lead to specified outcomes, only then can process measures act as proxy outcome measures. In developmental disability services this rarely applies, but most existing mechanisms for external evaluation, such as registration of residential and nursing homes, performance indicators and systems of accreditation, are still focused on process or output (e.g. incident forms or occupancy rates) rather than outcome.

The distinction between process and outcome is not always clear cut, and several indicators that are usually thought of as process measures, can equally be used in outcome measurement. For example, the quality of care is usually seen as a process, but the recipient may regard it as the most important outcome. What makes a measurement an outcome is not the nature of the instrument or measure, but the way that it is organized and its relationship to the problem and the intervention.

For people with developmental disabilities, there may be very specific interventions for particular conditions (such as medication or cognitive–behavioural approaches) or to build personal competence, but these are usually delivered in the context of services designed to improve quality of life, such as a community care service based on the 'five accomplishments' (O'Brien& Lyle, 1987). In reality, people usually receive several interventions concurrently or consecutively. Some of these may be medical but others, even if delivered by health professionals, may be directed at the social systems within which the person lives (Goldberg et al., 1995).

Sociological interventions, for example the policy and process of de-institutionalizing the residents of long-stay hospitals, are very difficult to define and the evaluation of different models of care is far from complete (Emerson & Hatton, 1994; Emerson et al., 1996). There are so many variables that affect the quality of care, and so many ways of measuring it, that it is very difficult to disentangle the significant factors. However, different types of care models can be compared through the use of surveys or observational studies (Dunn, 1996). There was a number of longitudinal studies that monitored the outcome of de-institutionalization (Bratt & Johnston,1988; Booth, Booth & Simons, 1990; Clare & Murphy, 1993) and another approach was to compare current hospital care with non-institutional community services (Felce, 1981; Davies, 1988).

As care has developed in the community, a range of support services has evolved, which also require evaluation. A recent study by Lowe, Felce and Blackman (1996) compared a challenging behaviour team with specialist workers to one with professionals without specialist experience in developmental disabilities.

Weaknesses of studies include selection bias and provider bias. Innovations are usually carried out by people who are enthusiasts, and Dunn (1996) points out that the service being used as a control may be run by demoralized and disillusioned staff who are well aware that they are just a comparison group for a new and interesting project.

The evaluation of services also presents the problem of multiple influences on outcome. Service users do not exist in isolation, but interact with each other and with the staff, and the nature of those relationships may be as influential as any specific therapies. There are many other features of staff organization and support that are thought to be significant in the delivery of good-quality services (Hatton & Emerson, 1993). After many years of attention to individuals, it is increasingly being recognized that a range of environmental factors contributes to the development or exacerbation of challenging behaviours (McGill, 1993), both directly and also by affecting the extent to which behavioural approaches can be successfully followed and maintained (Emerson et al., 1992; Holt & Oliver, 1997; Fig. 24.4B). Unless the link between an outcome and an intervention is clear, the outcome cannot be considered to be a measure of the effectiveness of that intervention.

Objectives and expectations

It is important to differentiate between ideal objectives, such as total cure, which may not be achievable, and realistic expectations for the person and the problem. The objective is often more ambitious and idealistic than realistic (Lindsey, 1997) and this is due to the various factors that can influence expectations (Fig. 24.5). Nevertheless, the identification of the ideal outcome can provide a useful criterion against which to measure the actual outcome. Many services providing social care for people with developmental disabilities have service aims that are usually based on the five accomplishments described by O'Brien and Lyle (1987). However, it is rare for any attempt to be made to measure the extent to which these aims have been achieved, and this leads to frequent criticisms of services that do not appear to live up to their objectives. Donlan (1997) points out that each agency should determine for itself what it intends to achieve for its service users and these aims should change to reflect the needs of the users.

Realistic expectations of change require information about the expected course of events if no intervention, or a different intervention, were to take place. Unfortunately, there is limited information on natural outcomes for people with developmental disabilities, and even when this information is available, the heterogeneity of the developmentally disabled population makes it particularly difficult to generalize these findings from one group to another.

It is also important to know the probability of achieving a particular outcome following a specific intervention. Initially, these probabilities can

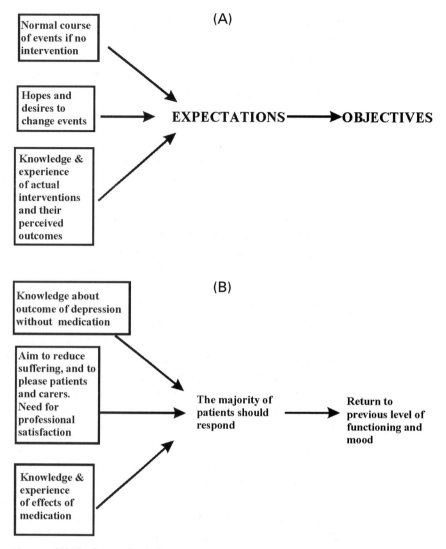

Fig. 24.5 (A) The factors that influence expectations. (B) Example of clinicians' expectations of the use of medication for clinical depression.

be sought from the literature on research findings. Over time they can be refined in the light of experience and outcome measurement. For people with developmental disabilities, the availability of this information varies from adequate for the short-term benefits of behavioural interventions for challenging behaviour (Lennox et al., 1988), to poor for the effectiveness of psychotropic medication for schizophrenia or challenging behaviour (Duggan & Brylewski, 1997).

Services may also be measured by setting criteria and standards for structure, processes and outcomes. Criteria are statements that define appropriate care and serve as benchmarks against which the actual care can be measured. They are usually determined by professionals on the basis of experience and research but, more recently, service users have made a more active contribution to this process. Standards are usually regarded as quantitative specifications of a criterion. For example, a criterion for the care of people with clinical depression might include appropriate medication in the correct dosage at specified times, with a standard of 100 per cent compliance.

Outcomes and their measurement

Planning and management of outcome measurement

When measuring outcomes, both benefits and costs must be identified to justify the use of the resources, to demonstrate that the measurement process is ethical, and to motivate staff. Issues of ethics, consent and confidentiality need to be addressed.

First, the areas for evaluation must be selected and the priorities determined. It can be useful to involve service users and staff (Simons, 1994; Whittaker, Gardner & Kershaw, 1991). Then, the issues relating to the sample size, the interventions being evaluated, and the objectives should be taken into account before finally deciding the outcomes to be measured. Both positive and negative outcomes should be considered, including the potential adverse effects of the intervention. For very specific conditions, the possible outcomes tend to be fewer in number than when there is a long-term course and a complex condition or need. There is a tendency to seek the ideal measure that will cover everything, but it will always be a compromise and it is better to monitor a few important items effectively.

When dealing with long-term disabilities, the time scale is very important. An initial response to an intervention may be followed by a relapse. The development of adaptive behaviours as alternatives to maladaptive behaviours can take time. Qureshi (1996) points out that outcomes may be viewed as a sequence of events and, for example, the final outcome of childhood interventions or care may only be seen in adulthood. Therefore, for some problems, it may be more useful to take a series of measures over a period of time to produce a response profile.

The process for information gathering must also be decided. It may be necessary to collect data routinely or an independent survey may be required. It is often better to start with a small number of simple measures so that the culture of their use becomes established. There is better motivation if participants are involved in the process of selecting or developing the measures and actively encouraged to collect data. The link with improvements in practice or other potential gains must be evident. Constructive feedback is vital if motivation for data collection is to be sustained.

Finally, the analysis of the information and the use of the results must be planned in advance. The results will require interpretation because there may be many possible explanations for the changes or lack of changes that are found.

Ideally, outcome measurement should be an ongoing process that can be adapted and improved by learning from the experience of self and others. Therefore, it should be designed in a way that is flexible enough to allow future changes to be made.

Selecting measures

Measurement scales should be valid and reliable. In addition, they must be sufficiently sensitive to record useful and significant changes in the outcomes of interest. Measures also have to be acceptable to the people who are using them, otherwise they will be poorly completed or totally rejected. Meyer and Janney (1989) also stress the importance of documentation processes that do not interrupt the flow of the normal procedures and that allow the sharing of meaningful observations. If there are operational data already available, it is tempting to use them even when their relationship to outcomes is unclear. However, relevant data can sometimes be captured as a by-product of routine operational systems, and this opportunity should be taken whenever possible.

Although a strong case can be made for structured measures, there is also the possibility of unexpected or unwanted outcomes. For example, open-ended exploratory approaches can be useful for discovering the important outcomes for service users and the ways that these are attributed to services.

Anecdotal accounts of outcomes can be a very powerful way of describing the potential of an intervention or service and are often more influential than the objective scientific evidence, even when this shows that an intervention is rarely effective.

Approaches to measurement

Measuring changes in symptoms or function

The level of functioning of a person is usually considered an important measure of outcome and there are a number of global functioning scales developed specifically for people with developmental disabilities. The most widely used of these include the Vineland Social Maturity Scale (Doll, 1965) and the Adaptive Behavior Scale (Nihira et al.,1974). Nevertheless, the completion of such scales is time consuming and they are not often used for outcome measurement. They are more often used to provide information about targets for intervention and can also provide a baseline against which selected changes can be measured. Often, services develop their own approach to information recording such as the semi-structured assessment procedure used by Kon and Bouras (1997) for the follow-up of clients who had been resettled from a large institution.

Some of the global function scales include maladaptive behaviours or symptoms of mental illness. The Adaptive Behavior Scale is in two sections: the first covers the level of development in ten areas of function, and the second is concerned with maladaptive behaviours in 14 different categories.

The Aberrant Behavior Checklist is an instrument used to rate inappropriate and maladaptive behaviours and can be used to measure change during treatment. It can be used across the range of developmental disability (Newton & Sturmey, 1988). The Health of the Nation Outcome Scales (Wing, Curtis & Beaver, 1996) that have been developed for mental illness have scales for social functioning, specific symptoms and behaviours. Attempts to use them with people with developmental disabilities have suggested that they are only applicable to people with mild developmental disability and mental health problems.

There are also measures based on direct observation and recording over time. These include measures of engagement in purposeful activity because this is regarded as a proxy measure for quality-of-life and quality-of-service delivery (Mansell et al., 1984). Such recording activities can be very labour intensive, require training of the observers, and they may not be practical as routine measures even if a time-sampling approach is used. They are more likely to be used in research. However, similar assessments can be developed for more routine use and with a much lower investment (Felce et al., 1979). Also, many simple recordings of less frequent events may be carried out routinely, such as observations on seizures, specific challenging behaviours, community activities (Lowe & de Paiva , 1991) and the use of medication.

Quality of life

Felce (1996) has suggested that the domains to be included in quality of life for people with developmental disabilities are physical well-being, material well-being, social well-being, development and activity, and emotional well-being. For each of these, he suggests indicators and illustrative studies.

Schalock et al. (1989; Schalock & Keith, 1993) have developed a quality-of-life scale specifically for people with developmental disabilities. It has ten questions in each of four sections: satisfaction, competence/productivity, empowerment/independence and social belonging/community integration. Cummins (1992) and his colleagues have also developed a useful quality-of-life scale that is based on an interview schedule.

Objective-based outcomes

Lindsey (1997) describes a system used to evaluate the work of clinical staff in a community developmental disability service. This rated the outcome against the objective set by the professional at the start of an intervention. It was difficult to separate poor outcomes from unrealistic expectations without the research evidence to show what could be achieved. The system was applicable to a range of problems and interventions but staff found it difficult to use because of the complexity of the approach and the difficulty in identifying the point at which outcome assessment should occur.

Individualized approaches

Many services for people with developmental disabilities already have systems in place for setting individual objectives. If these are carried out to a satisfactory standard, it should prove possible to monitor the extent to which the objectives are met. Donlan (1997) has described a system for monitoring predictive outcomes for individuals within the framework of the service objectives. Coded data are aggregated electronically to measure the effectiveness of the service.

Goal attainment scaling is an approach whereby a standardised scoring system is applied to individualized goals. Specific outcome measures are agreed and placed on a scale according to the degree of success or failure they represent. Goal attainment scaling can be used to evaluate a particular intervention, such as the effect of a communication on individuals with severe intellectual impairment and maladaptive behaviours (Danquah, Mate-Cole & Zehr, 1996), or as a more general quality-of-life measure (Rockwood, 1995).

Individual quality-of-life measures can also be developed (Hickey et al., 1996). These allow the subjects or their advocates to nominate the areas of life that are most important, to rate their level of functioning or satisfaction with each, and to indicate the relative importance of each to their overall quality of life.

Satisfaction and involvement of service users

Bowd (1989) noted that the criteria employed by adults with developmental disabilities to evaluate their quality of life differed from those of professionals. Professionals are likely to have more experience of managing a particular problem, but it is the service users who experience the consequences of any decisions made about their care.

Heal and Chadsey-Rusch (1985) developed a 29-item scale for people with developmental disabilities which includes satisfaction with residence, living arrangements, friends, neighbourhood, leisure and services. It was later developed to include work, recreation and relationships (Harner & Heal, 1993). The Quality of Life Questionnaire (Schalock et al., 1989; Schalock & Keith, 1993) is also directed at satisfaction with services.

Felce (1996) points out that satisfaction relates to expectations and the power to exercise choice. Where life experience and poor self-esteem have generated low expectations, and habituation to an impoverished lifestyle, then expressed satisfaction may be high for those service users, whereas the general population would be grossly dissatisfied with such circumstances (Flynn, 1989).

Felce, Taylor and Wright (1994) point out the difficulties when users are unable to understand or communicate about the services received, and suggest that considerable reliance may have to be placed on interviews with advocates or carers. However, with experience, it is possible to interview people with poor understanding and limited use of language (Flynn, 1986; Lowe & de Paiva, 1988).

Conclusion

Outcome measures may be objective or subjective, individualized or global. symptom specific or related to the quality of life. They must be developed and interpreted in the context of the target, the intervention and the objective. If scarce resources are to be used to provide the maximum possible benefit for service users, it is necessary for outcome measurement to inform service delivery. Sources of this information include research, professional and service user consensus, and operational measures of service outcomes, such as those obtained from audit. Practitioners should do their best to ensure that they learn from, and contribute to, this information base.

References

Bainton, D. (1992). A guide to outcome measurement for clinical managers. *The Clinician in Management*, **1**, 3, 9–12.

Booth, W., Booth, T. & Simons, K. (1990). Return journey: the relocation of adults from long-stay hospital into hostel accommodation. *British Journal of Mental Subnormality*, **36**, 87–97.

Bowd, A.D. (1989). Client satisfaction and normalisation of residential services for persons with developmental handicaps. *Canadian Journal of Community Mental Health*, **8**, 63–73.

Bratt, A. & Johnston, R. (1988). Changes in life style for young adults with profound handicaps following discharge from hospital care into a second generation housing project. *Mental Handicap Research* **1**, 49–74.

Clare, I. & Murphy, G. (1993). M.I.E.T.S (Mental Impairment Evaluation and Treatment Service): a service option for people with mild mental handicaps and challenging behaviour and/or psychiatric problems. *Mental Handicap Research* **6**, 70–91.

Cummins, R.A. (1992). *Comprehensive Quality of Life Scale – Intellectual Disability*. Melbourne: Psychology Research Centre, Deakin University.

Danquah, S., Mate-Cole, C. & Zehr, R. (1996). The effect of Danquah Communication System boards on maladaptive behaviours among individuals with severe intellectual impairment and non-verbal communication skills. *International Journal of Rehabilitation Research*, **19**(2), 143–56.

Davies, L. (1988). Community care: the costs and quality. *Health Services Management Research*, **1**, 145–55.

Doll, E.A. (1965). *The Vineland Scale of Social Maturity: Condensed Manual of Directions*. Minnesota: American Guidance Service.

Donlan, P. (1997). Measuring the outcome. In *Challenges and Change: Commissioning and Providing Services for People with Learning Disabilities*, ed. N. Bouras & P. Donlan, pp. 53–60. Brighton: Pavilion Publishing.

Duggan, L. & Brylewski, J. (1997). Systematic reviews of the effectiveness of anti-

psychotic medication for people with learning disability and either schizo-
phrenia or challenging behaviour. In *Proceedings of the Royal College of
Psychiatrists' Winter Meeting*, Cardiff, p. 14. London: Royal College of
Psychiatrists.

Dunn, G. (1996). Statistical methods for measuring outcomes. In *Mental Health
Outcome Measures*, ed. G. Thornicroft & M. Tansella, pp. 3–13. Berlin:
Springer-Verlag.

Emerson, E., Beasley, F., Offord, G. & Mansell, J. (1992). An evaluation of hospital-
based specialised staffed housing for people with seriously challenging
behaviours. *Journal of Intellectual Disability Research*, **36**, 291–307.

Emerson, E., Cullen, C., Hatton, C. & Cross, B. (1996). *Residential Provision for
People with Learning Disabilities: Summary Report*. Manchester: Hester
Adrian Research Centre, University of Manchester.

Emerson, E. & Hatton, C. (1994). *Moving out: Relocation from Hospital to
Community*. London: HMSO.

Felce, D. (1981). The capital costs of alternative residential facilities for mentally
handicapped people. *British Journal of Psychiatry* **139**, 230–7.

(1996). Ways to measure quality of outcome: an essential ingredient in quality
assurance. *Tizard Learning Disability Review*, **1**(2), 38–44.

Felce, D., Jenkins, J., Lunt, B., Powell, E. & Mansell, J. (1979). Measuring activity of
old people in residential care: testing a handbook for observers. *Evaluation
Review*, **4**(3), 371 -89.

Felce, D., Taylor, D. & Wright, K. (1994). People with learning disabilities. In
Health Care Needs Assessment, Vol. 2, Ed. A. Stevens & J. Raftery, pp.
412–50. Oxford: Radcliffe Medical Press.

Flynn, M. (1989). *Independent Living for Adults with a Mental Handicap: a Place of
my Own*. London: Cassell.

(1986). Adults who are mentally handicapped as consumers: issues and guidelines for interviewing. *Journal of Mental Deficiency Research*, **30**, 369–77.

Goldberg, D., Magril, L., Hale, J., Damaskinidou, K., Paul, J. & Tham, S. (1995).
Protection and loss: working with learning disabled adults and their families. *Journal of Family Therapy* **17**, 263–80.

Harner, C.J. & Heal, L.W. (1993). The Multifaceted Lifestyle Satisfaction Scale
(MLSS): psychometric properties of an interview schedule for assessing
personal satisfaction with residence, community setting and associated
services. *Applied Research in Mental Retardation*, **6**, 475–90.

Hatton, C. & Emerson, E. (1993). Organizational predictors of staff stress, satisfaction, and intended turnover in a service for people with multiple disabilities. *Mental Retardation*, **31**(6), 388–95.

Heal, L.W. & Chadsey-Rusch, J. (1985). The Lifestyle Satisfaction Scale (LSS):
assessing individual's satisfaction with residence, community setting and
associated services. *Applied Research in Mental Retardation*, **6**, 475–90.

Hickey, A., Bury, G., O'Boyle, C., Bradley, F., O'Kelly, F. & Shannon, W. (1996). A
new short form individual quality of life measure (SEIQoL-DW): application in a cohort of individuals with HIV/AIDS. *British Medical Journal*, **313**,
29–33.

Holt, G. & Oliver, B. (1997). Providing community care for people who challenge
services. In *Challenges and Change: Commissioning and Providing Services*

for People with Learning Disabilities, ed: N. Bouras & P. Donlan, pp. 45–52. Brighton: Pavilion Publishing.

Kon, Y. & Bouras, N. (1997). Psychiatric follow-up and health services utilisation for people with learning disabilities. *British Journal of Developmental Disabilities*, **43** (84), 20–6.

Lennox, D., Miltenberger, R., Spengler, P. & Erfanian, N. (1988). Decelerative treatment practices with persons who have mental retardation: a review of five years of the literature. *American Journal on Mental Retardation*, **92**, 492–501.

Lindsey, M. (1997). Measuring the outcome of services in the community. In *Challenges and Change: Commissioning and Providing Services for People with Learning Disabilities*, ed. N. Bouras & P. Donlan, pp. 61–70. Brighton: Pavilion Publishing.

Lotter, V. (1974). Factors related to outcome in autistic children. *Journal of Autism and Childhood Schizophrenia*, **4**, 263–77.

Lowe, K. & de Paiva, S. (1988). Canvassing the views of people with a mental handicap. *Irish Journal of Psychology*, **9**, 220–34.

(1991). *NIMROD: an Overview*. London: HMSO.

Lowe, K., Felce, D. & Blackman, D. (1996). Challenging behaviour: the effectiveness of specialist support teams. *Journal of Intellectual Disability Research*, **40**(4), 336–47.

Mansell, J., Jenkins, J., Felce, D. & de Kock, U. (1984). Measuring the activity of severely and profoundly mentally handicapped adults in ordinary housing. *Behaviour Research and Therapy*, **22**, 23–9.

McGill, P. (1993). Challenging behaviour, challenging environments and challenging needs. *Clinical Psychology Forum*, **56**, 14–8.

McGill, P., Clare, I. & Murphy, G. (1996). Understanding and responding to challenging behaviour: from theory to practice. *Tizard Learning Disability Review*, **1**(1), 9–17.

Meyer, L. & Janney, R. (1989). User-friendly measures of meaningful outcomes: evaluating behavioural interventions. *Journal of the Association for Persons with Severe Handicaps*, **14**(4), 263–70.

Newton, J.T. & Sturmey, P. (1988). The aberrant behavior checklist – a British replication and extension of its psychometric properties. *Journal of Mental Deficiency Research*, **32**, 87–92.

Nihira, K., Foster, R., Shellhaas, M. & Leland, J. (1974). *AAMD Adaptive Behaviour Scale, Revision*. Washington, DC: American Association on Mental Deficiency.

O'Brien, J. & Lyle, C. (1987). *Frameworks for Accomplishment*. Lithonia, GA: Responsive System Associates.

Qureshi, H. (1996). Outcomes in services for people with learning disabilities – the heart of the matter. *Tizard Learning Disability Review* **1**(3), 36–43.

Rockwood, K. (1995). Integration of research methods and outcome measures: comprehensive care for the frail elderly. *Canadian Journal on Aging*, **14**, (Suppl. 1), 151–64.

Schalock, R.L. & Keith, K.D. (1993). *Quality of Life Questionnaire*. Worthington, OH: IDS Publishing Corporation.

Schalock, R.L., Keith, K.D., Hoffman, K. & Karan, O.C. (1989). Quality of life: its measurement and use in human service programmes. *Mental Retardation* **27**, 25–31.

Shaw, C.D. (1989). Audit in internal medicine. *British Journal of Hospital Medicine*, **42**, 19.

Simons, K. (1994). Enabling research: people with learning difficulties. *Research, Policy and Planning*, **12**(2), 4–5.

Whittaker, A., Gardner, S. & Kershaw, J. (1991). *Service Evaluation by People with Learning Difficulties*. London: King's Fund.

Wing, J.K., Curtis, R.H. & Beaver, A.S. (1996). *HoNOS: Health of the Nation Outcome Scales. Report in Research and Development, July 1993–December 1995*. London: Royal College of Psychiatrists.

25 Staff stress

CHRIS HATTON

Introduction: the importance of staff

Staffing issues should be central to anyone interested in developing high-quality services for people with mental retardation (Reid, Parsons & Green, 1989; Rice & Rosen, 1991). The staff are the filling in the service sandwich, through which national policies are translated into practical action directly affecting the quality of life of people with mental retardation. As staff constitute the largest slice of revenue expenditure in services, increasing the quality of staff performance is crucial if scarce resources are optimally to benefit people with mental retardation.

There are several reasons why staff are crucial in promoting high-quality services. First, staff behaviour, particularly in the forms of assistance and positive contact, has a direct impact on the quality of life of people with mental retardation (Felce, 1996; Hatton et al., 1996). Second, other staff behaviours, such as absenteeism and turnover, have an indirect impact on the quality of life of people with mental retardation, by reducing organizational efficiency, the continuity of care for people using services, and the skills and experience of the work force (Maslach & Pines, 1977; Baumeister & Zaharia, 1986;). As in organizational psychology generally (Cooper & Payne, 1988; Arnold, Cooper & Robertson, 1995; Makin, Cooper & Cox, 1996), high staff stress has been implicated in both poor staff performance (Rose, Mullan & Fletcher, 1994) and other staff behaviours with negative consequences for services, such as staff absenteeism and turnover (Hatton & Emerson, 1993b; Hatton et al., 1997; Rose, 1995).

This chapter focuses on staff stress in services for people with mental retardation. General findings from organizational psychology are used to outline the concept of stress and the consequences of high stress for both staff and organizations. Next, research concerning services for people with mental retardation is examined to evaluate the extent to which these services show the characteristics of high-stress organizations. Factors that influence staff stress in services are discussed, and the chapter closes by discussing organizational strategies for reducing staff stress.

Stress at work

Organizational psychology (Cooper & Payne, 1988; Arnold et al., 1995) has generally examined workplace stress within a cognitive–behavioural framework (Lazarus & Folkman, 1984; Folkman & Lazarus, 1985). Briefly, this theory proposes that the relationship between potential stressors (e.g. life events, work situations) and actual levels of personal distress is not a direct one. Instead, people appraise potentially stressful situations in terms of whether they feel they have the resources (mental, physical, financial, social etc.) to deal with the situation to their advantage. If people feel that they do have sufficient resources, a stressful situation will be appraised as a *challenge*. People acting on this appraisal will use *problem-focused coping* strategies to try to alter the stressful situation directly to remove or reduce the source of stress, typically resulting in positive outcomes for themselves. Alternatively, they may feel that they do not have sufficient resources to deal with a stressful situation. In this case, they will appraise the situation as a *threat*, and will not try to alter the stressful situation, because they feel they do not have the resources to do so. Instead, they will use *emotion-focused coping* strategies to try to alter their painful emotions about the situation, typically resulting in negative outcomes for them.

This framework for understanding stress at work has a number of consequences. First, it recognizes that different people can respond differently to the same stressful situation. Second, it recognizes that a wide range of factors can have an impact on stress. Third, it recognizes that people and environments have a mutual impact upon each other. Finally, it recognizes that a person can use different coping strategies at different times, depending on the situation and the resources available. All of these aspects of the theory are useful when trying to understand staff stress in complex organizations.

It is worth noting that a certain amount of stress is positive. We all need challenges in our working lives to keep us motivated and to promote a sense of competence and well-being (indeed, a job without enough challenges can produce just as much distress as a job with too many challenges: Cox, 1980). It is only when situations become overwhelming and we feel we cannot cope that stress increases and becomes *distress*.

There is extensive evidence (Cooper & Payne, 1988; Arnold et al., 1995) that workplace distress has major short-term and long-term effects on both the well-being of individuals and the effective running of organizations. Table 25.1 lists some of the major effects of high stress on individuals and organizations. In the short term, high stress can have a number of negative effects on thinking, emotions and behaviour. In this context, it is worth noting that a workforce displaying these characteristics of high stress will be working very poorly with people with mental retardation. In addition, a group of staff who are cynical, not looking to solve problems and unwilling to take in new information is unlikely to absorb training or assiduously implement new programmes (they are, of course, also likely to resist inter-

Table 25.1 The short-term and long-term effects of high stress

Short-term effects

Cognitive	Emotional	Behavioural
Concentration and attention span decrease	Physical tensions increase	Speech problems increase
Distractability increases	Psychological tensions increase	Loss of interest and enthusiasm
Short-term and long-term memories worsen	Hypochondria increases	Increased absenteeism
Response speed becomes unpredictable	Personality traits change	Drug abuse increases
Error rate increases	Depression and helplessness appear	Lethargy and apathy appear
Organization and planning worsen	Self-esteem falls sharply	Sleep patterns are disrupted
New information is ignored		Increased cynicism
		Problems 'solved' superficially

Long-term effects

For individuals	For organizations
Heart disease	High absenteeism
High blood pressure	High staff turnover
Migraine and headaches	Poor staff performance
Asthma and allergies	Increased accidents
Intestinal problems, including ulcers	Difficulties in labour relations
Rheumatoid arthritis	Organizational costs associated with litigation and health care
Skin disorders	Increased training costs
Lung disease	Reduced organizational efficiency
Depression	
Anxiety	
Alcoholism	
Psychotic disorders	

Adapted from Arnold et al. (1995) and Fontana (1990).

ventions aimed at reducing staff stress). In the long term, the effects of high stress on individuals are very serious indeed, including serious physical and mental illness leading to increased mortality (Fletcher, 1988; Arnold et al., 1995). The long-term effects of high stress on organizations are also serious. For example, in 1984–85, 328 million days of work were lost in the UK due to stress-related illness on the part of employees (Arnold et al., 1995).

Staff stress in services for people with mental retardation

Research in organizational psychology clearly demonstrates the impact, for both individuals and organizations, of high staff stress on a number of important outcomes. There is increasing evidence that high workplace stress can be a major problem in UK services for people with mental retardation.

1. Approximately 30 per cent of staff in services for people with mental retardation report high levels of stress indicative of psychiatric problems
(Hatton & Emerson, 1993a; Hatton et al., 1995, 1997). There is some evidence that high stress may be more of a problem in services for people with
mental retardation than in similar services. For example, a recent survey of
512 staff in services for people with mental retardation (Hatton et al., 1997)
reported that 32.5 per cent of staff reported high levels of distress – using
the General Health Questionnaire (GHQ-12) a standard measure of distress, compared to 26.8 per cent of staff in general health services (Borrill et
al., 1996) and 16 per cent of English adults generally (Bennett et al., 1995).
However, there is wide variation in stress levels between individual services, with some services reporting very low levels of staff stress.
2. Levels of staff turnover vary widely between different services for people
with mental retardation, with annual turnover rates ranging from under 10
per cent to over 50 per cent (Hatton et al., 1995, for a summary). High staff
turnover and high absenteeism have been linked to high work stress in services for people with mental retardation (Hatton et al., 1997).
3. There is substantial variation between services in the amount of staff
contact received by people with mental retardation, with some residents of
community-based houses receiving very low levels of staff support, similar
to those found in institutions (Emerson & Hatton, 1994, 1996). This indicates very poor staff performance in some community-based housing services for people with mental retardation.

However, there is also wide variation between services in staff stress, turnover, and performance. Some services report low levels of staff stress and
turnover and good staff performance. This variation suggests that working
with people with mental retardation does not inevitably lead to high staff
stress. If we can understand which factors influence staff stress in this
context, then effective organizational interventions can be devised and
implemented to reduce it.

Factors influencing staff stress

Several studies have attempted to determine the characteristics of
service users, staff members and organizations that are associated with high
staff stress, poor staff morale and staff burnout. The list of factors can be
grouped into several domains (Arnold et al., 1995).

– Within-staff factors: these include anxiety and personal health (Browner et
al., 1987; Power & Sharp, 1988), staff beliefs about and emotional reactions
to challenging behaviour (Bromley & Emerson, 1995), and the coping strategies used by staff to deal with workplace problems (Thomson, 1987;
Hatton & Emerson, 1995; Hatton et al., 1997).
– Characteristics of service users: these focus on challenging behaviours
shown by service users (Bersani & Heifetz, 1985; Corrigan, 1993; Rose, 1993;
Bromley & Emerson, 1995; Hatton et al., 1995).

– Factors intrinsic to the job: these include work overload (Power & Sharp, 1988; Razza, 1993; Rose, 1993; Hatton et al., 1997), a lack of job variety (Allen, Pahl & Quine, 1990; Hatton & Emerson, 1993b), low income (Bersani & Heifetz, 1985), and the emotional impact of working with people with mental retardation (Hatton et al., 1995).

– Social support factors: these include feedback on job performance (Hatton & Emerson, 1993b), and both practical and emotional support from colleagues, supervisors and managers (Browner et al., 1987; Hatton & Emerson, 1993b; Razza, 1993; Rose, 1993, 1995; Hatton et al., 1995, 1997)

– Career development factors: these include lack of job security (Rose, 1995; Hatton et al., 1997), lack of promotion prospects (Hatton & Emerson, 1993b), and lack of further training and skill development (Hatton & Emerson, 1993b; Rose, 1995).

– Role in the organization: important factors here include role ambiguity (i.e. being unclear about what the job entails: Hatton & Emerson, 1993b; Hatton et al., 1997) and role conflict (i.e. receiving conflicting demands from others: Allen et al., 1990; Hatton & Emerson, 1993b; Razza, 1993; Hatton et al., 1997).

– Organizational structure and climate: factors here include hierarchical organizational structures (Hatton & Emerson, 1993b), lack of participation in organizational decision-making (Hatton & Emerson, 1993b; Hatton et al., 1997), and alienation from the organization (Hatton & Emerson, 1993b; Hatton et al., 1997). There is also some evidence implicating the role of the wider organizational climate in high staff stress, in terms of dissatisfaction with team climate (Rose, & Schlewa-Davies, 1997) and mismatches between the 'real' organizational climate as rated by staff and their 'ideal' organizational climate (Whybrow, 1994; Hatton et al., 1997).

– Work–home interface: some work has suggested a link between high staff stress and conflicting demands between work and home (Hatton et al., 1995, 1997; Rose, 1995).

As well as identifying factors implicated in staff stress and morale, this research has also begun to tease out which factors have the most impact on staff stress. For example, there is evidence that organizational factors, rather than aspects of user behaviour or service resources, are rated by staff as most stressful and are more closely linked to high staff stress (Browner et al., 1987; Allen et al., 1990; Rose, 1993; Bersani & Heifetz, 1995; Hatton et al., 1995, 1997). Of course, these findings should not be taken to mean that user characteristics or service resources are irrelevant to staff stress and well-being. All other things being equal, working with people with challenging behaviours and/or mental health problems in an under-resourced service is likely to be more stressful than working with more amenable people in a highly resourced service. It is simply that aspects of service organization, such as staff support, job design, and organizational culture, can all have a huge influence in either buffering against or exacerbating the effects of stressful user behaviour and poor service resources (Rose, 1995).

The body of research outlined above suggests that features of organizations have a crucial impact on staff stress and well-being and, by extension, on job performance, absenteeism and staff turnover. The next step is to establish what organizations can do to reduce staff stress.

Reducing staff stress

Given the importance of staff stress in services for people with mental retardation, there is a surprising lack of research evaluating stress reduction programmes or organizational interventions. This section of the chapter therefore draws on general organizational psychology principles to outline the range of possible organizational interventions and their likely impact on staff in services for people with mental retardation. Stress interventions can operate at three levels within organizations: the individual member of staff, the organization, or the individual/organizational interface (DeFrank & Cooper, 1987; Murphy, 1988). In practice, most organizations implement stress interventions at an individual level; this conveniently locates the problem of organizational stress within individual members of staff while avoiding more threatening and disruptive organizational change (Cooper & Cartwright, 1994; Makin et al., 1996).

DeFrank and Cooper (1987) present a framework for considering organizational stress interventions, based on their three levels of organizational intervention. This framework, adapted for organizations working with people with mental retardation, is presented in Table 25.2. Potential organizational interventions for improving staff stress and well-being will be discussed in relation to this framework.

Stress interventions focusing on the individual

A number of widely used interventions exists for reducing occupational stress at the level of the individual employee (Murphy, 1988; Arnold et al., 1995). Stress management programmes, for example, aim to help staff to identify sources and symptoms of stress and to cope better with stressful situations. Coping strategies taught on these programmes usually involve the improvement of emotion-focused coping strategies, such as cognitive coping strategies for dealing with stress. More rarely, the programmes focus on problem-focused coping strategies, such as time management and improving problem-solving skills. Another popular organizational approach is to offer personal counselling to highly stressed employees in an effort to improve the mental health of individuals. Finally, health promotion activities, such as providing exercise facilities and prohibiting workplace smoking, can also be used to reduce absenteeism and improve work performance.

These stress interventions can have positive effects, particularly on mental and physical health and absenteeism, although they appear to have little impact on staff commitment, work stress or job satisfaction (Sallis et al.,

Table 25.2 Levels of stress management interventions and outcomes

Interventions	Outcomes
Focus on individual	
Relaxation techniques	Improved depression and anxiety
Cognitive coping strategies	Fewer psychosomatic complaints
Time management	Less subjectively experienced stress
Health promotion	Less sleep disturbance
Personal counselling	Improved life satisfaction
Training	Reduced blood pressure, muscle tension
Focus on individual/organizational interface	
Relationships at work	Less job stress
Person–organization fit	More job satisfaction
Role issues	Less burnout
Participation and autonomy	Improved productivity and performance
	Less absenteeism
	Less turnover
Focus on organization	
Organizational structure	Improved productivity
Recruitment and retention	Less absenteeism
Work environment	Less turnover
	Success in recruitment and retention

Adapted from DeFrank & Cooper (1987).

1987; Cooper & Sadri, 1991). There is also some evidence that stress management programmes can reduce staff anxiety and depression, and improve staff performance, in services for people with mental retardation (Rose, 1997). However, stress interventions focusing on individuals alone are unlikely to have a lasting impact on staff because the sources of stress will remain unchanged (Arnold et al., 1995). For staff in services for people with mental retardation, stress interventions focusing on recognizing the symptoms of high stress and improving time management and problem-solving skills are likely to have the most lasting impact on staff morale and job performance (Rose, 1997).

Training can also be considered as a stress intervention programme. Whereas training on its own is unlikely to have a lasting effect on staff performance in services for people with mental retardation (Ziarnik & Bernstein, 1982; Repp, Felce & de Kock, 1987; Reid et al., 1989), in tandem with organizational interventions it may have long-term benefits for staff performance and staff morale (Reid et al., 1989).

Stress interventions focusing on the individual/organizational interface

Generally, there has been less focus on altering aspects of the individual/organizational interface, despite the obvious importance of these factors for staff stress and job performance.

In services for people with mental retardation, relationships at work are a crucial factor impacting on staff stress and well-being (Rose, 1995; Hatton et al., 1997). Services should recognize the central importance of supervisors, who need training in supervision skills and allotted time to supervise staff. Support from colleagues and team spirit could be fostered through the use of regular staff meetings, overlapping staff shifts, and staff support networks or mentoring systems. These issues are particularly important in dispersed community-based services, in which staff can work for long periods in isolation. Finally, regular contact with senior managers could do much to alleviate the feelings of alienation and powerlessness that many staff express.

Interventions aimed at improving person–organization fit, role conflict, role ambiguity and participation are all closely interlinked, and should have a major impact on staff morale, commitment and turnover (Hatton & Emerson, 1993c; Whybrow, 1994; Arnold et al., 1995; Hatton et al., 1997). First, services need to have a clear set of values, and a clear set of policies for putting these values into practice. These values and policies should be consistent with each other, and also consistent throughout all levels of the organization. This would help to reduce role conflict and role ambiguity, and also to clarify the aims of the organization for potential recruits. Second, services need to ensure that employees are in agreement with the values of the organization, and also in agreement with the methods the organization uses to implement its philosophy. Ways to achieve this include: ensuring at the recruitment stage that prospective employees are clear about organizational values and practices, and in agreement with them (possibly by including service users in the recruitment process: Townsley & Macadam, 1996); providing both values-based training and skills-based training to staff to inculcate organizational values and give staff the skills to implement those values; and giving staff at all levels in the organization a voice into the way the organization operates, both at the level of decisions about individuals and at the level of formulating organizational values and policies (Elkin & Rosch, 1990).

Stress interventions focusing on the organization

Again, relatively little attention has been paid to stress interventions focusing on the organization, particularly in services for people with mental retardation. Important interventions here are likely to concern altering the structure of organizations, looking at recruitment procedures, and altering the work environment, including working conditions and aspects of the job. With regard to organizational structure, services need to: ensure that they are not hierarchical; establish clear lines of communication and responsibility; and establish clear and achievable career development programmes to provide a continuing incentive for staff to improve skills (Hatton & Emerson, 1993a, 1993b, 1993c).

With regard to recruitment and retention, there is extensive evidence that younger, inexperienced staff are most likely to suffer high levels of stress and leave services for people with mental retardation (Allen et al., 1990; Hatton et al., 1995, 1997). Recruitment practices need to focus on gaining a balanced workforce in terms of age and experience. Additional support to young, inexperienced staff in the forms of induction training, ongoing skills training and supervision could improve stress, morale and turnover in this staff group (Hatton & Emerson, 1993c; Smith, Wun & Cumella, 1996).

Recruiting older staff, who are likely to have other commitments, also requires attention to be paid to working conditions. Changes here could include increasing the availability of part-time work and allowing more flexible shift structures. Given that long hours are associated with high staff stress and reduced work satisfaction (Hatton et al., 1997), restricting the number of additional hours staff are allowed to work could be beneficial, although this would require services to employ sufficient numbers of staff to cover holidays, sickness and emergencies. Reducing the length of shifts and increasing their predictability could also have an impact on a major source of general stress – conflicting demands between work and home (Hatton et al., 1995, 1997).

Finally, direct care staff, in particular, report that tedious and repetitive work is associated with high stress and reduced work satisfaction (Cox, 1980; Hatton et al., 1997). Whereas some of these tasks are an inevitable part of the job, organizations could pay more attention to alleviating some of the tedium associated with them. Services could consider giving staff more control over the timing of different tasks, providing positive reinforcement for the completion of tasks that are in themselves unrewarding (Reid et al., 1989), and increasing the variety of tasks undertaken by staff (Hatton et al., 1997).

Evaluating interventions

Given the lack of evidence concerning the effectiveness of stress interventions in services for people with mental retardation (Hatton & Emerson, 1993c; Rose, 1997), it is essential that organizations monitor levels of staff stress and work performance, both to evaluate the effectiveness of organizational interventions on staff, and also to identify staff who are exhibiting signs of high stress before major problems arise.

Conclusion: staff stress – an organizational responsibility

This chapter shows that high staff stress can be a major problem in services for people with mental retardation, and that it has serious consequences for staff, services and service users. However, high staff stress is not an inevitable consequence of working with people with mental retardation, and there are many ways in which organizations can intervene to improve staff stress and morale. As the final message of this chapter, it cannot be emphasized too strongly that staff stress in services for people with mental retardation is an organizational responsibility. All too often, staff experiencing high stress are made to feel that they are weak or incompetent, and are left unsupported by colleagues, supervisors and the organization generally. This is clearly unacceptable. If services are committed to improving the quality of life of people with mental retardation, then they have to be equally committed to improving the well-being of staff.

References

Allen, P., Pahl, J. & Quine, L. (1990). *Care Staff in Transition*. London: HMSO.

Arnold, J., Cooper, C.L. & Robertson, I.T. (1995). *Work Psychology: Understanding Human Behaviour in the Workplace, 2nd edn*. London: Pitman Publishing.

Baumeister, A.A. & Zaharia, E.S. (1986). Withdrawal and commitment of basic-care staff in residential programmes. In *Living Environemnts and Mental Retardation*, ed. S. Landesman, P.M. Vietze & M.J. Begab, pp. 269–87. Washington, DC: American Association on Mental Retardation.

Bennett, N., Dodd, T., Flatley, J., Freeth, S. & Bolling, K. (1995). *Health Survey for England 1993*. London: HMSO.

Bersani, H.A. & Heifetz, L.J. (1985). Perceived stress and satisfaction of direct-care staff members in community residences for mentally retarded adults. *American Journal of Mental Deficiency*, **90**, 289–95.

Borrill, C., Wall, T.D., West, M.A.et al. (1996). *Mental Health of the Workforce in NHS Trusts: Phase 1 Final Report*. Sheffield: Institute of Work Psychology.

Bromley, J. & Emerson, E. (1995). Beliefs and emotional reactions of care staff working with people with challenging behaviour. *Journal of Intellectual Disability Research*, **39**, 341–52.

Browner, C.H., Ellis, K.A., Ford, T., Silsby, J., Tampoya, J. & Yee, C. (1987). Stress, social support, and health of psychiatric technicians in a state facility. *Mental Retardation*, **25**, 31–8.

Cooper, C.L. & Cartwright, S. (1994). Healthy mind; healthy organization: a proactive approach to occupational stress. *Human Relations*, **47**, 455–71.

Cooper, C.L. & Payne, R. eds. (1988). *Causes, Coping and Consequences of Stress at Work*. Chichester: Wiley.

Cooper, C.L. & Sadri, G. (1991). The impact of stress counselling at work. *Journal of Social Behavior and Personality*, **6**, 411–33.

Corrigan, P.W. (1993). Staff stressors at a developmental center and state hospital. *Mental Retardation*, **31**, 234–8.

Cox, T. (1980). Repetitive work. In *Current Concerns in Occupational Stress*, ed. C.L. Cooper & R. Payne, pp. 23–4. Chichester: Wiley.

DeFrank, R.S. & Cooper, C.L. (1987). Worksite stress management interventions: their effectiveness and conceptualization. *Journal of Managerial Psychology*, **2**, 4–10.

Elkin, A.J. & Rosch, P.J. (1990). Promoting mental health at the workplace: the prevention side of stress management. *Occupational Medicine: State of the Art Review*, **5**, 739–54.

Emerson, E. & Hatton, C. (1994). *Moving Out: the Impact of Relocation from Hospital to Commuity on the Quality of Life of People with Learning Disabilities.* London: HMSO.

(1996). Deinstitutionalization in the UK and Ireland: outcomes for service users. *Journal of Intellectual and Developmental Disability*, **21**, 17–37.

Felce, D. (1996). Quality of support for ordinary living. In *Deinstitutionalization and Community Living: Intellectual Disability Services in Britain, Scandinavia and the USA*, ed. J. Mansell and K. Ericsson, pp. 117–33. London: Chapman and Hall.

Fletcher, B.C. (1988). The epidemiology of occupational stress. In *Causes, Coping and Consequences of Stress at Work*, ed. C.L. Cooper & R. Payne, pp. 3–50. Chichester: Wiley.

Folkman, S. & Lazarus, R.S. (1985). If it changes it must be a process: study of emotion and coping during three stages of a college examination. *Journal of Personality and Social Psychology*, **48**, 150–70.

Fontana, D. (1990). *Problems in Practice: Managing Stress.* London: BPS Books & Routledge.

Hatton, C., Brown, R., Caine, A. & Emerson, E. (1995). Stressors, coping strategies and stress-related outcomes among direct care staff in staffed houses for people with learning disabilities. *Mental Handicap Research*, **8**, 252–71.

Hatton, C. & Emerson, E. (1993a). *Staff Turnover, Stress and Morale at SENSE-in-the-Midlands. Report to the Department of Health.* Manchester: Hester Adrian Research Centre, University of Manchester.

(1993b). Organizational predictors of staff stress, satisfaction, and intended turnover in a service for people with multiple disabilities. *Mental Retardation*, **31**, 388–95.

(1993c). *The Effects of Organizational Change on Staff Turnover, Stress and Morale at SENSE-Midlands.* Manchester: Hester Adrian Research Centre, University of Manchester.

(1995). The development of a shortened 'ways of coping' questionnaire for use with direct care staff in learning disability services. *Mental Handicap Research*, **8**, 237–51.

Hatton, C., Emerson, E., Robertson, J., Henderson, D. & Cooper, J. (1996). Factors associated with staff support and resident lifestyle in services for people with multiple disabilities: a path analytic approach. *Journal of Intellectual Disability Research*, **40**, 466–77.

Hatton, C., Rivers, M., Mason, H. et al. (1997). *Staff in Services for People with Learning Disabilities: Report to the Department of Health.* Manchester: Hester Adrian Research Centre, University of Manchester.

Lazarus, R.S. & Folkman, S. (1984). *Stress, Appraisal and Coping.* New York: Springer-Verlag.

Makin, P., Cooper, C. & Cox, C. (1996). *Organizations and the Psychological Contract.* Leicester: BPS Books.

Maslach, C. & Pines, A. (1977). The burn-out syndrome in the day care setting. *Child Care Quarterly*, **6**, 100–13.

Murphy, L.R. (1988). Workplace interventions for stress reduction and prevention. In *Causes, Coping and Consequences of Stress at Work,* ed. C.L. Cooper & R. Payne, pp. 301–39. Chichester: Wiley.

Power, K.G. & Sharp, G.R. (1988). A comparison of sources of nursing stress and job satisfaction among mental handicap and hospice nursing staff. *Journal of Advanced Nursing,* **13,** 726–32.

Razza, N.J. (1993). Determinants of direct-care staff turnover in group homes for individuals with mental retardation. *Mental Retardation,* **31,** 284–91.

Reid, D.H., Parsons, M.B. & Green, C.W. (1989). *Staff Management in Human Services.* Springfield, IL: Charles C Thomas.

Repp, A.C., Felce, D. & de Kock, U. (1987). Observational studies of staff working with mentally retarded persons: A review. *Research in Developmental Disabilities,* **8,** 331–50.

Rice, D.M. & Rosen, M. (1991). Direct-care staff: a neglected priority. *Mental Retardation,* **29,** iii–iv.

Rose, J. (1993). Stress and staff in residential settings: the move from hospital to the community. *Mental Handicap Research,* **6,** 312–32.

(1995). Stress and residential staff: towards an integration of existing research. *Mental Handicap Research,* **8,** 220–36.

(1997). Stress and stress management. *Tizard Learning Disability Review,* **2,** 8–15.

Rose, J., Mullan, E. & Fletcher, B. (1994). An examination of the relationship between staff behaviour and stress levels in residential care. *Mental Handicap Research,* **7,** 312–28.

Rose, J. & Schelewa-Davies, D. (1997). Staff stress and team climate. *Journal of Learning Disabilities,* **1,** 19–24.

Sallis, J.F., Tervorrow, T.R., Johnson, C.C., Hovell, M.F. & Kaplan, R.M. (1987). Worksite stress management: a comparison of programmes. *Psychology and Health,* **1,** 237–55.

Smith, B., Wun, W.L. & Cumella, S. (1996). Training for staff caring for people with learning disability. *British Journal of Learning Disabilities,* **24,** 20–5.

Thomson, S. (1987). Stress in staff working with mentally handicapped people. In *Stress in Health Professionals,* ed. R. Payne and J. Firth-Cozens, pp. 151–65. Chichester: Wiley.

Townsley, R. & Macadam, M. (1996). *Choosing Staff: Involving People with Learning Difficulties in Staff Recruitment.* Bristol: Policy Press.

Whybrow, A. (1994). Staff in a Service for People with Learning Disabilities. PhD Thesis. Liverpool: University of Liverpool.

Ziarnik, J.P. & Bernstein, G.S. (1982). A critical examination of the effect of inservice training on staff performance. *Mental Retardation,* **20,** 109–14.

26 Professional training in the psychiatry of mental retardation in the UK

KENNETH DAY

Introduction

Recognition of the mental health problems and needs of people with mental retardation is a comparatively recent phenomenon and there is currently a worldwide paucity of specialist service provision. Lack of specialist staff, particularly psychiatrists, has been a major barrier to the development of services (Parmenter, 1988; Zarfas, 1988; Day, 1992; MHMR, 1993). The availability of specialist training varies markedly from country to country and, not surprisingly, bears a close relationship to the level of service development.

In the UK, the need for specialist mental health services for people with mental retardation with mental health problems, including behaviour disorders and offending, was recognized in the early 1970s (Royal College of Psychiatrists 1986a, 1989, 1996b; Department of Health, 1989, 1992, 1993a; Department of Health and Home Office, 1992; NHS Executive, 1998). A comprehensive network of specialist psychiatric services has been developed (Day 1993, 1994); there are well-established specialist training programmes for psychiatrists and nurses (Day & Jancar, 1991); and a number of initiatives has recently been introduced to address the training needs of other health care professionals including family doctors, community nurses and direct care staff.

The aim of this chapter is to provide an overview of current training of the main professional groups working with people with mental retardation with mental health problems in the UK. The focus is on psychiatrists, medical students, general practitioners and specialist nurses. Clinical psychologists, social workers and direct care staff are covered in less detail.

Psychiatrists

Mental retardation has been a recognized psychiatric specialty for 150 years in the UK, although, until recently, doctors working in the specialty fulfilled many roles and the more focused specialty of the 'psychiatry of mental handicap' was not borne until the early 1970s (Day & Jancar, 1991). Currently, there are approximately 200 consultants practising in the specialty and some 100 doctors in training, but the recommended norm of one whole-time consultant per 100 000 of the general population (Royal College of Psychiatrists, 1992a) has yet to be achieved. A substantial academic base has been created: the first Chair in the 'psychiatry of mental handicap' was established in London in 1980 and there are now six professorial chairs countrywide, with academic posts at senior lecturer level in all university teaching hospitals. The Royal College of Psychiatrists has a strong faculty of mental retardation and developmental disability and is active in developing and monitoring training programmes, organizing academic meetings, contributing to research and influencing national policy (Day & Jancar, 1991). The annual Blake Marsh lecture on mental retardation was established in 1966 (Day & Jancar, 1997), and the Burden Gold Medal and Research Prize was instituted in 1969 (Wiley, 1989). Several prizes and travelling scholarships in the specialty are available to trainees.

Psychiatric training in the UK takes a minimum of six years and follows a well-established pattern of a period of general professional training in psychiatry followed by a period of higher training in one of the recognized psychiatric specialities – general (adult) psychiatry, child and adolescent psychiatry, forensic psychiatry, old-age psychiatry, psychotherapy or mental retardation psychiatry (currently termed 'learning disability'). Responsibility for prescribing and monitoring training rests with the Royal College of Psychiatrists and the Joint Committee on Higher Psychiatric Training, whose educational policy (Royal College of Psychiatrists, 1997) has recently been revised to reflect the major changes in postgraduate medical education in the UK (Department of Health, 1993b) in line with European Community directives (European Specialist Medical Qualifications Order 1995). The main components of the training programme are summarized in Table 26.1 and described in more detail below.

General professional training

General professional training in psychiatry takes a minimum of three years and must be undertaken in a training scheme approved by the Royal College of Psychiatrists. The prescribed curriculum requires a course of not less than 30-half-days' academic lectures per term for a minimum of two years, and rotational clinical experience in a variety of service and clinical settings. Each scheme has a scheme organizer, is overseen by a training committee, and is regularly inspected by college approval teams. Consultants participating in training schemes must be approved as educational supervisors by the college. Trainees must have two to three sessions per week of protected time for academic study and a minimum of one hour per week consultant supervision during clinical placements. A clinical tutor system is in operation. Regularly updated reading lists are issued for each specialty.

Table 26.1 Specialist training in psychiatry in the UK

General professional training
Senior house officer

Three to four years supervised training in a scheme approved by the Royal College of Psychiatrists

Academic teaching and clinical experience in general (adult) psychiatry and other psychiatric specialties (including mental retardation)

Lectures in other topics relevant to the practice of psychiatry, e.g. psychology, neurology, social sciences, psychopathology, psychopharmacology, genetics, medical ethics, epidemiology

Membership of the Royal College of Psychiatrists (MRCPsych) by examination on completion

Higher training in a psychiatric specialty
Specialist registrar

Three to four years in a training scheme approved by the Joint Committee on Higher Psychiatric Training

Further development of general psychiatric skills and knowledge

Clinical placements of 12 to 18 months duration to provide a range of different service experience in chosen specialty

Academic: weekly academic meetings, opportunities to visit other services and to attend national and international conferences

Teaching and supervision: opportunities to teach medical undergraduates and other professional groups and to supervise trainee psychiatrists

Involvement in research and audit, including the planning and execution of an original research project and the acquisition of computer skills

Experience of management

Award of Certificate of Completion of Specialist Training (CCST) on satisfactory completion, inclusion on the Specialist Register (General Medical Council) and eligibility for consultant appointment and specialist practice

Clinical skills training is based on general adult psychiatry, in which there must be at least one year's full-time placement. Trainees are also expected to gain some experience in other psychiatric specialties. Up to one year of general professional training may be undertaken in general practice, general medicine or research. Academic courses are university based and cover the sciences basic to the practice of psychiatry: aetiology, diagnosis and management of the major psychiatric disorders, an introduction to the other psychiatric specialities, training in research methods and statistics, and the critical understanding of scientific literature and legal and ethical aspects. The majority of training schemes include a three to six-month full-time clinical placement and an academic course of 20 to 24 lectures in mental retardation.

Table 26.2 Summary curriculum for MRCPsych in Mental Retardation

Developmental
Neurology of brain development – effects of genetic and environmental factors
Common disorders, e.g. Down syndrome, fragile X syndrome, fetal alcohol syndrome, low-birth-weight babies
Specific disorders, e.g. autism, Asperger's syndrome
Influence of social factors on intellectual and emotional development

Classification and epidemiology
Historical perspectives
Modern systems of classification e.g. ICD-10, DSM-IV
Prevalence of mental retardation in the general population
Prevalence of psychiatric and behaviour disorders in mental retardation

Clinical
General characteristics of mental retardation
Aetiological factors
Developmental history taking
Presentation and diagnosis of psychiatric illness and behaviour disorders in mental retardation
Psychological methods of assessment
Psychological theories of behaviour disorders
Treatment of psychiatric and behaviour disorders including drug treatments, psychotherapy, behavioural therapy and cognitive therapy
Behavioural phenotypes
Impact on family – family psychodynamics
Assessment, management and treatment of offenders with mental retardation

Other
Broad understanding of relevant legislation
Principles of service provision
Provision and range of specialist psychiatric services for mental retardation

From Royal College of Psychiatrists (1997).

A recent survey indicates that 28 per cent of trainees undertake a clinical placement in mental retardation, whereas others gain some experience during child and adolescent placements. From the year 2000, it will be mandatory for all psychiatric trainees to undergo a six-month period of basic training in either the psychiatry of learning disability or child and adolescent psychiatry, or some combination of the two.

A list of recommended curriculum topics in mental retardation is given in Table 26.2. The aim at this level is to provide a broad introduction to all aspects of the care and treatment of people with mental retardation, with the focus on neuropsychiatry and management of the family, together with experience in both community and specialist hospital services. Exposure to the subject at this stage of training enhances the skill base of general psychiatrists, who are increasingly encountering people with mental retardation in their clinical practice, and facilitates recruitment to the specialty.

The postgraduate qualification in psychiatry in the UK is Membership of the Royal College of Psychiatrists (MRCPsych), which is obtained by examination. Part I of the examination, in basic clinical psychiatry, may be taken after one year's full-time training, and Part II, which may include questions on and a clinical examination in mental retardation, after satisfactory completion of training (Royal College of Psychiatrists, 1996a, 1997).

Higher psychiatric training

Higher training in a psychiatric specialty, e.g. mental retardation, is undertaken in an approved training scheme. The Joint Committee of Higher Psychiatric Training (JCHPT), which comprises representatives from the Royal College of Psychiatrist and the Association of University Teachers in Psychiatry, is responsible for prescribing training requirements and for the regular inspection and approval of higher training schemes (Joint Committee on Higher Psychiatric Training, 1995; Royal College of Psychiatrists, 1997). Higher psychiatric training schemes are usually organized on a regional basis to enable a sufficiently comprehensive and flexible programme to be developed to meet individual trainees' needs and interests. They are normally associated with university departments of psychiatry and regulated and overseen by a regional specialist training committee chaired by the postgraduate medical dean. Scheme organizers, who usually hold an academic appointment, are responsible for drawing up and co-ordinating training programmes. Consultants acting as trainers on schemes must be approved by the Royal College of Psychiatrists.

The prescribed programme for higher training in the psychiatry of mental retardation is summarized in Table 26.3. The aim is to increase further the core skills required by all psychiatrists (including leadership and management skills, multidisciplinary working , research and audit, teaching and supervision) and to impart an in-depth and expert knowledge and understanding of psychopathology, treatment measures and legal issues as they apply to the mentally retarded, together with a knowledge and understanding of the work of the relevant co-disciplines. Trainees must gain experience in hospital and community settings and across the full range of services, including adult mental retardation, child and adolescent mental retardation, and the management of forensic and other patients with special needs. Special interest sessions are allocated to enable trainees to obtain more experience in aspects of the service of particular interest to them or in disciplines relevant to the field such as neuropsychiatry, paediatrics or human genetics. Trainees must attend weekly academic meetings, gain experience in teaching and research (including the planning and execution of an original research project), participate in audit, and obtain some management experience by serving on committees. They are also

Table 26.3 Higher training in the psychiatry of mental retardation

Core clinical experience

Assessment, treatment and management of emotional and behaviour disorders, psychoses, epilepsy, and other psychiatric and developmental disorders

Full range of mental retardation – children, adolescents, adults and the elderly

Work with families, including dysfunctional families

Management of psychiatric emergencies, longer term problems, rehabilitation and resettlement, prevention

Knowledge of particular legal issues

Special interest

Forensic psychiatry, child psychiatry, psychotherapy, paediatrics, clinical genetics or neuropsychiatry, depending upon the trainee's needs and interests

Treatment methods

Experience in all types of treatment

Development of special skills in one or more through supervised practice

Treatment settings

Experience of a variety of hospital settings including admission/assessment, rehabilitation, secure units and continuing care

Experience of a full range of community settings, including residential homes, day services, education and joint work with community teams

Criminal justice settings

Multidisciplinary working – acting in a consultative capacity to non-health service facilities

Academic

Weekly academic meetings – lectures, case conferences, journal clubs

Content – psychiatric and behaviour disorders, child development, psychology, social services

From Joint Committee on Higher Psychiatric Training (1995).

encouraged to attend full-time or part-time courses outside their main training centre.

There must be at least one timetabled weekly supervision session with the consultant trainer in each clinical placement and regular meetings with the scheme organiser to discuss progress and problems. A formal review is carried out annually by a panel of the specialty training committee and recorded, together with the trainee's experience and progress to date and recommendations for further targeted training. There is no qualifying examination, but successful completion of higher training leads to the award of a Certificate of Completion of Specialist Training (CCST) by the Specialist Training Authority of the Medical Royal Colleges, inclusion on the Specialist Register of the General Medical Council, and eligibility for consultant appointment by competition (Department of Health, 1995c; NHS Executive, 1996).

The breadth and depth of higher training in mental retardation psychiatry have increased significantly in recent years as the knowledge base has grown and service provision has developed. All training schemes now provide a rich experience, with good supervision in well-developed and comprehensive services, and there has been a corresponding improvement in the recruitment and calibre of trainees. Increasing refinements in service provision are beginning to give rise to new specialisms – specifically, forensic mental retardation psychiatry and child and adolescent mental retardation psychiatry. The recommended minimum training for such posts is two years in mental retardation psychiatry and 18 months in either forensic or child and adolescent psychiatry (Joint Committee on Higher Psychiatric Training, 1995). However, there is recognition of the need for flexibility and latitude at the present time to enable these new specialisms to become properly established.

General practitioners and other medical specialties

The consequences of care in the community for the workload and training needs of general practitioners were recognized in the early 1980s (Howells, 1986; Kinnell, 1987), but it is only comparatively recently that the central role of the general practitioner and primary health care team in the management of the medical and psychiatric problems of people with mental retardation living in the community has come to be fully appreciated (Royal College of General Practitioners, 1990; Howells 1991; Department of Health, 1995a, Lennox & Kerr, 1997; NHS Executive, 1998). An average practice of four partners serving a population of 7000–8000 will be responsible for approximately 150 people with mental retardation (Kerr, 1997). Some also undertake specific responsibility for hostels and residential homes in their area and /or provide medical cover to hospital units. Only a minority of people with mental retardation are capable of properly using the medical and dental services (Whelan & Speake, 1977) or accessing health promotion facilities (Langan et al., 1993), and treatable medical conditions, including psychiatric problems, continue to go unobserved and untreated (Howells, 1986; Kinnell 1987; Wilson & Haire, 1990,). Many general practitioners still see the specialist psychiatrist as playing a global role in the provision of health care (Bernard & Bates, 1994) and few appear enthusiastic about organized health promotion and annual health screening (Kerr, Dunston & Thapar, 1996; Singh 1997; Bond et al., 1997).

During the past decade, numerous efforts have been made to address the training needs of family doctors. Locally organized postgraduate courses have met with varying degrees of success (Bicknell, 1985; Singh, 1997). The Royal Society of Medicine's Forum on Mental Retardation regularly runs conferences on a range of medical aspects of the care of the mentally retarded, and in 1990 the Royal College of General Practitioners published an excellent, eminently readable and practically orientated guide to the medical, social and legal aspects of the care of people with mental retardation for family doctors (Royal College of General Practitioners, 1990). More recently, the Department of Post Graduate Studies, University of Wales College of Medicine, has produced an in-depth *Distance Learning Work Book* for general practitioners covering identification, diagnosis, health surveillance, family, medical needs, morbidity associated with specific syndromes and health checks (Howells et al., 1993). Other positive developments include the publication of *Health of the Nation*; a strategy for people with learning disability (Department of Health, 1995a), and the *Welsh Health Gain Protocol for Learning Disability* (Welsh Health Planning Forum, 1992), which set targets and provide guidelines for the health care of people with mental retardation, the development of computer disk advice for general practitioners on the health problems of people with mental retardation, and the establishment of special registers of people with mental retardation and liaison posts with the specialist services in some practices (Singh, 1997). Vocational training placements that include some experience in mental retardation are also increasingly featuring in general practitioners vocational training schemes.

Such initiatives are, however, essentially ad hoc and depend very much upon the interests and enthusiasm of individual general practitioners, the local mental retardation services, and postgraduate training departments. A more systematic approach on a national basis is needed and there is evidence that many general practitioners would welcome this (Singh, 1997). Training should be tailored to meet specific needs: established general practitioners are likely to benefit most from occasional postgraduate sessions on a practical topic, whereas those with a special interest in or responsibility for people with mental retardation require more intensive training.

Similar training needs are now extending to all doctors, who are much more likely to encounter people with mental retardation in clinical practice than in the past – particularly those working in the fields of paediatrics, orthopaedic surgery, ENT and ophthalmology. A clinical attachment in child and adolescent psychiatry that offers some experience in mental retardation is an increasingly common option in the training of paediatricians and community physicians.

Medical undergraduates

Mental retardation has long featured in the curriculum of medical students in the UK, but until recently it was generally poorly co-ordinated and often limited to a parade of pathological specimens during an afternoon's visit to an institution, or carried out in paediatric departments with little opportunity for learning about adults (Holt & Huntley, 1973; Pilkington 1977; Shapira, Zeitlin & Sacks, 1978).

The growth of specialist academic departments, changes in the pattern of service delivery, and the increasing involvement of generic health services in the care of mentally retarded people have led to considerable improvements in teaching. A 1986 survey showed that British medical students received an average of 12 hours' specialist teaching in the subject, including 'hands-on' experience, video presentations, seminars and lectures, workshops, visits to services and role-play, with an examination at the end of the course in two-thirds of the teaching centres (Hollins & Bradley, 1987; Hollins 1988). Principal responsibility for training rests with departments of psychiatry, child health, family and community medicine.

Surveys of medical students (Pilkington, 1977; Holt & Bouras, 1988; Holt, Bouras & Brooks 1993) and young doctors three years post-qualification (Bradley, 1988) indicate a positive response to such teaching and an interest in learning more about both clinical aspects and the wider social issues in mental retardation. The value of face-to-face contact with people with mental retardation and their families, knowledge about services and how to access them, training in how to inform the family about the diagnosis, the diagnosis of mental illness in people with mental retardation, and the management of behaviour disorders and secondary handicaps were particularly emphasized. Learning about mental retardation is also of general value to medical practice, providing insights into living and coping with a chronic disability, the provision of services for the long-term disabled, crisis intervention and medical ethics. It also plays a vital role in recruitment to the specialty.

The Royal College of Psychiatrists' (1986b) guidelines on undergraduate teaching in mental retardation recommend a minimum core training of 12–15 hours and that the 'the primary aim should be to give the young doctor sufficient knowledge and understanding of the field of mental handicap to enable him to deal sensitively and knowledgeably with people with mental retardation and their families that they might encounter as a general practitioner or in hospital practice'. The list of suggested topics to be covered is given in Table 26.4. A senior academic presence in the field in each medical school is required to organize and co-ordinate the programme (Hollins, 1988).

Specialist nurses

Nurses working in the field of mental retardation in the UK have received specialist training leading to the qualification Registered Mental Handicap Nurse (RNMH) since 1919 (Day & Jancar, 1991). The content of training has varied over the years, reflecting changing service philosophies. During the 1970s and 1980s, there was a major shift of emphasis from the medical to the social aspects of care, and the specialty of mental retardation nursing was all but destroyed by an over-interpretation of normalization

Table 26.4 Recommended topics for medical undergraduate teaching in mental retardation

Epidemiology of mental retardation
Classification
Aetiology
Prevention
Clinical features and associated disorders
Social and family aspects
Assessment and care of the individual
Concepts of care and services systems
Where to get or refer for help
Major ethical issues

From Royal College of Psychiatrists (1986b).

philosophy, the closure of long-stay mental retardation hospitals, and calls for a 'new caring profession' – a hybrid of social care and nursing (Department of Health and Social Security, 1979). The Royal College of Psychiatrists campaigned strongly for the specialist mental handicap nurse, pointing out that nurses remaining in the hospital service would be principally concerned with psychiatric aspects of care, and called for a thorough review of training to ensure that future nurses would be adequately equipped for this role (Royal College of Psychiatrists, 1987).

The debate continues, but recent years have seen an increasing acknowledgement of the need for the specialist nurse in mental retardation whose remit includes mental health care (Chief Nursing Officers of the United Kingdom, 1991; Brown, 1994; Department of Health 1995a, 1995b; Matthews, 1996). Disappointingly, however, training still remains focused primarily on community nursing and general health care and there is little or no specific training in the psychiatry of mental retardation A continuing bias towards the social aspects of care and the blurring of professional roles in community mental handicap teams have been further emphasized by the introduction of joint training and a dual qualification in nursing and social care (CCETSW, 1992a) and similar proposals in relation to occupational therapy (Sainsbury Centre for Mental Health, 1997).

The situation has been further complicated by a recent national re-organization of nurse training in the UK that requires all trainee nurses to undertake a common foundation course on basic nursing for a minimum of 18 months, followed by 18 months' specialist training in one of the five recognized branches of nursing – of which mental handicap nursing is one (United Kingdom Central Council for Nursing, Midwifery and Health Visiting, 1986). This has generated concerns about the lack of exposure to mental retardation during the common foundation course, the potentially deleterious consequences for recruitment to the specialty and the adequacy of the duration of specialist training, and has led to calls for a return to single specialty training (Sines, 1993; Brown, 1994).

Some nurses working in specialist psychiatric services for people with mental retardation are dually qualified in both mental health and mental handicap nursing, but the majority obtain further training and experience on an in-service basis and by attending specialist courses on specific aspects of mental health care in mental retardation organized by colleges of health and the professional organizations. One way forward is through the specialist nurse practitioner – a qualified nurse who has undertaken specialist post basic training and obtained post – basic nursing experience in a particular area of nursing (United Kingdom Central Council for Nursing, Midwifery and Health Visiting, 1986). Whereas this is at present limited to general mental handicap nursing, it is to be hoped that it will not be long before the specialist nurse practitioner in the psychiatry of mental retardation is established and appropriate training programmes developed. Another positive development is the growing availability to nurses and other disciplines of diploma or masters degree courses on specific aspects of care – two recent examples being forensic practice and mental health studies in mental retardation.

Clinical psychologists and professions allied to medicine

Currently, there are some 350 qualified clinical psychologists working in the UK in the mental retardation services (not all exclusively so), a thriving Special Interest Group in the British Psychological Society, and eight academic or research professorial chairs.

Training in clinical psychology is undertaken at postgraduate level in a three-year university course, approved by the British Psychological Society, leading to a doctoral degree in clinical psychology (British Psychological Society, 1994). Entry requirements are an honours degree in psychology, recognized by the British Psychological Society, and typically two year's practical experience in the health service as an assistant psychologist or research assistant. The course comprises systematic academic teaching integrated with periods of practical clinical experience under the direct supervision of approved senior professional staff in a variety of service specialties and across the full age spectrum. Students must also learn research skills and carry out at least one clinically relevant piece of original research. Successful completion of training and graduation entitles the individual to be entered on the Register of Chartered Psychologists and to practise as a clinical psychologist in the health, teaching or research field (Watts, 1985; Clearing House for PCCP, 1997).

The academic course includes lectures on mental retardation, covering development in relation to mental retardation, causes and characteristics, aspects of care (assessment and monitoring, interventions, skills development), and service issues – normalization, staff support, service provision, organization and policy (Powell, Young & Frosh, 1993). There is also a mandatory six-month clinical placement in mental retardation services that must provide both community and hospital experience and a minimum of 55 contact hours' work with individuals or small groups (client, carer, family) and work at a system/organizational/policy level. Students intending to work with the mentally retarded usually obtain one year's practical experience in the field as an assistant psychologist or research assistant before embarking on a higher degree, and can opt for further clinical placements of up to one year in mental retardation services during the course. Further training and experience are obtained as part of general professional development.

The professions allied to medicine – physiotherapists, occupational therapists and speech therapists – receive a brief introduction to mental retardation during their academic course and may undertake a clinical placement, but receive no specific training in mental health aspects of care. The possibility of shared courses with nurses and perhaps social workers for some aspects of training has been mooted for the future (Sainsbury Centre for Mental Health, 1997).

Social workers

The role of the social services in the care of people with mental retardation has grown considerably during the last two decades and there has been a corresponding expansion in the role of field social workers. These changes have occurred in the context of the emergence of the generic social worker with a general remit and training. One response has been a move towards joint training and qualifications with the nursing profession (CCETSW, 1992a), but there is also a growing minority view in favour of a return to specialisms in social work practice and training.

The Diploma in Social Work (DipSW) is the professional social work qualification for social workers in all settings and sectors in the UK. It is awarded after a minimum of two years' training at higher education level in a programme approved by the Central Council for Education and Training in Social Work (CCETSW). The training requirements published by CCETSW on the knowledge, skills and values required for competent social work practice are couched in broad principles and make little mention of specific client groups (CCETSW, 1996). Guidance on the mental health dimension in social work makes no specific mention of mental health issues in mental retardation (CCETSW, 1994), nor is there any mention of the topic in the training recommendations for approved social workers/mental health officers who undertake special responsibilities in relation to the Mental Health Acts (CCETSW, 1993). In practice, however, most courses touch on the topic, if only briefly, in the academic programme, and during their second year students must undertake two supervised service placements of 50 to 80 days each in an area of particular social work practice, one or both of which may be mental retardation. Growing awareness of the importance of mental health issues in mental retardation is likely to increase its profile in future training programmes.

As with all other professional groups, there is a continuing need for social work practitioners with special expertise and training in mental retardation. Currently, there are few hospital-based social workers in mental retardation and their dwindling number is a matter of great concern to psychiatrists and other professionals working in these services. A joint CCETSW/ Royal College of Psychiatrists conference in 1989 attempted to address this problem and concluded that training for social workers in the mental health problems of people with mental retardation was important, but most appropriately undertaken at post-qualification level in locally based settings, and noted the scope presented in the context of approved social worker training (CCETSW, 1992b). The recently introduced Advanced Award in Social Work presents an excellent opportunity to take this forward, but so far detailed curriculum guidance has only been developed in relation to forensic social work – which, interestingly, also makes no specific mention of mental retardation (CCETSW, 1995b). It is to be hoped that a curriculum can soon be developed for social workers wishing to specialize in the mental health aspects of mental retardation.

Direct care staff

Latterly, attention has focused on the training needs of first-level care workers in community day and residential facilities (Holt, 1995). Currently, these workers receive little or no training in the psychiatric aspects of mental retardation, with the consequence that psychiatric illness amongst their clients frequently goes unrecognized and untreated (Patel, Goldberg & Moss, 1993).

The training of direct care staff in this aspect of care has been pioneered in the UK by Bouras and his colleagues, who have produced a comprehensive training package, 'Mental Health in Learning Disabilities' (Bouras & Holt, 1997). This comprises an introductory video, a training pack with facilitators' notes, handouts, case studies, exercise sheets and overheads and a handbook covering the presentation, assessment and treatment of mental health problems, challenging behaviour, epilepsy and autism in mentally retarded people of all ages, service provision, and legal and ethical issues. Another useful development is the production of a checklist specifically designed to help care staff to screen for mental health problems in their mentally retarded clients and to make informed referrals (Moss et al., 1997; Prosser et al., 1997).

Continuing professional development

Continuing professional development – the maintenance and development of knowledge and skills throughout the whole of an individual's professional career – is now enshrined in medical, nursing and social work practice in the UK and is gradually extending to all other professional groups. Professional bodies such as the Royal College of Psychiatrists, the British Psychological Society, the Central Council for the Education and Training in Social Work, and the English National Board of Nursing organize numerous educational activities on the mental health aspects of mental retardation exclusively for their members. But there is an increasing trend towards interdisciplinary initiatives. In a pioneering move in the 1980s, the Royal Society of Medicine established the Forum on Mental Retardation and opened its doors to a wide range of professionals. The British Institute of Learning Disabilities, founded in 1971, offers a wide range of educational conferences and workshops and a one-year certificate course in learning disability studies, available to all disciplines. A growing number of universities are offering diploma and masters degree courses in the mental health aspects of mental retardation.

Conclusion

Good-quality and effective services for people with mental retardation and mental health problems are crucially dependent upon the availability of properly trained and experienced staff at all levels. The UK has an excellent record in the training of psychiatrists, psychologists and nurses, but recent changes in service philosophy and provision require that much more attention be paid to the education and training of non-specialist staff, particularly primary health and direct care staff.

Current debate is focusing around the future training needs of *all* professional groups in the light of radically changing patterns of service and care and changing and sometimes overlapping professional roles (Weinstein, 1994). A recent review of the future roles and training of mental health staff emphasized the need to establish the core competencies required by all staff working in the service and the distinctive competencies required by each professional group, and proposed a mix of shared learning and separate professional development as the way forward for some groups (Sainsbury Centre for Mental Health, 1997) – conclusions that seem equally pertinent in the field of mental retardation.

Acknowledgements

Grateful thanks are due to Professor John Cox, Dean of the Royal College of Psychiatrists, Dr Derek Milne, Senior Lecturer in Clinical

Psychology, University of Newcastle upon Tyne, and Peter Matthias, Director, Central Council for the Education and Training in Social Work for their guidance in the preparation of this chapter.

References

Bernard, S.E. & Bates, R.E. (1994). The role of the psychiatrist in learning disability: how it is perceived by the G.P. *Psychiatric Bulletin*, **18**, 205–6.

Bicknell J. (1985). Educational programmes for general practitioners and clinical assistants in the mental handicap service. *Bulletin of the Royal College of Psychiatrists*, 8 154–55.

Bond, L., Kerr, M., Dunstan, F. & Thapar, A. (1997). Attitudes of general practitioners towards the health care of people with intellectual disability and the factors underlying these attitudes. *Journal of Intellectual Disability Research*, **41**, 391– 400.

Bouras, N. & Holt, G. (1997). *Mental Health in Learning Disabilities: Training Package*, 2nd edn. Brighton: Pavilion Publishing.

Bradley, E. (1988). Preparing medical undergraduates for their increasing role with patients who also have a mental handicap: a retrospective study. *Medical Teacher*, **10**, 283–88.

British Psychological Society (1994). *Every thing You Need to Know about Training in Psychology*. Leicester: British Psychological Society.

Brown, J. (1994). *Analysis of Responses to the Consensus Statement on the Future of the Specialist Nurse Practitioner in Learning Disabilities*. Report commissioned by the Chief Nursing Officer for England. York: University of York, SPSW Publishing.

CCETSW (1992a). *Learning Together: Shaping New Services for People with Learning Disabilities*. London: Central Council for Education and Training in Social Work.

(1992b). *A Double Challenge: working with People Who have Both Learning Difficulties and a Mental Illness*. Paper No 19.27. London: Central Council for Education and Training in Social Work.

(1993). *Regulations and Guidance for the Training of Social Workers to be considered for Approval in England and Wales under the Mental Health Act 1989*. Paper 19.19. London: Central Council for Education and Training in Social Work.

(1994). *The Mental Health Dimension in Social Work: Guidance for the Dip SW Programmes*. Paper 16. London: Central Council for Education and Training and Social Work.

(1995a). *Assuring Quality in the Diploma of Social Work – 1: Rules and Requirements for the Dip SW*. London: Central Council for Education and Training in Social Work.

(1995b). *Achieving Competence in Forensic Social Work: Guidance for the Advanced Award in Social Work*. London: Central Council for Education and Training in Social Work.

(1996). *Assessing Quality: Rules and Requirements for the DipSW*. London: Central Council for Educational Training in Social Work.

Chief Nursing Officers of the United Kingdom (1991). *Caring for People – Mental Handicap Nursing (Cullen Report). Health Publications Unit.* Lancashire: Heywood.

Clearing House for PCCP 1997). *Handbook: Postgraduate Courses in Clinical Psychology.* Leeds: Leeds University.

Day, K. (1992). Mental health care for the mentally handicapped in four European countries: the argument for specialised services. *Italian Journal of Intellectual Impairment,* **5,** 3–11.

   (1993). Mental Health Services for People with Mental Retardation: A Framework for the Future. *Journal of Intellectual Disability Research,* **37** Suppl. 1, 7–16.

   (1994). Psychiatric services in mental retardation: Generic of specialised provision? In *Mental Health in Mental Retardation,* ed. Bouras N, pp. 275–92. Cambridge: Cambridge University Press.

Day, K. & Jancar, J. (1991). Mental handicap and the Royal Medico Psychological Association: a historical association 1841–1991. In *150 Years of British Psychiatry 1841–1991,* ed. G.E. Berrios & H. Freeman, pp. 268–78. London: Gaskell Press.

   (1997). Dr Blake Marsh and the Blake Marsh lectures. *Psychiatric Bulletin,* **21,** 26–9.

Department of Health (1989). N*eeds and Responses: Services for Adults with Mental Handicap who are Mentally Ill, Who have Behaviour Problems or who Offend.* Report of a Department of Health Study Team. Stanmore, Middlesex: Department of Health Leaflets Unit.

   (1992). *Health Services for People with Learning Disabilities (Mental Handicap).* NHSME Health Service Guidelines HSG (92) 42. Heywood, Lancashire: Health Publications Unit.

   (1993a). *Services for People with Learning Disabilities and Challenging Behaviour or Mental Health Needs.* London: HMSO.

   (1993b). *Hospital Doctors: Training for the Future.* The Report of the Working Group on Specialist Medical Training (The Calman Report). Heywood, Lancashire Department of Health.

   (1995a). *The Health of the Nation: A Strategy for People with Learning Disabilities.* London: Department of Health.

   (1995b). *Continuing the Commitment: Report of the Learning Disability Nursing Project.* London: HMSO.

   (1995c). *Implementing the Reforms to Specialist Medical Training (PL CMO(95)3).* Wetherby: DH Publications.

Department of Health and Home Office (1992). *Review of Health and Social Services for Mentally Disordered Offenders and Others Requiring Similar Services.* Final Summary Report. CM2088. London: HMSO.

Department of Health and Social Security (1979). *Report of the Committee of Enquiry into Mental Handicap Nursing and Care (Jay Report).* CMNO 7468. London: HMSO.

Hollins, S. (1988). How mental handicap is taught in UK medical schools. *Medical Teacher,* **10,** 289–96.

Hollins, S. & Bradley, E. (1987). Mental handicap in context: medical undergraduate education. *Bulletin of the Royal College of Psychiatrists,* **11,** 389–91.

Holt, A.S. & Huntley, R.M.C. (1973). Mental subnormality: medical training in the UK. *British Journal of Medical Education,* **7,** 197–203.

Holt G. (1995). Training staff on mental health in mental retardation. In *Proceedings of the International Congress II on the Dually Diagnosed,* pp. 109–11. New York: National Association for Dually Diagnosed.

Holt, G. & Bouras, N. (1988) Attitudes of medical students to mental health. *Medical Teacher,* **10,** 305–7.

Holt G. & Bouras, N. eds. (1997). *Mental Health in Learning Disabilities: Handbook,* 2nd edn. Brighton: Pavilion Publishing.

Holt, G., Bouras, N. & Brooks, D. (1993). Medical students' evaluation of their experience of the psychiatry of mental handicap. *Psychiatric Bulletin,* **17,** 21–2.

Howells, G. (1986). Are the medical needs of mentally handicapped adults being met? *Journal of the Royal College of General Practitioners* **36,** 449–53.

(1991). Mental handicap: care in the community. *British Journal of General Practice,* **41,** 2–4.

Howells, G., Kerr, M. & Lervy, D. (1993). *Learning Disability (Mental Handicap): Distance Learning Work Book for General Practitioners.* Swansea: University of Wales College of Medicine, School of Post Graduate Studies.

Joint Committee on Higher Psychiatric Training (1995). *Higher Training Schemes in Mental Handicap Psychiatry. Handbook,* 7th edn, pp. 37–9. Occasional Paper OP27. London: JCHPT and Royal College of Psychiatrists.

Kerr, M. (1997). A primary health care perspective. In *Challenges and Change: Commissioning and Providing Services for People with Learning Disabilities,* eds. N. Bouras & T. Donlan, pp. 25–9. Brighton: Pavilion Publishers.

Kerr, M., Dunston, F. & Thapar, A. (1996). Attitudes of general practitioners to caring for people with learning disability. *British Journal of General Practice,* **46,** 92–4.

Kinnell, H.G. (1987). Community medical care of people with mental handicaps: room for improvement. *Mental Handicap* **15,** 146–51.

Langan, J., Russell, O. & Whitfield, M. (1993). *Community Care and the General Practitioner: Primary Care for People with Learning Disabilities.* Bristol: Norah Fry Research Centre.

Lennox, N.G. & Kerr, M.P. (1997). Review: primary health care and people with an intellectual disability: the evidence base. *Journal of Intellectual Disability Research,* **41,** 365–72.

Matthews, D.R. (1996). Learning disabilities: the challenge for nursing. *Nursing Times,* **92,** 36–8.

MHMR (1993). Symposium of the European Association for Mental Health in Mental Retardation. The mental health of Europeans with learning disabilities. *Journal of Intellectual Disability of Research,* **37,** Suppl. 1.

Moss, S.C., Prosser, H. Simpson, N. & Patel, P. (1997). *The PAS–ADD Checklist.* Manchester: Hester Adrian Research Centre, University of Manchester.

NHS Executive (1996). *A Guide to Specialist Registrar Training.* Wetherby: DH Publications.

(1998). *Signposts for Success in Commissioning and Providing Health Services for People with Learning Disabilities.* Wetherby: DH Publications.

Parmenter, T.R. (1988). Analysis of Australian mental health services for people with mental retardation. *Australian and New Zealand Journal of Developmental Disabilities,* **14,** 9–13.

Patel, P., Goldberg, D. & Moss, S.C. (1993). Psychiatric morbidity in older people with moderate and severe learning disability. II. The prevalence study. *British Journal of Psychiatry,* **163,** 481–91.

Pilkington, T.L .(1977). Teaching medical students about mental handicap. *Developmental Medicine and Child Neurology,* **19,** 652–58.

Powell, G.E., Young, R. & Frosh, S. (1993). *Curriculum in clinical psychology.* Leicester: British Psychological Society Publications.

Prosser, H., Moss, S.C., Costello, H., Simpson, N. & Patel, P. (1997). *The Mini PAS–ADD: a Preliminary Assessment Schedule for the Detection of Mental Health Needs in Adults with Learning Disability.* Manchester: Hester Adrian Research Centre, University of Manchester.

Royal College of General Practitioners (1990). *Primary Care for People with a Mental Handicap.* Occasional Paper no. 47. London: Royal College of General Practitioners.

Royal College of Psychiatrists (1986a). Psychiatric services for mentally handicapped adults and young people. *Bulletin of the Royal College of Psychiatrists,* **10,** 321–2.

(1986b). Undergraduate training in mental handicap. Section for the psychiatry of mental handicap. *Bulletin of The Royal College of Psychiatrists,* **10,** 292.

(1987). Mental handicap nurses: training in psychiatric aspects of care. Section for psychiatry of mental handicap. *Bulletin of The Royal College of Psychiatrists,* **11.**

(1989). Training requirements required to provide a psychiatric service for children and adolescents with mental handicap. *Bulletin of The Royal College of Psychiatrists,* **13,** 326–8.

(1992a). *Mental Health of the Nation: the Contribution of Psychiatry.* Council Report CR16. London: Royal College of Psychiatrists.

(1992b). *Psychiatric Services for Children and Adolescents with Mental Handicap.* London: Royal College of Psychiatrists.

(1996a). *The Basic Sciences and Clinical Curricula for the Royal College of Psychiatrists Examinations.* London: Royal College of Psychiatrists.

(1996b). *Meeting the Mental Health Needs of Adults with Mild Learning Disabilities.* London: Royal College of Psychiatrists.

(1997). *Educational Policy.* Occasional Paper OP 36. London: Royal College of Psychiatrists.

Sainsbury Centre for Mental Health (1997). *Pulling Together: the Future Roles and Training of Mental Health Staff.* London: Sainsbury Centre.

Shapiro, A., Zeitlin, H. & Sacks, B. (1978). *Teaching of Mental Handicap to Undergraduates in London University. Report of a Working Party to the Psychiatric Subcommittee of the Board of Study in Medicine.* London: University of London.

Sines, D. (1993). Opportunities for Change: *a New Direction for People with Learning Disabilities.* Discussion paper. London: Department of Health.

Singh, P. (1997). *Prescription for Change: A MENCAP Report on the Role of GPs and*

Carers in the Provision of Primary Care for People with Learning Disabilities.
London: MENCAP.

United Kingdom Central Council for Nursing, Midwifery and Health Visiting
(1986). *Project 2000*, London: UKCC.

Watts, F.N. (1985). Clinical psychology. *Health Trends* 17, 28–31.

Weinstein, J. (1994). *Sewing the Seams for a Seamless Service: a Review of
Developments in Interprofessional Education and Training.* London: Central
Council for Education and Training in Social Work.

Welsh Health Planning Forum (1992). *Protocol for investment in Health Gain:
Mental Handicap (Learning Disabilities).* Cardiff: Welsh Office NHS
Directorate.

Whelan, E. & Speake, B., (1977). *Adult Training Centres in England and Wales:
Report of the First National Survey.* Manchester: National Association of
Teachers of the Mentally Handicapped Hester Adrian Research Centre.

Wiley, Y.V. (1989). Burden Research Medal and Prize (1969–1989). *Psychiatric
Bulletin,* **13**, 701.

Wilson, D. & Haire, A. (1990). Health scanning for people with mental handicap
living in the community. *British Medical Journal,* **301**, 1379–80.

Zarfas, D.E. (1988). Mental health systems for people with mental retardation: a
Canadian perspective. *Australian and New Zealand Journal of
Developmental Disabilities,* **14**, 3–7.

Index